CREATIVE
HOMEOWNER®

BEST-SELLING

1-STORY HOME PLANS

CREATIVE HOMEOWNER®, Upper Saddle River, New Jersey

CREATIVE
HOMEOWNER®
A Division of Federal Marketing Corp.
Upper Saddle River, NJ

Home Plans Editor: Kenneth D. Stuts, CPBD

Design and Layout: iiCREATiVE (David Kroha, Cindy DiPierdomenico, Judith Kroha)

Cover Design: David Geer

Vice President and Publisher: Timothy O. Bakke
Production Coordinator: Sara M. Markowitz

Current Printing (last digit)
10 9 8 7 6 5 4 3 2 1

Manufactured in the United States of America

Best-Selling 1-Story Home Plans
Library of Congress Control Number: 2009934269
ISBN-10: 1-58011-482-2
ISBN-13: 978-1-58011-482-0

CREATIVE HOMEOWNER®
A Division of Federal Marketing Corp.
24 Park Way
Upper Saddle River, NJ 07458
www.creativehomeowner.com

Note: The homes as shown in the photographs and renderings in this book may differ from the actual blueprints. When studying the house of your choice, please check the floor plans carefully.

PHOTO CREDITS

Front cover: *main image* plan 441002, page 125; *left to right* plan 161224, page 259; plan 161002, page 117; plan 121053, page 231 **page 1:** plan 151140, page 246 **page 3:** *top* 121053, page 231; *center* plan 271074, page 228; *bottom* plan 661004, page 228 **page 4:** plan 131002, page 89 **page 5:** plan 121009, page 40 **page 6:** *top* plan 441015, page 278; *bottom* plan 161002, page 117 **page 7:** plan 161224, page 259 **page 8:** plan 131047, page 114 **page 52:** Charles Mann **page 53:** Carolyn L. Bates, design & installation: Paul Wieczoreck, Champlain Valley Landscaping **page 54:** Mark Samu **page 55:** Mark Lohman, design: Stout Landscaping **page 56:** *all* John Parsekian/CH **page 57:** Mark Lohman, design: Maraya Droney Design **page 58:** *all* Charles Mann **page 59:** *top* Mark Samu; *bottom* Mark Lohman, design: Maraya Droney Design **page 134:** *top* courtesy of Thomasville; *bottom both* courtesy of Rubbermaid **page 135:** courtesy of IKEA **page 136:** courtesy of Closetmaid **page 137:** *top* courtesy of Closetmaid; *bottom* courtesy of Rubbermaid **pages 138–139:** *all* courtesy of Rubbermaid **pages 140–141:** courtesy of Diamond Cabinets **page 182:** Mark Samu, courtesy of Hearst Magazines **page 183:** Mark Samu, design: Paula Yedyank **page 184:** *left* Mark Lohman, design: Janet Lohman Interior Design; *right* Mark Samu, design: Jean Stoffer **page 185:** Mark Lohman, design: Cheryl Hamilton-Gray **pages 186–187:** *top* Anne Gummerson, design: Gina Fitzsimmons, Fitzsimmons Design Associates; *bottom right* davidduncanlivingston.com; *bottom center* Tony Giammarino/Giammarino & Dworkin; *bottom left* Mark Samu, design: Ken Kelly **page 188:** Mark Samu, design: Ken Kelly **page 189:** *top both* Mark Samu, design: Jean Stoffer; *bottom* Mark Samu **page 234:** Jessie Walker **pages 235–237:** *all* courtesy of Hostetler Patio Enclosures, Inc. **page 238:** *illustrations by* Mario Ferro **page 239:** Roger Bruhn **page 240:** *top left* Jessie Walker; *top right* Jessie Walker, design: Adele Lampert/Interiors II; *bottom* Roger Holmes **page 241:** Jessie Walker **page 279:** plan 161093, page 227 **page 283:** *top* plan 151383, page 244; *center* 161037, page 232; *bottom* plan 271079, page 213 **page 288:** *top* 151004, page 195; *center* plan 271073, page 145; *bottom* plan 211002, page 105 **Back cover:** *bottom left to right* plan 101022, page 162; plan 661007, page 248; plan 481154, page 146

Planet Friendly Publishing
✓ Made in the United States
✓ Printed on Recycled Paper
Text: 10% Cover: 10%
Learn more: www.greenedition.org

At Creative Homeowner we're committed to producing books in an earth-friendly manner and to helping our customers make greener choices.

Manufacturing books in the United States ensures compliance with strict environmental laws and eliminates the need for international freight shipping, a major contributor to global air pollution.

And printing on recycled paper helps minimize our consumption of trees, water, and fossil fuels. *Best-Selling 1-Story Home Plans* was printed on paper made with 10% post-consumer waste. According to the Environmental Defense Fund Paper Calculator, by using this innovative paper instead of conventional papers we achieved the following environmental benefits:

Trees Saved: 14
Water Saved: 6,448 gallons
Solid Waste Eliminated: 392 pounds
Greenhouse Gas Emissions Eliminated: 1,339 pounds

For more information on our environmental practices, please visit us online at www.creativehomeowner.com/green

Contents

Getting Started

Maybe you can't wait to bang the first nail. Or you may be just as happy leaving town until the windows are cleaned. The extent of your involvement with the construction phase is up to you. Your time, interests, and abilities can help you decide how to get the project from lines on paper to reality. But building a house requires more than putting pieces together. Whoever is in charge of the process must competently manage people as well as supplies, materials, and construction. He or she will have to

- Make a project schedule to plan the orderly progress of the work. This can be a bar chart that shows the time period of activity by each trade.
- Establish a budget for each category of work, such as foundation, framing, and finish carpentry.
- Arrange for a source of construction financing.
- Get a building permit and post it conspicuously at the construction site.
- Line up supply sources and order materials.
- Find subcontractors and negotiate their contracts.
- Coordinate the work so that it progresses smoothly with the fewest conflicts.
- Notify inspectors at the appropriate milestones.
- Make payments to suppliers and subcontractors.

Acting as the builder, above, requires the ability to hire and manage subcontractors.

Building a home, opposite, includes the need to schedule building inspections at the appropriate milestones.

You as the Builder

You'll have to take care of every logistical detail yourself if you decide to act as your own builder or general contractor. But along with the responsibilities of managing the project, you gain the flexibility to do as much of your own work as you want and subcontract out the rest. Before taking this path, however, be sure you have the time and capabilities. Do you also have the time and ability to schedule the work, hire and coordinate subs, order materials, and keep ahead of the accounting required to manage the project successfully? If you do, you stand to save the amount that a general contractor would charge to take on these responsibilities, normally 15 to 30 percent of the construction cost. If you take this responsibility on but mismanage the project, the potential savings will erode and may even cost you more than if you had hired a builder in the first place. A subcontractor might charge extra for having to return to the site to complete work that was originally scheduled for an earlier date. Or perhaps because you didn't order the windows at the beginning, you now have to pay for a recent cost increase. (If you had hired a builder in the first place, he or she would absorb the increase.)

Hiring a Builder to Handle Construction

A builder or general contractor will manage every aspect of the construction process. Your role after signing the construction contract will be to make regular progress payments and ensure that the work for which you are paying has been completed. You will also consult with the builder and agree to any changes that may have to be made along the way.

Leads for finding builders might come from friends or neighbors who have had contractors build, remodel, or add to their homes. Real-estate agents and bankers may have some names handy but are more likely familiar with the builder's ability to complete projects on time and budget than the quality of the work itself.

The next step is to narrow your list of candidates to three or four who you think can do a quality job and work harmoniously with you. Phone each builder to see whether he or she is interested in being considered for your project. If so, invite the builder to an interview at your home. The meeting will serve two purposes. You'll be able to ask the candidate about his or her experience, and you'll be able to see whether or not your personalities are compatible. Go over the plans with the builder to make certain that he or she understands the scope of the project. Ask if they have constructed similar houses. Get references, and check the builder's standing with the Better Business Bureau. Develop a short list of builders, say three, and ask them to submit bids for the project.

Contracts

Lump-Sum Contracts

A lump-sum, or fixed-fee, contract lets you know from the beginning just what the project will cost, barring any changes made because of your requests or unforeseen conditions. This form works well for projects that promise few surprises and are well defined from the outset by a complete set of contract documents. You can enter into a fixed-price contract by negotiating with a single builder on your short list or by obtaining bids from three or four builders. If you go the latter route, give each bidder a set of documents and allow at least two weeks for them to submit their bids. When you get the bids, decide who you want and call the others to thank them for their efforts. You don't have to accept the lowest bid, but it probably makes sense to do so since you have already honed the list to builders you trust. Inform this builder of your intentions to finalize a contract.

Cost-Plus-Fee Contracts

Under a cost-plus-fee contract, you agree to pay the builder for the costs of labor and materials, as verified by receipts, plus a fee that represents the builder's overhead and profit. This arrangement is sometimes referred to as "time and materials." The fee can range between 15 and 30 percent of the incurred costs. Because you ultimately pick up the tab—whatever the costs—the contractor is never at risk, as he is with a lump-sum contract. You won't know the final total cost of a cost-plus-fee contract until the project is built and paid for. If you can live with that uncertainty, there are offsetting advantages. First, this form allows you to accommodate unknown conditions much more easily than does a lump-sum contract. And rather than being tied down by the project documents, you will be free to make changes at any point along the way. This can be a trap, though. Watching the project take shape will spark the desire to add something or do something differently. Each change costs more, and the accumulation can easily exceed your budget. Because of the uncertainty of the final tab and the built-in advantage to the contractor, you should think twice before entering into this form of contract.

Contract Content

The conditions of your agreement should be spelled out thoroughly in writing and signed by both parties, whatever contractual arrangement you make with your builder. Your contract should include provisions for the following:

- The names and addresses of the owner and builder.
- A description of the work to be included ("As described in the plans and specifications dated . . .").
- The date that the work will be completed if time is of the essence.
- The contract price for lump-sum contracts and the builder's allowed profit and overhead costs for changes.
- The builder's fee for cost-plus-fee contracts and the method of accounting and requesting payment.
- The criteria for progress payments (monthly, by project milestones) and the conditions of final payment.
- A list of each drawing and specification section that is to be included as part of the contract.
- Requirements for guarantees. (One year is the standard period for which contractors guarantee the entire project, but you may require specific guarantees on

When submitting bids, all of the builders should base their estimates on the same specifications. Once the work begins, communicate with your builder to keep the work proceeding smoothly.

Inspect your newly built home, if possible, before the builder closes it up and finishes it.

certain parts of the project, such as a 20-year guarantee on the roofing.)

- Provisions for insurance.
- A description of how changes in the work orders will be handled.

The builder may have a standard contract that you can tailor to the specifics of your project. These contain complete specific conditions with blanks that you can fill in to fit your project and a set of "general conditions" that cover a host of issues from insurance to termination provisions. It's always a good idea to have an attorney review the draft of your completed contract before signing it.

Working with Your Builder

The construction phase officially begins when you have a signed copy of the contract and copies of any insurance required from the builder. It's not unheard of for a builder to request an initial payment of 10 to 20 percent of the total cost to cover mobilization costs, those costs associated with obtaining permits and getting set up to begin the actual construction. If you agree to this, keep a careful eye on the progress of the work to ensure that the total paid out at any one time doesn't get too far out of sync with the actual work completed.

What about changes? From here on, it's up to you and your builder to proceed in good faith and to keep the channels of communication open. Even so, changes of one sort or another beset every project, and they usually add to its cost.

Light at the End of the Tunnel.

The builder's request for a final inspection marks the end of the construction phase—almost. At the final inspection meeting, you and the builder will inspect the work, noting any defects or incomplete items on a "punch list." When the builder tidies up the punch list items, you should reinspect. Sometimes, builders go on to another job and take forever to clean up the last few details, so only after all items on the list have been completed satisfactorily should you release the final payment, which often accounts for the builder's profit.

Some Final Words

Having a positive attitude is important when undertaking a project as large as building a home. A positive attitude can help you ride out the rigors and stress of the construction process.

Stay Flexible. Expect problems, because they certainly will occur. Weather can upset the schedule you have established for subcontractors. A supplier may get behind on deliveries, which also affects the schedule. An unexpected pipe may surprise you during excavation. Just as certain, every problem that comes along has a solution if you are open to it.

Be Patient. The extra days it may take to resolve a construction problem will be forgotten once the project is completed.

Express Yourself. If what you see isn't exactly what you thought you were getting, don't be afraid to look into changing it. Or you may spot an unforeseen opportunity for an improvement. Changes usually cost more money, though, so don't make frivolous decisions.

Finally, watching your home go up is exciting, so stay upbeat. Get away from your project from time to time. Dine out. Take time to relax. A positive attitude will make for smoother relations with your builder. An optimistic outlook will yield better-quality work if you are doing your own construction. And though the project might seem endless while it is under way, keep in mind that all the planning and construction will fade to a faint memory at some time in the future, and you will be getting a lifetime of pleasure from a home that is just right for you.

Ten Steps You Should Do Before Submitting Your Plans For a Permit

1. Check Your Plans to Make Sure That You Received What You Ordered

You should immediately check your plans to make sure that you received exactly what you ordered. All plans are checked for content prior to shipping, but mistakes can happen. If you find an error in your plans call 1-800-523-6789. All plans are drawn on a particular type of foundation and all details of the plan will illustrate that particular foundation. If you ordered an alternate foundation type, it should be included immediately after the original foundation. Tell your builder which foundation you wish to use and disregard the other foundation.

2. Check to Make Sure You Have Purchased the Proper Plan License

If you purchased prints, your plan will have a round red stamp stating, "If this stamp is not red it is an illegal set of plans." This license grants the purchaser the right to build one home using these construction drawings. It is illegal to make copies, doing so is punishable up to $150,000 per offense plus attorney fees. If you need more prints, call 1-800-523-6789. The House Plans Market Association monitors the home building industry for illegal prints.

It is also illegal to modify or redraw the plan if you purchased a print. If you purchased prints and need to modify the plan, you can upgrade to the reproducible master, PDF files, or CAD files — call 1-800-523-6789. If you purchased a reproducible master, PDF files, or CAD file you have the right to modify the plan and make up to 10 copies. A reproducible master, PDF files, or CAD files comes with a license that you must surrender to the printer or architect making your changes.

3. Complete the "Owner Selection" Portion of the Building Process

The working drawings are very complete, but there are items that you must decide upon. For example, the plans show a toilet in the bathroom, but there are hundreds of models from which to choose. Your individual selection should be made based upon the color, style, and price you wish to pay. This same thing is true for all of the plumbing fixtures, light fixtures, appliances, and interior finishes (for the floors, walls, and ceilings) and exterior finishes. The selection of these items is required in order to obtain accurate competitive bids for the construction of your home.

4. Complete Your Permit Package by Adding Other Documents That May Be Required

Your permit department, lender, and builder will need other drawings or documents that must be obtained locally. These items are explained in the next three items.

5. Obtain a Heating & Cooling Calculation and Layout

The heating and cooling system must be calculated and designed for your exact home and your location. Even the orientation of your home can affect the system size. This service is normally provided free of charge by the mechanical company that is supplying the equipment and installation. However, to get an unbiased calculation and equipment recommendation, we suggest employing the services of a mechanical engineer.

6. Obtain a Site Plan

A site plan is a document that shows the relationship of your home to your property. It may be as simple as the document your surveyor provides, or it can be a complex collection of drawings such as those prepared by a landscape architect. Typically, the document prepared by a surveyor will only show the property boundaries and the footprint of the home. Landscape architects can provide planning and drawings for all site amenities, such as driveways and walkways, outdoor structures such as pools, planting plans, irrigation plans, and outdoor lighting.

7. Obtain Earthquake or Hurricane Engineering if You Are Planning to Build in an Earthquake or Hurricane Zone

If you are building in an earthquake or hurricane zone, your permit department will most likely require you to submit calculations and drawings to illustrate the ability of your home to withstand those forces. This information is never included with pre-drawn plans because it would penalize the vast majority of plan purchasers who do not build in those zones. A structural engineer licensed by the state where you are building usually provides this information.

8. Review Your Plan to See Whether Modifications Are Needed

These plans have been designed to assumed conditions and do not address the individual site where you are building. Conditions can vary greatly, including soil conditions, wind and snow loads, and temperature, and any one of these conditions may require some modifications of your plan. For example, if you live in an area that receives snow, structural changes may be necessary. We suggest:

(i)Have your soil tested by a soil-testing laboratory so that subsurface conditions can be determined at your specific building site. The findings of the soil-testing laboratory should be reviewed by a structural engineer to determine if the existing plan foundation is suitable or if modifications are needed.

(ii)Have your entire plan reviewed by your builder or a structural engineer to determine if other design elements, such as load bearing beams, are sized appropriately for the conditions that exist at your site.

Now that you have the complete plan, you may discover items that you wish to modify to suit your own personal taste or decor. To change the drawings, you must have the reproducible masters, PDF files, or CAD files (see item 2). We can make the changes for you. For complete information regarding modifications, including our fees, go to www.ultimateplans.com and click the "resources" button on the home page; then click on "our custom services."

9. Record Your Blueprint License Number

Record your blueprint license number for easy reference. If you or your builder should need technical support, the license number is required.

10. Keep One Set of Plans as Long as You Own the Home

Be sure to file one copy of your home plan away for safe keeping. You may need a copy in the future if you remodel or sell the home. By filing a copy away for safe keeping, you can avoid the cost of having to purchase plans later.

Plan #191030

Dimensions: 33' W x 36' D
Levels: 1
Heated Square Footage: 864
Bedrooms: 2
Bathrooms: 1
Foundation: Crawl space or slab
Materials List Available: No
Price Category: A

Images provided by designer/architect.

Enjoy the view from the spacious front porch of this cozy cottage, which is ideal for a retirement home, vacation retreat, or starter home.

Features:

- Porch: This 6-ft.-wide porch, which runs the length of the home, gives you plenty of space to set up a couple of rockers next to a potted herb garden.
- Living/Dining Room: This huge living and dining area gives you many options for design. The snack bar that it shares with the kitchen is a practical touch.
- Kitchen: The first thing you'll notice in this well-planned kitchen is how much counter and storage space it offers.
- Laundry Room: Opening to the backyard, this room also features ample storage space.
- Bedrooms: Both rooms have good closet space and easy access to the large, luxurious bath.

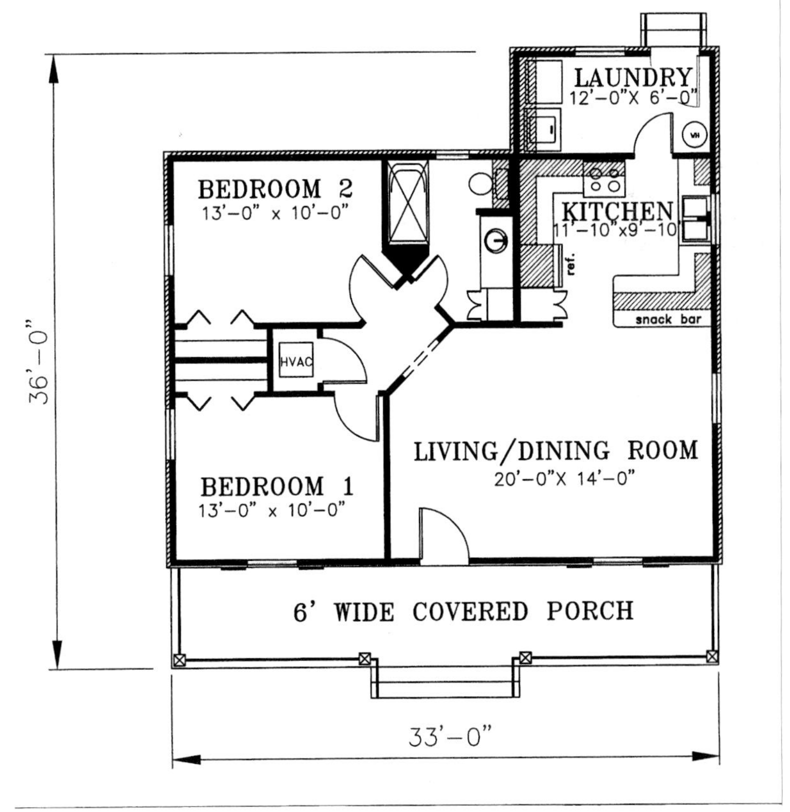

Copyright by designer/architect.

Images provided by designer/architect.

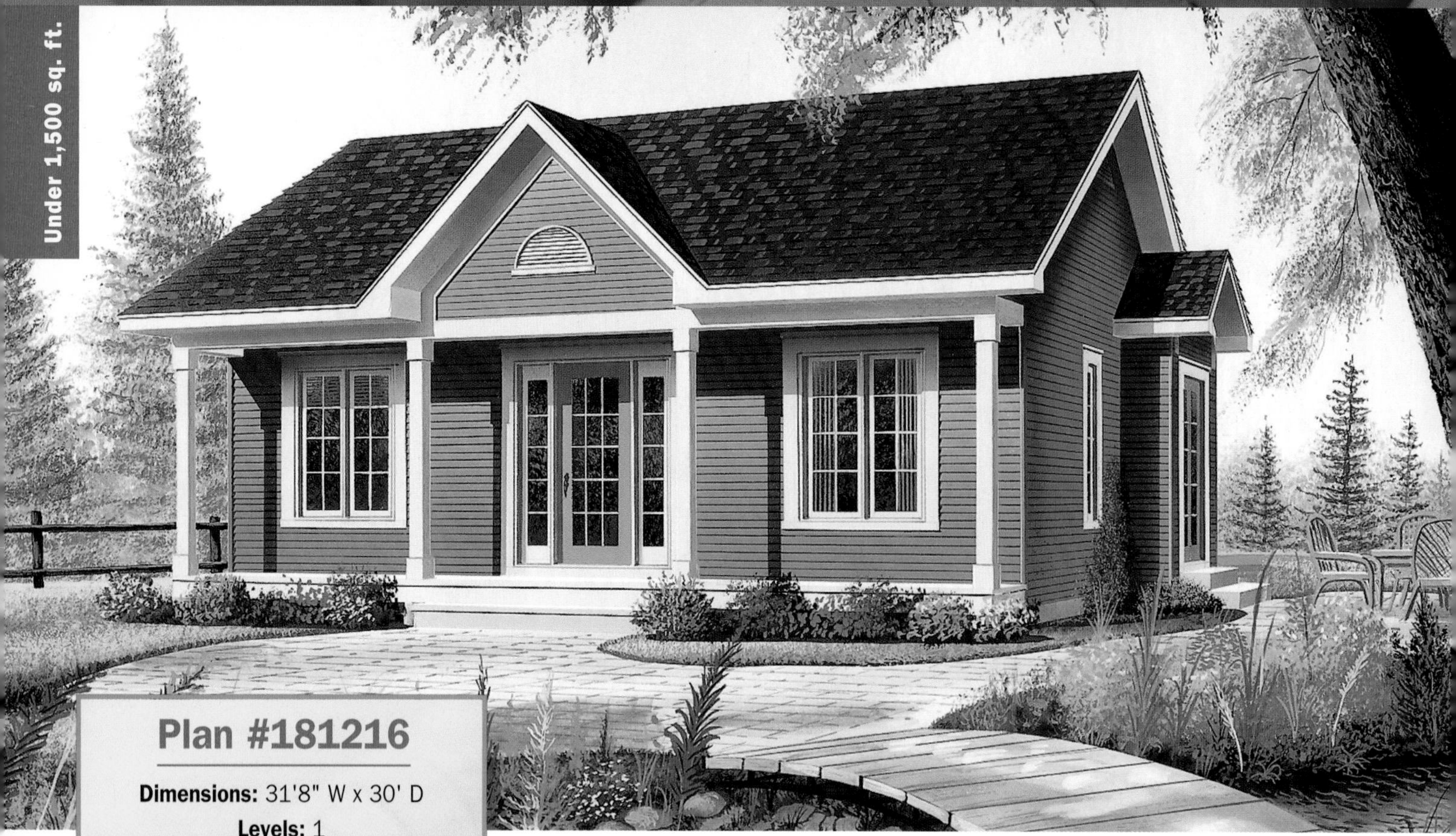

Plan #181216

Dimensions: 31'8" W x 30' D
Levels: 1
Heated Square Footage: 910
Bedrooms: 2
Bathrooms: 1
Foundation: Basement
Materials List Available: Yes
Price Category: A

CAD FILE AVAILABLE

A lot of creativity goes into creating this comfortable home. It begins with a Creole-style covered front porch that lines up across the entire front of the house, beckoning folks to laze awhile in the cool summer shade.

Features:

- Front Door: This entry door has something special—transom and sidelight windows to brighten the interior with natural light.
- Family Room: This large and open room eases to other important rooms—including the great-sized kitchen.
- Kitchen: This large eat-in kitchen has hearty cabinet and counter space.
- Bedrooms: A roomy full bathroom pampers two full-sized bedrooms, which are enhanced by unusual windows and excellent closet space.

Copyright by designer/architect.

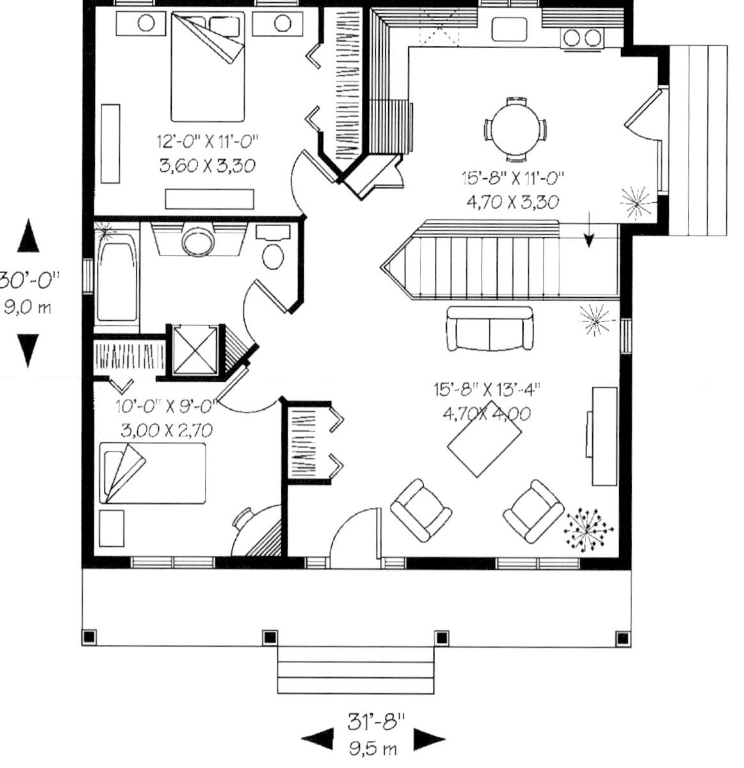

Plan #341146

Dimensions: 40' W x 29'4" D
Levels: 1
Heated Square Footage: 960
Bedrooms: 3
Bathrooms: 2
Foundation: Crawl space, slab, basement, or walkout
Materials List Available: No
Price Category: A

Images provided by designer/architect.

CAD FILE CAD AVAILABLE

59'-10"
34'-10"
PORCH
GREAT ROOM 17'-7" X 19'-5"
CLOS
BEDROOM 1 13'-0" X 15'-5"
CLOSET
BATH 1
GARDEN TUB
SHWR.
BATH 2
W. D. WH
UTILITIES 9'-4" X 8'-5"
PAN.
REF
COATS LINENS
CLOSET
DINING 11'-0" X 13'-7"
EAT-AT BAR
FOYER
CLOSET
BEDROOM 3 11'-7" X 11'-5"
BEDROOM 2 11'-5" X 11'-5"
D/W
KITCHEN 14'-0" X 15'-5"
BUILT-IN SHELVES
PORCH

Copyright by designer/architect.

Plan #341026

Dimensions: 39'9" W x 26' D
Levels: 1
Heated Square Footage: 1,009
Bedrooms: 3
Bathrooms: 2
Foundation: Crawl space; slab or basement for fee
Materials List Available: Yes
Price Category: B

Illustration provided by designer/architect.

Copyright by designer/architect.

39'-9"
26'-0"
BATH
D
W
DINING
BEDROOM 11'-6" X 11'-4"
W.H.
KITCHEN 15'-0" X 11'-4"
BATH
R
LINEN
CLOS.
CLOS.
CLOS.
BEDROOM 11'-4" X 9'-10"
BEDROOM 9'-0" X 9'-10"
LIVING ROOM 15'-0" X 11'-4"
CLOS.
STOOP

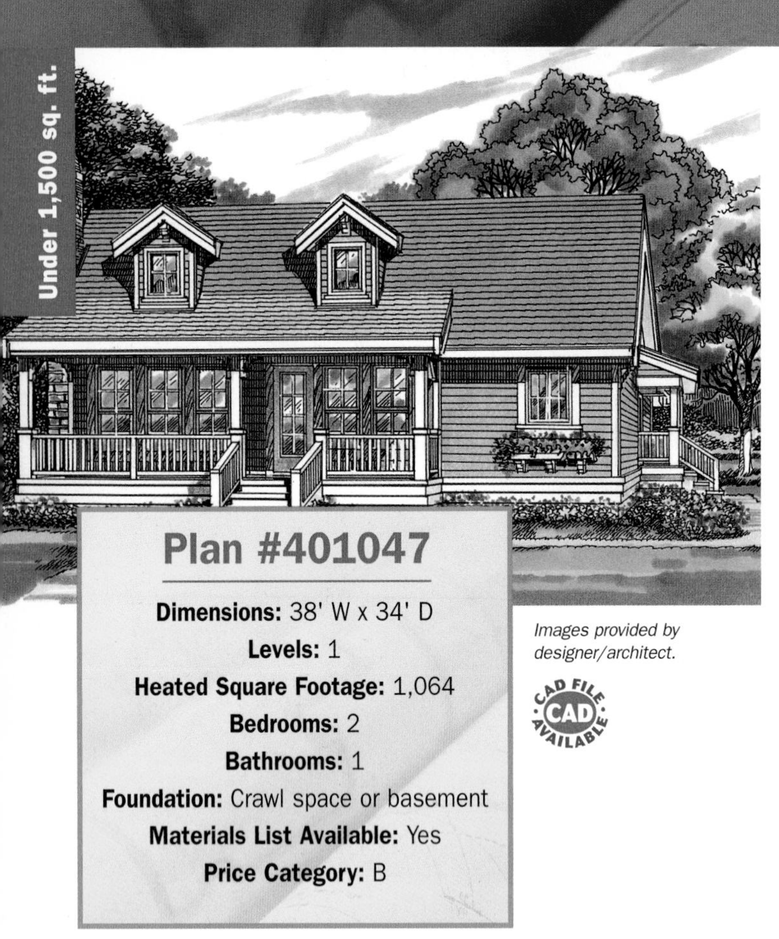

Plan #401047

Dimensions: 38' W x 34' D

Levels: 1

Heated Square Footage: 1,064

Bedrooms: 2

Bathrooms: 1

Foundation: Crawl space or basement

Materials List Available: Yes

Price Category: B

Images provided by designer/architect.

CAD FILE AVAILABLE

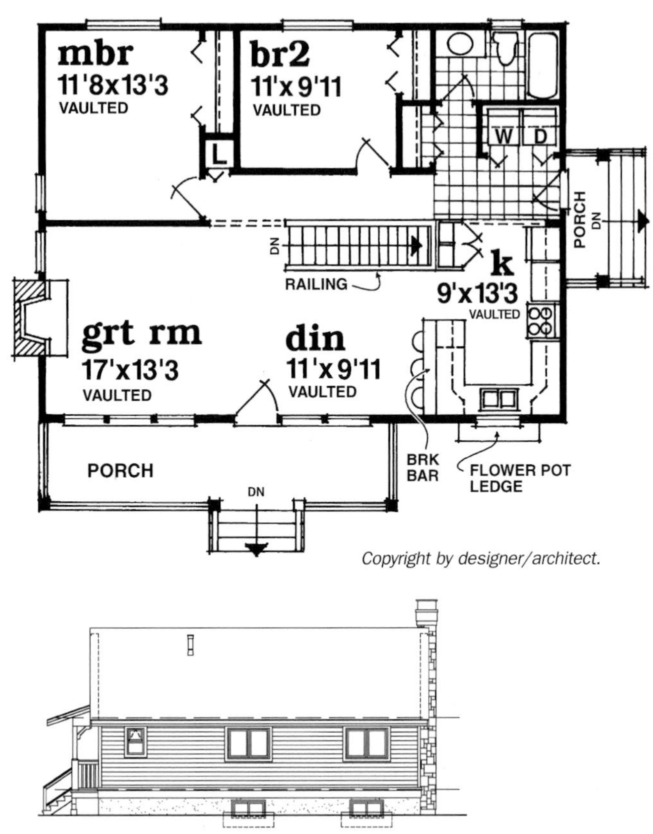

Copyright by designer/architect.

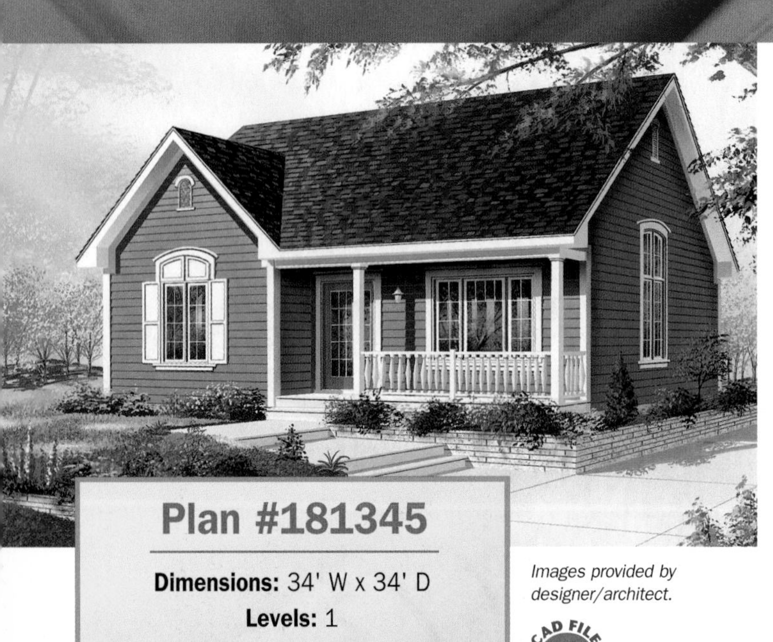

Plan #181345

Dimensions: 34' W x 34' D

Levels: 1

Heated Square Footage: 1,079

Bedrooms: 2

Bathrooms: 1

Foundation: Crawl space or slab; basement or walkout for fee

Materials List Available: Yes

Price Category: B

Images provided by designer/architect.

CAD FILE AVAILABLE

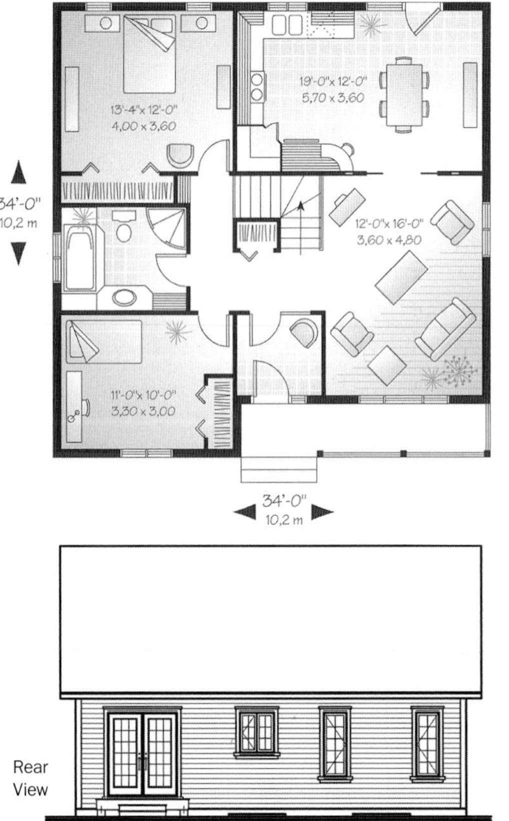

Copyright by designer/architect.

Plan #181148

Dimensions: 36' W x 34' D
Levels: 1
Heated Square Footage: 1,174
Bedrooms: 3
Bathrooms: 1
Foundation: Full basement
Materials List Available: Yes
Price Category: B

Images provided by designer/architect.

CAD FILE AVAILABLE

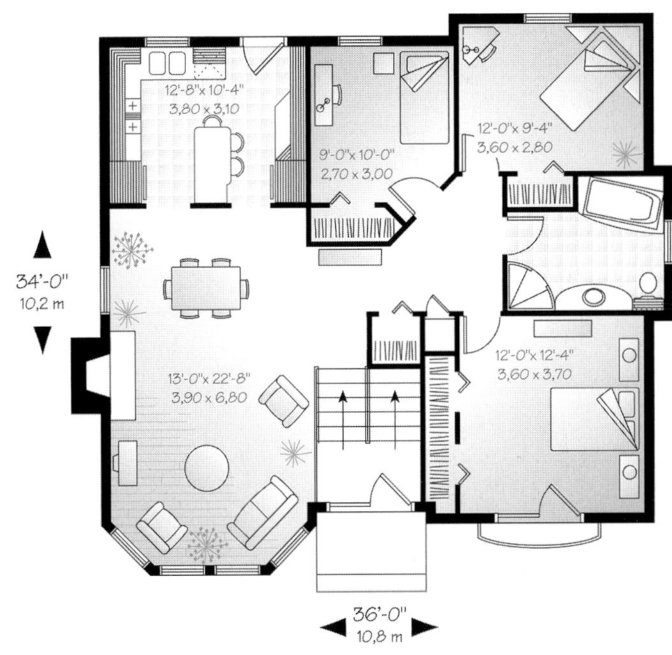

Copyright by designer/architect.

Plan #211016

Dimensions: 44'6" W x 59' D
Levels: 1
Heated Square Footage: 1,191
Bedrooms: 3
Bathrooms: 2
Foundation: Slab; crawl space for fee
Materials List Available: Yes
Price Category: B

Images provided by designer/architect.

CAD FILE AVAILABLE

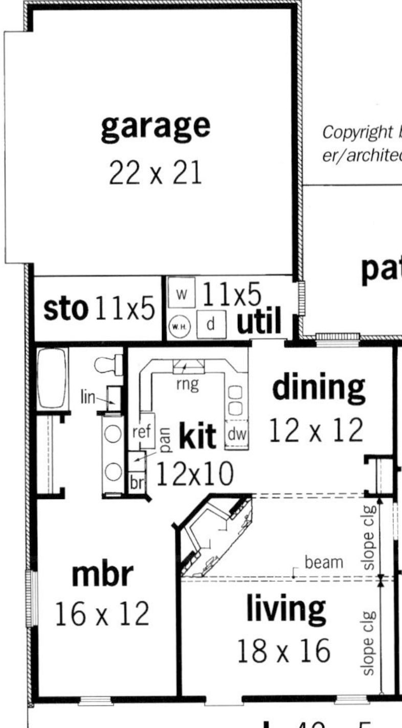

Copyright by designer/architect.

Plan #341004

Dimensions: 56'10" W x 28'6" D

Levels: 1

Heated Square Footage: 1,101

Bedrooms: 3

Bathrooms: 2

Foundation: Crawl space; slab or basement for fee

Materials List Available: Yes

Price Category: B

Images provided by designer/architect.

CAD FILE AVAILABLE

You'll love the romantic feeling that the gables and front porch give to this well designed home, with its family-oriented layout.

Features:

- Living Room: The open design between this spacious room and the kitchen/dining area makes this home as ideal for family activities as it is for entertaining.
- Outdoor Living Space: French doors open to the back deck, where you're sure to host alfresco dinners or easy summer brunches.
- Kitchen: Designed for the cook's convenience, this kitchen features ample work area as well as excellent storage space in the nearby pantry.
- Laundry Area: Located behind closed doors to shut out the noise, this laundry closet is conveniently placed.
- Master Suite: With triple windows, a wide closet, and a private bath, this is a luxurious suite.

SMARTtip

Creating Depth with Wall Frames

Wall frames create an illusion of depth and density because 1) they are three-dimensional and 2) they divide the wall area into smaller, denser segments. The three-dimensional quality of wall frames is fundamentally different from that of the alternative treatment: raised panels. Despite the name, raised panels actually produce a concave-like, or receding, effect whereas wall frames are more convex, protruding outward. In terms of sculpture, concave units create negative space while convex units create positive space. Raised panels, therefore, deliver a uniform sense of volume, mass, and density, while wall frames create a higher level of tension and dramatic interest.

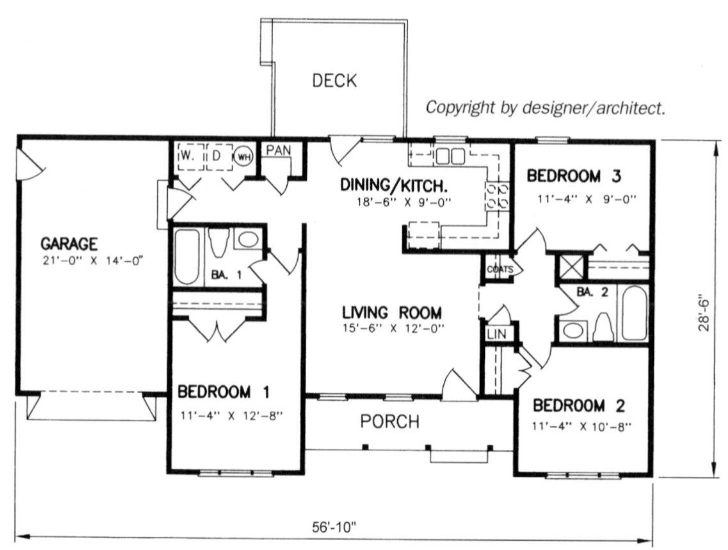

Copyright by designer/architect.

Plan #181021

Dimensions: 37' W x 44' D
Levels: 1
Heated Square Footage: 1,124
Bedrooms: 2
Bathrooms: 1
Foundation: Basement
Materials List Available: Yes
Price Category: B

Images provided by designer/architect.

This cozy country cottage is enhanced by lattice trim details over the porch and garage.

Features:

- Ceiling Height: 8 ft.
- Living Room: This living room gets extra architectural interest from a sunken floor. The room, located directly to the left of the entry hall, has plenty of space for entertaining.
- Dining Room: This dining room is located in center of the home. It's adjacent to the kitchen to make it easy to serve meals.
- Kitchen: This bright and efficient kitchen is a real pleasure in which to work. It includes a pantry and double sinks. There's a breakfast bar that will see plenty of informal meals for families on the go.
- Covered Porch: This is the perfect place to which to retire after dinner on a warm summer evening.
- Bedrooms: Each of the two bedrooms has its own closet. They share a full bathroom.

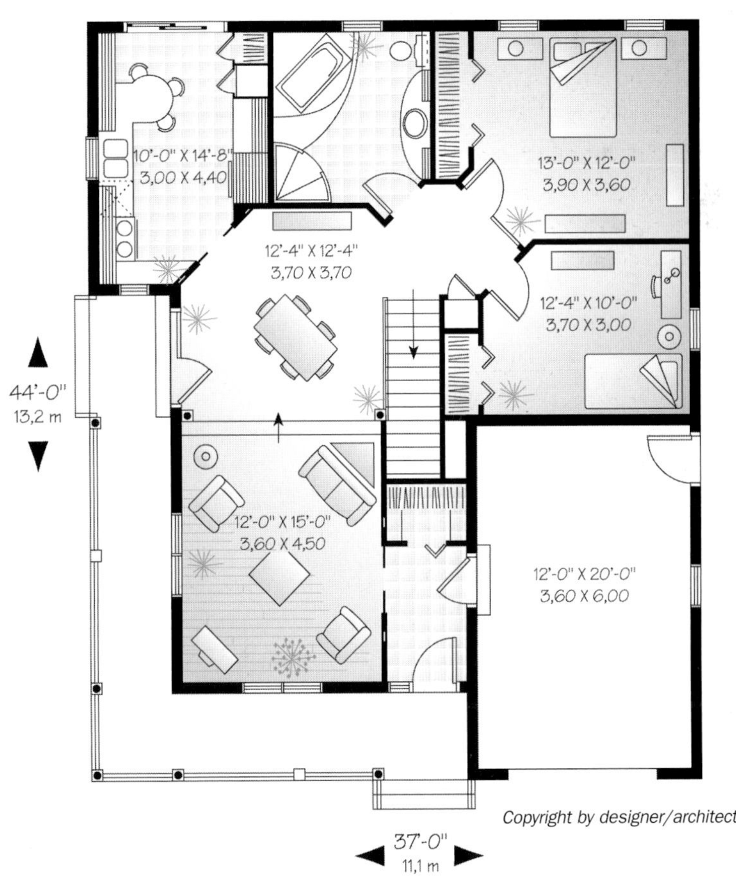

Copyright by designer/architect.

Images provided by designer/architect.

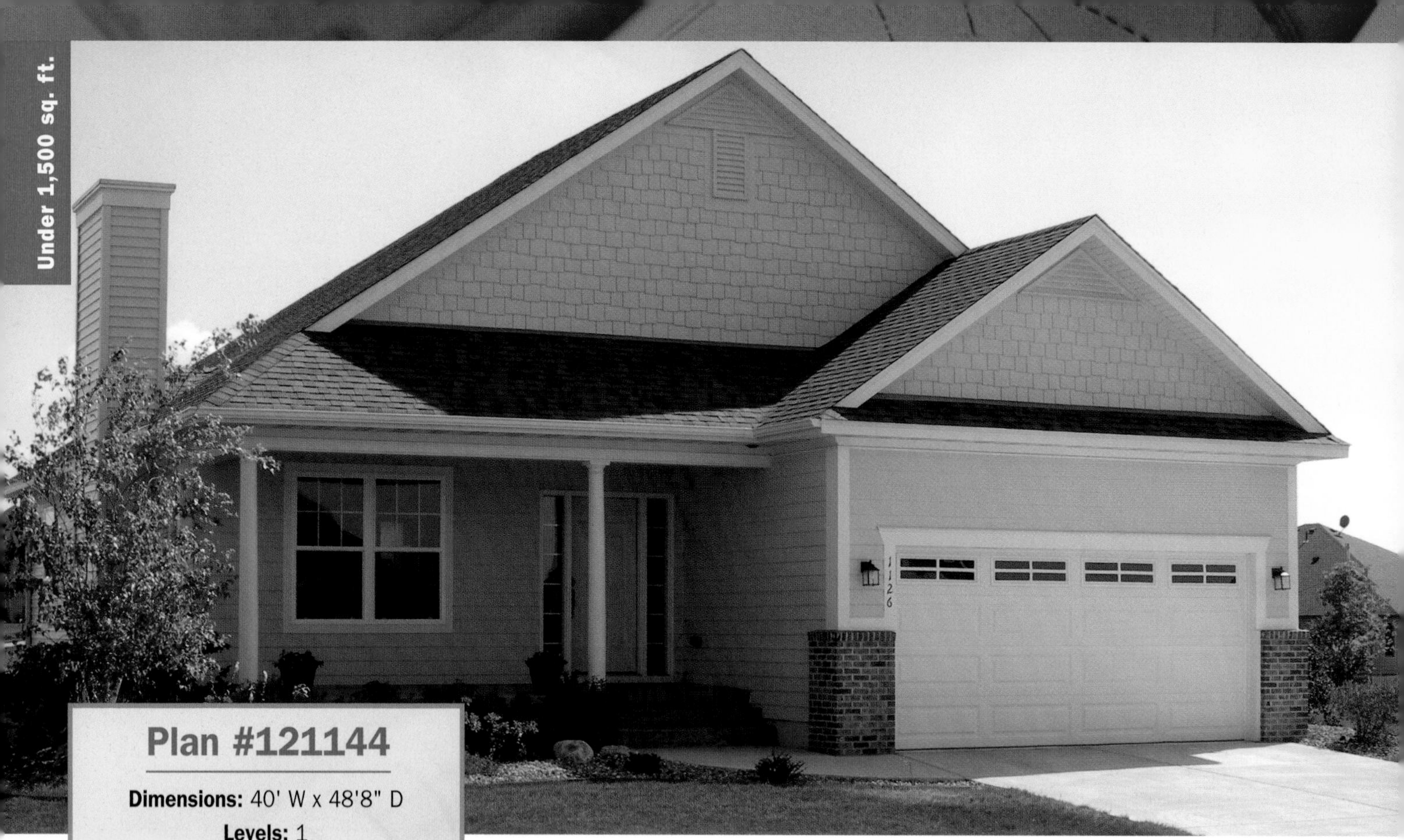

Plan #121144

Dimensions: 40' W x 48'8" D
Levels: 1
Heated Square Footage: 1,195
Bedrooms: 3
Bathrooms: 2
Foundation: Basement; crawl space for fee
Materials List Available: Yes
Price Category: B

CAD FILE AVAILABLE

This is the right design if you want a home that will be easy to expand as your family grows.

Features:

- Front Porch: Hang baskets of plants from the roof of this porch, which is just the right size for a couple of comfortable rocking chairs and a side table.
- Family Room: This family room welcomes you as you enter the home. A crackling fire enhances the ambiance of the room.
- Kitchen: This intelligently designed kitchen has an efficient U-shape layout. A serving bar open to the dining area is a feature that makes entertaining easier.
- Master Suite: This is a compact space that is designed to feel large, and it includes a walk-in closet. The master bath is an added bonus.

Copyright by designer/architect.

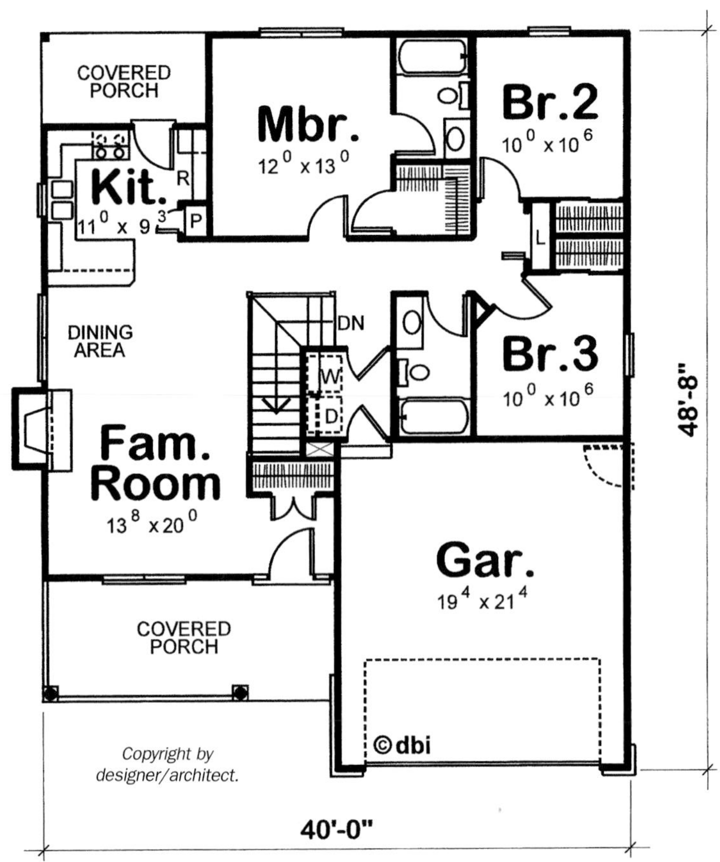

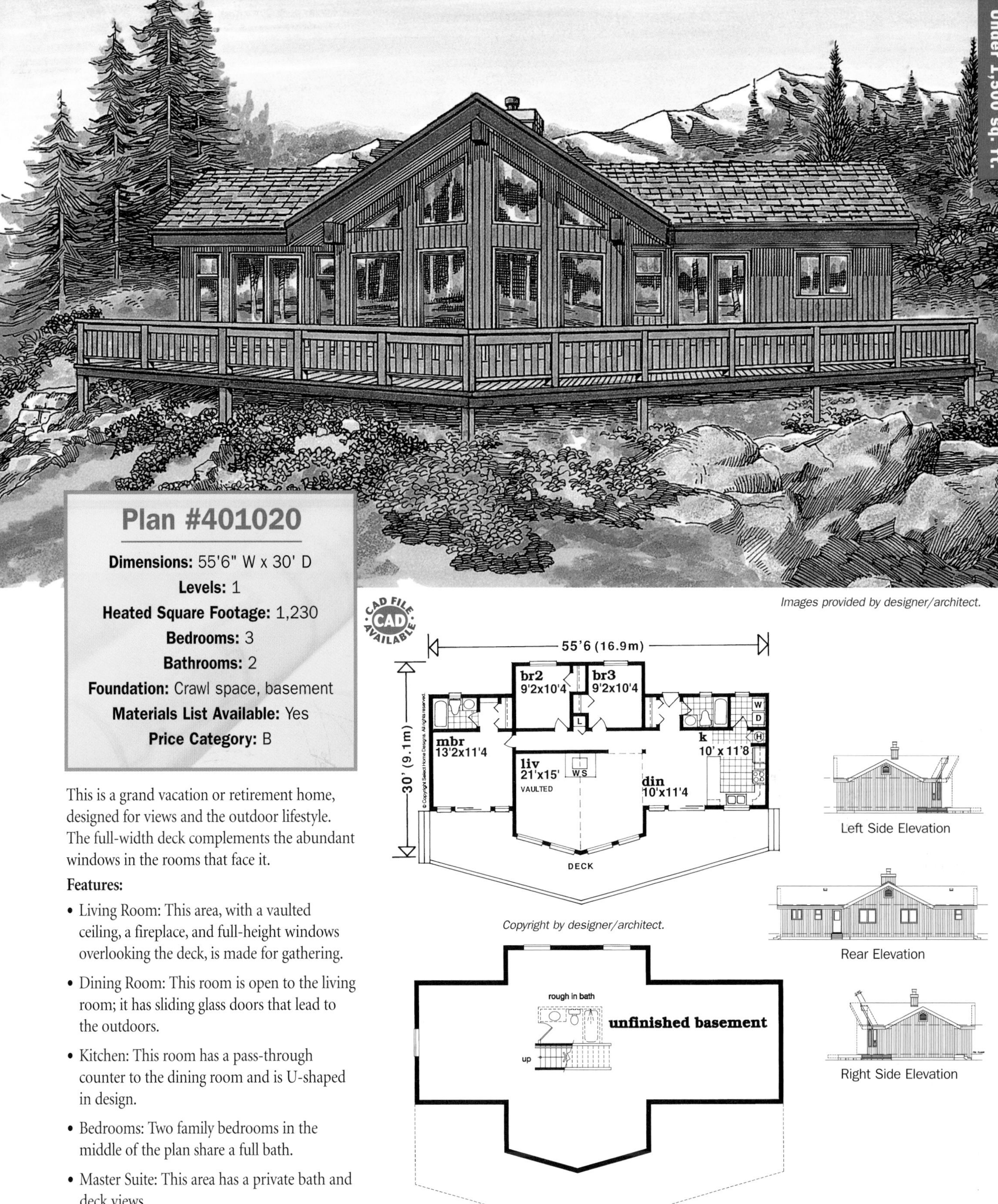

Plan #401020

Dimensions: 55'6" W x 30' D
Levels: 1
Heated Square Footage: 1,230
Bedrooms: 3
Bathrooms: 2
Foundation: Crawl space, basement
Materials List Available: Yes
Price Category: B

Images provided by designer/architect.

Copyright by designer/architect.

Optional Basement Level Floor Plan

This is a grand vacation or retirement home, designed for views and the outdoor lifestyle. The full-width deck complements the abundant windows in the rooms that face it.

Features:

- Living Room: This area, with a vaulted ceiling, a fireplace, and full-height windows overlooking the deck, is made for gathering.
- Dining Room: This room is open to the living room; it has sliding glass doors that lead to the outdoors.
- Kitchen: This room has a pass-through counter to the dining room and is U-shaped in design.
- Bedrooms: Two family bedrooms in the middle of the plan share a full bath.
- Master Suite: This area has a private bath and deck views.

Plan #181714

Dimensions: 38' W x 36'4" D
Levels: 1
Heated Square Footage: 1,244
Bedrooms: 2
Bathrooms: 1
Foundation: Basement; crawl space or slab for fee
Materials List Available: Yes
Price Category: B

Images provided by designer/architect.

CAD FILE AVAILABLE

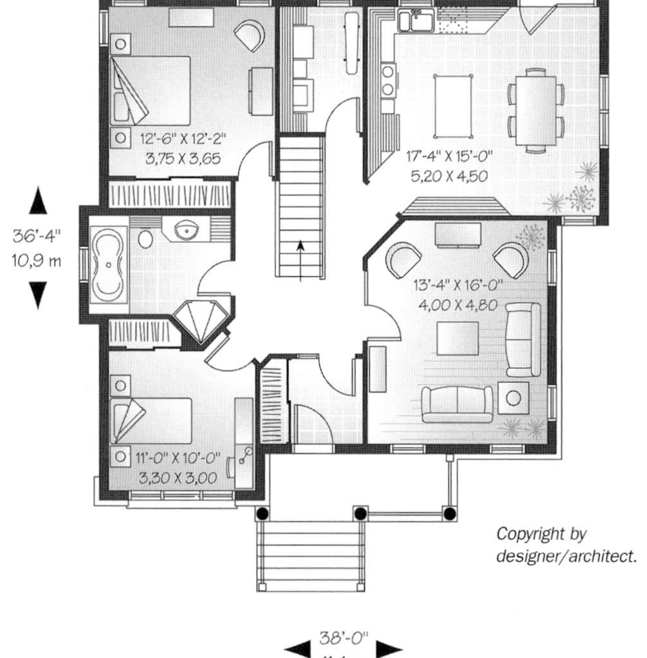

Copyright by designer/architect.

Plan #341304

Dimensions: 40' W x 35'4" D
Levels: 1
Heated Square Footage: 1,248
Bedrooms: 3
Bathrooms: 2
Foundation: Crawl space, slab, basement, or walkout
Materials List Available: Yes
Price Category: B

Images provided by designer/architect.

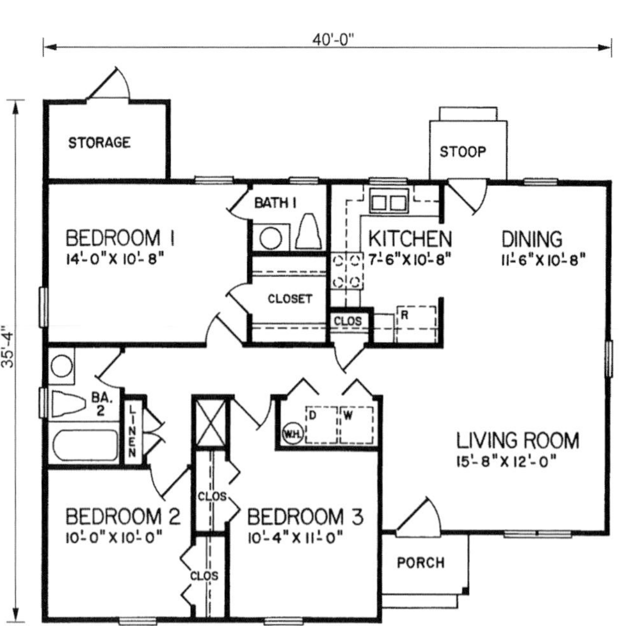

Copyright by designer/architect.

Plan #131008

Dimensions: 45'4" W x 36'4" D
Levels: 1
Heated Square Footage: 1,299
Bedrooms: 3
Bathrooms: 2
Foundation: Crawl space, basement
Materials List Available: Yes
Price Category: C

Images provided by designer/architect.

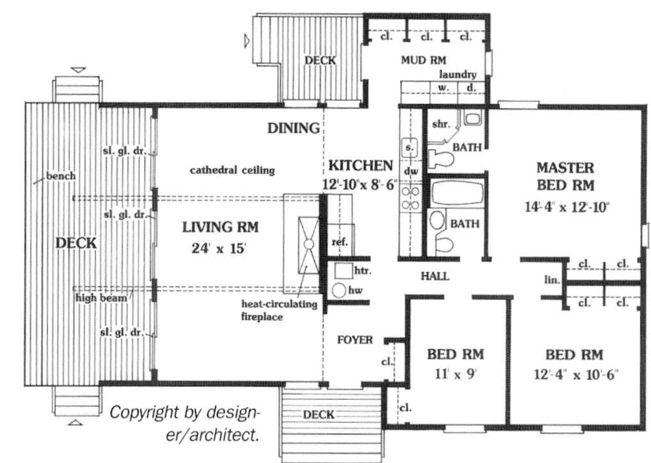

Copyright by designer/architect.

Rear View

Plan #371093

Dimensions: 50' W x 45' D
Levels: 1
Heated Square Footage: 1,300
Bedrooms: 3
Bathrooms: 2
Foundation: Crawl space, slab, or basement
Materials List Available: No
Price Category: B

Images provided by designer/architect.

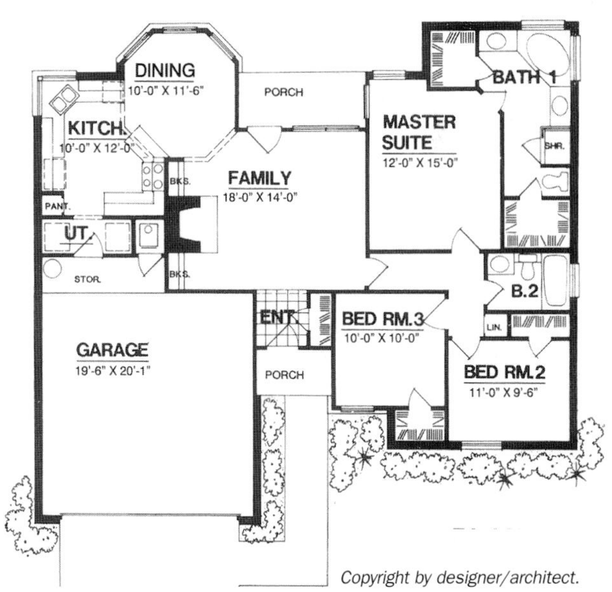

Copyright by designer/architect.

Optional Basement Level Floor Plan

Plan #341028

Dimensions: 40' W x 32' D
Levels: 1
Heated Square Footage: 1,248
Bedrooms: 3
Bathrooms: 2
Foundation: Crawl space; slab or basement for fee
Materials List Available: Yes
Price Category: B

Images provided by designer/architect.

This home's efficient layout and comfortable living spaces all add up to a charming design that is perfect for many first-time homebuyers.

CAD FILE AVAILABLE

Features:

- Living Room: This spacious living room features a fireplace and twin windows.
- Kitchen/Dining Room: This kitchen/dining room provides a pantry and convenient access to the deck at the back of the home.
- Master Suite: You will love this master suite's dual-sink vanity and spacious walk-in closet.
- Utility Room: A separate utility room reduces the noise created by the washer and dryer.

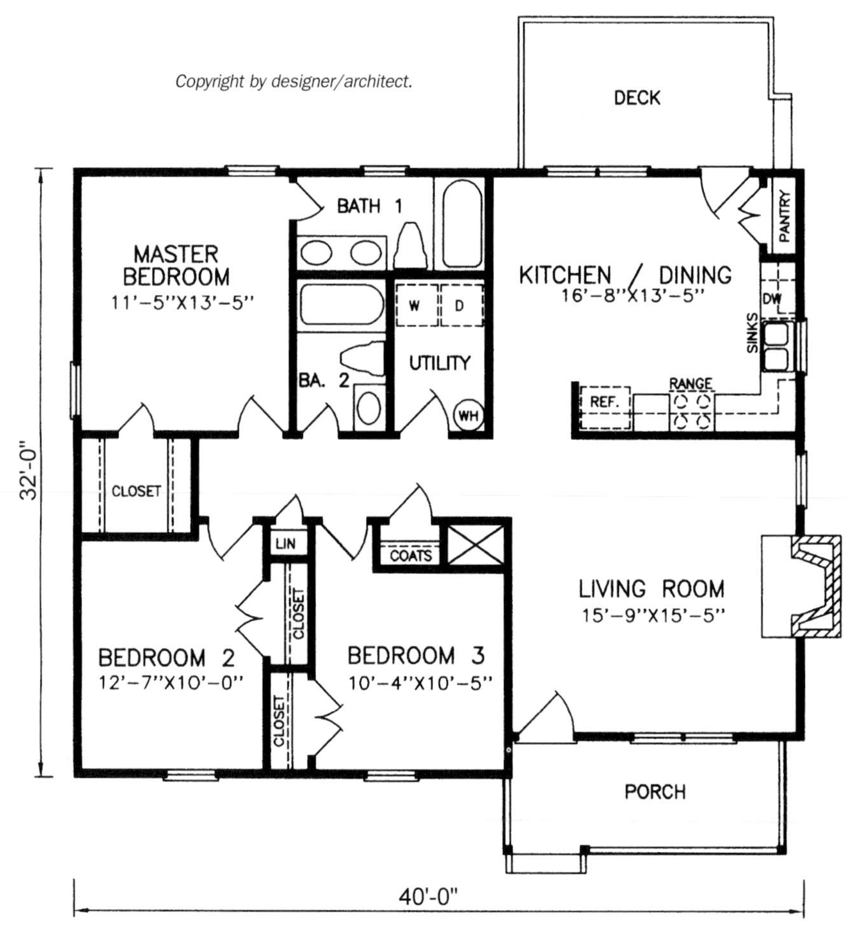

Images provided by designer/architect.

Plan #251001

Dimensions: 61'3" W x 40'6" D
Levels: 1
Heated Square Footage: 1,253
Bedrooms: 3
Bathrooms: 2
Foundation: Crawl space or slab
Materials List Available: Yes
Price Category: B

This charming country home has a classic full front porch for enjoying summertime breezes.

Features:

- Ceiling Height: 8 ft.
- Foyer: Guests will walk through the front porch into this foyer, which opens to the family room.
- Screened Porch: A second porch is screened and is located at the rear of the home off the dining room, so your guests can step out for a bit of fresh air after dinner.
- Family Room: Family and friends will be drawn to this large open space, with its handsome fireplace and sloped ceiling.
- Kitchen: This open and airy kitchen is a pleasure in which to work. It has ample counter space and a pantry.
- Master Bedroom: This master bedroom features a large walk-in closet. It has its own master bath with a single vanity, a tub, and a walk-in shower.
- Garage: This attached garage provides plenty of extra storage space, as well as parking for two cars.

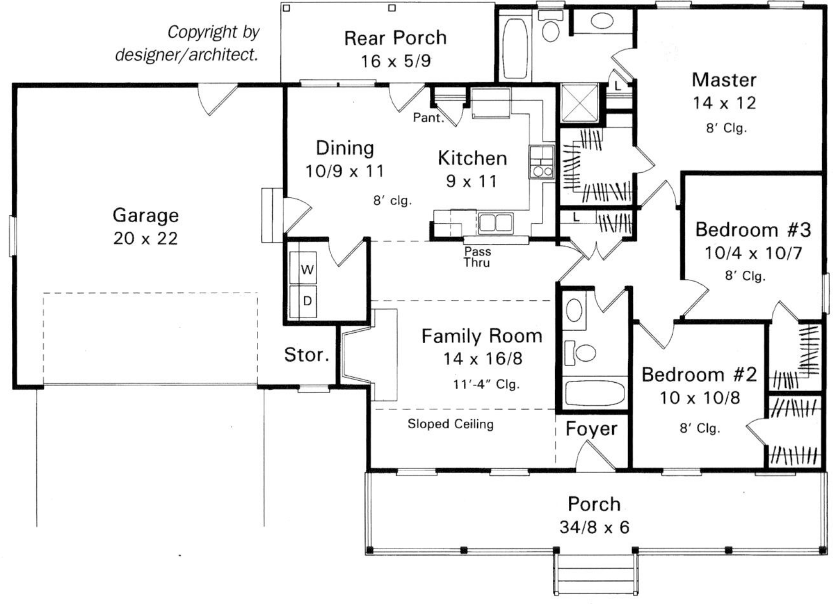

Images provided by designer/architect.

Plan #321033

Dimensions: 38' W x 46' D
Levels: 1
Heated Square Footage: 1,268
Bedrooms: 3
Bathrooms: 2
Foundation: Basement
Materials List Available: Yes
Price Category: D

CAD FILE AVAILABLE

Clean lines and a layout fit for contemporary living create a graceful and efficient update to a simple cottage design that is perfect for families just starting out.

Features:

- Great Room: At the center of everything, this great room will be the heart of the home. Its unhampered transition into the dining areas and kitchen creates a feeling of openness that will welcome guests into your home.
- Kitchen: This kitchen maximizes space and efficiency with simple transitions and plenty of workspace. The laundry room is adjacent for easy cleanup; the dining room and breakfast area are just steps away; and a snack bar provides the only barrier between the kitchen and great room. Cookouts are also simplified by easy access to the back patio.
- Master Suite: Everyone knows that the master bath makes the master suite, and this home is no different. His and her sinks, a large tub with a view, and a separate standing shower combine to create both a retreat and a remedy for hectic mornings.
- Secondary Bedrooms: Bedroom 2 has plenty of closet space and would be perfect for a nursery or even a converted office. Bedroom 3 also has ample closet space and is opened up by a vaulted ceiling. Both are in a space of their own with a nearby full bathroom.

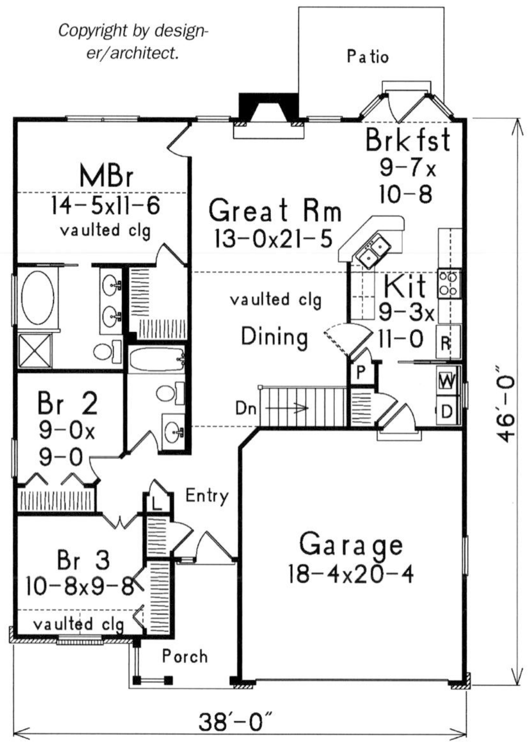

Plan #171001

Dimensions: 44' W x 41' D
Levels: 1
Heated Square Footage: 1,277
Bedrooms: 3
Bathrooms: 2
Foundation: Crawl space or slab
Materials List Available: Yes
Price Category: B

Images provided by designer/architect.

You'll love this design if you're looking for a compact ranch with rustic, country styling and plenty of well designed family areas.

Features:

- Porch: Set a couple of rockers and containers of blooming plants and fragrant herbs on this lovely front porch.
- Great Room: A substantial fireplace is the focal point of this large room. Fill it with a dried floral bouquet in summer, and gather chairs around its warmth in winter.
- Dining Room: This room adjoins the great room for easy entertaining in any season and opens to the large screened porch for summer parties.
- Kitchen: With good counter space and an open layout, this kitchen is built for efficiency.
- Master Bedroom: Split from the other two bedrooms for privacy, this quiet retreat features a large walk-in closet and lovely window area.

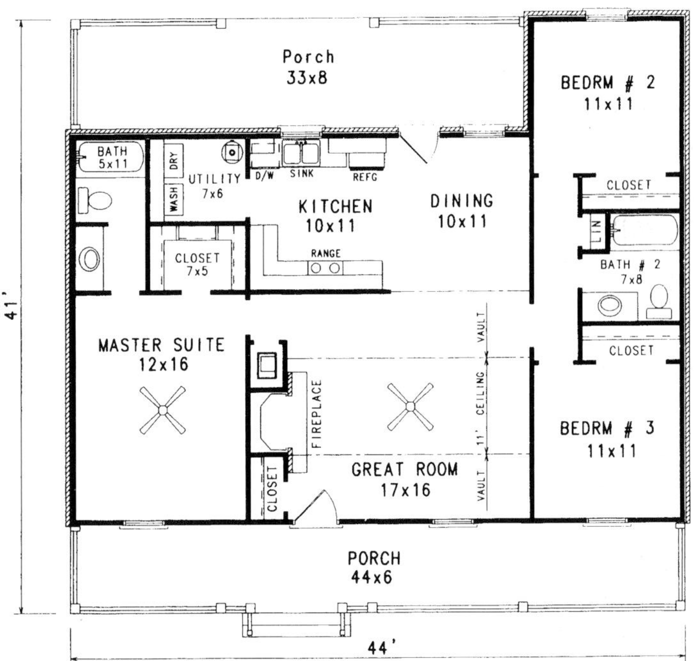

Copyright by designer/architect.

Plan #121012

Dimensions: 40' W x 48'8" D
Levels: 1
Heated Square Footage: 1,195
Bedrooms: 3
Bathrooms: 2
Foundation: Basement
Materials List Available: Yes
Price Category: B

Images provided by designer/architect.

This home, as shown in the photograph, may differ from the actual blueprints. For more detailed information, please check the floor plans carefully.

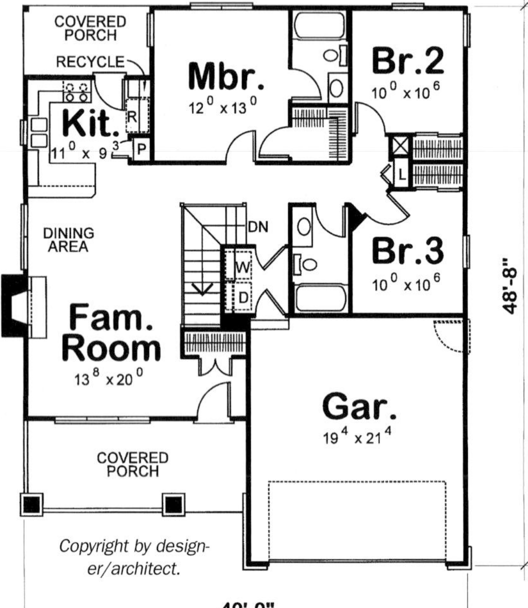

Copyright by designer/architect.

This compact one-level home uses an open plan to make the most of its square footage.

Features:

- Ceiling Height: 8 ft.
- Covered Porch: This delightful area, located off the kitchen, provides a private spot to enjoy some fresh air.
- Open Plan: The family room, dining area and kitchen share a big open space to provide a sense of spaciousness. Moving so easily between these interrelated areas provides the convenience demanded by a busy lifestyle.
- Master Suite: An open plan is convenient, but it is still important for everyone to have their private space. The master suite enjoys its own bath and walk-in closet. The secondary bedrooms share a nearby bath.
- Garage: Here you will find parking for two cars and plenty of extra storage space as well.

Rendering reflects floor plan

Images provided by designer/architect.

Plan #271007

Dimensions: 51'5" W x 40'9" D
Levels: 1
Heated Square Footage: 1,283
Bedrooms: 3
Bathrooms: 2
Foundation: Basement
Materials List Available: Yes
Price Category: B

This charming traditional home has an appealing exterior and is full of exceptional interior features.

Features:

- Great Room: This room is just off the front foyer and boasts a dramatic vaulted ceiling and inviting fireplace.
- Dining room: Open to the great room, this area overlooks the delightful rear deck.
- Kitchen: This area is efficiently designed with a pantry and a sunny vaulted breakfast nook, which leads to the deck, making breakfast alfresco a daily option.

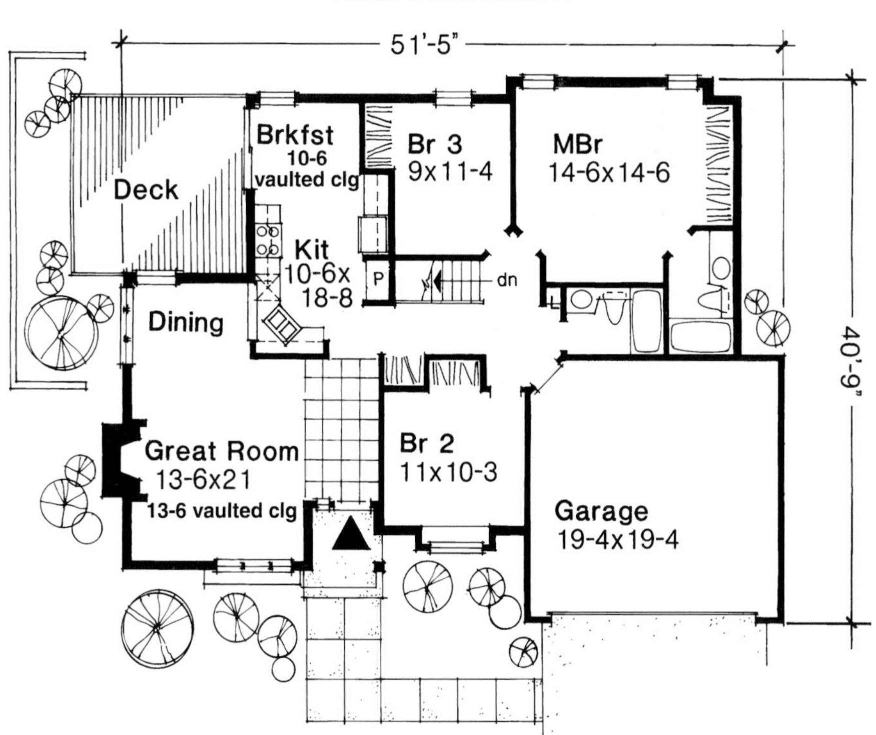

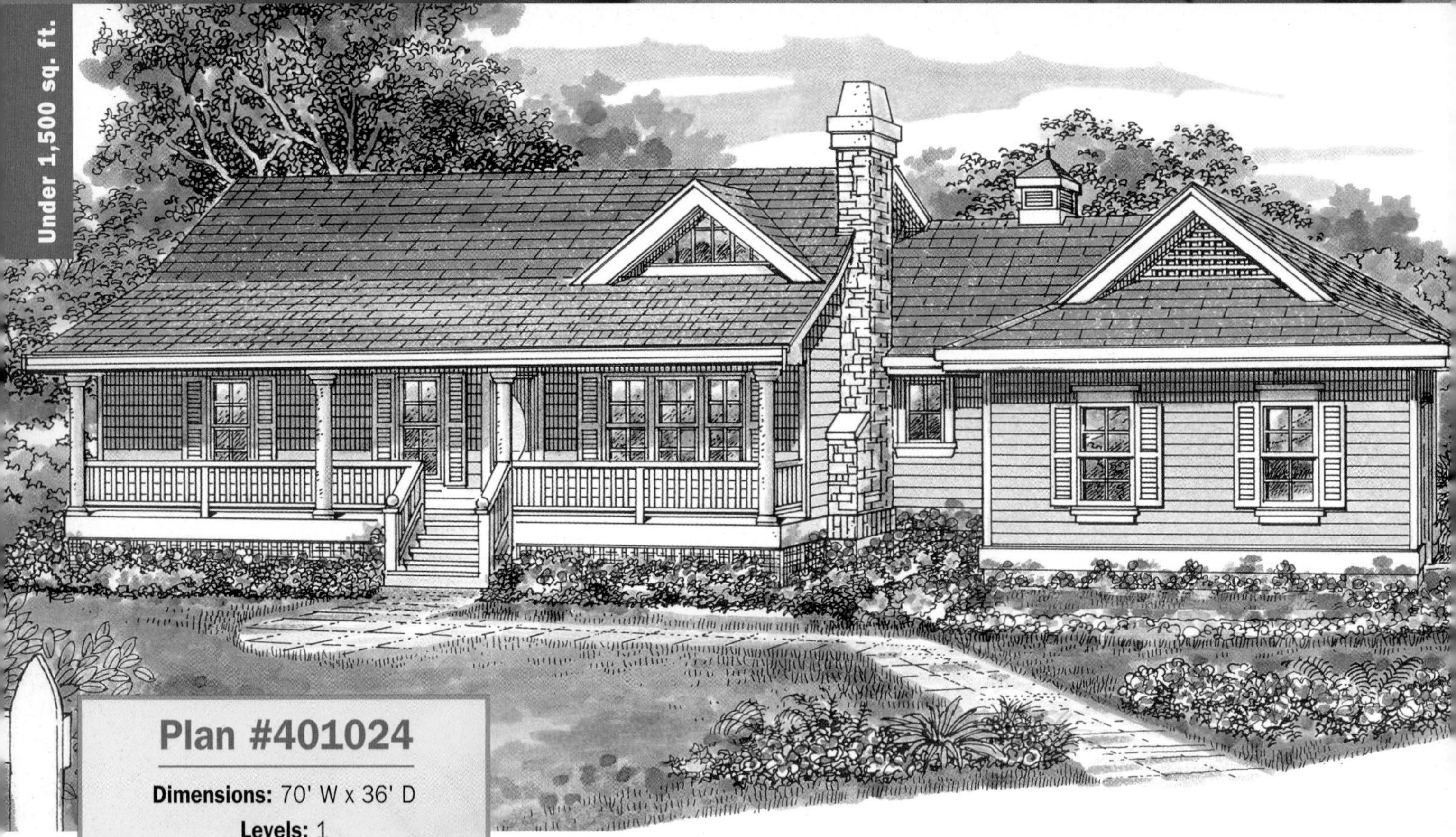

Plan #401024

Dimensions: 70' W x 36' D
Levels: 1
Heated Square Footage: 1,298
Bedrooms: 3
Bathrooms: 2
Foundation: Basement
Materials List Available: Yes
Price Category: B

CAD FILE AVAILABLE

A front veranda, cedar lattice, and a solid-stone chimney enhance the appeal of this one-story country-style home.

Features:

- Great Room: The open plan begins with this great room, which includes a fireplace and a plant ledge over the wall separating the living space from the country kitchen.
- Kitchen: This U-shaped kitchen provides an island work counter and sliding glass doors to the rear deck and screened porch.
- Master Suite: This area has a wall closet and a private bath with window seat.

Images provided by designer/architect.

Copyright by designer/architect.

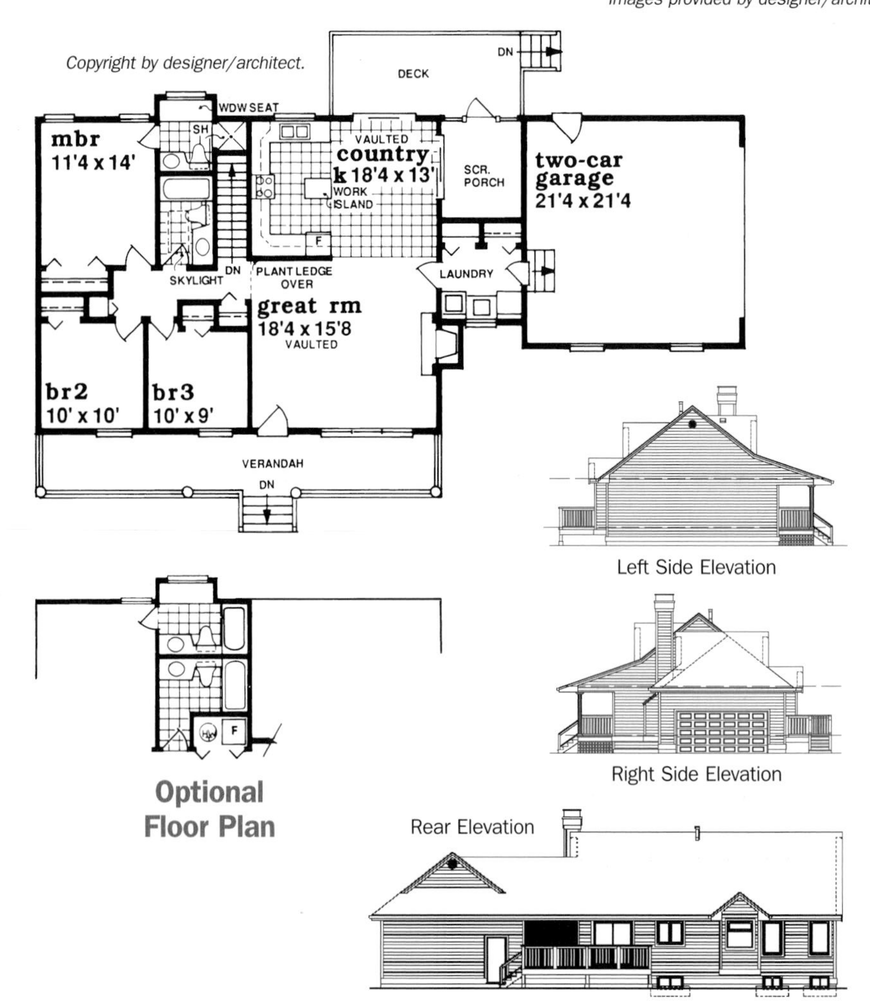

Optional Floor Plan

Left Side Elevation

Right Side Elevation

Rear Elevation

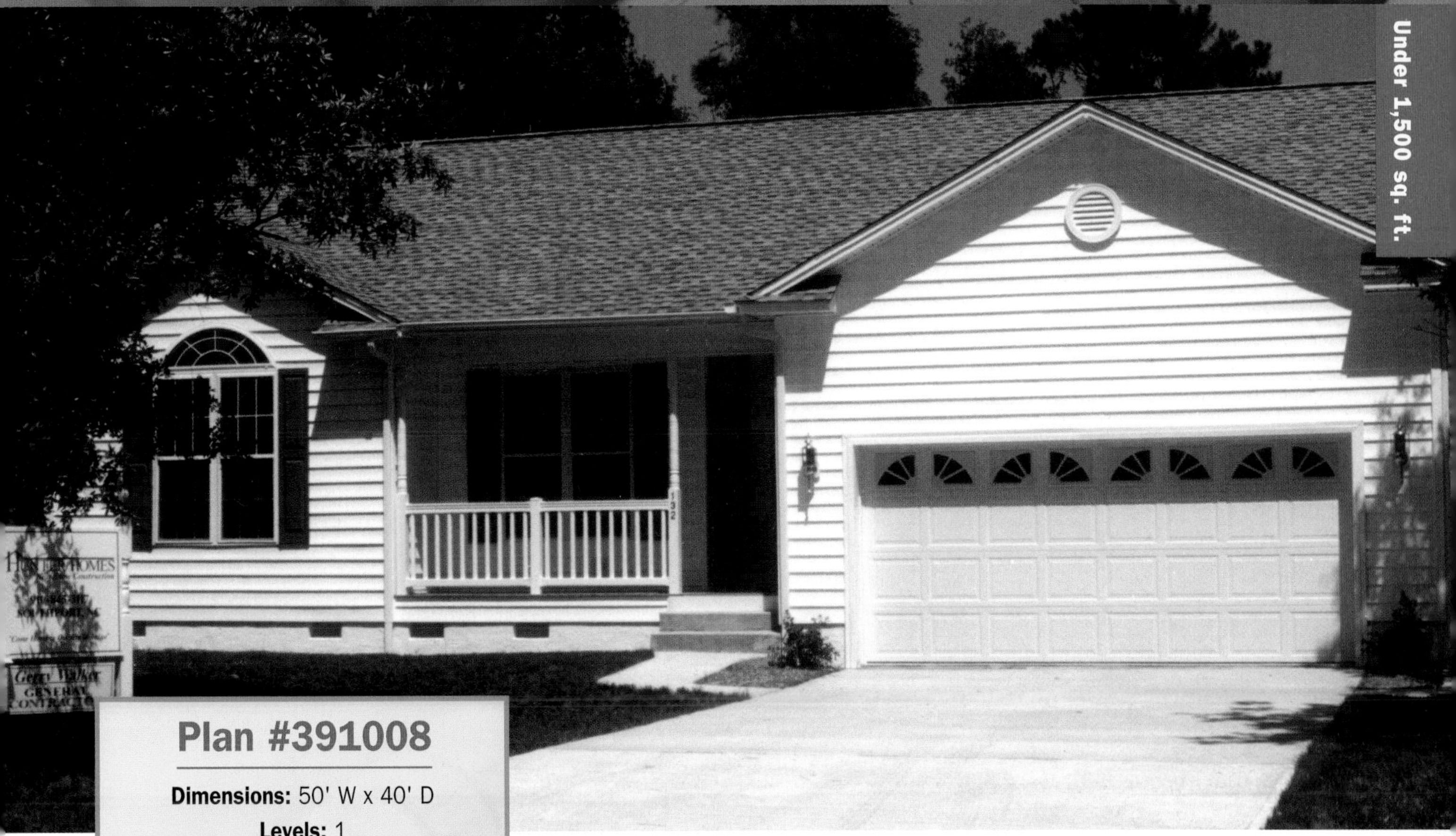

Plan #391008

Dimensions: 50' W x 40' D
Levels: 1
Heated Square Footage: 1,312
Bedrooms: 3
Bathrooms: 2
Foundation: Crawl space, slab, or basement
Materials List Available: Yes
Price Category: B

Images provided by designer/architect.

Here's the sum of brains and beauty, which will please all types of families, from starters and nearly empty nesters to those going golden.

Features:

- Entry: This restful fresh-air porch and formal foyer bring you graciously toward the great room, with its fireplace and vaulted ceiling.
- Dining Room: This adjacent dining room features sliding doors to the deck and smooth open access to the U-shaped kitchen.
- Laundry Room: The laundry area has its own separate landing from the garage, so it's conveniently out of the way.
- Master Suite: This master suite with tray ceilings features nearly "limitless" closet space, a private bath, and large hall linen closet.
- Bedrooms: The two secondary bedrooms, also with roomy closets, share a full bath. Bedroom 3 easily becomes a home office with direct foyer access and a window overlooking the porch.

Copyright by designer/architect.

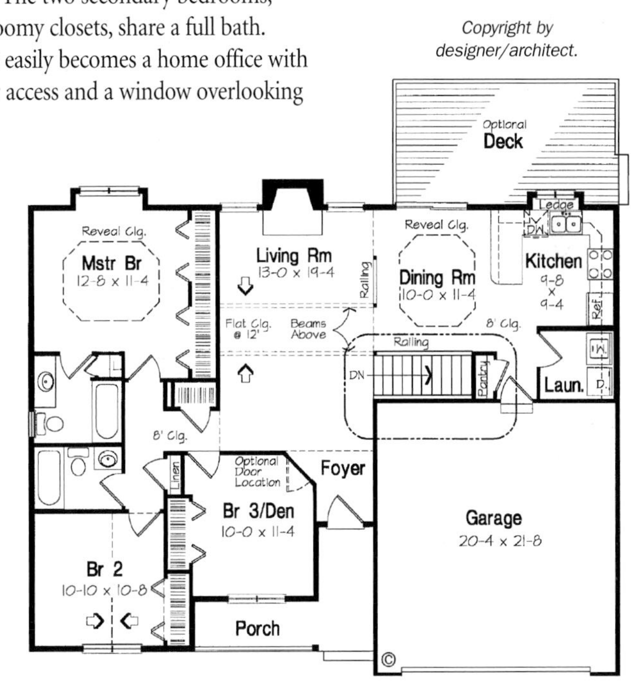

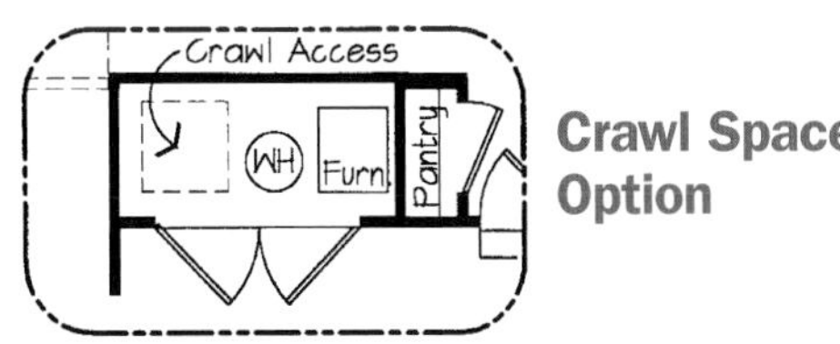

Crawl Space Option

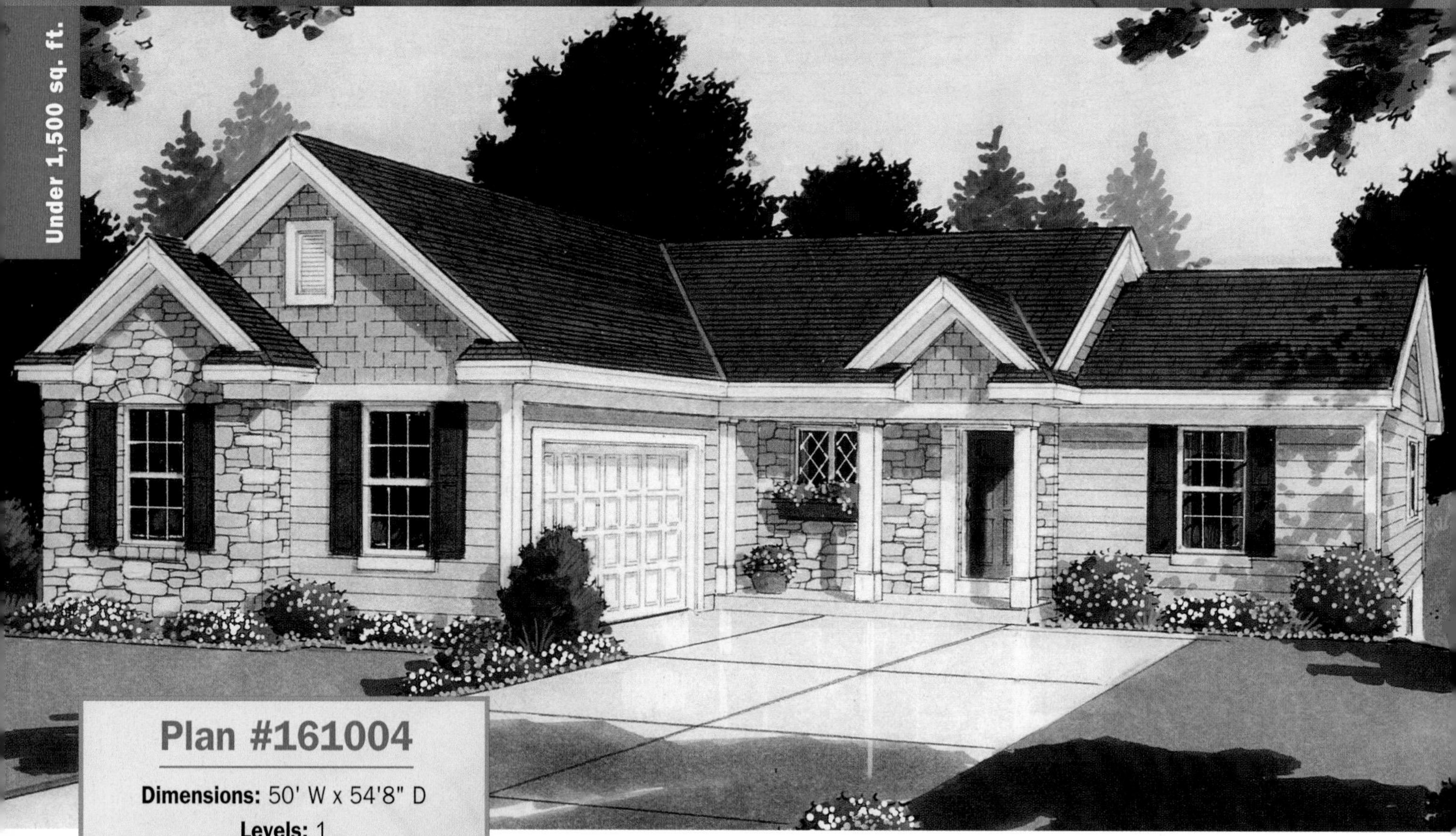

Plan #161004

Dimensions: 50' W x 54'8" D
Levels: 1
Heated Square Footage: 1,315
Bedrooms: 3
Bathrooms: 2
Foundation: Basement
Materials List Available: Yes
Price Category: B

Images provided by designer/architect.

This multi-featured ranch has a covered porch, a ceiling that slopes to an 11-ft. height, an optional library, and a full basement to enhance your living enjoyment.

Features:

- Great Room: Experience the expansive entertainment area created by this open great room and the dining area. Enjoy the lovely fireplace, with full glass on both sides.
- Kitchen: This kitchen is designed for total convenience and easy work patterns with immediate access to the first-floor laundry area.
- Master Bedroom: This master bedroom, split from the other bedrooms, offers privacy and features tray ceiling design.
- Basement: Designed with the future in mind, this full basement has open stairs leading to it and can be updated to expand your living space.

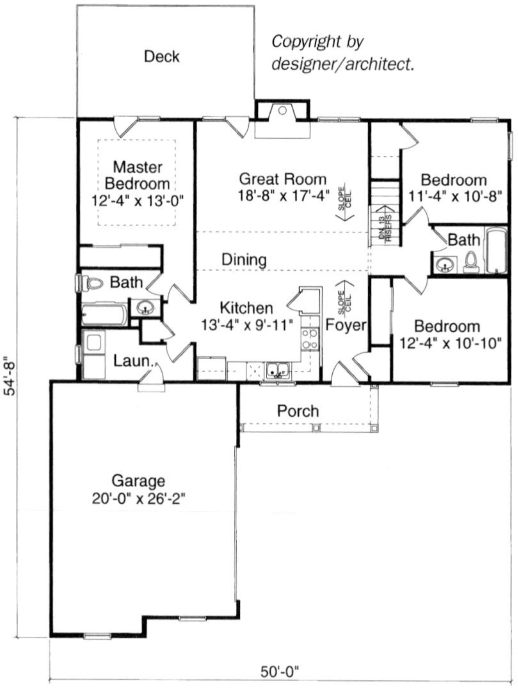

Deck
Copyright by designer/architect.
Master Bedroom 12'-4" x 13'-0"
Great Room 18'-8" x 17'-4"
Bedroom 11'-4" x 10'-8"
Bath
Dining
Bath
Kitchen 13'-4" x 9'-11"
Foyer
Bedroom 12'-4" x 10'-10"
Laun.
Porch
Garage 20'-0" x 26'-2"
54'-8"
50'-0"

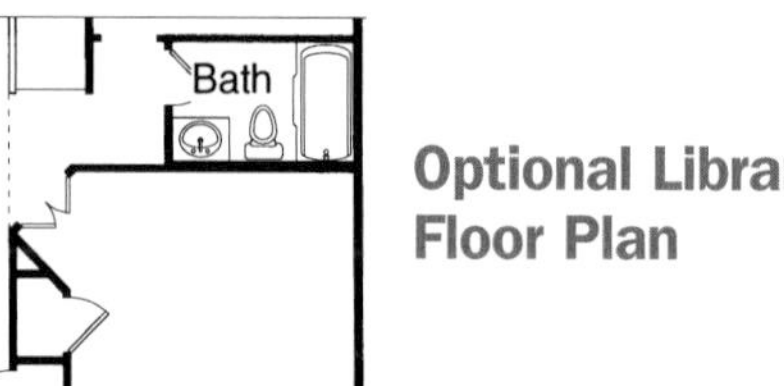

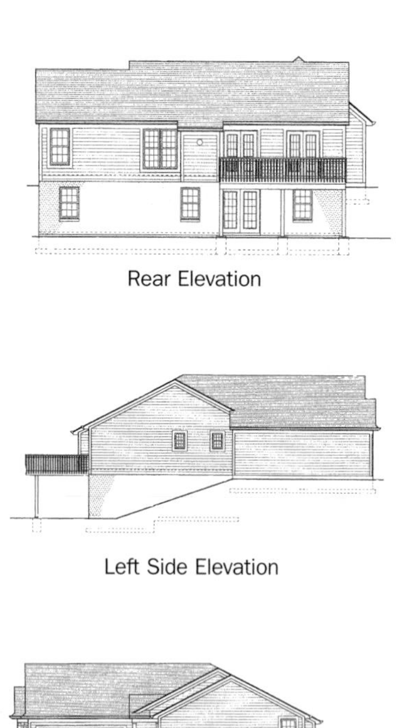

Rear Elevation

Left Side Elevation

Right Side Elevation

Bath
Optional Library Floor Plan

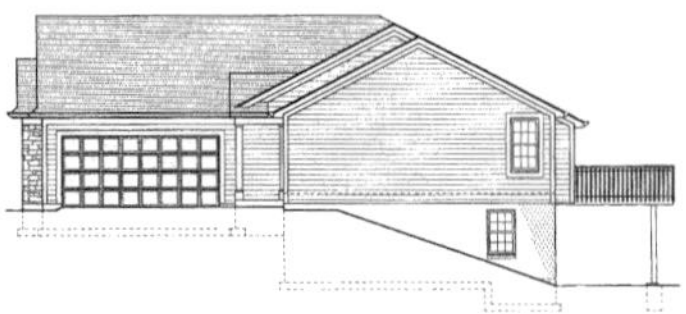

Plan #121121

Dimensions: 47'4" W x 45'8"D
Levels: 1
Heated Square Footage: 1,341
Bedrooms: 3
Bathrooms: 2
Foundation: Basement; crawl space for fee
Materials List Available: Yes
Price Category: C

Images provided by designer/architect.

This traditional home is charming and bound to make your life simpler with all its amenities.

Features:

- Great Room: Already equipped with an entertainment center, bookcase and a fireplace by which you can enjoy those books, this room has endless possibilities. This is a room that will bring the whole family together.
- Kitchen: This design includes everything you need and everything you want: a pantry waiting to be filled with your favorite foods, plenty of workspace, and a snack bar that acts as a useful transition between kitchen and breakfast room.
- Breakfast Room: An extension of the kitchen, this room will fill with the aroma of coffee and a simmering breakfast, so you'll be immersed in your relaxing morning. With peaceful daylight streaming in through a window-lined wall, this will easily become the best part of your day.
- Master Suite: Plenty of breathing room for both of you, there will be no fighting for sink or closet space in this bedroom. The full master bath includes dual sinks, and the walk-in closet will hold everything you both need. Another perk of this bathroom is the whirlpool bathtub.
- Garage: This two-car garage opens directly into the home, so there is no reason to get out of your warm, dry car and into unpleasant weather.

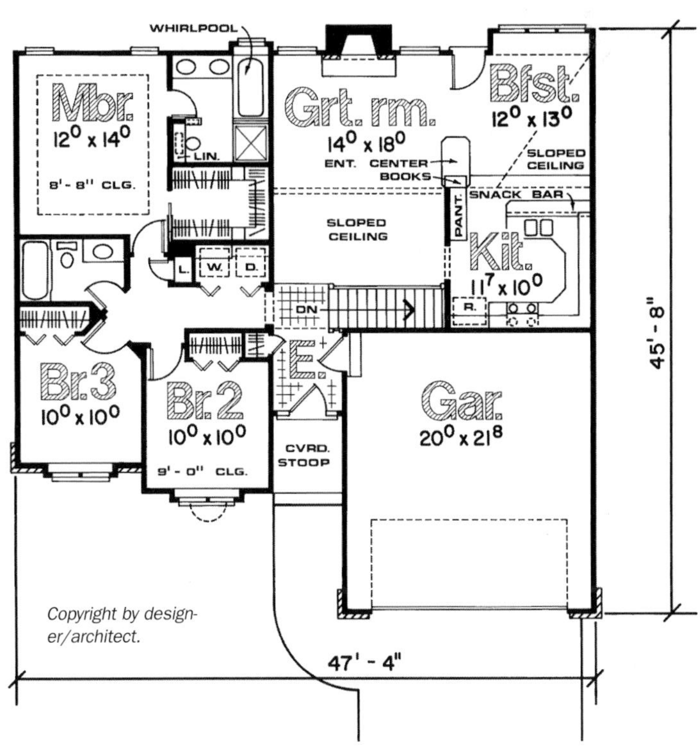

Plan #181727

Dimensions: 60' W x 30' D
Levels: 1
Heated Square Footage: 1,350
Bedrooms: 3
Bathrooms: 1
Foundation: Basement
Materials List Available: Yes
Price Category: B

Images provided by designer/architect.

CAD FILE AVAILABLE

Copyright by designer/architect.

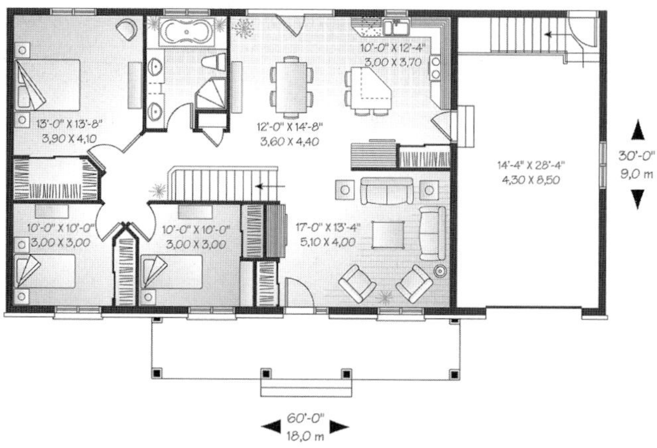

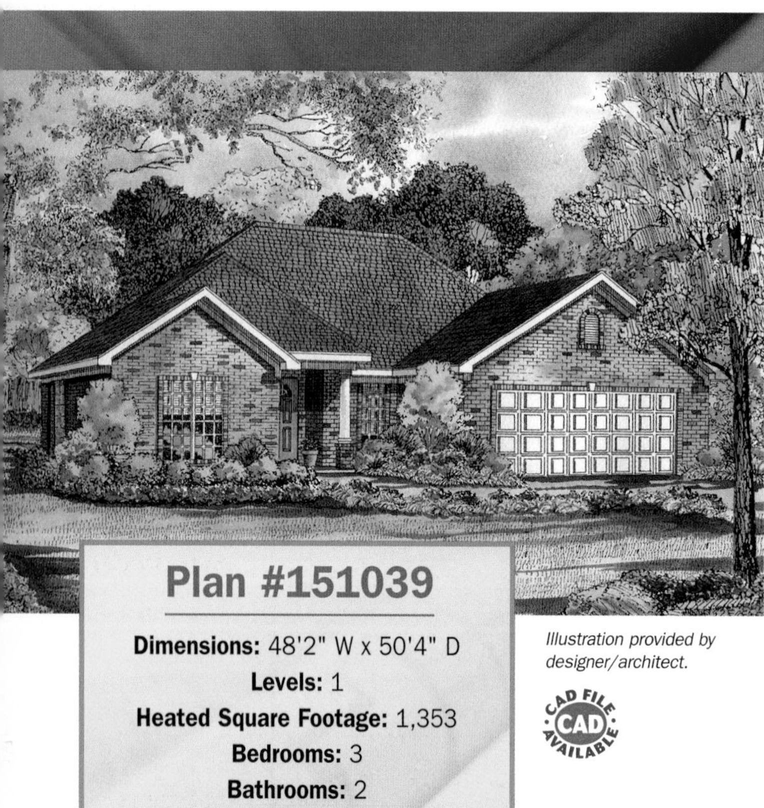

Plan #151039

Dimensions: 48'2" W x 50'4" D
Levels: 1
Heated Square Footage: 1,353
Bedrooms: 3
Bathrooms: 2
Foundation: Crawl space, slab or basement
CompleteCost List Available: Yes
Price Category: B

Illustration provided by designer/architect.

CAD FILE AVAILABLE

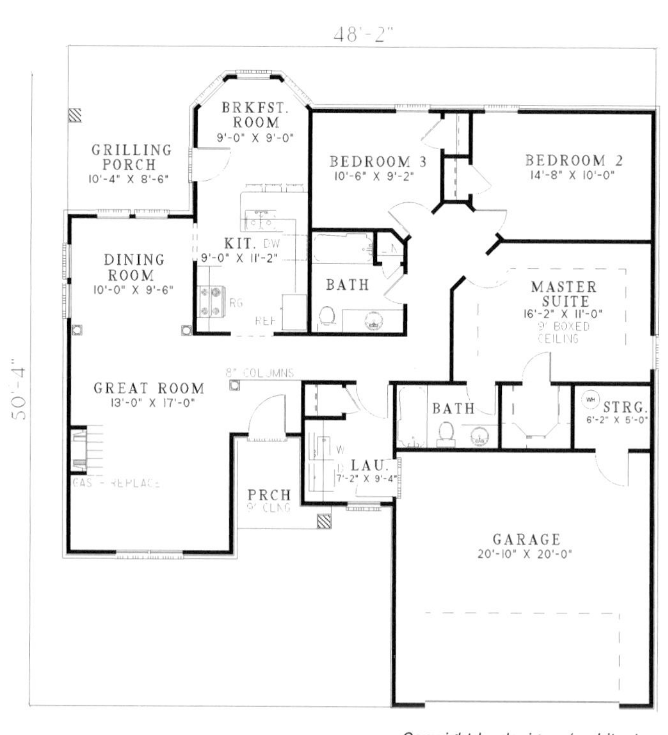

Copyright by designer/architect.

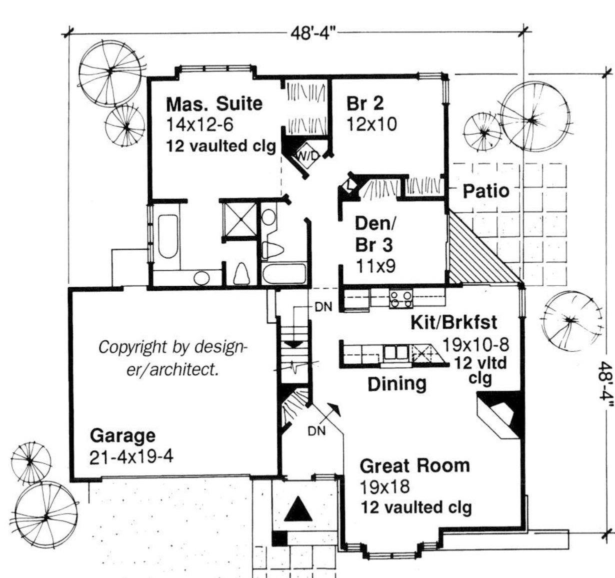

Plan #271005

Dimensions: 48'4" W x 48'4" D
Levels: 1
Heated Square Footage: 1,368
Bedrooms: 3
Bathrooms: 2
Foundation: Basement
Materials List Available: Yes
Price Category: B

Images provided by designer/architect.

SMARTtip

Design with Computers

Consider using a computer-aided design (CAD) program to plan your deck. Some programs let you see three-dimensional views of your design complete with railings, stairs, planters, hot tubs, and the surrounding landscaping.

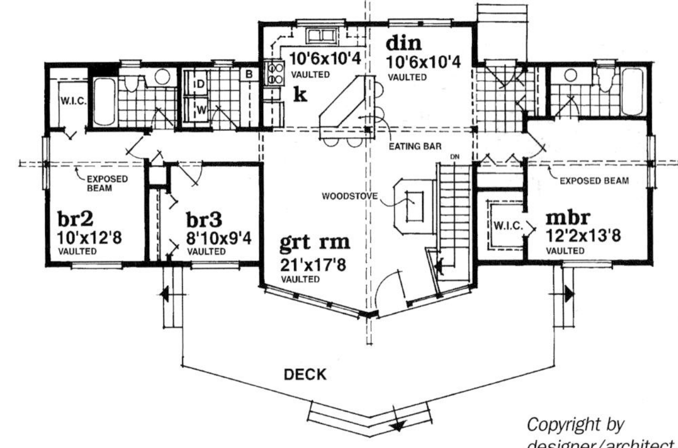

Copyright by designer/architect.

Plan #401033

Dimensions: 62' W x 29' D
Levels: 1
Heated Square Footage: 1,405
Bedrooms: 3
Bathrooms: 2
Foundation: Crawl space or basement
Materials List Available: Yes
Price Category: B

Images provided by designer/architect.

CAD FILE AVAILABLE

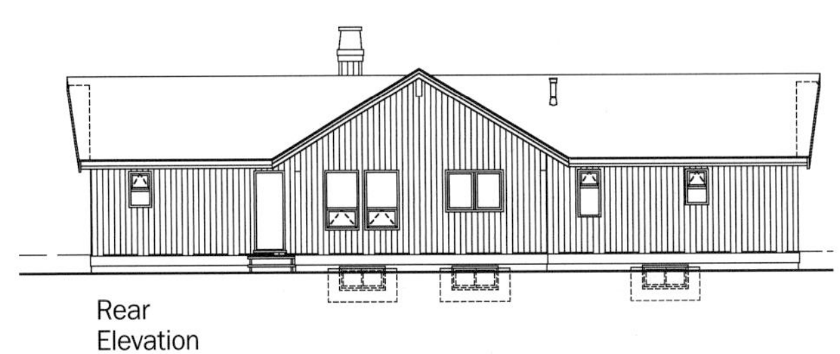

Rear Elevation

Images provided by designer/architect.

Plan #321013

Dimensions: 68' W x 30' D
Levels: 1
Heated Square Footage: 1,360
Bedrooms: 3
Bathrooms: 2
Foundation: Basement
Materials List Available: Yes
Price Category: B

CAD FILE AVAILABLE

This efficiently designed home has an abundance of space for the growing family.

Features:

- Covered Porch: This large covered porch welcomes you home, providing the perfect place to sit and relax.
- Family Room: With its large size, cozy fireplace, and convenient connection to the kitchen, this family room is wonderful for both entertaining and relaxing.
- Kitchen: You will love to cook in this beautiful kitchen, which features a pantry and an island.
- Master Suite: Located in the rear of the home, this spacious master suite features a spacious bath and a walk-in closet. Window placement allows for many possible furniture arrangements.
- Secondary Bedrooms: Equal-size rooms will help eliminate quarrels on who has the larger room. Both rooms feature large closets.

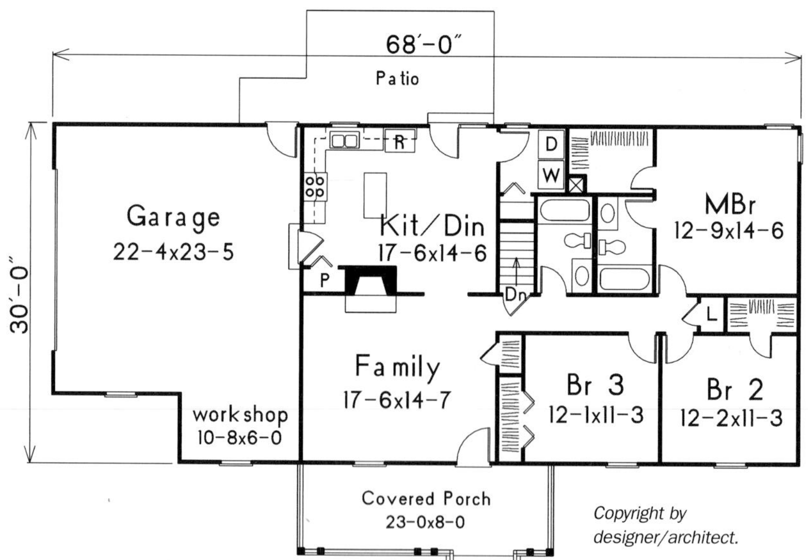

Copyright by designer/architect.

Images provided by designer/architect.

Plan #251003

Dimensions: 42' W x 42' D
Levels: 1
Heated Square Footage: 1,393
Bedrooms: 3
Bathrooms: 2
Foundation: Crawl space or slab
Materials List Available: Yes
Price Category: B

Come home to this three-bedroom home with front porch and unattached garage.

Features:

- Family Room: This room feels large and warm, with its high ceiling and cozy fireplace.
- Kitchen: This island kitchen with dining area has plenty of cabinet space.
- Master Bedroom: This large master bedroom features a walk-in closet and a view of the backyard.
- Master Bath: Located in the rear of the home, this master bath features a soaking tub and a separate shower.

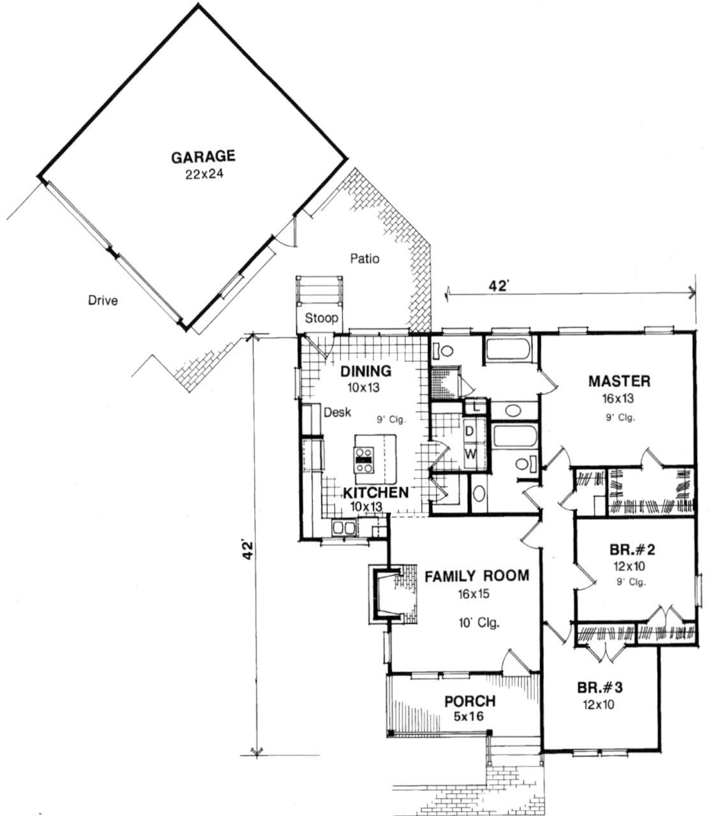

Copyright by designer/architect.

Plan #131014

Dimensions: 48' W x 43'4" D
Levels: 1
Heated Square Footage: 1,380
Bedrooms: 3
Bathrooms: 2
Foundation: Crawl space, slab, or basement
Materials List Available: Yes
Price Category: C

CAD FILE AVAILABLE

Images provided by designer/architect.

The exterior of this home looks formal, thanks to its twin dormers, gables, and the bay windows that flank the columned porch, but the inside is contemporary in both design and features.

Features:

- Great Room: Centrally located, this great room has a 10-ft. ceiling. A fireplace, built-in cabinets, and windows that overlook the rear covered porch make it as practical as it is attractive.
- Dining Room: A bay window adds to the charm of this versatile room.
- Kitchen: This U-shaped room is designed to make cooking and cleaning jobs efficient.
- Master Suite: With a bay window, a walk-in closet, and a private bath with an oval tub, the master suite may be your favorite area.
- Additional Bedrooms: Located on the opposite side of the house from the master suite, these rooms share a full bath in the hall.

Living Room

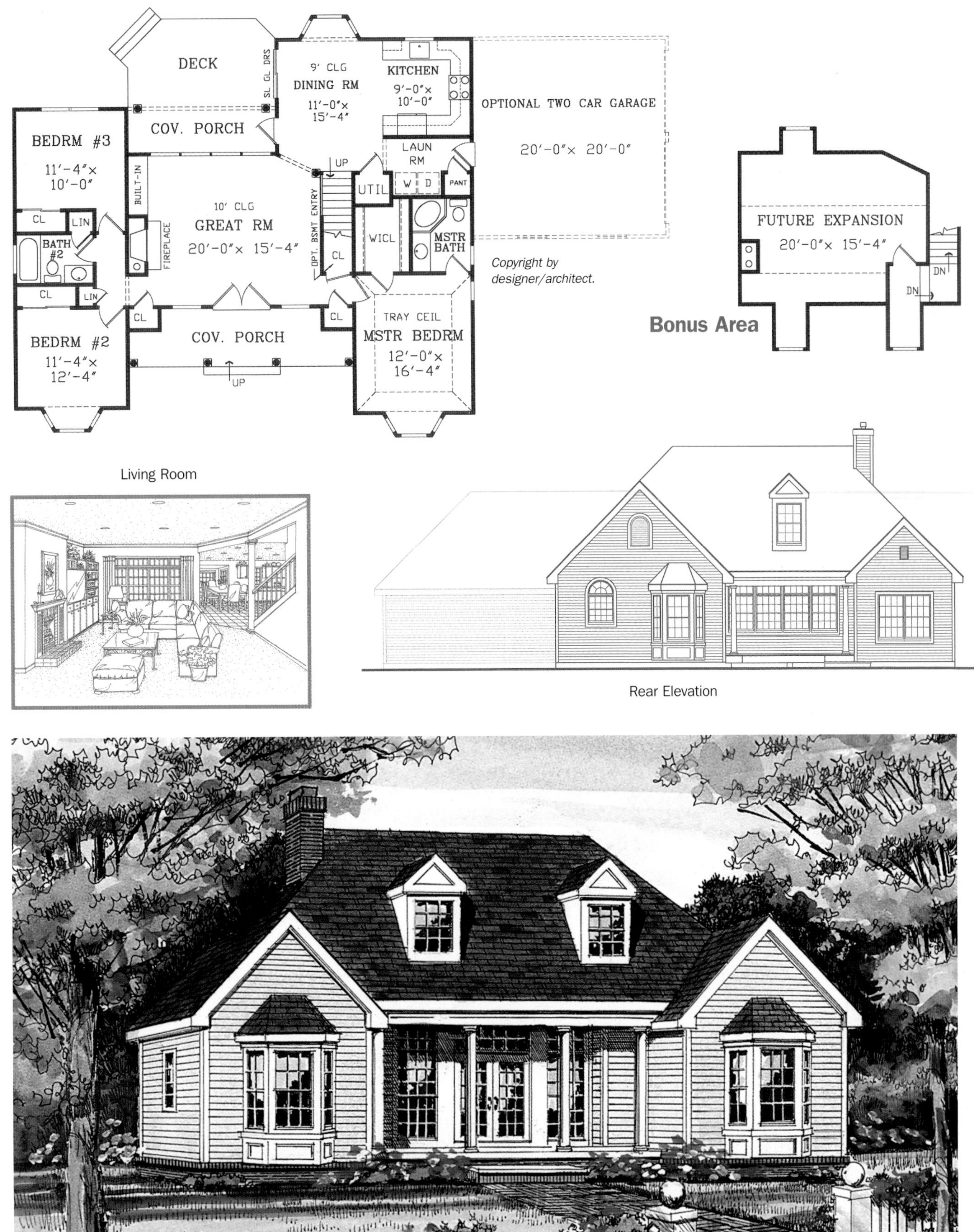

Copyright by designer/architect.

Bonus Area

Living Room

Rear Elevation

Plan #321002

Dimensions: 72' W x 28' D
Levels: 1
Heated Square Footage: 1,400
Bedrooms: 3
Bathrooms: 2
Foundation: Crawl space, basement
Materials List Available: Yes
Price Category: D

Images provided by designer/architect.

CAD FILE AVAILABLE

If you're looking for a well-designed compact home with contemporary amenities, this could be the home of your dreams.

Features:

- Porch: Just the right size for some rockers and a swing, this porch could become your outdoor living area when the weather is fine.
- Living Room: A vaulted ceiling adds to the spacious feeling in this room, where friends and family are sure to gather.
- Kitchen: This space-saving design, in combination with the ample counter and cabinet space, makes cooking a pleasure.
- Utility Room: This large room is fitted with cabinets for extra storage space. You'll find storage space in the large garage, too.
- Master Bedroom: This room is somewhat secluded for privacy, making it an ideal place for some quiet time at the end of the day.

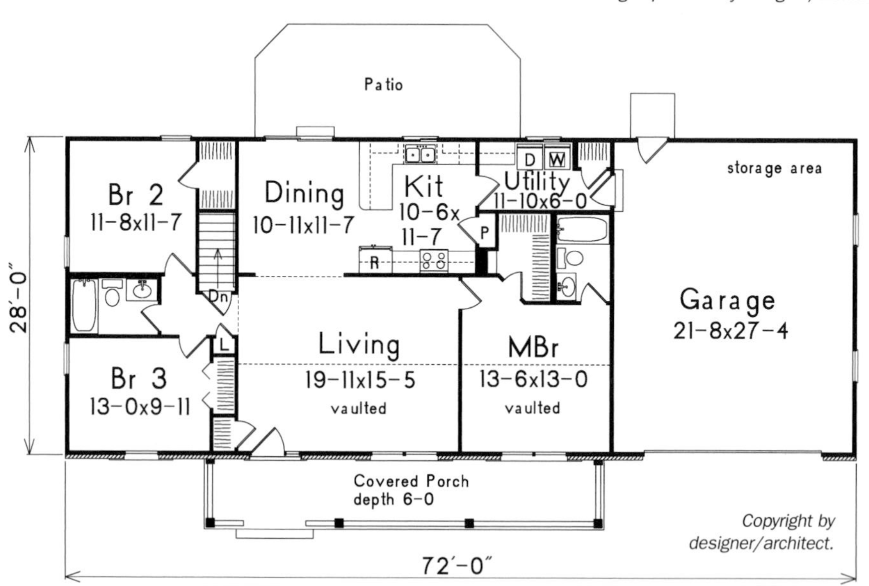

Copyright by designer/architect.

SMARTtip

Fabric Draping Ability

Test a fabric's draping ability by looking at a large piece in a fabric store. Gather at least two to three yards of material, holding one end in your hand. Check how it drapes. Does it fall into folds easily? Also look at the pattern when it is gathered. Does the design become lost in the folds? Ask a salesclerk or a friend to hold the fabric, and look at it from a few feet away.

Plan #351009

Dimensions: 54' W x 47' D
Levels: 1
Heated Square Footage: 1,400
Bedrooms: 3
Bathrooms: 2
Foundation: Crawl space, slab, or basement
Materials List Available: Yes
Price Category: D

CAD FILE AVAILABLE

Images provided by designer/architect.

This design offers a great value in space planning by using the open concept, with split bedrooms, in a layout that is easy to build.

Features:

- Ceilings: All ceilings are a minimum of 9-ft. high.
- Great Room: This large gathering area provides room for family activities as well as being open to the kitchen and dining area.
- Master Suite: This oversized private area provides a great bathroom arrangement for busy couples as well as a large walk-in closet.
- Bedrooms: The split bedroom layout provides zoned privacy and improved noise control.
- Patio: This area is the perfect place to enjoy the afternoons grilling out or relaxing with friends and family.

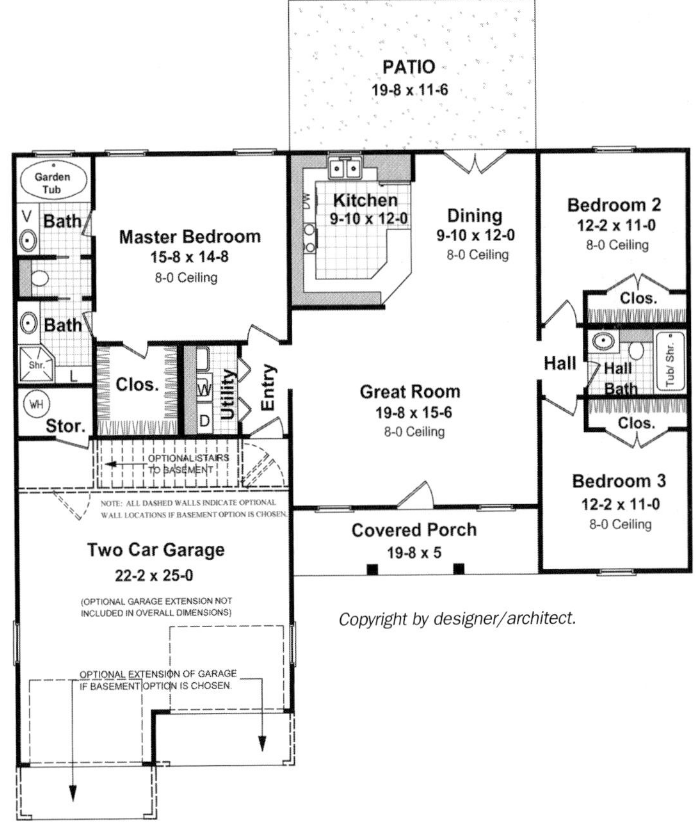

Copyright by designer/architect.

DECK
SOAKER TUB
BOX WINDOW
WORKSHOP
LDR
country k 18'11 x 13'4 vaulted
WORK ISLAND
RAILING
mbr 12' x 14'4
SKYLIGHT
DN
POT LEDGE OVER CLOSETS
ART NICHE
two-car garage 21'6 x 19'6
grt rm 20' x 13'4 vaulted
br3 12' x 10'
br2 12' x 10'
VERANDAH
RAILING

Plan #401025

Dimensions: 70' W x 34' D
Levels: 1
Heated Square Footage: 1,408
Bedrooms: 3
Bathrooms: 2
Foundation: Crawl space, basement
Materials List Available: Yes
Price Category: B

Images provided by designer/architect.

CAD FILE AVAILABLE

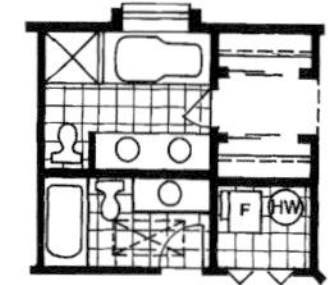

Optional Floor Plan

Copyright by designer/architect.

Rear Elevation

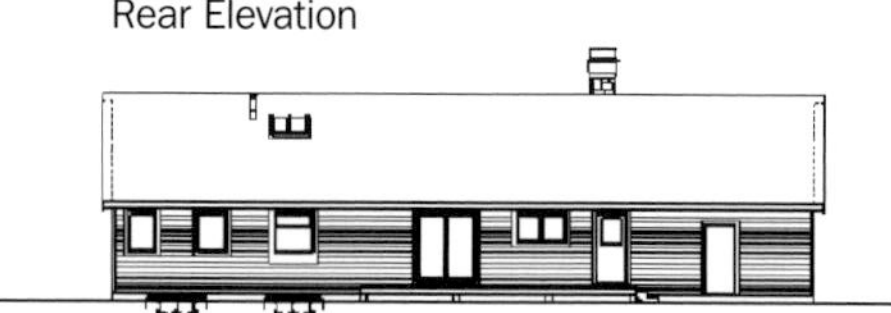

Plan #341128

Dimensions: 76'10" W x 40'10" D
Levels: 1
Heated Square Footage: 1,410
Bedrooms: 3
Bathrooms: 2
Foundation: Crawl space, slab, basement, or walkout
Materials List Available: Yes
Price Category: B

Images provided by designer/architect.

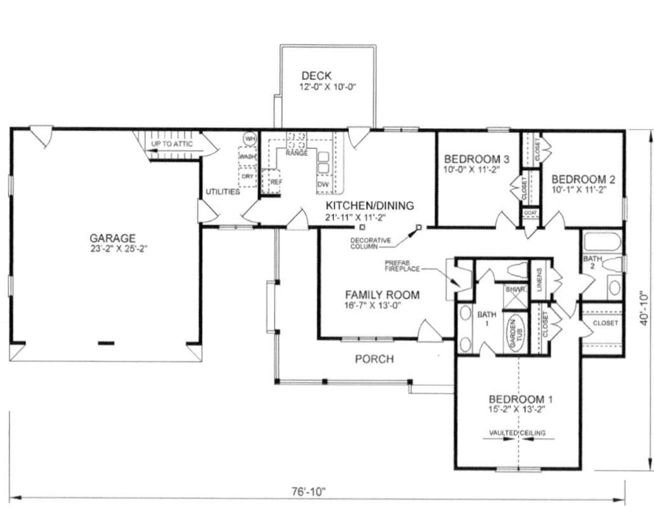

Copyright by designer/architect.

Plan #321330

Dimensions: 66' W x 30' D
Levels: 1
Heated Square Footage: 1,414
Bedrooms: 3
Bathrooms: 2
Foundation: Crawl space, slab or basement
Materials List Available: Yes
Price Category: B

Images provided by designer/architect.

CAD FILE AVAILABLE

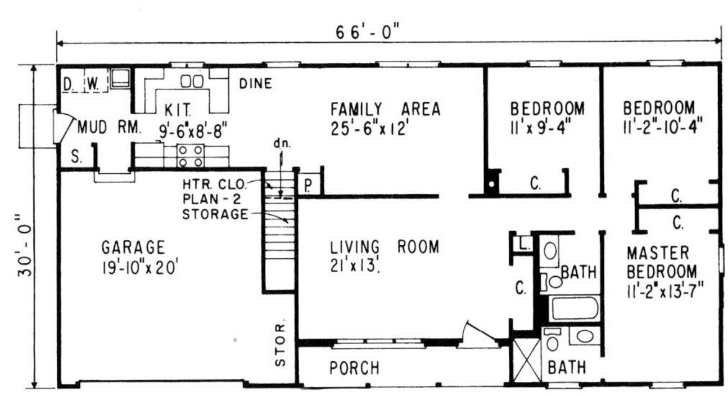

Copyright by designer/architect.

Plan #211024

Dimensions: 61' W x 44' D
Levels: 1
Heated Square Footage: 1,418
Bedrooms: 3
Bathrooms: 2
Foundation: Slab
Materials List Available: Yes
Price Category: B

Images provided by designer/architect.

CAD FILE AVAILABLE

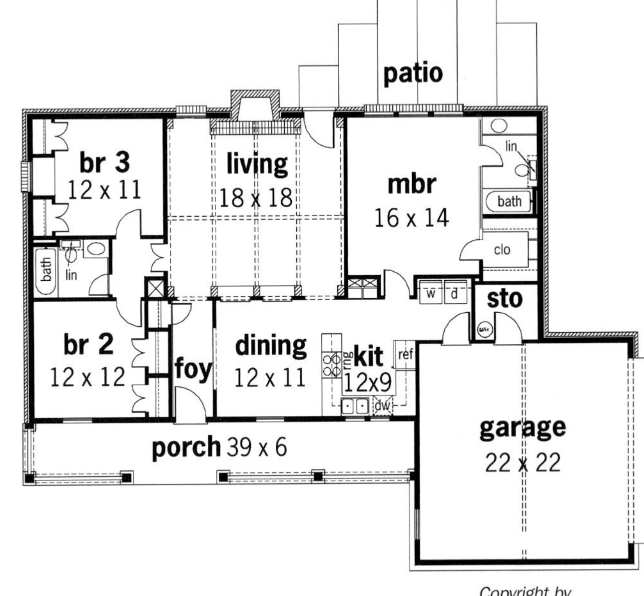

Copyright by designer/architect.

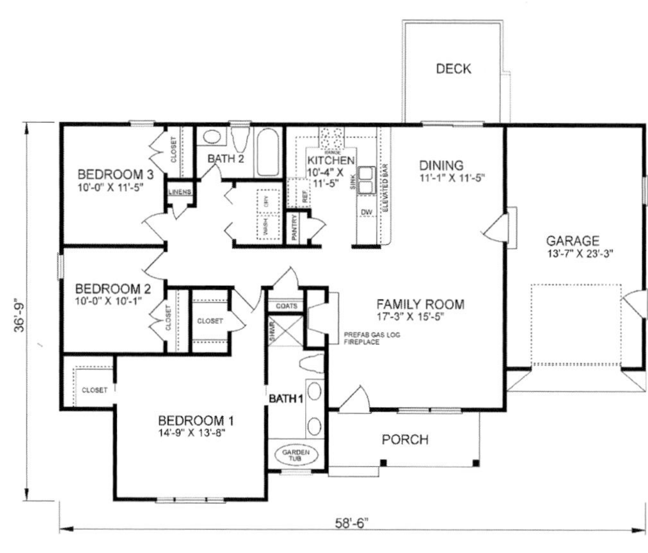

Plan #341064

Dimensions: 58'6" W x 36'9" D
Levels: 1
Heated Square Footage: 1,418
Bedrooms: 3
Bathrooms: 2
Foundation: Crawl space, slab, basement, or walkout
Materials List Available: Yes
Price Category: B

Images provided by designer/architect.

CAD FILE AVAILABLE

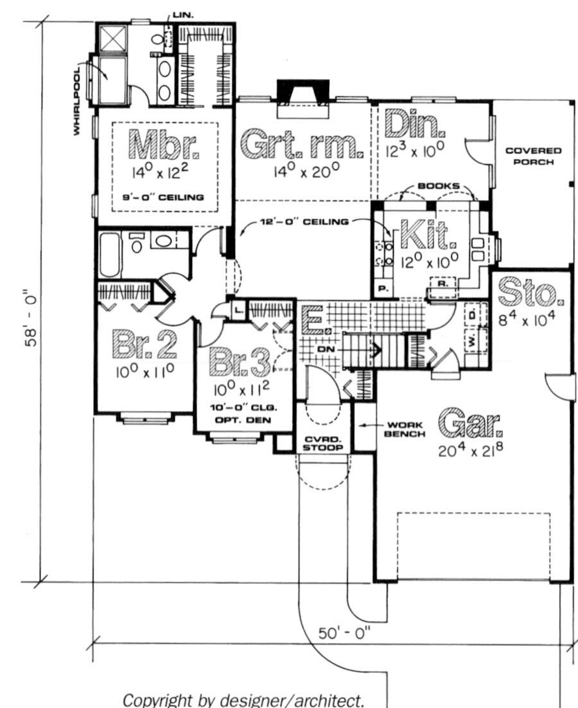

Plan #121009

Dimensions: 50' W x 58' D
Levels: 1
Heated Square Footage: 1,422
Bedrooms: 3
Bathrooms: 2
Foundation: Basement; crawl space or slab for fee
Materials List Available: Yes
Price Category: B

Images provided by designer/architect.

CAD FILE AVAILABLE

Plan #371030

Dimensions: 38'10" W x 64'4" D
Levels: 1
Heated Square Footage: 1,434
Bedrooms: 3
Bathrooms: 2
Foundation: Slab
Materials List Available: No
Price Category: B

Images provided by designer/architect.

Copyright by designer/architect.

Plan #371049

Dimensions: 52' W x 45' D
Levels: 1
Heated Square Footage: 1,440
Bedrooms: 3
Bathrooms: 2
Foundation: Slab
Materials List Available: No
Price Category: B

Images provided by designer/architect.

52'-0"
45'-0"
10'-0" HIGH CLG.
DINING RM.
10'-0" x 11'-2"
PORCH
CLG. SLOPES TO 10'-0"
MASTER SUITE
12'-0" X 14'-0"
MARBLE TUB
BATH 1
GLASS SHR.
SINK
D.W.
KITCH.
11'-4" x 12'-0"
REF.
10'-0" HIGH CLG.
LIVING RM.
20'-0" X 14'-2"
BKS.
HEARTH
FIRE PLACE
W.
D.
UT.
PANTRY
STORAGE
LIN.
B.2
ENT.
W/H
BED RM.3
11'-6" X 11'-0"
BED RM.2
11'-0" X 11'-0"
GARAGE
19'-6" X 20'-0"
P.

Copyright by designer/architect.

Plan #221016

Dimensions: 56' W x 42' D
Levels: 1
Heated Square Footage: 1,461
Bedrooms: 3
Bathrooms: 2
Foundation: Basement
Materials List Available: No
Price Category: B

Images provided by designer/architect.

The interesting roofline and classic siding give this traditional ranch home an instant appeal.

CAD FILE CAD AVAILABLE

Features:

- Ceiling Height: 8 ft.
- Great Room: From the entry, you'll look into this great room, where a handsome fireplace with large flanking windows makes you feel at home.
- Dining Room: Open to the great room, this room features access to the rear deck. An eating island shared with the kitchen allows the whole living area to flow together.
- Kitchen: The step-saving layout and ample counter space will delight the family chef.
- Master Suite: With a large walk-in closet and deluxe bath with a whirlpool tub, separate shower, and two-sink vanity, this private area will become a real retreat at the end of the day.
- Additional Bedrooms: Add the optional door from the entry to transform bedroom #2 into a quiet den, or use it as a bedroom.

Rear Elevation

Copyright by designer/architect.

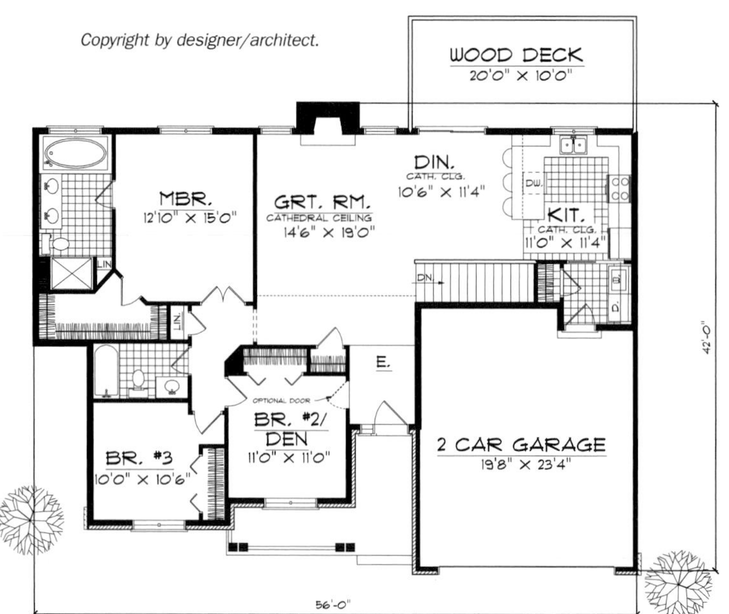

Plan #131003

Dimensions: 60' W x 39'10" D
Levels: 1
Heated Square Footage: 1,466
Bedrooms: 3
Bathrooms: 2
Foundation: Crawl space, slab or basement
Materials List Available: Yes
Price Category: C

Images provided by designer/architect.

Copyright by designer/architect.

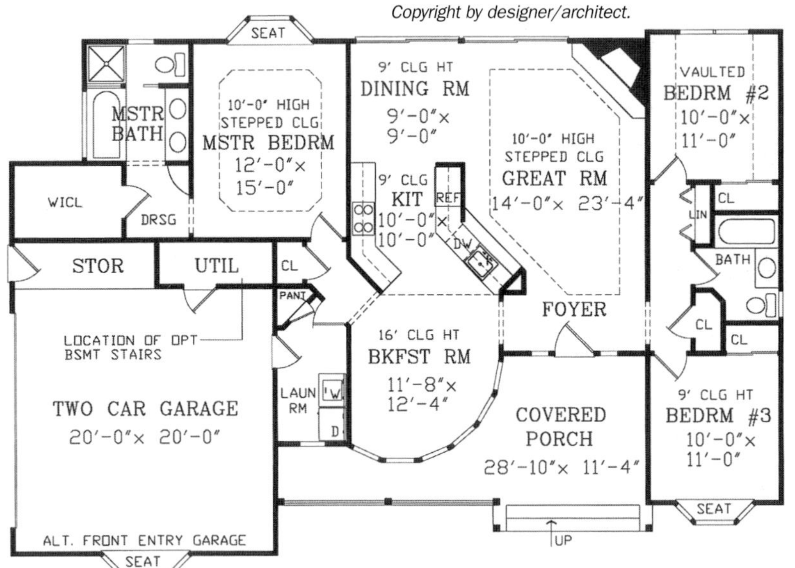

Victorian styling adds elegance to this compact and easy-to-maintain ranch design.

Features:

- Ceiling Height: 8 ft.
- Foyer: Bridging between the front door and the great room, this foyer is a surprise feature.
- Great Room: A 10-ft. ceiling adds to the spacious feeling of this room, while the corner fireplace gives it an intimate feeling. Sliding glass doors at the rear of the room open to the backyard.
- Dining Room: This formal room adjoins the great room, allowing guests and family to flow between the rooms.
- Breakfast Room: Turrets add a Victorian feeling to this room that's just off the kitchen and overlooks the front porch.
- Master Suite: Privacy is assured in this suite, which is separated from the main part of the house. A compartmented bath and large walk-in closet add convenience to its beauty.

Breakfast Room

Plan #151529

Dimensions: 43' W x 66'6" D
Levels: 1
Heated Square Footage: 1,474
Bedrooms: 2
Bathrooms: 2
Foundation: Crawl space or slab
CompleteCost List Available: Yes
Price Category: B

Images provided by designer/architect.

This elegant design is reflective of the Arts and Crafts era. Copper roofing and carriage style garage doors warmly welcome guests into this split-bedroom plan.

Features:

- Great Room: With access to the grilling porch as a bonus, this large gathering area features a 10-ft.-high ceiling and a beautiful fireplace.
- Kitchen: This fully equipped island kitchen has a raised bar and a built-in pantry. The area is open to the great room and dining room, giving an open and airy feeling to the home.
- Master Suite: Located on the opposite side of the home from the secondary bedroom, this retreat offers a large sleeping area and two large closets. The master bath features a spa tub, a separate shower, and dual vanities.
- Bedroom: This secondary bedroom has a large closet and access to the full bathroom in the hallway.

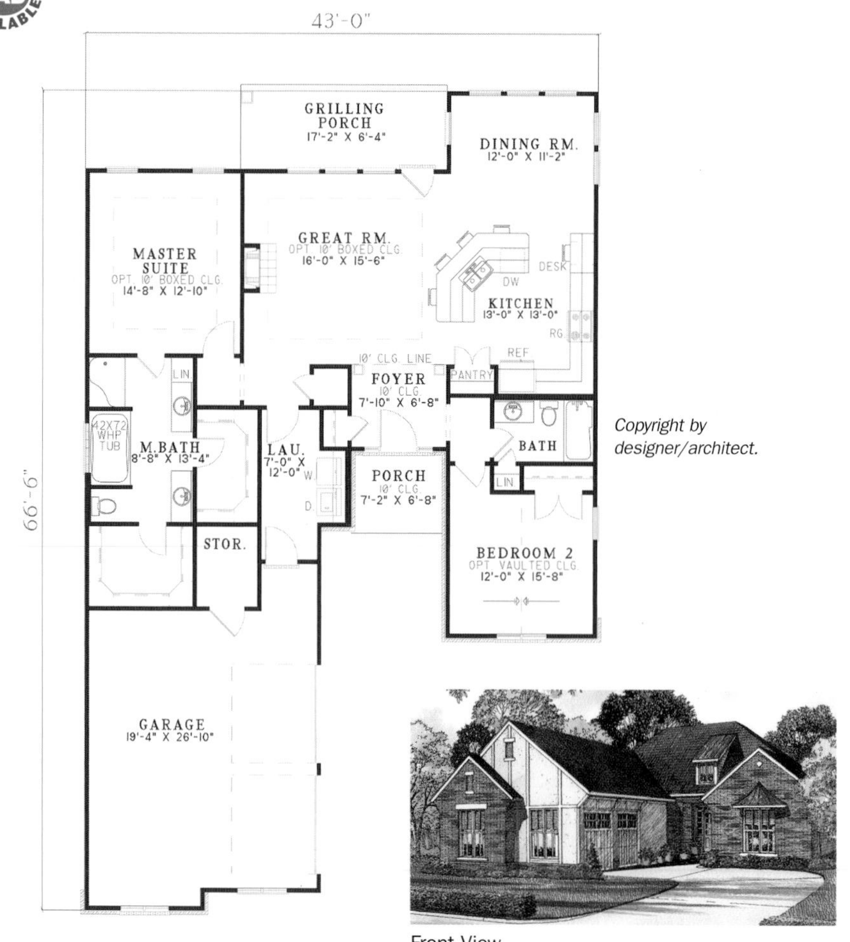

Copyright by designer/architect.

Front View

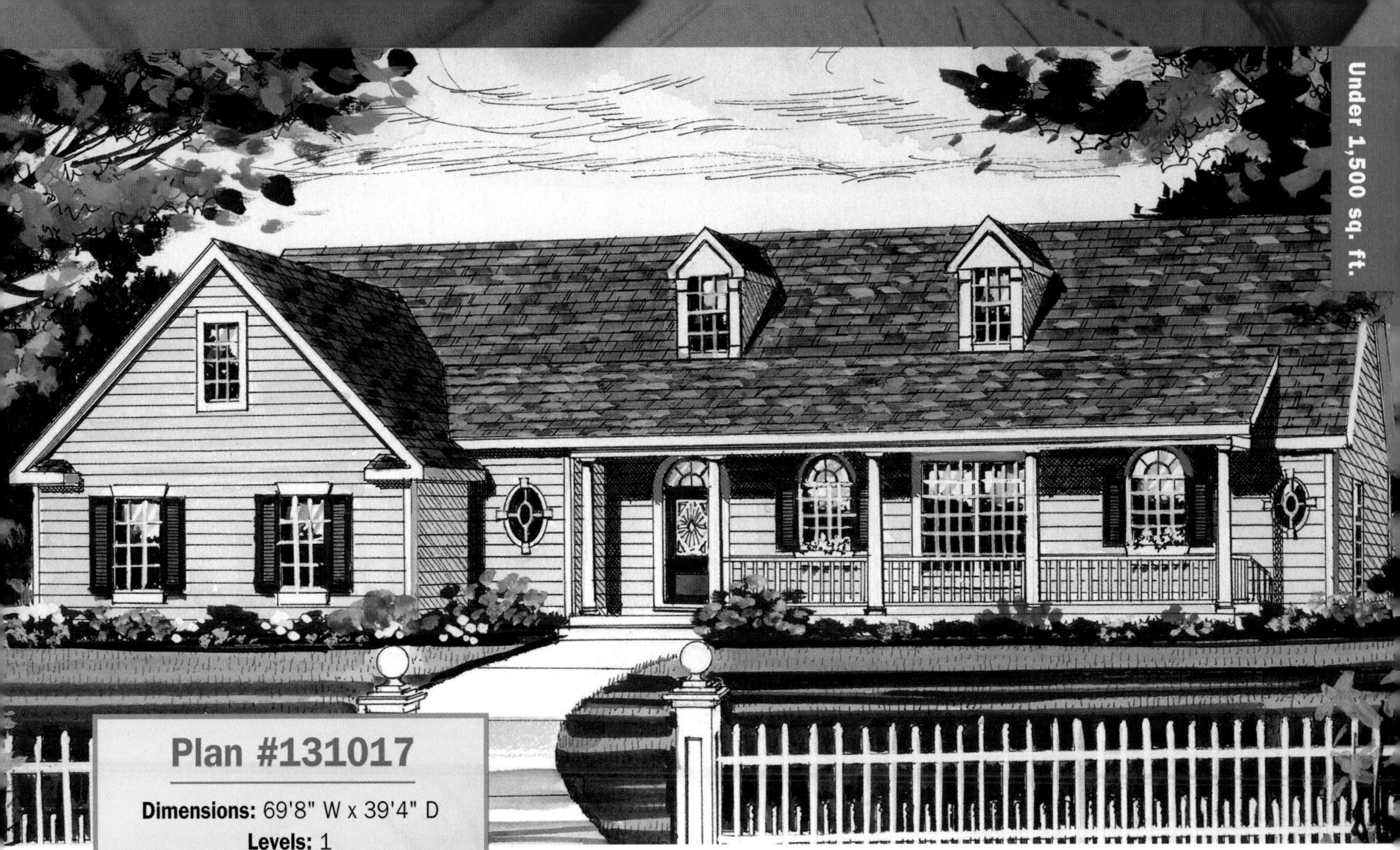

Plan #131017

Dimensions: 69'8" W x 39'4" D
Levels: 1
Heated Square Footage: 1,480
Bedrooms: 3
Bathrooms: 2
Foundation: Crawl space, slab, or basement
Materials List Available: Yes
Price Category: C

Images provided by designer/architect.

This fully accessible home is designed for wheelchair access to every area, giving everyone true enjoyment and freedom of movement.

Features:

- Great Room: Facing towards the rear, this great room features a volume ceiling that adds to the spacious feeling of the room.
- Kitchen: Designed for total convenience and easy work patterns, this kitchen also offers a view out to the covered front porch.
- Master Bedroom: Enjoy the quiet in this room which is sure to become your favorite place to relax at the end of the day.
- Additional Bedrooms: Both rooms have easy access to a full bath and feature nicely sized closet spaces.
- Garage: Use the extra space in this attached garage for storage.

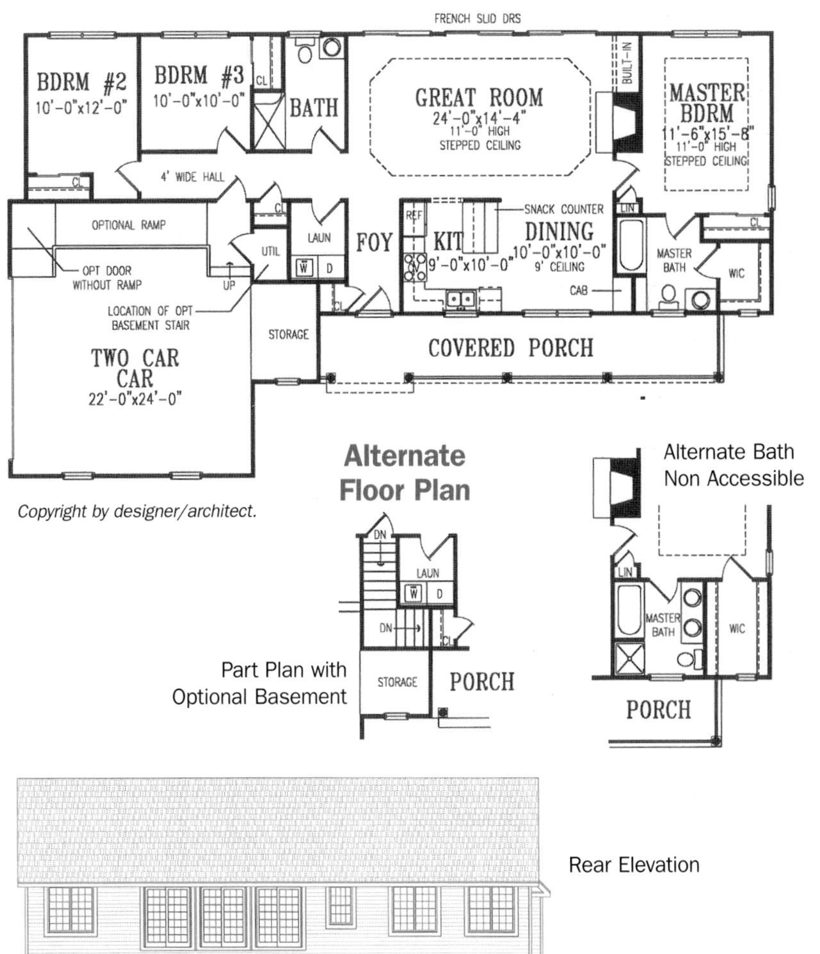

Copyright by designer/architect.

Alternate Floor Plan

Part Plan with Optional Basement

Alternate Bath Non Accessible

Rear Elevation

Plan #341023

Dimensions: 72'7" W x 34' D
Levels: 1
Heated Square Footage: 1,469
Bedrooms: 3
Bathrooms: 2
Foundation: Crawl space, slab, or basement
Materials List Available: Yes
Price Category: B

Images provided by designer/architect.

Copyright by designer/architect.

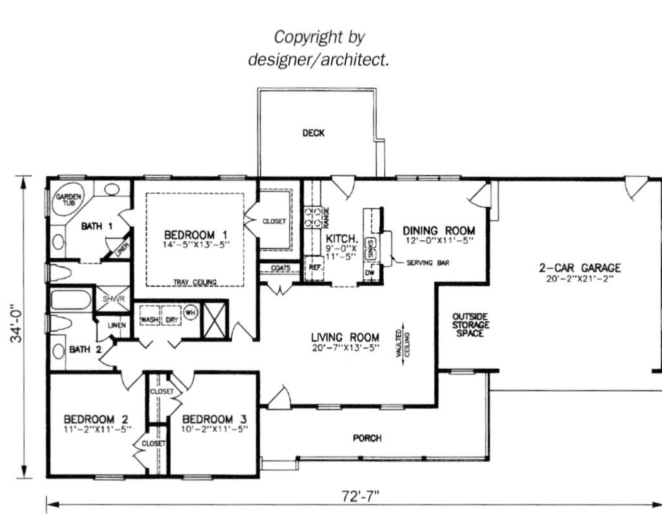

Plan #181153

Dimensions: 46' W x 34' D
Levels: 1
Heated Square Footage: 1,478
Bedrooms: 3
Bathrooms: 1
Foundation: Full basement
Materials List Available: Yes
Price Category: B

Images provided by designer/architect.

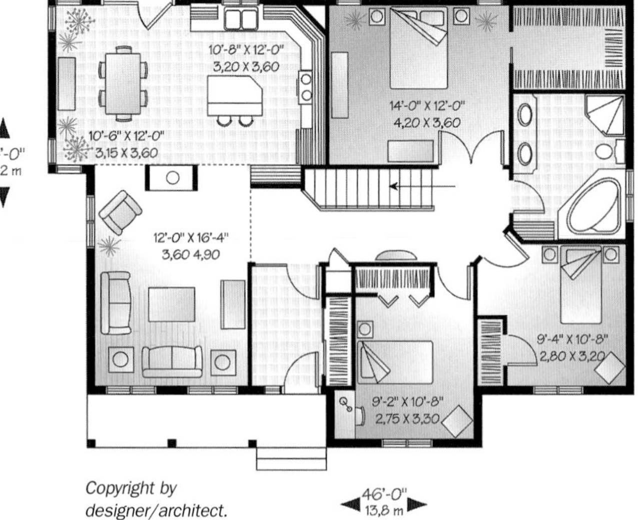

Copyright by designer/architect.

Plan #281031

Dimensions: 48' W x 58' D
Levels: 1
Heated Square Footage: 1,493
Bedrooms: 3
Bathrooms: 2
Foundation: Basement or walkout
Materials List Available: Yes
Price Category: B

Images provided by designer/architect.

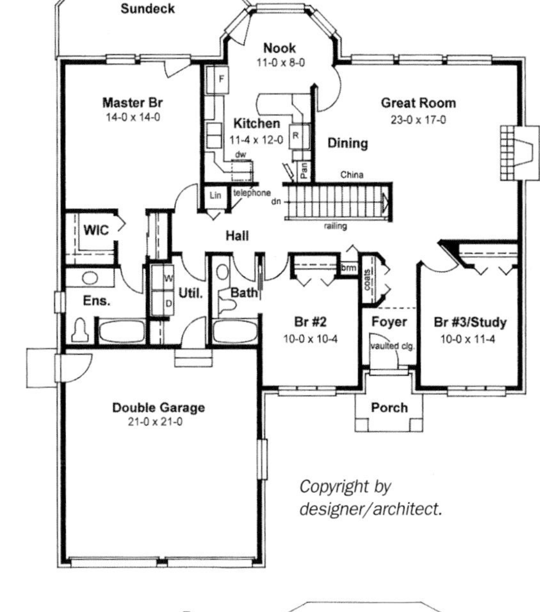

Copyright by designer/architect.

Rear Elevation

Plan #221013

Dimensions: 48' W x 58'8" D
Levels: 1
Heated Square Footage: 1,495
Bedrooms: 3
Bathrooms: 2
Foundation: Basement
Materials List Available: No
Price Category: B

Illustration provided by designer/architect.

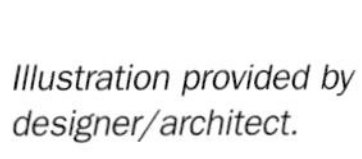

SCREEN PORCH 12'8" x 12'0"
DIN. CATHEDRAL CEILING 12'8" x 12'0"
BR.#3 10'8" x 10'4"
GRT. RM. CATHEDRAL CEILING 12'8" x 19'8"
KIT. 10'0" x 10'6"
MBR. TRAY CEILING 13'2" x 15'2"
BR.#2 CATHEDRAL CEILING 10'10" x 10'4"
E.
2 CAR GAR. 20'0" x 20'0"
48'-0"
58'-8"

Rear Elevation

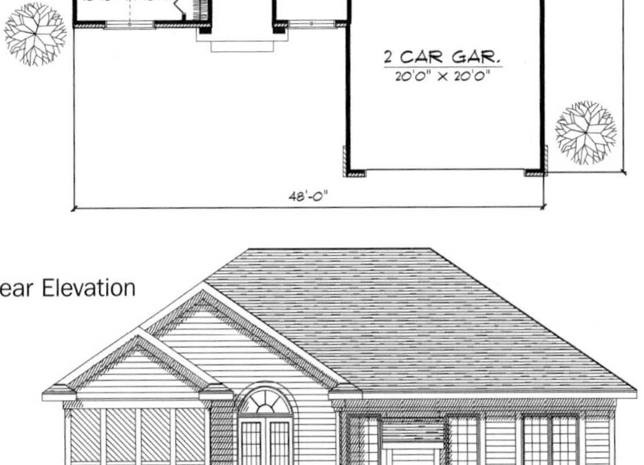

Plan #351020

Dimensions: 54' W x 48' D
Levels: 1
Heated Square Footage: 1,488
Bedrooms: 3
Bathrooms: 2
Foundation: Crawl space, slab, or basement
Materials List Available: Yes
Price Category: D

CAD FILE AVAILABLE

Images provided by designer/architect.

This is a lot of house for its size and is an excellent example of the popular split bedroom layout.

Features:

- Great Room: This large room is open to the dining room.
- Kitchen: This fully equipped kitchen has a peninsula counter and is open into the dining room.
- Master Suite: This private area, located on the other side of the home from the secondary bedrooms, features large walk-in closets and bath areas.
- Bedrooms: The two secondary bedrooms have large closets and share a hall bathroom.

Copyright by designer/architect.

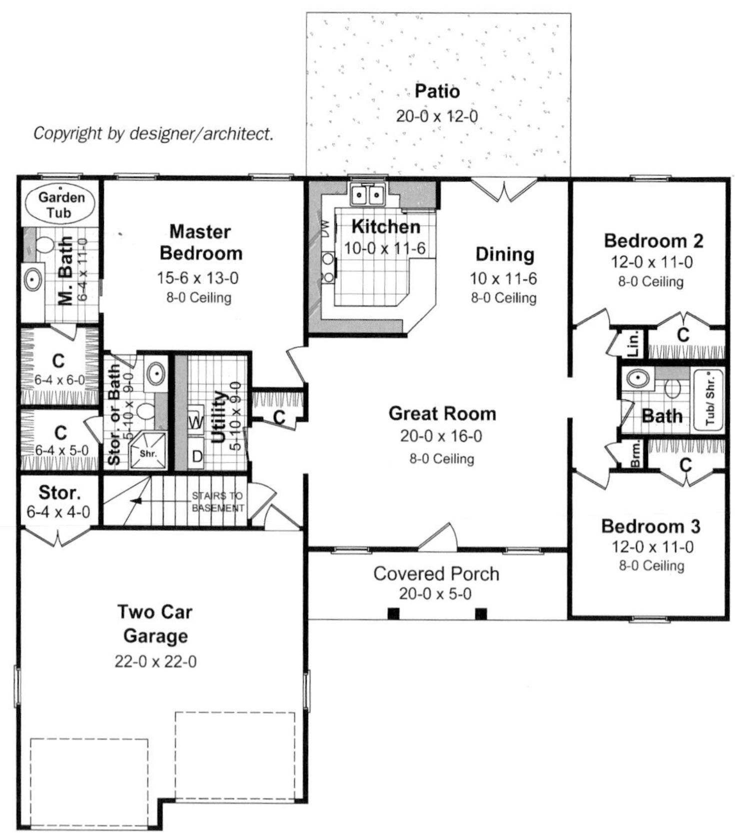

Plan #311024

Dimensions: 56' W x 45' D
Levels: 1
Heated Square Footage: 1,492
Bedrooms: 3
Bathrooms: 2
Foundation: Crawl space, slab, or basement
Materials List Available: Yes
Price Category: B

Images provided by designer/architect.

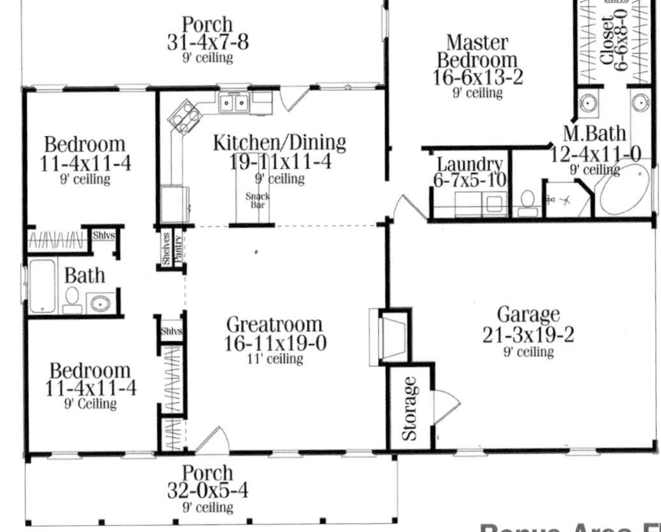

With its uncomplicated layout, this charming, traditional house is a perfect starter or retirement home.

Features:

- Porches: Front and back covered porches allow you to enjoy the outdoors without leaving home. Sit out on warm summer evenings, enjoying the breeze and greeting passersby.
- Kitchen: This efficient layout includes a snack bar, which can act as a transition or buffet for the adjacent formal dining room.
- Master Suite: Enjoy a private entry to the porch, a walk-in closet, and a large master bath with his and her vanities, a large whirlpool tub, and a separate shower.
- Secondary Bedrooms: Two additional bedrooms have ample closet space and access to a shared bathroom, all tucked away from the main area of the home.

Rear View

Bonus Area Floor Plan

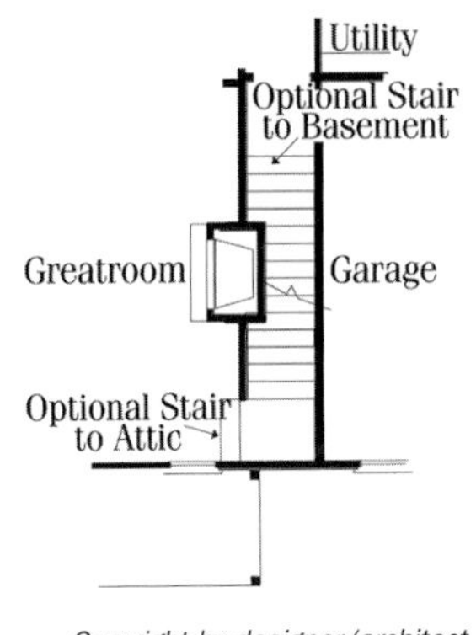

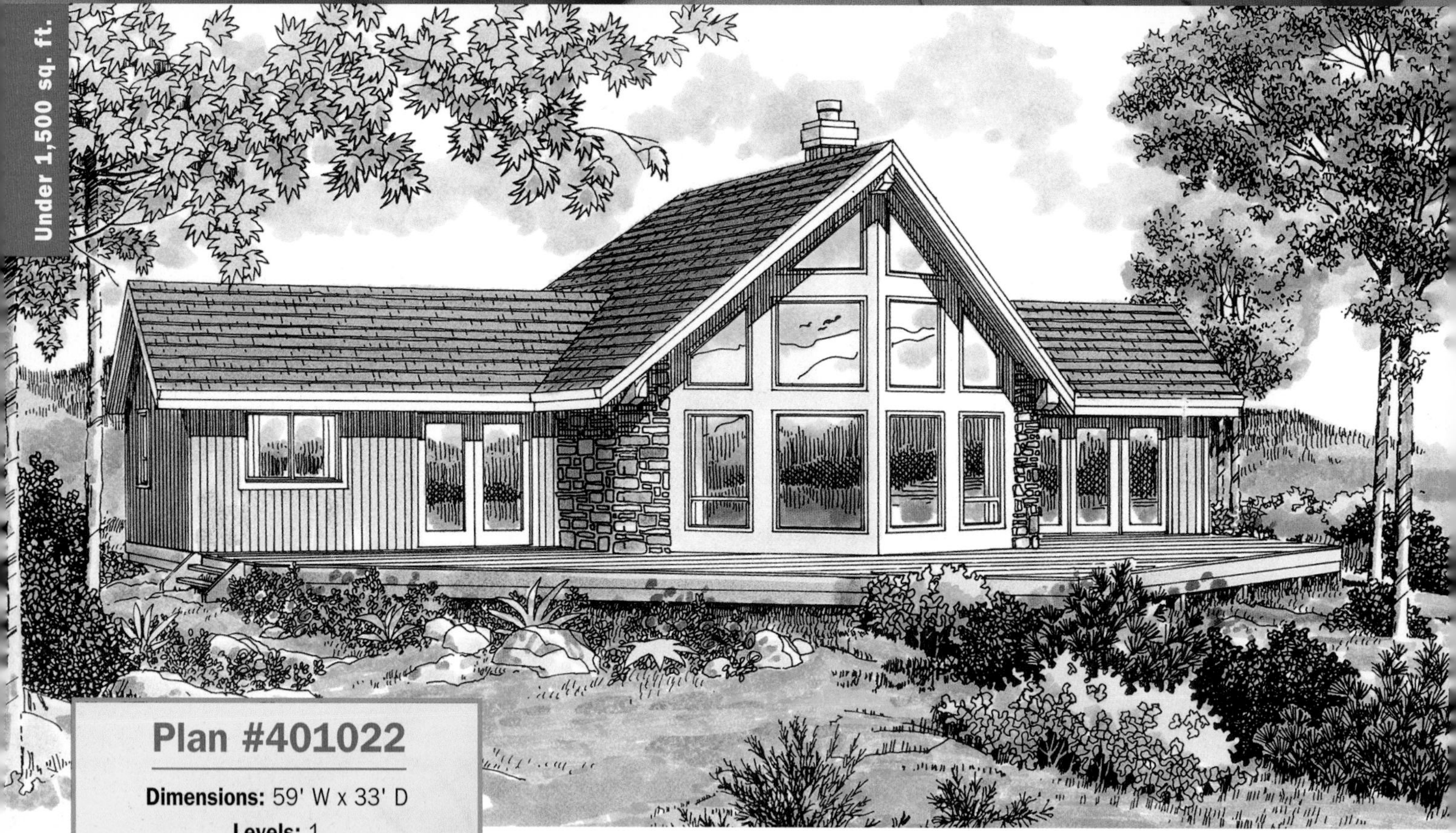

Plan #401022

Dimensions: 59' W x 33' D
Levels: 1
Heated Square Footage: 1,495
Bedrooms: 3
Bathrooms: 2
Foundation: Basement
Materials List Available: Yes
Price Category: B

Images provided by designer/architect.

CAD FILE AVAILABLE

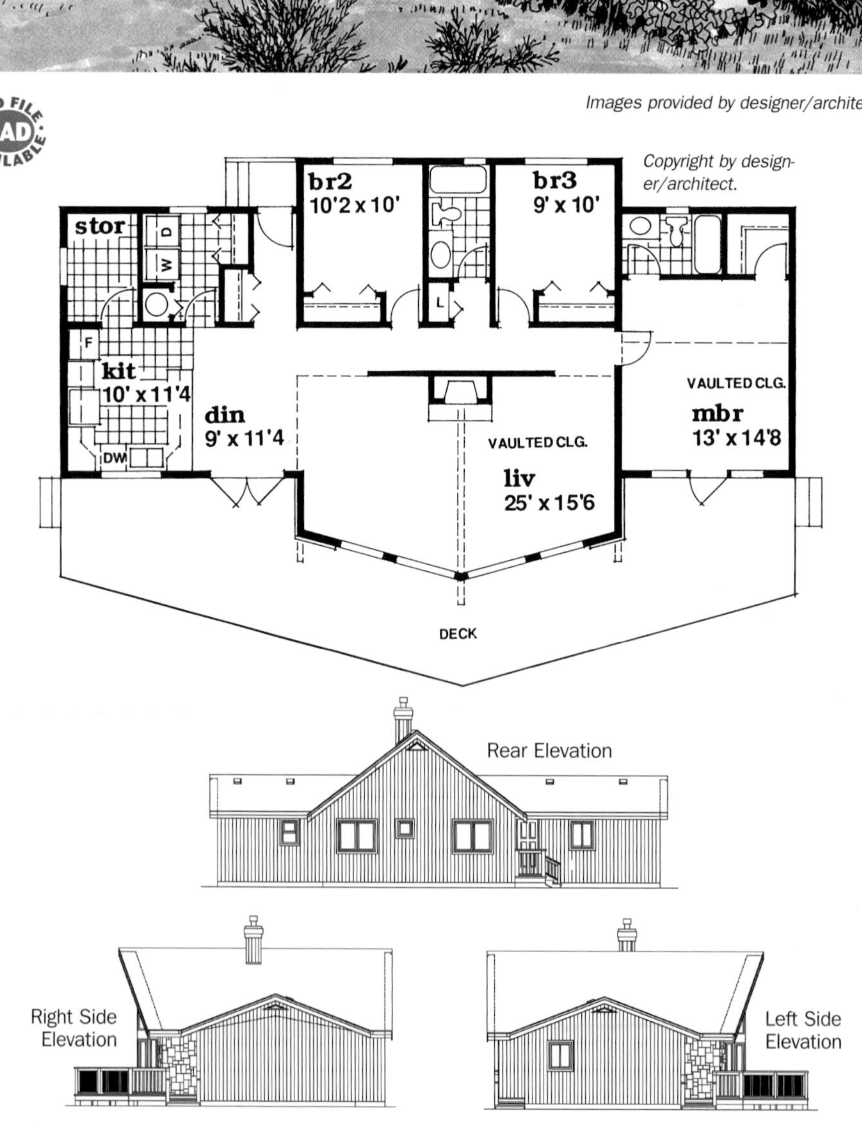

This three-bedroom cottage has just the right rustic mix of vertical wood siding and stone accents. Inside, the living is pure resort-style comfort.

Features:

- High Ceilings: Vaulted ceilings are featured throughout the living room and master bedroom.
- Living Room: This room has a fireplace and full-height windows overlooking the deck.
- Dining Room: This room features double-door access to the deck
- Master Bedroom: This principal sleeping area has a single door that opens to the deck.
- Bedrooms: Two family bedrooms share a bathroom that is situated between them.

Rear Elevation

Right Side Elevation

Left Side Elevation

Plan #161079

Dimensions: 66'4" W x 44'10" D
Levels: 1
Heated Square Footage: 1,498
Bedrooms: 3
Bathrooms: 2
Foundation: Basement
Materials List Available: Yes
Price Category: B

Images provided by designer/architect.

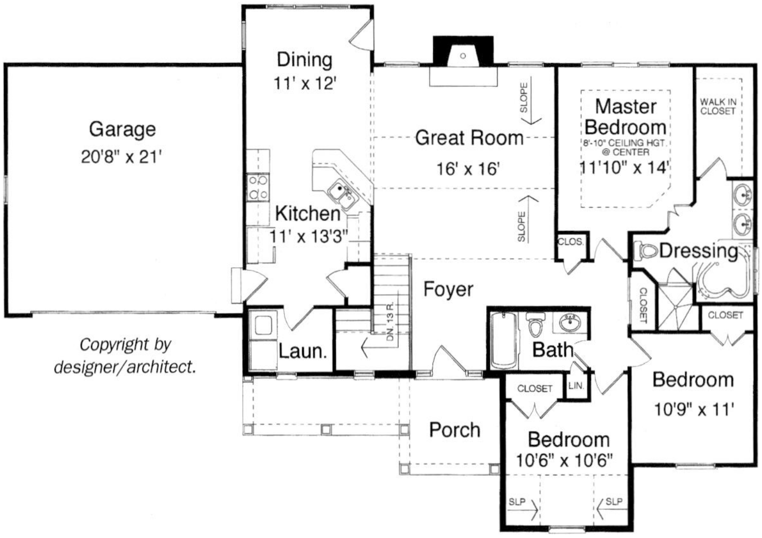

This three-bedroom one-story house enjoys step-saving convenience, plus a beautiful stone-and-siding facade with a covered porch.

Features:

- Great Room: This gathering area, with a gas fireplace and sloped ceiling, is visible from the foyer, breakfast room, and kitchen, creating a large open area.
- Kitchen: This large kitchen, with its snack bar, and the breakfast area both open generously to the great room for a continuous traffic flow.
- Master Suite: This suite enjoys a luxurious bath, large walk-in closet, and raised ceiling.
- Basement: This full basement shows a rough-in for a bathroom and offers space for a future living area.

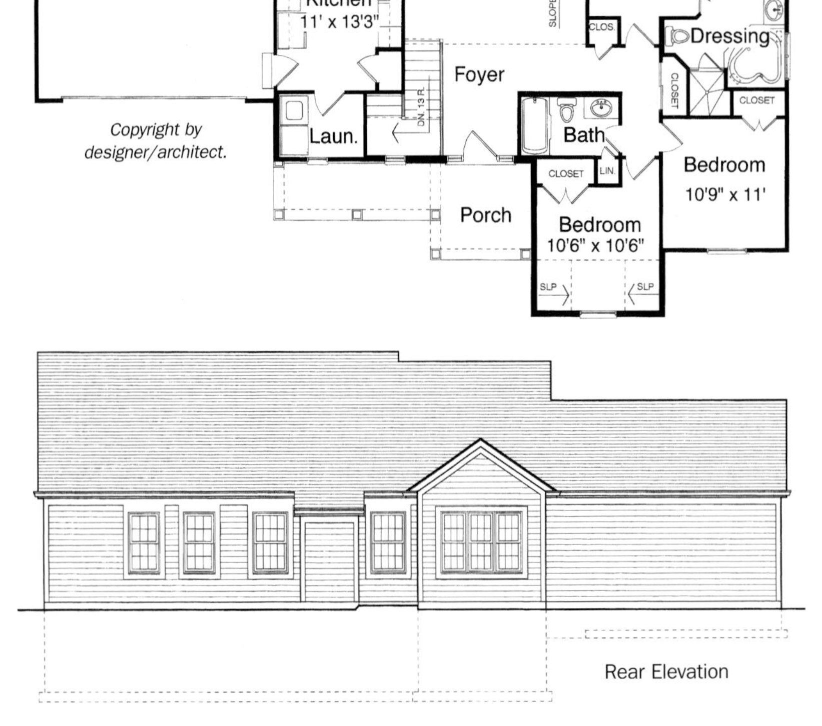

Rear Elevation

The following article was reprinted from *Landscaping with Stone 2nd edition* (Creative Homeowner 2009).

Retaining Wall

Retaining walls let you alter the grade or slope of the land to create level areas that you can use for planting, adding a patio, or any one of a number of uses. They also protect the slope from eroding or collapsing. As with freestanding stone walls, you can build a dry-laid wall or a mortared version. Dry-laid walls are informal and do not require a concrete footing, so they are easier to build than mortared retaining walls. Mortared walls offer more stability, but they tend to be more difficult to build.

The walls in the sunken garden, shown below, are a good example of retaining wall construction. With thoughtful, creative planning you can build a dry-laid retaining wall that is handsome, durable, and an asset to your landscape.

A loose-laid wall, opposite, provides an informal touch by softening the perimeter of this garden.

Retaining walls create a sunken garden room, below, that extends the normal growing season.

Preparing the Site

Begin by calculating the height of the wall. Usually, the angle of the slope determines the height of the wall—the steeper the slope the taller the wall. There are exceptions to this rule. For example, privacy walls are usually tall no matter how steep the slope against which they are built. You may want a wall at a specific height so that you can get access to a garden bed.

Tall walls are more difficult and more costly to build. Structural and drainage issues are more critical for walls more than 3 feet tall and, if you have no prior experience, should not be attempted without professional advice or assistance. The visual mass of a tall wall can also present problems. Rather than build one tall wall, consider adding terraces and building a series of shorter walls.

Walls and Permits

Before you start digging, find out whether you need a permit to build a dry-laid stone retaining wall.

Terracing a Slope. Farmers have been terracing hillsides for thousands of years. For a homeowner, the incentive usually comes from a desire to turn an otherwise uninspiring or difficult-to-maintain hillside into accessible and attractive gardens.

The shorter walls typical of terraces require less skill to fabricate, and you can construct them in stages. Terraces are also less expensive to construct than one tall wall, and they create an inviting destination. All the steps that apply to retaining walls apply to terracing a natural hillside or constructed berm. If the slope is steep and you want wide terraces, then you will have extra fill to remove from the site.

Excavation. Once you know the location and height of the wall, you are ready to begin excavating the site. Short walls with little slope behind them may require nothing more than removing the sod and excavating down 4 to 6 inches. On sloped ground, excavation is usually a cut-and-fill process. As you cut into the slope, you use the soil to level off another area.

Plan on excavating more soil than may appear necessary. You will need space for the wall, space to work, room for gravel backfill, and space for additional backfill to minimize pressure on the wall—an important consideration for walls that front steep, tall slopes.

In many cases, you will end up with more soil than you can use on the current project. Try to find some other landscaping use for the removed soil.

The Base of the Wall. Because they can shift with the movement of the earth, dry-laid retaining walls do not require a concrete footing. In gravelly soil that drains well, remove the sod and 4 to 6 inches of topsoil. Slope the grade in the trench ¼ to ½ inch per foot into the hill. In sandy or wet soils, excavate an additional 4 to 12 inches; lay down landscape fabric; and backfill the trench with gravel that compacts and drains.

The height of the wall will determine the width of your trench. Use this guide: for walls under 3 feet tall, make the width of the wall at its base equal to one-half the finished height of the wall; for taller walls, the width of the base should be closer to two-thirds the height of the wall. A 3-foot-tall wall should have a 2-foot-wide base. Consult a professional mason or landscape contractor when planning on a wall that is taller than 3 feet.

Mortared walls require a concrete footing. Local building codes determine the depth and width of the footing.

Drainage. Runoff from the slope will seep out between the stones of a dry-laid retaining wall. Typically, these types of walls do not require an additional drainage system. But if the

Use retaining walls to create level areas for planting, as shown opposite. The height of some parts of the wall makes it easy to tend to the plants.

Building with large, rounded stones is challenging and best used on short walls, left.

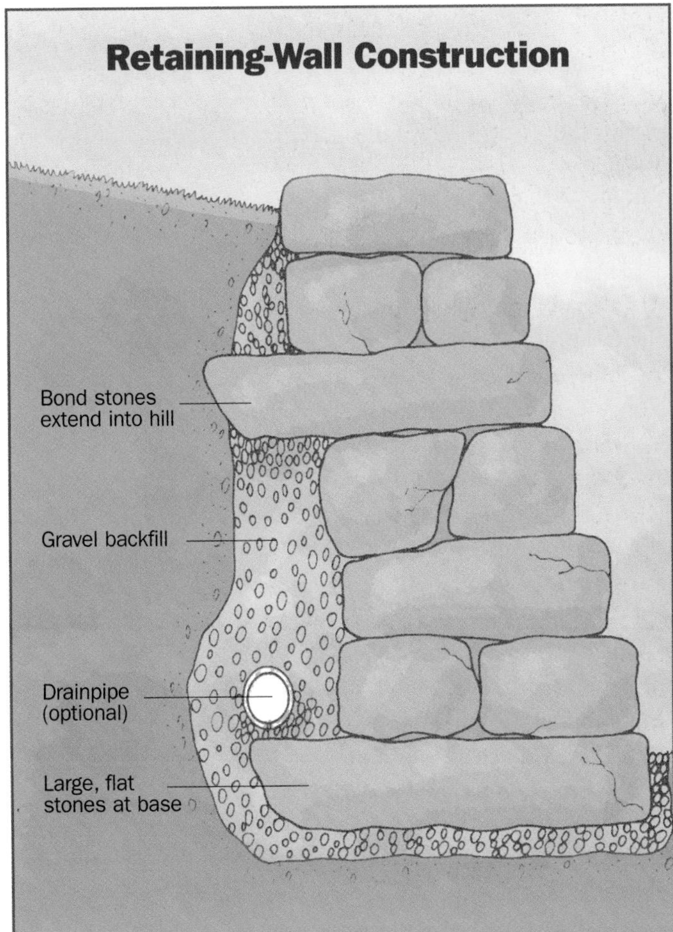

site is wet and you want to minimize seepage through the wall, add a drainpipe that can move the water away from the wall. Backfilling with a few inches of coarse gravel minimizes erosion and loss of soil through the wall. For greater stability, particularly with steep slopes, lay landscape fabric between the soil and the backfill gravel.

If you are planning a mortared wall, you must provide a drainage system. Without weep holes or some other drainage system, runoff from the slope will exert tremendous pressure against the wall, resulting in buckling of the wall.

Building the Wall

When the stone is delivered to the site, sort it as you would for a freestanding wall: larger stones for the base, bond stones to span between wythes, rubble for fill between the wythes, and cap stones or coping for the top of the wall. Unlike freestanding walls, retaining walls need only one good face. If your wall is short and there isn't a lot of pressure on it, you can build the wall one stone wide provided your stones are large and good building stone, that is, they fit together well.

Calculate the Batter. Retaining walls lean back into the slope they support. This lean is called the batter. Retaining walls typically have about a 2-inch batter for every foot of height. If a wall is short and the stone is at least semidressed, you can reduce or eliminate the batter.

Lay the Base Course. Use your largest and flattest stones for the base course. Place bond stones at each end of the wall and at 4- to 6-foot intervals along the wall. Ideally, the bond stones should be long enough to extend into the slope. Between the bond stones, lay wall stones, one in front of the other, to create a double-wythe wall. Fill any gaps between these stones with smaller stones or rubble.

Tilt all the main wall stones into the hill. After laying the first course, you can backfill along the front of the wall and firmly tamp the soil in 2-inch layers. If you are going to install perforated drainpipe, now is the time to lay it along the backside of the wall. Slope the pipe to facilitate drainage.

Add the Remaining Courses. Place the next course, setting it back slightly from the first. Stagger the location of the bond stones, offsetting them from the bond stones in the first course. Lay stones so that all joints between courses are staggered.

After the second course is laid, backfill with gravel and fill almost to the top of the second course. Firmly tamp the gravel in 2-inch layers. Continue laying up courses in the same manner, checking the angle of the face with your batter gauge periodically and backfilling after every two courses.

Cap the Wall. Cap stones usually span the width of the wall and protrude slightly over it. Because water can move through a dry-laid wall, the water-shedding function of the cap stones isn't as crucial. For stability, especially if the wall is located somewhere where it will be used as seating, you may want to mortar the capstones.

Finish Backfilling and Grading. After laying the capstones, backfill with gravel up to within 4 inches or so of the top of the wall. Lay landscape fabric over the top of the gravel, and finish backfilling with soil or mulch.

SMARTtip

Make a Batter Gauge

Stone walls should slope inward from bottom to top. To check the inward slope as you build, construct a batter gauge from 1x2s joined at one end and spread apart at the other. **1.** The distance between the two ends is the slope you want to maintain. To use the gauge, hold the sloping 1x2 against the wall, and place a level on the other board. **2.** You are maintaining the right amount of batter when the level reads plumb.

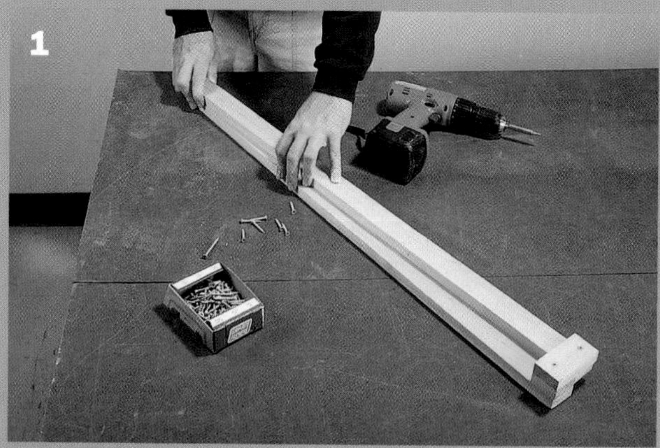

Retaining walls lean back into the slope. Plan on a 2-in. batter for every foot of height.

This charming water feature, left, is enclosed by an informal-looking stone retaining wall.

Instead of a single high wall, consider building a series of stepped layers, bottom left, that you can then plant.

To facilitate drainage for walls such as the one shown bottom right, as you set the stones, backfill with gravel behind the wall.

Lay retaining wall stones so that all joints between courses are staggered, above.

Runoff from the slope will seep out between the stones of a dry-laid retaining wall, right.

Plan #151215

Dimensions: 53' W x 56'6" D
Levels: 1
Heated Square Footage: 1,519
Bedrooms: 3
Bathrooms: 2
Foundation: Crawl space or slab
CompleteCost List Available: Yes
Price Category: C

Images provided by designer/architect.

This brick home, with a front-loading garage, is the perfect home for a young family.

Features:

- Great Room: This large entertainment area has a corner fireplace and entry to the grilling porch.
- Kitchen: Designed with a walk-through layout, this kitchen is open to the breakfast room.
- Master Suite: This private area, located on the opposite side of the home from the secondary bedrooms, features a master bathroom with large his and her walk-in closets.
- Bedrooms: The two secondary bedrooms share a common bathroom.

CAD FILE AVAILABLE

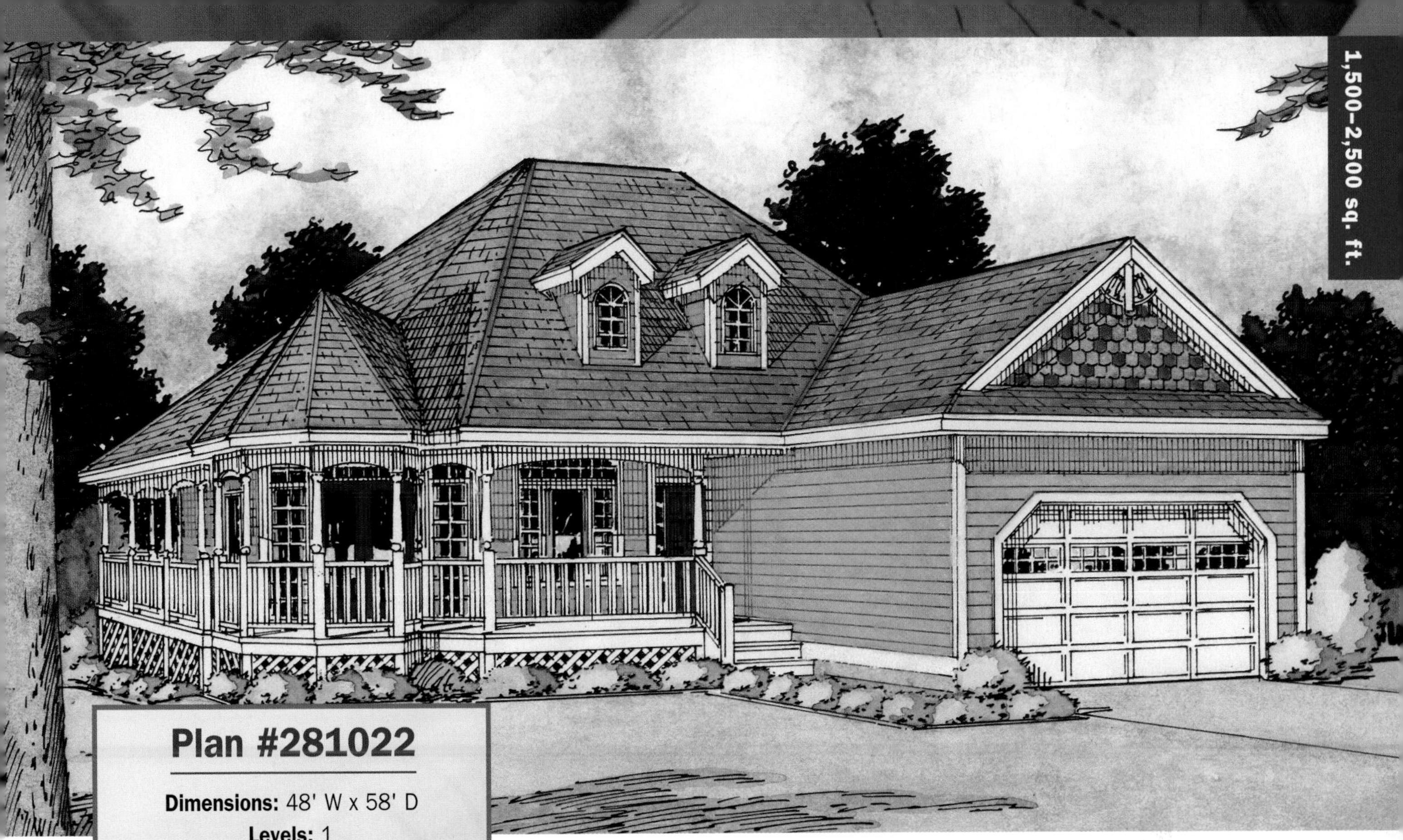

Plan #281022

Dimensions: 48' W x 58' D
Levels: 1
Heated Square Footage: 1,506
Bedrooms: 3
Bathrooms: 2
Foundation: Basement
Materials List Available: Yes
Price Category: C

Images provided by designer/architect.

You'll spend hours enjoying the sunshine on this home's wraparound porch and gazebo.

Features:

- Porch: Stretching from the front to the back of the house, this porch has a gazebo on one corner and becomes a covered deck at the back.
- Great Room: This beautiful great room includes a three-sided fireplace and French doors that open out onto the porch by the gazebo.
- Kitchen: Divided from the dining room and great room by an island with a raised snack bar, this kitchen also has French doors nearby that open out to the covered deck, a wonderful location for outdoor meals.
- Master Suite: Close to the secondary bedrooms, this master suite includes a spacious walk-in closet, a whirlpool tub, and a dual-sink vanity.

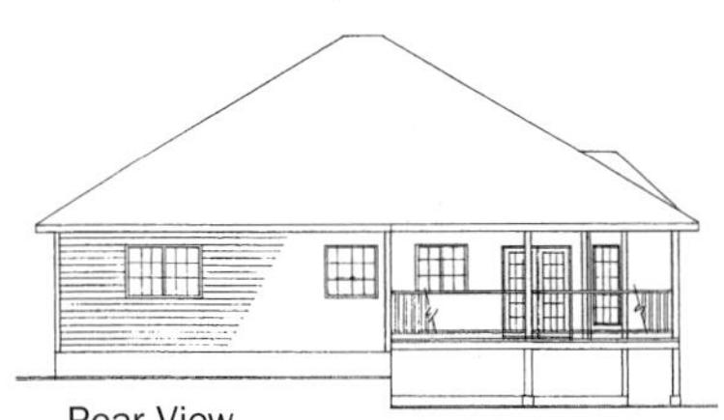

Rear View

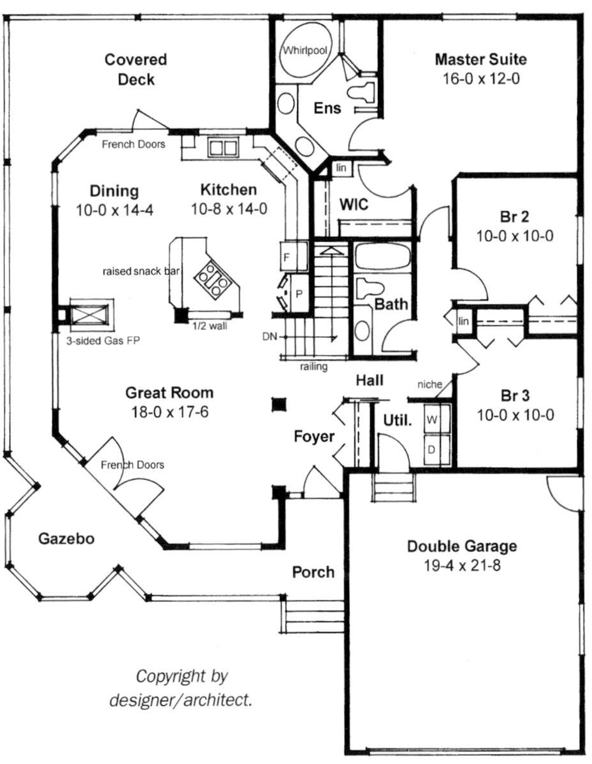

Plan #351062

Dimensions: 51'8" W x 51'2" D
Levels: 1
Heated Square Footage: 1,502
Bedrooms: 3
Bathrooms: 2
Foundation: Crawl space or slab
Materials List Available: Yes
Price Category: E

Images provided by designer/architect.

CAD FILE CAD AVAILABLE

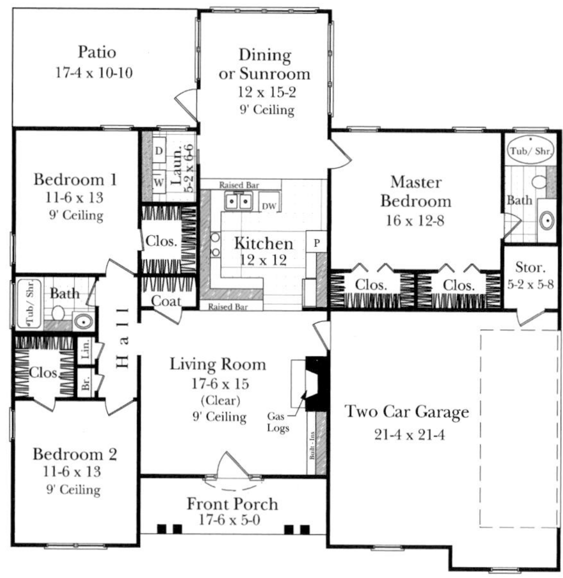

Copyright by designer/architect.

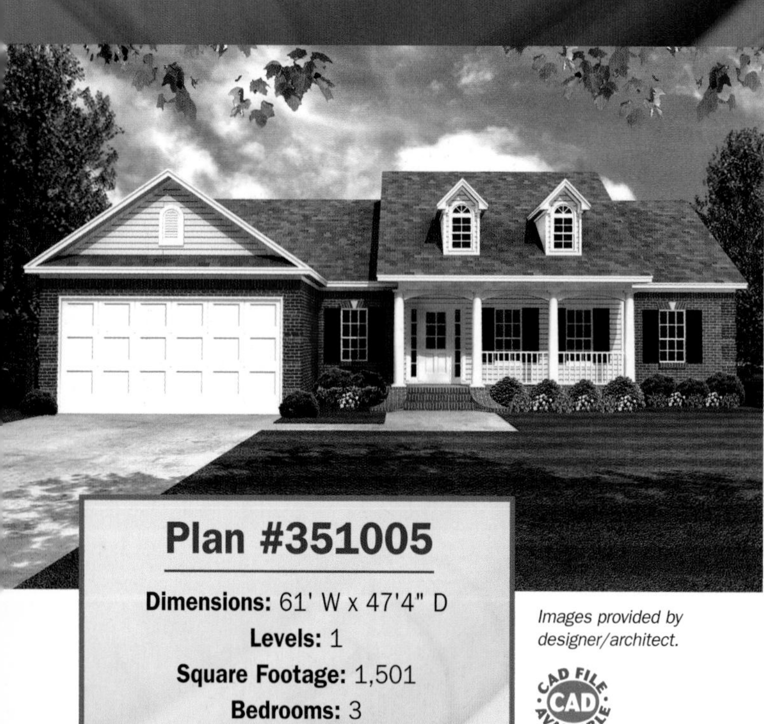

Plan #351005

Dimensions: 61' W x 47'4" D
Levels: 1
Square Footage: 1,501
Bedrooms: 3
Bathrooms: 2
Foundation: Crawl space, slab, or basement
Materials List Available: Yes
Price Category: E

Images provided by designer/architect.

CAD FILE CAD AVAILABLE

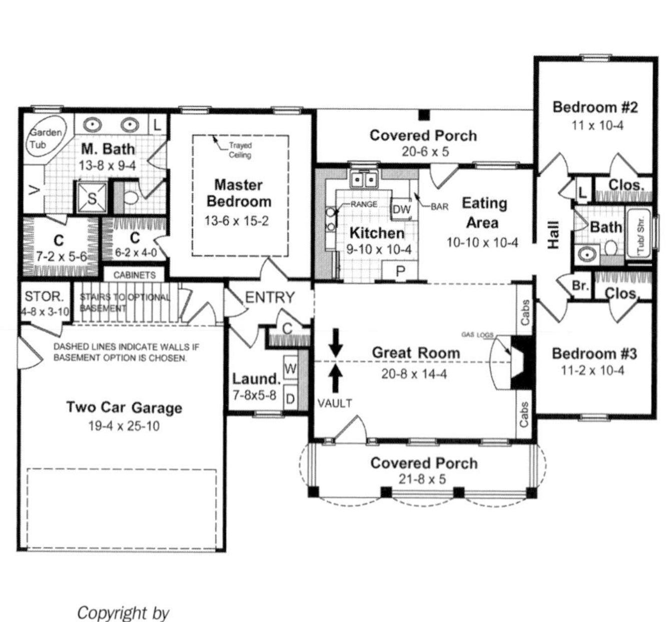

Copyright by designer/architect.

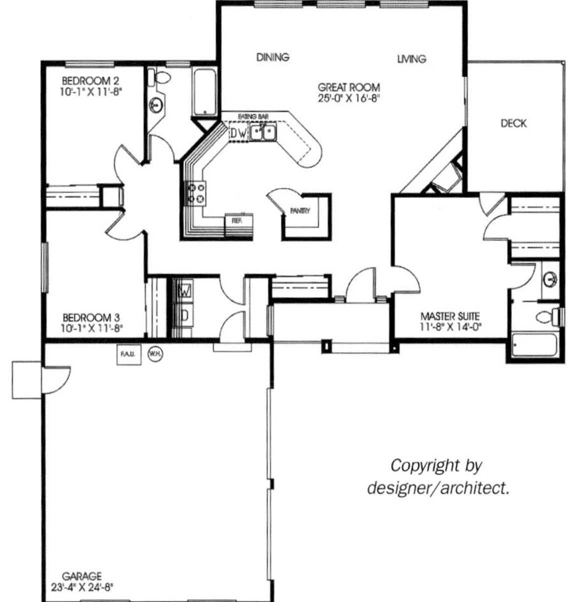

Plan #501549

Dimensions: 54' W x 60' D
Levels: 1
Heated Square Footage: 1,502
Bedrooms: 3
Bathrooms: 2
Foundation: Crawl space
Materials List Available: Yes
Price Category: C

Images provided by designer/architect.

Copyright by designer/architect.

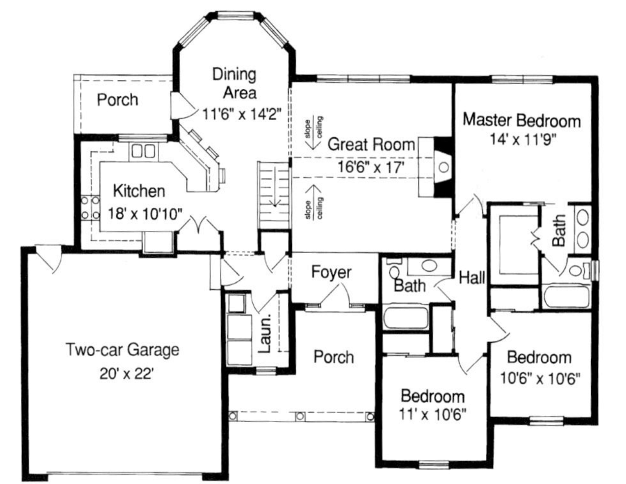

Plan #161003

Dimensions: 60' W x 47' D
Levels: 1
Heated Square Footage: 1,508
Bedrooms: 3
Bathrooms: 2
Foundation: Basement
Materials List Available: Yes
Price Category: C

Images provided by designer/architect.

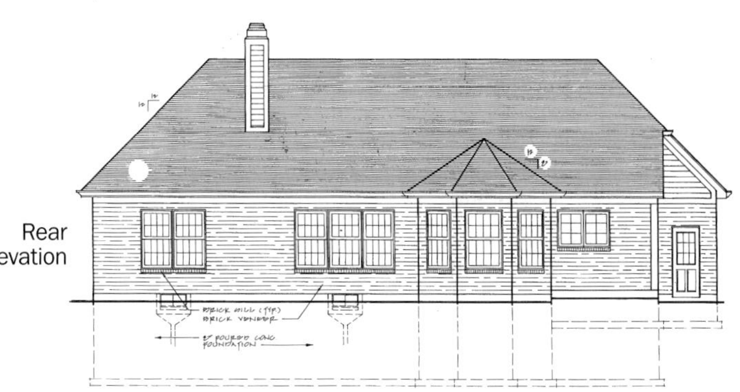

Rear Elevation

Images provided by designer/architect.

Copyright by designer/architect.

Plan #161013

Dimensions: 59'4" W x 46'4" D
Levels: 1
Heated Square Footage: 1,509
Bedrooms: 3
Bathrooms: 2
Foundation: Basement
Materials List Available: Yes
Price Category: C

The unique roofline and stone accents make this home stand apart from the rest.

Features:

- Foyer: Just off the front porch, this entry opens to the great room.
- Great Room: This room warms up with a fireplace and is open to the dining area.
- Kitchen: This kitchen features a peninsula with a raised bar, creating more seating space for the adjacent dining room.
- Master Suite: This suite features a private bathroom with a walk-in closet and double vanities.
- Bedrooms: Two secondary bedrooms have large closets and share a hall bathroom.

Plan #151169

Dimensions: 51'6" W x 49'10" D
Levels: 1
Heated Square Footage: 1,525
Bedrooms: 3
Bathrooms: 2
Foundation: Crawl space, slab, basement, or daylight basement
CompleteCost List Available: Yes
Price Category: C

CAD FILE AVAILABLE

Images provided by designer/architect.

This comfortable home is filled with amenities that will thrill both friends and family.

Features:

- Great Room: This spacious room has a gas fireplace in the corner, 9-ft. boxed ceiling, and convenient door to the rear covered porch.
- Dining Room: Bay windows look out to the rear porch and let light flood into this room.
- Kitchen: An angled work and snack bar and large pantry are highlights in this well-planned room.
- Breakfast Room: A door to the rear porch, wide windows, and computer desk are highlights here.
- Master Suite: You'll feel pampered by the 9-ft. boxed ceiling and bath with two huge closets, whirlpool tub, separate shower, and dual vanity.
- Additional Bedrooms: Transform bedroom 3 into a study or home office if you can, and add the optional door to the foyer for total convenience.

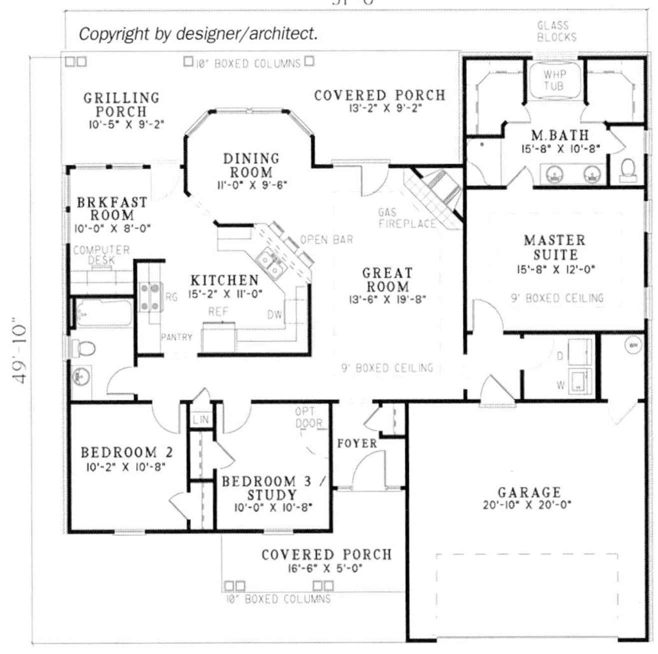

Rear View

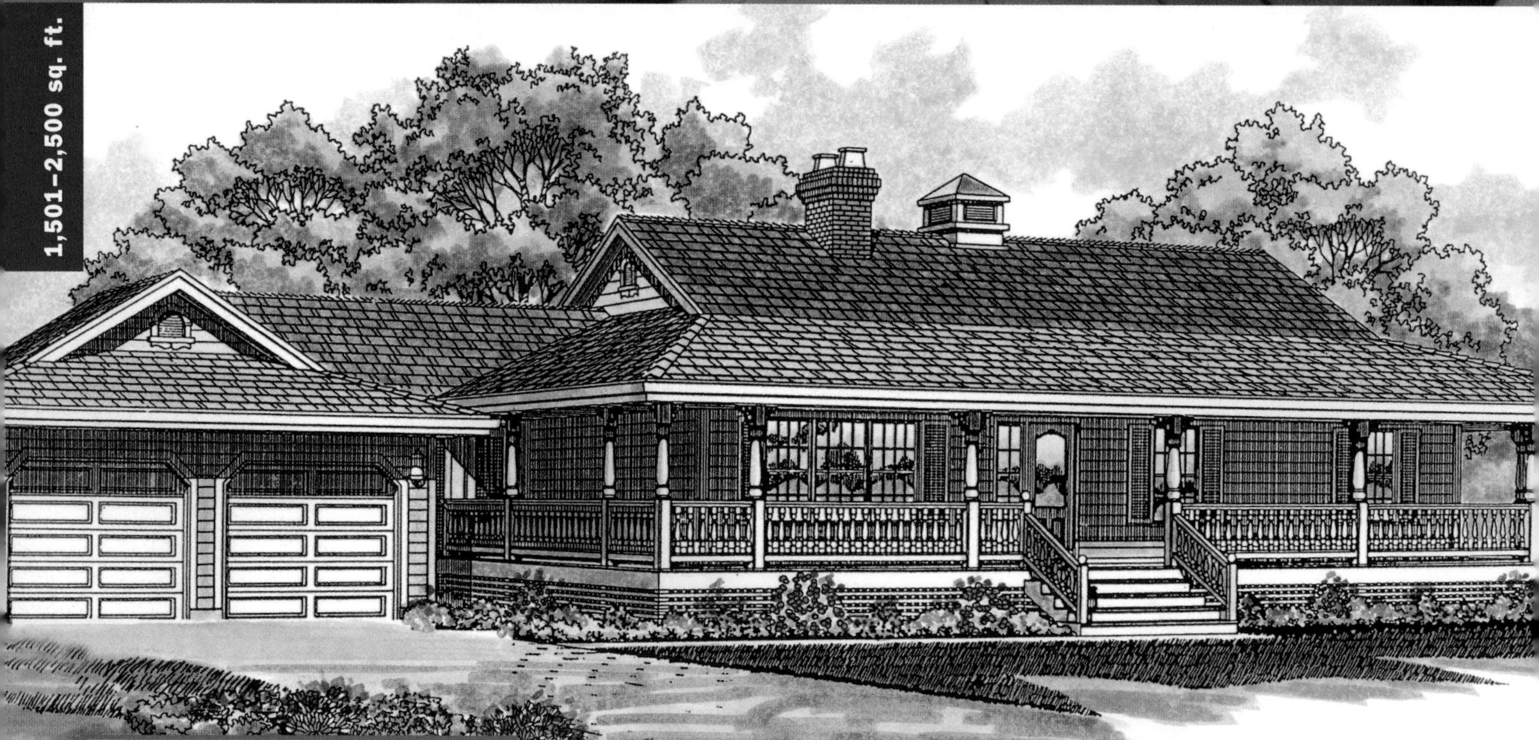

Plan #401008

Dimensions: 87' W x 44' D
Levels: 1
Heated Square Footage: 1,541
Bedrooms: 3
Bathrooms: 2
Foundation: Basement
Materials List Available: Yes
Price Category: C

CAD FILE AVAILABLE

This popular design begins with a wraparound covered porch made even more charming by turned wood spindles.

Features:

- Great Room: The entry opens directly into this great room, which is warmed by a woodstove.
- Dining Room: This room offers access to a screened porch for outdoor after-dinner leisure.
- Kitchen: This country kitchen features a center island and a breakfast bay for casual meals.
- Bedrooms: Family bedrooms share a full bath that includes a soaking tub.

Images provided by designer/architect.

Copyright by designer/architect.

1541 sq. ft.

Rear Elevation

Left Side Elevation

Right Side Elevation

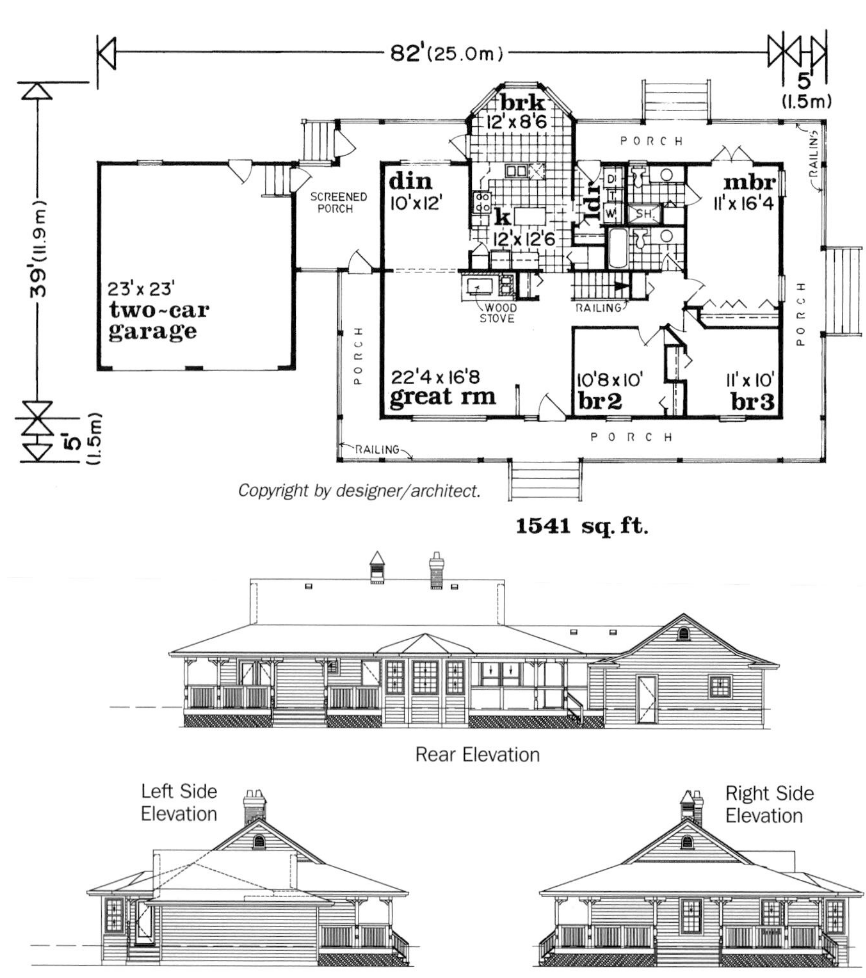

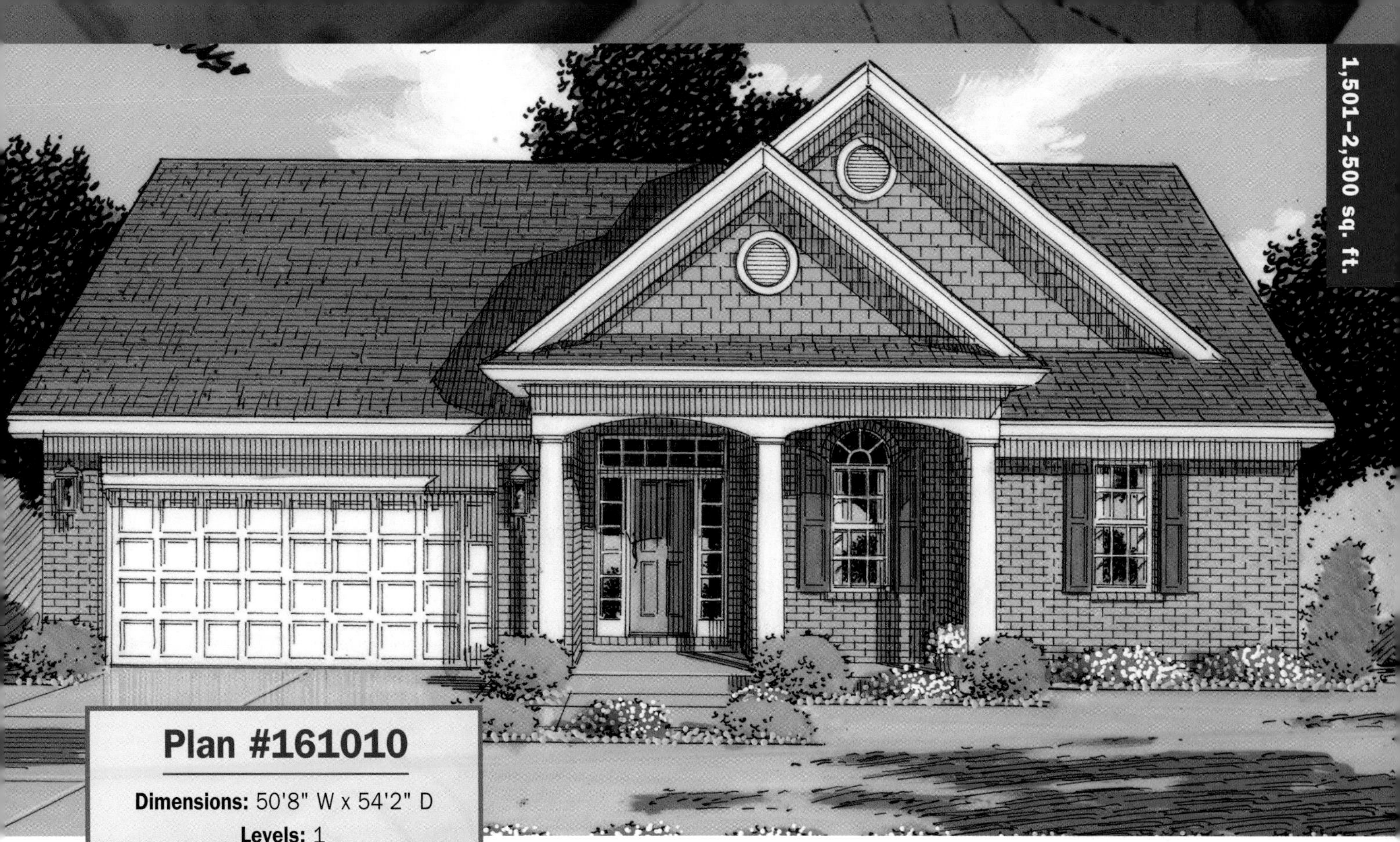

Plan #161010

Dimensions: 50'8" W x 54'2" D
Levels: 1
Heated Square Footage: 1,544
Bedrooms: 3
Bathrooms: 2
Foundation: Basement
Materials List Available: Yes
Price Category: C

Images provided by designer/architect.

Right Side Elevation

Rear Elevation

Left Side Elevation

This one-story home's many distinctive and elegant features—including arched openings and sloped ceilings—will surprise and excite you at every turn.

Features:

- Great Room: Decorative columns frame the entrance from the foyer to this great room and are repeated at the opening to the formal dining area.
- Kitchen: Designed for quick meals or to accommodate an oversized crowd, this kitchen features a curved countertop with seating that functions as a delightful bar.
- Master Bedroom: This master bedroom is split to afford you more privacy and features a compartmented bath that forms a separate vanity area.
- Additional Bedrooms: Take advantage of the double doors off the foyer to allow one bedroom to function as a library.

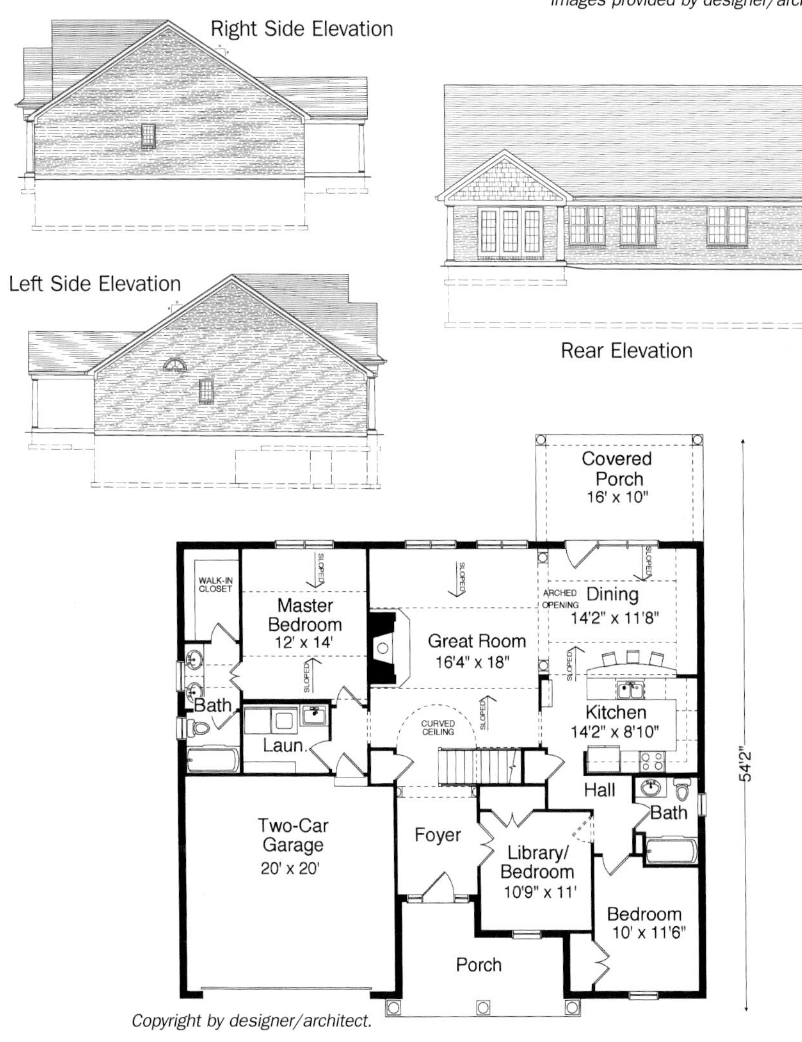

Copyright by designer/architect.

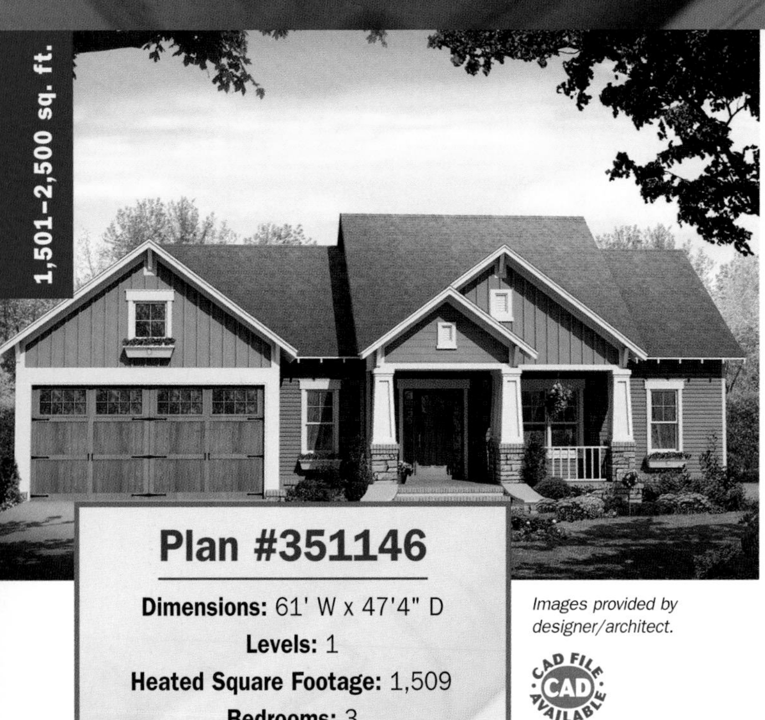

Plan #351146

Dimensions: 61' W x 47'4" D
Levels: 1
Heated Square Footage: 1,509
Bedrooms: 3
Bathrooms: 2
Foundation: Crawl space, slab or basement
Materials List Available: Yes
Price Category: C

Images provided by designer/architect.

CAD FILE AVAILABLE

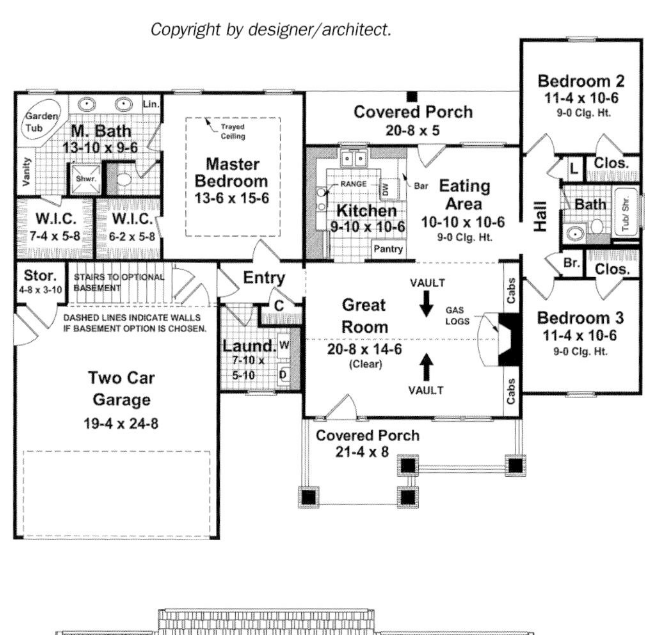

Rear View

Plan #321224

Dimensions: 47' W x 45' D
Levels: 1
Heated Square Footage: 1,519
Bedrooms: 4
Bathrooms: 2
Foundation: Crawl space, slab or basement
Materials List Available: Yes
Price Category: C

Images provided by designer/architect.

CAD FILE AVAILABLE

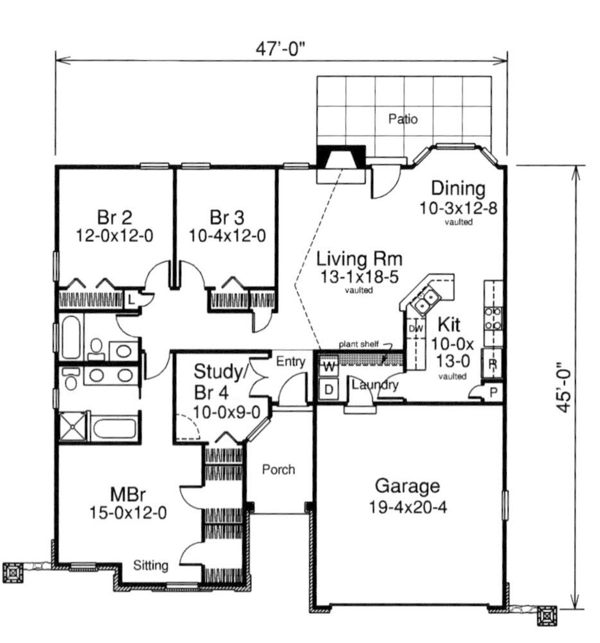

Plan #151037

Dimensions: 50' W x 56' D
Levels: 1
Heated Square Footage: 1,538
Bedrooms: 3
Bathrooms: 2
Foundation: Crawl space, slab, or basement
CompleteCost List Available: Yes
Price Category: C

Images provided by designer/architect.

CAD FILE AVAILABLE

Copyright by designer/architect.

Plan #391039

Dimensions: 50' W x 45'4" D
Levels: 1
Heated Square Footage: 1,539
Bedrooms: 3
Bathrooms: 2
Foundation: Crawl space, basement, slab
Materials List Available: Yes
Price Category: C

Images provided by designer/architect.

Copyright by designer/architect.

Plan #251004

Dimensions: 50'9" W x 42'1" D
Levels: 1
Heated Square Footage: 1,550
Bedrooms: 3
Bathrooms: 2
Foundation: Crawl space, slab
Materials List Available: Yes
Price Category: C

Images provided by designer/architect.

CAD FILE AVAILABLE

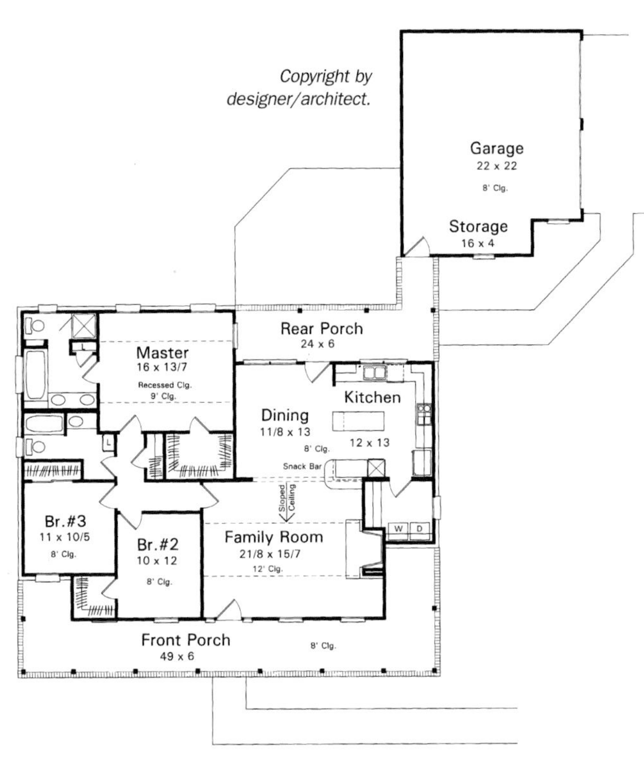

Plan #291001

Dimensions: 63' W x 37' D
Levels: 1
Heated Square Footage: 1,550
Bedrooms: 3
Bathrooms: 2
Foundation: Basement
Materials List Available: No
Price Category: C

Images provided by designer/architect.

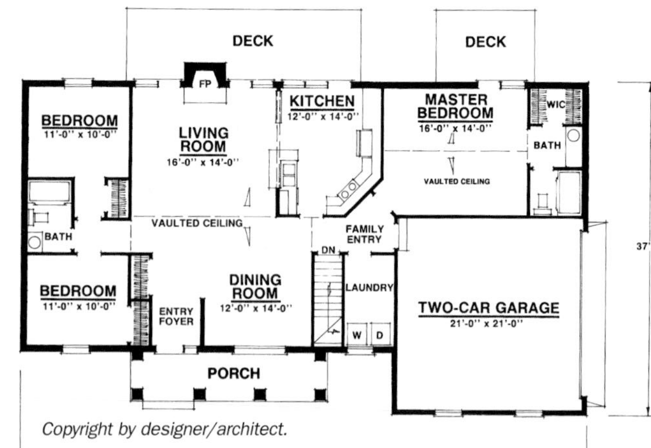

Rear View

Plan #391021

Dimensions: 54' W x 48'4" D

Levels: 1

Heated Square Footage: 1,568

Bedrooms: 3

Bathrooms: 2

Foundation: Crawl space, basement, slab

Materials List Available: Yes

Price Category: C

Images provided by designer/architect.

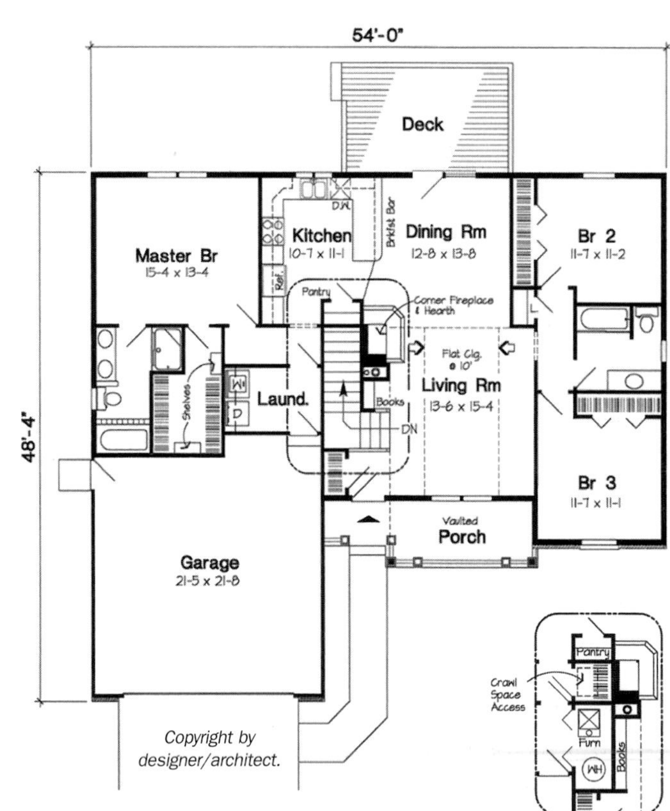

Copyright by designer/architect.

Plan #151463

Dimensions: 48'6" W x 56'8" D

Levels: 1

Heated Square Footage: 1,574

Bedrooms: 3

Bathrooms: 2

Foundation: Crawl space or slab; basement or walkout for fee

CompleteCost List Available: Yes

Price Category: C

Images provided by designer/architect.

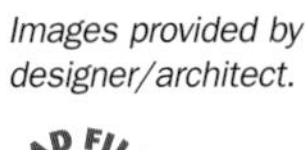

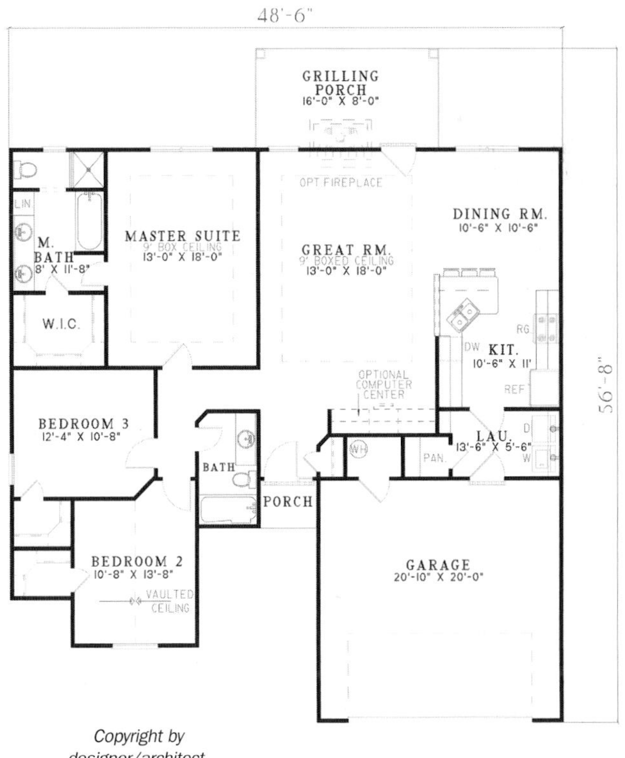

Copyright by designer/architect.

Plan #191037

Dimensions: 57'4" W x 65' D
Levels: 1
Heated Square Footage: 1,575
Bedrooms: 3
Bathrooms: 2
Foundation: Crawl space, slab
Materials List Available: No
Price Category: C

Images provided by designer/architect.

Living Room

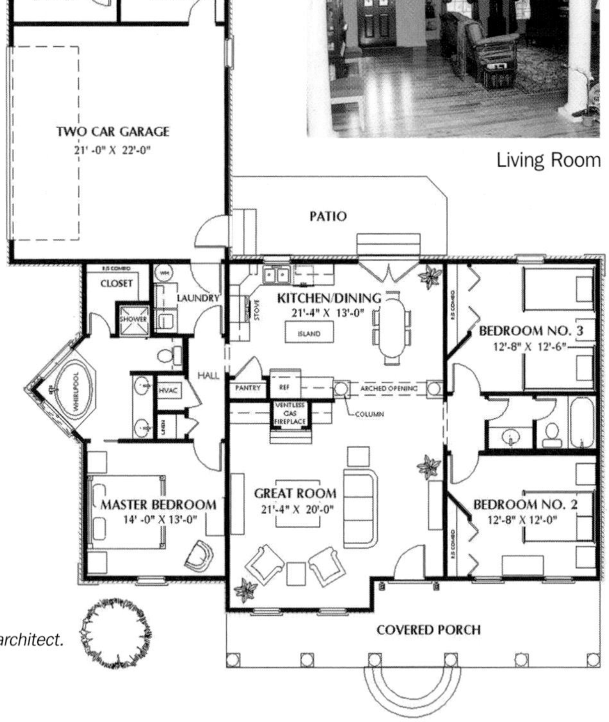

Copyright by designer/architect.

Plan #151608

Dimensions: 49'6" W x 55' D
Levels: 1
Heated Square Footage: 1,576
Bedrooms: 3
Bathrooms: 2
Foundation: Crawl space or slab
CompleteCost List Available: Yes
Price Category: C

Images provided by designer/architect.

CAD FILE AVAILABLE

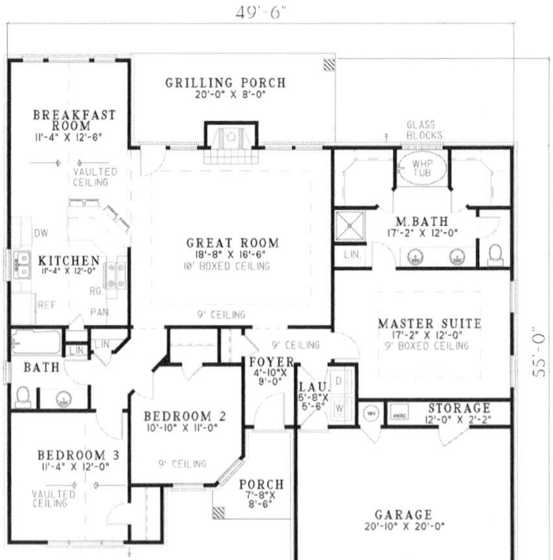

Copyright by designer/architect.

Plan #131007

Dimensions: 59'10" W x 47'8" D
Levels: 1
Heated Square Footage: 1,595
Bedrooms: 3
Bathrooms: 2
Foundation: Crawl space, slab, basement, or walkout
Materials List Available: Yes
Price Category: D

Images provided by designer/architect.

SCREENED PORCH 13'-4"x 12'-8"
TRAY CEIL GREAT RM 14'-0"x 22'-8"
TRAY CEIL MSTR BEDRM 12'-0"x 18'-0"
MSTR BATH
WICL
DRSG
BEDRM #3 13'-4"x 11'-0"
WET BAR
W D
STOR
UTIL
LOCATION OF OPT BSMT STAIR
CL
BATH
DINING RM 10'-0"x 13'-0"
KITCHEN 10'-0"x 11'-0"
REF
DW
FOY
TWO CAR GARAGE 20'-0"x 21'-4"
BEDRM #2 11'-0"x 14'-0"
COV. PORCH

Copyright by designer/architect.

Rear Elevation

Plan #211030

Dimensions: 75' W x 37' D
Levels: 1
Heated Square Footage: 1,595
Bedrooms: 3
Bathrooms: 2
Foundation: Slab
Materials List Available: Yes
Price Category: D

Images provided by designer/architect.

SMARTtip

Brackets in Window Treatments

Although it is rarely noticed, a bracket plays an important role in supporting rods and poles. If a treatment rubs against a window frame, an extension bracket solves the problem. It projects from the wall at an adjustable length, providing enough clearance. A hold-down bracket anchors a cellular shade or a blind to the bottom of a door, preventing the treatment from moving when the door is opened or closed.

Copyright by designer/architect.

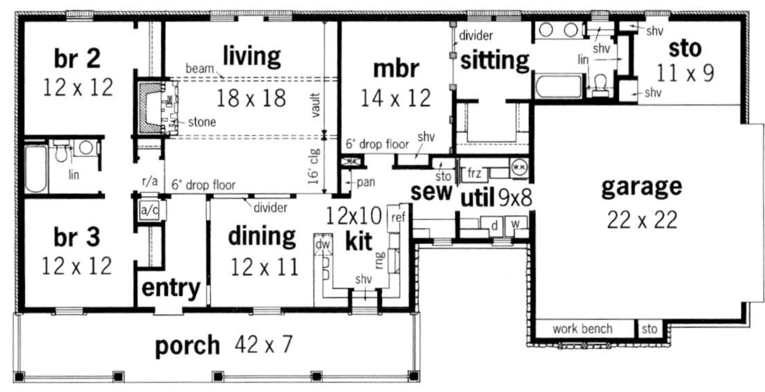

Plan #441003

Dimensions: 50' W x 48' D
Levels: 1
Heated Square Footage: 1,580
Bedrooms: 3
Bathrooms: 2½
Foundation: Crawl space; slab or basement available for fee
Materials List Available: No
Price Category: C

CAD FILE AVAILABLE

Images provided by designer/architect.

Craftsman styling with modern floor planning—that's the advantage of this cozy design. Covered porches at front and back enhance both the look and the livability of the plan.

Features:

- Great Room: This vaulted entertaining area boasts a corner fireplace and a built-in media center. The area is open to the kitchen and the dining area.
- Kitchen: This large, open island kitchen will please the chef in the family. The raised bar is open to the dining area and the great room.
- Master Suite: Look for luxurious amenities such as double sinks and a separate tub and shower in the master bath. The master bedroom has a vaulted ceiling and a walk-in closet with built-in shelves.
- Bedrooms: Two secondary bedrooms are located away from the master suite. Each has a large closet and access to a common bathroom.

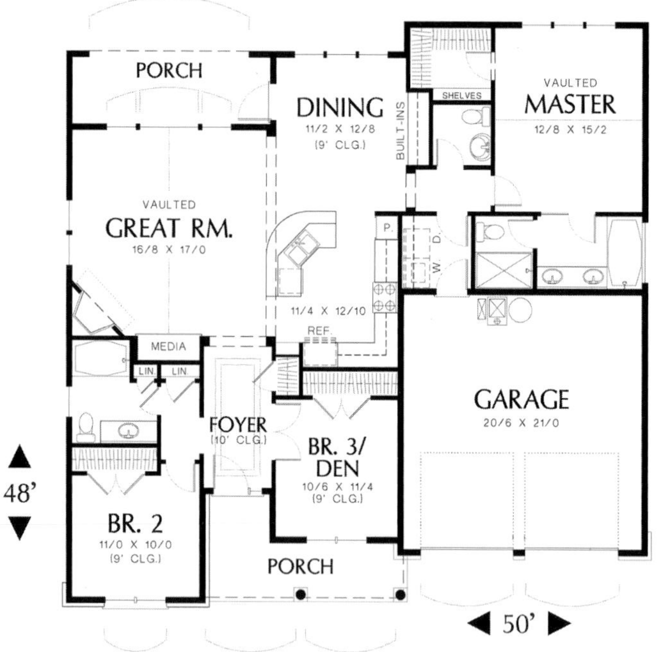

Copyright by designer/architect.

Rear Elevation

Plan #131005

Dimensions: 70' W x 37'4" D
Levels: 1
Heated Square Footage: 1,595
Bedrooms: 3
Bathrooms: 2
Foundation: Crawl space, slab, or basement
Materials List Available: Yes
Price Category: D

Images provided by designer/architect.

With the finest features of an open design in the main living areas, this home gives privacy where you need it. Best of all, it's wheelchair accessible.

Features:

- Foyer: A high ceiling gives this area real presence and serves to blend it seamlessly with the great room and the dining room.
- Great Room: The open design allows you to use this room as an extension of the dining room or, if you wish, furnish it to create a private reading nook or visually separate media center.
- Breakfast Room: Both this room and the adjacent well-appointed kitchen flow into the rest of the living area. However, access to the rear porch, where you can sit out and enjoy the weather while you eat, distinguishes this room.
- Master Suite: Located in the same wing as the other bedrooms, this suite has a separate entrance and features a vaulted ceiling, three closets, and a compartmented bath.

SMARTtip

Create a Courtyard

Create a private walled-garden retreat with fences covered by climbing vines. Add height with trellises, and divide spaces with clipped boxwood hedges. Include an (almost) instant patio by digging away an area of sod and then covering it with a layer of sand and landscaping mesh to discourage weeds. Then cover it with pea gravel, and add a garden bench, statuary, and perhaps an antique or two. The result? European ambiance for even the most nondescript suburban yard.

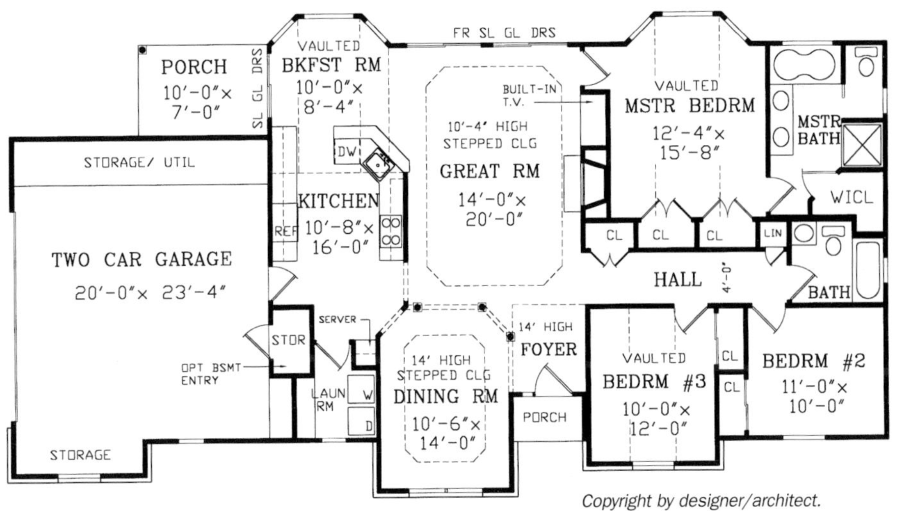

Copyright by designer/architect.

Images provided by designer/architect.

Plan #351023

Dimensions: 61'8" W x 45'8" D
Levels: 1
Heated Square Footage: 1,600
Bedrooms: 3
Bathrooms: 2
Foundation: Crawl space, slab, or basement
Materials List Available: Yes
Price Category: E

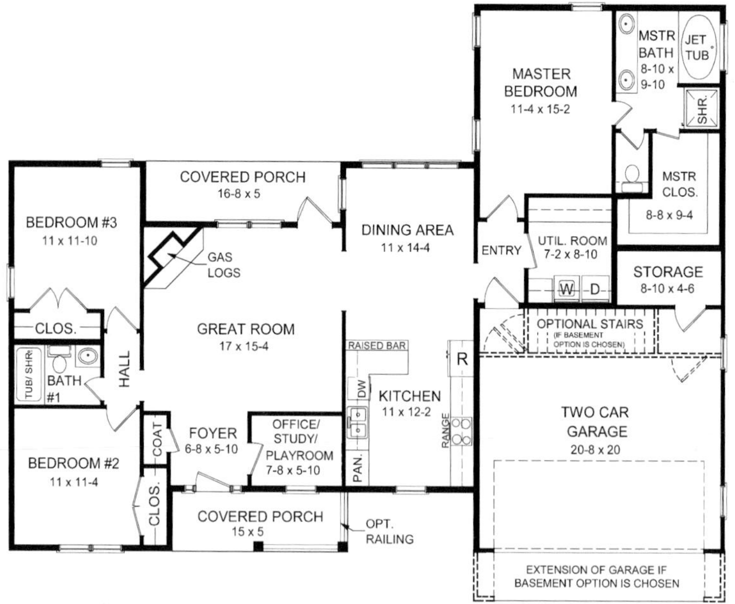

Copyright by designer/architect.

This beautiful three-bedroom home has everything your family needs to live the comfortable life.

Features:

- Great Room: Just off the foyer is this large room. It features a cozy fireplace and access to the rear covered porch.
- Dining Room: This formal room has large windows with a view of the backyard.
- Kitchen: This kitchen has an abundance of cabinets and counter space. It is open to the dining room.
- Master Suite: This isolated suite, with its jetted tub, separate shower, large closet, and dual vanities, is a perfect retreat.
- Bedrooms: The two secondary bedrooms have large closets and share a hall bathroom.

Plan #161007

Dimensions: 66'4" W x 43'10" D
Levels: 1
Heated Square Footage: 1,611
Bedrooms: 3
Bathrooms: 2
Foundation: Basement; crawl space option for fee
Materials List Available: Yes
Price Category: C

CAD FILE AVAILABLE

Images provided by designer/architect.

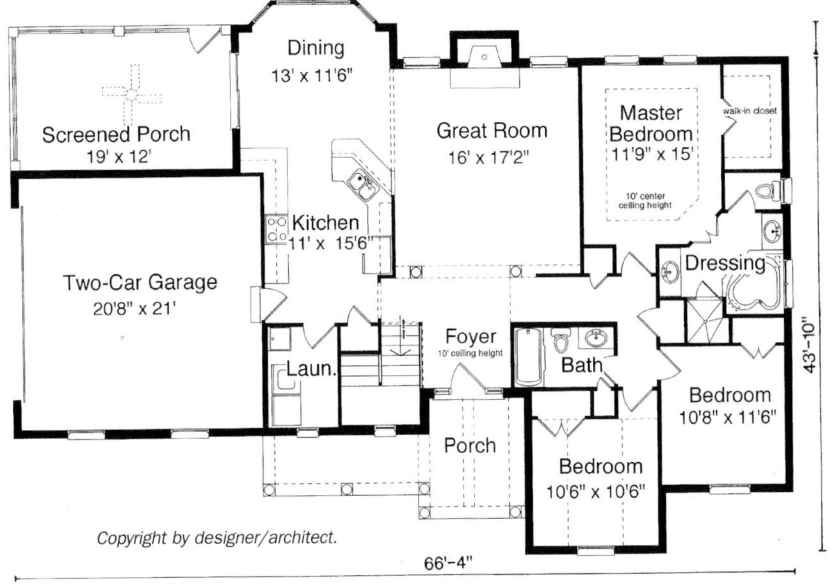

Copyright by designer/architect.

Rear Elevation

A lovely front porch and an entry with sidelights invite you to experience the impressive amenities offered in this exceptional ranch home.

Features:

- Great Room: Grand openings, featuring columns from the foyer to this great room and continuing to the bayed dining area, convey an open, spacious feel. The fireplace and matching windows on the rear wall of the great room enhance this effect.
- Kitchen: This well-designed kitchen offers convenient access to the laundry and garage. It also features an angled counter with ample space and an abundance of cabinets.
- Master Suite: This deluxe master suite contains many exciting amenities, including a lavishly appointed dressing room and a large walk-in closet.
- Porch: Sliding doors lead to this delightful screened porch for relaxing summer interludes.

Plan #131001

Dimensions: 72'4" W x 32'4" D
Levels: 1
Heated Square Footage: 1,615
Bedrooms: 3
Bathrooms: 2
Foundation: Crawl space, slab, basement, or walkout
Materials List Available: Yes
Price Category: D

Images provided by designer/architect.

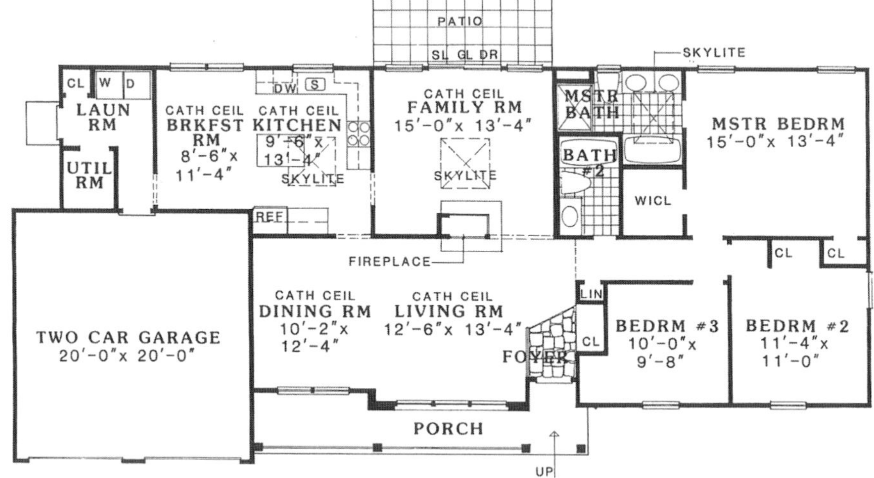

Copyright by designer/architect.

Cathedral ceilings and illuminating skylights add drama and beauty to this practical ranch house.

Features:

- Ceiling Height: 8 ft.
- Front Porch: Watch the rain in comfort from the covered front porch.
- Foyer: The stone-tiled foyer flows into the living areas.
- Living Room: Oriented towards the front of the house, the living room opens to the dining room and shares a lovely three-sided fireplace with the family room.
- Family Room: Conveniently located to share the fireplace with the living room, this room is bright and cheery thanks to its skylights as well as the sliding glass doors that open onto the rear patio.
- Kitchen: An island makes this sunny room both efficient and attractive.
- Breakfast Nook: Located just off the kitchen, this area can serve double-duty as a spot for kitchen visitors to sit.
- Dining Room: The open design between the dining and living rooms adds to the spacious feeling that the cathedral ceiling creates in this area.
- Laundry Room: This area opens from the kitchen for convenience.
- Master Suite: A walk-in closet makes this room practical, but the master bathroom with a skylight, dual-sink vanity, soaking tub, and separate shower makes it luxurious.
- Bedrooms: The two additional bedrooms share a bathroom.

Images provided by designer/architect.

Plan #351033

Dimensions: 64' W x 39' D
Levels: 1
Heated Square Footage: 1,654
Bedrooms: 3
Bathrooms: 2
Foundation: Crawl space, slab, or basement
Materials List Available: Yes
Price Category: E

CAD FILE AVAILABLE

This gorgeous three-bedroom brick home would be the perfect place to raise your family.

Features:

- Great Room: This terrific room has a gas fireplace with built-in cabinets on either side.
- Kitchen: This island kitchen with breakfast area is open to the great room.
- Master Suite: This private room features a vaulted ceiling and a large walk-in closet. The bath area has a walk-in closet, jetted tub, and double vanities.
- Bedrooms: The two additional bedrooms share a bathroom located in the hall.

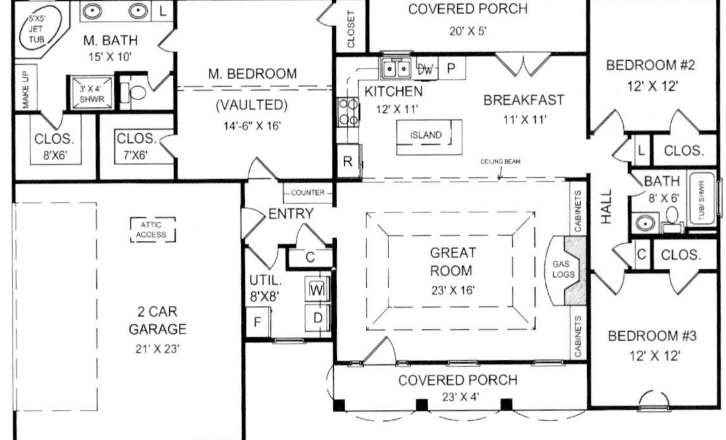

Copyright by designer/architect.

Plan #131010

Dimensions: 70' W x 34'4" D
Levels: 1
Heated Square Footage: 1,667
Bedrooms: 3
Bathrooms: 2
Foundation: Basement, crawl space, or slab
Materials List Available: Yes
Price Category: D

Images provided by designer/architect.

CAD FILE AVAILABLE

You'll love this affordable ranch house, with its open floor plan that gives so much usable space, and its graceful layout.

Features:

- Living Room: Adjacent to the dining room, this living room features a pass-through fireplace that is open to the family room beyond.
- Family Room: A vaulted ceiling with a sky light gives character to this room, where everyone will gather on weekend afternoons and in the evening, to relax.
- Kitchen: Also lit from above by a skylight, this kitchen features an island work space.
- Breakfast Room: Just off the kitchen, this breakfast room is sure to be a popular spot at any time of day.
- Master Bedroom: Get away from it all in this lovely room, with space to spread out and relax in private.

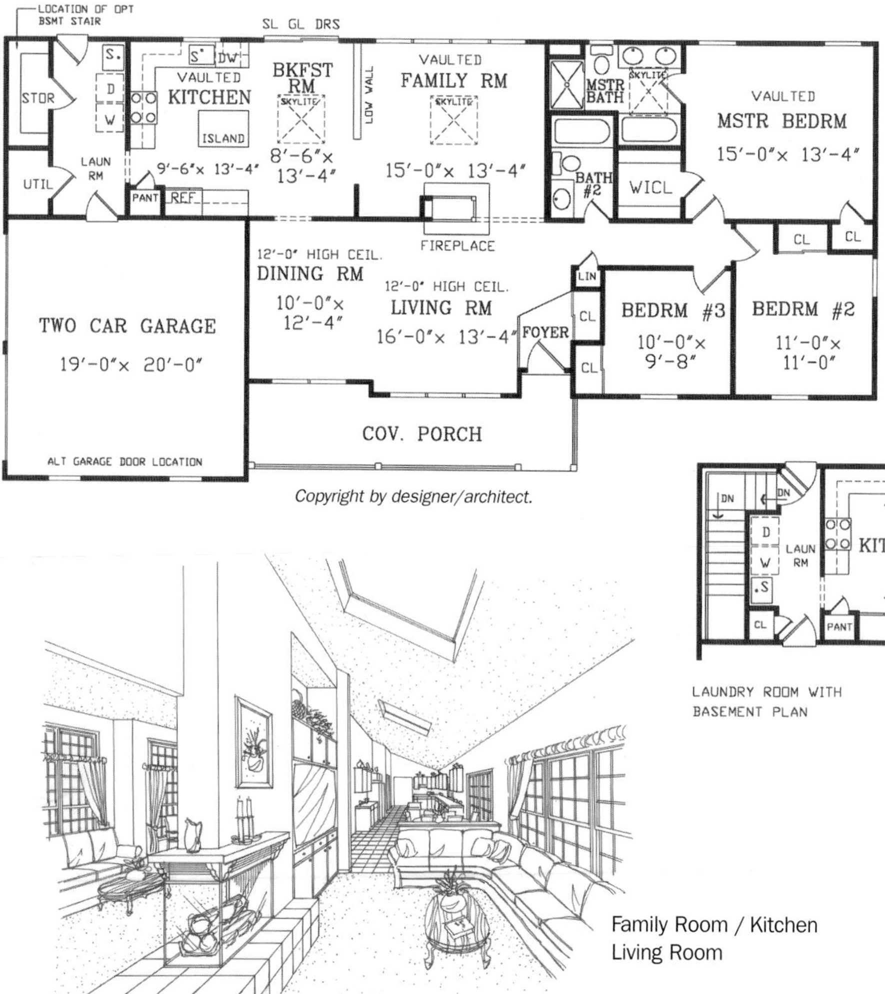

Copyright by designer/architect.

LAUNDRY ROOM WITH BASEMENT PLAN

Family Room / Kitchen
Living Room

Plan #241005

Dimensions: 53' W x 55'9" D
Levels: 1
Heated Square Footage: 1,670
Bedrooms: 3
Bathrooms: 2
Foundation: Crawl space or slab; basement option for fee
Materials List Available: No
Price Category: C

Images provided by designer/architect.

This charming starter home, in split-bedroom format, combines big-house features in a compact design.

Features:

- Great Room: With easy access to the formal dining room, kitchen, and breakfast area, this great room features a cozy fireplace.
- Kitchen: This big kitchen, with easy access to a walk-in pantry, features an island for added work space and a lovely plant shelf that separates it from the great room.
- Master Suite: Separated for privacy, this master suite offers a roomy bath with whirlpool tub, dual vanities, a separate shower, and a large walk-in closet.
- Additional Rooms: Additional rooms include a laundry/utility room—with space for a washer, dryer, and freezer—a large area above the garage, well-suited for a media or game room, and two secondary bedrooms.

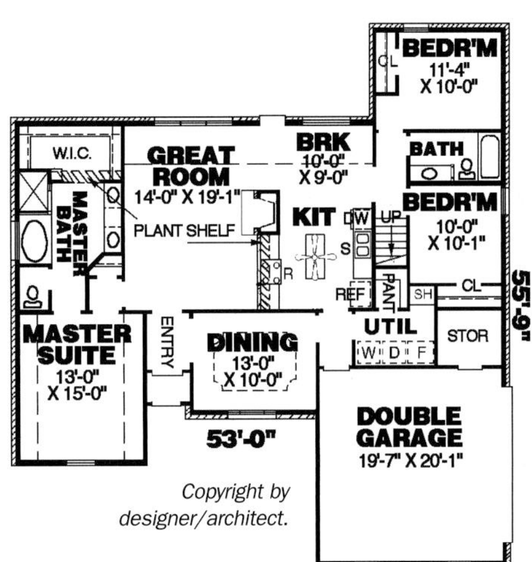

Copyright by designer/architect.

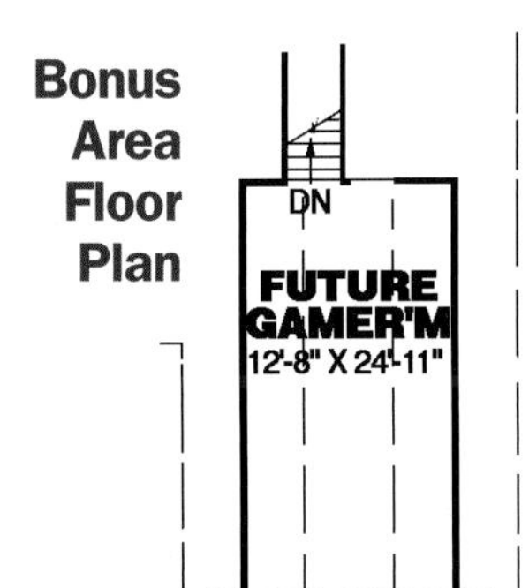

Bonus Area Floor Plan

SMARTtip

Window Scarf

The best way to wrap a window scarf around a pole is as follows:

- Lay out the material on a large, clean surface. Gather the fabric at the top of each jabot, and use elastic to hold it together.
- Swing one jabot into place over the pole and, starting from there, wind the swag portion as many times as you need around the pole until you reach the elastic at the second jabot, which should have landed at the opposite pole end.
- Readjust wraps along the pole. Generally, wrapped swags just touch or slightly overlap.
- For a dramatic effect, stuff the wrapped swags with tissue paper or thin foam, depending on the translucence and weight of fabric.
- Release elastics at tops of jabots.

Plan #241041

Dimensions: 65' W x 45' D
Levels: 1
Heated Square Footage: 1,612
Bedrooms: 3
Bathrooms: 2
Foundation: Slab
Material List Available: No
Price Category: C

Images provided by designer/architect.

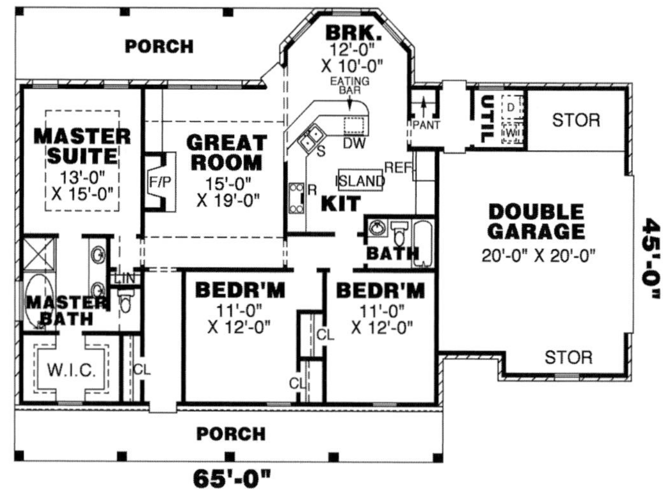

Copyright by designer/architect.

Plan #151043

Dimensions: 53' W x 64' D
Levels: 1
Heated Square Footage: 1,636
Bedrooms: 3
Bathrooms: 2
Foundation: Crawl space, slab; basement option for fee
CompleteCost List Available: Yes
Price Category: E

Images provided by designer/architect.

CAD FILE AVAILABLE

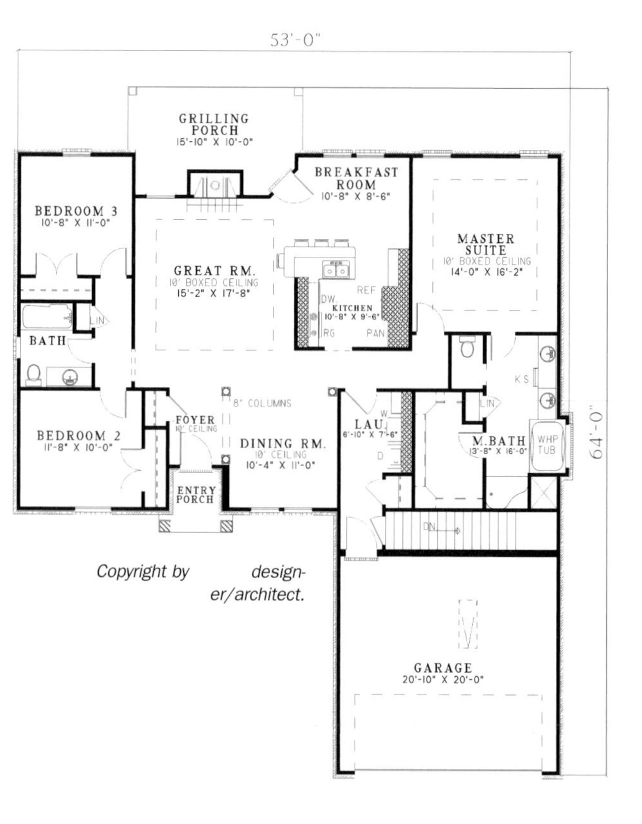

Copyright by designer/architect.

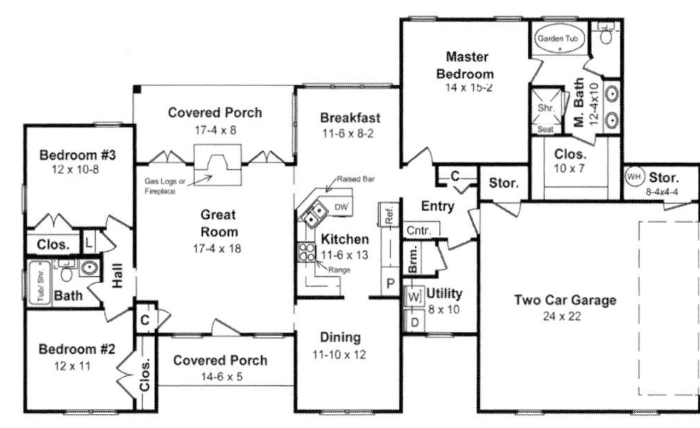

Plan #351006

Dimensions: 64' W x 39' D
Levels: 1
Heated Square Footage: 1,638
Bedrooms: 3
Bathrooms: 2
Foundation: Crawl space, slab, or basement
Materials List Available: Yes
Price Category: E

Images provided by designer/architect.

CAD FILE AVAILABLE

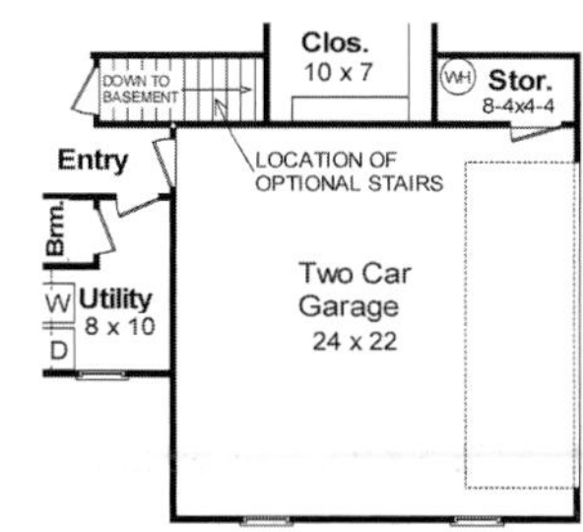

Stair Location for Basement Option

Copyright by designer/architect.

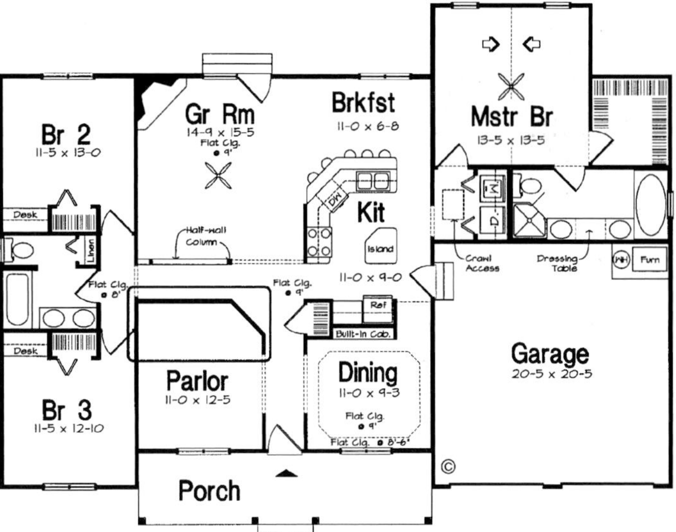

Plan #391038

Dimensions: 59' W x 44' D
Levels: 1
Heated Square Footage: 1,642
Bedrooms: 3
Bathrooms: 2
Foundation: Crawl space, slab, or basement
Materials List Available: Yes
Price Category: C

Images provided by designer/architect.

CAD FILE AVAILABLE

Copyright by designer/architect.

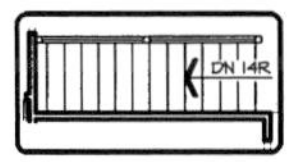

Optional Basement Stairs

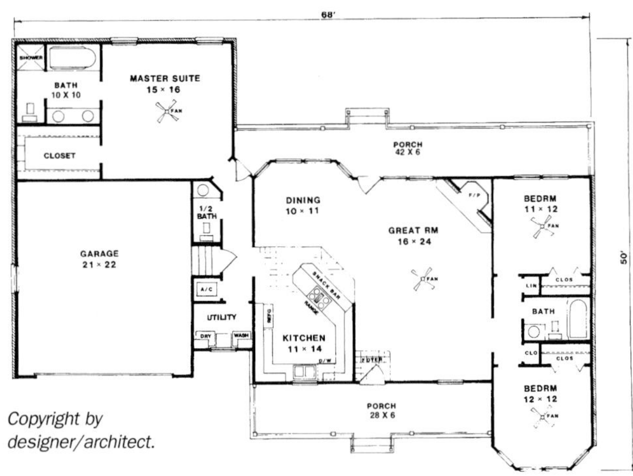

Copyright by designer/architect.

Plan #171006

Dimensions: 68' W x 50' D
Levels: 1
Heated Square Footage: 1,648
Bedrooms: 3
Bathrooms: 2½
Foundation: Crawl space, slab
Materials List Available: Yes
Price Category: C

Images provided by designer/architect.

SMARTtip

Window Shades

While decorative hems add interest to roller shades, they also increase the cost. If you're handy with a glue gun, choose one of the trims available at fabric and craft stores, and consider attaching it yourself. Give your shades fancy pulls for an inexpensive dash of pizzazz.

Plan #121008

Dimensions: 62' W x 56' D
Levels: 1
Heated Square Footage: 1,651
Bedrooms: 2
Bathrooms: 2
Foundation: Basement; crawl space or slab for fee
Materials List Available: Yes
Price Category: C

Images provided by designer/architect.

CAD FILE AVAILABLE

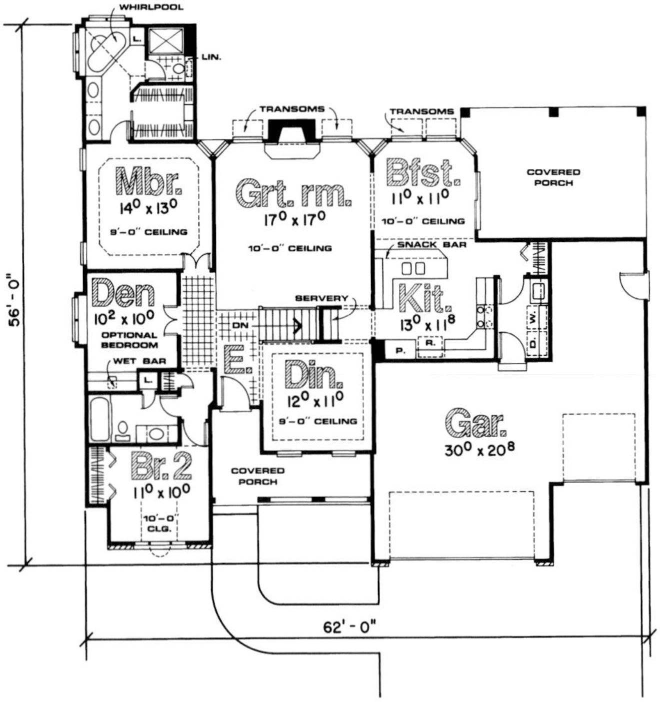

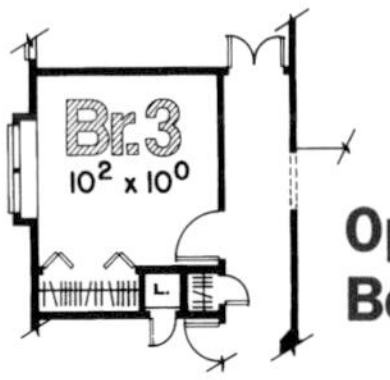

Optional Bedroom

Copyright by designer/architect.

Plan #161009

Dimensions: 60'9" W x 49' D
Levels: 1
Heated Square Footage: 1,651
Bedrooms: 3
Bathrooms: 2
Foundation: Basement
Materials List Available: No
Price Category: C

Images provided by designer/architect.

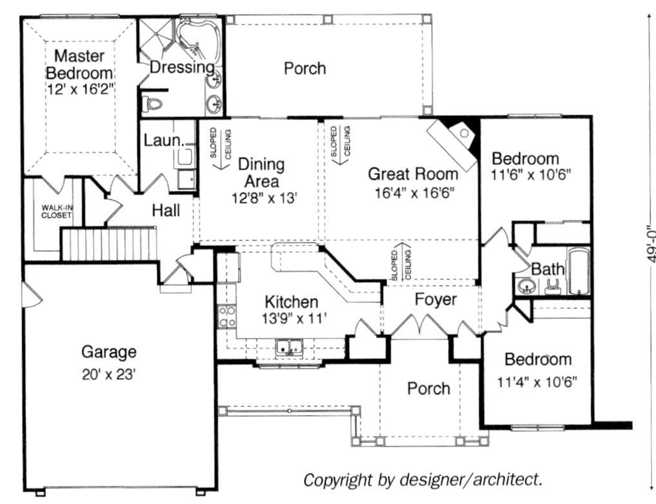

Copyright by designer/architect.

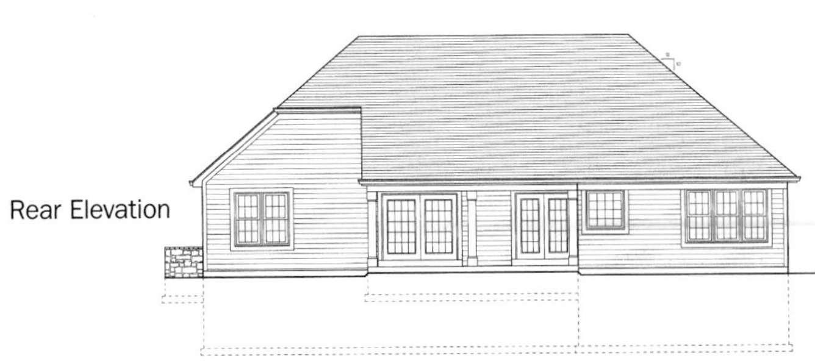

Rear Elevation

Plan #171008

Dimensions: 72' W x 40' D
Levels: 1
Heated Square Footage: 1,652
Bedrooms: 3
Bathrooms: 2
Foundation: Crawl space, slab
Materials List Available: Yes
Price Category: C

Images provided by designer/architect.

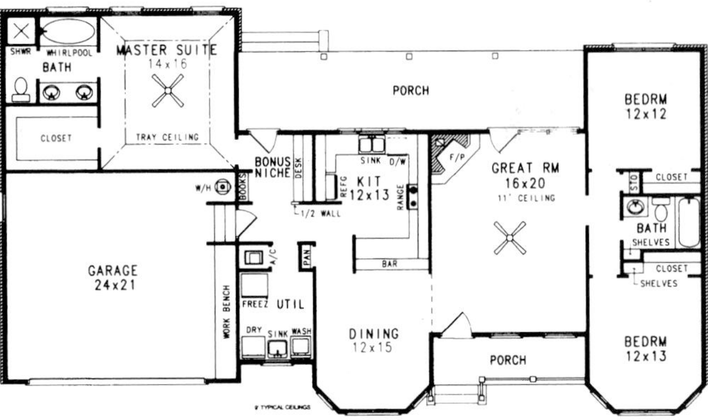

SMARTtip

Lighting for Decorative Shadows

Use lighting to create decorative shadows. For interesting, undefined shadows, set lights at ground level aiming upward in front of a shrub or tree that is close to a wall. For silhouetting, place lights directly behind a plant or garden statue that is near a wall. In both cases, using a wide beam will increase the effect.

Plan #341030

Dimensions: 52' W x 40' D

Levels: 1

Heated Square Footage: 1,660

Bedrooms: 3

Bathrooms: 2

Foundation: Crawl space or slab; basement for fee

Materials List Available: Yes

Price Category: C

Images provided by designer/architect.

CAD FILE AVAILABLE

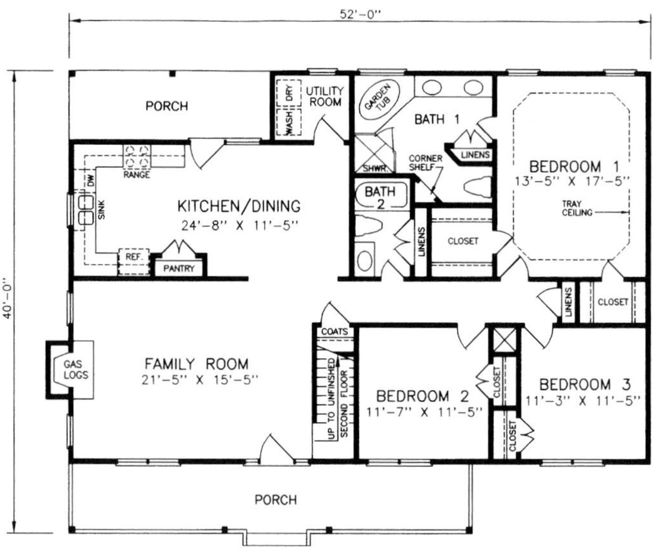

Copyright by designer/architect.

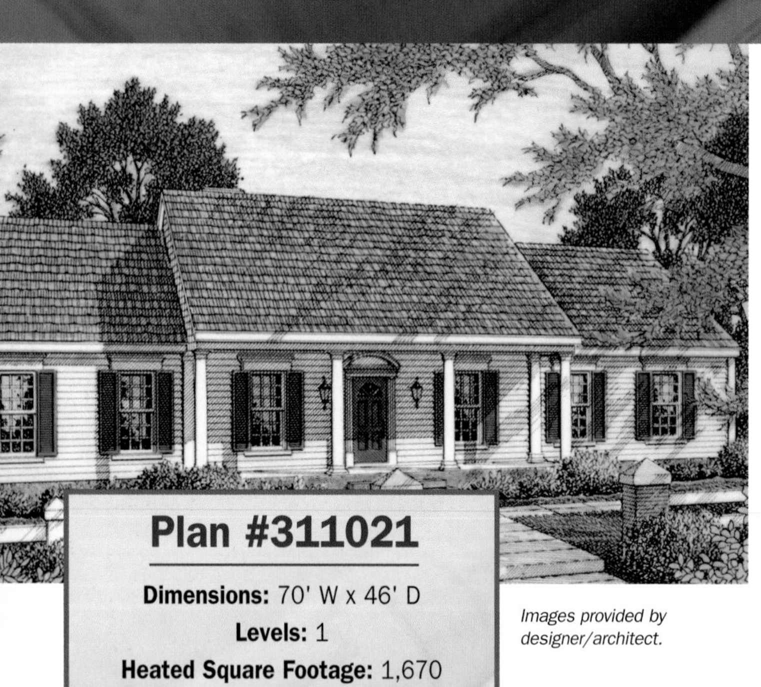

Plan #311021

Dimensions: 70' W x 46' D

Levels: 1

Heated Square Footage: 1,670

Bedrooms: 3

Bathrooms: 2

Foundation: Crawl space, slab, or basement

Materials List Available: Yes

Price Category: C

Images provided by designer/architect.

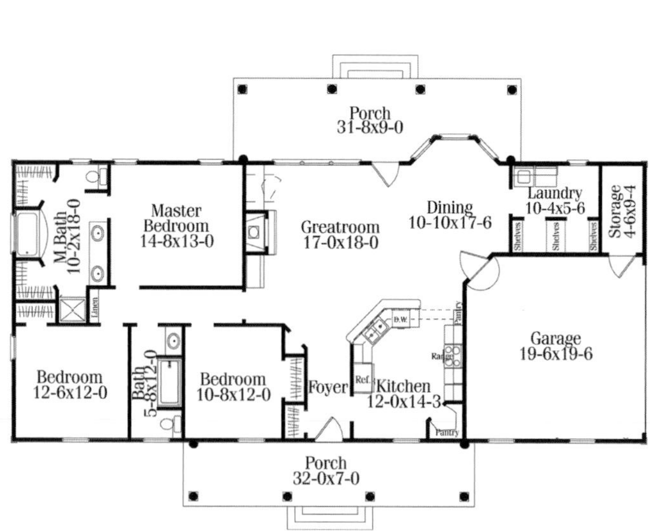

Stair Location for Basement Option

Copyright by designer/architect.

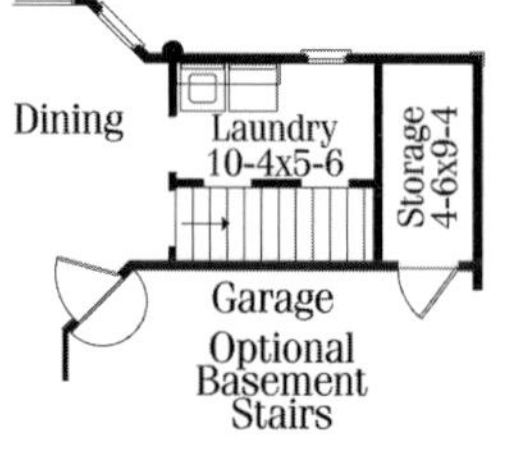

Plan #311051

Dimensions: 56'6" W x 68'6" D
Levels: 1
Heated Square Footage: 1,680
Bedrooms: 3
Bathrooms: 2
Foundation: Crawl space, slab, or basement
Material List Available: Yes
Price Category: C

Images provided by designer/architect.

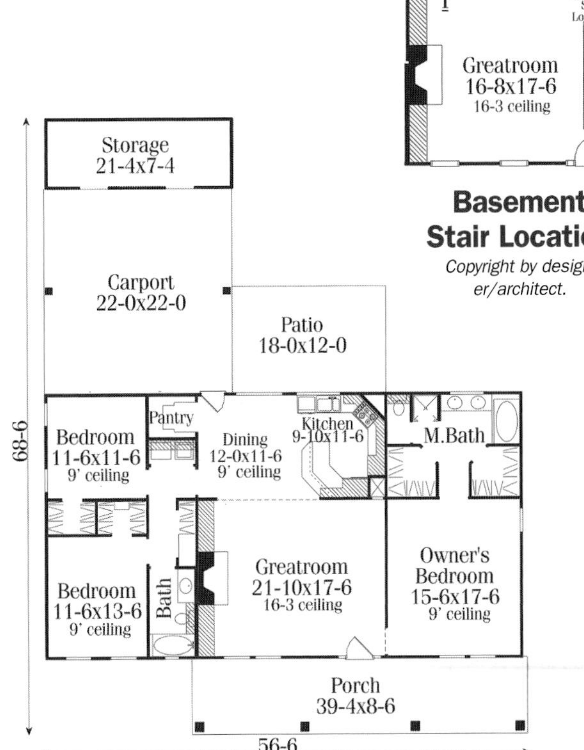

Basement Stair Location

Copyright by designer/architect.

Plan #341035

Dimensions: 60' W x 28' D
Levels: 1
Heated Square Footage: 1,680
Bedrooms: 4
Bathrooms: 2
Foundation: Crawl space, slab; basement option for fee
Materials List Available: Yes
Price Category: C

Images provided by designer/architect.

CAD FILE AVAILABLE

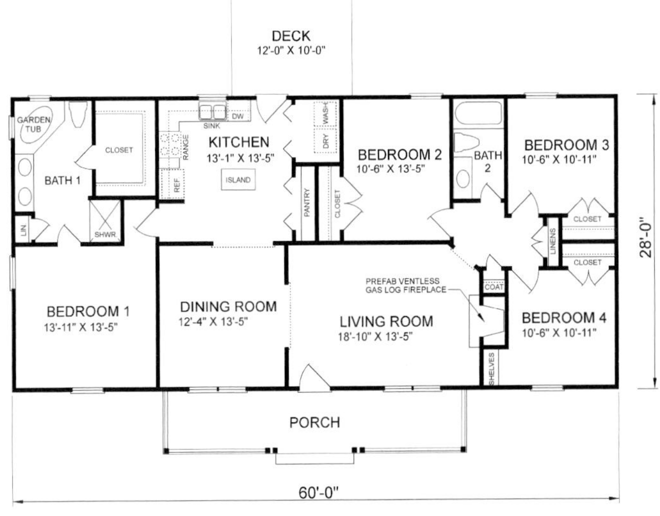

Copyright by designer/architect.

Plan #171023

Dimensions: 74' W x 41' D
Levels: 1
Heated Square Footage: 1,684
Bedrooms: 3
Bathrooms: 2
Foundation: Crawl space or slab
Materials List Available: Yes
Price Category: C

Images provided by designer/architect.

This beautifully designed home will be a perfect place to raise your family.

Features:

- Great Room: This large gathering area features a corner fireplace and an 11-ft.-high ceiling. Its direct access to the rear porch enables the room to expand on nice summer days.
- Kitchen: Featuring plenty of workspace and storage, this kitchen is adjacent to the dining room, simplyfying mealtime transitions.
- Master Suite: This spacious area features a walk-in closet to simplify the process of getting ready in the morning. The master bath features a stall shower and a garden tub.
- Secondary Bedrooms: Both of the two additional bedrooms have ample closet space and access to a full bathroom.

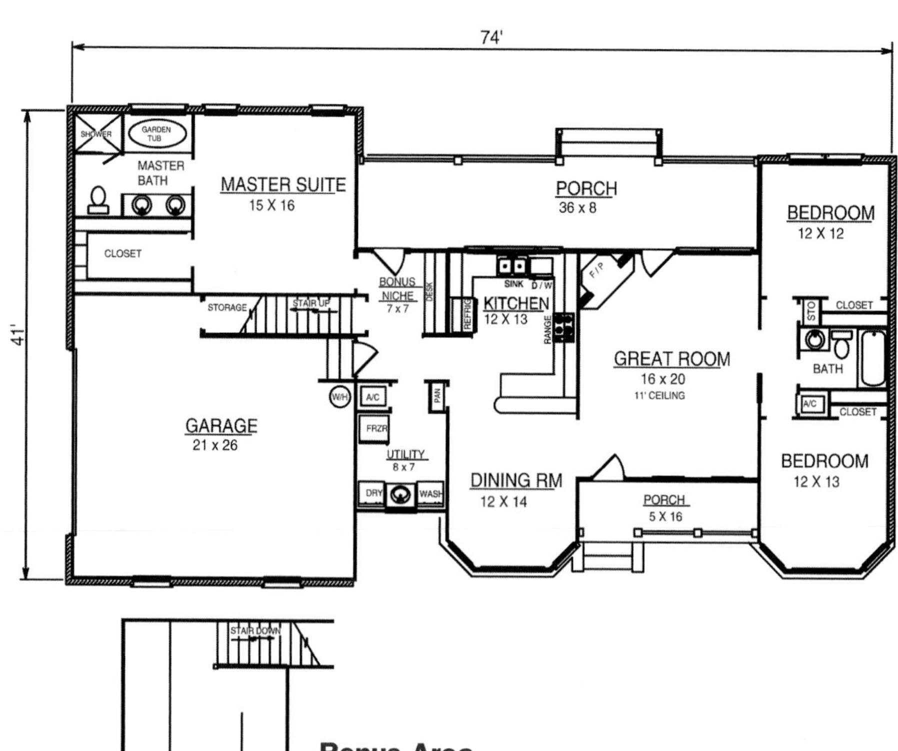

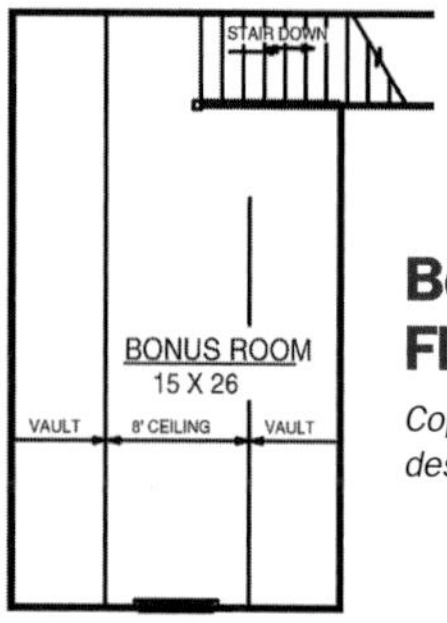

Bonus Area Floor Plan

Copyright by designer/architect.

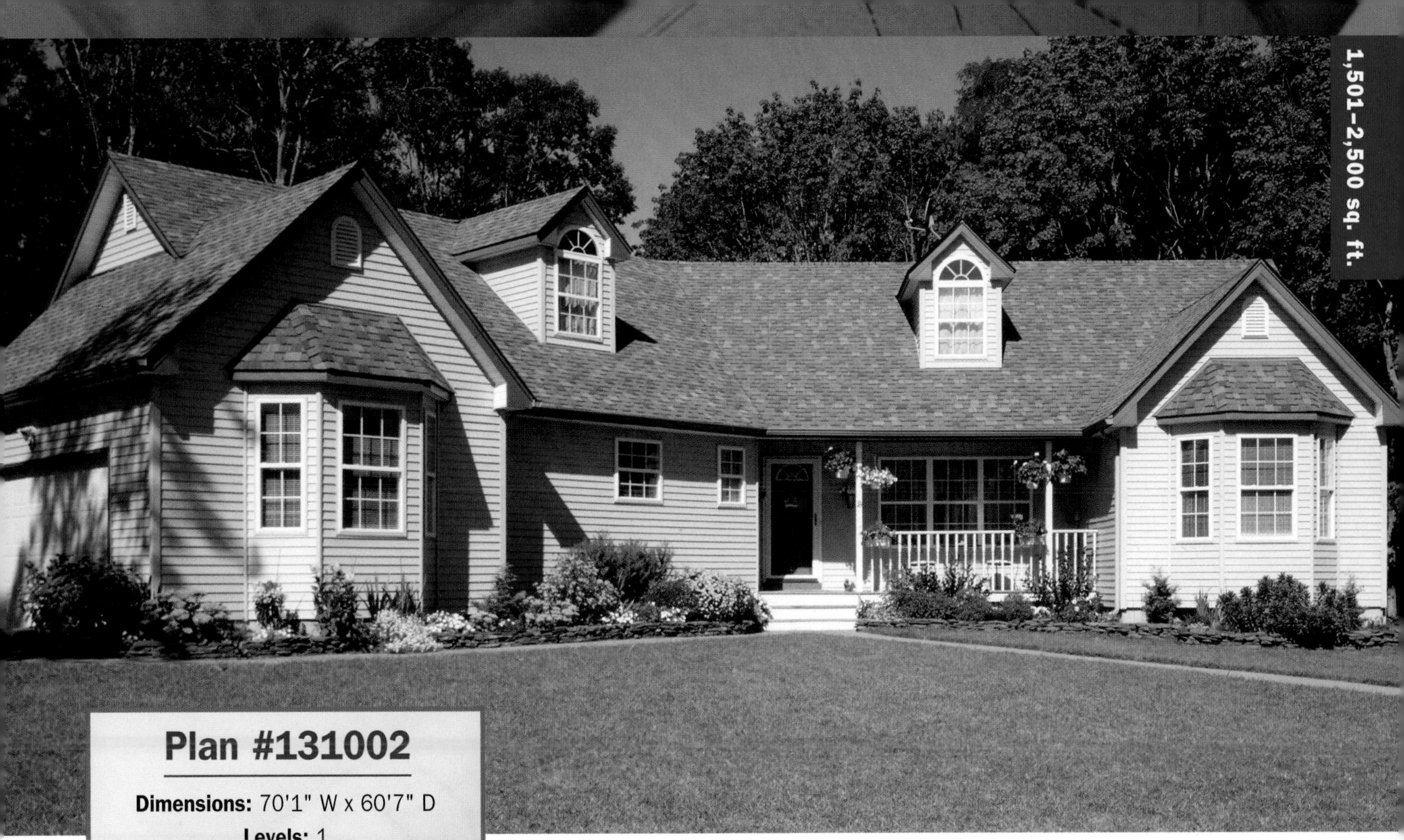

Plan #131002

Dimensions: 70'1" W x 60'7" D
Levels: 1
Heated Square Footage: 1,709
Bedrooms: 3
Bathrooms: 2½
Foundation: Slab or basement
Materials List Available: Yes
Price Category: D

Images provided by designer/architect.

CAD FILE AVAILABLE

Copyright by designer/architect.

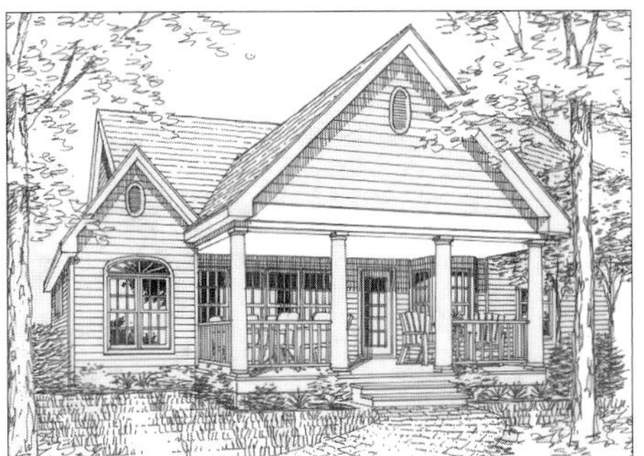

Rear View

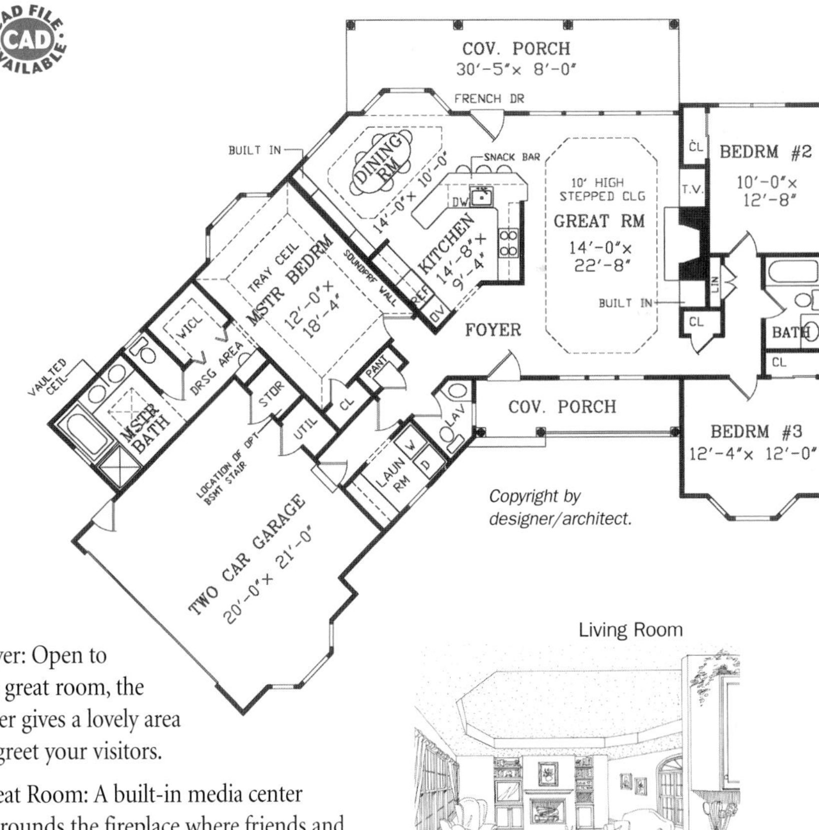

You'll love the way this angled ranch brings out the best in a corner lot or on a slope.

Features:

- Ceiling Height: 8 ft.
- Front Porch: Hang baskets of plants from the roof of this porch, which is just the right size for a couple of rockers and a side table.
- Dining Room: Well-placed windows flood this room with sunlight during the day and a built-in cabinet gives ample storage space for all your china, linens, and collectables.
- Foyer: Open to the great room, the foyer gives a lovely area to greet your visitors.
- Great Room: A built-in media center surrounds the fireplace where friends and family are sure to gather.
- Master Suite: You'll love the privacy of this somewhat isolated but easily accessed room. Decorate to show off the large bay window and tray ceiling, and enjoy the luxury of a separate toilet room.

Living Room

Plan #321001

Dimensions: 83' W x 42' D
Levels: 1
Heated Square Footage: 1,721
Bedrooms: 3
Bathrooms: 2
Foundation: Crawl space, slab, or walkout
Materials List Available: Yes
Price Category: E

Images provided by designer/architect.

Rear View

Front View

CAD FILE AVAILABLE

You'll love the atrium, which creates a warm, naturally lit space inside this gracious home, as well as the roof dormers that give the house wonderful curb appeal from the outside.

Features:

- Great Room: Bathed in light from the atrium window wall, this room, with its vaulted ceiling, will be the hub of your family life.
- Dining Room: This room also has a vaulted ceiling and is lit by the atrium, but you can draw drapes at night to create a cozy, warm feeling.
- Kitchen: Designed for functionality, this step-saving kitchen is easy to organize and makes cooking a pleasure.
- Breakfast Room: For convenience, this room is located between the kitchen and the rear covered porch.
- Master Suite: Retire with pleasure to this lovely retreat, with its luxurious bath.

Copyright by designer/architect.

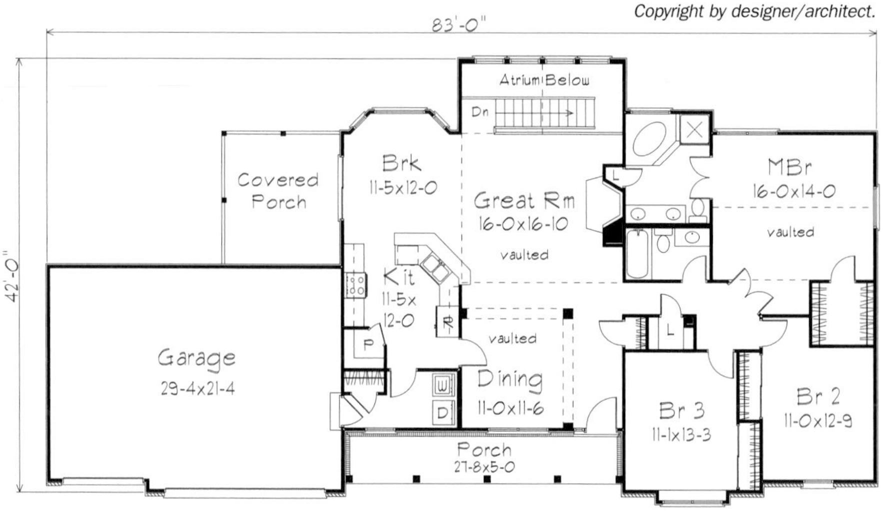

83'-0"
42'-0"
Atrium Below
Dn
Covered Porch
Brk 11-5x12-0
Great Rm 16-0x16-10 vaulted
MBr 16-0x14-0 vaulted
Kit 11-5x12-0
vaulted
Dining 11-0x11-6
Garage 29-4x21-4
Br 3 11-1x13-3
Br 2 11-0x12-9
Porch 27-8x5-0

Plan #371033

Dimensions: 73' W x 33' 4" D
Levels: 1
Heated Square Footage: 1,724
Bedrooms: 3
Bathrooms: 2
Foundation: Crawl space or slab
Materials List Available: No
Price Category: C

CAD FILE CAD AVAILABLE

Images provided by designer/architect.

This beautiful brick-and-stone country home will be the envy of the neighborhood.

Features:

- Front Porch: This charming yet functional porch welcomes you home.
- Family Room: This large room, with its cathedral ceiling and cozy fireplace, is ideal for entertaining.
- Kitchen: This gourmet kitchen has all the necessities you will ever need, including a raised bar area.
- Master Suite: This cozy area features a stepped ceiling. The luxurious bath boasts a marble tub and two walk-in closets.

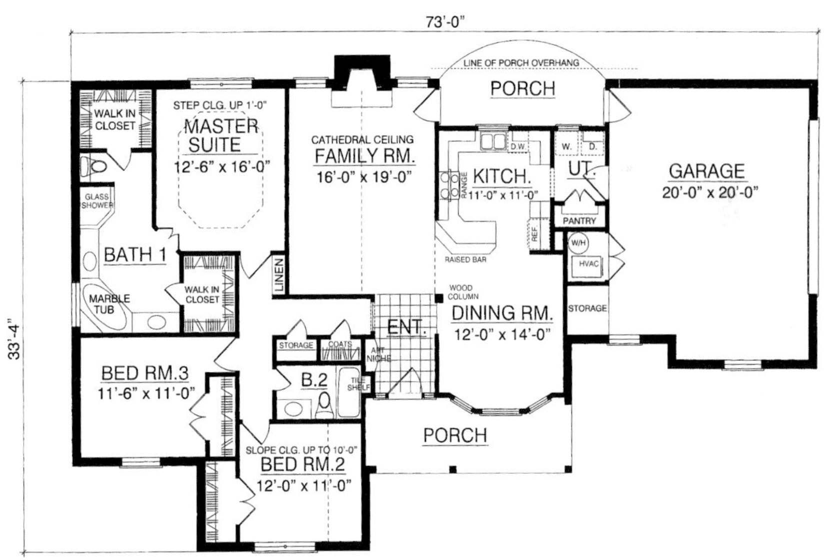

Copyright by designer/architect.

Plan #371011

Dimensions: 55'4" W x 49'10" D
Levels: 1
Heated Square Footage: 1,681
Bedrooms: 3
Bathrooms: 2½
Foundation: Crawl space, slab or basement
Materials List Available: No
Price Category: C

Images provided by designer/architect.

CAD FILE AVAILABLE

Copyright by designer/architect.

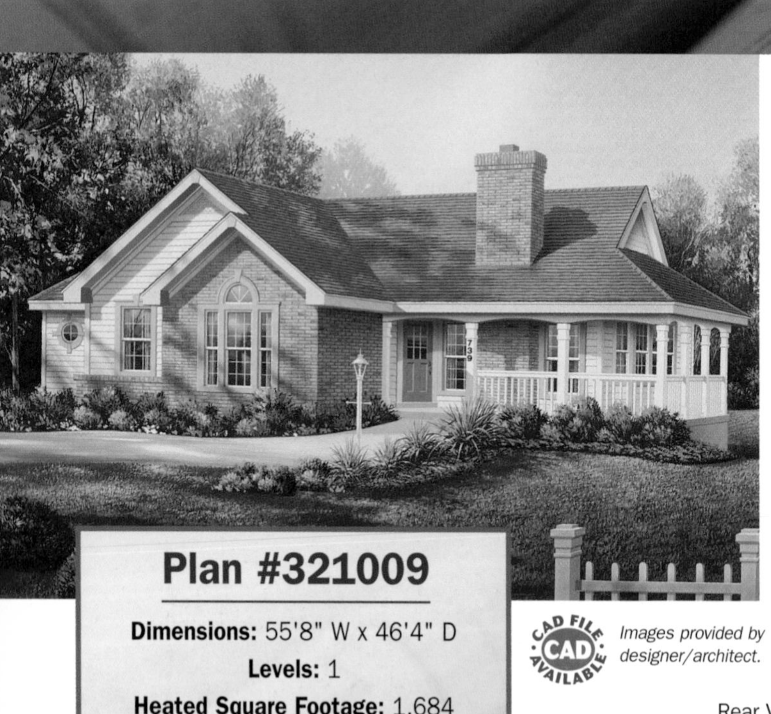

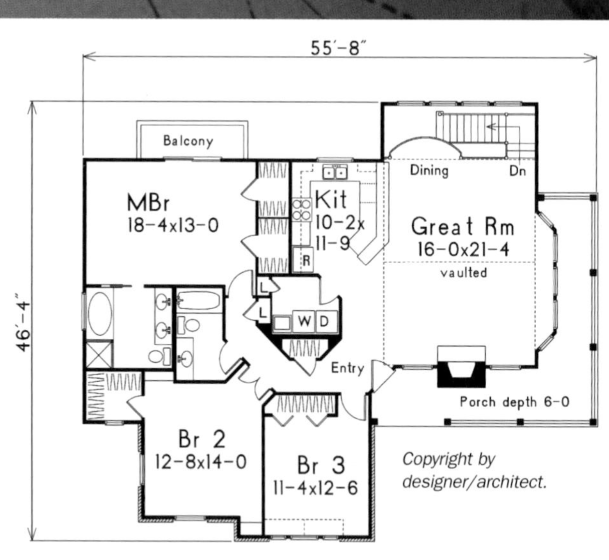

Copyright by designer/architect.

Plan #321009

Dimensions: 55'8" W x 46'4" D
Levels: 1
Heated Square Footage: 1,684
Bedrooms: 3
Bathrooms: 2
Foundation: Walkout
Materials List Available: Yes
Price Category: E

CAD FILE AVAILABLE

Images provided by designer/architect.

Rear View

Optional Basement Level Floor Plan

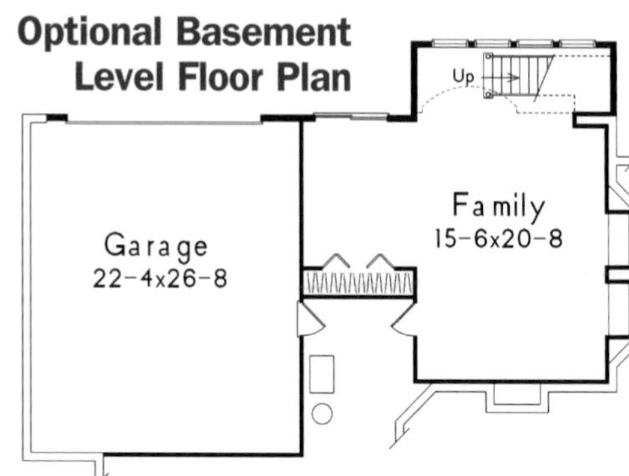

Plan #311008

Dimensions: 70'1" W x 48' D
Levels: 1
Heated Square Footage: 1,688
Bedrooms: 3
Bathrooms: 2
Foundation: Basement, crawl space, or slab
Materials List Available: Yes
Price Category: C

Images provided by designer/architect.

Porch 31-4x8-0
Master Bedroom 13-6x15-6
Bath
Bath
Greatroom 15-4x19-5
Breakfast 9-10x10-6
Kitchen 9-6x11-6
Laundry 8-6x9-4
Storage 8-6x9-4
Garage 21-6x21-6
Bedroom 13-6x11-6
Bedroom 10-11x11-6
Foyer
Dining 12-0x11-6
Porch 31-4x8-0

Rear View

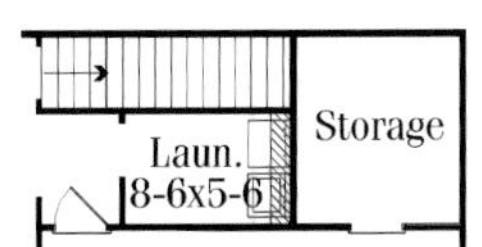

Basement Stair Option

Plan #121118

Dimensions: 42' W x 59'8" D
Levels: 1
Heated Square Footage: 1,636
Bedrooms: 3
Bathrooms: 2
Foundation: Basement; crawl space for fee
Materials List Available: Yes
Price Category: C

Images provided by designer/architect.

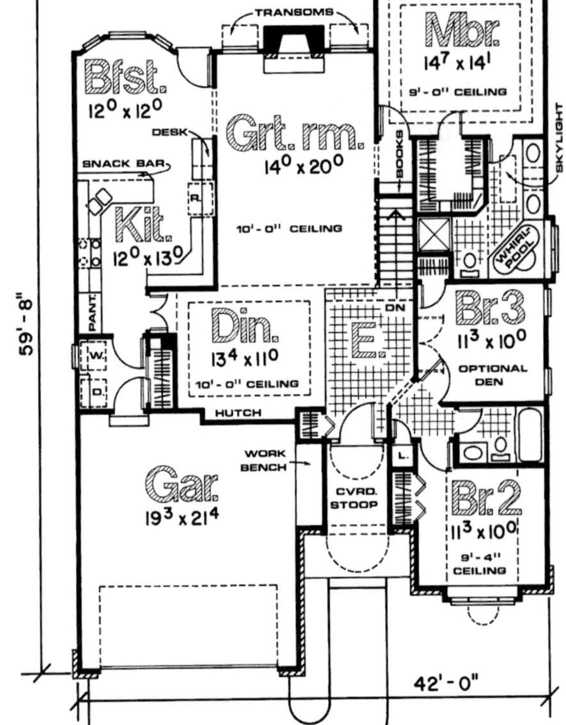

Copyright by designer/architect.

Plan #161014

Dimensions: 51'8" W x 49'8" D
Levels: 1
Heated Square Footage: 1,698
Bedrooms: 3
Bathrooms: 2
Foundation: Basement; crawl space for fee
Materials List Available: Yes
Price Category: C

Images provided by designer/architect.

Porch 12' x 12'
Master Bedroom 15' x 13'2"
Tray Ceiling
Walk-in Closet
Bath
Great Room - Dining 28'8" x 16'11" Irr.
Stepped Ceiling
Kitchen 12' x 12' Irr.
Pantry
Laun. 7'4" x 6'
Down
Hall
Bath
Foyer
Bedroom/Den 10'2" x 11'6"
Bedroom 11'4" x 12'
Porch
Two-Car Garage 20' x 21'

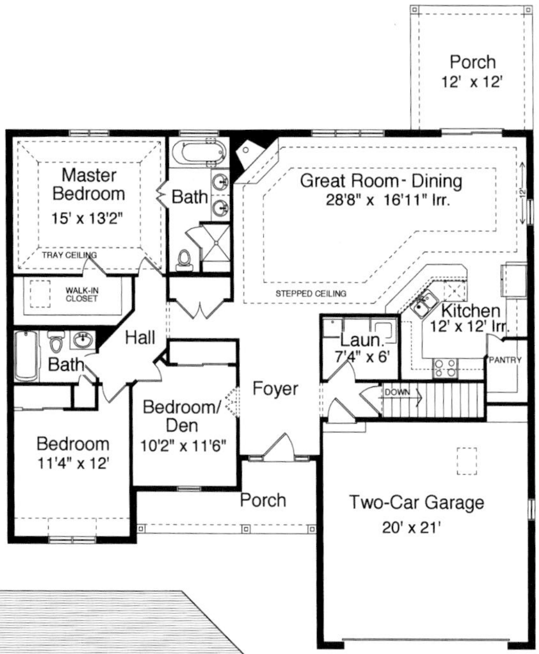

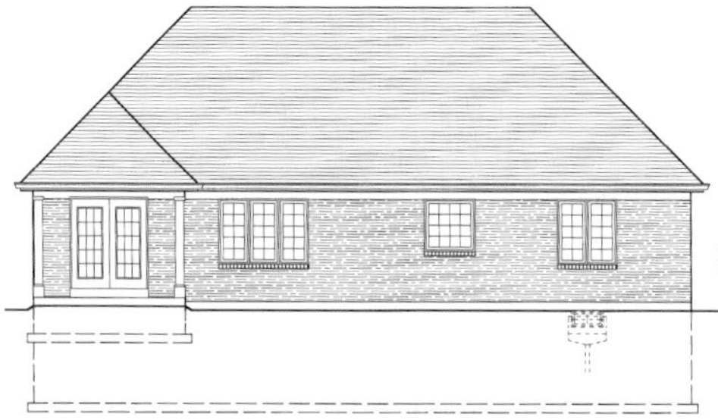

Rear Elevation

Plan #321026

Dimensions: 67' W x 42'4" D
Levels: 1
Heated Square Footage: 1,712
Bedrooms: 3
Bathrooms: 2½
Foundation: Crawl space
Materials List Available: Yes
Price Category: C

Images provided by designer/architect.

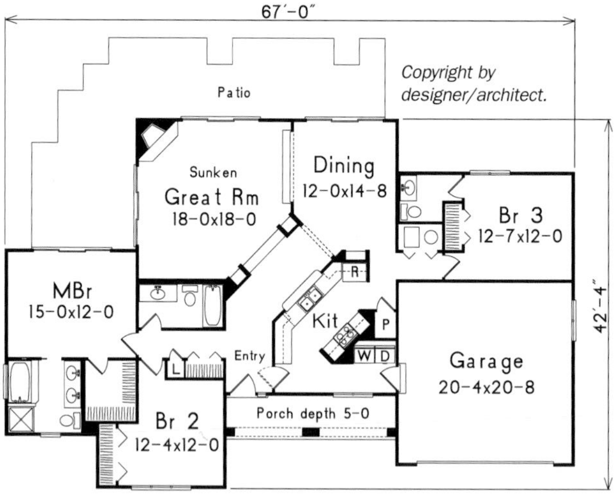

67'-0"
Copyright by designer/architect.
Patio
Sunken Great Rm 18-0x18-0
Dining 12-0x14-8
Br 3 12-7x12-0
MBr 15-0x12-0
Kit
R
P
W D
Entry
Garage 20-4x20-8
Br 2 12-4x12-0
L
Porch depth 5-0
42'-4"

SMARTtip

Deck Design with Computers

Consider using a computer-aided design (CAD) program to plan your deck. Some programs let you see three-dimensional views of your design complete with railings, stairs, planters, hot tubs, and the surrounding landscaping.

Plan #341029

Dimensions: 49' W x 57' D

Levels: 1

Heated Square Footage: 1,737

Bedrooms: 3

Bathrooms: 2

Foundation: Crawl space; slab or basement for fee

Materials List Available: Yes

Price Category: C

Images provided by designer/architect.

CAD FILE AVAILABLE

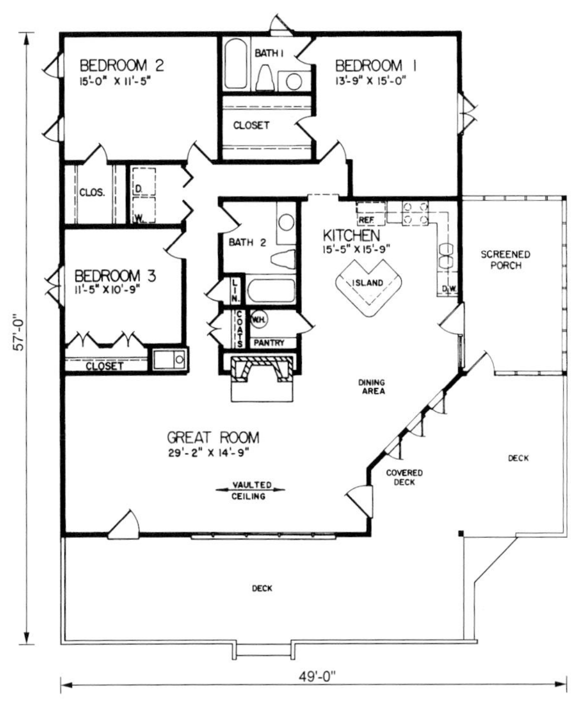

Copyright by designer/architect.

Plan #391034

Dimensions: 72'4" W x 43' D

Levels: 1

Heated Square Footage: 1,737

Bedrooms: 3

Bathrooms: 2

Foundation: Crawl space, slab, or basement

Materials List Available: Yes

Price Category: C

Images provided by designer/architect.

This home, as shown in the photograph, may differ from the actual blueprints. For more detailed information, please check the floor plans carefully.

Rear View

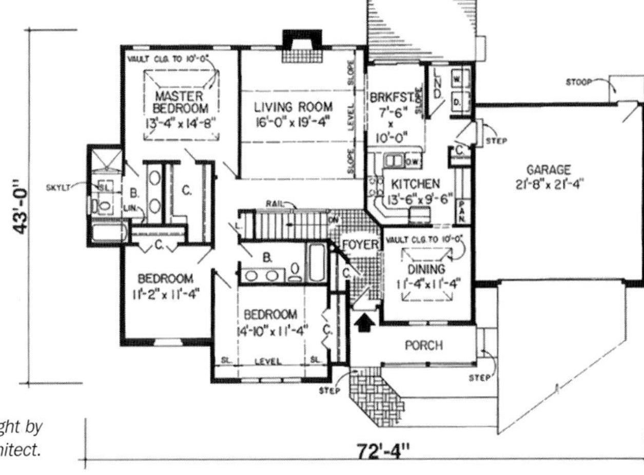

Copyright by designer/architect.

Images provided by designer/architect.

Plan #441004

Dimensions: 55' W x 48' D

Levels: 1

Heated Square Footage: 1,728

Bedrooms: 2

Bathrooms: 2

Foundation: Crawl space; slab or basement available for fee

Materials List Available: No

Price Category: C

CAD FILE AVAILABLE

Empty nesters and first-time homeowners will adore the comfort within this charming home. Rooms benefit from the many windows, which welcome light into the home.

Features:

- Great Room: This vaulted room is equipped with a media center and fireplace. Windows span across the back of the room and the adjoining dining room, extending the perceived area and offering access to the covered patio.
- Kitchen: Taking advantage of corner space, this kitchen provides ample cabinets and countertops to store goods and prepare meals. Every chef will appreciate the extra space afforded by the pantry.
- Master Suite: This luxurious escape has a large sleeping area with views of the backyard. The master bath features a spa tub, dual vanities, and a walk-in closet.
- Garage: This front-loading two-car garage has a shop area located in the rear.

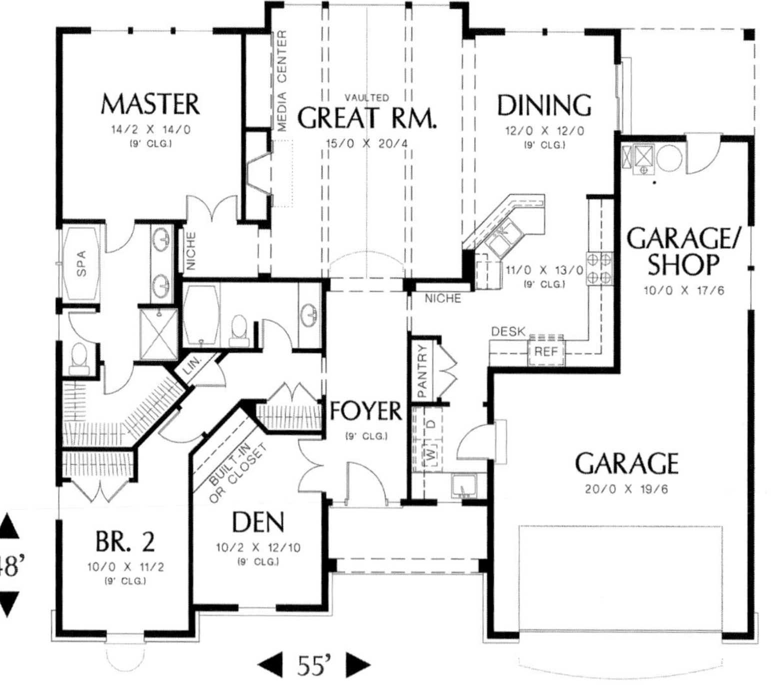

Copyright by designer/architect.

Rear Elevation

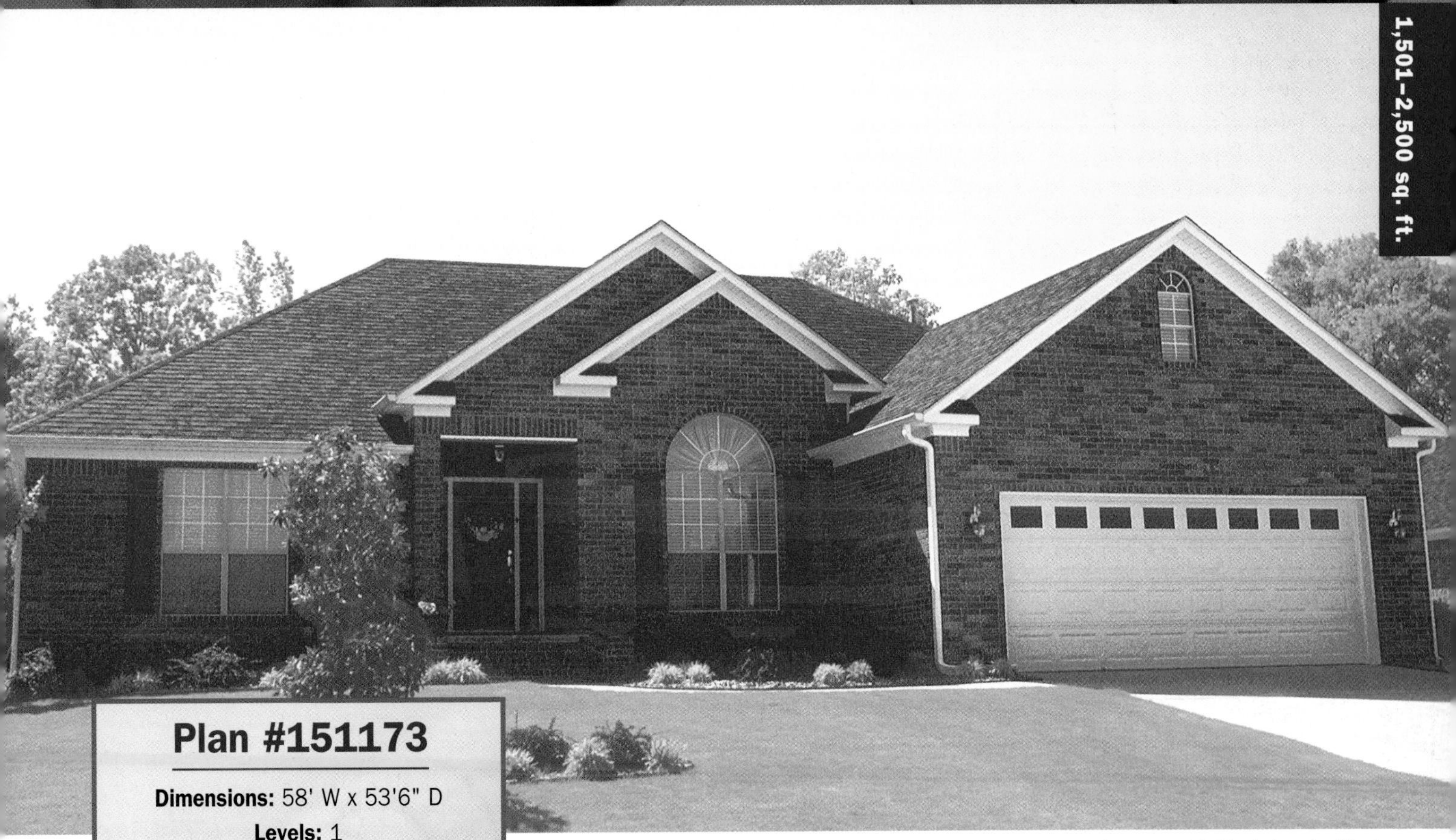

Images provided by designer/architect.

Plan #151173

Dimensions: 58' W x 53'6" D
Levels: 1
Heated Square Footage: 1,739
Bedrooms: 3
Bathrooms: 2
Foundation: Crawl space, slab, basement, or walkout
CompleteCost List Available: Yes
Price Category: C

CAD FILE AVAILABLE

You'll love the charming architectural features and practical contemporary design of this ranch-style home.

Features:

- Great Room: Perfect for entertaining guests or just cozying up to the glowing fireplace with loved-ones, this great room is conveniently located in the center of everything.
- Kitchen: This highly efficient design, complete with island and plenty of workspace and storage, is just steps away from the sunlit breakfast room and the formal dining room, simplifying meal transitions.
- Master Suite: A romantic getaway in itself, this spacious master bedroom adjoins his and her walk-in closets, and a large compartmentalized master bath with a whirlpool tub, dual vanities, and a standing shower. The room also includes a private entrance to the back porch.
- Secondary Bedrooms: In a remote space of their own, these two nicely sized bedrooms share access to a full bathroom.

Copyright by designer/architect.

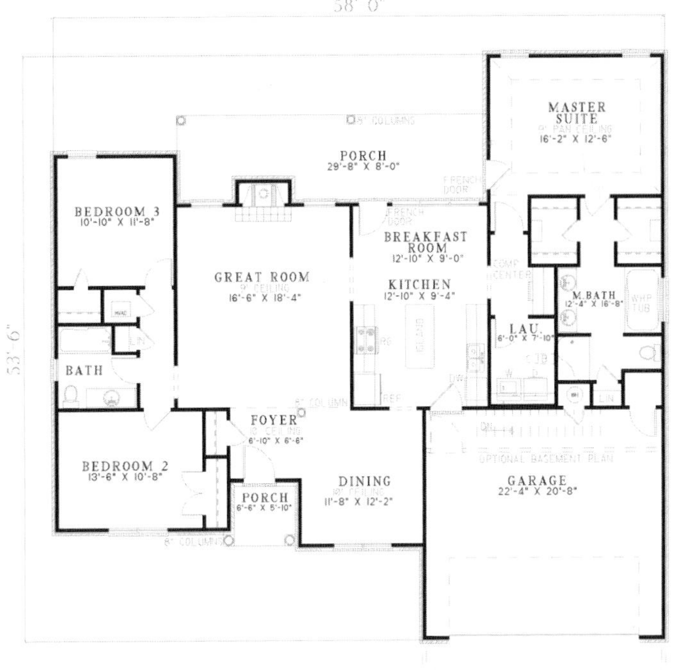

Plan #321008

Dimensions: 57' W x 52'2" D
Levels: 1
Heated Square Footage: 1,761
Bedrooms: 4
Bathrooms: 2
Foundation: Basement
Materials List Available: Yes
Price Category: C

CAD FILE AVAILABLE

Images provided by designer/architect.

Copyright by designer/architect.

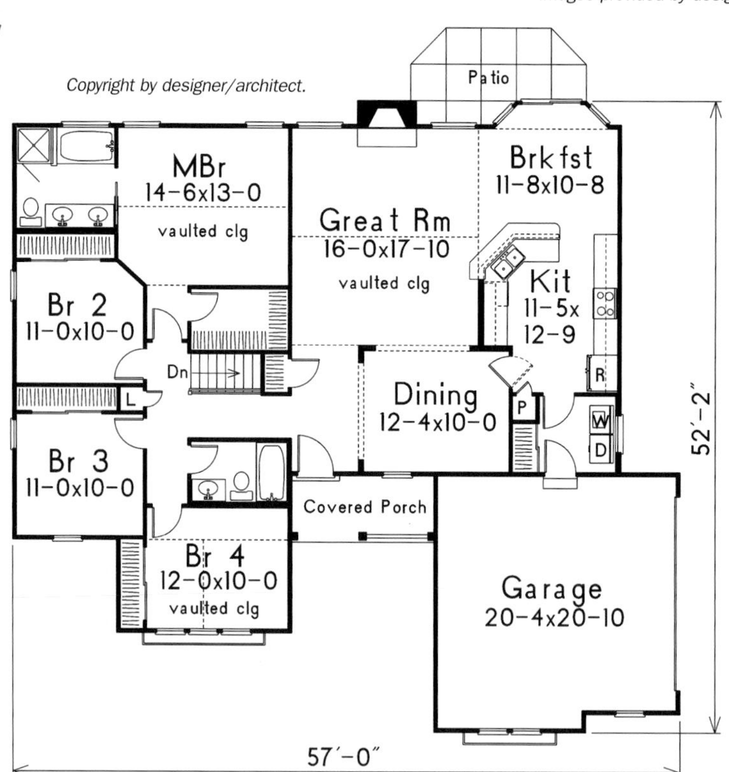

One look at the roof dormers and planter boxes that grace the outside of this ranch, and you'll know that the interior is planned for comfortable family living.

Features:

- Great Room: A vaulted ceiling in this room points up its generous dimensions. Put a grouping of chairs near the fireplace to take advantage of the cozy spot it creates in chilly weather.
- Kitchen: Open to the great room, this kitchen has been planned for convenience. It features a pass-through to the dining area for easy serving when you've got a crowd to feed.
- Master Bedroom: A vaulted ceiling here makes you feel especially pampered, and the walk-in closet and amenity-filled bath add to that feeling.
- Additional Bedrooms: Great closet space characterizes all the rooms in this home, making it easy for children of any age to keep it organized and tidy.

SMARTtip

Hanging Wallpaper

Use liner paper to smooth out a damaged wall and to provide uniform support for expensive paper.

Plan #121006

Dimensions: 46' W x 58' D
Levels: 1
Heated Square Footage: 1,762
Bedrooms: 3
Bathrooms: 2
Foundation: Slab; crawl space or basement for fee
Materials List Available: Yes
Price Category: C

CAD FILE AVAILABLE

Images provided by designer/architect.

The entry has a trio of arched openings that leads you to other areas of this amenity-packed home.

Features:

- Ceiling Height: 8 ft. except as noted.
- Eating Bar: Conveniently located between the kitchen and family room, this is sure to be a favorite spot for informal entertaining and family gatherings.
- Family room: A wall of windows, a fireplace, and a vaulted ceiling stretching to 11 ft. work together to make this a bright and warm room.
- Kitchen: There's no shortage of counter space in this well-planned kitchen that features a center island in addition to the eating bar.
- Master Suite: Luxuriate at the end of the day in this large bedroom with its decorative tray ceiling and walk-in closet. Enjoy the pampering bath with its sunlit corner whirlpool flanked by vanities.
- Garage: Two bays provide room for cars and plenty of storage as well.

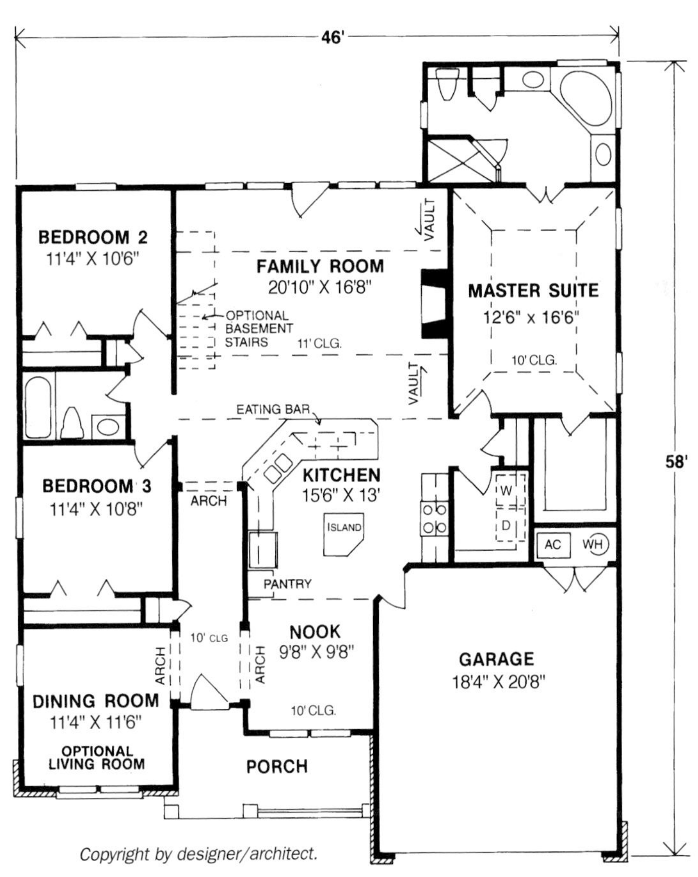

Copyright by designer/architect.

Plan #351002

Dimensions: 64' W x 45'10" D
Levels: 1
Heated Square Footage: 1,752
Bedrooms: 3
Bathrooms: 2
Foundation: Crawl space, slab, or basement
Materials List Available: Yes
Price Category: E

Images provided by designer/architect.

This is a beautiful classic traditional home with a European touch.

Features:

- Great Room: This gathering area has a gas log fireplace that is flanked by two built-in cabinets. The area has a 10-ft.-tall tray ceiling.
- Kitchen: This L-shaped island kitchen has a raised bar and is open to the eating area and great room. The three open spaces work together as one large room.
- Master Suite: Located on the opposite side of the home from the secondary bedrooms, this suite has a vaulted ceiling. The master bath has dual vanities and a garden tub.
- Bedrooms: The two secondary bedrooms share a hall bathroom and have ample closet space.

Great Room

Kitchen

Master Bathroom

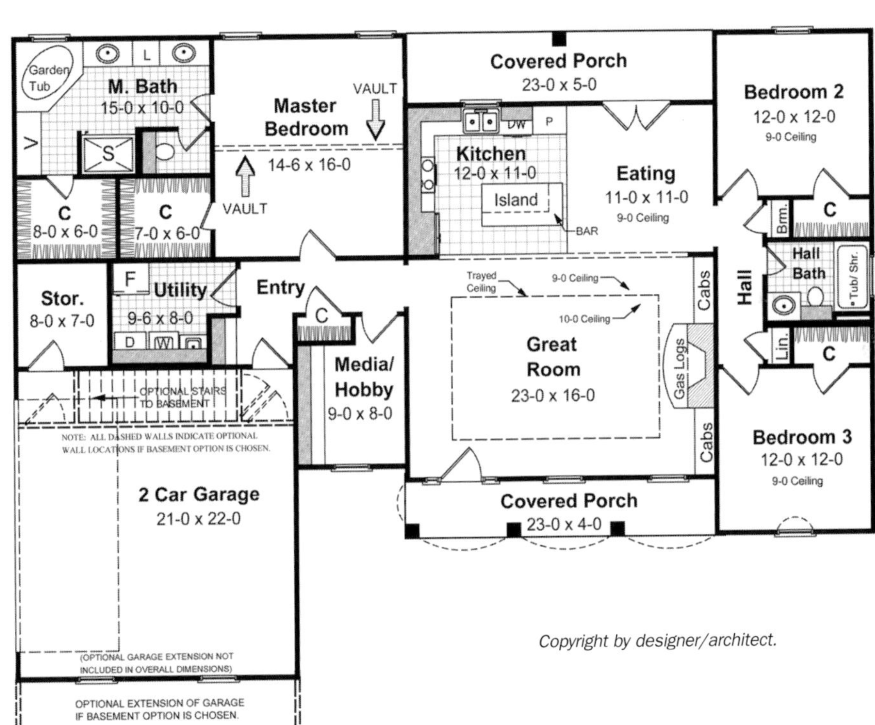

Plan #151054

Dimensions: 67' W x 54'10" D

Levels: 1

Heated Square Footage: 1,746

Bedrooms: 3

Bathrooms: 2

Foundation: Crawl space or slab; basement for fee

CompleteCost List Available: Yes

Price Category: C

Images provided by designer/architect.

SMARTtip

Mixing and Matching Windows

Windows, both fixed and operable, are made in various styles and shapes. While mixing styles should be carefully avoided, a variety of interesting window sizes and shapes may nevertheless be combined to achieve symmetry, harmony, and rhythm on the exterior of a home.

Plan #221011

Dimensions: 59' W x 58' D

Levels: 1

Heated Square Footage: 1,756

Bedrooms: 3

Bathrooms: 2

Foundation: Basement

Materials List Available: No

Price Category: C

Images provided by designer/architect.

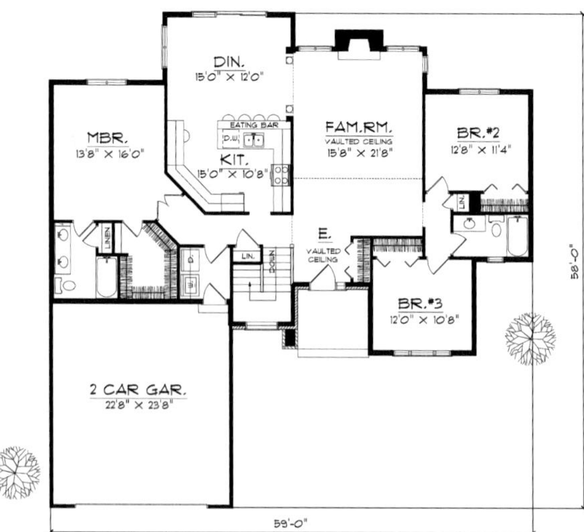

Rear Elevation

Plan #121331

Dimensions: 62' W x 48' D
Levels: 1
Heated Square Footage: 1,763
Bedrooms: 3
Bathrooms: 2½
Foundation: Basement
Materials List Available: Yes
Price Category: G

Images provided by designer/architect.

CAD FILE AVAILABLE

Copyright by designer/architect.

Plan #171009

Dimensions: 68' W x 50' D
Levels: 1
Heated Square Footage: 1,771
Bedrooms: 3
Bathrooms: 2
Foundation: Crawl space, slab
Materials List Available: Yes
Price Category: C

Images provided by designer/architect.

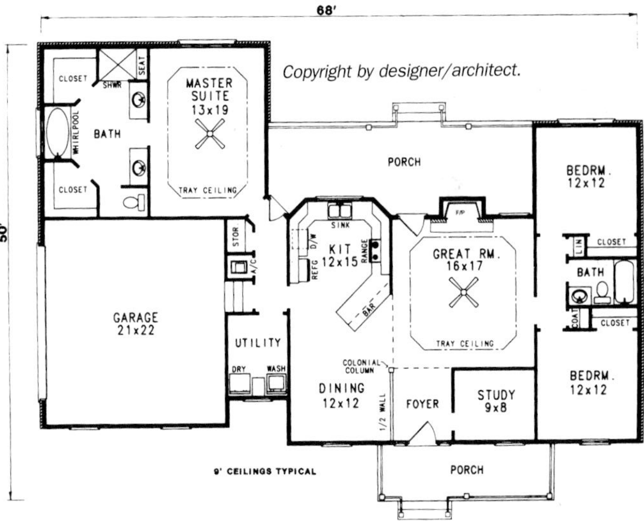

Copyright by designer/architect.

SMARTtip

Deck Awnings

Awnings come in bright colors. As light filters through, it will cast a hue to anything under the deck. Warm colors, such as red or pink, will create a rosy glow; cool colors, such blues or greens, will enhance the shade.

Plan #191003

Dimensions: 56' W x 42' D

Levels: 1

Heated Square Footage: 1,785

Bedrooms: 3

Bathrooms: 3

Foundation: Crawl space, slab, or basement

Materials List Available: No

Price Category: C

Images provided by designer/architect.

56'-0" Width

Plan #271077

Dimensions: 69'6" W x 53' D

Levels: 1

Heated Square Footage: 1,786

Bedrooms: 1

Bathrooms: 1½

Foundation: Basement or daylight basement

Materials List Available: No

Price Category: C

Images provided by designer/architect.

CAD FILE AVAILABLE

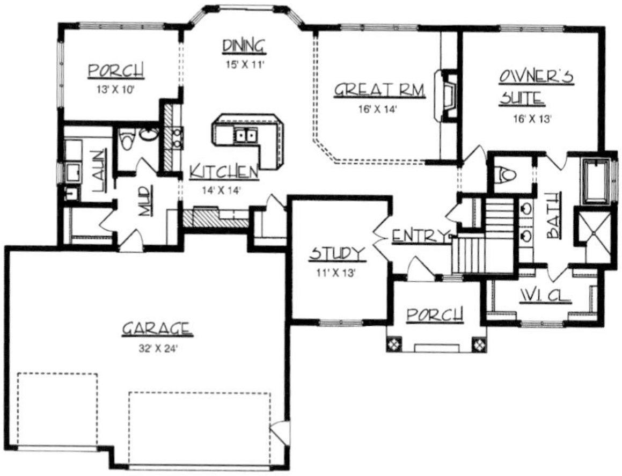

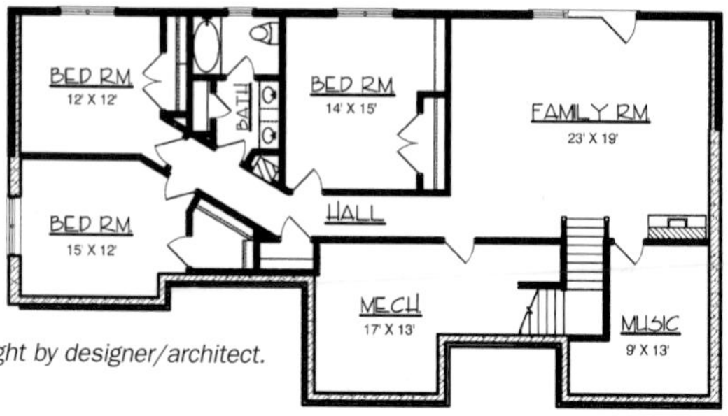

Optional Basement Level Floor Plan

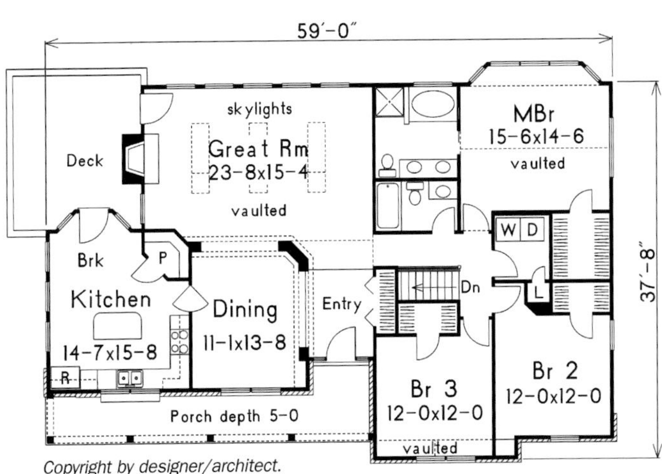

Copyright by designer/architect.

Plan #321010

Dimensions: 59' W x 37'8" D
Levels: 1
Heated Square Footage: 1,787
Bedrooms: 3
Bathrooms: 2
Foundation: Basement, or walkout
Materials List Available: Yes
Price Category: C

Images provided by designer/architect.

CAD FILE AVAILABLE

SMARTtip

Country Décor in Your Bathroom

Collections are often part of a country decor, even in the bathroom. All you need is three or more of anything that have size, shape, or color in common. You can mass them on walls, on shelves, on the windowsills, or even along the edge of the tub.

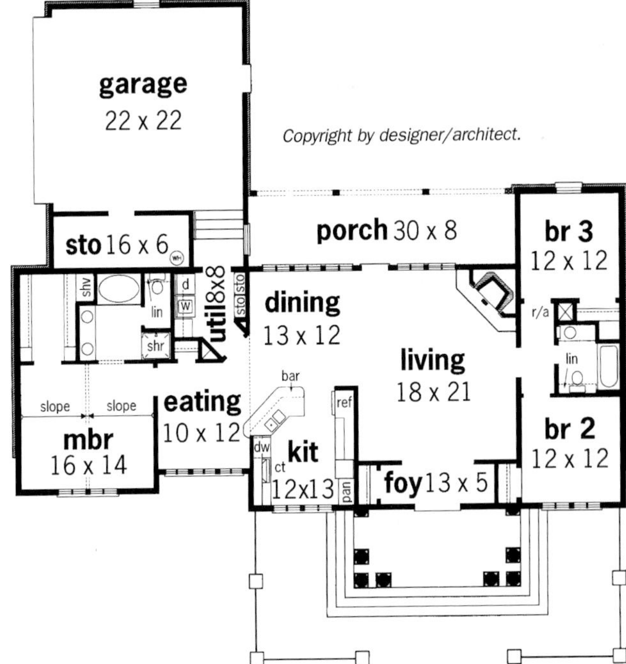

Copyright by designer/architect.

Plan #211002

Dimensions: 68' W x 62' D
Levels: 1
Heeated Square Footage: 1,792
Bedrooms: 3
Bathrooms: 2
Foundation: Crawl space
Materials List Available: Yes
Price Category: C

Images provided by designer/architect.

Plan #351003

Dimensions: 64' W x 45'10" D
Levels: 1
Heated Square Footage: 1,751
Bedrooms: 3
Bathrooms: 2
Foundation: Crawl space, slab, or basement
Materials List Available: Yes
Price Category: D

CAD FILE AVAILABLE

Images provided by designer/architect.

This beautiful three-bedroom brick house with a covered porch is perfect for today's family.

Features:

- Great Room: This gathering room features a tray ceiling, a gas fireplace, and built-in cabinets.
- Kitchen: This island kitchen with a raised bar is open to the great room and eating area.
- Master Suite: This primary bedroom features a vaulted ceiling and large walk-in closet. The private bath boasts a double vanity, corner tub, and walk-in closet.
- Bedrooms: Two additional bedrooms are located on the other side of the home from the master suite and share a common bathroom.

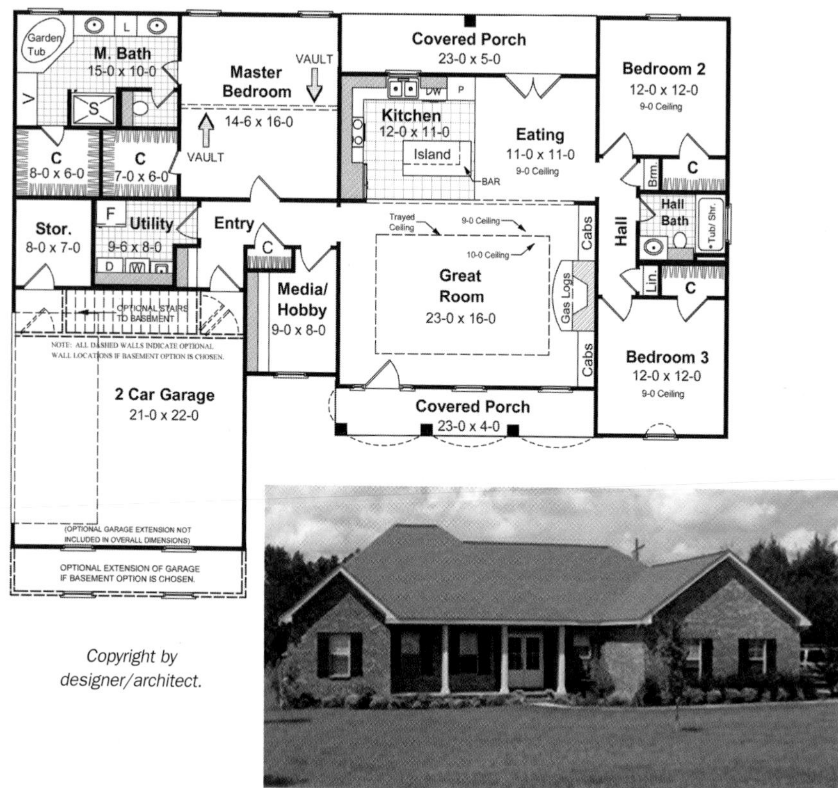

Copyright by designer/architect.

Dining Room

Kitchen

Great Room

Master Bathroom

Rear View

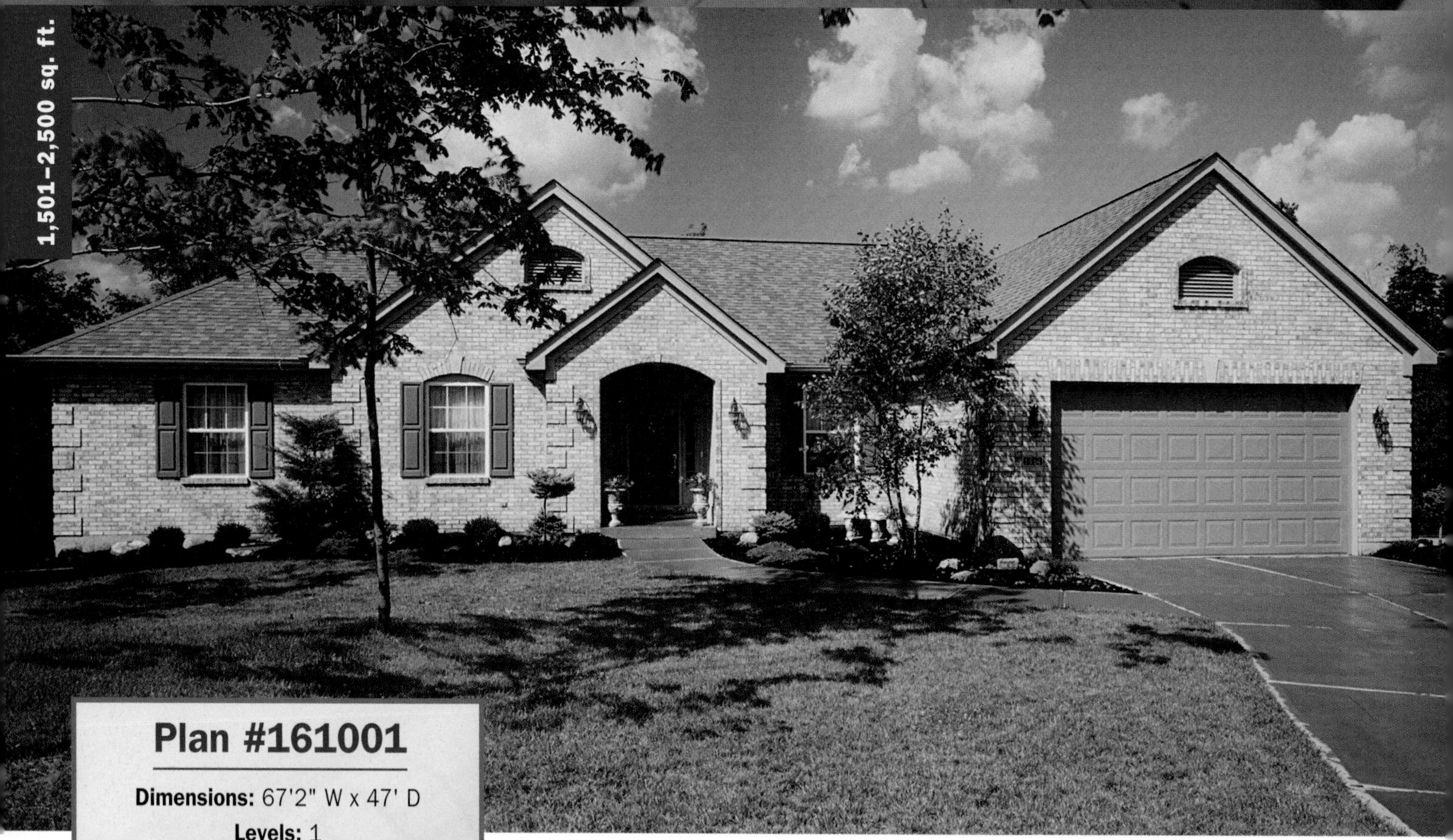

Plan #161001

Dimensions: 67'2" W x 47' D

Levels: 1

Heated Square Footage: 1,782

Bedrooms: 3

Bathrooms: 2

Foundation: Basement

Materials List Available: Yes

Price Category: C

Images provided by designer/architect.

Copyright by designer/architect.

CAD FILE AVAILABLE

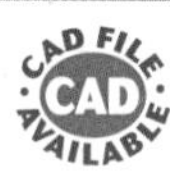

An all-brick exterior displays the solid strength that characterizes this gracious home.

Features:

- Great Room: A feeling of spaciousness permeates the gathering area created by the foyer, great room, and dining room. Multiple windows provide natural light that dances along a sloped ceiling, spilling onto decorative columns and a fireplace.
- Breakfast Area: A continuation of the sloped ceiling leads to the breakfast area where French doors open to a screened porch.
- Kitchen: An abundance of cabinets and counter space are the hallmarks of this large kitchen with its easy access to a spacious laundry room and storage area.
- Master Suite: A tray ceiling and spacious walk-in closet in the master bedroom, along with a whirlpool tub and double-bowl vanity in the bathroom, enable you to pamper yourself.

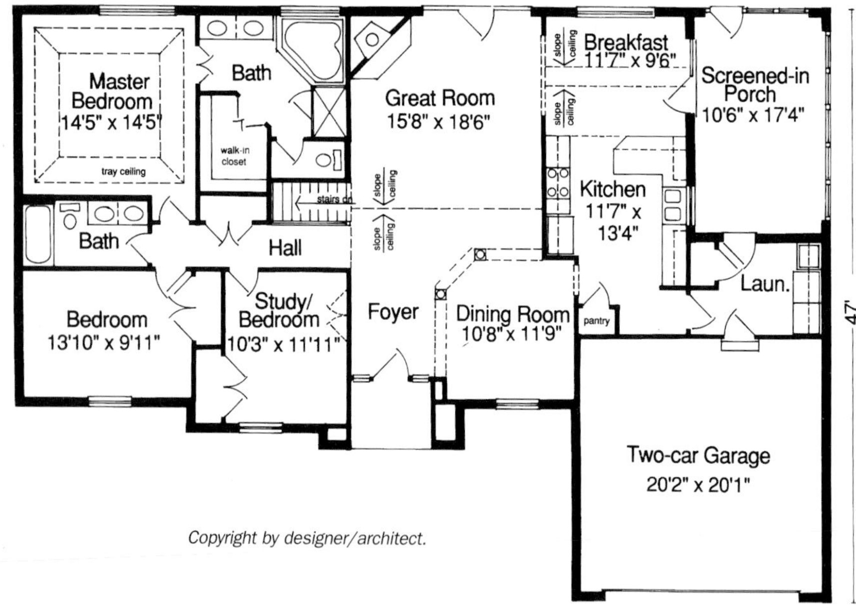

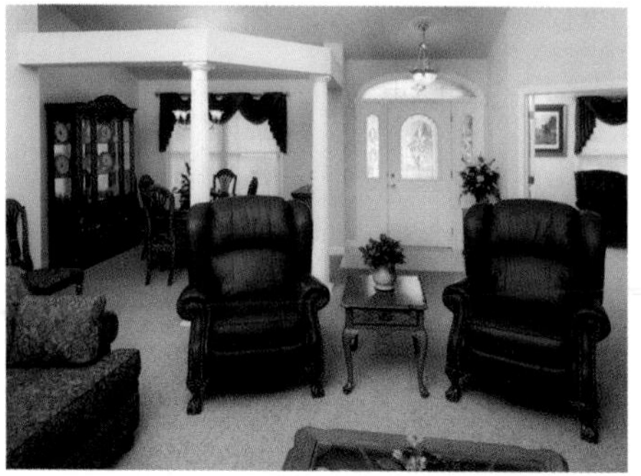

Great Room/Foyer

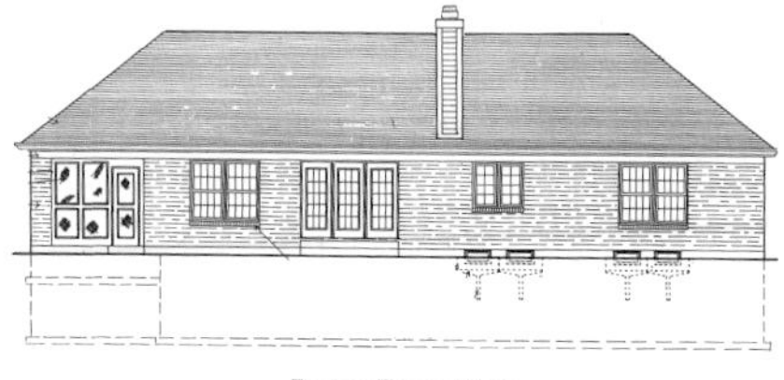

Rear Elevation

Plan #101004

Dimensions: 55'8" W x 56'6" D

Levels: 1

Heated Square Footage: 1,787

Bedrooms: 3

Bathrooms: 2

Foundation: Crawl space, slab, or basement

Materials List Available: Yes

Price Category: D

CAD FILE AVAILABLE

Images provided by designer/architect.

This carefully designed ranch provides the feel and features of a much larger home.

Features:

- Ceiling Height: 9 ft. unless otherwise noted.
- Entry: Guests will step up onto the inviting front porch and into this entry, with its impressive 11-ft. ceiling.
- Dining Room: Open to the entry and to its left is this elegant dining room, perfect for entertaining or informal family gatherings.
- Family Room: This family gathering place features an 11-ft. ceiling to enhance its sense of spaciousness.
- Kitchen: This intelligently designed kitchen has an open plan. A breakfast bar and a serving bar are features that add to its convenience.
- Master Suite: This suite is loaded with amenities, including a double-step tray ceiling, direct access to the screened porch, a sitting room, deluxe bath, and his and her walk-in closets.

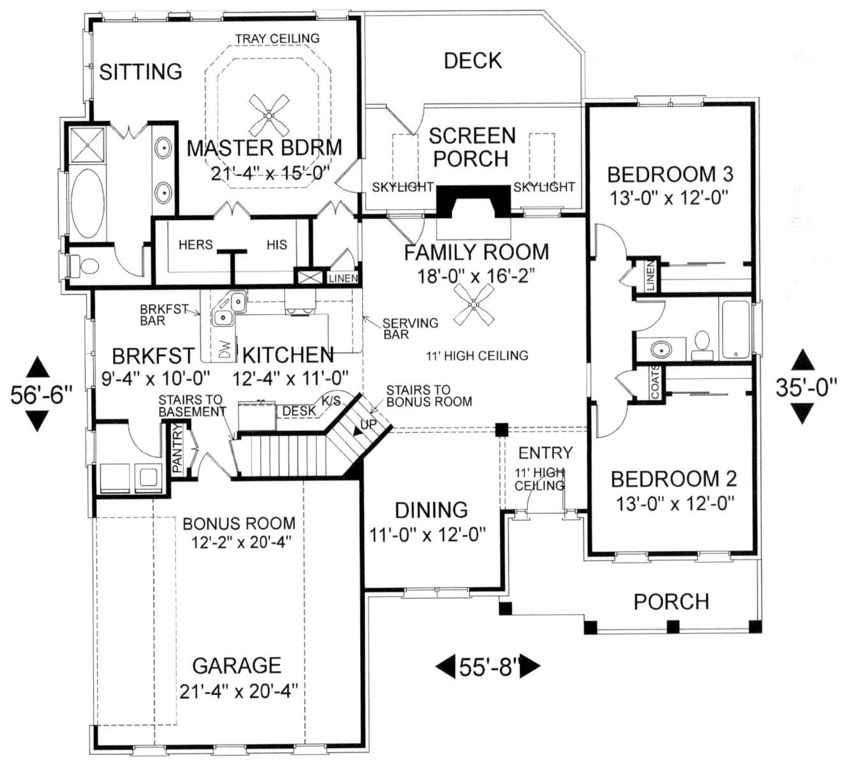

Copyright by designer/architect.

Plan #151007

Dimensions: 54'2" W x 56'2" D
Levels: 1
Heated Square Footage: 1,787
Bedrooms: 3
Bathrooms: 2
Foundation: Crawl space, slab, basement, or walkout
CompleteCost List Available: Yes
Price Category: C

CAD FILE CAD AVAILABLE

Images provided by designer/architect.

This home, as shown in the photograph, may differ from the actual blueprints. For more detailed information, please check the floor plans carefully.

This compact, well-designed home is graced with amenities usually reserved for larger houses.

Features:

- Foyer: A 10-ft. ceiling creates unity between the foyer and the dining room just beyond it.
- Dining Room: 8-in. boxed columns welcome you to this dining room, with its 10-ft. ceilings.
- Great Room: The 9-ft. boxed ceiling suits the spacious design. Enjoy the fireplace in the winter and the rear-grilling porch in the summer.
- Breakfast Room: This bright room is a lovely spot for any time of day.
- Master Suite: Double vanities and a large walk-in closet add practicality to this quiet room with a 9-ft. pan ceiling. The master bath includes whirlpool tub with glass block and a separate shower.
- Bedrooms: Bedroom 2 features a bay window, and both rooms are convenient to the bathroom.

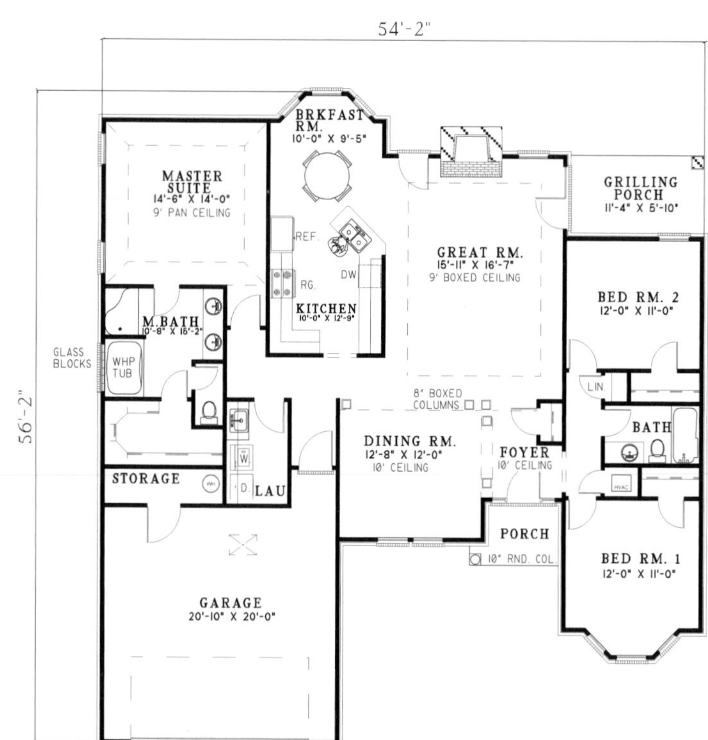

Copyright by designer/architect.

Plan #321003

Dimensions: 67'4" W x 48' D
Levels: 1
Heated Square Footage: 1,791
Bedrooms: 4
Bathrooms: 2
Foundation: Basement
Materials List Available: Yes
Price Category: E

CAD FILE AVAILABLE

Images provided by designer/architect.

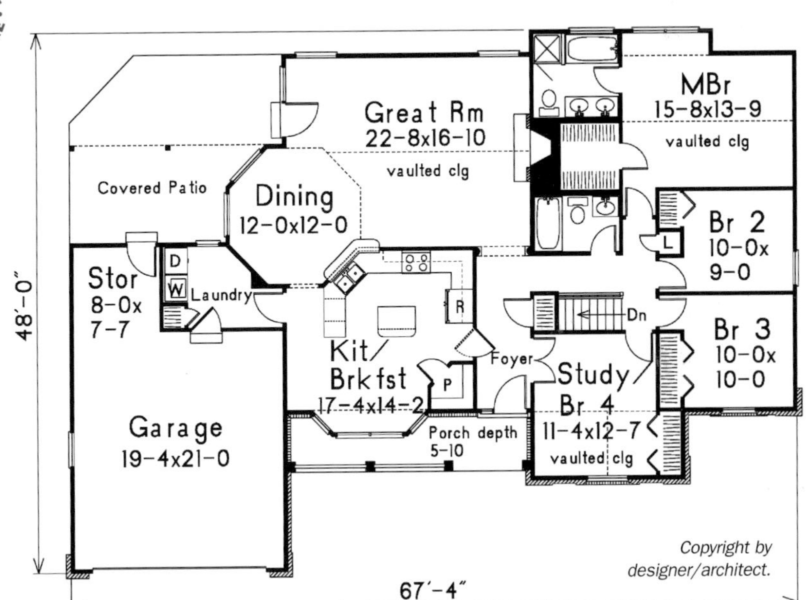

Copyright by designer/architect.

The traditional good looks of the exterior of this home are complemented by the stunning contemporary design of the interior.

Features:

- Great Room: With a vaulted ceiling to highlight its spacious dimensions, this room is certain to be the central gathering spot for friends and family.
- Dining Room: Also with a vaulted ceiling, this room has an octagonal shape for added interest. Windows here and in the great room look out to the covered patio.
- Kitchen: A center island gives a convenient work space in this well-designed kitchen, which features a pass-through to the dining room for easy serving, and large, walk-in pantry for storage.
- Breakfast Room: A bay window lets sunshine pour in to start your morning with a smile.
- Master Bedroom: A vaulted ceiling and a sitting area make you feel truly pampered in this room.

SMARTtip

Bay & Bow Windows

Occasionally too little room exists between the window frame (if there is one) and the ceiling. In this situation you might be able to use ceiling-mounted hardware. Alternatively, a cornice across the top and a rod mounted inside the cornice will give you the dual benefit of visually lowering the top of the window and concealing the hardware.

Plan #391019

Dimensions: 56' W x 32' D
Levels: 1
Heated Square Footage: 1,792
Bedrooms: 3
Bathrooms: 2
Foundation: Basement
Materials List Available: Yes
Price Category: C

Images provided by designer/architect.

This southern-style cottage with sociable porch fits in almost anywhere, from a leafy lane to hillside or curbside and renders a lot of living space and hospitality.

Features:

- Family Room: This room features a central stone fireplace, plus two walls of windows to usher in the light. Sloping ceilings and decorative beams boost its rustic charm. An enormously generous space, it opens wide to the corner kitchen.
- Dining Room: This room has its own level of sophistication, including entry outside to the deck.
- Utility Areas: The family-sized pantry and laundry area are set off by themselves to avoid interference with everyday living.
- Master Suite: A leisurely hall leads to the master bedroom and private full bath, wide walk-in closets, and a trio of windows.
- Bedrooms: Across the hall the two secondary bedrooms share a roomy bath and a view of the front porch.

Front View

Side/Rear View

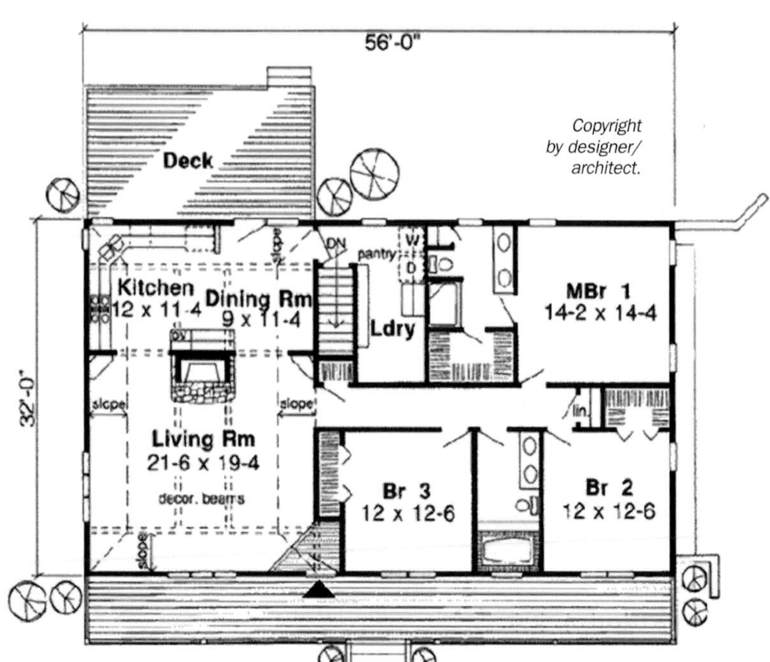

Plan #431001

Dimensions: 58'8" W x 62' D
Levels: 1
Heated Square Footage: 1,792
Bedrooms: 3
Bathrooms: 2½
Foundation: Crawl space or basement
Materials List Available: Yes
Price Category: C

Images provided by designer/architect.

Your neighbors will envy this Southern-style home.

Features:

- Great Room: The entry overlooks this room, where a fireplace warms gatherings on chilly evenings. A large window and French doors allow a view of the yard.
- Kitchen: The primary workstation in this kitchen is a peninsula, which faces the fireplace in the great room. The peninsula is equipped with a sink and snack counter.
- Master Suite: This private space is located on the other side of the home from the other bedrooms. It contains expansive his and her walk-in closets, a spa tub, and a double vanity area in the salon.
- Bedrooms: Two additional bedrooms are separated from the master suite. Both bedrooms have large closets and share a hall bathroom.

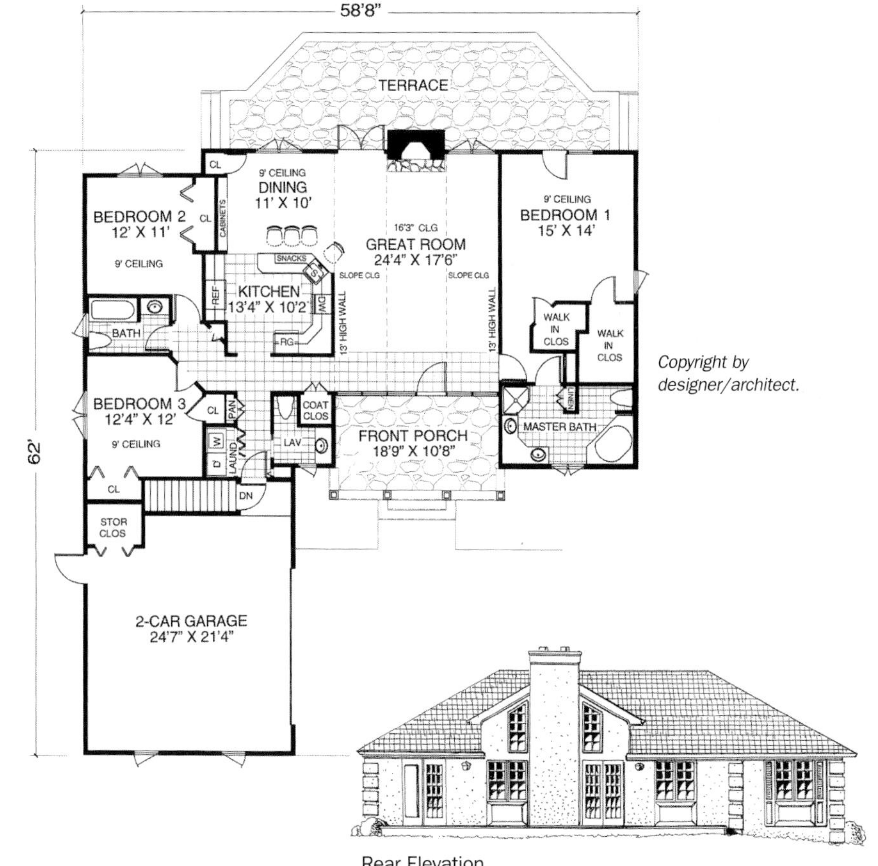

Copyright by designer/architect.

Rear Elevation

Plan #131047

Dimensions: 69'10" W x 51'8" D
Levels: 1
Heated Square Footage: 1,793
Bedrooms: 3
Bathrooms: 2
Foundation: Crawl space, slab, or basement
Materials List Available: Yes
Price Category: D

Images provided by designer/architect.

The country charm of this well-designed home is mixed with the convenience and luxury normally reserved for more contemporary plans.

Features:

- Great Room: The spaciousness of this great room is enhanced by the 11-ft. stepped ceiling. A fireplace makes it cozy on cool evenings or on chilly winter days, and two sets of French sliding glass doors open to the back porch.
- Kitchen: In addition to the convenient layout of this design, you'll also love its bright, airy position. It includes an old-fashioned pantry, a sink under a window, and a sunny breakfast area that opens to the wraparound porch.
- Master Suite: You'll find 11-ft. ceilings in both the master bedroom and the bayed sitting area that the suite includes. In the bath, the circular spa tub is surrounded by a glass-block wall.
- Bonus Space: A permanent staircase leads to an unfinished bonus space on the upper level.

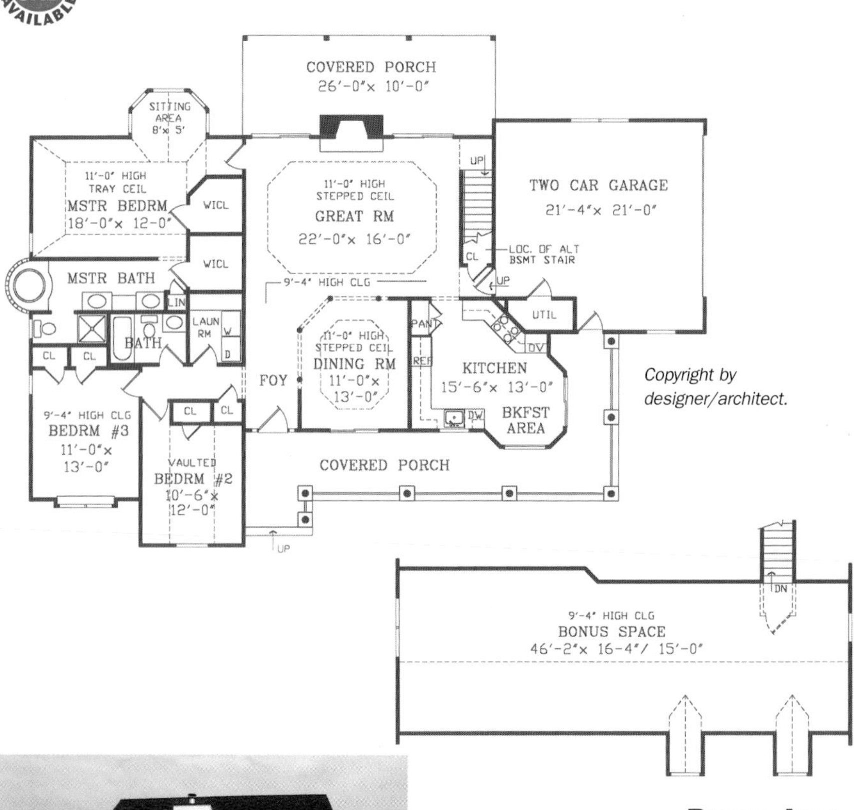

Copyright by designer/architect.

Images provided by designer/architect.

Plan #151196

Dimensions: 89' W x 49'4" D
Levels: 1
Heated Square Footage: 1,800
Bedrooms: 3
Bathrooms: 2
Foundation: Crawl space or slab; basement for fee
CompleteCost List Available: Yes
Price Category: C

CAD FILE AVAILABLE

This charming home, with its wide front porch, is perfect on a little piece of land or a quiet suburban street.

Features:

- Screened Porch: This screened-in porch creates extra living space where you can enjoy warm summer breezes in a bug-free atmosphere.
- Great Room: Make a "great" first impression by welcoming guests into this spacious, fire-light-illuminated great room.
- Kitchen: This efficient area is surrounded on all sides by workspace and storage. A snack bar, adjacent dining room, and attached grilling porch create plenty of mealtime options.
- Master Suite: This master suite creates a stress-free environment with its, large walk-in closet, whirlpool tub, standing shower, and his and her vanities.

Copyright by designer/architect.

Images provided by designer/architect.

Plan #441005

Dimensions: 50' W x 59' D
Levels: 1
Heaetd Square Footage: 1,800
Bedrooms: 3
Bathrooms: 2
Foundation: Crawl space; slab or basement for fee
Materials List Available: No
Price Category: D

CAD FILE AVAILABLE

This home looks as if it's a quaint little abode—with its board-and-batten siding, cedar shingle detailing, and column-covered porch—but even a quick peek inside will prove that there is much more to this plan than meets the eye.

Features:

- Foyer: This entry area rises to a 9-ft.-high ceiling. On one side is a washer-dryer alcove with a closet across the way; on the other is another large storage area. Just down the hallway is a third closet.
- Kitchen: This kitchen features a center island, built-in desk/work center, and pantry. This area and the dining area also boast 9-ft.-high ceilings and are open to a vaulted great room with corner fireplace.
- Dining Room: Sliding doors in this area lead to a covered side porch, so you can enjoy outside dining.
- Master Suite: This suite has a vaulted ceiling. The master bath is wonderfully appointed with a separate shower, spa tub, and dual sinks.
- Bedrooms: Three bedrooms (or two plus an office) are found on the right side of the plan.

Rear Elevation

Copyright by designer/architect.

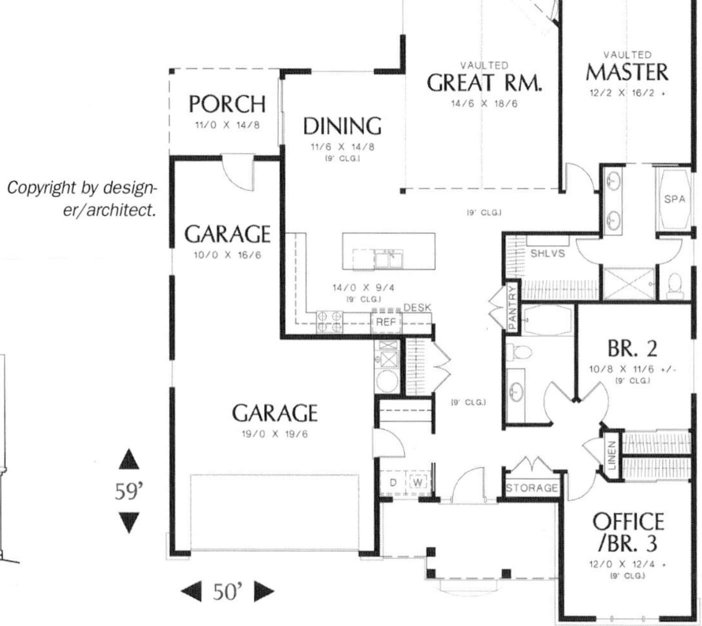

Plan #161002

Dimensions: 64'2" W x 44'2" D
Levels: 1
Heated Square Footage: 1,860
Bedrooms: 3
Bathrooms: 2
Foundation: Basement
Materials List Available: Yes
Price Category: D

Images provided by designer/architect.

The brick, stone, and cedar shake facade provides color and texture to the exterior, while the unique nooks and angles inside this delightful one-level home give it character.

Features:

- Great Room/Dining Room: This spacious great room is furnished with a wood-burning fireplace, a high ceiling, and French doors. Wide entrances to the breakfast room and dining room expand its space to comfortably hold large gatherings.
- Kitchen: The breakfast bar offers additional seating. The covered porch lets you enjoy a view of the landscape and is conveniently located for outdoor meals off this kitchen and breakfast area.
- Master Suite: The master suite is a private retreat. An alcove creates a comfortable sitting area, and an angled entry leads to the bath with whirlpool and a double-bowl vanity.

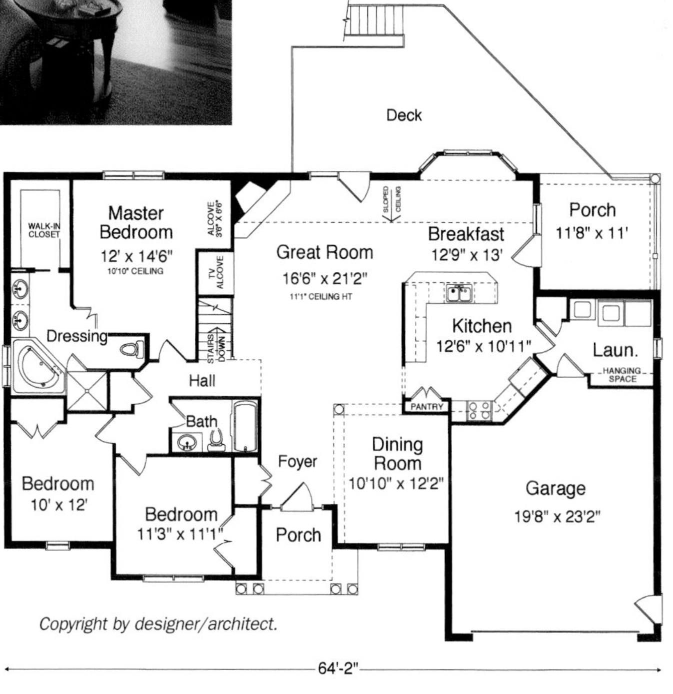

Great Room/Foyer

Rear Elevation

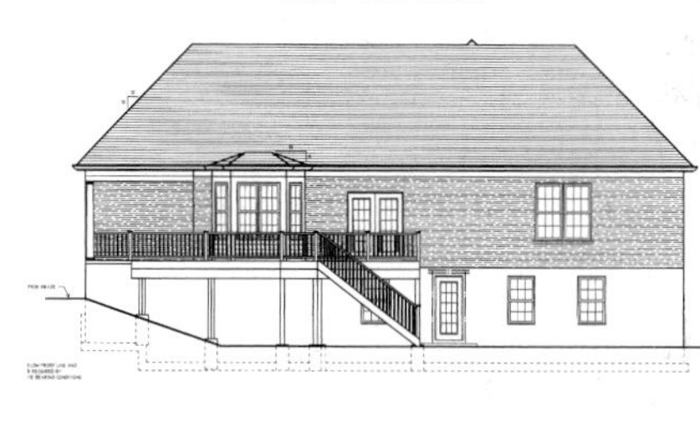

Deck
Master Bedroom 12' x 14'6" 10'10" CEILING
WALK-IN CLOSET
ALCOVE
TV ALCOVE
Great Room 16'6" x 21'2" 11'1" CEILING HT
SLOPED CEILING
Breakfast 12'9" x 13'
Porch 11'8" x 11'
Kitchen 12'6" x 10'11"
Laun.
HANGING SPACE
PANTRY
Dressing
STAIRS DOWN
Hall
Bath
Foyer
Dining Room 10'10" x 12'2"
Garage 19'8" x 23'2"
Bedroom 10' x 12'
Bedroom 11'3" x 11'1"
Porch
44'-2"
64'-2"

Copyright by designer/architect.

Copyright by designer/architect.

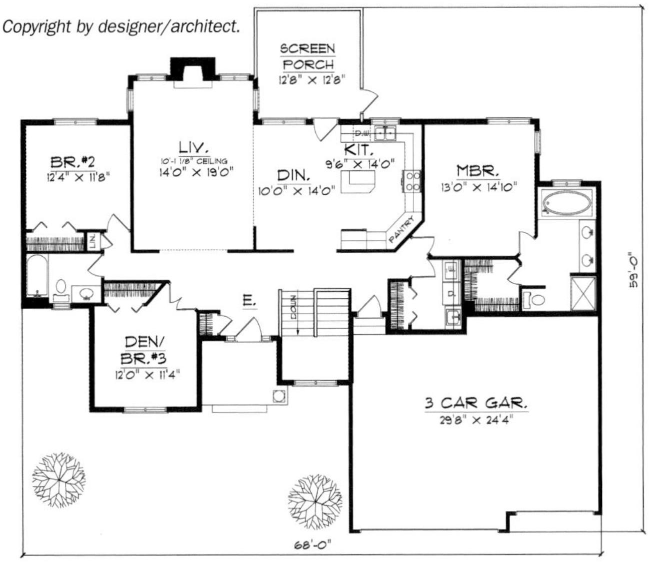

SCREEN PORCH 12'8" x 12'8"
LIV. 10'-1 1/8" CEILING 14'0" x 19'0"
BR.#2 12'4" x 11'8"
KIT. 9'6" x 14'0"
DIN. 10'0" x 14'0"
MBR. 13'0" x 14'10"
E.
DEN/ BR.#3 12'0" x 11'4"
3 CAR GAR. 29'8" x 24'4"
68'-0"
59'-0"

Plan #221009

Dimensions: 68' W x 59' D
Levels: 1
Heated Square Footage: 1,795
Bedrooms: 3
Bathrooms: 2
Foundation: Basement
Materials List Available: No
Price Category: C

Images provided by designer/architect.

CAD FILE AVAILABLE

Rear Elevation

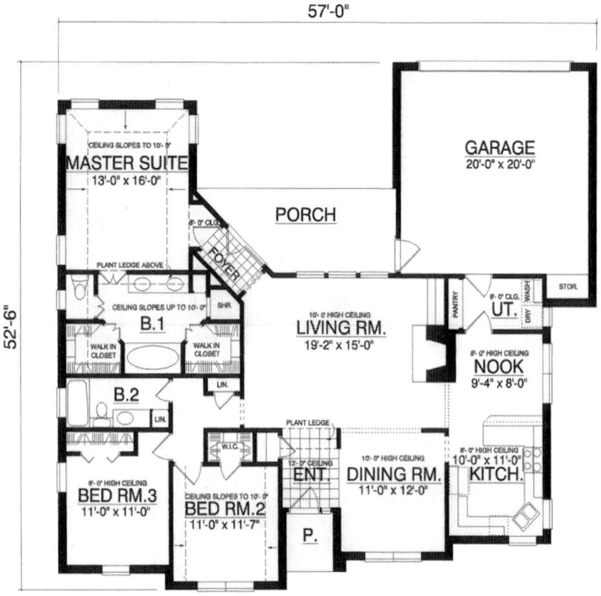

57'-0"
52'-6"
MASTER SUITE 13'-0" x 16'-0"
PORCH
GARAGE 20'-0" x 20'-0"
FOYER
B.1
LIVING RM. 19'-2" x 15'-0"
UT.
NOOK 9'-4" x 8'-0"
B.2
ENT.
DINING RM. 11'-0" x 12'-0"
KITCH. 10'-0" x 11'-0"
BED RM.3 11'-0" x 11'-0"
BED RM.2 11'-0" x 11'-7"
P.

Plan #371104

Dimensions: 57' W x 52'6" D
Levels: 1
Heated Square Footage: 1,795
Bedrooms: 3
Bathrooms: 2
Foundation: Crawl space or slab
Materials List Available: No
Price Category: C

Images provided by designer/architect.

Copyright by designer/architect.

Plan #351038

Dimensions: 65' W x 50' D

Levels: 1

Heated Square Footage: 1,800

Bedrooms: 3

Bathrooms: 2

Foundation: Crawl space, slab, or basement

Materials List Available: Yes

Price Category: E

Images provided by designer/architect.

CAD FILE AVAILABLE

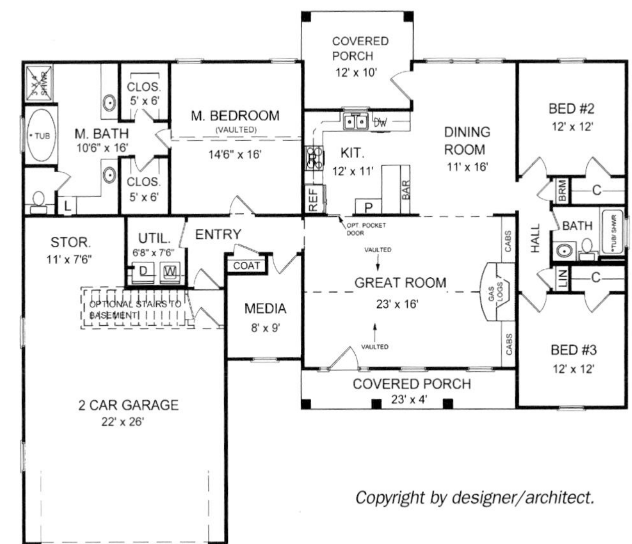

Copyright by designer/architect.

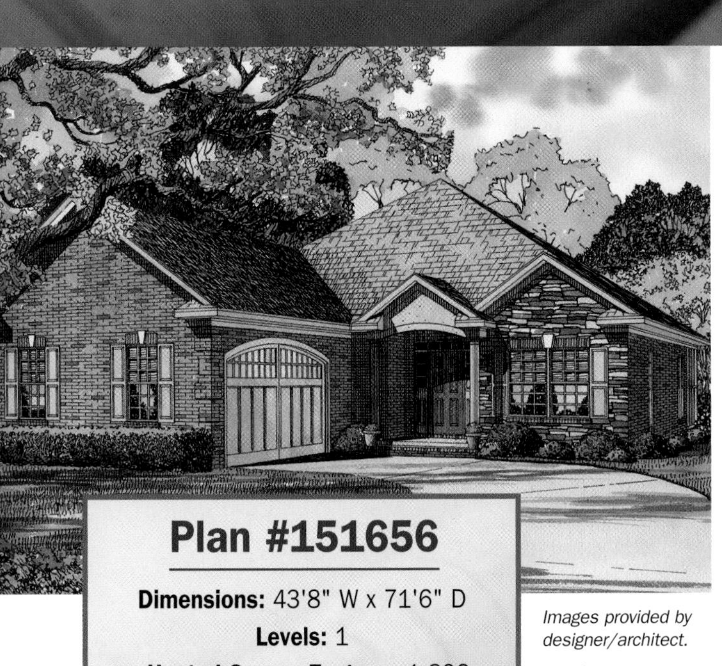

Plan #151656

Dimensions: 43'8" W x 71'6" D

Levels: 1

Heated Square Footage: 1,806

Bedrooms: 3

Bathrooms: 2

Foundation: Crawl space or slab

CompleteCost List Available: Yes

Price Category: D

Images provided by designer/architect.

CAD FILE AVAILABLE

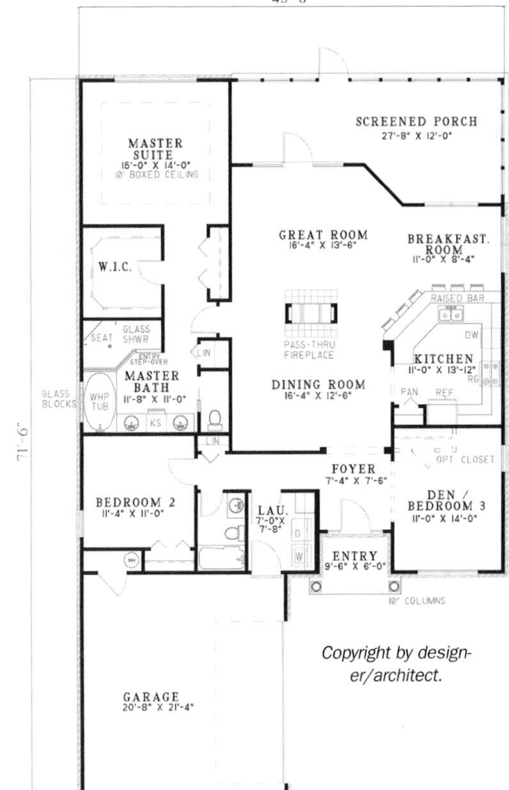

Copyright by designer/architect.

Plan #221099

Dimensions: 63' W x 53' D
Levels: 1
Heated Square Footage: 1,829
Bedrooms: 2
Bathrooms: 2
Foundation: Basement
Materials List Available: No
Price Category: D

Images provided by designer/architect.

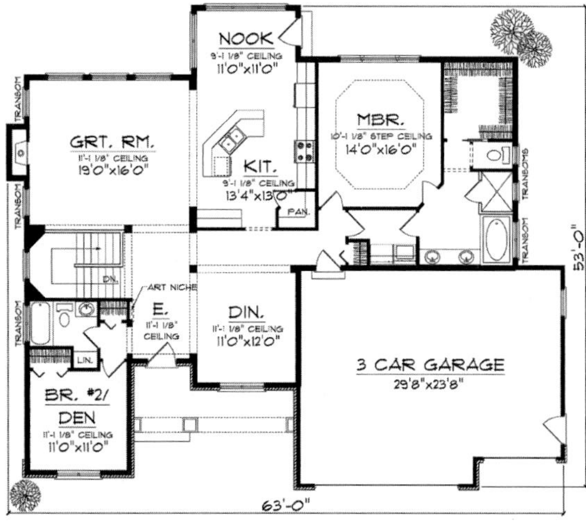

Copyright by designer/architect.

Rear Elevation

Plan #311012

Dimensions: 65'8" W x 55' D
Levels: 1
Heated Square Footage: 1,836
Bedrooms: 3
Bathrooms: 2
Foundation: Basement, crawl space, or slab
Materials List Available: Yes
Price Category: D

Images provided by designer/architect.

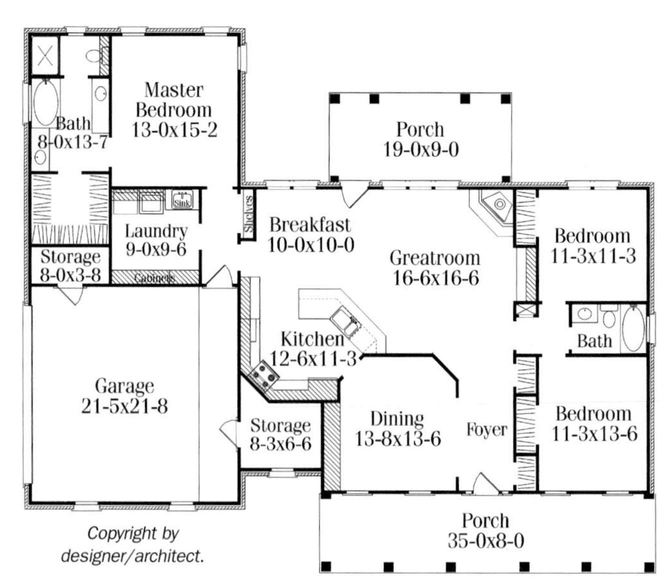

Copyright by designer/architect.

Basement Stair Location

Porch
12/4 x 14/3
Vaulted Ceiling
Master
18 x 14
Recessed Ceiling
Breakfast
12/4 x 10/8
Desk
9' Ceiling
Br. #2
12 x 11
9' Ceiling
Family Room
20 x 15/3
11'-7" Ceiling
Kitchen
14/4 x 9/8
Utility
9/8 x 8/10
W D
Br. #3
12 x 11
9' Ceiling
Foyer
8/8 x 11/7
Dining
13/4 x 11/7
11'-7" Ceiling
Garage
24 x 24
Porch
11/4 x 6

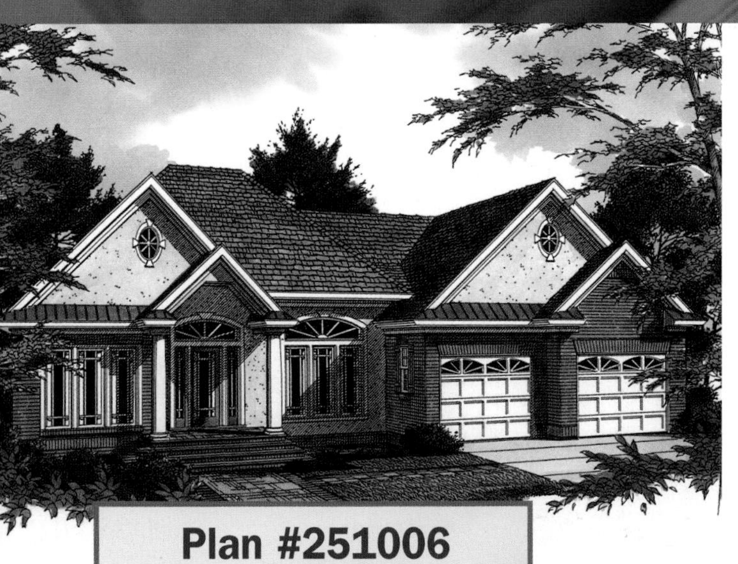

Plan #251006

Dimensions: 65'5" W x 59'11" D
Levels: 1
Heated Square Footage: 1,849
Bedrooms: 3
Bathrooms: 2
Foundation: Crawl space or slab
Materials List Available: Yes
Price Category: D

Images provided by designer/architect.

Copyright by designer/architect.

Copyright by designer/architect.

SHLVS
MASTER
12/8 X 15/4 +/-
(9' CLG.)
DINING
10/0 X 11/4
(9' CLG.)
MEDIA CENTER
GREAT RM.
14/10 X 19/2 +/-
(9' CLG.)
BR. 2
12/0 X 10/0
(9' CLG.)
LINEN
BR. 3
12/0 X 10/0
(9' CLG.)
10/2 X 13/10+/-
(9' CLG.)
(9' CLG.)
REF
PAN
W D
BUILT-IN
FOYER
(10' CLG.)
(9' CLG.)
VAULTED
DEN
13/0 X 13/2+
WINDOW SEAT
GARAGE
20/0 X 21/6
68'
44'

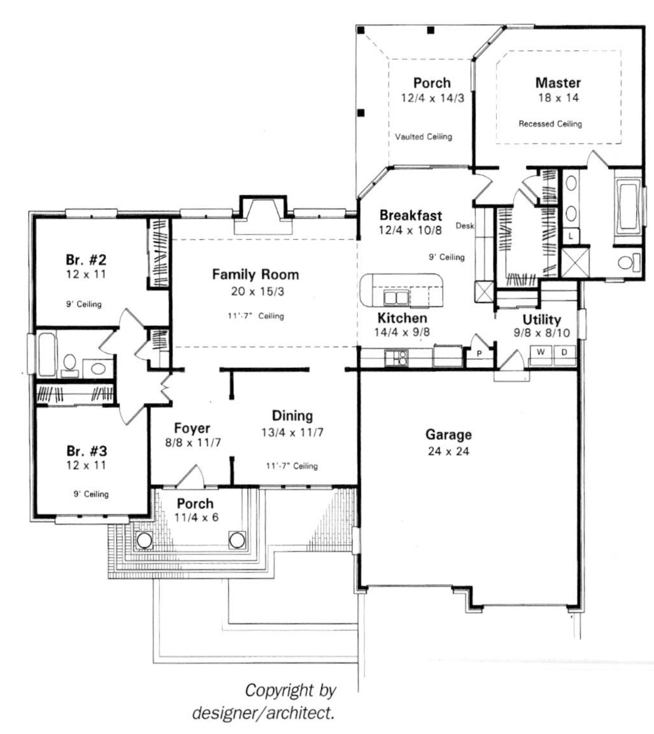

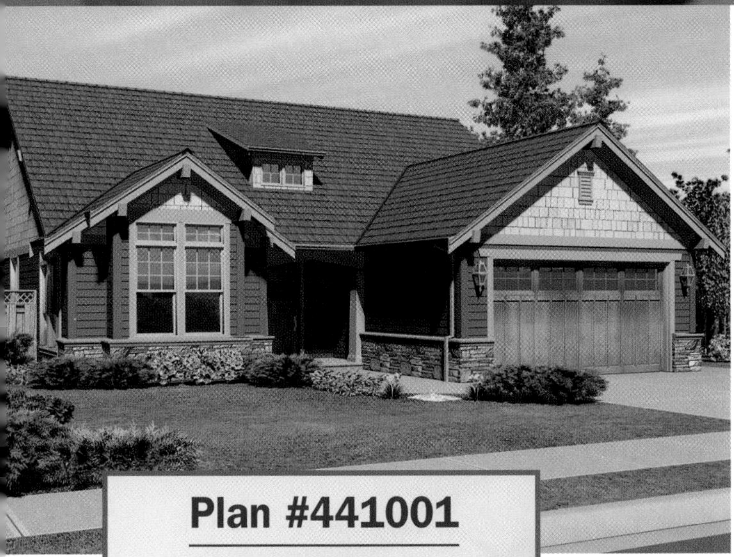

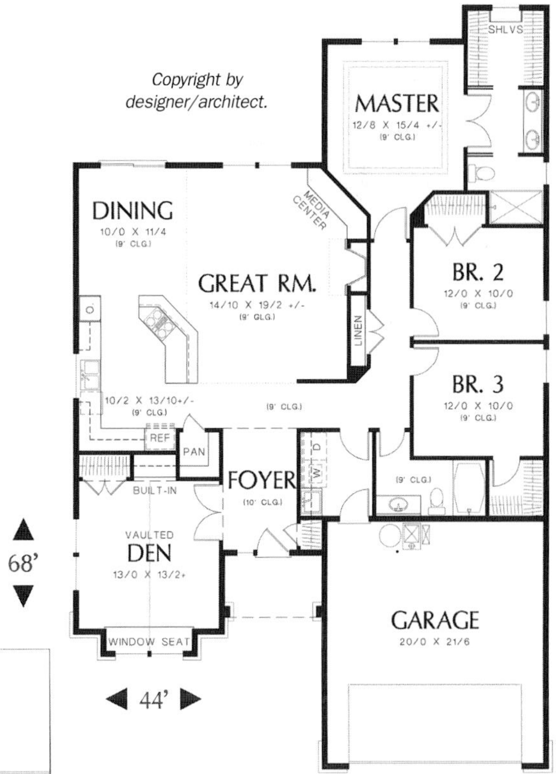

Plan #441001

Dimensions: 44' W x 68' D
Levels: 1
Heated Square Footage: 1,850
Bedrooms: 3
Bathrooms: 2
Foundation: Crawl space; slab or basement for fee
Materials List Available: No
Price Category: D

CAD FILE AVAILABLE

Images provided by designer/architect.

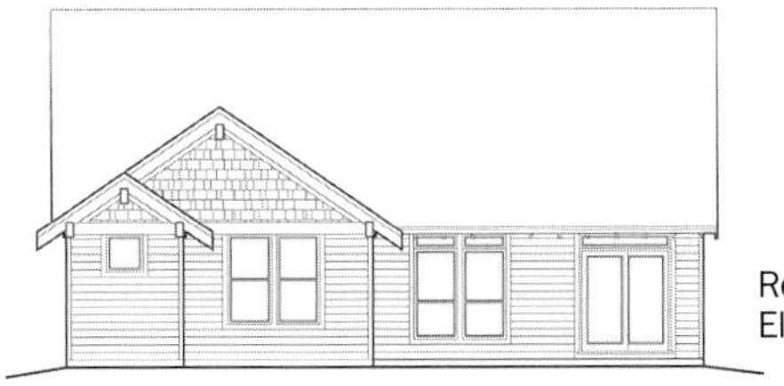

Rear Elevation

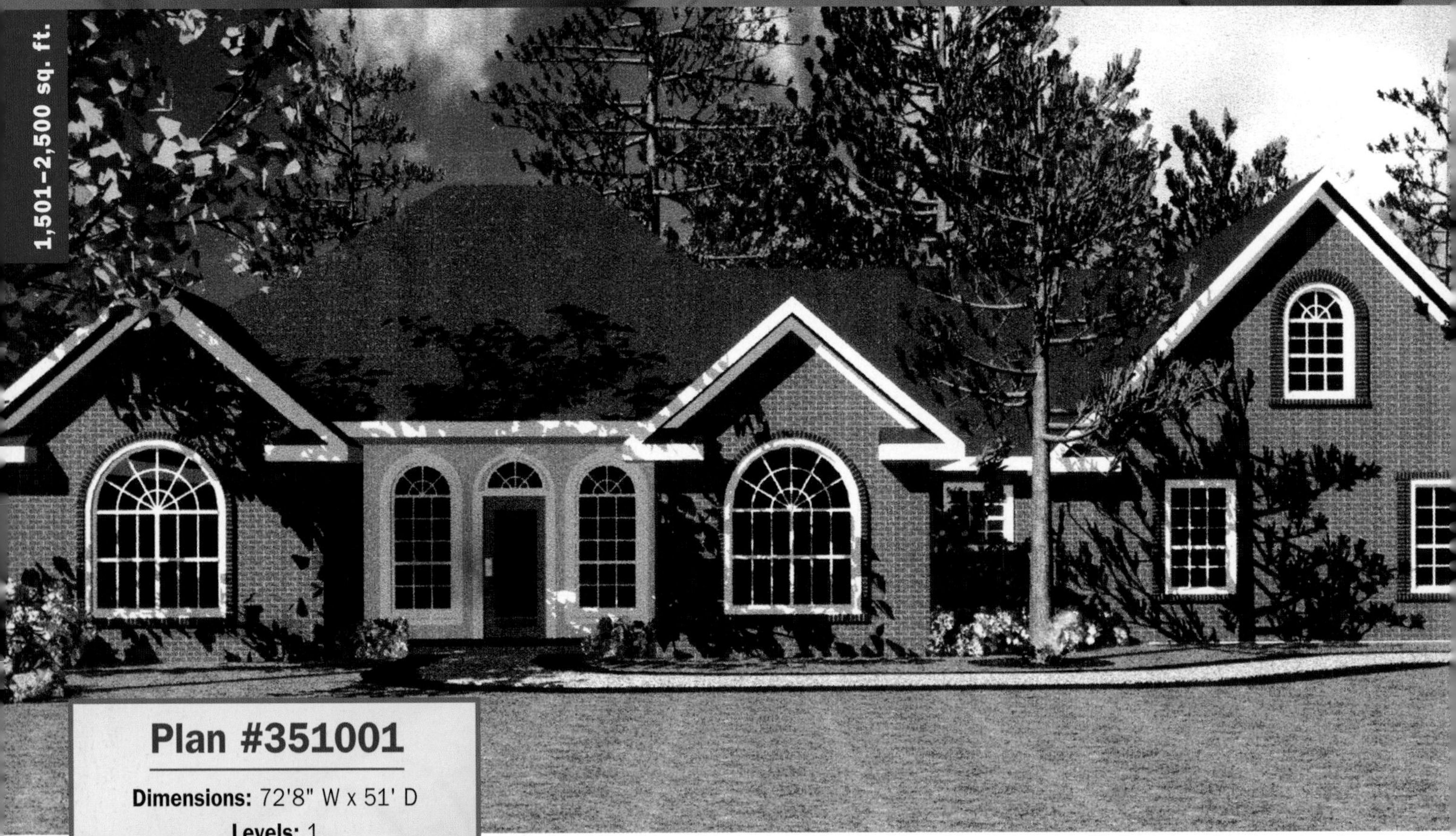

Plan #351001

Dimensions: 72'8" W x 51' D
Levels: 1
Heated Square Footage: 1,855
Bedrooms: 3
Bathrooms: 2½
Foundation: Crawl space, slab, or basement
Materials List Available: Yes
Price Category: E

CAD FILE AVAILABLE

Images provided by designer/architect.

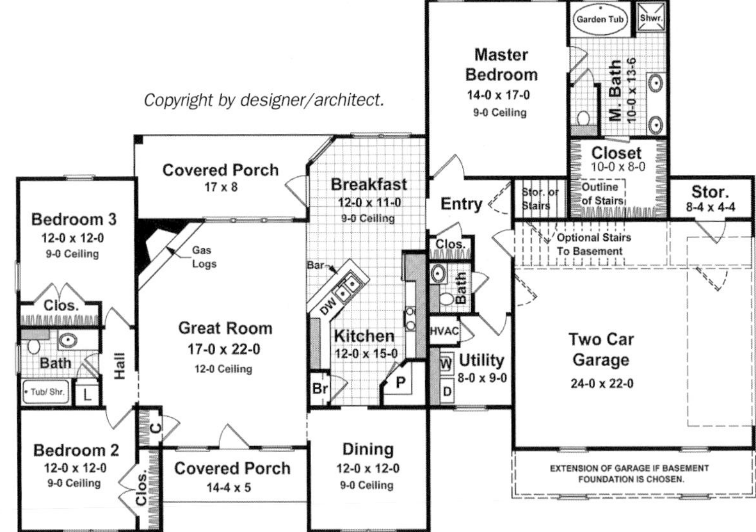

From the lovely arched windows on the front to the front and back covered porches, this home is as comfortable as it is beautiful.

Features:

- Great Room: Come into this room with 12-ft. ceilings, and you're sure to admire the corner gas fireplace and three windows overlooking the porch.
- Dining Room: Set off from the open design, this room is designed to be used formally or not.
- Kitchen: You'll love the practical walk-in pantry, broom closet, and angled snack bar here.
- Breakfast Room: Brightly lit and leading to the covered porch, this room will be a favorite spot.
- Bonus Room: Develop a playroom or study in this area.
- Master Suite: The large bedroom is complemented by the private bath with garden tub, separate shower, double vanity, and spacious walk-in closet.

Copyright by designer/architect.

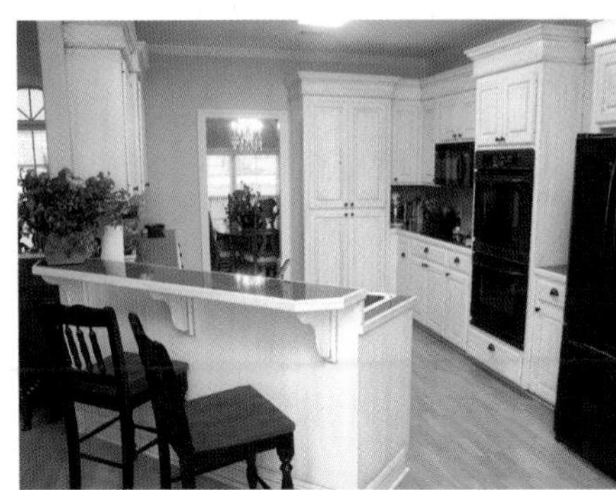

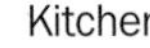

Kitchen

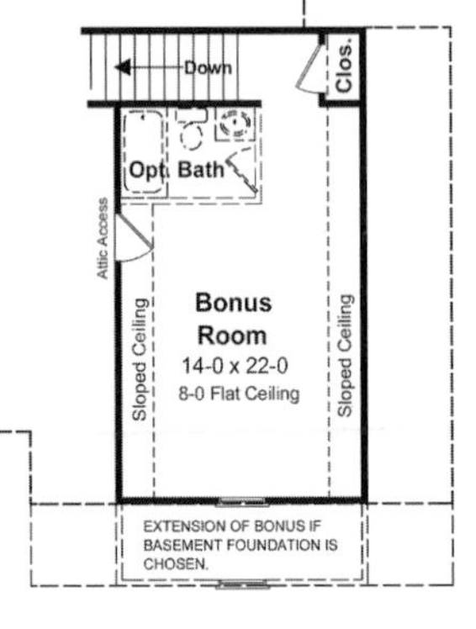

Bonus Area Floor Plan

Plan #131015

Dimensions: 57'4" W x 56'10" D

Levels: 1

Heated Square Footage: 1,860

Bedrooms: 3

Bathrooms: 2

Foundation: Crawl space, slab, or basement

Materials List Available: Yes

Price Category: E

Images provided by designer/architect.

The mixture of country charm and formal elegance is sure to thrill any family looking for a distinctive and comfortable home.

Features:

- Great Room: Separated from the dining room by a columned arch, this spacious room has a stepped ceiling, a built-in media center, and a fireplace. French doors within a rear bay lead to the large backyard patio at the rear of the house.
- Dining Room: Graced by a bay window, this formal room has an impressive 11-ft. 6-in.-high stepped ceiling.
- Breakfast Room: With a 12-ft. sloped ceiling, this room shares an eating bar with the kitchen.
- Master Bedroom: The 10-ft. tray ceiling and bay window contribute elegance, and the walk-in closet and bath with a bayed nook, whirlpool tub, and separate shower make it practical.

This home, as shown in the photograph, may differ from the actual blueprints. For more detailed information, please check the floor plans carefully.

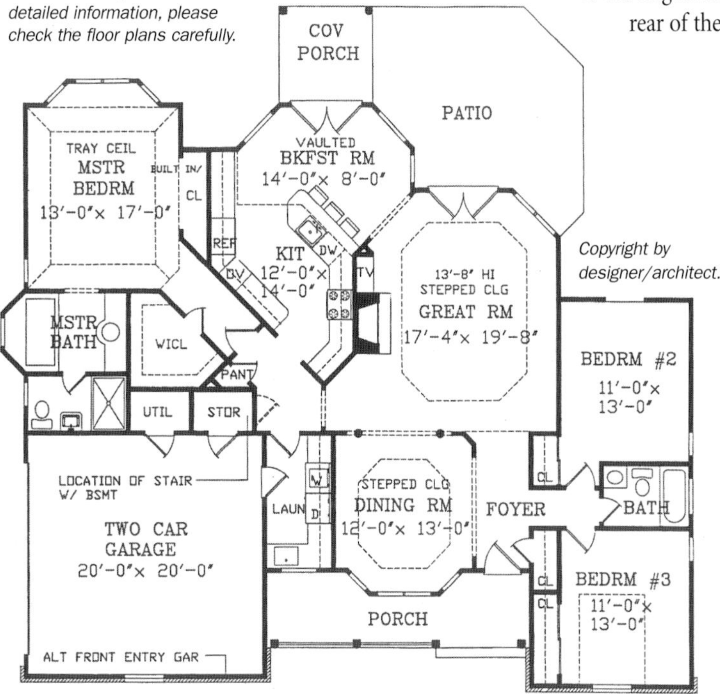

Copyright by designer/architect.

Rear Elevation

Great Room

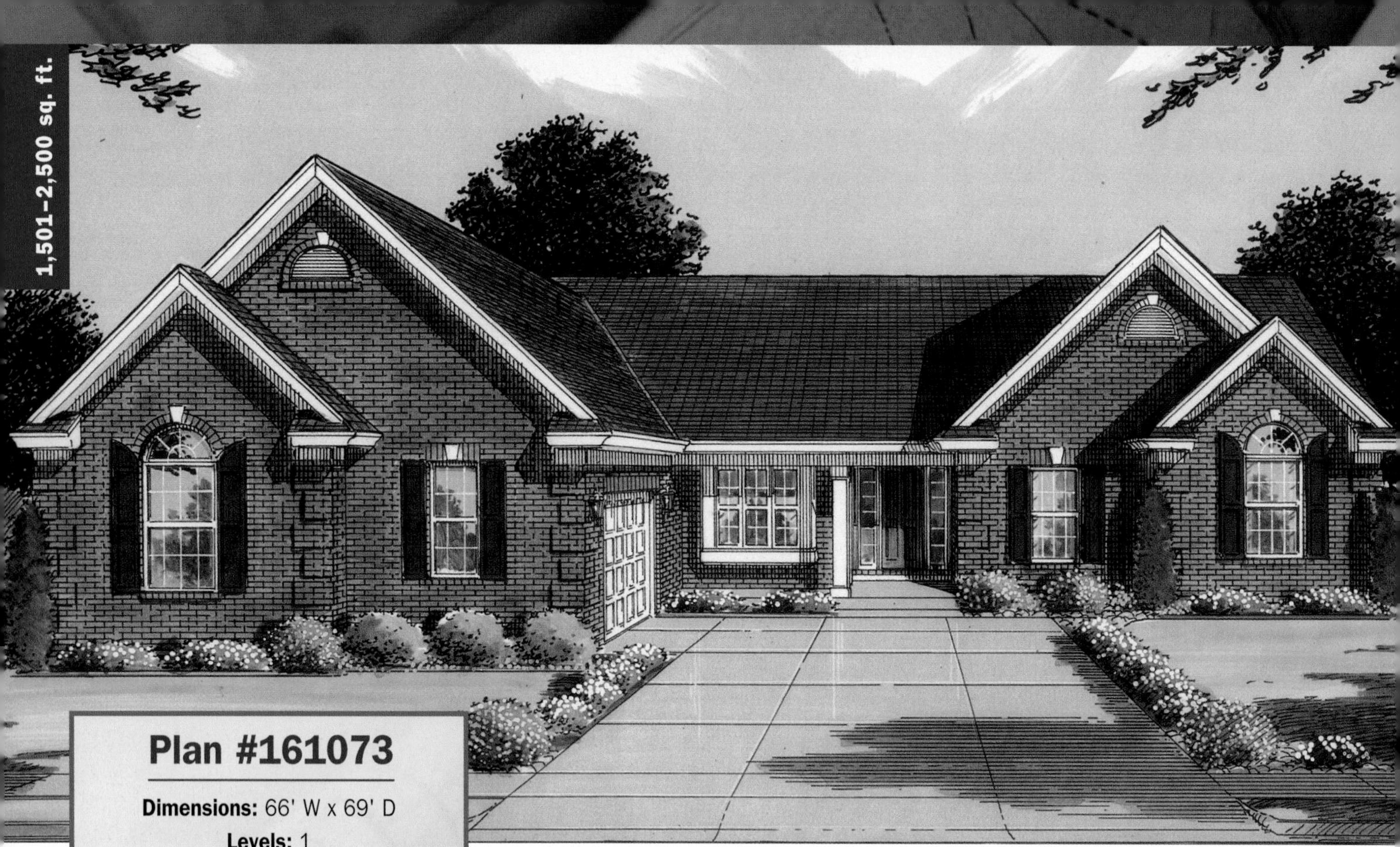

Plan #161073

Dimensions: 66' W x 69' D
Levels: 1
Heated Square Footage: 1,895
Bedrooms: 3
Bathrooms: 2
Foundation: Basement
Materials List Available: No
Price Category: D

Images provided by designer/architect.

The brick exterior with quoins, arched windows, and wood trim creates a rich, solid look in this delightful one-level home.

Features:

- Great Room: This large gathering area is decorated by a gas fireplace and offers a view of the rear yard.
- Dining Room: This open room is topped with a sloped ceiling that reaches 12-ft. high.
- Kitchen: This large kitchen, with its snack bar, and the breakfast area both open generously to the great room for a continuous traffic flow.
- Master Suite: This luxurious suite enjoys a whirlpool tub, double-bowl vanity, and shower enclosure.

Copyright by designer/architect.

Rear Elevation

Right Side Elevation

Left Side Elevation

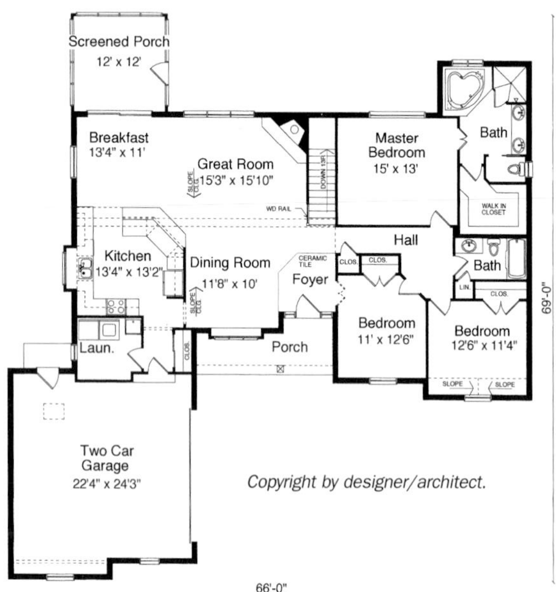

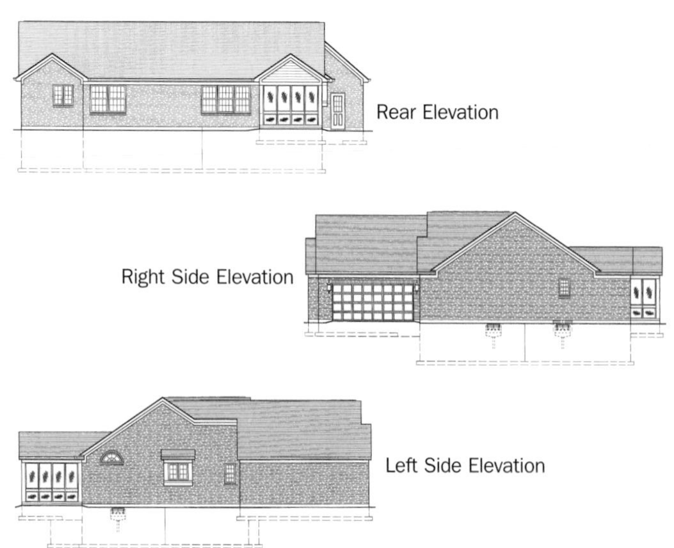

Plan #441002

Dimensions: 70' W x 51' D
Levels: 1
Heated Square Footage: 1,873
Bedrooms: 3
Bathrooms: 2
Foundation: Crawl space
Materials List Available: No
Price Category: D

Images provided by designer/architect.

CAD FILE AVAILABLE

Shutters flank tall windows to adorn the front of this charming home. A high roofline gives presence to the façade and allows vaulted ceilings in all the right places inside.

Features:

- Great Room: The entry hall overlooks this room, where a fireplace warms gatherings on chilly evenings and built-in shelves, to the right of the fireplace, add space that might be used as an entertainment center. A large three-panel window wall allows for a rear-yard view.
- Dining Room: This area is connected directly to the great room and features double doors to a covered porch.
- Kitchen: This open work area contains ample counter space with an island cooktop and large pantry.
- Bedrooms: The bedrooms are split, with the master suite in the back and additional bedrooms at the front.
- Master Suite: This suite boasts a 9-ft.-high ceiling and is graced by a luxurious bathroom and a walk-in closet.

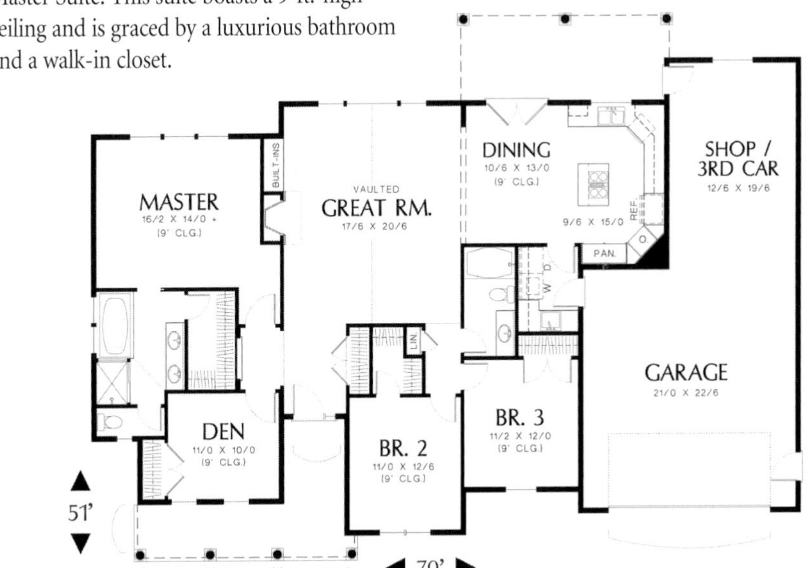

Copyright by designer/architect.

Rear Elevation

Rear Elevation

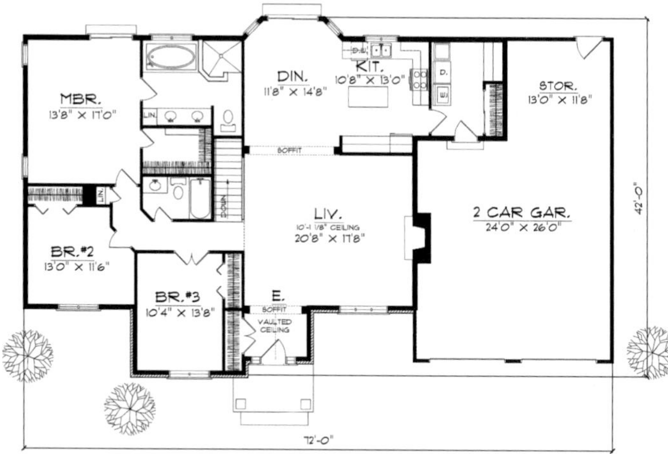

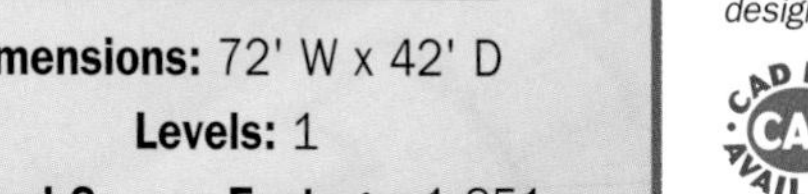

Plan #221005

Dimensions: 72' W x 42' D
Levels: 1
Heated Square Footage: 1,851
Bedrooms: 3
Bathrooms: 2
Foundation: Basement
Materials List Available: No
Price Category: D

Images provided by designer/architect.

CAD FILE AVAILABLE

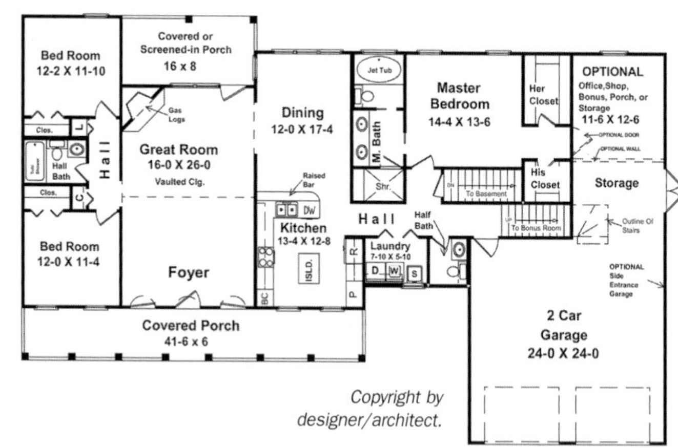

Copyright by designer/architect.

Plan #351004

Dimensions: 78' W x 49'6" D
Levels: 1
Heated Square Footage: 1,852
Bedrooms: 3
Bathrooms: 2½
Foundation: Crawl space, slab, or basement
Materials List Available: Yes
Price Category: D

CAD FILE AVAILABLE

Images provided by designer/architect.

Rear View

Bonus Room

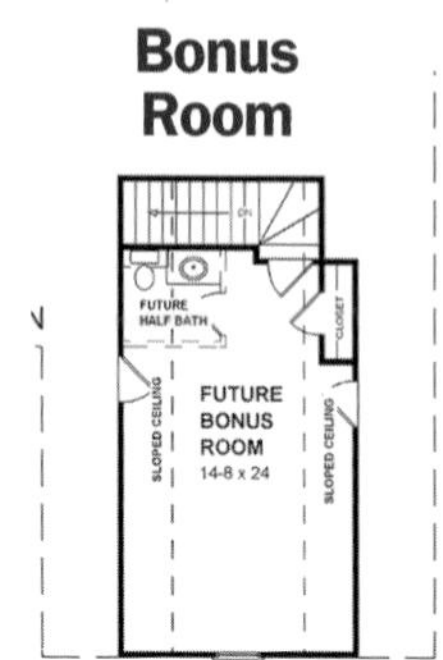

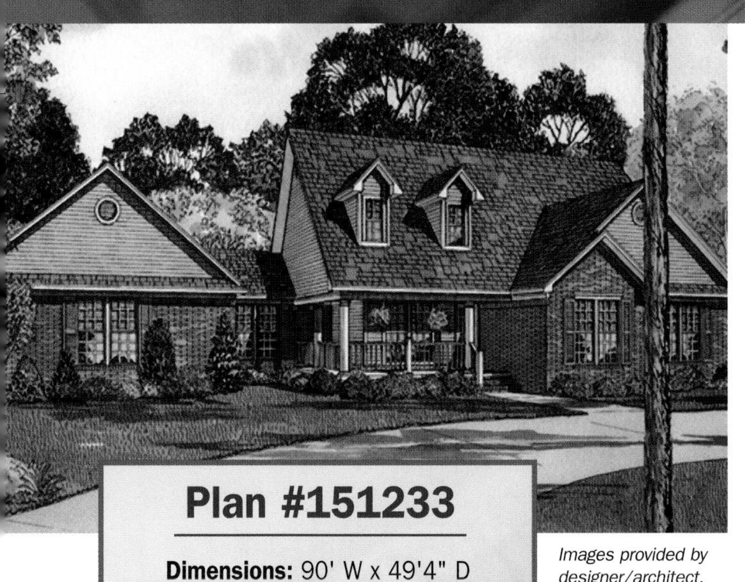

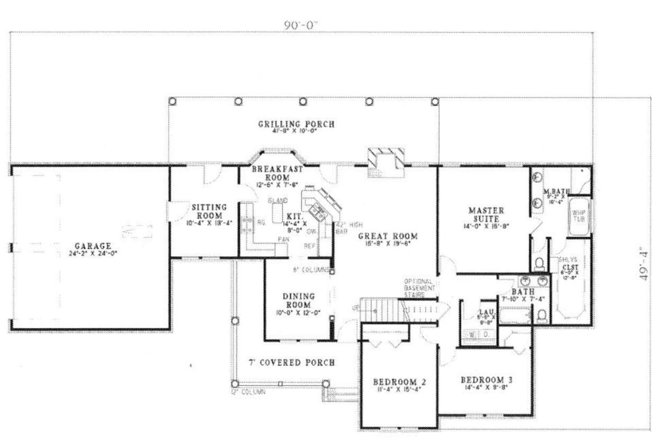

Plan #151233

Dimensions: 90' W x 49'4" D
Levels: 1
Heated Square Footage: 1,853
Bedrooms: 3
Bathrooms: 2
Foundation: Crawl space or slab; basement or walkout for fee
CompleteCost List Available: Yes
Price Category: D

Images provided by designer/architect.

CAD FILE AVAILABLE

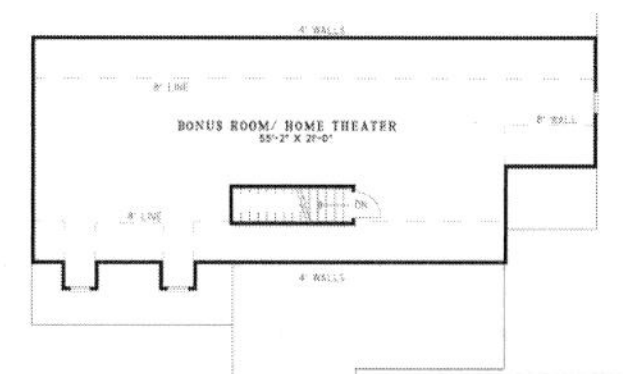

Bonus Area Floor Plan

Copyright by designer/architect.

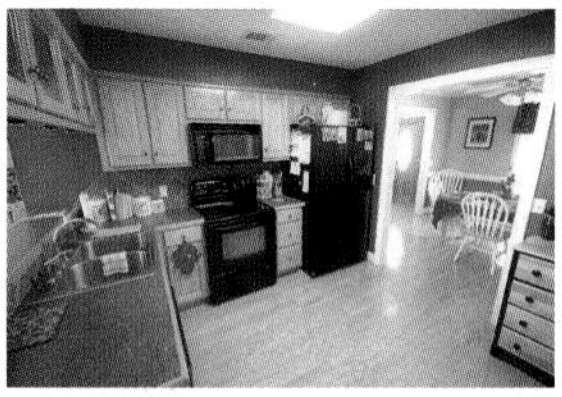

Kitchen

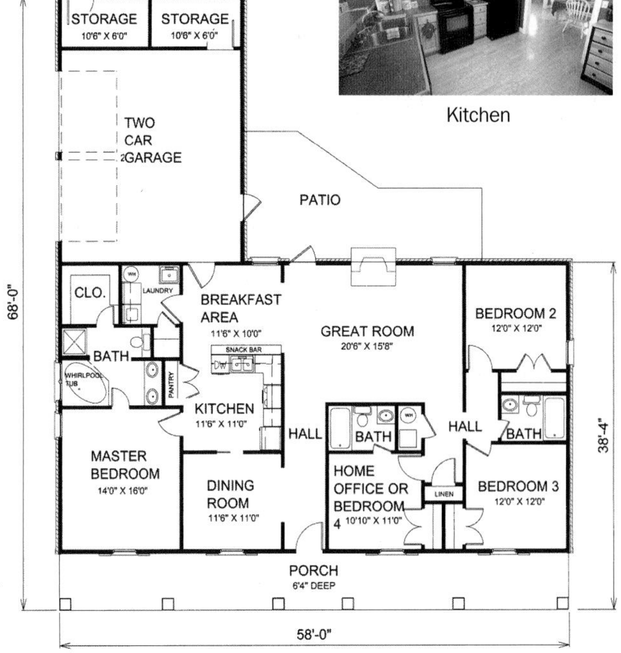

STORAGE 10'6" X 6'0"
STORAGE 10'6" X 6'0"
TWO CAR GARAGE
PATIO
CLO.
LAUNDRY
BREAKFAST AREA 11'6" X 10'0"
GREAT ROOM 20'6" X 15'8"
BEDROOM 2 12'0" X 12'0"
BATH
WHIRLPOOL TUB
PANTRY
SNACK BAR
KITCHEN 11'6" X 11'0"
HALL
BATH
HALL
BATH
MASTER BEDROOM 14'0" X 16'0"
DINING ROOM 11'6" X 11'0"
HOME OFFICE OR BEDROOM 4 10'10" X 11'0"
LINEN
BEDROOM 3 12'0" X 12'0"
PORCH 6'4" DEEP
68'-0"
38'-4"
58'-0"

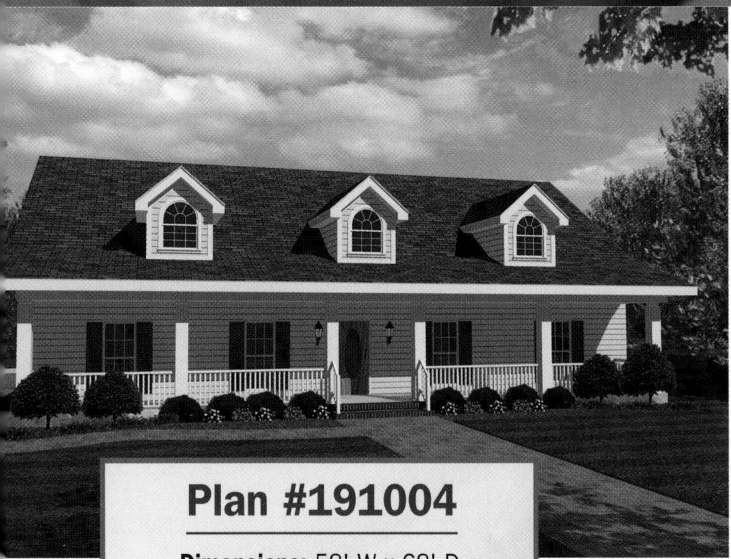

Plan #191004

Dimensions: 58' W x 68' D
Levels: 1
Heated Square Footage: 1,856
Bedrooms: 3
Bathrooms: 3
Foundation: Crawl space
Materials List Available: No
Price Category: D

Images provided by designer/architect.

Copyright by designer/architect.

Plan #211039

Dimensions: 62' W x 64' D
Levels: 1
Heated Square Footage: 1,868
Bedrooms: 3
Bathrooms: 2
Foundation: Slab
Materials List Available: Yes
Price Category: D

Images provided by designer/architect.

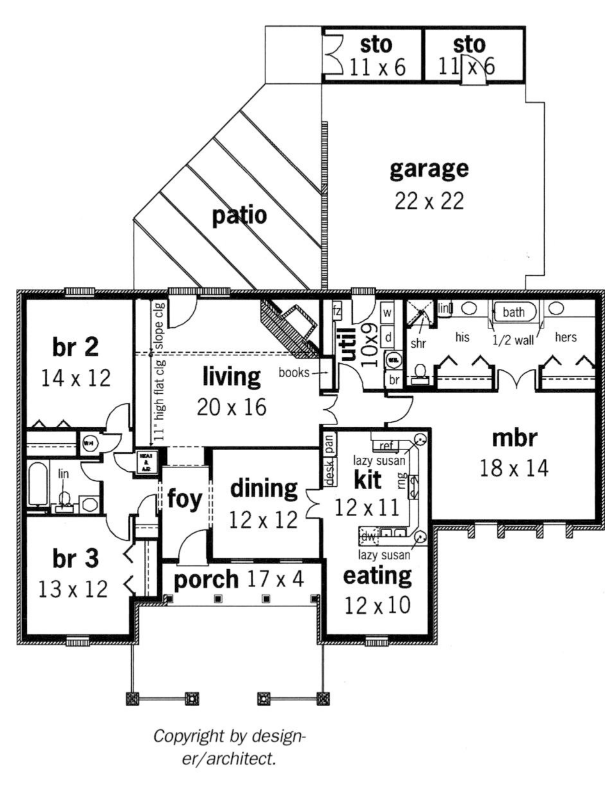

Copyright by designer/architect.

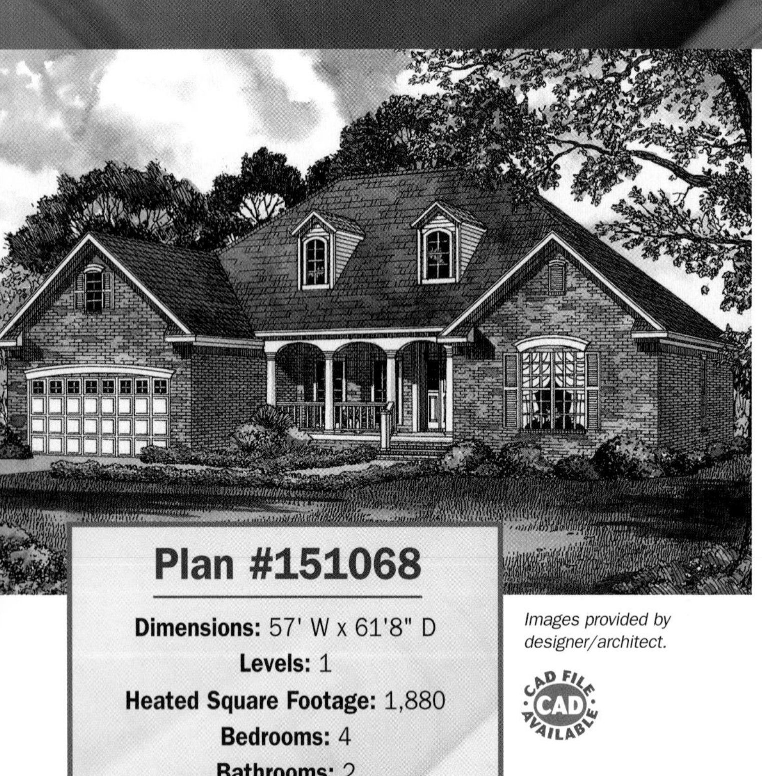

Plan #151068

Dimensions: 57' W x 61'8" D
Levels: 1
Heated Square Footage: 1,880
Bedrooms: 4
Bathrooms: 2
Foundation: Crawl space, slab, basement or walkout
CompleteCost List Available: Yes
Price Category: D

Images provided by designer/architect.

CAD FILE AVAILABLE

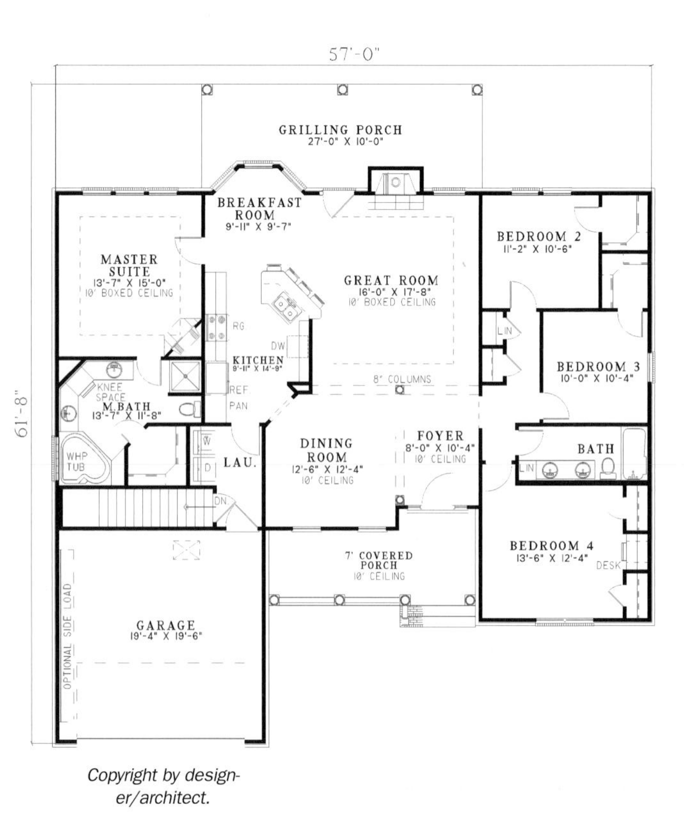

Copyright by designer/architect.

Plan #381010

Dimensions: 62' W x 87'6" D
Levels: 1
Heated Square Footage: 1,905
Bedrooms: 3
Bathrooms: 2
Foundation: Crawl space
Materials List Available: Yes
Price Category: E

Images provided by designer/architect.

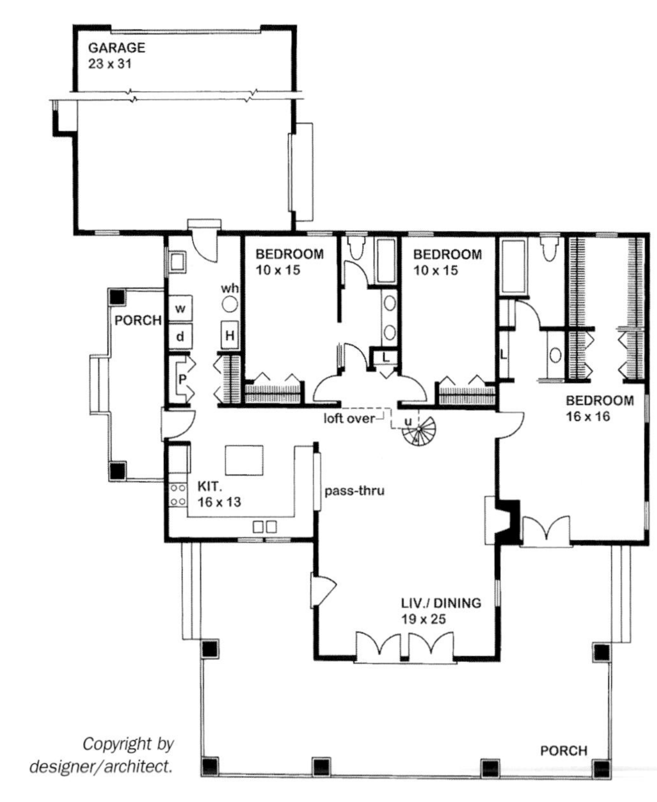

Plan #151075

Dimensions: 56' W x 64'4" D
Levels: 1
Heated Square Footage: 1,909
Bedrooms: 3
Bathrooms: 2
Foundation: Crawl space, slab (basement option for fee)
CompleteCost List Available: Yes
Price Category: D

Images provided by designer/architect.

CAD FILE AVAILABLE

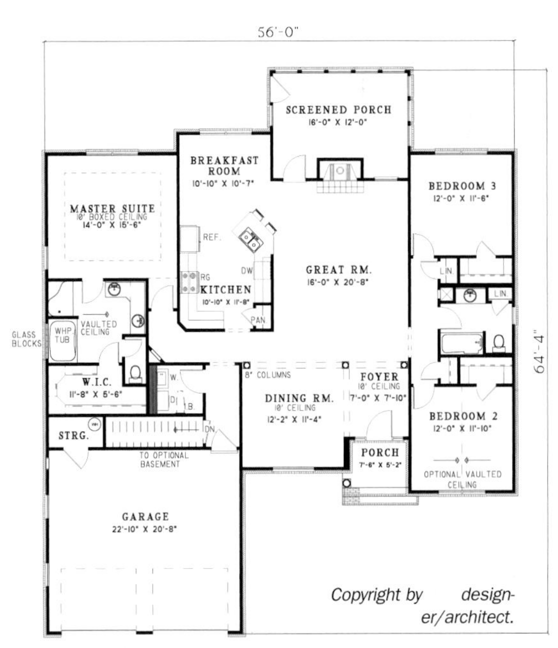

Images provided by designer/architect.

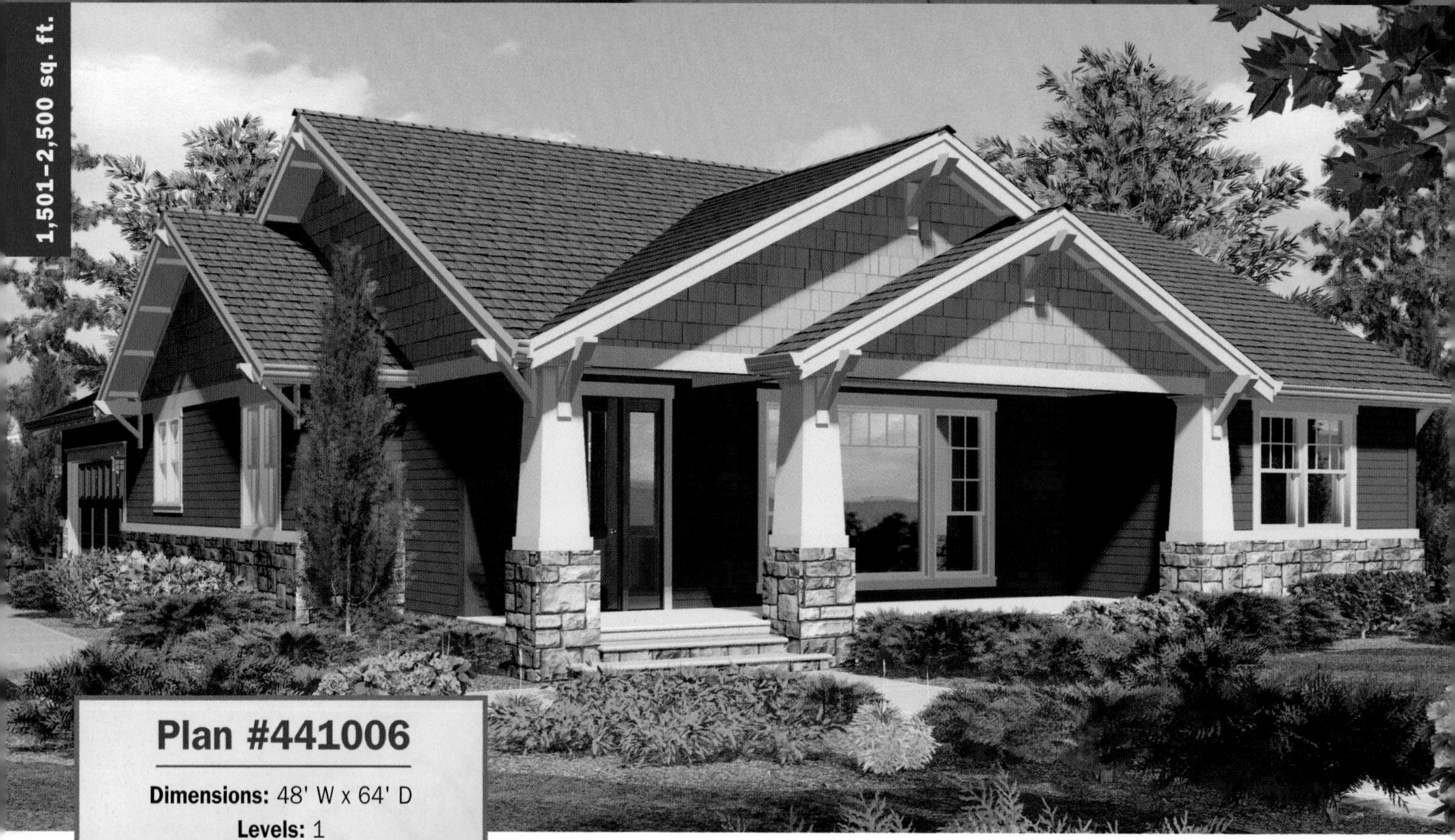

Plan #441006

Dimensions: 48' W x 64' D
Levels: 1
Heated Square Footage: 1,891
Bedrooms: 3
Bathrooms: 2
Foundation: Crawl space; slab or basement for fee
Materials List Available: Yes
Price Category: D

CAD FILE AVAILABLE

Copyright by designer/architect.

Rear Elevation

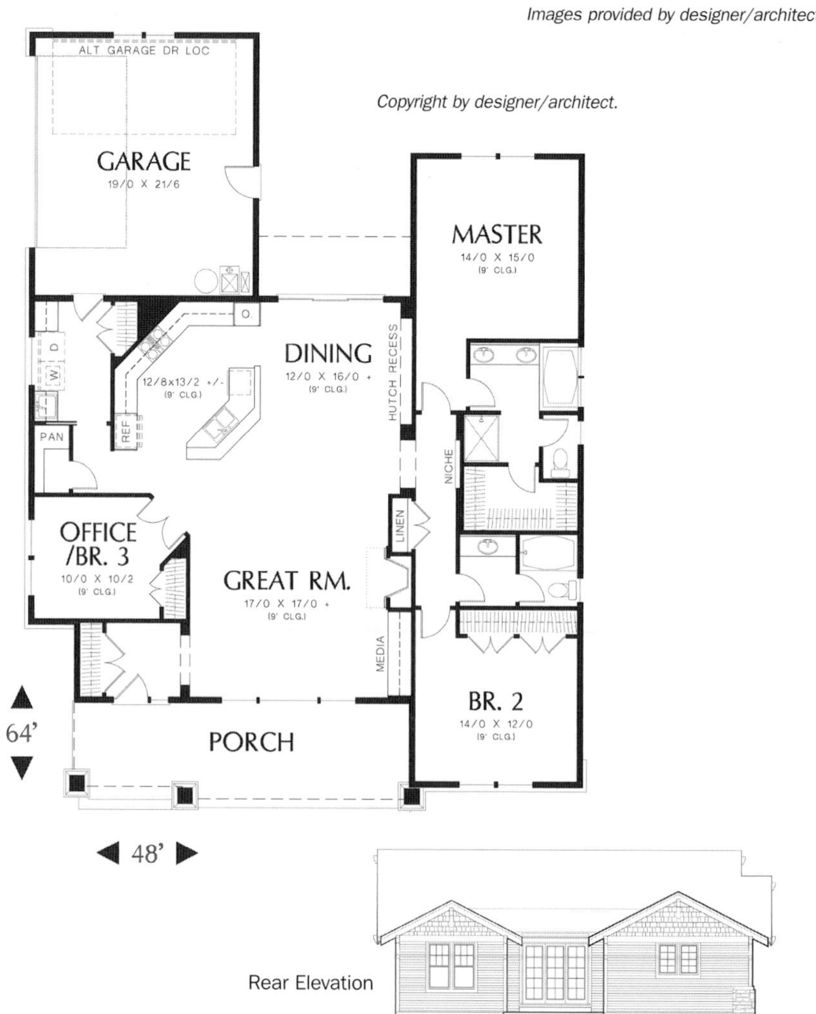

If you prefer the look of Craftsman homes, you'll love the details this plan includes. Wide-based columns across the front porch, Mission-style windows, and a balanced mixture of exterior materials add up to true good looks.

Features:

- Great Room: A built-in media center and a fireplace in this room make it distinctive.
- Kitchen: A huge skylight over an island eating counter brightens this kitchen. A private office space opens through double doors nearby.
- Dining Room: This room has sliding glass doors opening to the rear patio.
- Bedrooms: Two bedrooms with two bathrooms are located on the right side of the plan. One of the bedrooms is a master suite with a vaulted salon and a bath with a spa tub.
- Garage: You'll be able to reach this two-car garage via a service hallway that contains a laundry room, a walk-in pantry, and a closet.

Plan #131011

Dimensions: 75'2" W x 60'9" D
Levels: 1
Heated Square Footage: 1,897
Bedrooms: 4
Bathrooms: 2
Foundation: Crawl space, slab, or basement
Materials List Available: Yes
Price Category: E

Images provided by designer/architect.

You'll love this home if you're looking for a plan for a sloping lot or flat one or if you want to orient the rear porch to face into or away from the sun.

Features:

- Ceiling Height: 8 ft.
- Living Area: The whole family will find it easy to congregate in this lovely room.
- Kitchen: The angle of the home makes the kitchen especially convenient while also giving it an unusual amount of character.
- Study: Located near the front door, this room can serve as a home office or fourth bedroom as easily as it does a private study.
- Master Suite: Located at the opposite end of the home from the other two bedrooms, this master suite offers privacy and quiet.
- Additional Bedrooms: These two bedrooms share a distinctive hall bathroom.

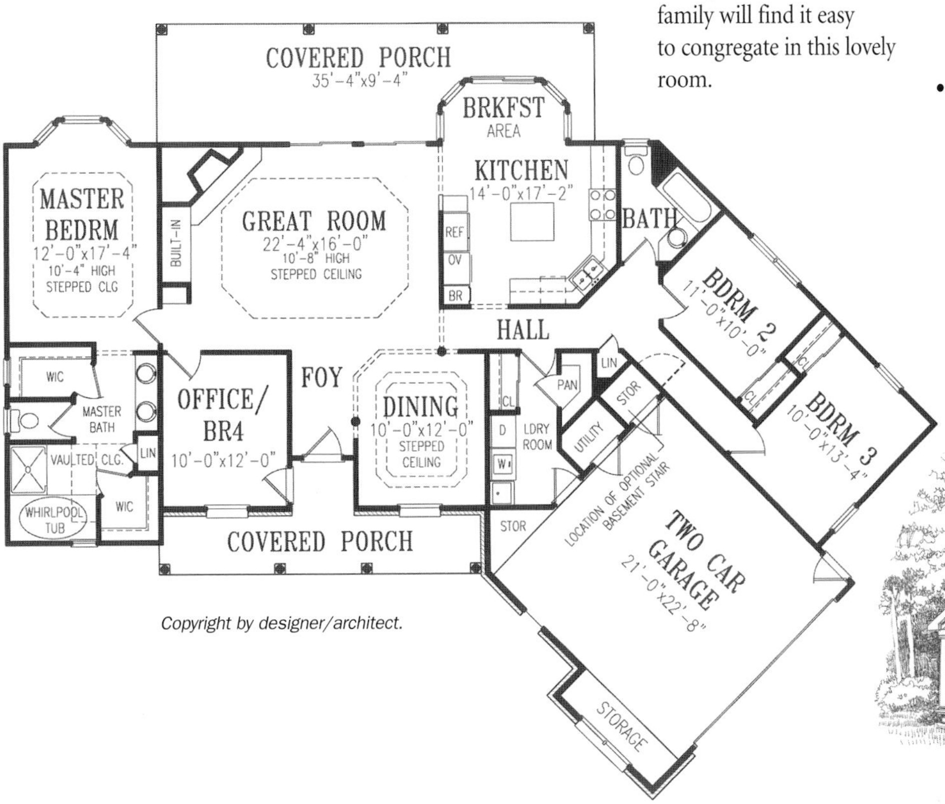

Rear View

Images provided by designer/architect.

Plan #131016

Dimensions: 75' W x 45' D
Levels: 1
Heated Square Footage: 1,902
Bedrooms: 3
Bathrooms: 2
Foundation: Crawl space, slab, or basement
Materials List Available: Yes
Price Category: E

If traditional country looks appeal to you, you'll be delighted by the wraparound covered porch that forms the entryway to this comfortable home.

Features:

- Great Room: Sit by the fireplace in this room with feature walls so large that they'll suit a home theater or large media center.
- Kitchen: Overlooking the great room, this well-designed kitchen has great cabinets and ample counter space to make all your cooking and cleaning a pleasure.
- Master Suite: A large bay window makes the bedroom in this private suite sophisticated, and two walk-in closets make it practical. You'll love to relax in the master bath, whether in the whirlpool tub or the separate shower. A dual-sink vanity completes the amenities in this room.
- Garage: Find extra storage space in this two-bayed, attached garage.

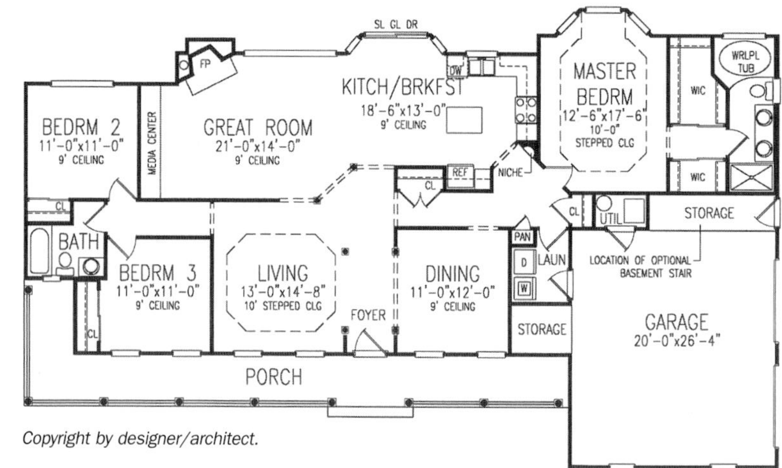

Copyright by designer/architect.

Great Room

Plan #121001

Dimensions: 56' W x 58' D
Levels: 1
Heated Square Footage: 1,911
Bedrooms: 3
Bathrooms: 2
Foundation: Basement
Materials List Available: Yes
Price Category: D

Images provided by designer/architect.

CAD FILE AVAILABLE

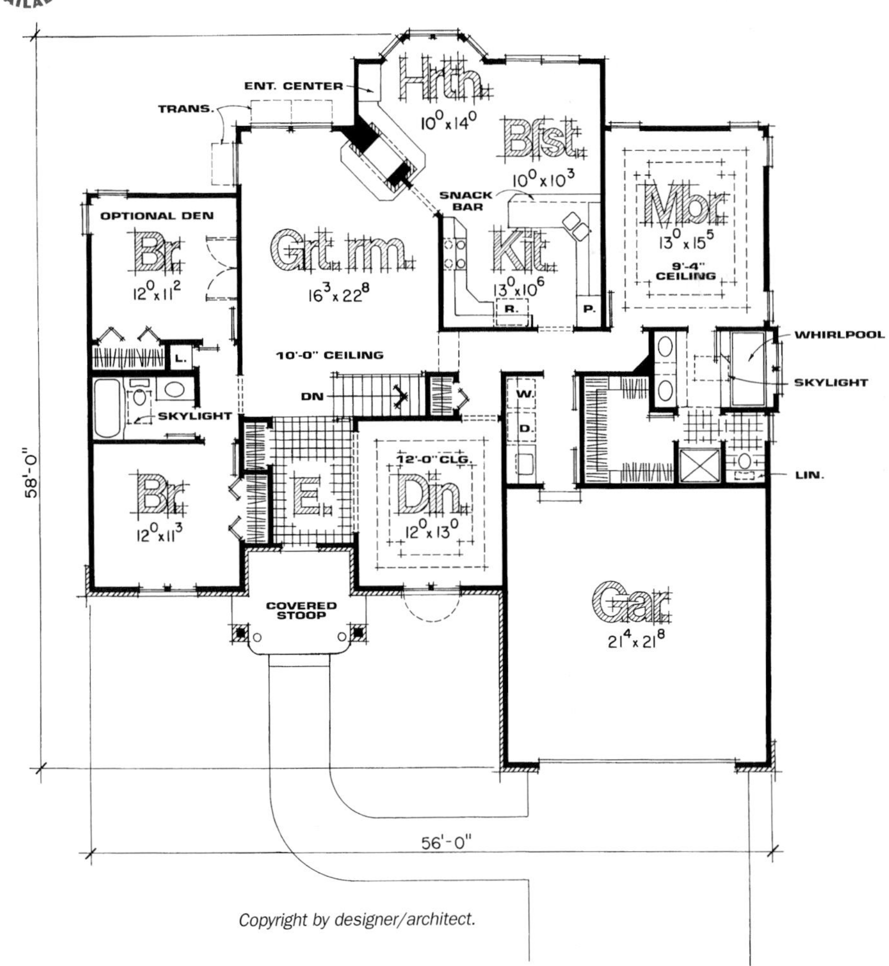

Copyright by designer/architect.

Detailed, soaring ceilings and top-notch amenities set this distinctive home apart.

Features:

- Ceiling Height: 8 ft. except as noted.
- Formal Dining Room: The entry enjoys a pleasing view of this dining room's detailed 12-ft. ceiling and picture window.
- Great Room: At the back of the home, a see-through fireplace in this great room is joined by a built-in entertainment center.
- Hearth Room: This bayed room shares the see-through fireplace with the great room.
- Master Suite: Enjoy the stars and the sun in the private bath's whirlpool and separate shower. The bath features the same decorative ceiling as the dining room.

Storage Options for Your Home

One of the great things about moving into a new home is all that new, uncluttered closet space you gain. But if you are like most homeowners, storage of all types will quickly become scarce, especially in a smaller home. Here are some tips for expanding and organizing storage space.

Home offices require a mix of storage options: open shelving, drawers, and file cabinets.

Shelving Types

Shelving is an easy and economical way to add extra storage space in almost any part of your home—along walls, inside closets, and even in the basement or garage. Building shelves doesn't usually require a lot of skill or specialized tools, so this is one project just about any do-it-yourselfer can handle. And unless you decide to use hardwood—which looks great but costs a bundle—it won't cost a lot to install them either.

Solid wood shelving is the way to go when you want to show off the wood or your work.

Plywood and particleboard offer a couple of advantages when it comes to shelving, though. They cost less than solid wood, and can be bought faced with decorative surfaces. They also come in sheets, which makes them ideal for a really wide shelf. Inexpensive, manufactured storage units ready for assembly often are made from melamine-coated particleboard.

Wood trim will help match your new shelves to the rest of the room or add some interesting detail. Trim is also a handy way to hide seams, gaps, exposed edges of plywood, and other blemishes. You can get trim in either hardwood or softwood. If you plan on finishing a project with stain or sealer, make sure the trim matches the wood you used for the rest of the project.

Ready-made shelving offers a quick alternative to building your own shelves.

Bracket Options

There are two basic types of ready-to-hang shelving supports: stationary shelf brackets and shelving standards. Stationary brackets come in many sizes and styles, and range from utilitarian to decorative. Shelving standards are slotted metal strips that support various types of shelf brackets.

Mounting Brackets

For maximum strength, anchor shelf supports to wall studs. If your shelf will carry a light load, you can anchor its supports between studs with mollies or toggle bolts. Attaching supports directly to the studs is always better, though, because sooner or later something heavy will wind up on the shelf. Use masonry anchors to attach shelf supports to brick or concrete. You can also attach shelf supports to a ledger attached to wall studs with 3-inch drywall screws.

Mud rooms and areas near the entrance the family uses most should have storage for coats, hats, and boots.

Shelf Standards. Metal shelf standards can be mounted directly to walls or, for a more decorative look, you can insert the standards in grooves routed into the wood itself or into hardwood strips.

Cut the standards to fit with a hacksaw, and attach them to wall studs with 3-inch drywall screws. Use a carpenter's level to make sure that both standards are plumb and that the corresponding mounting slots are level. Mount standards 6 inches from the ends of shelving to prevent sagging. For long wall shelves, install standards every 48 inches.

Many kitchen and closet storage systems use wire grids that attach to walls with molded plastic brackets. If you anticipate light loads, you can mount these brackets to drywall using the screws and expansion anchors usually included with such systems. But for heavier loads, use drywall screws to fasten the brackets directly to the wall studs.

Customized Storage

Built-in storage units are an excellent way to make the most of existing storage space in your home. Ready-made or custom-made built-in shelving units, entertainment centers, kitchen cabinets, medicine cabinets, window seats, and under-bed drawers are not only inexpensive and easy to assemble, they allow you to add a unique, personalized touch to your living spaces.

Built-in Shelving

A built-in shelving unit can create valuable storage capacity from an overlooked wall space, such as the area between windows or between a door and its adjacent corner. To construct the shelving, you'll need 1×10 or 1×12 lumber for side panels, top and base panels, and shelves; four 2×2 strips for spreaders; trim molding to conceal gaps along the top and bottom of the unit; 12d common nails and 6d finishing nails. If the unit will be bearing heavy loads, use hardwood boards, and make sure that the shelves span no more than 36 inches. To make installation easier, cut the side pieces an inch shorter than the ceiling height. (This way, you'll be able to tilt the unit into position without scraping the ceiling.) Paint or stain the wood pieces before assembling the unit. Hang the shelves from pegs or end clips inserted into holes drilled in the side pieces.

Adding Closet Space

What homeowner, even a new homeowner, hasn't complained about having too little closet space? Fortunately, there are almost always ways to find a bit more closet space or to make the closet space you have more efficient. Often, it isn't the space that is lacking but how the space is organized that is the problem. The trick is to find ways to help you organize the space.

Ventilated closet systems help keep your belongings neat and within easy reach.

Organizing Systems. The easiest and most obvious solution is one of the many commercial closet organizing systems now on the market. There are a number of configurations available, and you can customize most systems to meet your needs. Constructing your own version of a commercial closet organizer is another option. With a combination of shelves and plywood partitions, you can divide a closet into storage zones, with a single clothes pole on one side for full-length garments; double clothes poles on the other side for half-length garments like jackets, skirts, or slacks; a column of narrow shelves between the two for folded items or shoes; and one or more closet-wide shelves on top.

Before designing a closet system, above, inventory all of the items you want to store in the closet.

Metal shelf standards, left, can provide a quick solution for creating shelving in areas where it is needed.

Cedar Closets

Both solid cedar boards and composite cedar panels have only moderate resistance to insects, and are used more for their pleasant aroma and appearance. The sheets of pressed red and tan particles are no less aromatic than solid wood, but the panels are 40 to 50 percent less expensive, and are easier to install. Solid boards require more carpentry work, and are likely to produce a fair amount of waste unless you piece the courses and create more joints. To gain the maximum effect, every inside surface should be covered, including the ceiling and the back of the door. The simplest option is to use ¼-inch-thick panels, which are easy to cut into big sections that cover walls in one or two pieces. Try to keep cedar seams in boards or panels from falling over drywall seams. No stain, sealer, or clear finish is needed; just leave the wood raw. The cedar aroma will fade over the years as natural oils crystallize on the

For garages and basements, you'll find a combination of shelving and hanging hooks keeps tools and equipment organized, opposite top.

Storage for basements, garages, and workshops, opposite bottom, should include a cabinet that locks for storage of dangerous chemicals.

Specialized storage accessories, such as the sports storage system shown at right, not only keeps items organized but they also keep them in ready-to-play condition.

surface. But you can easily regenerate the scent from the panels by scuffing the surface with fine sandpaper.

Ideas for Basements, Garages, and Workshops

Workshops and other utility areas such as garages, attics, and basements can benefit from storage upgrades as much as any other room in the home—perhaps even more so, as utility areas are prone to clutter. Convenience, flexibility, and safety are the things to keep in mind when reorganizing your work space. Try to provide storage space for tools and hardware as near as possible to where they'll be used. In addition to a sturdy workbench, utility shelving is a mainstay in any workshop. You can buy ready-to-assemble units or make your own using ¾-inch particleboard or plywood shelves and ¾ × 1½-inch (1×2) hardwood stock for cleats (nailed to the wall), ribs (nailed to the front underside of the shelves), and vertical shelf supports.

DIY Utility Storage. Don't forget about pegboard. To make a pegboard tool rack, attach washers to the back of the pegboard with hot glue, spacing the washers to coincide with wall studs. Position the pegboard so that the rear washers are located over studs. Drive drywall screws through finish washers and the pegboard into studs. (Use masonry anchors for concrete walls.)

Finally, try to take advantage of any otherwise wasted space. The area in your garage above your parked car is the ideal spot for a U-shaped lumber storage rack, made of 1×4 stock and connecting plates. The space in front of the car could be used for a storage cabinet or even a workbench.

Instant Storage. To utilize the overhead space in your garage, build deep storage platforms supported by ledgers screwed to wall studs and threaded rods hooked to ceiling joists or rafters. You can also hang tools from the walls by mounting pegboard. You can buy sets with a variety of hooks and brackets for tools. For small items, such as jars of nails, make shallow shelves by nailing 1×4

GREENS
SPA FOOD
CLASSICS
GRILLING
HARBOR
BREAD MIX
COLAVITA
EXTRA VIRGIN OLIVE OIL
al dente

Kitchen Storage

The type of storage in a kitchen is almost as important as the amount. Some people like at least a few open shelves for displaying attractive china or glassware; others want absolutely everything tucked away behind doors.

What are your storage needs? The answer depends partly on your food shopping habits and partly on how many pots, pans, and other pieces of kitchen equipment you have or would like to have. A family that goes food shopping several times a week and prepares mostly fresh foods needs more refrigerator space, less freezer capacity, and fewer cabinets than a family that prefers packaged or prepared foods and makes only infrequent forays to the local supermarket.

Storage accessories, such as the pullout pot holder above, come as options from some cabinet manufacturers, or you can install them later yourself. Notice how the side rails hold the pot lids in place. The cabinet below features space for small baskets.

Planning

To help clarify your needs, mentally walk yourself through a typical meal and list the utensils used to prepare food, where you got them, and your progress throughout the work area. And don't limit yourself to full-scale meals. Much kitchen work is devoted to preparing snacks, reheating leftovers, and making lunches for the kids to take to school.

Food Preparation. During food preparation, the sink and stove come into use. Some families rely heavily on the microwave for reheating. Using water means repeated trips to the sink, so that area might be the best place to keep a steamer, salad spinner, and coffee and tea canisters, as well as glassware and cups. Near the stove you may want storage for odd-shaped items such as a fish poacher or wok. You can hang frequently used pans and utensils from a convenient rack; stow other items in cabinets so that they do not collect grease.

During the Meal. When the food is ready, you must take it to the table. If the eating space is nearby, a work counter might turn into a serving counter. If the dining space is in another room, a pass-through facilitates serving.

After the Meal. When the meal ends, dishes must go from the table to the sink or dishwasher, and leftovers to storage containers and the refrigerator. Now the stove and counters need to be wiped down and the sink scoured. When the dishwasher finishes its cycle, everything must be put away.

Open versus Closed Storage. Shelves, pegboards, pot racks, cup hooks, magnetic knife racks, and the like put your utensils on view, which is a good way to personalize your kitchen.

But open storage has drawbacks. Items left out in the open can look messy unless they are kept neatly arranged. Another option is to install glass doors on wall cabinets. This handily solves the dust problem

Plan #151089

Dimensions: 84" W x 55'6" D
Levels: 1
Heated Square Footage: 1,921
Bedrooms: 3
Bathrooms: 3
Foundation: Crawl space, slab, or basement
CompleteCost List Available: Yes
Price Category: E

Images provided by designer/architect.

CAD FILE AVAILABLE

If your family loves to combine indoor and outdoor living, this home's fabulous porches and deck space make it perfect.

Features:

- Porches: A huge wraparound front porch, sizable rear porch, and deck that joins them give you space for entertaining or simply lounging.
- Living Room: A fireplace and built-in media center could be the focal points in this large room.
- Hearth Room: Open to both the living room and kitchen, this hearth room also features a fireplace.
- Kitchen: This step-saving kitchen includes ample storage and work space, as well as an angled bar it shares with the hearth room. Atrium doors lead to the rear porch.
- Bonus Upper Level: A large game room and a full bath make this area a favorite with the children.

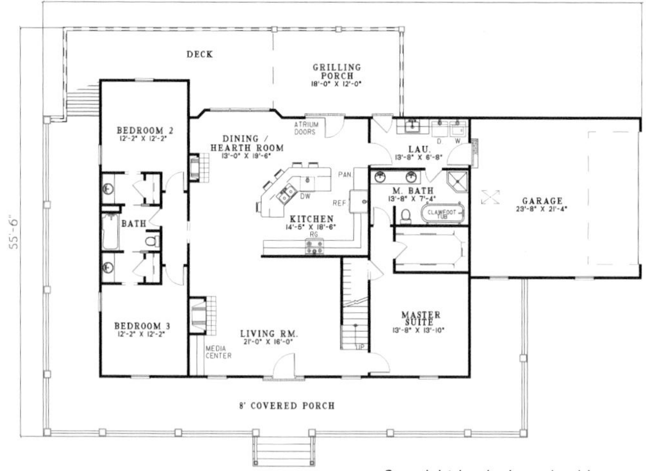

Copyright by designer/architect.

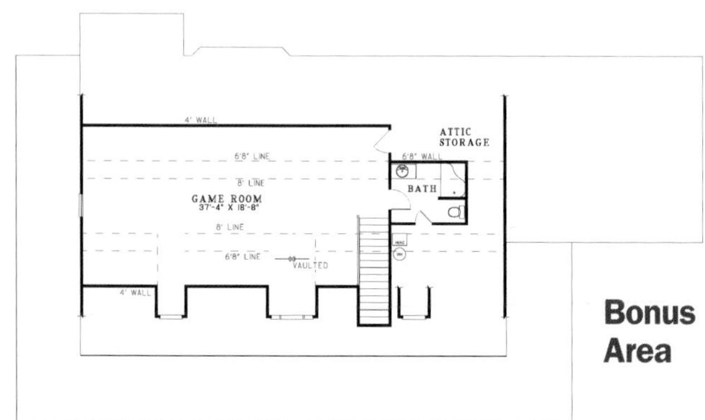

Bonus Area

Plan #221015

Dimensions: 69'8" W x 46' D
Levels: 1
Heated Square Footage: 1,926
Bedrooms: 3
Bathrooms: 2½
Foundation: Basement; walkout basement for fee
Materials List Available: No
Price Category: D

CAD FILE AVAILABLE

Images provided by designer/architect.

Rear Elevation

You'll love the open plan in this lovely ranch and admire its many features, which are usually reserved for much larger homes.

Features:

- Ceiling Height: 8 ft.
- Great Room: A vaulted ceiling and tall windows surrounding the centrally located fireplace give distinction to this handsome room.
- Dining Room: Positioned just off the entry, this formal room makes a lovely spot for quiet dinner parties.
- Dining Nook: This nook sits between the kitchen and the great room. Central doors in the bayed area open to the backyard.
- Kitchen: An island will invite visitors while you cook in this well-planned kitchen, with its corner pantry and ample counter space.
- Master Suite: A tray ceiling, bay window, walk-in closet, and bath with whirlpool tub, dual-sink vanity, and standing shower pamper you here.

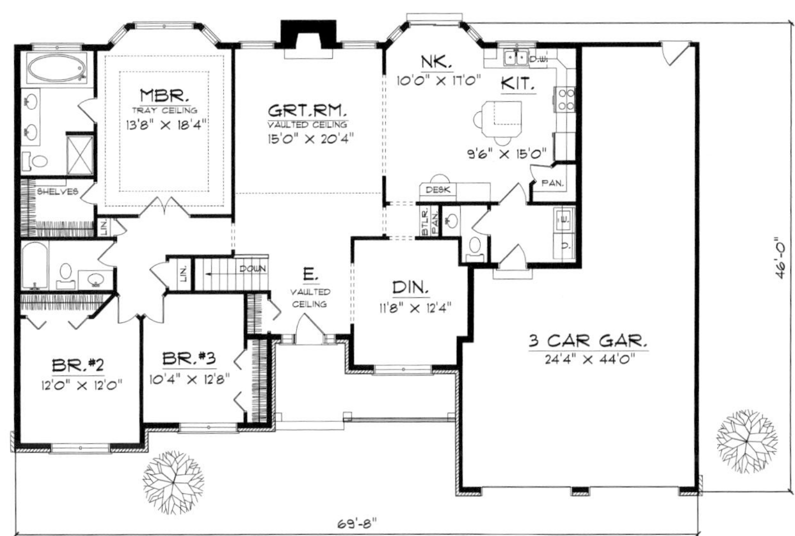

Copyright by designer/architect.

Images provided by designer/architect.

Plan #301005

Dimensions: 71' W x 42' D
Levels: 1
Heated Square Footage: 1,930
Bedrooms: 3
Bathrooms: 2
Foundation: Crawl space, slab
Materials List Available: Yes
Price Category: D

This home features an old-fashioned rocking-chair porch that enhances the streetscape.

Features:

- Ceiling Height: 8 ft.
- Dining Room: When the weather is warm, guests can step through French doors from this elegant dining room and enjoy a breeze on the rear screened porch.
- Family Room: This family room is a warm and inviting place to gather, with its handsome fireplace and built-in bookcases.
- Kitchen: This kitchen offers plenty of counter space for preparing your favorite recipes. Its U-shape creates a convenient open traffic pattern.
- Master Suite: You'll look forward to retiring at the end of the day in this truly luxurious master suite. The bedroom has a fireplace and opens through French doors to a private rear deck. The bath features a corner spa tub, a walk-in shower, double vanities, and a linen closet.

WOOD DECK 12-0 x 10-0
SCR. PORCH 12-0 x 10-0
WOOD DECK 11-0 x 10-0
MASTER BEDROOM 18-2 x 17-0
BATH
KITCHEN 11-6 x 11-4
DINING 16-0 x 11-4
LAUNDRY 10-0 x 11-4
BATH
HALL
GREAT ROOM 16-0 x 21-8
GARAGE 21-8 x 21-8
BEDROOM 13-0 x 12-0
BEDROOM 13-2 x 12-0
PORCH 28-0 x 8-0
71'-0"
42'-0"

SMARTtip

Light With Shutters

For the maximum the amount of light coming through shutters, use the largest panel possible on the window. Make sure the shutters have the same number of louvers per panel so that all of the windows in the room look unified. However, don't choose a panel that is over 48 inches high, because the shutter becomes unwieldy. Also, any window that is wider than 96 inches requires extra framing to support the shutters.

Plan #271073

Dimensions: 69' W x 56' D
Levels: 1
Heated Square Footage: 1,920
Bedrooms: 3
Bathrooms: 2½
Foundation: Walkout basement
Materials List Available: No
Price Category: D

Images provided by designer/architect.

A great floor plan and plenty of space make this home perfect for people who welcome family members back home to visit.

Features:

- Great Room: This vaulted space shares a see-through fireplace with a cozy hearth room.
- Kitchen: An angled island and a step-in pantry are the highlights of this room.
- Study: Double doors introduce this versatile space, which shows off a nice bay window.
- Master Suite: Double doors lead to the bedroom. The private bath hosts a whirlpool tub and a separate shower.
- Basement: This level contains more bedrooms and family spaces for visiting relatives.

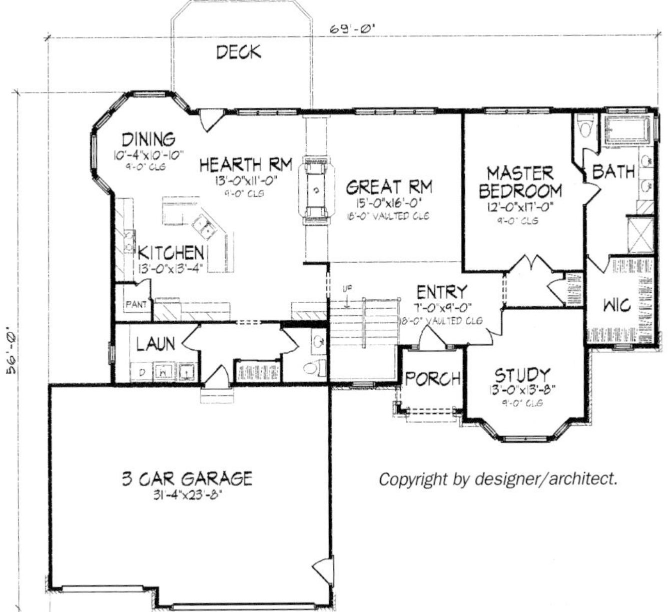

Copyright by designer/architect.

Basement Level Floor Plan

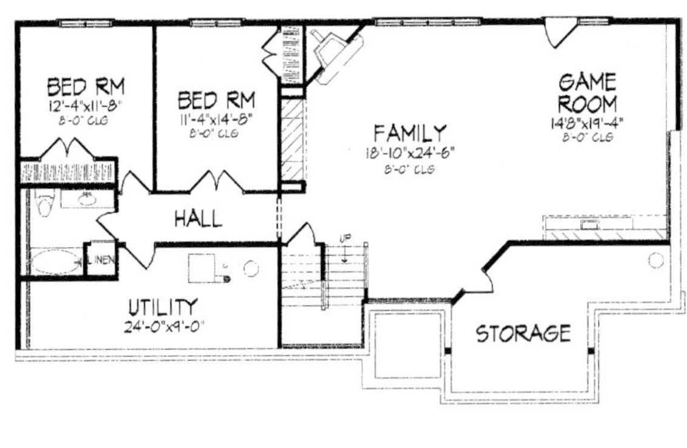

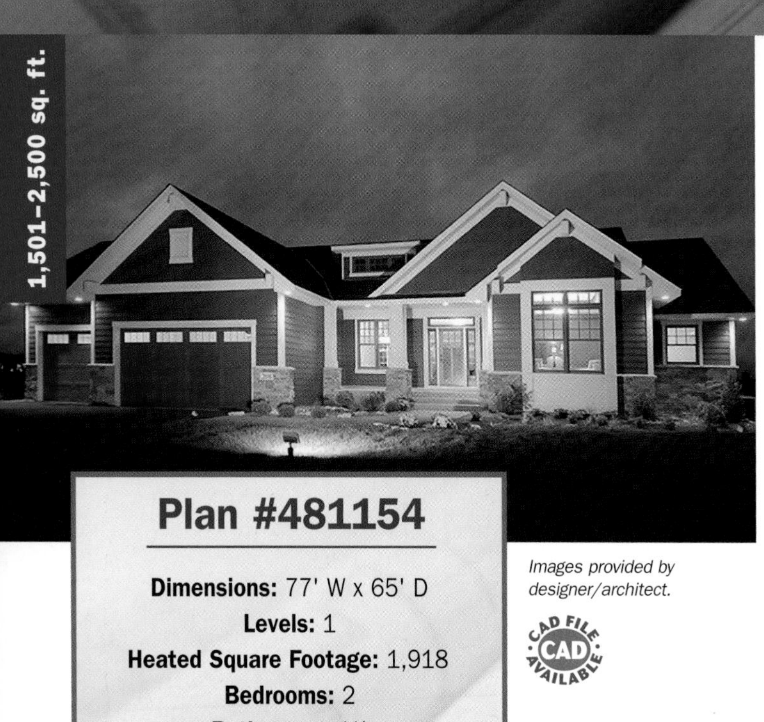

Plan #481154

Dimensions: 77' W x 65' D
Levels: 1
Heated Square Footage: 1,918
Bedrooms: 2
Bathrooms: 1½
Foundation: Walkout
Material List Available: No
Price Category: D

Images provided by designer/architect.

CAD FILE AVAILABLE

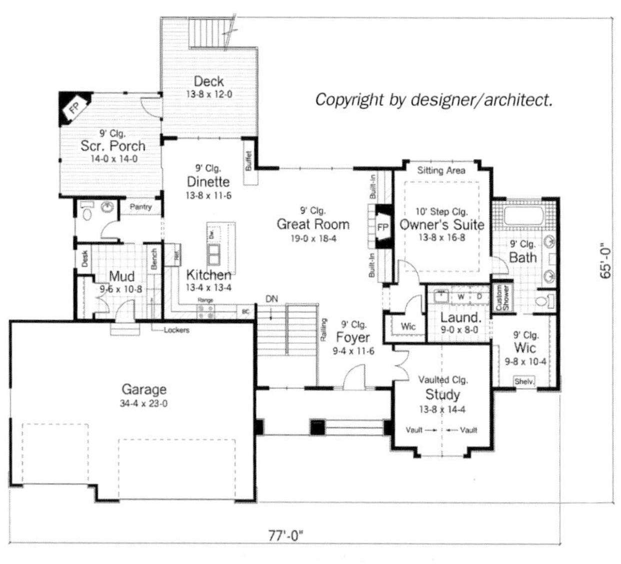

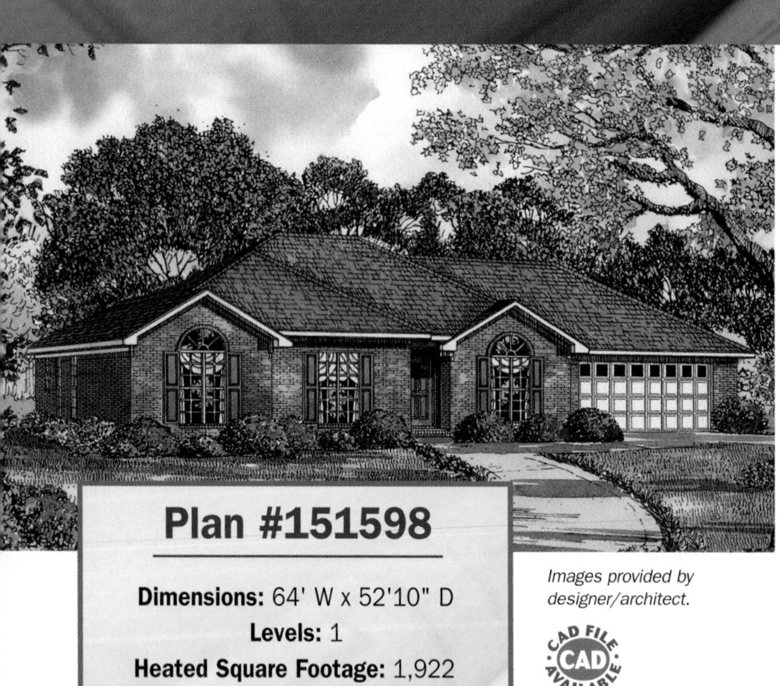

Plan #151598

Dimensions: 64' W x 52'10" D
Levels: 1
Heated Square Footage: 1,922
Bedrooms: 3
Bathrooms: 2
Foundation: Crawl space or slab
CompleteCost List Available: Yes
Price Category: D

Images provided by designer/architect.

CAD FILE AVAILABLE

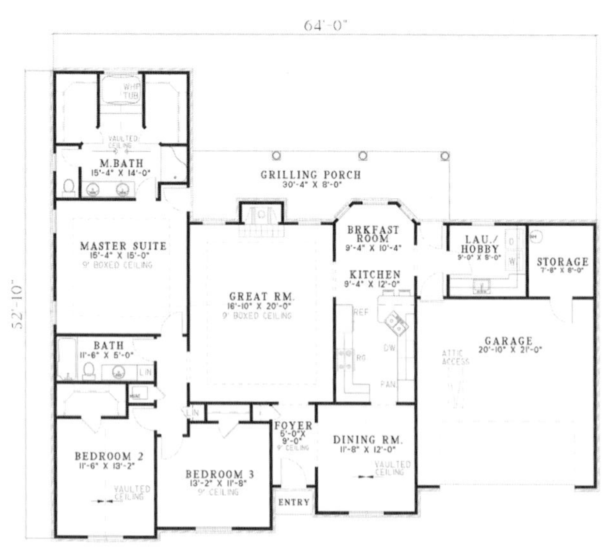

Copyright by designer/architect.

Plan #351186

Dimensions: 68' W x 59'10" D
Levels: 1
Heated Square Footage: 1,924
Bedrooms: 3
Bathrooms: 2
Foundation: Basement
Materials List Available: Yes
Price Category: D

Images provided by designer/architect.

CAD FILE AVAILABLE

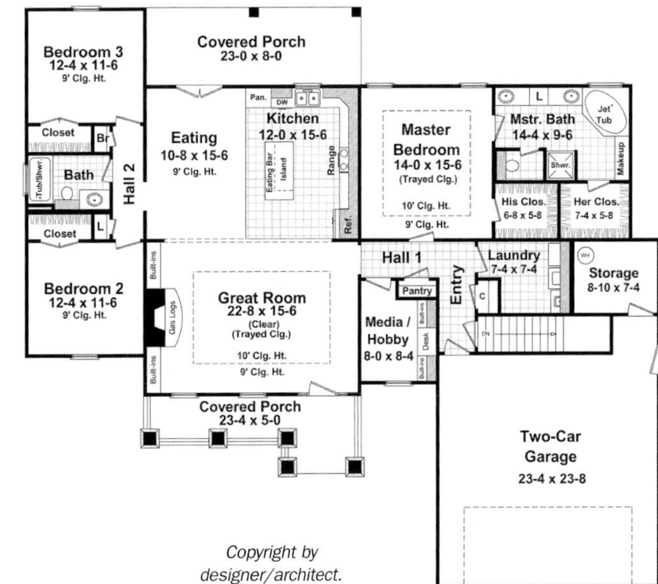

Copyright by designer/architect.

Plan #351205

Dimensions: 70'8" W x 60' D
Levels: 1
Heated Square Footage: 1,934
Bedrooms: 3
Bathrooms: 2
Foundation: Crawl space or slab
Materials List Available: Yes
Price Category: D

Images provided by designer/architect.

CAD FILE AVAILABLE

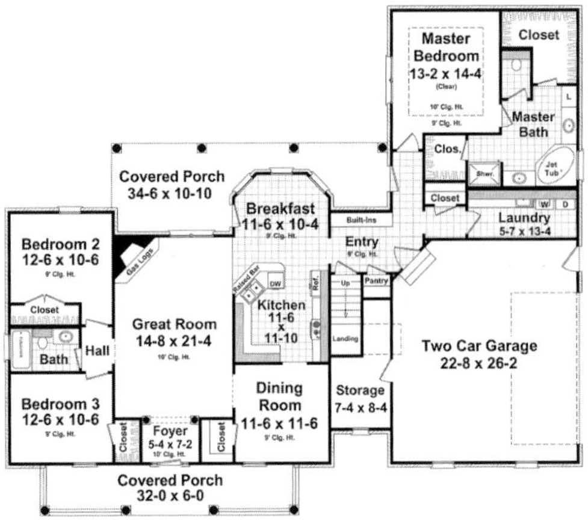

Rear Elevation

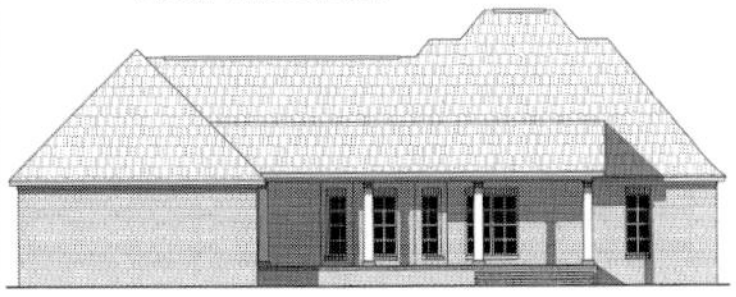

Bonus Area

Copyright by designer/architect.

Plan #371007

Dimensions: 72'10" W x 49'1" D
Levels: 1
Heated Square Footage: 1,944
Bedrooms: 4
Bathrooms: 2
Foundation: Crawl space, slab or basement
Materials List Available: No
Price Category: D

Images provided by designer/architect.

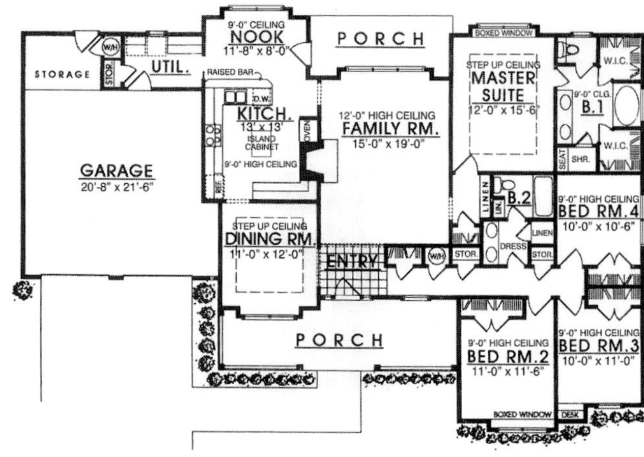

Copyright by designer/architect.

Plan #151056

Dimensions: 56'8" W x 58'4" D
Levels: 1
Heated Square Footage: 1,950
Bedrooms: 3
Bathrooms: 2
Foundation: Crawl space, slab
CompleteCost List Available: Yes
Price Category: D

Images provided by designer/architect.

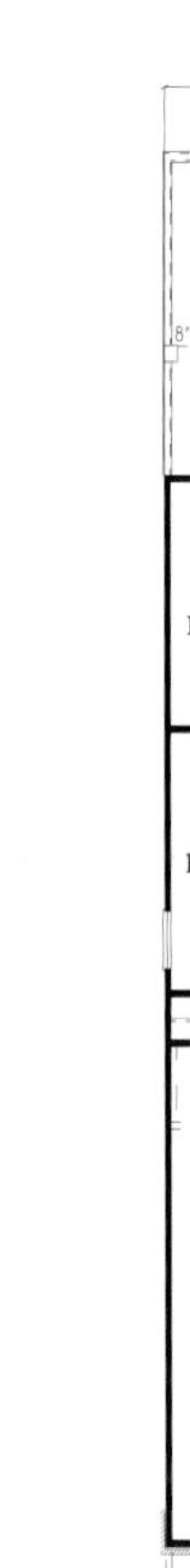

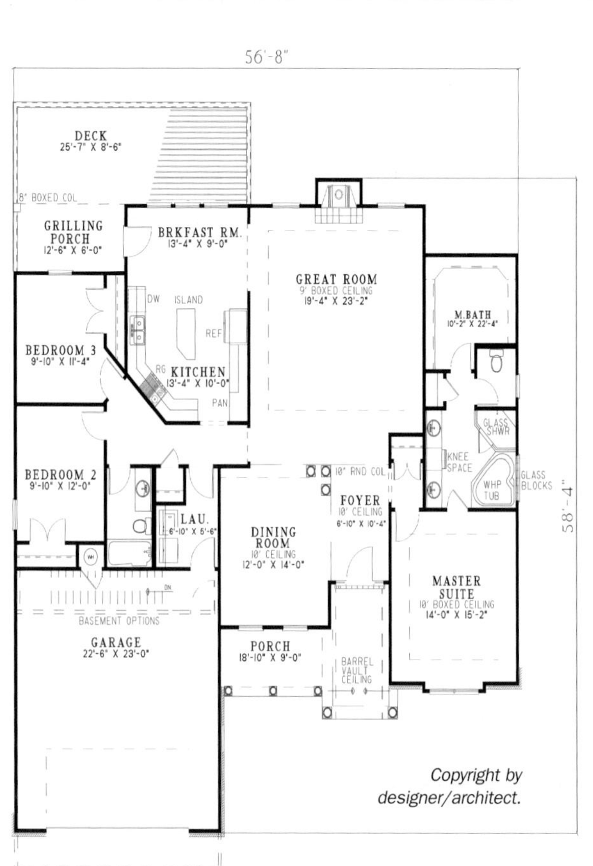

Copyright by designer/architect.

Storage
17-4x5-8
Garage
20-4x21-4
Porch
17-4x10-0
Master
Bedroom
17-4x13-6
Laundry
7-4x6-3
1/2 Bath
Pantry
Greatroom
17-4x17-4
Bath
M.Bath
Kitchen/
Breakfast
13-3x20-5
Dining
11-3x13-4
Foyer
Bedroom
11-3x10-1
Bedroom
11-4x11-4
Porch
31-0x8-0

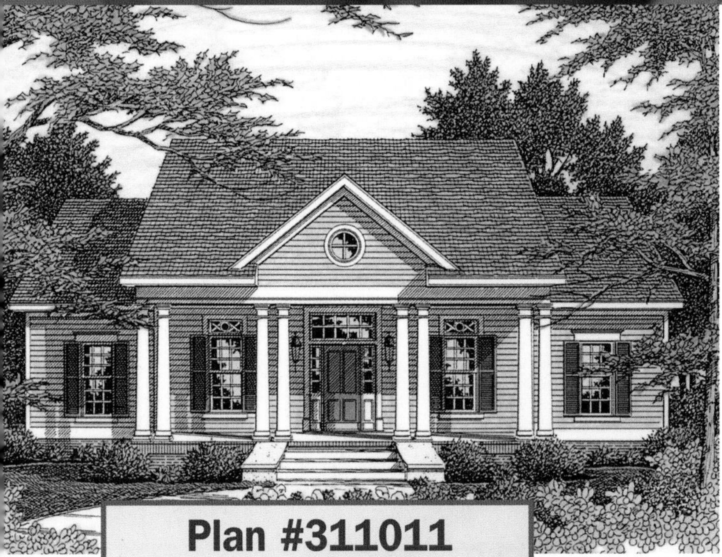

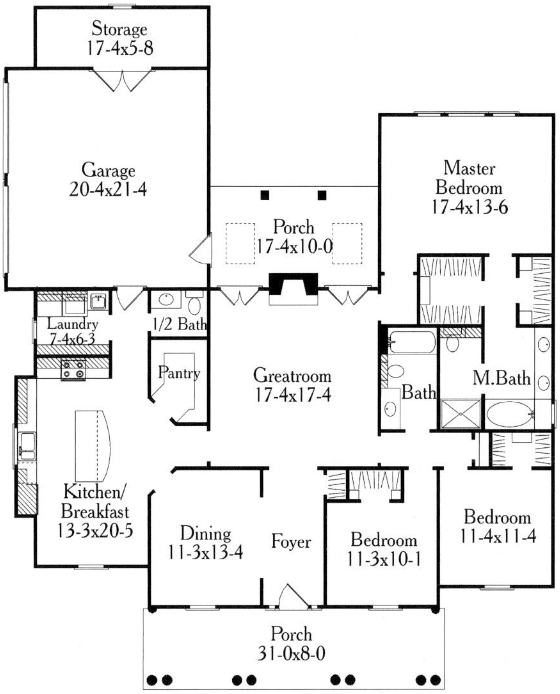

Plan #311011

Dimensions: 56'4" W x 67'4" D
Levels: 1
Heated Square Footage: 1,955
Bedrooms: 3
Bathrooms: 2½
Foundation: Crawl space, slab, or basement
Materials List Available: Yes
Price Category: D

Images provided by designer/architect.

1/2
Bath
Greatroom
Kitchen

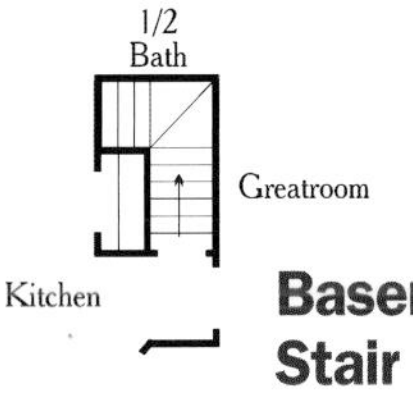

Basement Stair Location

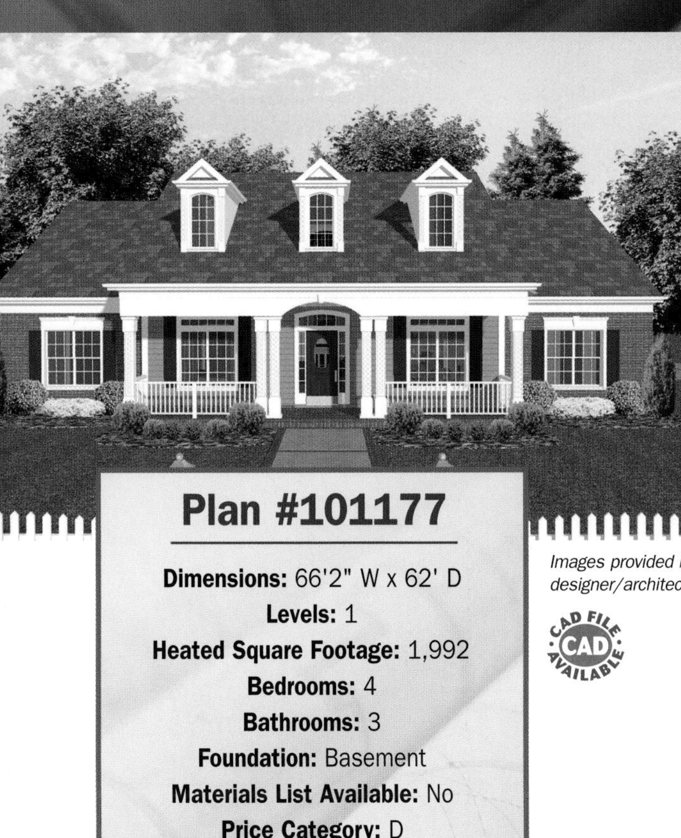

Plan #101177

Dimensions: 66'2" W x 62' D
Levels: 1
Heated Square Footage: 1,992
Bedrooms: 4
Bathrooms: 3
Foundation: Basement
Materials List Available: No
Price Category: D

Images provided by designer/architect.

CAD FILE CAD AVAILABLE

Copyright by designer/architect.

BONUS ROOM
10'-7" x 22'-6"
GARAGE
22'-0" x 22'-6"
DECK
21'-1" x 13'-8"
OUTDOOR FIREPLACE
SCREENED PORCH
24'-10" x 12'-0"
MECH.
BREAKFAST
8'-6" x 11'-0"
MASTER BEDROOM
19'-0" x 15'-0"
HIS
HERS
SITTING
FAMILY ROOM
16'-0" x 21'-11"
KITCHEN
17'-3" x 12'-6"
BEDROOM 2
11'-0" x 14'-0"
LIVING / BEDROOM 3
11'-0" x 12'-0"
DINING
13'-8" x 12'-0"
MEDIA / OFFICE
13'-8" x 11'-0"
PORCH
33'-4" x 6'-0"
66'-2"
62'-0"

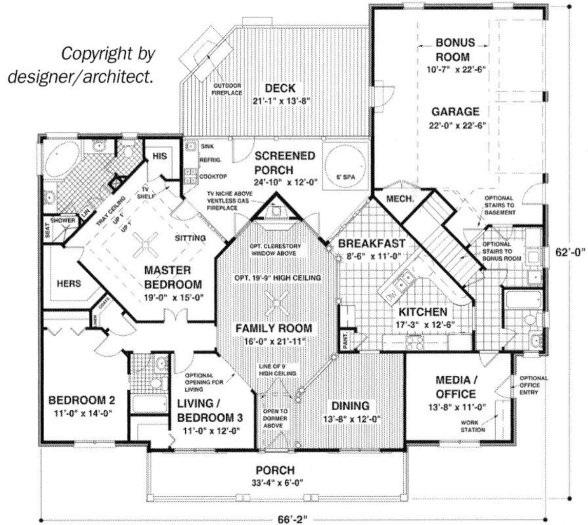

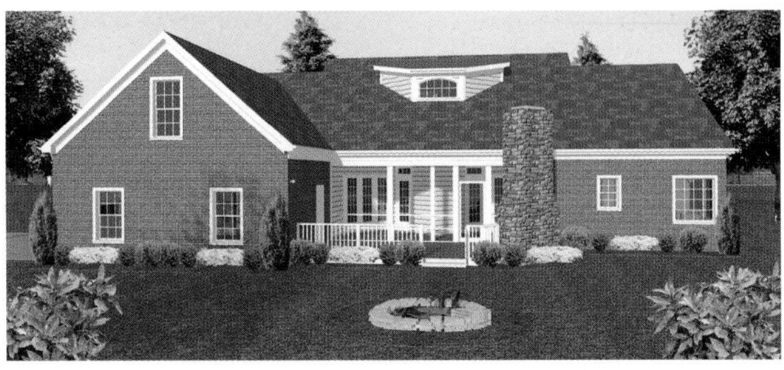

Rear View

Plan #151117

Dimensions: 66' W x 55' D
Levels: 1
Heated Square Footage: 1,957
Bedrooms: 3
Bathrooms: 3
Foundation: Crawl space, slab, or basement
CompleteCost List Available: Yes
Price Category: D

CAD FILE AVAILABLE

Images provided by designer/architect.

Copyright by designer/architect.

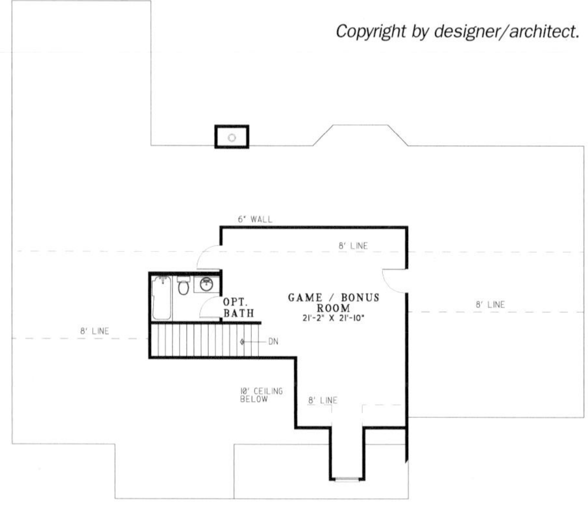

Bonus Area Floor Plan

You'll love this home if you have a family-centered lifestyle and enjoy an active social life.

Features:

- Foyer: A 10-ft. ceiling sets the tone for this home.
- Great Room: A 10-ft. boxed ceiling and fireplace are the highlights of this room, which also has a door leading to the rear covered porch.
- Dining Room: Columns mark the entry from the foyer to this lovely formal dining room.
- Study: Add the French doors from the foyer to transform bedroom 3, with its vaulted ceiling, into a quiet study.
- Kitchen: This large kitchen includes a pantry and shares an eating bar with the adjoining, bayed breakfast room.
- Master Suite: You'll love the access to the rear porch, as well as the bath with every amenity, in this suite.

Images provided by designer/architect.

Plan #101028

Dimensions: 57'8" W x 57'6" D
Levels: 1
Heated Square Footage: 1,963
Bedrooms: 3
Bathrooms: 2
Foundation: Basement
Materials List Available: No
Price Category: D

This elegant brick-and-stone home is a real eye-catcher.

Features:

- Dining Room: Just off the foyer, this formal area is open to the family room.
- Family Room: This large gathering area has a cozy fireplace and flows into the screened in porch.
- Kitchen: This U-shaped "heart of the home" is open to the breakfast area.
- Master Suite: This private retreat has everything; his and her closets, a tray ceiling, a sitting area, and a large bathroom with double vanities.
- Bedrooms: Located on the opposite side of the home from the master suite, the two secondary bedrooms have walk-in closets and share a bathroom.

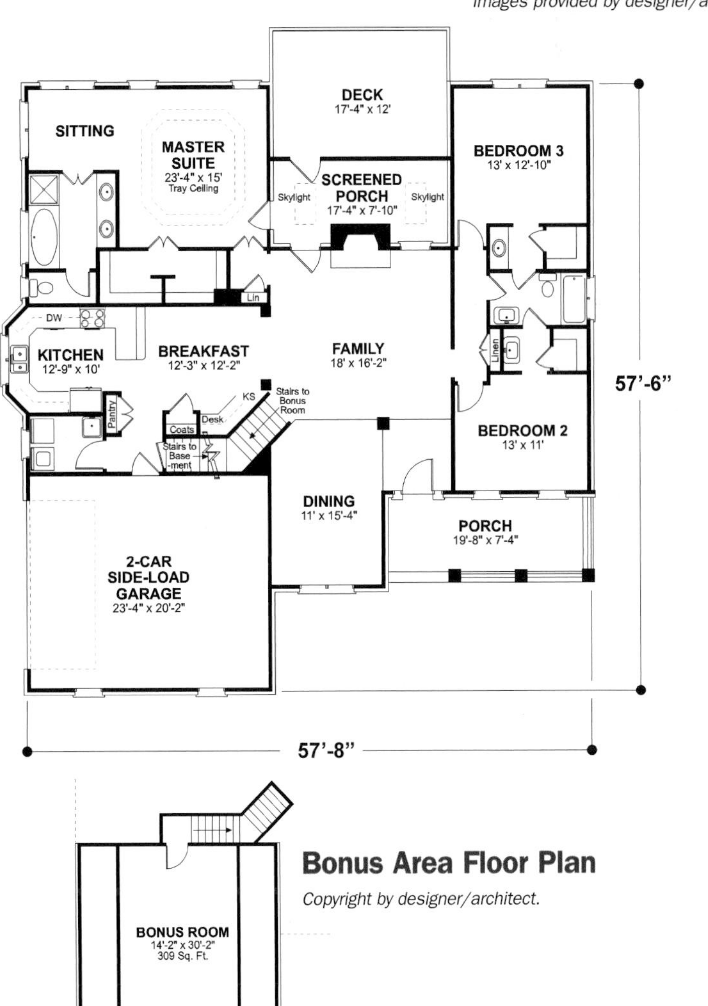

Bonus Area Floor Plan

Copyright by designer/architect.

Plan #151170

Dimensions: 57' W x 64'4" D
Levels: 1
Heated Square Footage: 1,965
Bedrooms: 4
Bathrooms: 2
Foundation: Crawl space, slab; basement or daylight basement for fee
CompleteCost List Available: Yes
Price Category: E

CAD FILE AVAILABLE

Images provided by designer/architect.

The clean lines of the open floor plan and high ceilings match the classic good looks of this home's exterior.

Features:

- Foyer: The 10-ft. ceiling here sets the stage for the open, airy feeling of this lovely home.
- Dining Room: Set off by columns from the foyer and great room, this area is ideal for entertaining.
- Great Room: Open to the breakfast room beyond, this great room features a masonry fireplace and a door to the rear grilling porch.
- Breakfast Room: A deep bay overlooking the porch is the focal point here.
- Kitchen: Planned for efficiency, the kitchen has an angled island with storage and snack bar.
- Master Suite: A boxed ceiling adds elegance to the bedroom, and the bath features a whirlpool tub, double vanity, and separate shower.

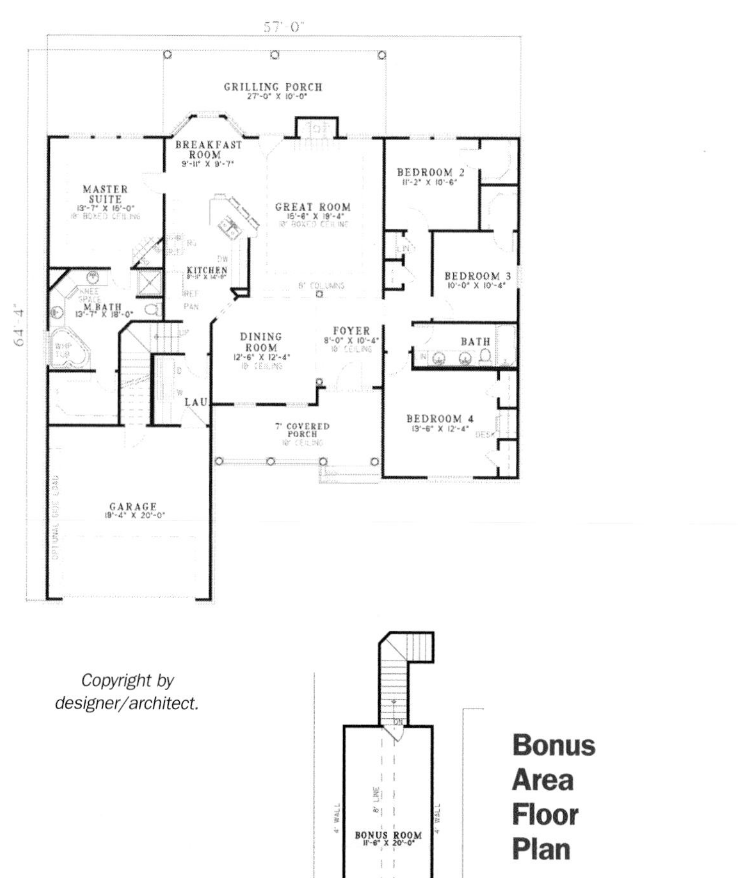

Copyright by designer/architect.

Bonus Area Floor Plan

Images provided by designer/architect.

Plan #311017

Dimensions: 72' W x 55'2" D
Levels: 1
Heated Square Footage: 1,974
Bedrooms: 3
Bathrooms: 2½
Foundation: Crawl space, slab or basement
Materials List Available: Yes
Price Category: D

This charming home features an efficient design that allows for large rooms contained in a modest footprint.

Features:

- Great Room: There's plenty of room for all kinds of family activities in this large room that features a soaring cathedral ceiling. The fireplace adds character and warmth to this gathering area.
- Kitchen: The family chef will have plenty of space to work in this large kitchen. An abundance of cabinets and counter space makes this room a dream come true.
- Master Suite: Separated from the secondary bedrooms for privacy, this oasis will help you relax after a busy day. The master bath and large walk-in closet are just the right size.
- Secondary Bedrooms: Two large bedrooms are close to the main full bathroom. One bedroom has direct access to the rear patio.

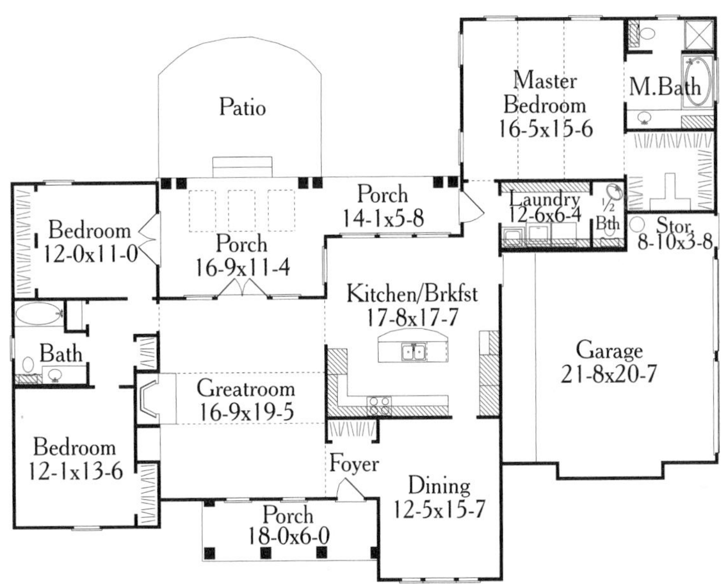

Copyright by designer/architect.

Plan #101006

Dimensions: 63' W x 58' D
Levels: 1
Heated Square Footage: 1,982
Bedrooms: 3
Bathrooms: 2½
Foundation: Crawl space, slab, basement, or walkout
Materials List Available: Yes
Price Category: D

CAD FILE AVAILABLE

Images provided by designer/architect.

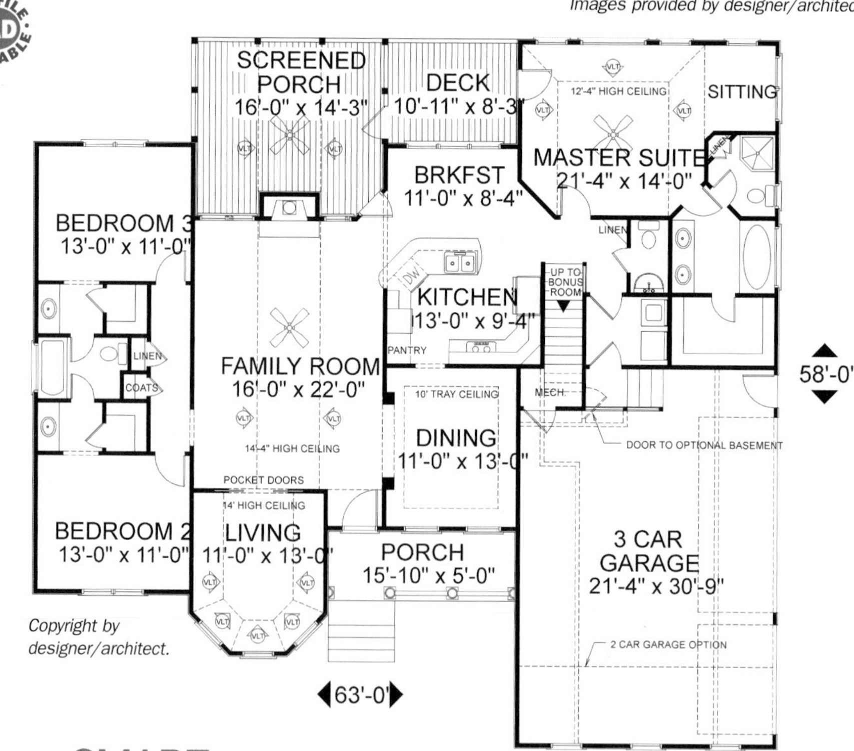

Copyright by designer/architect.

Radius-top windows and siding accented with wood shingles give this home a distinctive look.

Features:

- Ceiling Height: 9 ft. unless otherwise noted.
- Family Room: This room is perfect for all kinds of informal family activities. A vaulted ceiling adds to its sense of spaciousness.
- Dining Room: This room, with its tray ceiling, is designed for elegant dining.
- Porch: When the weather gets warm, you'll enjoy stepping out onto this large screened porch to catch a breeze.
- Master Suite: You'll love ending your day and getting up in the morning in this exquisite master suite, with its vaulted ceiling, sitting area, and large walk-in closet.
- Bonus Room: Just off the kitchen are stairs leading to this enormous bonus room, offering more than 330 sq. ft. of future expansion space.

SMARTtip

Art in Pools

The tiled walls and floor of a pool make great canvases for art, so incorporate a serious or whimsical design. Also, make the stairs wide and shallow to form a wading area for kids.

Plan #181159

Dimensions: 37' W x 31' D
Levels: 1
Heated Square Footage: 1,992
Main Level Sq. Ft.: 996
Lower Level Sq. Ft.: 996
Bedrooms: 3
Bathrooms: 2
Foundation: Walkout basement
Materials List Available: Yes
Price Category: D

CAD FILE AVAILABLE

Images provided by designer/architect.

Ideal for the family who loves the outdoors, this charmer features a wraparound porch that creates a covered pavilion and roofed terrace.

Features:

- Ceiling Height: 9-ft. ceilings enhance the airy feeling given by the many windows here.
- Family Rooms: These family rooms (one on each floor) allow a busy family adequate space for entertaining a crowd.
- Kitchen: Designed for efficient work patterns, this kitchen features ample work and storage space, as well as an island that can double as a
- Bedrooms: Each bedroom features a large, walk-in closet and easy access to a large, amenity-filled bathroom with a double vanity, tub, enclosed shower, and private toilet.
- Porch: Enjoy the panoramic view from this spacious covered porch at any time of day.

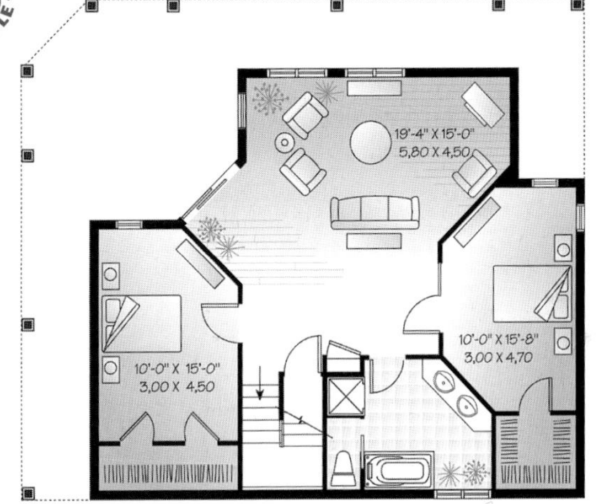

Lower Level Floor Plan

Copyright by designer/architect.

Main Level Floor Plan

Plan #101005

Dimensions: 63' W x 57'2" D
Levels: 1
Heated Square Footage: 1,992
Bedrooms: 3
Bathrooms: 2½
Foundation: Crawl space, slab, or basement
Materials List Available: Yes
Price Category: D

CAD FILE AVAILABLE

Images provided by designer/architect.

Rear View

This midsized ranch is accented with Palladian windows and inviting front porch.

Features:

- Ceiling Height: 9 ft. unless otherwise noted.
- Special Ceilings: Tray or vaulted ceilings adorn the living room, family room, dining room, and master suite.
- Kitchen: This bright and airy kitchen is designed to be a pleasure in which to work. It shares a big bay window with the contiguous breakfast room.
- Breakfast Room: The light streaming in from the bay window makes this the perfect place to linger with coffee and the Sunday paper.
- Master Suite: This lovely suite is exceptional, with its sitting area and direct access to the deck, as well as a full-featured bath and spacious walk-in closet.
- Secondary Bedrooms: The other bedrooms each measure about 13 ft. x 11 ft. They have walk-in closets and share a "Jack-and-Jill" bath.

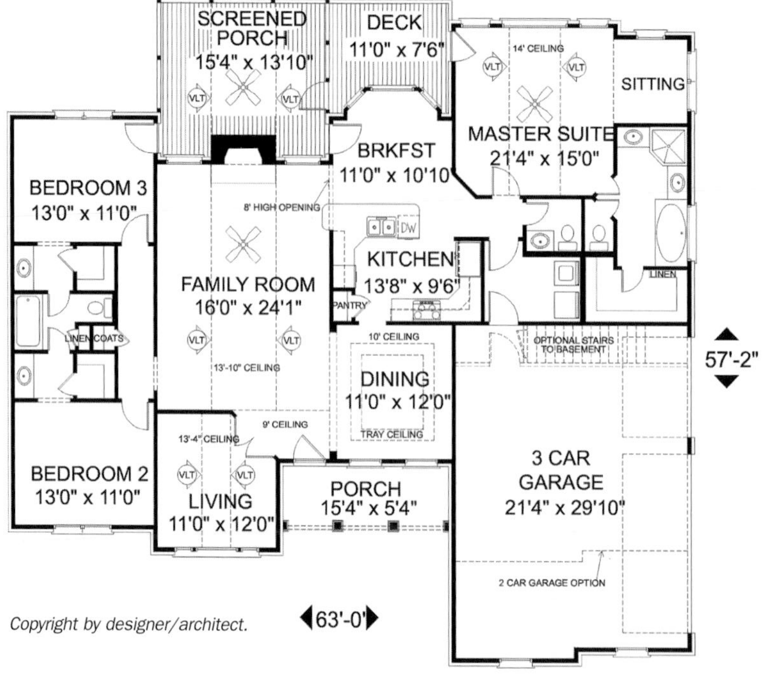

Copyright by designer/architect.

Kitchen

Living Room

Dining Room

Family Room

Master Bedroom

Master Bath

Plan #131044

Dimensions: 57'6" W x 42'4" D
Levels: 1
Heated Square Footage: 1,994
Bedrooms: 4
Bathrooms: 2
Foundation: Crawl space, slab, or basement
Materials List Available: Yes
Price Category: E

Images provided by designer/architect.

Under a covered porch, Victorian-detailed bay windows grace each side of the brick-faced facade at the center of this ranch-style home, giving it a formal air.

Features:

- Ceiling Height: 10-ft. ceilings grace the central living area and the master bedroom of this home.
- Foyer: Round-top windows make this area and the flanking rooms bright and cheery.
- Great Room: A fireplace and built-ins that are visible from anywhere in this large room make it a natural gathering place for friends and family.
- Optional Office: Use the room just off the central hall as a home office, fourth bedroom, or study.
- Master Suite: You'll love the bay window, tray ceiling, two walk-in closets, and private bath.
- Bonus Space: Finish this large area in the attic for extra living space, or use it for storage.

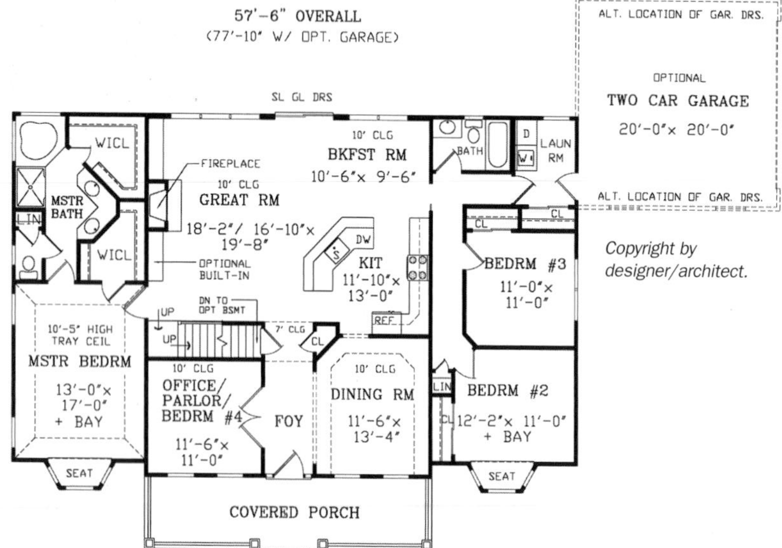

Copyright by designer/architect.

Rear Elevation

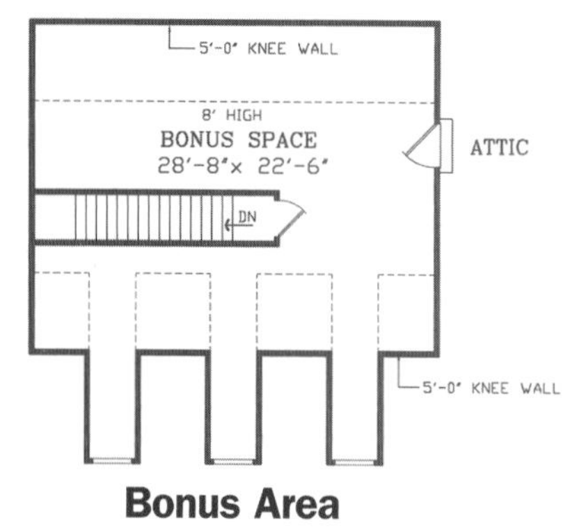

Bonus Area

Plan #121050

Dimensions: 64' W x 50' D
Levels: 1
Heated Square Footage: 1,996
Bedrooms: 2
Bathrooms: 2
Foundation: Basement; crawl space for fee
Materials List Available: Yes
Price Category: D

Images provided by designer/architect.

This compact design includes features usually reserved for larger homes and has styling that is typical of more-exclusive home designs.

Features:

- Entry: As you enter this home, you'll see the formal living and dining rooms—both with special ceiling detailing—on either side.
- Great Room: Located in the rear of the home for convenience, this great room is likely to be your favorite spot. The fireplace is framed by transom-topped windows, so you'll love curling up here, no matter what the weather or time of day.
- Kitchen: Ample counter and cabinet space make this kitchen a dream in which to work.
- Master Suite: A tray ceiling and lovely corner windows create an elegant feeling in the bedroom, and two walk-in closets make it easy to keep this space tidy and organized. The private bath has a skylight, corner whirlpool tub, and two separate vanities.

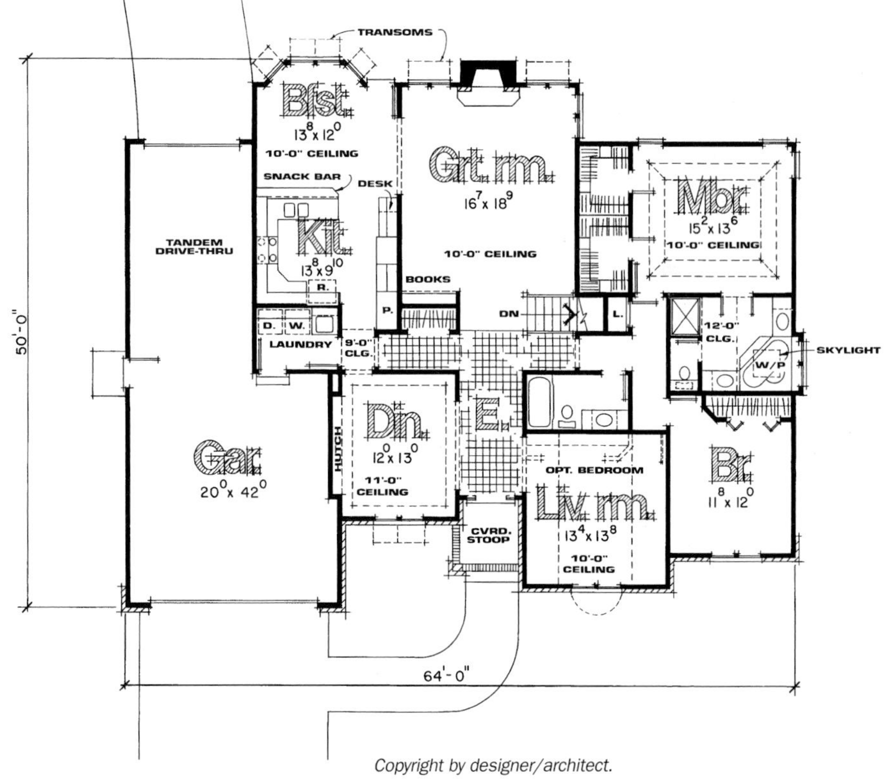

Copyright by designer/architect.

Plan #371042

Dimensions: 71'6" W x 49' D
Levels: 1
Heated Square Footage: 1,999
Bedrooms: 3
Bathrooms: 2
Foundation: Crawl space, slab or basement
Materials List Available: No
Price Category: D

CAD FILE AVAILABLE

Images provided by designer/architect.

Ornate windows accent the exterior of this elegant French-style home—a dream come true.

Features:

- Entry: The raised porch will lead you into this beautiful tiled entry, with a barrel ceiling and columns separating it from a formal dining room.
- Living Room: This massive room has a double stepped-up ceiling and access to the rear porch. There is a built-in media center and charming fireplace.
- Kitchen: This gourmet kitchen with breakfast nook has a serving bar, which opens into the living room.
- Master Suite: This suite also has a stepped-up ceiling and a luxurious master bath with his and her vanities and walk-in closets.
- Bedrooms: Two additional large bedrooms share a convenient hall bathroom.

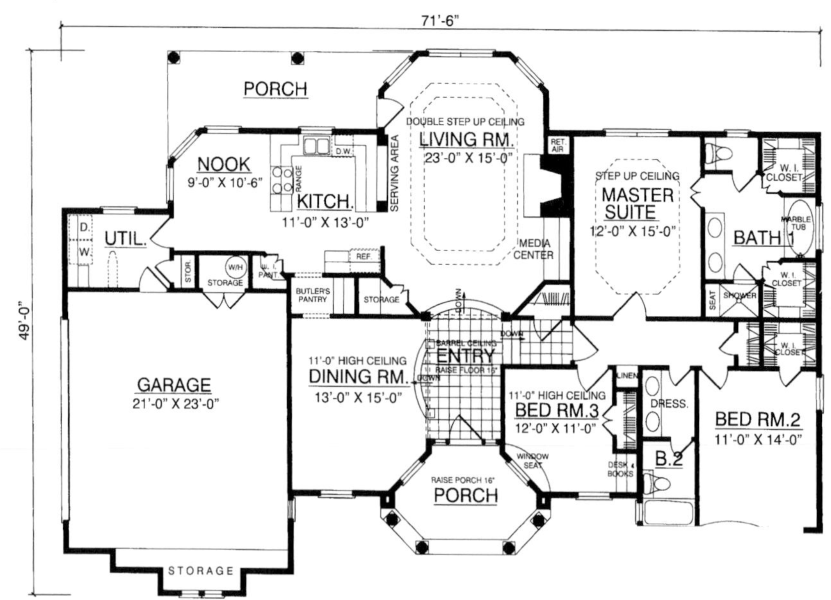

Copyright by designer/architect.

Plan #211005

Dimensions: 68' W x 64' D
Levels: 1
Heated Square Footage: 2,000
Bedrooms: 3
Bathrooms: 2
Foundation: Slab
Materials List Available: Yes
Price Category: D

Images provided by designer/architect.

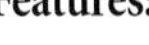

A brick veneer exterior complements the columned porch to make this a striking home.

CAD FILE AVAILABLE

Features:

- Ceiling Height: 9 ft. unless otherwise noted.
- Living Room: From the front porch, the foyer unfolds into this expansive living room. Family and friends will be drawn to the warmth of the living room's cozy fireplace.
- Formal Dining Room: This elegant room is designed for dinner parties of any size.
- Kitchen: Located between the formal dining room and the dinette, the kitchen can serve formal meals as easily as quick family repasts.
- Master Suite: There's plenty of room to unwind at the end of a long day in the huge master bedroom. Luxuriate in the private bath, with its spa tub, separate shower, dual sinks, and two walk-in closets.
- Home Office: The home office, accessible from the master bedroom, is the perfect quiet spot to work, study, or pay the bills.

SMARTtip

Do-It-Yourself Ponds

To avoid disturbing utility lines, contact your utility companies before doing any digging. Locate a freestanding container pond on your deck near an existing (GFCI) outlet. For an in-ground pond, have an electrician run a buried line and install a GFCI outlet near the pond so you can plug in a pump or fountain.

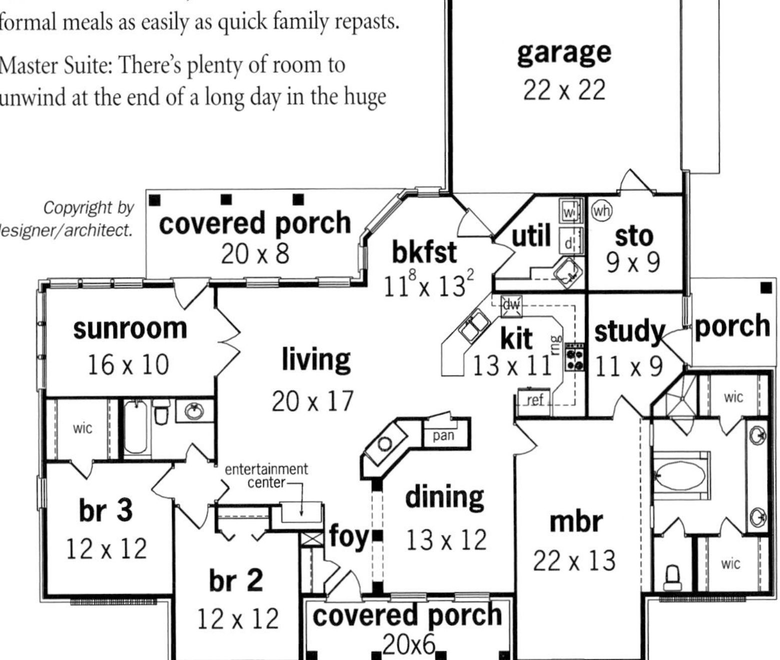

Plan #101022

Dimensions: 66'2" W x 62' D

Levels: 1

Heated Square Footage: 1,992

Bedrooms: 3

Bathrooms: 3

Foundation: Crawl space, slab, or basement

Materials List Available: Yes

Price Category: D

Images provided by designer/architect.

The exterior of this lovely home is traditional, but the unusually shaped rooms and amenities are contemporary.

Features:

- Foyer: This two-story foyer is open to the family room, but columns divide it from the dining room.
- Family Room: A gas fireplace and TV niche, flanked by doors to the covered porch, sit at the rear of this seven-sided, spacious room.
- Breakfast Room: Set off from the family room by columns, this area shares a snack bar with the kitchen and has windows looking over the porch.
- Bedroom 3: Use this room as a living room if you wish, and transform the guest room to a media room or a family bedroom.
- Master Suite: The bedroom features a tray ceiling, has his and her dressing areas, and opens to the porch. The bath has a large corner tub, separate shower, linen closet, and two vanities.

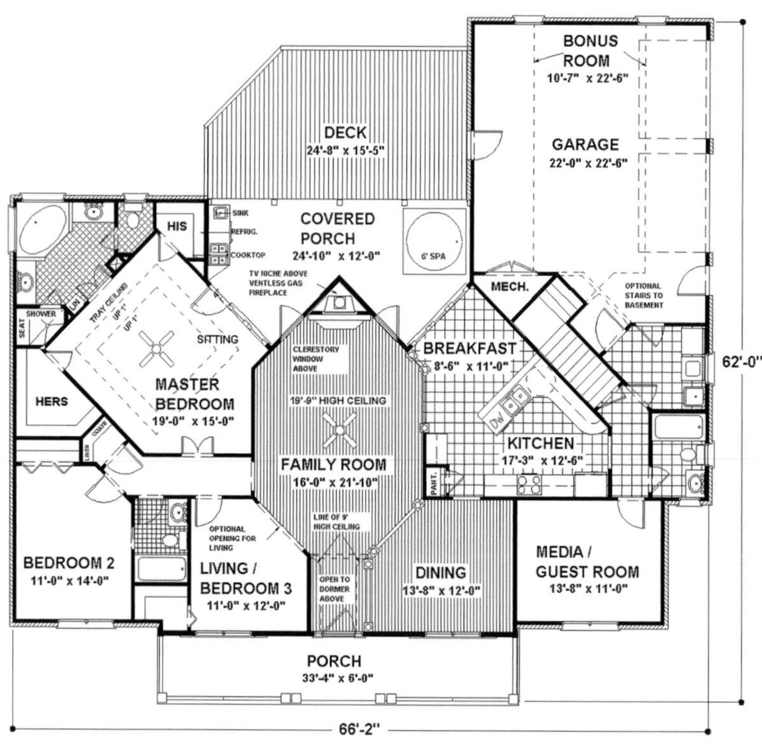

Copyright by designer/architect.

Kitchen

Great Room

Dining Room

Hearth Room

Master Bedroom

Study

Plan #351047

Dimensions: 64' W x 54'4" D
Levels: 1
Heated Square Footage: 2,001
Bedrooms: 3
Bathrooms: 2
Foundation: Crawl space, slab, or basement
Materials List Available: Yes
Price Category: F

Images provided by designer/architect.

This home incorporates a unique design that maximizes every inch of its usable space to give you more for less.

Features:

- Great Room: This large room features a vaulted ceiling and a gas fireplace that has built-in cabinets on each side.
- Kitchen: This kitchen has a raised bar and is open to the sunroom and dining room.
- Dining Room: This gracious room has a view of the backyard and a raised ceiling.
- Master Suite: This area boasts a raised ceiling and a walk-in closet. There is also a private master bath with walk-in closet.
- Bedrooms: These two additional bedrooms share a bathroom located in the hall.

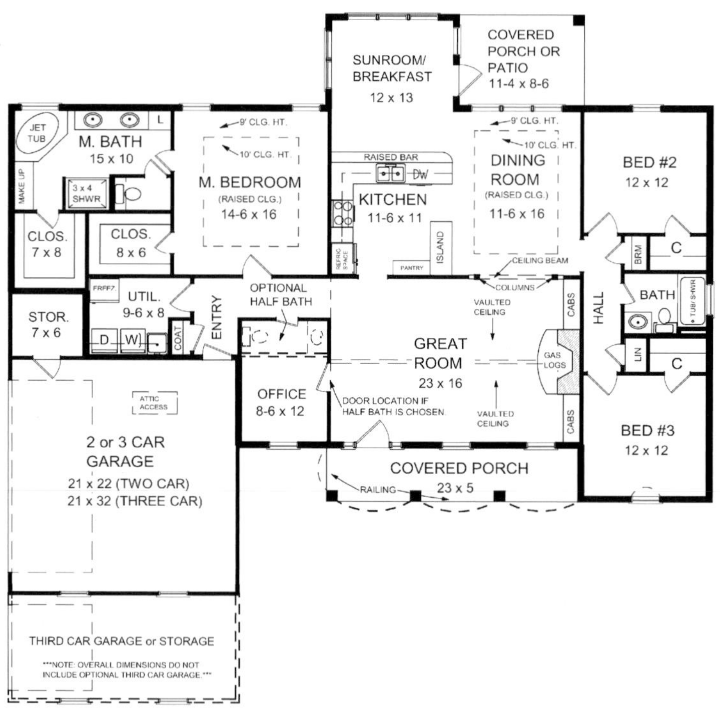

Copyright by designer/architect.

Plan #151138

Dimensions: 53' W x 49'4" D
Levels: 1
Heated Square Footage: 2,010
Bedrooms: 3
Bathrooms: 2
Foundation: Basement or walkout
CompleteCost List Available: Yes
Price Category: C

Images provided by designer/architect.

This versatile offering fits anywhere. Its design is as comfortable in the city as it is in the country.

Features:

- Porches: Two porches-a covered porch at the front of the home and a grilling porch at the back-are wonderful for entertaining or relaxing.
- Great Room: This beautiful great room is a wonderful, versatile space, with its vaulted ceiling and fireplace.
- Kitchen: In this kitchen, there is space for cooks and diners alike, thanks to the spacious countertop and raised eating bar. For a more formal setting, there is an adjoining dining room.
- Master Suite: Spacious areas define this wonderful master suite, with its large bedroom area and sizable walk-in closet.

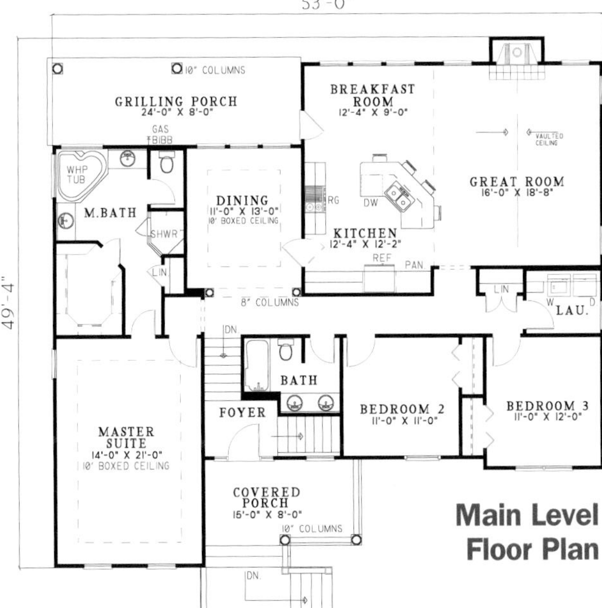

Main Level Floor Plan

Copyright by designer/architect.

Lower Level Floor Plan

Plan #211049

Dimensions: 73' W x 66' D
Levels: 1
Heated Square Footage: 2,023
Bedrooms: 3
Bathrooms: 2
Foundation: Slab
Materials List Available: Yes
Price Category: D

Images provided by designer/architect.

CAD FILE AVAILABLE

This European-style home features an open floor plan that maximizes use and flexibility of space.

Features:

- Ceiling Height: 8 ft. unless otherwise noted.
- Living/Dining Area: This combined living-and-dining area features high ceilings, which make the large area seem even more spacious. Corner windows will fill the room with light. The wet bar and cozy fireplace make this the perfect place for entertaining.
- Backyard Porch: This huge covered backyard porch is accessible from the living/dining area, so the entire party can step outdoors on a warm summer night.
- Kitchen: More than just efficient, this modern kitchen is actually an exciting place to cook. It features a dramatic high ceiling and plenty of work space.
- Utility Area: Located off the kitchen, this area has extra freezer space, a walk-in pantry, and access to the garage.
- Eating Nook: Informal family meals will be a true delight in this nook that adjoins the kitchen and faces a lovely private courtyard.

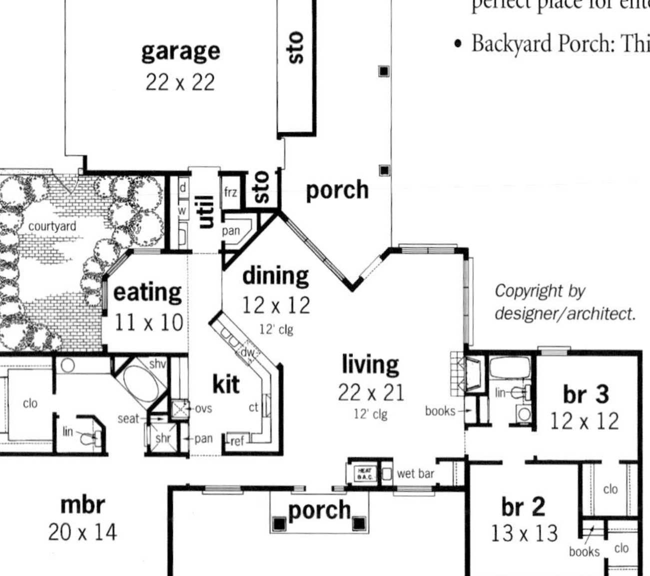

Copyright by designer/architect.

SMARTtip

Outdoor Lighting Safety

Lighting is necessary for walkways, paths, stairways, and transition areas (from the deck to the yard, hot tub, or pool) to prevent accidents. Choose from low-voltage rail, path, and post lighting for these areas. The corners of planters or built-in seating should also be delineated with lighting. Consider installing floodlights near doorways or large open spaces for security reasons.

Plan #351008

Dimensions: 64'6" W x 61'4" D
Levels: 1
Heated Square Footage: 2,002
Bedrooms: 3
Bathrooms: 2
Foundation: Crawl space or basement
Materials List Available: Yes
Price Category: F

Images provided by designer/architect.

This home has the charming appeal of a quaint cottage that you might find in an old village in the English countryside. It's a unique design that maximizes every inch of its usable space.

Features:

- Great Room: This room has a vaulted ceiling and built-in units on each side of the fireplace.
- Kitchen: This kitchen boasts a raised bar open to the breakfast area; the room is also open to the dining room.
- Master Suite: This bedroom retreat features a raised ceiling and a walk-in closet. The bathroom has a double vanity, large walk-in closet, and soaking tub.
- Bedrooms: Two bedrooms share a common bathroom and have large closets.

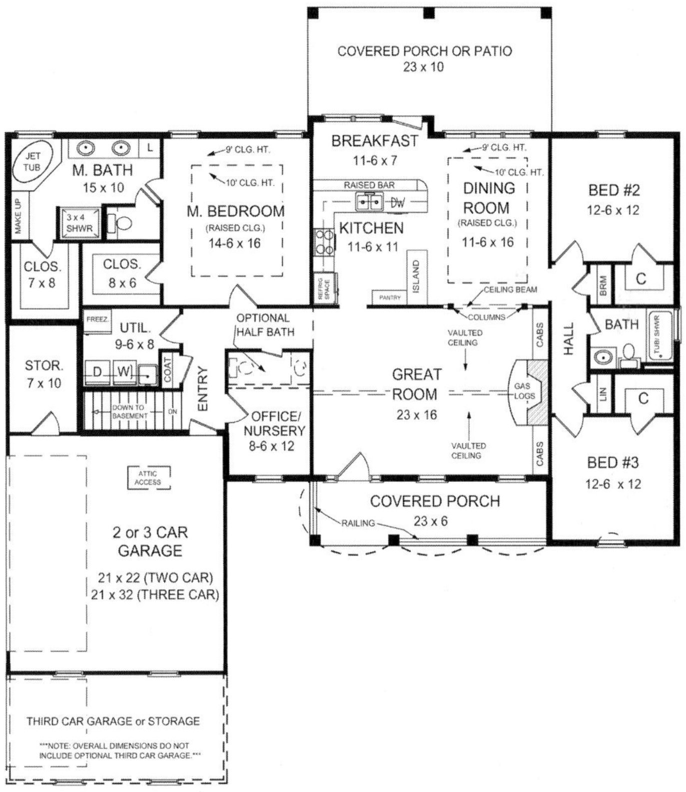

Copyright by designer/architect.

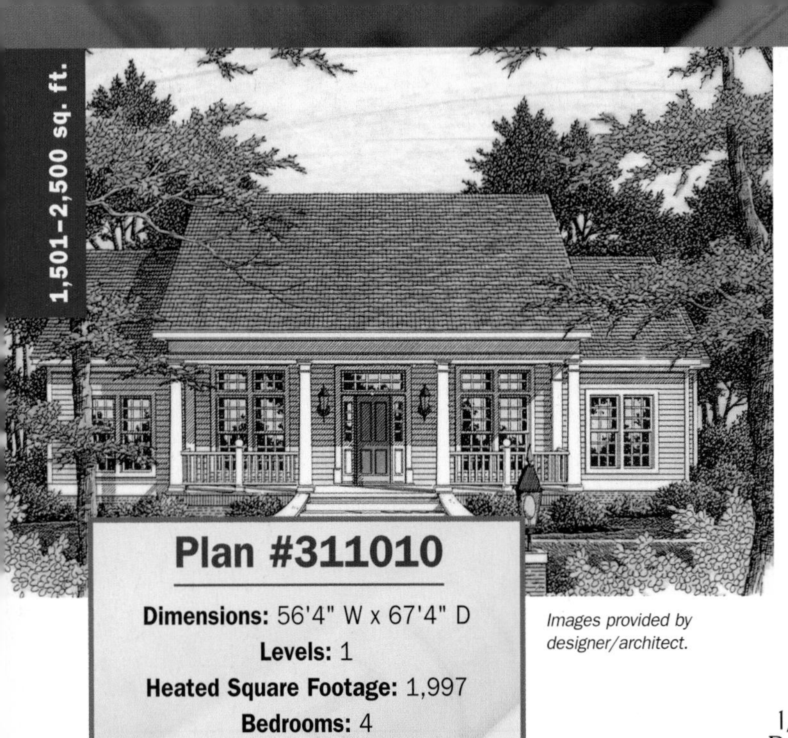

Plan #311010

Dimensions: 56'4" W x 67'4" D
Levels: 1
Heated Square Footage: 1,997
Bedrooms: 4
Bathrooms: 2½
Foundation: Basement, crawl space, or slab
Materials List Available: Yes
Price Category: D

Images provided by designer/architect.

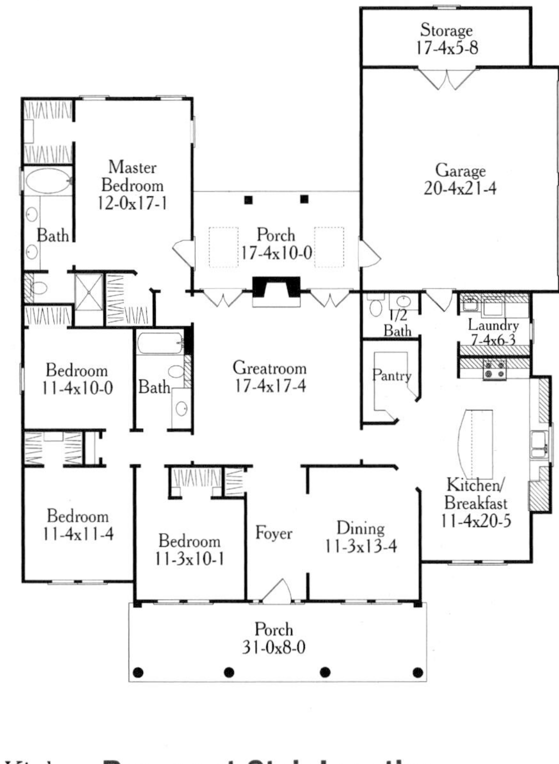

1/2 Bath
Greatroom
Kitchen

Basement Stair Location

Plan #101169

Dimensions: 63' W x 62'8" D
Levels: 1
Heated Square Footage: 2,000
Bedrooms: 3
Bathrooms: 2½
Foundation: Basement
Materials List Available: No
Price Category: D

Images provided by designer/architect.

SCREENED PORCH 16'-0" x 13'-8"
DECK 10'-8" x 10'-2"
MASTER SUITE 21'-4" x 15'-6"
SITTING
BEDROOM SUITE #2 13'-0" x 11'-0"
CASUAL DINING 11'-0" x 12'-5"
FAMILY ROOM 16'-0" x 21'-0"
KITCHEN 11'-0" x 13'-3"
LAUNDRY 8'-0" x 7'-2"
MASTER BATH 9'-4" x 12'-6"
COFFEE CORNER 11'-0" x 8'-0"
BEDROOM SUITE #3 13'-0" x 11'-0"
OFFICE / LIVING / BEDROOM 4 11'-6" x 10'-8"
PORCH 15'-4" x 5'-4"
3 CAR GARAGE 21'-4" x 33'-4"
62'-8"
63'-0"

Copyright by designer/architect.

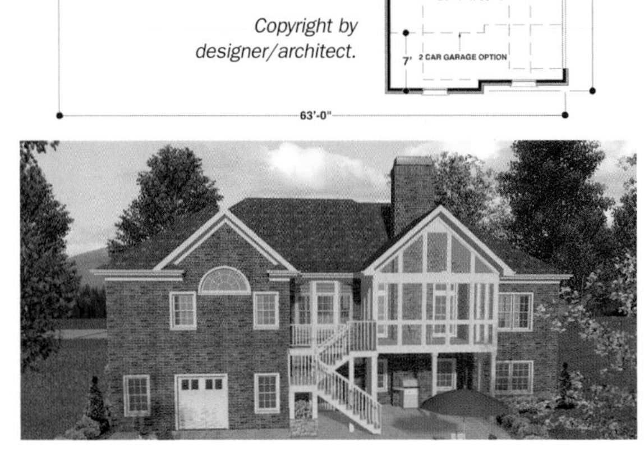

Rear View

Plan #351102

Dimensions: 67' W x 56' D
Levels: 1
Heated Square Footage: 2,000
Bedrooms: 3
Bathrooms: 2½
Foundation: Crawl space, slab or basement
Materials List Available: Yes
Price Category: F

Images provided by designer/architect.

CAD FILE CAD AVAILABLE

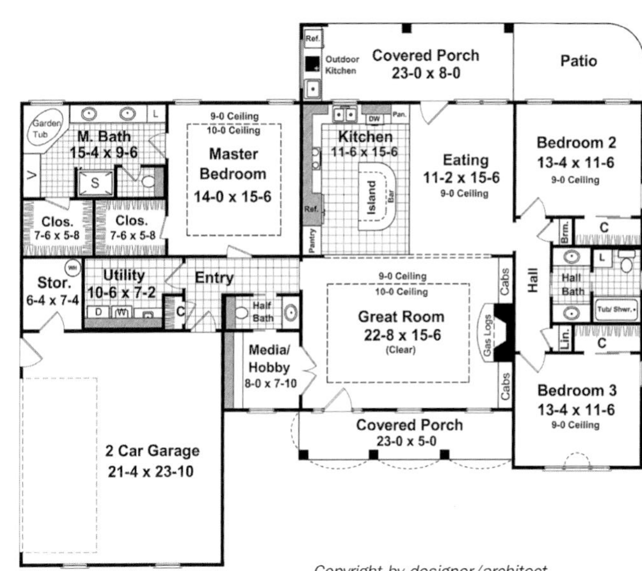

Copyright by designer/architect.

Plan #441008

Dimensions: 60' W x 50' D
Levels: 1
Heated Square Footage: 2,001
Bedrooms: 3
Bathrooms: 2
Foundation: Crawl space; slab or basement available for fee
Materials List Available: No
Price Category: D

Images provided by designer/architect.

SPA
VAULTED MASTER 16/6 X 13/0
DINING 12/8 X 14/0
VAULTED GREAT RM. 17/6 X 20/0
GARAGE/ SHOP 11/6 X 15/6
GARAGE 19/0 X 22/0
FOYER
DEN 10/0 X 13/2
BR. 3 11/8 X 12/2
BR. 2 10/0 X 13/2
50'
60'

Copyright by designer/architect.

Rear Elevation

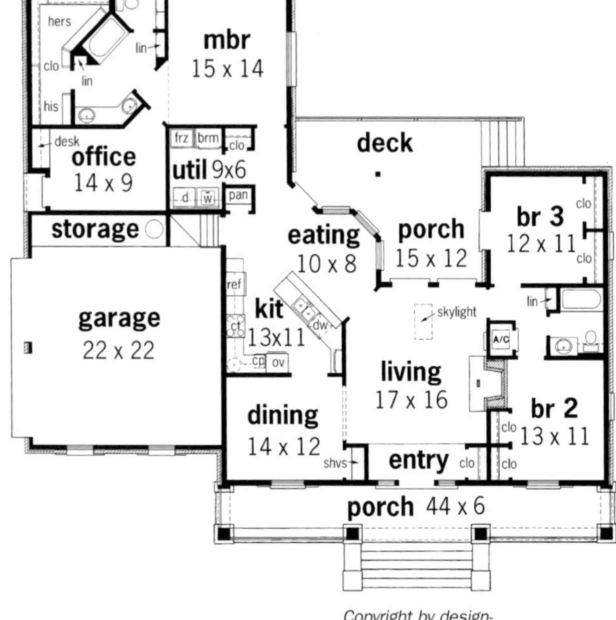

Images provided by designer/architect.

Copyright by designer/architect.

Plan #211048

Dimensions: 66' W x 60' D
Levels: 1
Heated Square Footage: 2,002
Bedrooms: 3
Bathrooms: 2
Foundation: Crawl space; slab for fee
Materials List Available: Yes
Price Category: D

Copyright by designer/architect.

Plan #221018

Dimensions: 67' W x 53' D
Levels: 1
Heated Square Footage: 2,007
Bedrooms: 3
Bathrooms: 2
Foundation: Basement
Materials List Available: No
Price Category: D

Images provided by designer/architect.

CAD FILE AVAILABLE

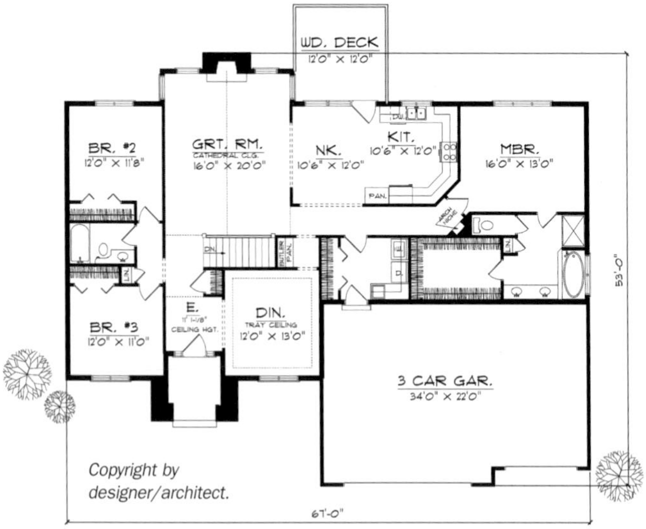

Rear Elevation

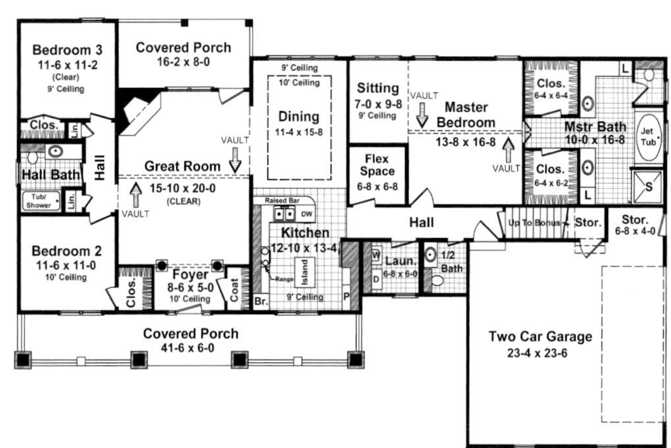

Plan #351069

Dimensions: 78' W x 49'6" D
Levels: 1
Heated Square Footage: 2,008
Bedrooms: 3
Bathrooms: 2½
Foundation: Crawl space or slab
Materials List Available: Yes
Price Category: F

Images provided by designer/architect.

CAD FILE AVAILABLE

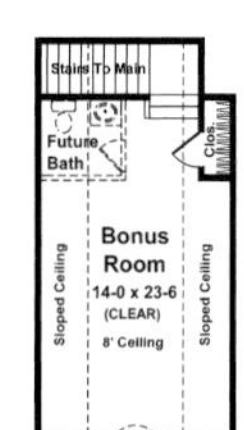

Bonus Level Floor Plan

Copyright by designer/architect.

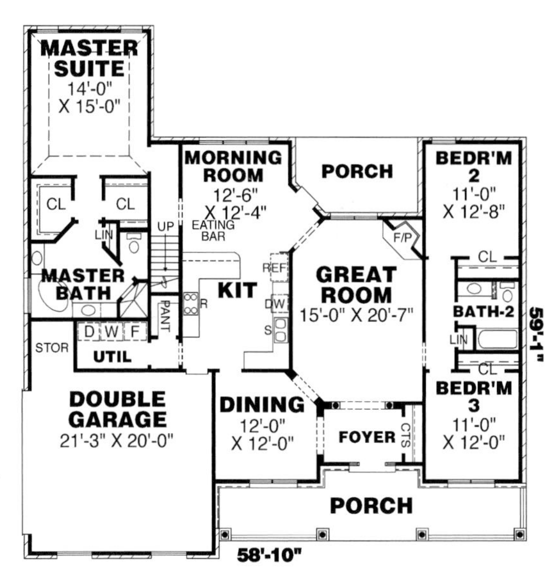

Plan #241007

Dimensions: 58'10" W x 59'1" D
Levels: 1
Heated Square Footage: 2,036
Bedrooms: 3
Bathrooms: 2
Foundation: Crawl space, slab
Materials List Available: No
Price Category: D

Images provided by designer/architect.

Bonus Area Floor Plan

Copyright by designer/architect.

Plan #321030

Dimensions: 61' W x 51' D
Levels: 1
Heated Square Footage: 2,029
Bedrooms: 4
Bathrooms: 2
Foundation: Crawl space, slab, basement, or walkout
Materials List Available: Yes
Price Category: D

CAD FILE AVAILABLE

Images provided by designer/architect.

Two covered porches and a rear patio make this lovely home fit right into a site with a view.

Features:

- Great Room: Boxed entryway columns, a vaulted ceiling, corner fireplace, widowed wall, and door to the patio are highlights in this spacious room.
- Study: Tucked into the back of the house for privacy, the study also opens to the rear patio.
- Dining Area: The windowed alcove lets natural light flow into this room, which adjoins the kitchen.
- Kitchen: A central island, deep pantry, and ample counter area make this room a cook's delight.
- Master Suite: You'll love the two walk-in closets, decorative bedroom window, and double doors opening to the private porch. The bath includes a garden tub, a separate shower, and two vanities.
- Additional Bedrooms: Both bedrooms have a walk-in closet.

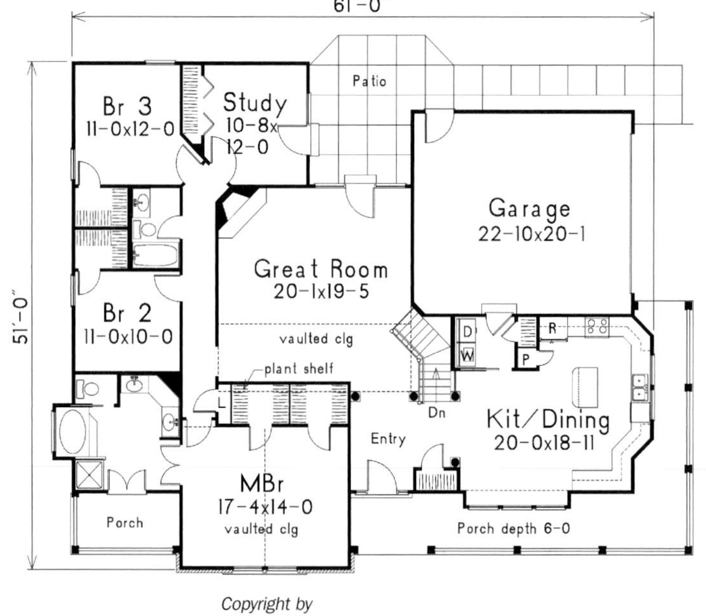

Copyright by designer/architect.

Plan #151105

Dimensions: 60'6" W x 91'4" D
Levels: 1
Heated Square Footage: 2,039
Bedrooms: 4
Bathrooms: 2
Foundation: Crawl space, slab, or optional basement
CompleteCost List Available: Yes
Price Category: D

Images provided by designer/architect.

If you've always wanted a wraparound porch with columns, this could be your dream home.

Features:

- Great Room: Just off the foyer, this spacious room features a handsome fireplace where friends and family are sure to gather.
- Dining Room: Columns set off this dining room, and the large window area allows natural lighting during the day.
- Kitchen: Open to the dining room, this well-planned kitchen features a large central island with a sink and a dishwasher on one side and an eating bar on the other.
- Breakfast Room: You'll love the unusual shape of this room and its windows overlooking the rear porch. Access to the porch is from a hallway here.
- Master Suite: Enjoy two walk-in closets, plus a bath with a corner whirlpool tub, glass shower, linen closet, vanity, and compartmentalized toilet.

CAD FILE AVAILABLE

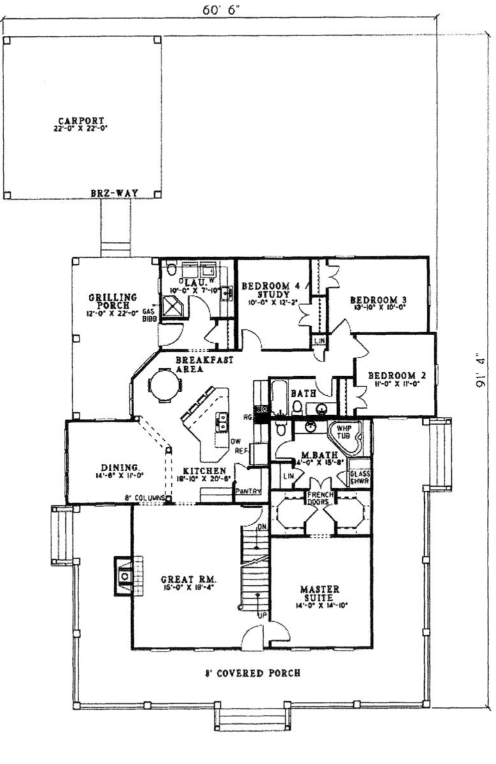

Bonus Area

Copyright by designer/architect.

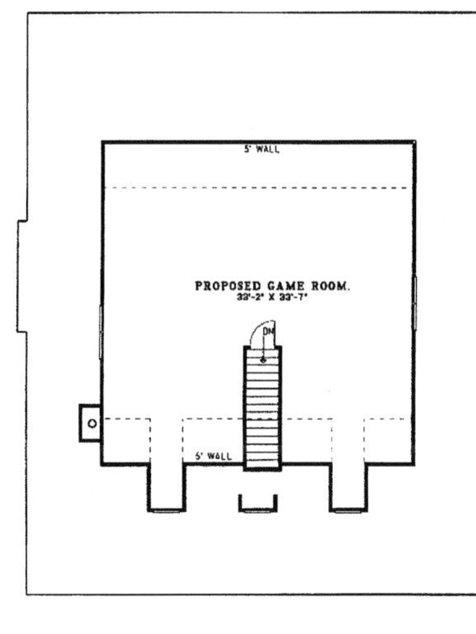

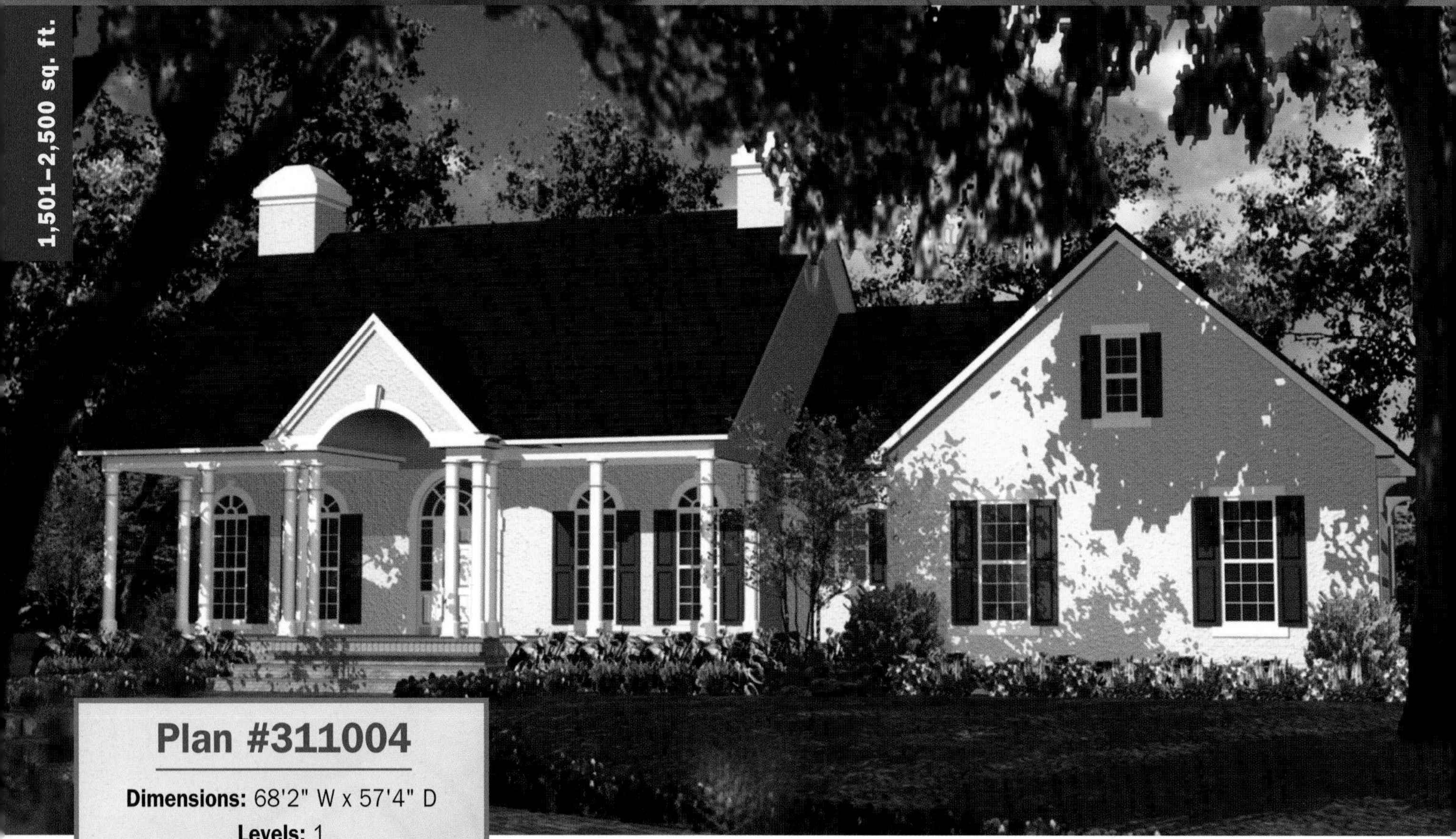

Plan #311004

Dimensions: 68'2" W x 57'4" D
Levels: 1
Heated Square Footage: 2,046
Bedrooms: 3
Bathrooms: 2½
Foundation: Crawl space, slab, or basement
Materials List Available: Yes
Price Category: D

Images provided by designer/architect.

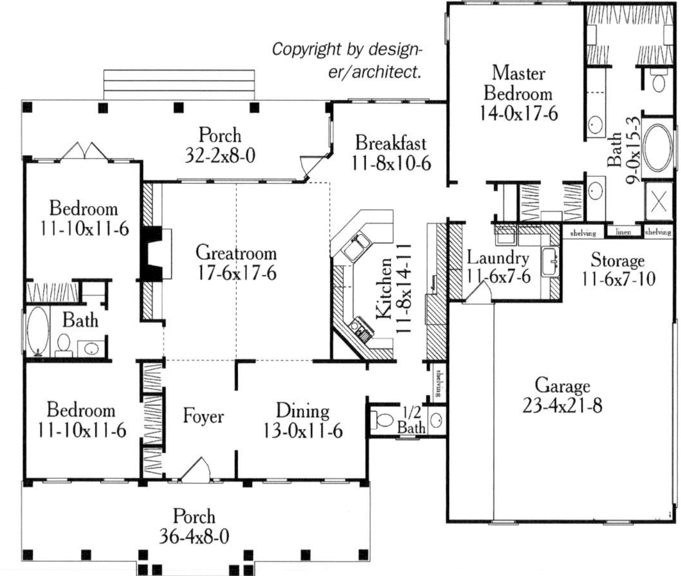

The open design of the public spaces in this home makes it ideal for an active family life or frequent entertaining.

Features:

- Great Room: Open to the foyer, this spacious room has a fireplace flanked by built-ins and a bank of windows at the rear.
- Dining Room: This large front room is convenient to the kitchen but isolated enough to be just right for a formal dinner party or a casual family meal.
- Kitchen: The angled work space creates efficient traffic patterns, and the snack bar makes it easy for small visitors to share the news of their day.
- Breakfast Room: The expansive window area lights this room, and the door to the rear porch makes outside entertaining easy.
- Master Suite: You'll feel coddled by the large window area, two walk-in closets, and bath with two vanities, tub, and shower.

Copyright by designer/architect.

Rear View

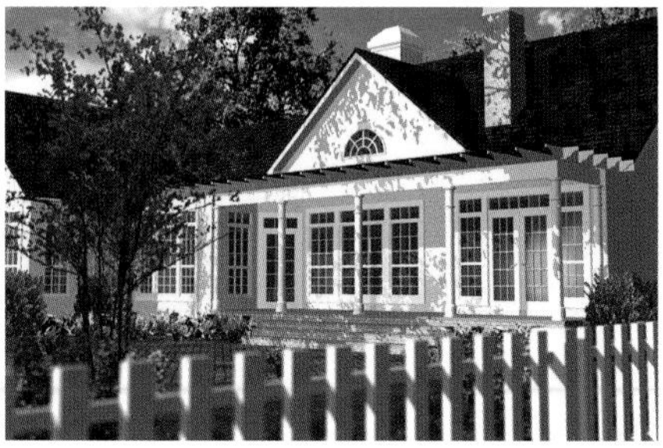

Plan #101030

Dimensions: 63' W x 63' D
Levels: 1
Heated Square Footage: 2,071
Bedrooms: 3
Bathrooms: 2½
Foundation: Crawl space or basement
Materials List Available: No
Price Category: E

This lovely three-bedroom brick home with an optional bonus room above the three-car garage is just what you've been looking for.

Features:

- Family Room: This large room, with its high ceiling and cozy fireplace, is great for entertaining.
- Kitchen: This kitchen boasts a built-in pantry and a peninsula opening into the breakfast nook.
- Master Suite: This suite, with its 14-ft.-high ceiling and private sitting area, is a perfect place to relax after a long day. The bath has a double vanity, large walk-in closet, and soaking tub.
- Bedrooms: Two additional bedrooms feature walk-in closets and share a private bathroom.

CAD FILE AVAILABLE

Images provided by designer/architect.

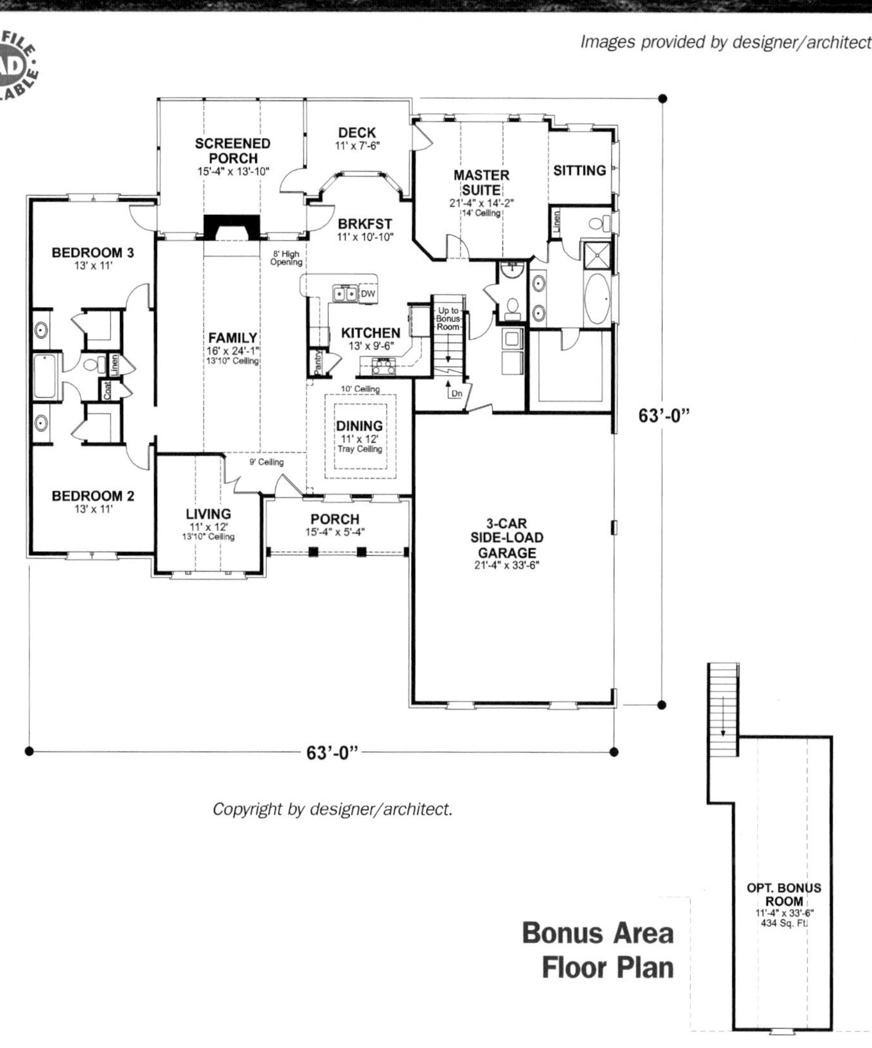

Copyright by designer/architect.

Bonus Area Floor Plan

Plan #351105

Dimensions: 69' W x 59'10" D
Levels: 1
Heated Square Footage: 2,000
Bedrooms: 3
Bathrooms: 2½
Foundation: Crawl space, slab or basement
Materials List Available: Yes
Price Category: F

Images provided by designer/architect.

This inviting home has rustic styling with upscale features.

CAD FILE AVAILABLE

Features:

- Outdoor Living: The front and rear covered porches add plenty of usable outdoor living space and include that much-requested outdoor kitchen.
- Great Room: This expansive great room includes a beautiful trayed ceiling and features built-in cabinets and a gas fireplace.
- Kitchen: This spacious kitchen features an oversize island with a large eating bar and breakfast area.
- Master Suite: The master bedroom has a raised ceiling and opens into the well-equipped bath that includes dual sinks, oversize corner jet tub, and large his and her walk-in closets.
- Flex Space: There is a storage area off of the garage for projects and storage. The media/hobby space could be used as a home office, dining room, or playroom.

Kitchen

Master Bathroom

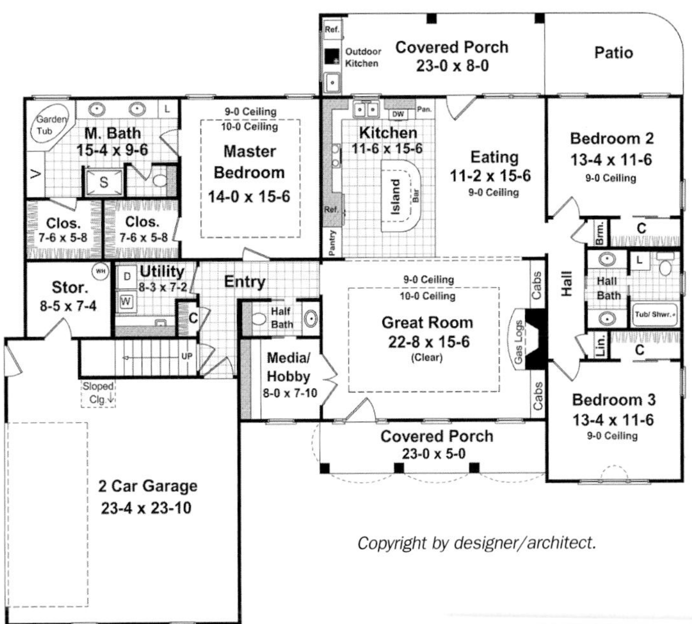

Copyright by designer/architect.

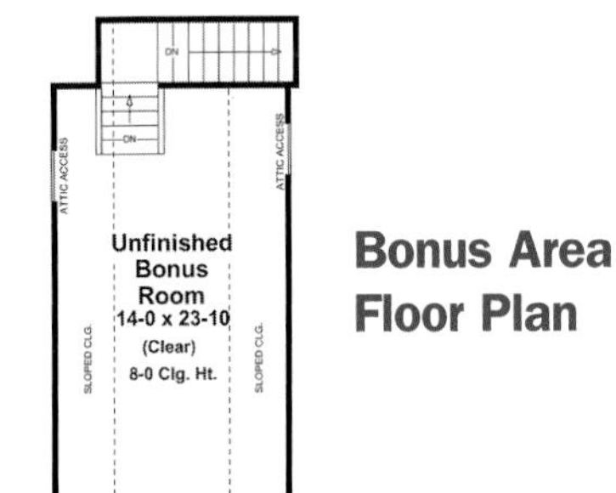

Bonus Area Floor Plan

Rear View

Plan #161026

Dimensions: 67'6" W x 63'6" D
Levels: 1
Heated Square Footage: 2,041
Bedrooms: 3
Bathrooms: 2
Foundation: Basement
Materials List Available: No
Price Category: D

Images provided by designer/architect.

Basement Level Floor Plan

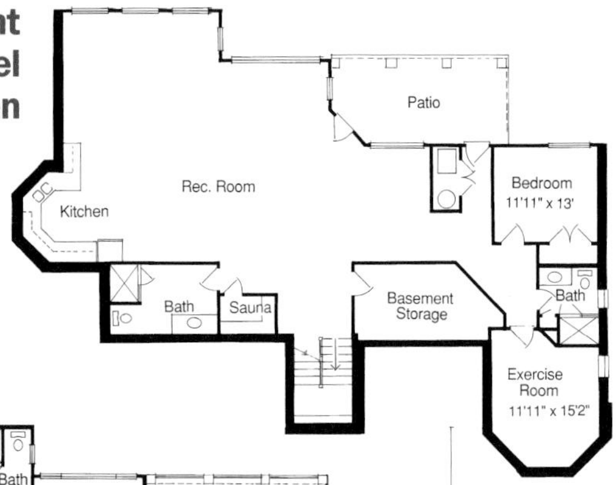

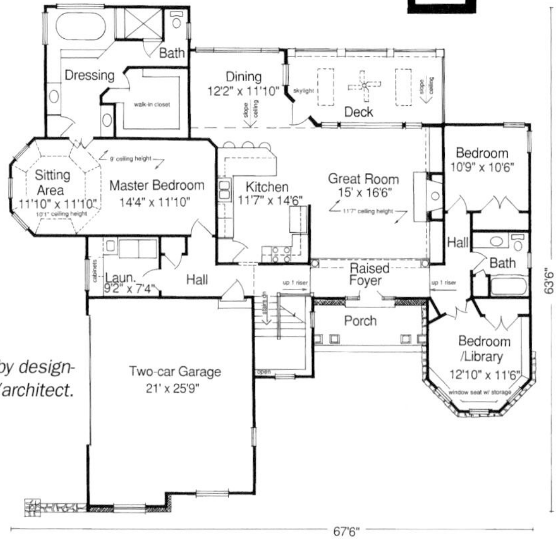

Copyright by designer/architect.

Plan #351126

Dimensions: 69' W x 63'10" D
Levels: 1
Heated Square Footage: 2,021
Bedrooms: 3
Bathrooms: 2½
Foundation: Crawl space, slab or basement
Materials List Available: Yes
Price Category: F

Images provided by designer/architect.

CAD FILE AVAILABLE

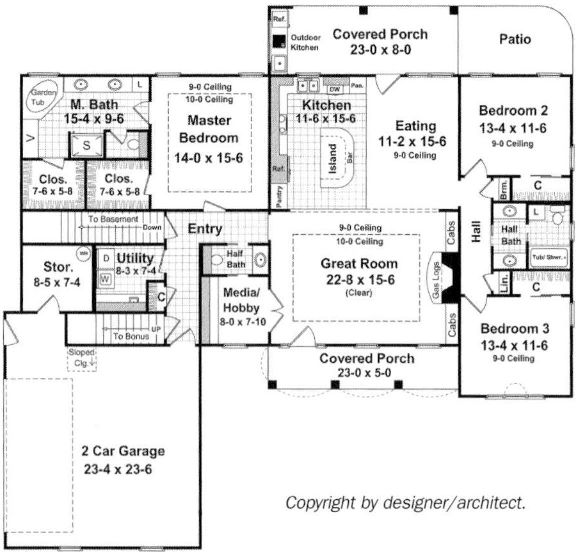

Copyright by designer/architect.

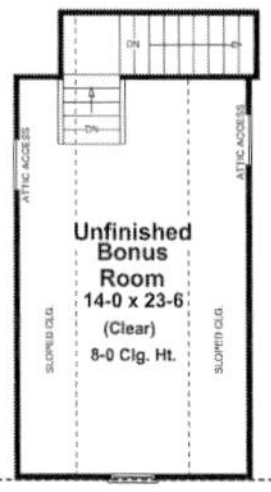

Bonus Area Floor Plan

Plan #661073

Dimensions: 60'4" W x 56' D
Levels: 1
Heated Square Footage: 2,041
Bedrooms: 4
Bathrooms: 2
Foundation: Slab
Materials List Available: No
Price Category: D

Images provided by designer/architect.

CAD FILE AVAILABLE

Bedroom 4 13⁴ · 9⁴
Bath 2
Covered Patio
Master Suite 14⁸ · 16⁸
Nook
Bedroom 3 11⁰ · 11⁰
Family Rm. 18⁴ · 14⁴
w.i.c.
Master Bath
Kitchen
Laun.
Bedroom 2 11⁰ · 11⁰
Living Rm. 10¹⁰ · 13²
Foyer
Dining Rm. 10¹⁰ · 13²
Entry
2 Car Garage 20⁰ · 20⁸

Copyright by designer/architect.

Front View

Plan #271082

Dimensions: 71' W x 62' D
Levels: 1
Heated Square Footage: 2,074
Bedrooms: 4
Bathrooms: 2
Foundation: Crawl space or slab
Materials List Available: No
Price Category: D

Images provided by designer/architect.

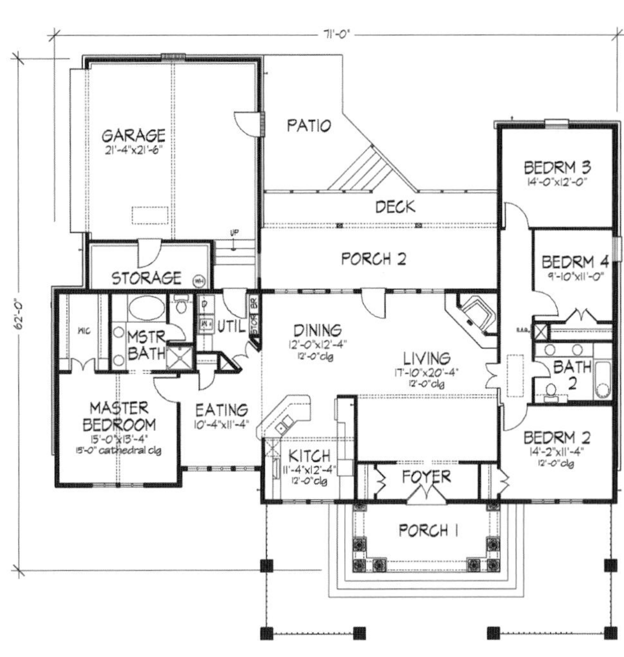

Copyright by designer/architect.

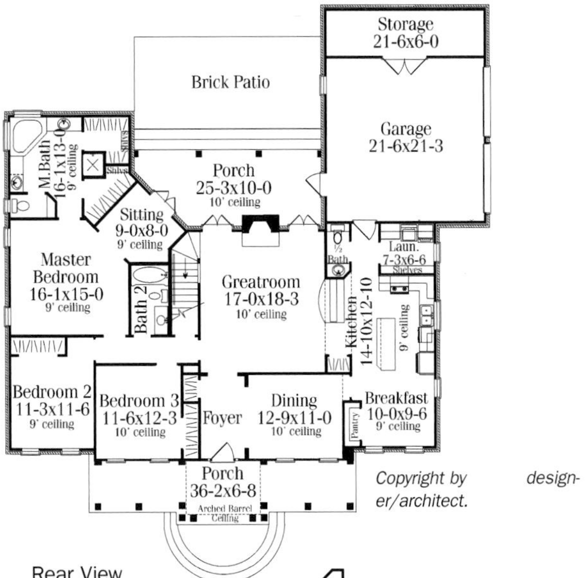

Plan #311001

Dimensions: 65'11" W x 67'9" D
Levels: 1
Heated Square Footage: 2,085
Bedrooms: 3
Bathrooms: 2½
Foundation: Crawl space, slab, or basement
Materials List Available: No
Price Category: D

Images provided by designer/architect.

Rear View

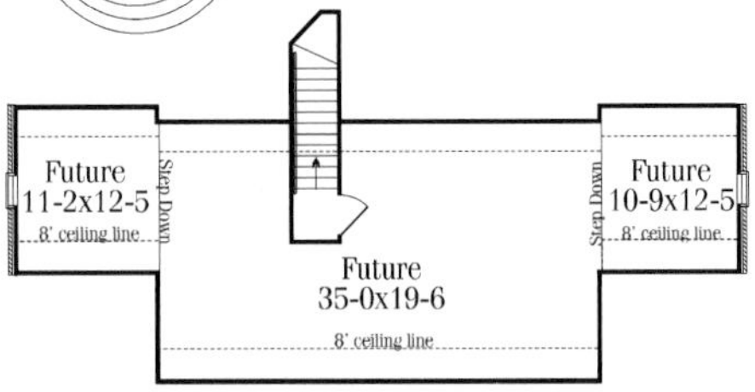

Storage 21-6x6-0
Brick Patio
Garage 21-6x21-3
M.Bath 16-1x13-0 9' ceiling
Porch 25-3x10-0 10' ceiling
Sitting 9-0x8-0 9' ceiling
Master Bedroom 16-1x15-0 9' ceiling
Bath 2
Greatroom 17-0x18-3 10' ceiling
½ Bath
Laun. 7-3x6-6
Kitchen 14-10x12-10 9' ceiling
Bedroom 2 11-3x11-6 9' ceiling
Bedroom 3 11-6x12-3 10' ceiling
Foyer
Dining 12-9x11-0 10' ceiling
Breakfast 10-0x9-6 9' ceiling
Pantry
Porch 36-2x6-8
Arched Barrel Ceiling

Copyright by designer/architect.

Future 11-2x12-5 8' ceiling line
Step Down
Future 35-0x19-6 8' ceiling line
Step Down
Future 10-9x12-5 8' ceiling line

Optional Bonus Area

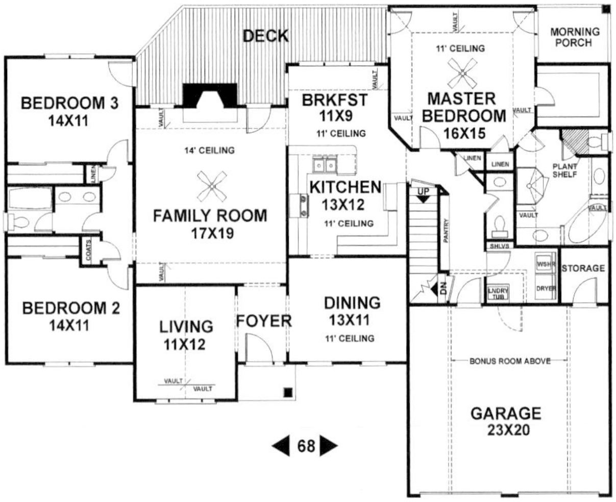

Plan #101008

Dimensions: 68' W x 53' D
Levels: 1
Heated Square Footage: 2,088
Bedrooms: 3
Bathrooms: 2½
Foundation: Crawl space, slab, or basement
Materials List Available: Yes
Price Category: E

Images provided by designer/architect.

CAD FILE CAD AVAILABLE

Copyright by designer/architect.

DECK
MORNING PORCH
BEDROOM 3 14X11
14' CEILING
FAMILY ROOM 17X19
BRKFST 11X9 11' CEILING
KITCHEN 13X12 11' CEILING
11' CEILING
MASTER BEDROOM 16X15
PLANT SHELF
STORAGE
BEDROOM 2 14X11
LIVING 11X12
FOYER
DINING 13X11 11' CEILING
BONUS ROOM ABOVE
GARAGE 23X20
68
53

SMARTtip

Accentuating Your Bathroom with Details

No matter how big or small the room, details will pull the style together. Some of the best details that you can include are the smallest—drawer pulls from an antique store or shells in a glass jar or just left on the countertop. Add period flavor with crown molding, or dress up contemporary fixtures with polished stone fittings.

Plan #171015

Dimensions: 79' W x 46' D
Levels: 1
Heated Square Footage: 2,089
Bedrooms: 3
Bathrooms: 2½
Foundation: Crawl space or slab
Materials List Available: Yes
Price Category: D

Images provided by designer/architect.

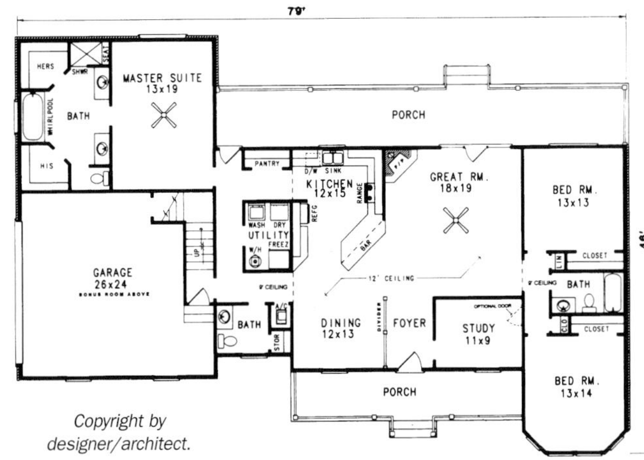

Copyright by designer/architect.

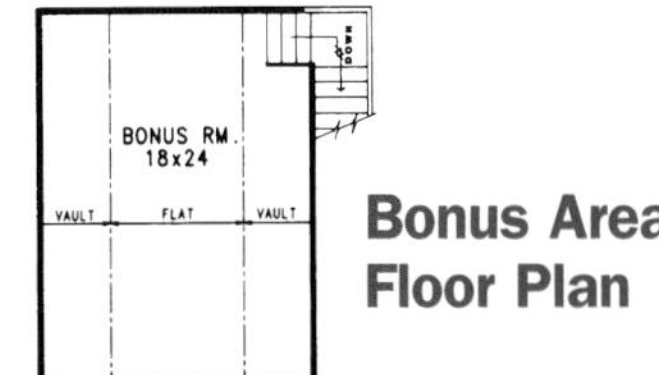

Bonus Area Floor Plan

Plan #191032

Dimensions: 80'4" W x 52' D
Levels: 1
Heated Square Footage: 2,091
Bedrooms: 3
Bathrooms: 2
Foundation: Slab
Materials List Available: No
Price Category: D

Images provided by designer/architect.

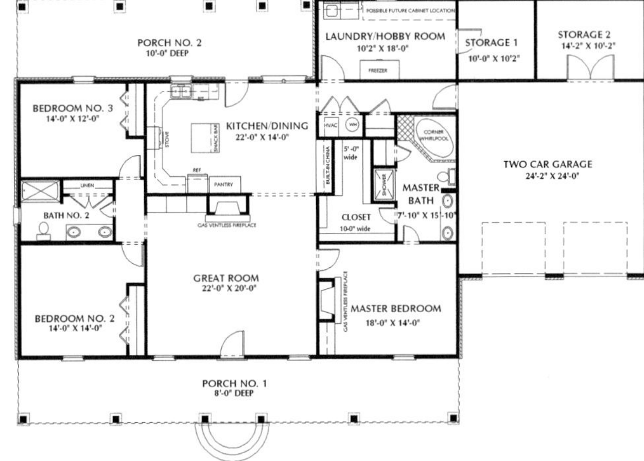

Copyright by designer/architect.

Choosing Kitchen Cabinets

Who can't relate to this scenario: you turn on the oven to preheat it, but wait, did you take out the large roasting pan first? How about the lasagna dish, muffin tins, pizza stone, and cookie sheets that are in there, too? Now where can you put everything that was in the oven while the casserole is baking, and the countertop is laden with the rest of tonight's dinner ingredients?

The oven, it seems, has become the catch-all for the big, awkward stuff that you can't fit into kitchen cabinets but is just too ugly to display. Besides, the countertop is where you keep the toaster oven, food processor, coffeemaker, canisters, hand mixer, portable TV, notepad, coupon file, bills, hand lotion, car keys, and your vitamins! Wouldn't life be grand if there was a place for everything and everything was in its place? Good cabinetry

The following article was reprinted from *The Smart Approach to Home Decorating* (Creative Homeowner 2007).

Shorter cabinets directly over the cooktop and sink open up the room, provide a safe distance between cabinetry and heat, and allow for decorative lighting in the form of fluorescent sconces, opposite.

To break up the monotony of cabinets, install some alternative storage, such as these drawer-like baskets. Take advantage of the easy access by filling them with things you use often, left.

outfitted with an assortment of organizing options can help you there. It can make your kitchen more efficient and a whole lot neater while establishing a style, or "look," for the room. Keep in mind, however, that cabinetry will also consume about 40 percent of your kitchen design budget, according to the NKBA. So before making any expensive decisions—or costly mistakes—investigate all of the various cabinetry options that are available to you.

Cabinet Construction

Basically, cabinets are constructed in one of two ways: framed or frameless. Framed cabinets have a traditional look, with a full frame across the face of the cabinet box that may show between closed doors. This secures adjacent cabinets and strengthens wider cabinet boxes with a center rail. Hinges on framed cabinets may or may not be visible around doors when they are closed. The door's face may be ornamented with raised or recessed panels, trimmed or framed panels, or a framed-glass panel with or without muntins (the narrow vertical and horizontal strips of wood that divide panes of glass).

Frameless cabinets—also known as European-style cabinets, although American manufacturers also make them—are built without a face frame and sport a clean, contemporary look. There's no trim or molding with this simple design. Close-fitting doors cover the entire front of the box; no ornamentation appears on the face of the doors; and hinges are typically hidden inside the cabinet box.

Choosing one type over another is generally a matter of taste, although framed units offer slightly less interior space. But the quality of construction is a factor that should always be taken into consideration. How do you judge it? Solid wood is too expensive for most of today's budgets, but it might be used on just the doors and frames. More typical is plywood box construction, which offers good structural support and solid wood on the doors and frames. To save money, cabinetmakers sometimes use strong plywood for support elements, such as the box and frame, and medium-density fiberboard for other parts, such as doors and drawer fronts. In yet another alternative, good-quality laminate cabinets can be made with high-quality, thick particleboard underneath the laminate finish.

There are other things to look for in cabinet construction. They include dovetail or mortise-and-tenon joinery and solidly mortised hinges. Also, make sure that the interior of every cabinet is well finished, with adjustable shelves that are a minimum ⅝ inch thick to prevent bowing.

Unless you have the time and skill to build the cabinets yourself or can hire someone else to do it, you'll have to purchase them in one of four ways. Knockdown cabinetry (also known as RTA, ready to assemble) is shipped flat and, sometimes, unfinished because you put the pieces together. Stock cabinetry comes in standard sizes but limited styles and colors; it is often available on the spot or can be delivered quickly. Like stock, semi-custom cabinetry comes in standard styles, but it is manufactured to fit a homeowner's specific size and finish needs. Custom cabinetry is not limited in terms of style or size because it is built to the designer's specifications.

Cabinet Accessories & Options

Most people would agree that no matter how much storage space they have, they need even more. The problem often isn't the amount, it's the inaccessible placement and inefficient configuration of the storage space. One of the greatest benefits today's designers and manufacturers offer is fitted and accessorized interiors that maximize even the smallest nook and cranny inside cabinets and drawers. These accommodations not

Color makes all the difference in a room. Here, a variety of creamy colors throughout the kitchen adds personality. Pretty green and blue cabinets are a nice change from plain white.

An updated country style, cabinets with sleeker lines and elegant granite counters intermingle here with the usual down-home charm and informal mix of woods and hardware.

only expand the use of space, but increase convenience and accessibility. Among them are the following:

Appliance Garages. Appliance garages make use of dead space in a corner, but they can be installed anywhere in the vertical space between the wall-mounted cabinet and the countertop. A tambour (rolltop) door hides small appliances such as a food processor or anything else you want within reach but hidden from view. This form of minicabinet can be equipped with an electrical outlet and can even be divided into separate sections to store more than one item. Reserve part of the appliance garage for cookbook storage, or outfit it with small drawers for little items or spices. Customize an appliance garage any way you like.

Lazy Susans and Carousel Shelves. These rotating shelves maximize dead corner storage and put items such as dishes or pots and pans within easy reach. A Lazy Susan rotates 360 degrees, so just spin it to find what you're looking for. Carousel shelves, which attach to two right-angled doors, rotate 270 degrees; open the doors and the shelves, which are actually attached to the doors, put any item within hand reach. Pivoting shelves are a variation on the carousel design and may or may not be door-mounted. In addition, units may be built into taller cabinets, creating a pantry that can store a lot in a small amount of space.

Fold-Down Mixer Shelf. This spring-loaded shelf swings up and out of a base cabinet for use, then folds down and back

These custom cabinets add unique options, such as pullout storage for dish linens and angled cabinets that make use of small spaces.

into the cabinet when the mixer is no longer needed, which reduces clutter by keeping the countertop clear of appliances.

Slide-Outs and Tilt-Outs. Installed in base cabinets, slide-out trays and racks store small appliances, linens, cans, or boxed items, while slide-out bins are good for holding onions, potatoes, grains, pet food, or potting soil—even garbage or recycling containers. A tilt-out tray is located in the often-wasted area just below the lip of the countertop in front of the sink and above base cabinet doors. It looks like a drawer but tilts open to provide a neat nook for sponges and scouring pads that look messy when left on the counter.

Built-in Pantry Units. These fold-out or slide-out units can be fitted into narrow areas that might otherwise remain wasted. Store dry or canned goods here. Fold-out units have door-mounted shelves and an in-cabinet shelf that pivots; slide-out units fit multiple shelves in a cabinet.

In addition to these options, check out everything that a cabinet manufacturer has to offer to make the most of a cabinet's storage capacity. Other items to look for include special racks for trays and cookie sheets, drawer inserts for organizing spices and utensils, watertight recycling bins, wine racks, fold-down recipe book rests, sliding pot racks, built-in canister drawers, and plate racks.

Unique two-toned cabinetry adds interest in a country kitchen, left. The appliances are integrated with the same two-toned panels and the hardware echoes the geometric design.

Glass-fronted bins are a colorful and convenient way to store pasta and dried beans, opposite bottom left.

Personalize your kitchen with cabinets made from exotic wood and finished with a custom-mixed high-gloss lacquer, opposite bottom right.

Cabinetry with the look of fine furniture integrates this kitchen almost seamlessly into an adjacent living space, below.

If you decide to add cabinets without a lot of built-ins, consider refitting them with cabinet organizers. These plastic, plastic-coated wire, or enameled-steel racks and hangers are widely available at department stores and home centers.

Beware of the temptation to over-specialize your kitchen storage. Sizes and needs for certain items change, so be sure to allot at least 50 percent of your kitchen's storage to standard cabinets with one or more movable shelves.

The Decorative Role of Cabinets

The look you create in your kitchen will be largely influenced by the cabinetry you select. Finding a style that suits you and how you will use your new kitchen is similar to shopping for furniture. In fact, don't be surprised to see many furniture details dressing up the cabinets on view in showrooms and home centers today.

Besides architectural elements such as fluted pilasters, corbels, moldings, and bull's-eye panels, look for details such as fretwork, rope motifs, gingerbread trim, balusters, composition ornamentation (it looks like carving), even footed cabinets that mimic freestanding furniture pieces.

If your taste runs toward less-fussy design, you'll also find handsome door and drawer styles that feature minimal or no decoration. Woods and finishes are just as varied, and range from informal looks in birch, oak, ash, and maple to rich mahogany and cherry. Laminate finishes, though less popular than they were a decade ago, haven't completely disappeared from the marketplace, but an array of colors has replaced the once-ubiquitous almond and white finishes.

Color

Color is coming on strong on wood cabinetry, too. Accents in one, two, or more hues are pairing with natural wood tones. White-painted cabinets take on a warmer glow with tinted shades of this always popular neutral. Special "vintage" finishes, such as translucent color glazes, continue to grow in popularity, as do distressed finishing techniques, such as wire brushing and rubbed-through color that add both another dimension and the appeal of handcraftmanship, even on mass-produced items. Contemporary kitchens, which historically favor an all-white palette, are warming up with earthier neutral shades, less sterile off-whites, and wood.

If you're shy about using color on such a high-ticket item as cabinetry, try it as an accent on molding, door trim, or island cabinetry. Just as matched furniture suites have become passé in other rooms of the house, the same is true for the kitchen, where mixing several looks can add sophistication and visual interest.

Hardware

Another way to emphasize your kitchen's decorative style is with hardware. From exquisite reproductions in brass, pewter, wrought iron, or ceramic to handsome bronze, chrome, nickel, glass, steel, plastic, rubber, wood, or stone creations, a smorgasbord of shapes and designs is available. Some pieces are highly polished; others are matte-finished, smooth, or hammered. Some are abstract or geometrical; others are simple, elegant shapes. Whimsical designs take on the forms of animals or teapots, vegetables or flowers. Even just one or two great-looking door or drawer pulls can be showstoppers in a kitchen that may otherwise be devoid of much personality. Like mixing cabinet finishes, a combination of two hardware styles—perhaps picked up from other materials in the room—makes a big design statement. As the famed architect Mies Van der Rohe once stated, "God is in the details," and the most perfect detail in your new kitchen may be the artistic hardware that you select.

Besides looks, consider the function of a pull or knob. You have to be able to grip it easily and comfortably. If your fingers or hands get stiff easily, select C- or U-shaped pulls. If you like a knob, try it out in the showroom to make sure it isn't slippery or awkward when you grab it. Knobs and pulls can be inexpensive if you can stick to unfinished ones that you can paint in an accent color picked up from the tile or wallpaper. If you want to save money at first, you can start with simple knobs and pulls and change them later. Replacing the hardware can redefine the style of the cabinets. The right knob or pull can suggest any one of a number of vintage looks or decorative styles.

This cabinet color, opposite, was chosen to echo one of the colors in the granite countertop and backsplash.

Satin-finish hardware looks great against paint with a soft metallic sheen, while the center of each handle reflects the granite countertop, top left.

Unique braided handles personalize plain cabinetry, top right.

The homeowner matched this pattern in the adjacent accessories. Adding natural-wood accents, such as these drawer handles, helps balance the traditional and modern styles that are both in play in this kitchen, below.

Plan #151050

Dimensions: 69'2" W x 74'10" D
Levels: 1
Heated Square Footage: 2,096
Bedrooms: 3
Bathrooms: 2½
Foundation: Crawl space, slab, basement or walkout
CompleteCost List Available: Yes
Price Category: F

CAD FILE AVAILABLE

Images provided by designer/architect.

You'll love this spacious home for both its elegance and its convenient design.

Features:

- Ceiling Height: 8 ft.
- Great Room: A 9-ft. boxed ceiling complements this large room, which sits just beyond the front gallery. A fireplace and door to the rear porch make it a natural gathering spot.
- Kitchen: This well-designed kitchen includes a central work island and shares an angled eating bar with the adjacent breakfast room.
- Breakfast Room: This room's bay window is gorgeous, and the door to the garage is practical.
- Master Suite: You'll love the 9-ft. boxed ceiling in the bedrom and the vaulted ceiling in the bath, which also includes two walk0in closets, a corner whirlpool tub, split vanities, a shower, and a separate toilet room.
- Workshop: A hugh workshop with half-bath is ideal for anyone who loves to build or repair.

Kitchen

Master Bedroom

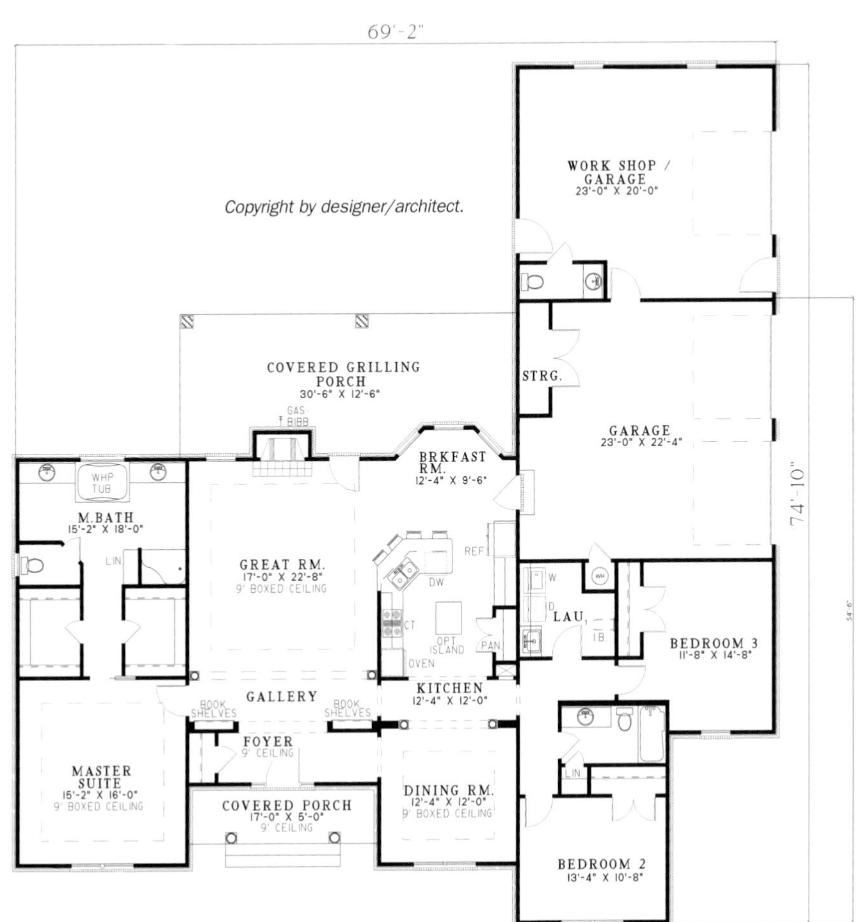

Images provided by designer/architect.

Plan #151850

Dimensions: 66' W x 52' D

Levels: 1

Heated Square Footage: 2,075

Bedrooms: 4

Bathrooms: 3

Foundation: Crawl space, slab; basement or walkout for fee

CompleteCost List Available: Yes

Price Category: D

This European-style home has beautiful details both inside and outside.

Features:

- Courtyard: Upon walking up the path to the entry of this home, you are greeted by a courtyard, where you can plant flowers and set up an area to relax in the sun.
- Great Room: Entertain your friends and family in this great room, which features access to the grilling porch at the rear of the home, a fireplace, and a connection to the kitchen.
- Kitchen: This kitchen was created with many wonderful details, including a pantry, an eating bar, and an attached breakfast room.
- Master Suite: Featuring access to the grilling porch, a spacious walk-in closet, a dual-sink vanity, and a whirlpool tub, this master suite is a great place to relax after a long day.

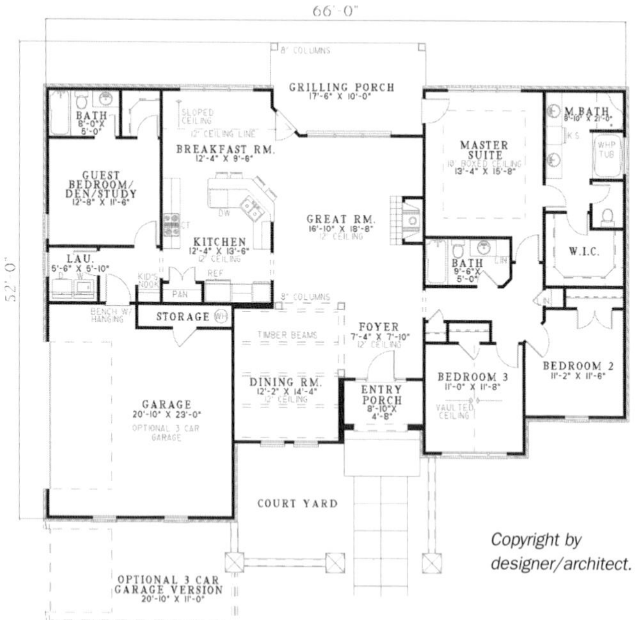

Copyright by designer/architect.

Plan #101009

Dimensions: 70'2" W x 59' D
Levels: 1
Heated Square Footage: 2,097
Bedrooms: 3
Bathrooms: 3
Foundation: Crawl space, slab, or basement
Materials List Available: Yes
Price Category: E

Images provided by designer/architect.

CAD FILE AVAILABLE

Round columns enhance this country porch design, which will nestle into any neighborhood.

Features:

- Ceiling Height: 9 ft. unless otherwise noted.
- Family Room: This large family room seems even more spacious, thanks to the vaulted ceiling. It's the perfect spot for all kinds of family activities.
- Dining Room: This elegant dining room is adorned with a decorative round column and a tray ceiling.
- Kitchen: You'll love the convenience of this enormous 14-ft.-3-in. x 22-ft.-6-in. country kitchen, which is open to the family room.
- Screened Porch: A French door leads to this breezy porch, with its vaulted ceiling.
- Master Suite: This sumptuous suite includes a double tray ceiling, a sitting area, a large walk-in closet, and a luxurious bath.
- Patio or Deck: This area is accessible from both the screened porch and master suite.

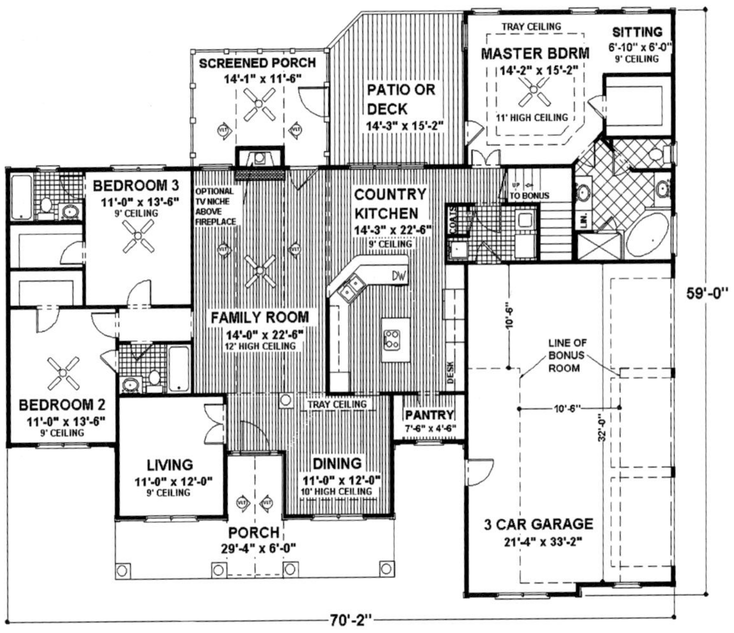

Copyright by designer/architect.

SMARTtip

Single-Level Decks

A single-level deck can use a strong vertical element, such as a pergola or a gazebo, to make it interesting. A simple and less-expensive option is a potted conical shrub or a clematis growing on a trellis.

Plan #151703

Dimensions: 69'2" W x 74'10" D
Levels: 1
Heated Square Footage: 2,096
Bedrooms: 3
Bathrooms: 2½
Foundation: Crawl space, slab, basement or walkout
CompleteCost List Available: Yes
Price Category: D

Images provided by designer/architect.

Main Level Floor Plan

Optional Main Level Floor Plan

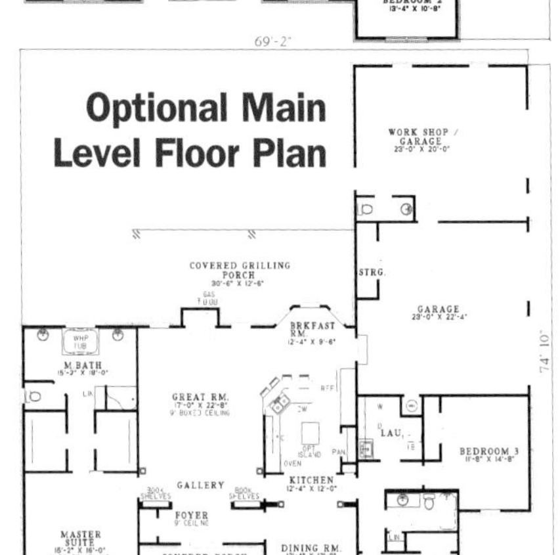

Copyright by designer/architect.

Plan #351053

Dimensions: 79'4" W x 53'6" D
Levels: 1
Heated Square Footage: 2,100
Bedrooms: 3
Bathrooms: 3
Foundation: Crawl space, slab or basement
Materials List Available: Yes
Price Category: F

Images provided by designer/architect.

Bonus Area Floor Plan

Copyright by designer/architect.

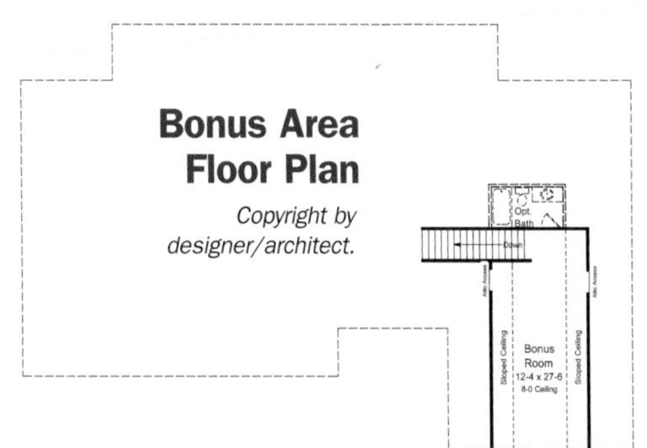

Plan #151004

Dimensions: 64'8" W x 62'1" D
Levels: 1
Heated Square Footage: 2,107
Bedrooms: 4
Bathrooms: 2½
Foundation: Crawl space, slab, or basement
CompleteCost List Available: Yes
Price Category: E

Images provided by designer/architect.

This home, as shown in the photograph, may differ from the actual blueprints. For more detailed information, please check floor plans carefully.

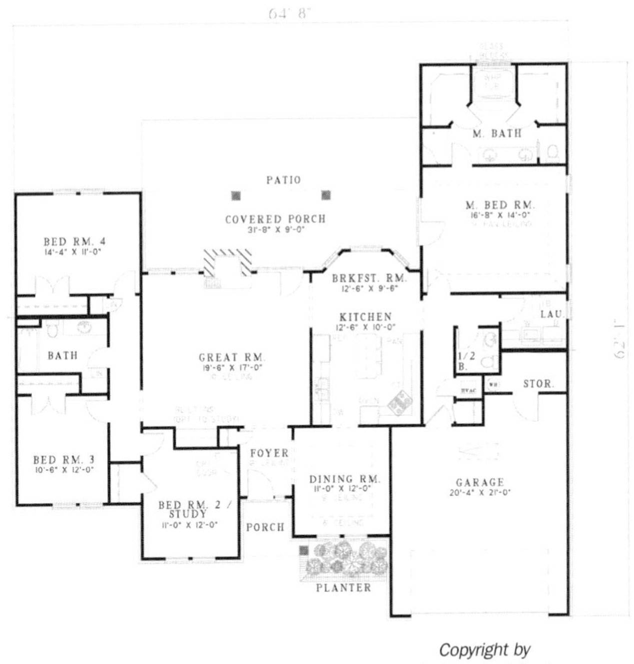

Copyright by designer/architect.

Plan #161092

Dimensions: 92'6" W x 56'8" D
Levels: 1
Heated Square Footage: 2,110
Bedrooms: 3
Bathrooms: 2
Foundation: Walkout basement
Materials List Available: Yes
Price Category: D

Images provided by designer/architect.

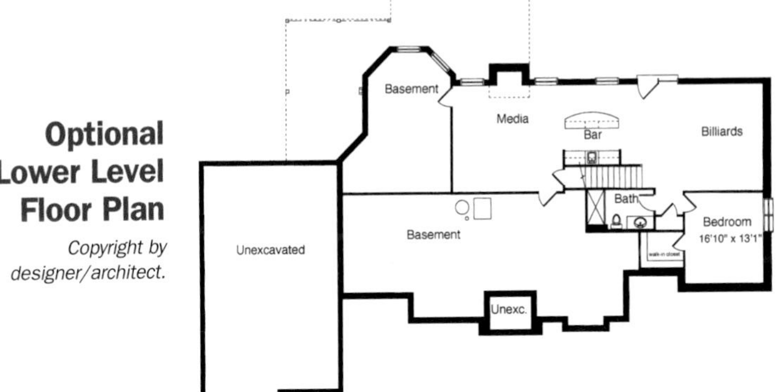

Optional Lower Level Floor Plan

Copyright by designer/architect.

Plan #151495

Dimensions: 67'2" W x 64'8" D
Levels: 1
Heated Square Footage: 2,121
Bedrooms: 3
Bathrooms: 2
Foundation: Slab
CompleteCost List Available: Yes
Price Category: D

Images provided by designer/architect.

CAD FILE AVAILABLE

Copyright by designer/architect.

Plan #191055

Dimensions: 60' W x 76' D
Levels: 1
Heated Square Footage: 2,123
Bedrooms: 3
Bathrooms: 2½
Foundation: Crawl space or slab
Materials List Available: No
Price Category: D

Images provided by designer/architect.

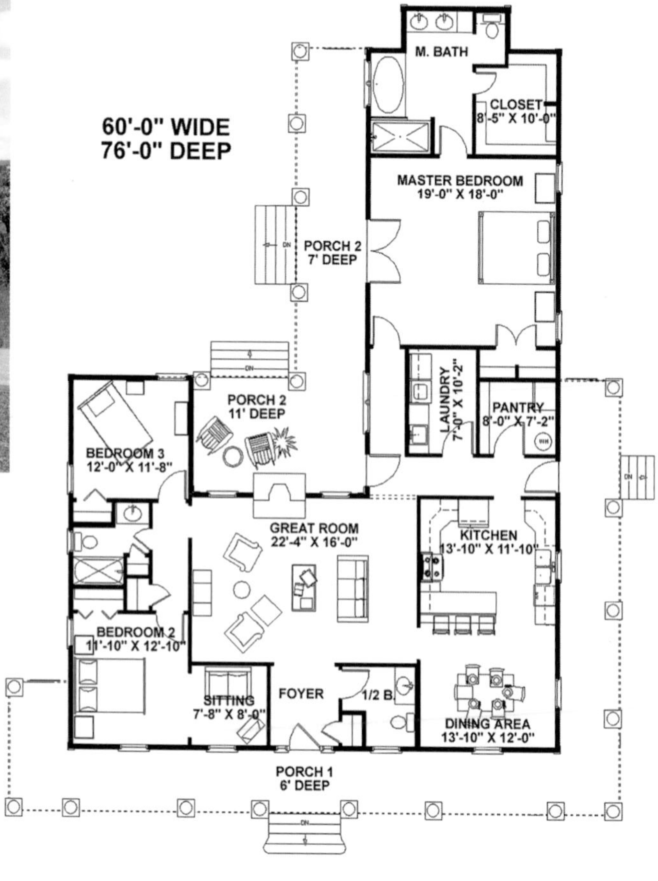

Copyright by designer/architect.

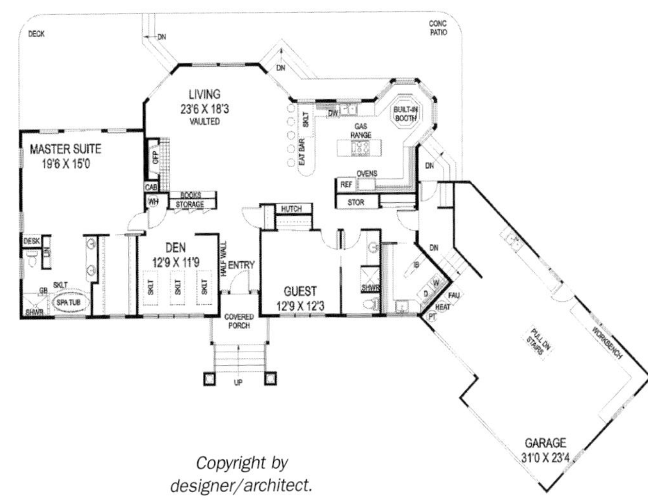

Plan #501723

Dimensions: 101'9" W x 63'9" D
Levels: 1
Heated Square Footage: 2,125
Bedrooms: 2
Bathrooms: 2
Foundation: Crawl space
Materials List Available: No
Price Category: D

Images provided by designer/architect.

CAD FILE AVAILABLE

Copyright by designer/architect.

Plan #151842

Dimensions: 60'4" W x 64'4" D
Levels: 1
Heated Square Footage: 2,135
Bedrooms: 4
Bathrooms: 2
Foundation: Crawl space or slab; basement or walkout for fee
CompleteCost List Available: Yes
Price Category: D

Images provided by designer/architect.

CAD FILE AVAILABLE

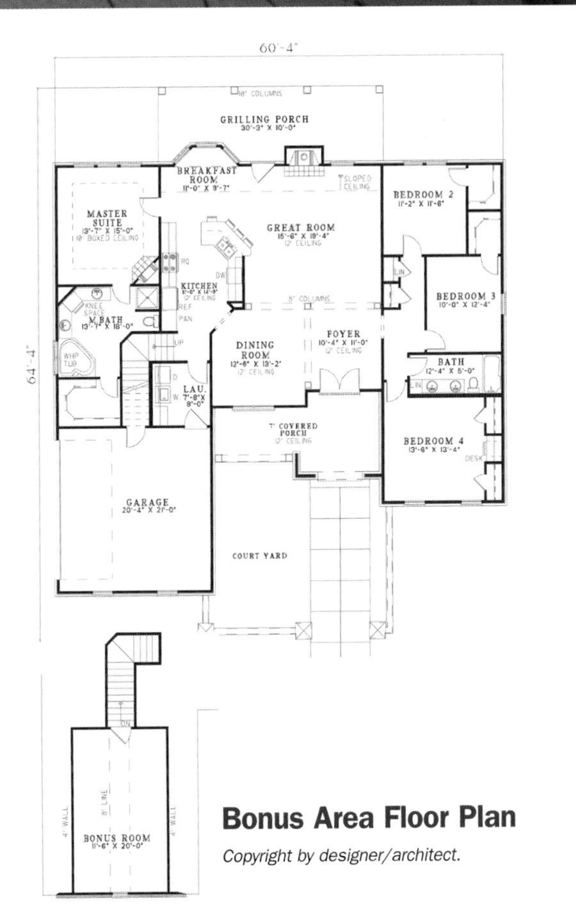

Bonus Area Floor Plan

Copyright by designer/architect.

Images provided by designer/architect.

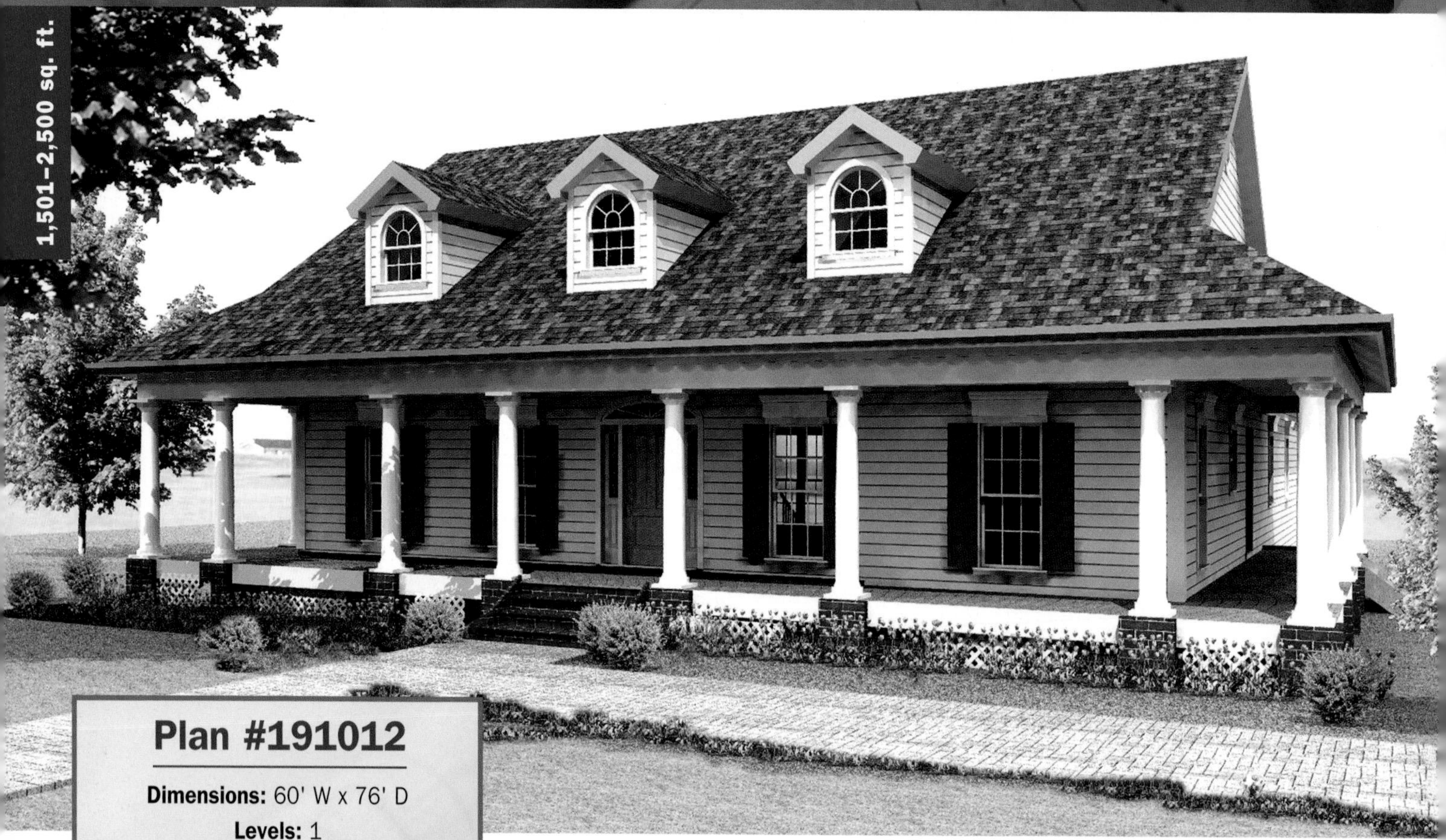

Plan #191012

Dimensions: 60' W x 76' D
Levels: 1
Heated Square Footage: 2,123
Bedrooms: 3
Bathrooms: 2½
Foundation: Crawl space or slab
Materials List Available: No
Price Category: D

The wraparound porch adds to the charm of this home.

Features:

- Porches: The front wraparound porch will be the perfect spot to greet neighbors as they stroll by. The rear porch is a private place to relax and enjoy a beautiful day.
- Great Room: This large gathering area features a 10-ft.-high ceiling and large windows, which offer a view of the backyard. There is even room for a formal dining table.
- Master Suite: Located on the opposite side of the home from the secondary bedrooms, this retreat offers a large sleeping area. The master bath will pamper you with an oversize shower, a tub, and dual vanities.
- Secondary Bedrooms: Two similarly sized bedrooms have ample closet space and share a full bathroom.

Kitchen

Copyright by designer/architect.

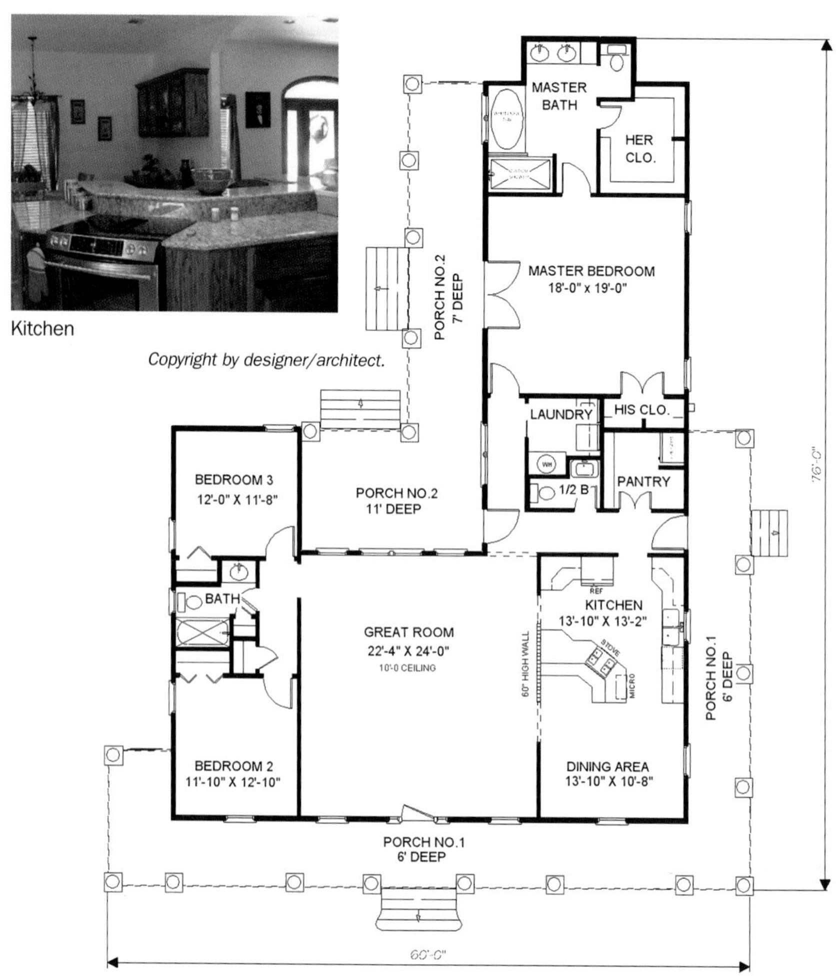

Images provided by designer/architect.

Plan #151171

Dimensions: 63'10" W x 72'2" D
Levels: 1
Heated Square Footage: 2,131
Bedrooms: 3
Bathrooms: 2½
Foundation: Crawl space, slab; basement or daylight basement for fee
CompleteCost List Available: Yes
Price Category: D

CAD FILE AVAILABLE

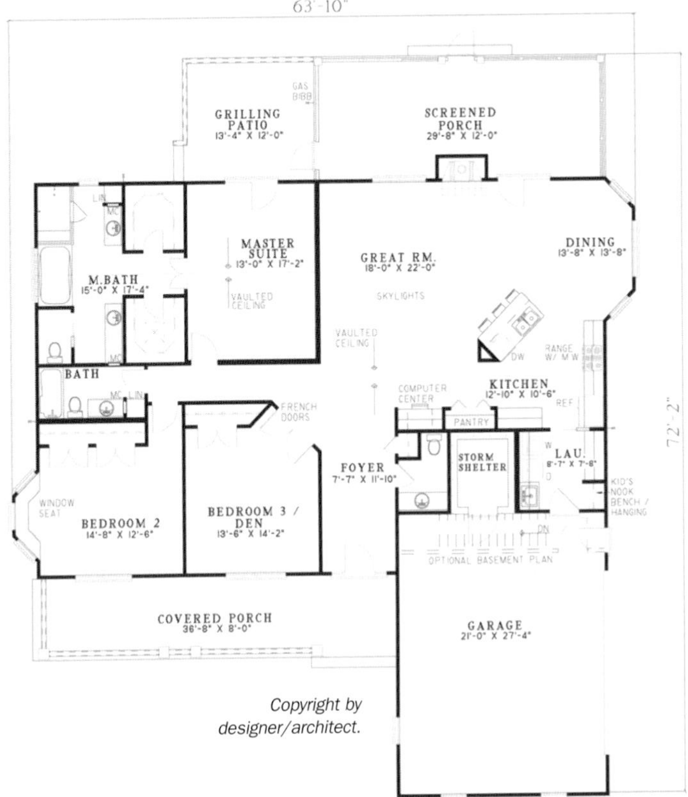

Copyright by designer/architect.

This home has everything an active family could possibly want—beauty, luxury, and plenty of space to relax and entertain, both inside and out.

Features:

- Great Room: Skylights in the vaulted ceiling, a fireplace, and the door to the rear screened porch make this a favorite place to spend time.
- Dining Area: Bay windows let light flood the area.
- Kitchen: The central island and snack bar, pantry, computer center, and ample counter and cabinet space make a great working area.
- Storm Shelter: You'll be happy to have this room, and even happier not to have to use it.
- Master Suite: The vaulted ceiling, door to the grilling patio, two walk-in closets, and luxury bath combine to create a suite you'll love.
- Additional Bedrooms: A window seat in one room is a child's dream, and you'll love the big closets.

Plan #151034

Dimensions: 58'6" W x 64'6" D
Levels: 1
Heated Square Footage: 2,133
Bedrooms: 3
Bathrooms: 2
Foundation: Crawl space, slab, basement, or walkout
CompleteCost List Available: Yes
Price Category: D

This home, as shown in the photograph, may differ from the actual blueprints. For more detailed information, please check the floor plans carefully.

Images provided by designer/architect.

You'll love the high ceilings, open floor plan, and contemporary design features in this home.

Features:

- Great Room: A pass-through tiled fireplace between this lovely large room and the adjacent hearth room allows you to notice the mirror effect created by the 10-ft. boxed ceilings in both rooms.
- Dining Room: An 11-ft. ceiling and 8-in. boxed column give formality to this lovely room, where you're certain to entertain.
- Kitchen: If you're a cook, this room may become your favorite spot in the house, thanks to its great design, which includes plenty of work and storage space, and a very practical layout.
- Master Suite: A 10-ft. boxed ceiling gives elegance to this room. A pocket door opens to the private bath, with its huge walk-in closet, glass-blocked whirlpool tub, separate glass shower, and private toilet room.

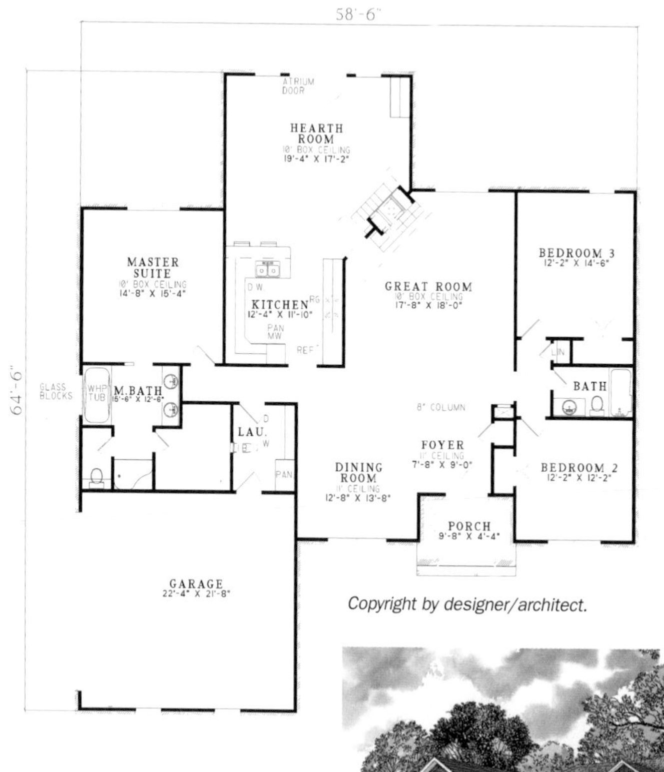

Copyright by designer/architect.

Rendering reflects floor plan

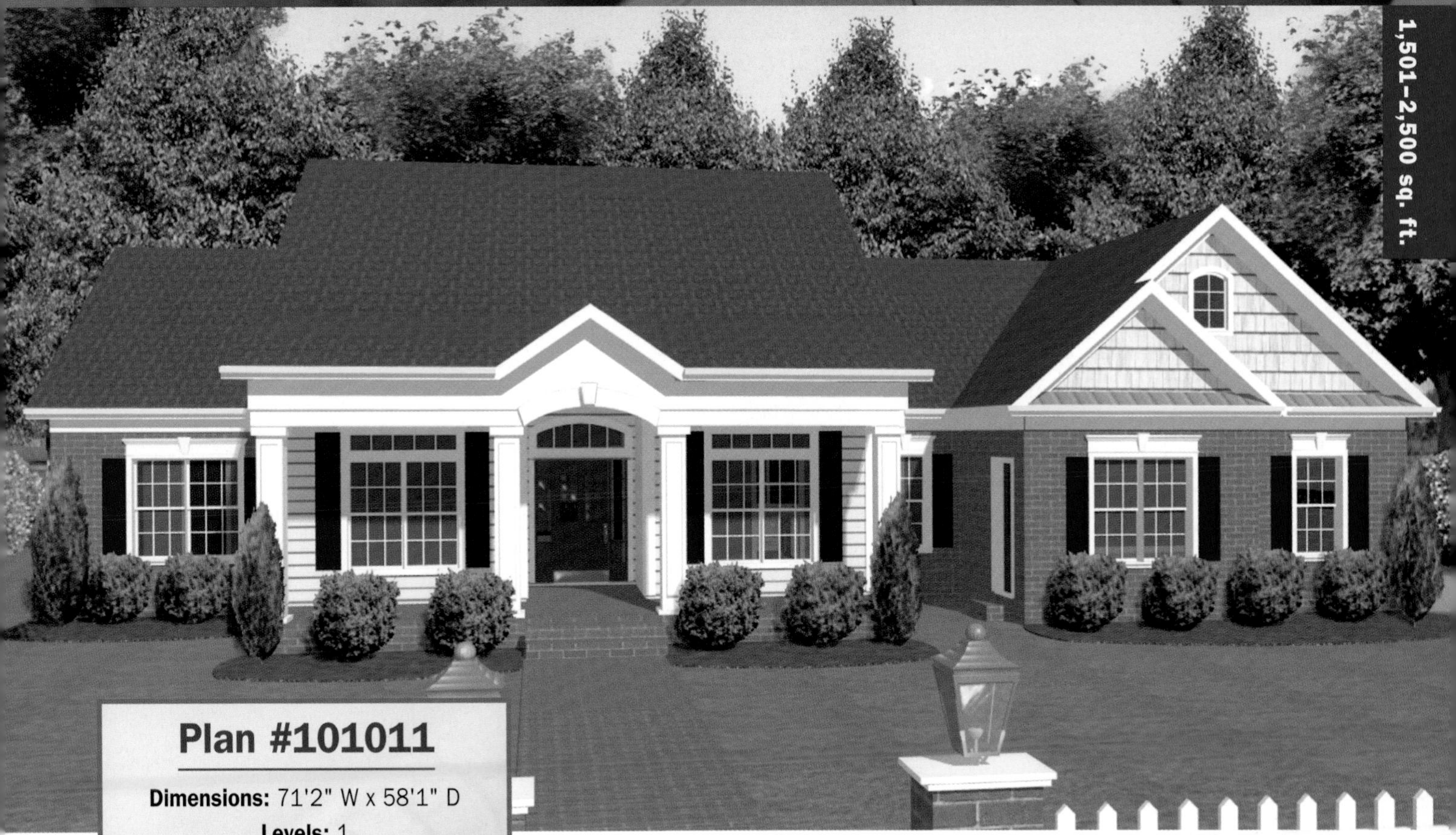

Images provided by designer/architect.

Plan #101011

Dimensions: 71'2" W x 58'1" D
Levels: 1
Heated Square Footage: 2,184
Bedrooms: 3
Bathrooms: 3
Foundation: Crawl space, slab, basement, or walkout
Materials List Available: Yes
Price Category: E

A classic design and spacious interior add up to a flexible design suitable to any modern lifestyle.

Features:

- Ceiling Height: 9 ft. unless otherwise noted.
- Dining Room: A decorative square column and a tray ceiling adorn this elegant dining room.
- Screened Porch: Enjoy summer breezes in style by stepping out of the French doors into this vaulted screened porch.
- Kitchen: Does everyone want to hang out in the kitchen while you are cooking? No problem. True to the home's country style, this huge 14-ft.-3-in. x 22-ft.-6-in. kitchen has plenty of room for helpers. This area is open to the vaulted family room.
- Patio or Deck: This pleasant outdoor area is accessible from both the screened porch and the master bedroom.
- Master Suite: This luxurious suite includes a double tray ceiling, a sitting area, two walk-in closets, and an exquisite bath.

Kitchen

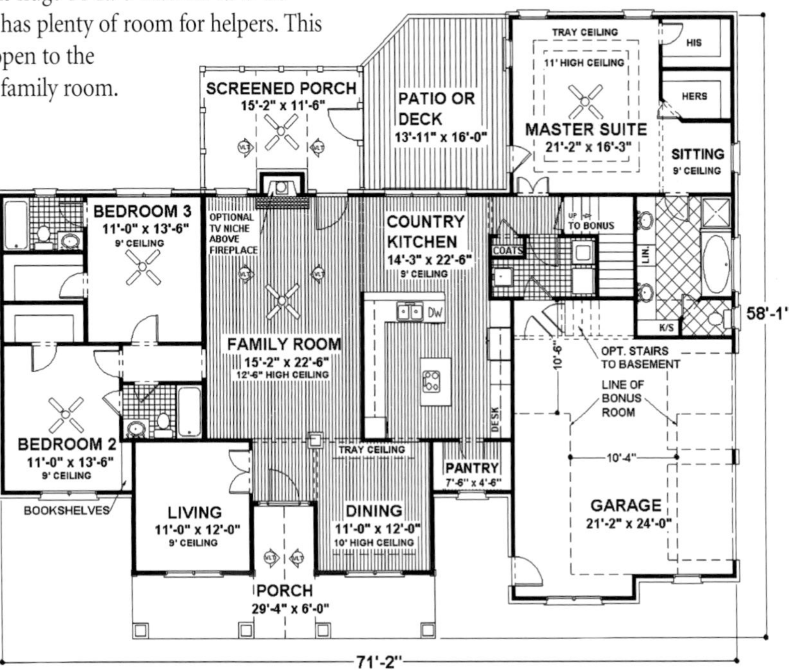

Plan #351206

Dimensions: 71' W x 77' D

Levels: 1

Heated Square Footage: 2,140

Bedrooms: 4

Bathrooms: 2½

Foundation: Crawl space, slab or basement

Materials List Available: Yes

Price Category: D

Images provided by designer/architect.

CAD FILE AVAILABLE

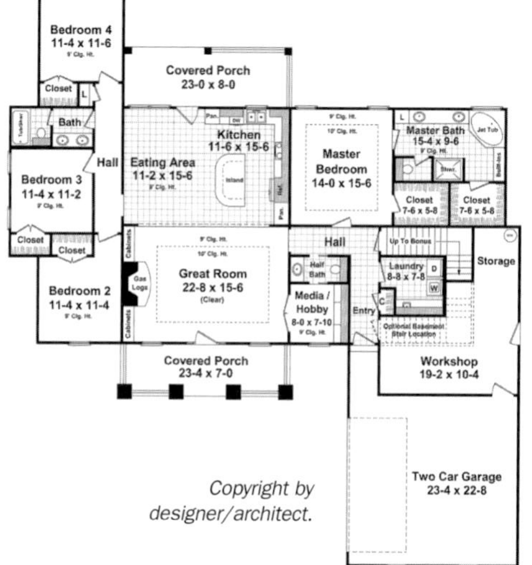

Copyright by designer/architect.

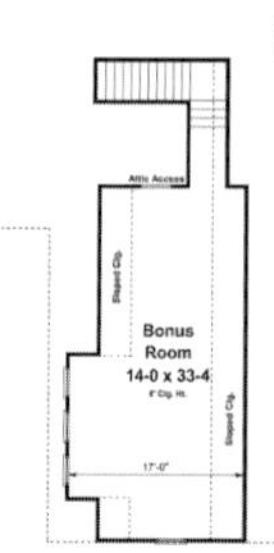

Bonus Area Floor Plan

Plan #121176

Dimensions: 67' W x 52' D

Levels: 1

Heated Square Footage: 2,144

Bedrooms: 4

Bathrooms: 2

Foundation: Slab; basement for fee

Materials List Available: Yes

Price Category: D

Images provided by designer/architect.

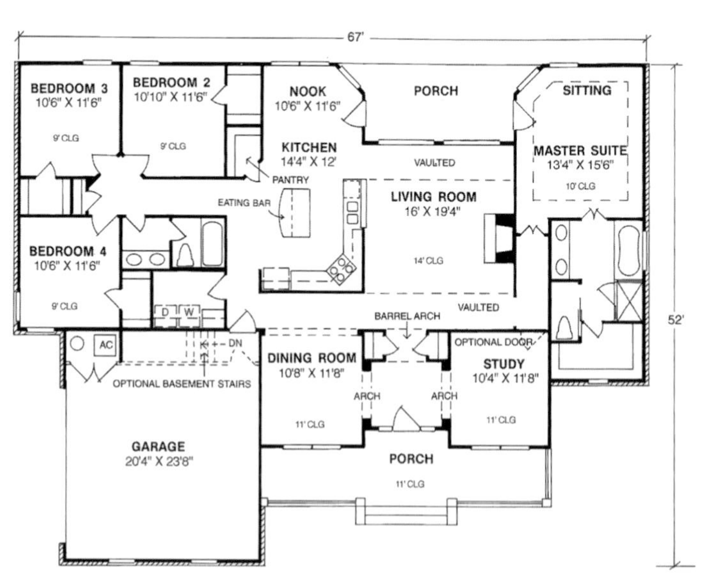

Copyright by designer/architect.

Plan #191001

Dimensions: 62' W x 72' D

Levels: 1

Heated Square Footage: 2,156

Bedrooms: 4

Bathrooms: 3

Foundation: Crawl space, slab, or basement

Materials List Available: No

Price Category: D

Images provided by designer/architect.

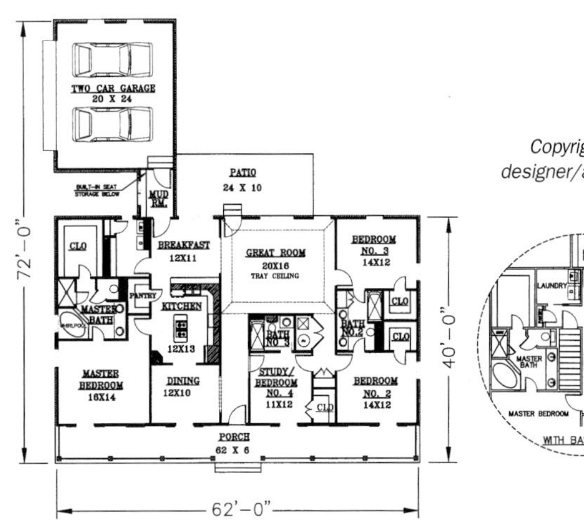

Copyright by designer/architect.

Front View

Plan #121117

Dimensions: 76' W x 46' D

Levels: 1

Heated Square Footage: 2,172

Bedrooms: 4

Bathrooms: 3

Foundation: Basement; crawl space for fee

Materials List Available: Yes

Price Category: D

Images provided by designer/architect.

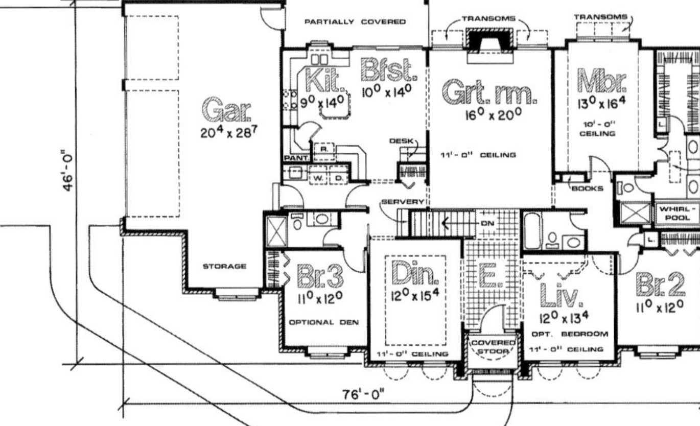

Copyright by designer/architect.

Plan #191009

Dimensions: 62' W x 76' D
Levels: 1
Heated Square Footage: 2,172
Bedrooms: 4
Bathrooms: 2
Foundation: Crawl space, slab
Materials List Available: No
Price Category: D

Images provided by designer/architect.

This charming home is equally attractive in a rural or a settled area, thanks to its classic lines.

Features:

- Porches: Covered front and back porches emphasize the comfort you'll find in this home.
- Great Room: A tray ceiling gives elegance to this spacious room, where everyone is sure to gather. A fireplace makes a nice focal point, and French doors open onto the rear covered porch.
- Dining Room: Arched openings give distinction to this room, where it's easy to serve meals for the family or host a large group.
- Kitchen: You'll love the cooktop island, walk-in pantry, wall oven, snack bar, and view out of the windows in the adjoining breakfast area.
- Master Suite: The large bedroom here gives you space to spread out and relax, and the bath includes a corner whirlpool tub, shower, and dual sinks. An 8-ft. x 10-ft. walk-in closet is off the bath.

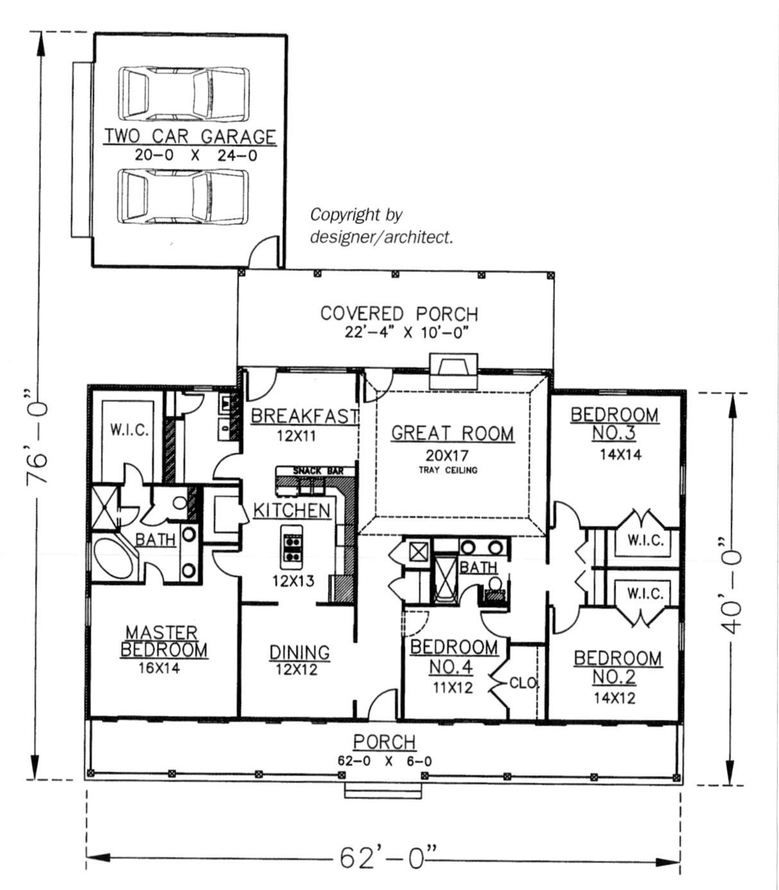

Plan #271076

Dimensions: 69' W x 57' D
Levels: 1
Heated Square Footage: 2,188
Bedrooms: 1
Bathrooms: 1½
Foundation: Walk-out basement
Materials List Available: No
Price Category: D

Images provided by designer/architect.

CAD FILE AVAILABLE

This stunning home, with its optional finished basement plan to add two more bedrooms, would be perfect for your growing family.

Features:

- Great Room: This room with tray ceiling has a fireplace with built-in cabinets on either side.
- Kitchen: This island kitchen, with dinette area, is open to the great room.
- Master Bedroom: This room features a tray ceiling and a view of the backyard.
- Master Bath: This private bath has a walk-in closet and double vanities.

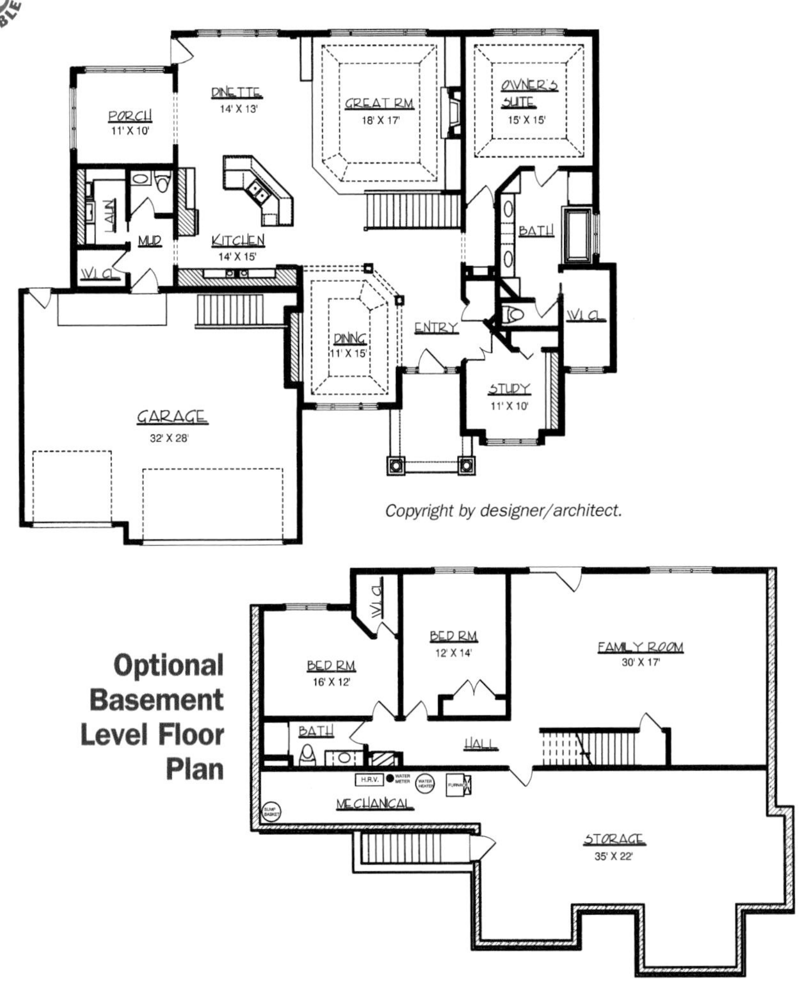

Copyright by designer/architect.

Optional Basement Level Floor Plan

Images provided by designer/architect.

Plan #391138

Dimensions: 76' W x 75' D
Levels: 1
Heated Square Footage: 2,194
Bedrooms: 3
Bathrooms: 2
Foundation: Crawl space or basement
Materials List Available: Yes
Price Category: D

A truly sensational layout! A beautiful brick courtyard and a swimming pool anchor this unusual design.

Features:

- Living Room: This area is the interior highlight of the home. The large, exciting space features a skylight and large windows that flood the room with light.
- Kitchen: This large U-shaped kitchen has a raised bar, which is open to the living room. A pocket door leads to the dining area.
- Master Suite: This private retreat is located in a wing of its own. The suite has access to the rear patio. The master bath features dual vanities and a glass shower.
- Bedrooms: Two bedrooms are located on the opposite side of the home to give those in the master suite privacy. The family room will act as a playroom for the kids.

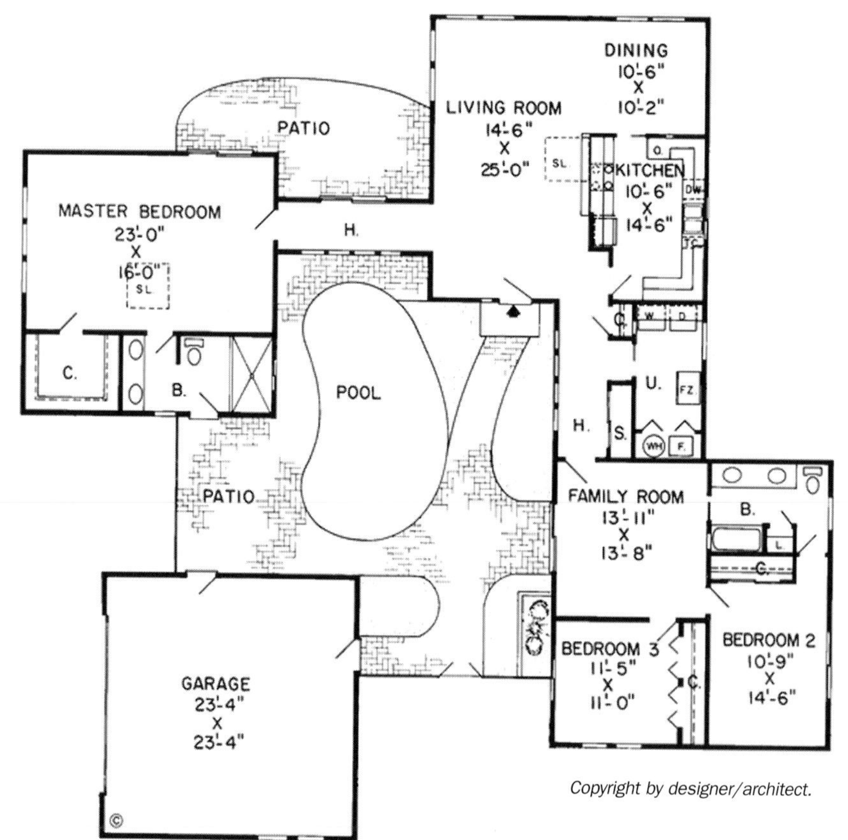

Plan #311015

Dimensions: 72'10" W x 56'6" D
Levels: 1
Heated Square Footage: 2,197
Bedrooms: 3
Bathrooms: 2½
Foundation: Crawl space, slab or basement
Materials List Available: No
Price Category: D

Images provided by designer/architect.

The elegant exterior of this home will enhance any neighborhood.

Features:

- Porches: Two porches, one at the front and one at the back of the home, are wonderful for enjoying fresh air and relaxing.
- Great Room: This beautiful great room has a cathedral ceiling, a fireplace flanked by built-in cabinets, and access to the porch at the rear of the home.
- Kitchen: Surrounded by counter space, you'll always have room to prepare meals in this kitchen. The adjoining breakfast room shares a door to the porch with the great room, which is perfect for meals outside.
- Master Suite: Located away from the busier areas of the home, this master suite features a large bedroom area, two spacious closets, and two vanities.

Copyright by designer/architect.

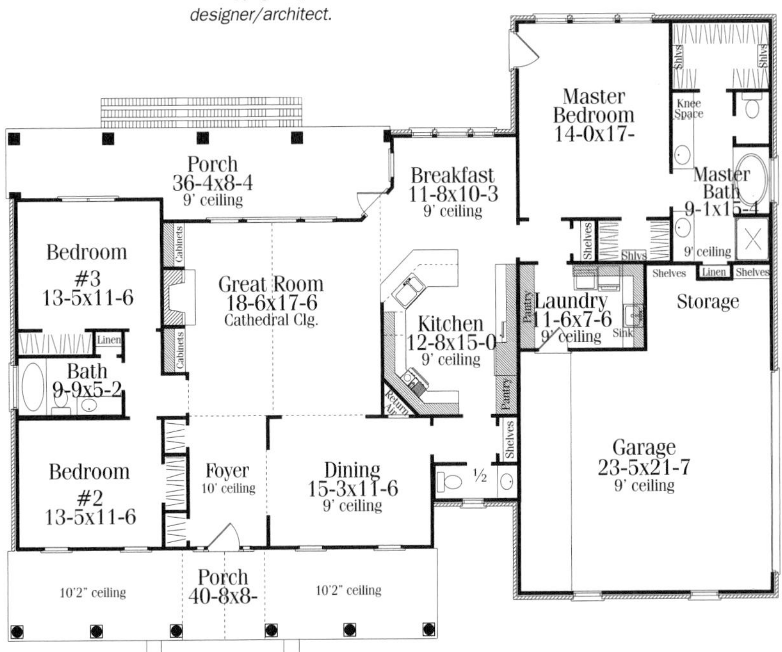

Plan #151113

Dimensions: 62'10" W x 91'4" D
Levels: 1
Heated Square Footage: 2,186
Bedrooms: 4
Bathrooms: 3
Foundation: Crawl space, slab, or basement
CompleteCost List Available: Yes
Price Category: D

Images provided by designer/architect.

CAD FILE AVAILABLE

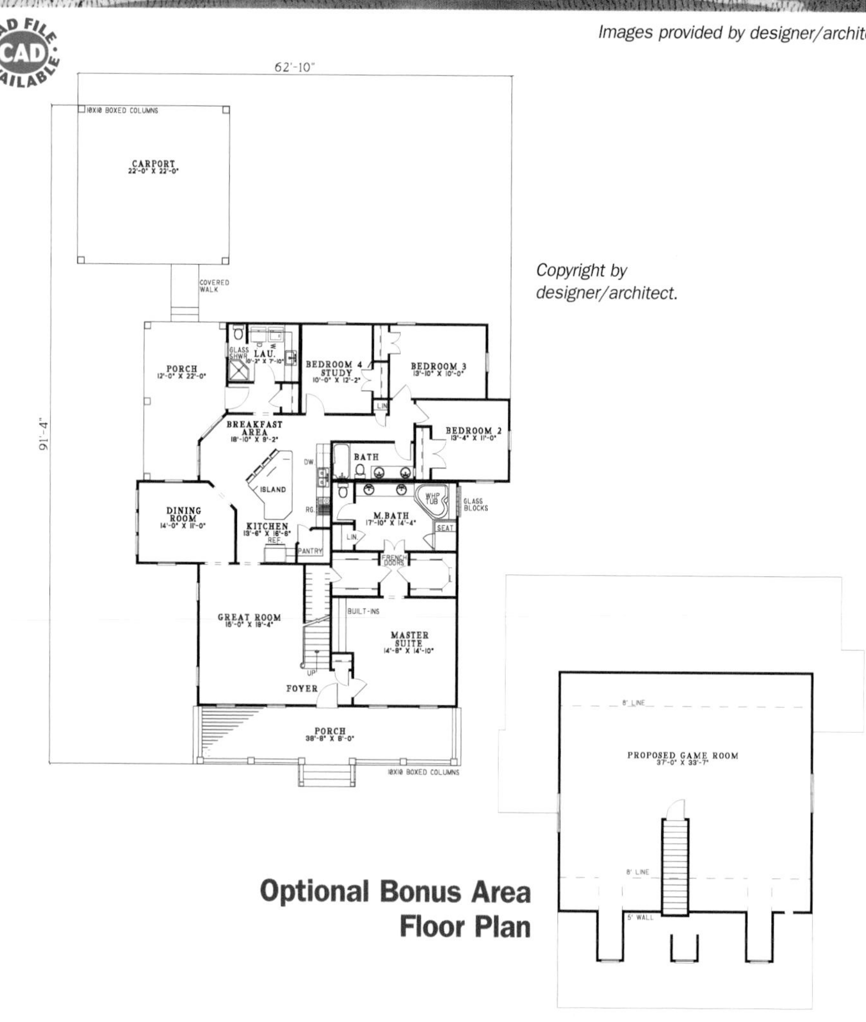

Copyright by designer/architect.

Optional Bonus Area Floor Plan

The porch on this four-bedroom ranch welcomes you home.

Features:

- Great Room: You'll find this large room just off the foyer.
- Dining Room: This room, with a view of the side yard, is located adjacent to the kitchen and the great room.
- Kitchen: This island kitchen, with a built-in pantry, is open to the breakfast area.
- Master Suite: This suite features his and her walk-in closets and a private bathroom with double vanities and whirlpool tub.
- Bedrooms: Three secondary bedrooms have large closets and share a hall bathroom.

Plan #131019

Dimensions: 83'6" W x 53'4" D
Levels: 1
Heated Square Footage: 2,243
Bedrooms: 3
Bathrooms: 2½
Foundation: Crawl space, slab, or basement
Materials List Available: Yes
Price Category: F

Images provided by designer/architect.

Drama marks this contemporary, angled ranch-style home which can be placed to suit any site, even the most difficult.

CAD FILE AVAILABLE

Features:

- Great Room: Imagine having an octagonal great room! The shape alone makes it spectacular, but the view to the backyard from its four exterior sides adds to the impression it creates, and you'll love its 16-ft. tray ceiling, fireplace, and wall designed to fit a large entertainment center.
- Kitchen: This room is adjacent to and visually connected to the great room but has excellent features of its own that make it an easy place to cook or clean.
- Master Suite: Separated from the other bedrooms, this suite is planned for privacy. You'll love the bath here and look forward to the quiet you can find at the end of the day.
- Additional Bedrooms: In a wing of their own, the other two bedrooms share a bath.

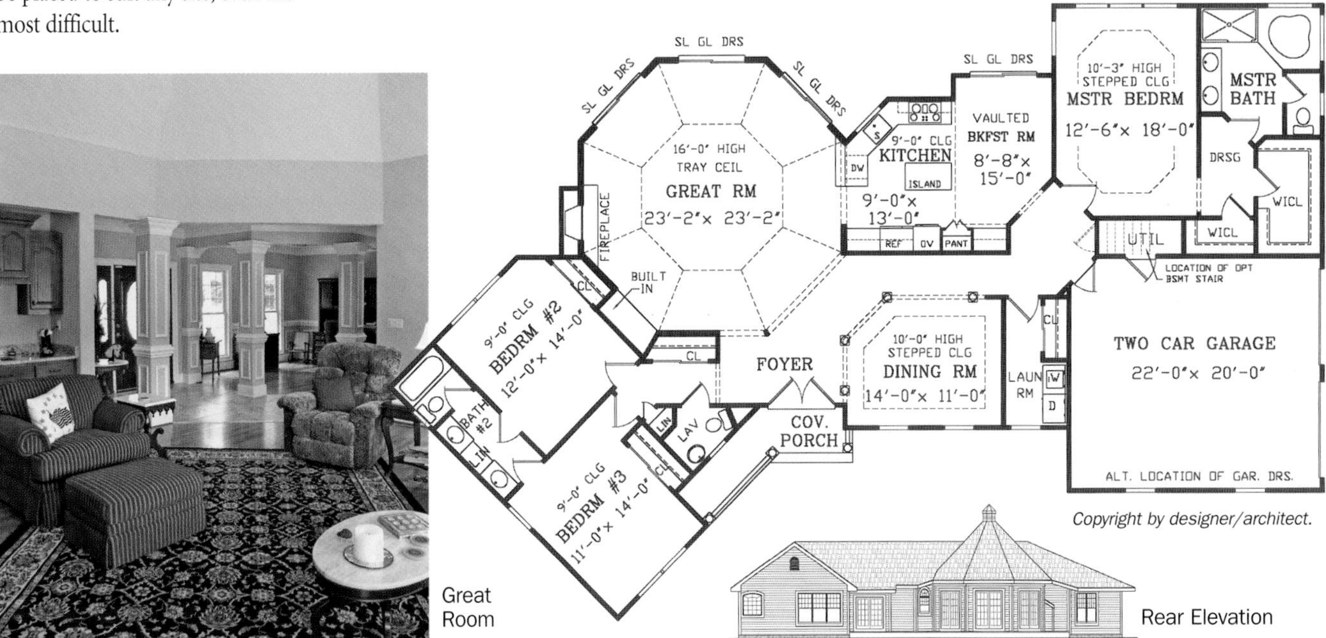

Great Room

Copyright by designer/architect.

Rear Elevation

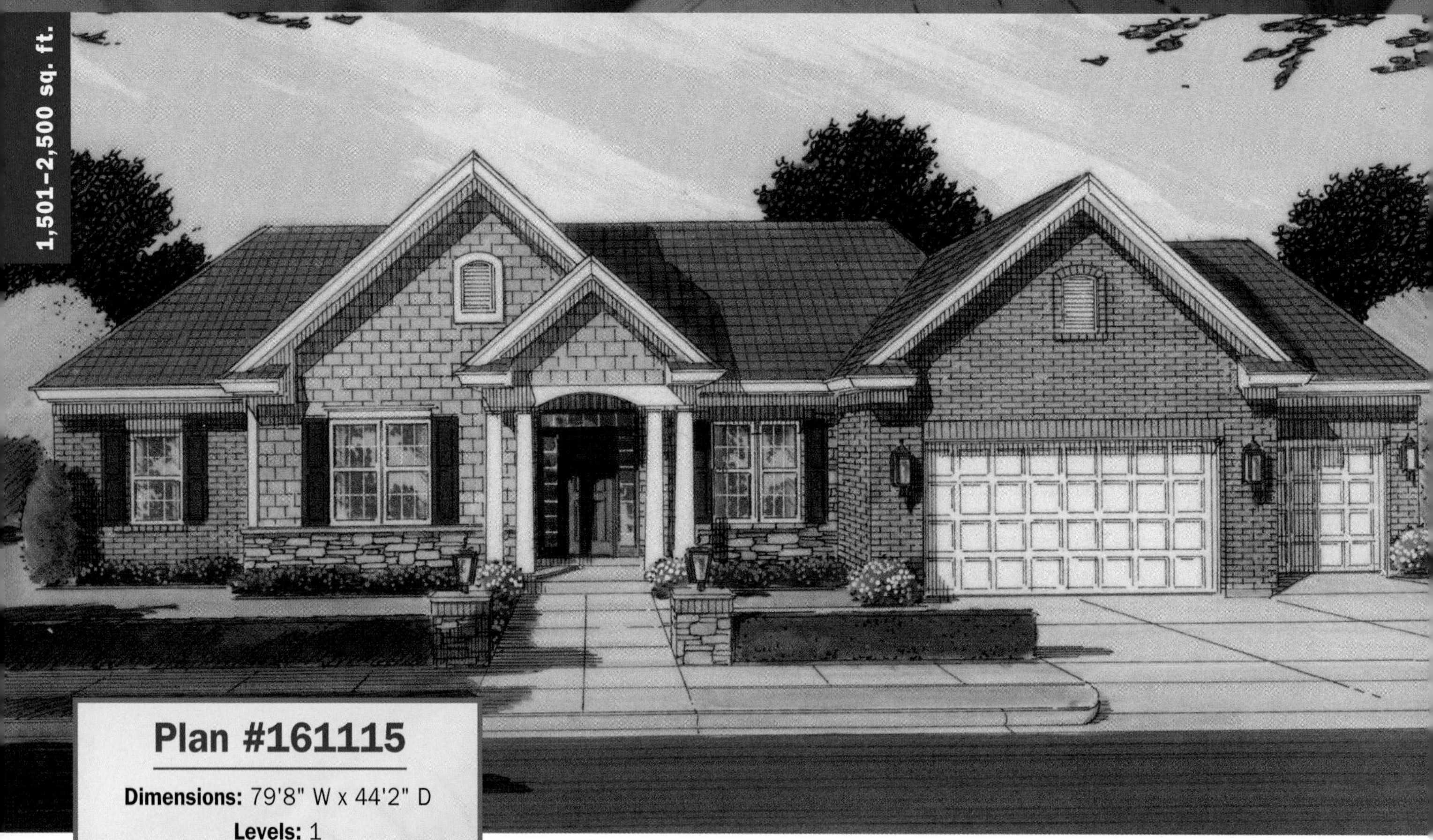

Plan #161115

Dimensions: 79'8" W x 44'2" D
Levels: 1
Heated Square Footage: 2,253
Bedrooms: 4
Bathrooms: 3
Foundation: Walkout basement
Materials List Available: Yes
Price Category: E

Images provided by designer/architect.

This one-level home offers a beautiful exterior of brick and stone with shake siding.

Features:

- Great Room: This open gathering area features an 11-foot-high ceiling and access to the rear yard. Turn on the corner gas fireplace, and fill the room with warmth and charm.
- Kitchen: This peninsula kitchen with built-in pantry and counter seating offers easy access to both formal and informal dining. The laundry facilities and the garage are just a few steps away. A magnificent bay window decorates the breakfast room and brings natural light into the area.
- Master Suite: This retreat offers a furniture alcove in the sleeping area and a walk-in closet. The private bath features a double-bowl vanity and a whirlpool tub.
- Guest Suite: This private bedroom suite is located behind the three-car garage and offers a welcoming environment for your overnight guests.
- Basement: This full walkout basement expands the living space of the delightful home.

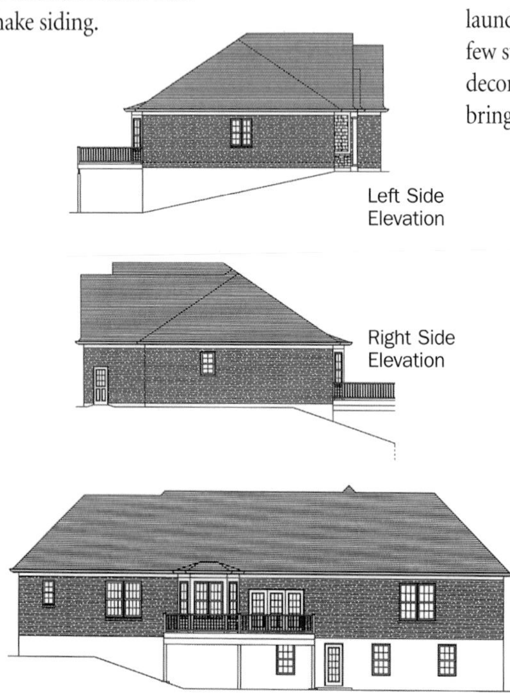

Left Side Elevation

Right Side Elevation

Copyright by designer/architect.

Rear Elevation

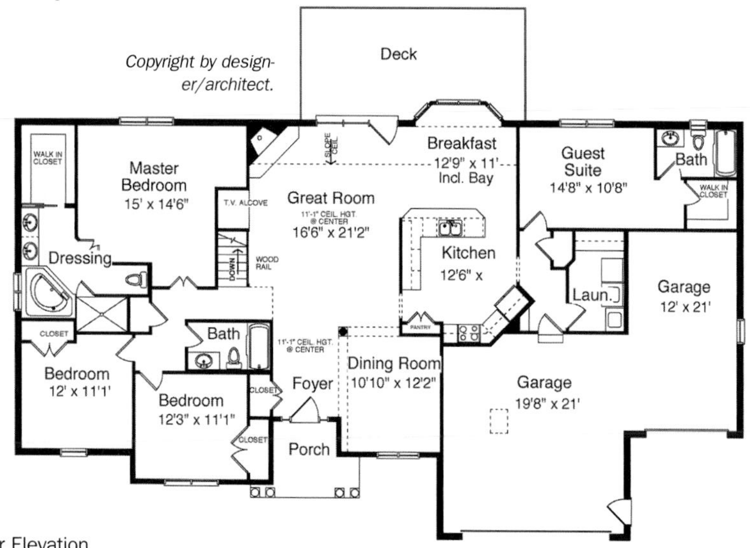

Plan #171004

Dimensions: 72' W x 52' D
Levels: 1
Heated Square Footage: 2,256
Bedrooms: 3
Bathrooms: 2
Foundation: Crawl space, slab
Materials List Available: Yes
Price Category: E

Images provided by designer/architect.

This home greets you with a front porch featuring a high roofline and stucco columns.

Features:

- Ceiling Height: 9 ft. unless otherwise noted.
- Foyer: Step through the front porch into this impressive foyer, which opens to the formal dining room and the study.
- Dining Room: This dining room's 12-ft. ceiling enhances its sense of spaciousness, with plenty of room for large dinner parties.
- Family Room: With plenty of room for all kinds of family activities, this room also has a 12-ft. ceiling, a fireplace, and two paddle fans.
- Kitchen: This kitchen has all the counter space you'll need to prepare your favorite recipes. There's a pantry, desk, and angled snack bar.
- Master Bedroom: This master retreat is separate from the other bedrooms for added privacy. It has an elegant, high step-up ceiling and a paddle fan.
- Master Bath: This master bath features a large walk-in closet, deluxe corner bath, walk-in shower, and his and her vanities.

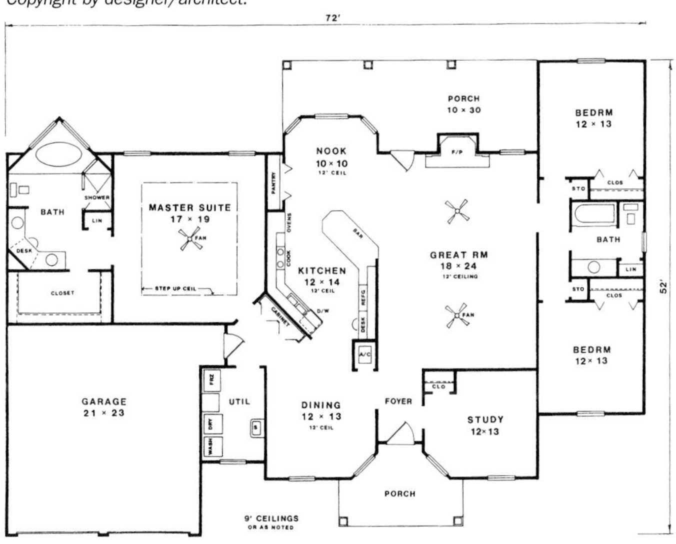

SMARTtip

Windows – Privacy

You can easily stencil a work of art onto a windowpane, perhaps only as a border around the edge. Choose or create a design that gives you as little or as much privacy and light control as you need. Use a ready-made stencil or a piece of openwork fabric such as lace, or mask a design onto the glass using tape and a razor knife. Then apply glass paint or frosted glass spray, referring to the instructions and guidelines that come with the product.

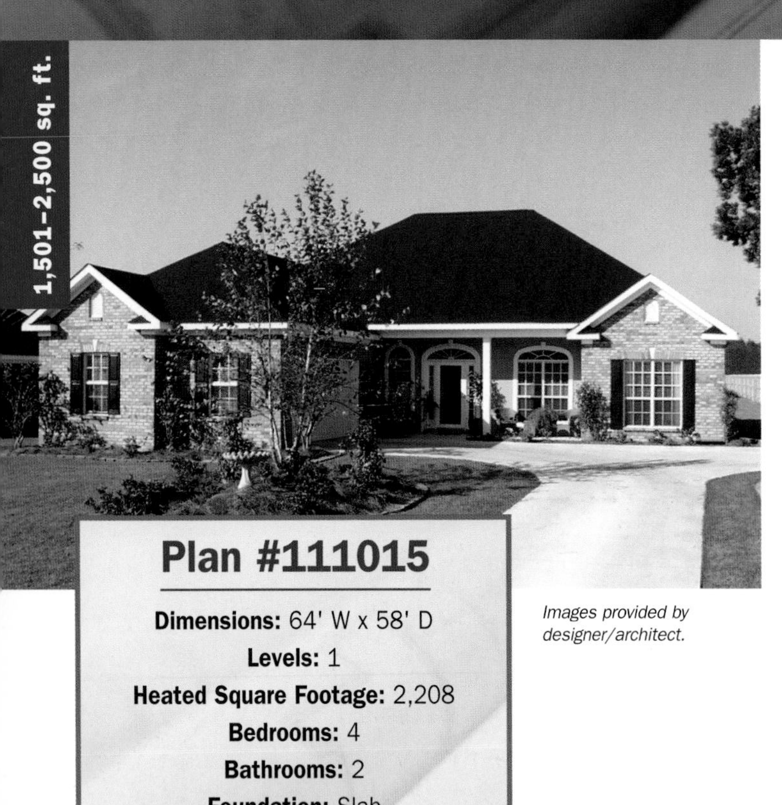

Plan #111015

Dimensions: 64' W x 58' D
Levels: 1
Heated Square Footage: 2,208
Bedrooms: 4
Bathrooms: 2
Foundation: Slab
Materials List Available: No
Price Category: F

Images provided by designer/architect.

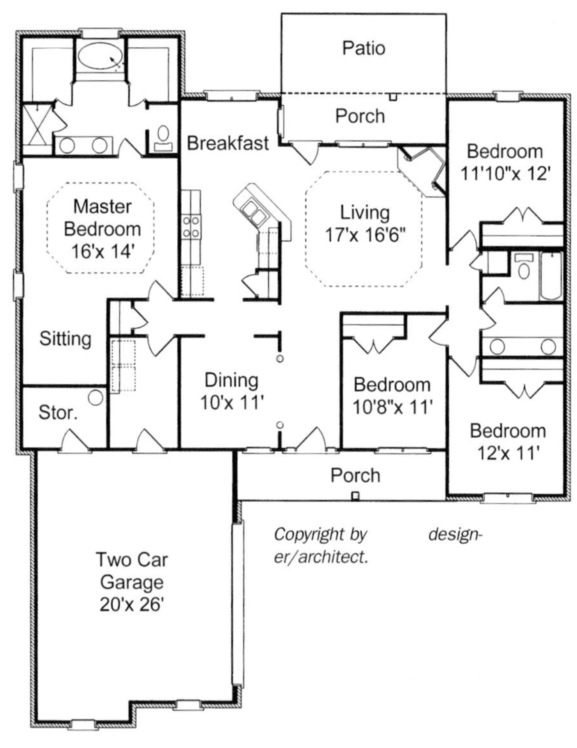

Copyright by designer/architect.

Plan #121034

Dimensions: 92'8" W x 59'4" D
Levels: 1
Heated Square Footage: 2,223
Bedrooms: 1
Bathrooms: 2½
Foundation: Basement; crawl space for fee
Materials List Available: Yes
Price Category: E

Images provided by designer/architect.

CAD FILE AVAILABLE

Covered Deck
Eating Area
Hearth Room
Great Room
Mbr.
Workshop
Dining Room
Garage
Covered Stoop
Flex Room
59'-4"
92'-8"

Copyright by designer/architect.

Optional Basement Level Floor Plan

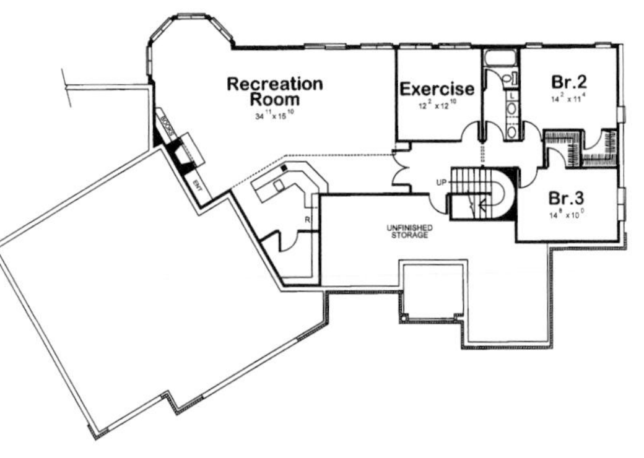

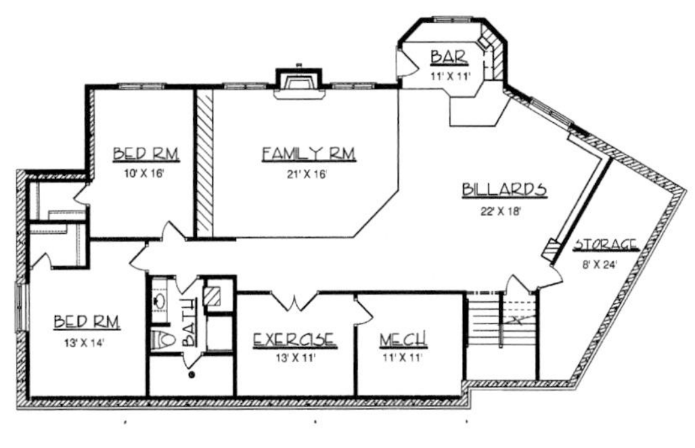

Optional Basement Level Floor Plan

Plan #271079

Dimensions: 104' W x 55' D
Levels: 1
Heated Square Footage: 2,228
Bedrooms: 1-3
Bathrooms: 1½
Foundation: Daylight basement
Materials List Available: No
Price Category: E

Images provided by designer/architect.

CAD FILE AVAILABLE

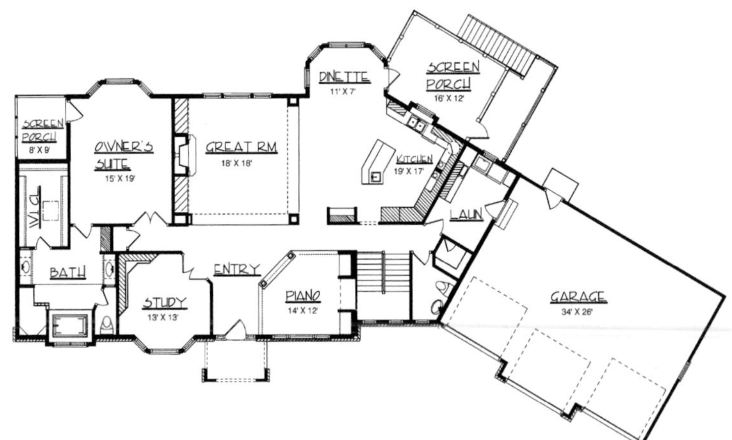

Copyright by designer/architect.

Plan #371059

Dimensions: 77'8" W x 56'6" D
Levels: 1
Heated Square Footage: 2,240
Bedrooms: 4
Bathrooms: 2½
Foundation: Slab; crawl space for fee
Materials List Available: No
Price Category: E

Images provided by designer/architect.

CAD FILE AVAILABLE

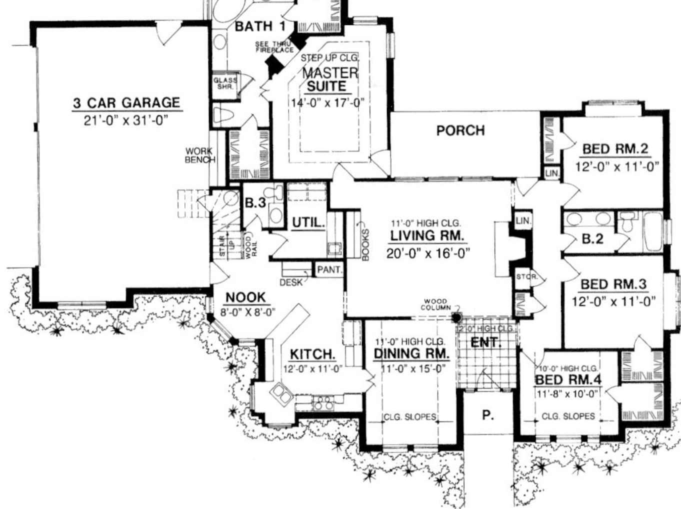

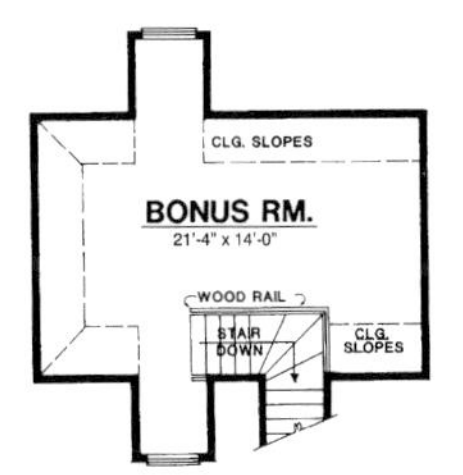

Bonus Area Floor Plan

Copyright by designer/architect.

Plan #161249

Dimensions: 80'2" W x 51'8" D
Levels: 1
Heated Square Footage: 2,246
Bedrooms: 3
Bathrooms: 2
Foundation: Basement; crawl space, slab or walkout for fee
Materials List Available: Yes
Price Category: E

Images provided by designer/architect.

CAD FILE AVAILABLE

Copyright by designer/architect.

Plan #351007

Dimensions: 73'8" W x 53'2" D
Levels: 1
Heated Square Footage: 2,251
Bedrooms: 3
Bathrooms: 2½
Foundation: Crawl space, slab, or basement
Materials List Available: Yes
Price Category: F

Images provided by designer/architect.

CAD FILE AVAILABLE

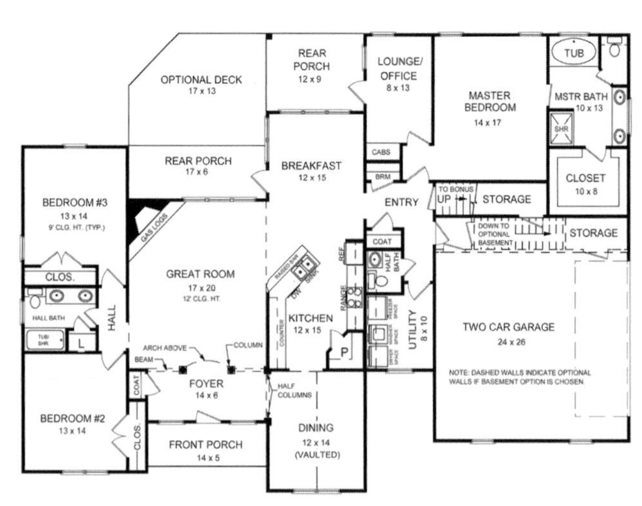

Bonus Area Floor Plan

Copyright by designer/architect.

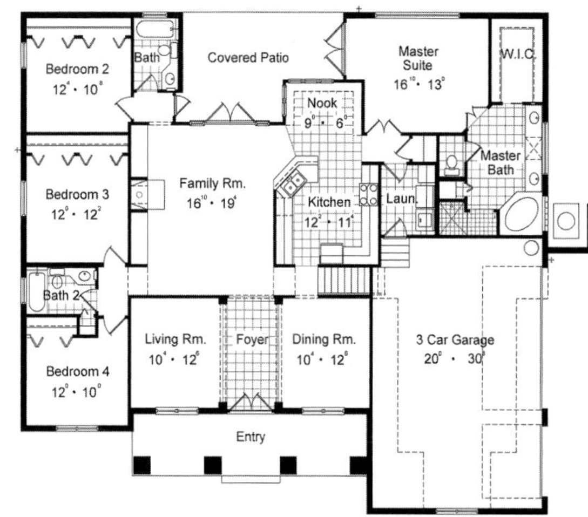

Plan #661160

Dimensions: 62'4" W x 57' D
Levels: 1
Heated Square Footage: 2,258
Bedrooms: 4
Bathrooms: 3
Foundation: Slab
Materials List Available: No
Price Category: F

Images provided by designer/architect.

CAD FILE AVAILABLE

Bonus Area Floor Plan

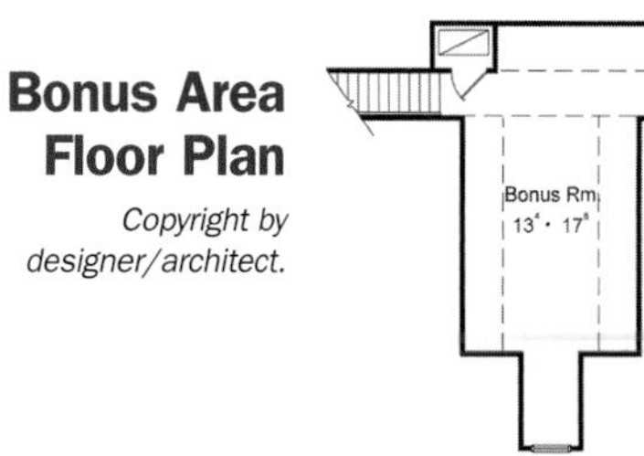

Copyright by designer/architect.

Plan #101033

Dimensions: 62' W x 69'2" D
Levels: 1
Heated Square Footage: 2,260
Bedrooms: 3
Bathrooms: 3
Foundation: Basement
Materials List Available: No
Price Category: E

Images provided by designer/architect.

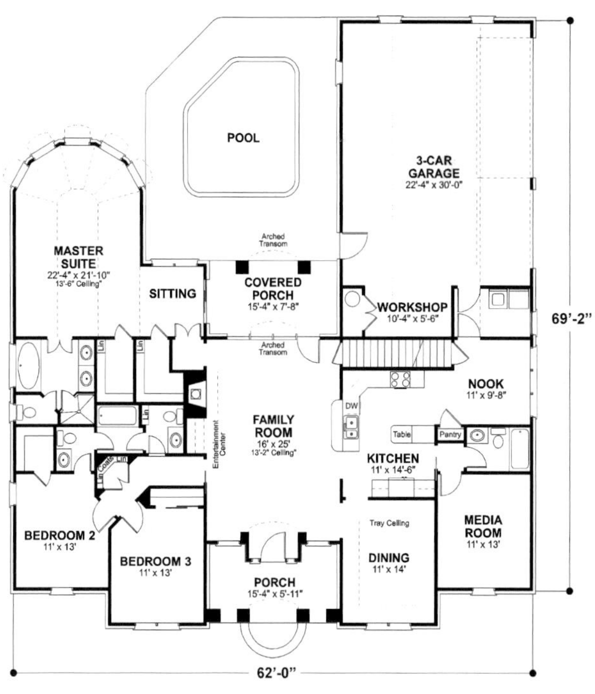

Copyright by designer/architect.

Plan #311007

Dimensions: 71'2" W x 62' D
Levels: 1
Heated Square Footage: 2,267
Bedrooms: 4
Bathrooms: 2½
Foundation: Crawl space, slab or basement
Materials List Available: Yes
Price Category: E

Images provided by designer/architect.

Master Bedroom 13-0x20-2
M.Bath
Porch 20-3x8-0
Breakfast 10-2x11-8
Laun. 5-6x7-5
Stor.
Bedroom 11-9x13-5
Greatroom 15-9x17-5
Kitchen 12-6x13-9
Garage 21-6x21-6
Bedroom 11-6x11-6
Bedroom 11-6x11-6
Foyer
Dining 13-5x11-6
Porch 33-9x8-0

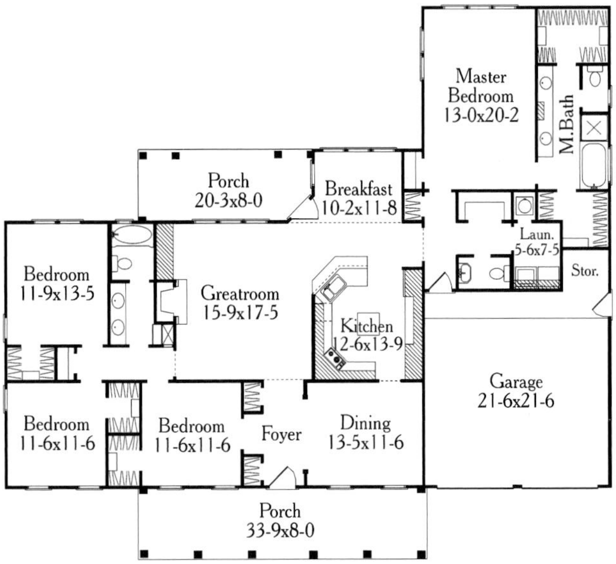

Basement Stair Location

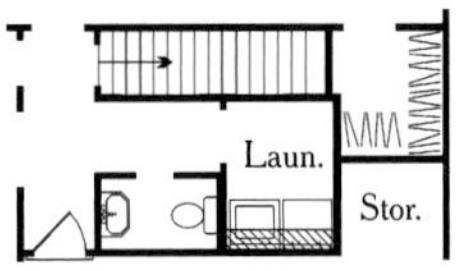

Laun.
Stor.

Plan #121116

Dimensions: 72' W x 56' D
Levels: 1
Heated Square Footage: 2,276
Bedrooms: 3
Bathrooms: 2½
Foundation: Basement; crawl space for fee
Materials List Available: Yes
Price Category: E

Images provided by designer/architect.

Transoms
Bfst. 13⁰ x 11⁰
Transoms
Mbr. 13⁰ x 15⁵
Grt. rm. 16⁰ x 19⁸
9'-4" ceilings
Desk
Wet bar
Snack bar
Br. 2 12⁰ x 11⁰
Kit. 13⁰ x 10⁵
Dresser/Ent. center
DN
Br. 3 12⁰ x 11⁶
Whirlpool
Glass block
Din. 13⁰ x 13⁷
10'-8" ceiling
Den 13³ x 13³
10'-8" ceiling
E.
Covered stoop
Transoms
Transoms
Gar. 31³ x 23⁸
56'-0"
72'-0"

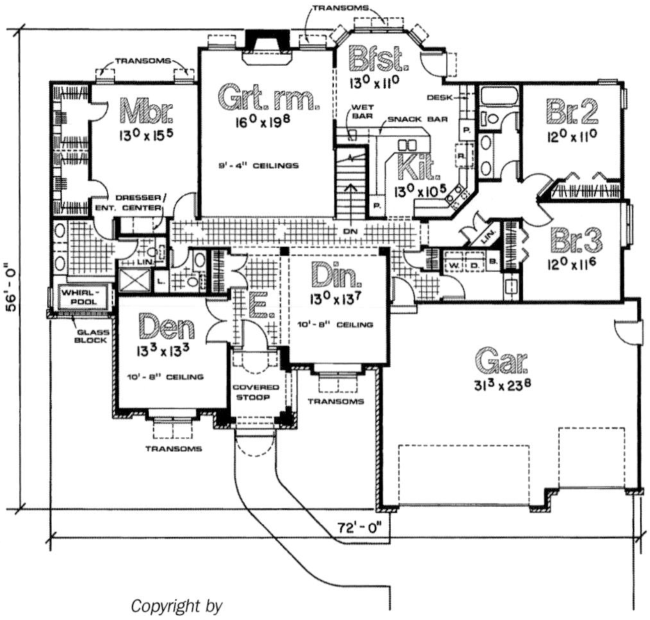

Copyright by designer/architect.

Plan #151634

Dimensions: 70' W x 73'8" D
Levels: 1
Heated Square Footage: 2,285
Bedrooms: 4
Bathrooms: 2
Foundation: Crawl space or slab
CompleteCost List Available: Yes
Price Category: E

Images provided by designer/architect.

CAD FILE AVAILABLE

Copyright by designer/architect.

Plan #311030

Dimensions: 76'10" W x 55'6" D
Levels: 1
Heated Square Footage: 2,286
Main Level Sq. Ft.: 2,286
Opt. Bonus Sq. Ft.: 443
Bedrooms: 3
Bathrooms: 2½
Foundation: Basement, crawl space, or slab
Materials List Available: Yes
Price Category: E

Images provided by designer/architect.

Rear View

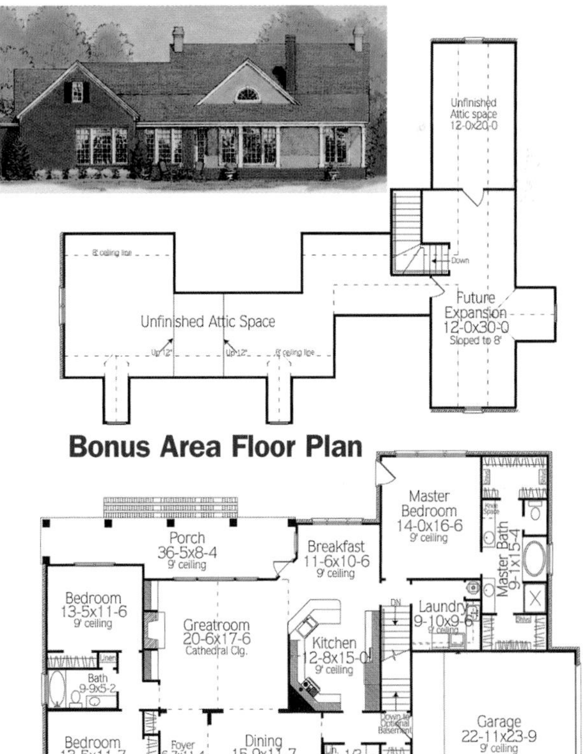

Copyright by designer/architect.

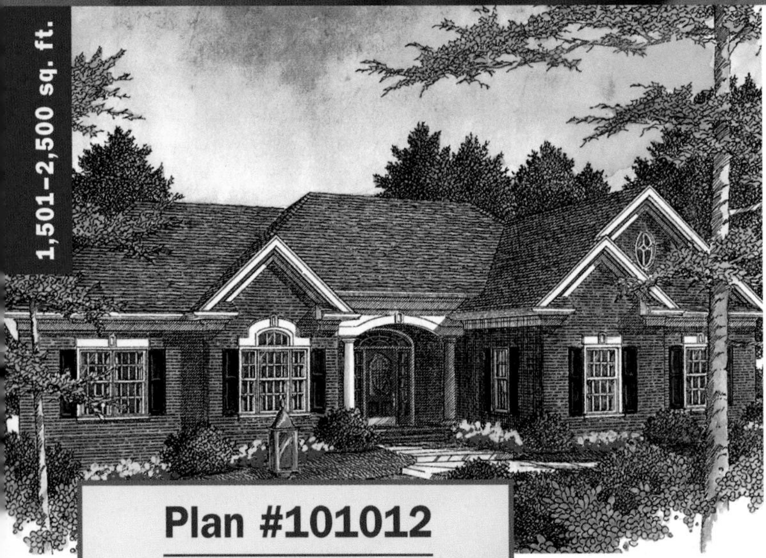

Plan #101012

Dimensions: 69'4" W x 62'9" D
Levels: 1
Heated Square Footage: 2,288
Bedrooms: 3
Bathrooms: 2½
Foundation: Crawl space, slab, basement, or walkout
Materials List Available: No
Price Category: E

Images provided by designer/architect.

CAD FILE AVAILABLE

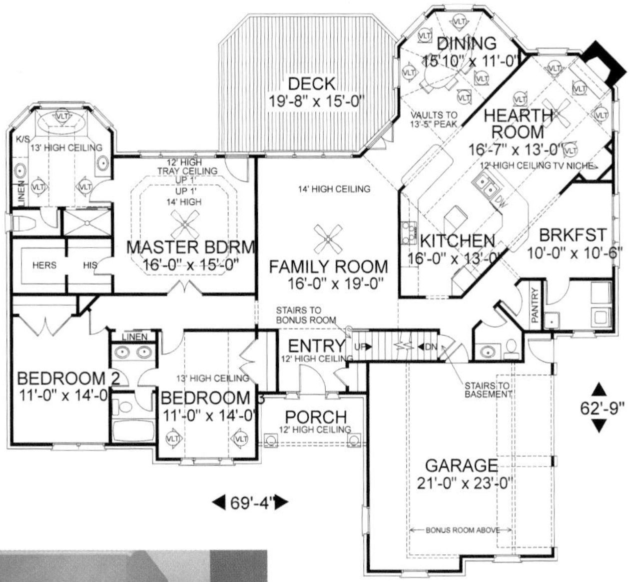

DECK 19'-8" x 15'-0"
DINING 15'10" x 11'-0"
HEARTH ROOM 16'-7" x 13'-0"
MASTER BDRM 16'-0" x 15'-0"
FAMILY ROOM 16'-0" x 19'-0"
KITCHEN 16'-0" x 13'-0"
BRKFST 10'-0" x 10'-6"
ENTRY
BEDROOM 2 11'-0" x 14'-0"
BEDROOM 3 11'-0" x 14'-0"
PORCH
GARAGE 21'-0" x 23'-0"
69'-4"
62'-9"

Copyright by designer/architect.

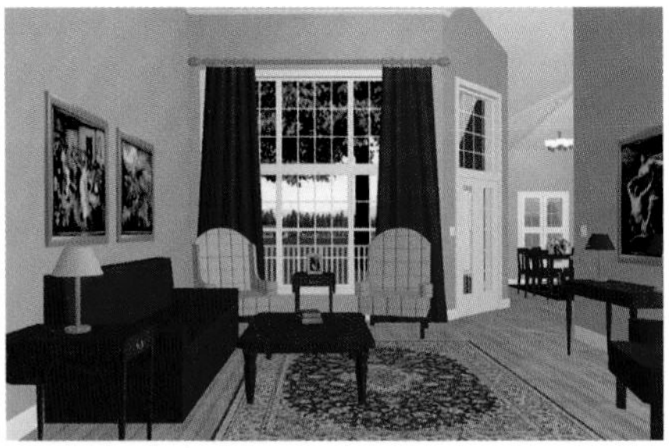

Living Room

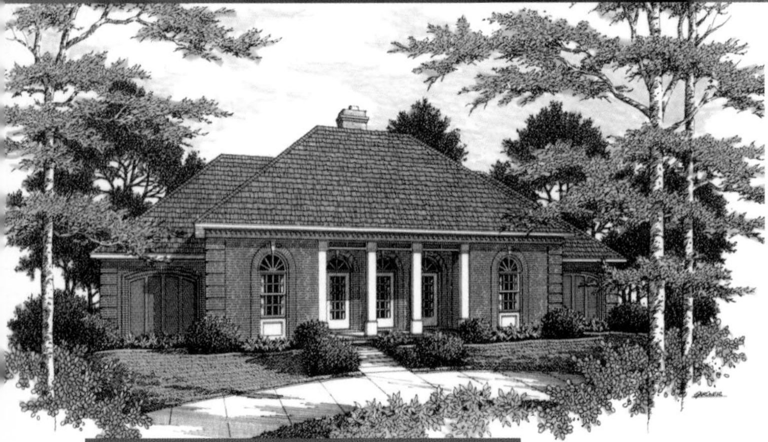

Plan #211059

Dimensions: 68' W x 84' D
Levels: 1
Heated Square Footage: 2,299
Bedrooms: 3
Bathrooms: 2
Foundation: Slab or basement
Materials List Available: No
Price Category: E

Images provided by designer/architect.

CAD FILE AVAILABLE

sto 18 x 6
garage 22 x 22
porch 20 x 8
dinette
study / home off 16 x 13
sun rm 16 x 10
kit
living 20 x 20
br 3 12 x 12
br 2 12 x 12
foy
dining 13 x 12
mbr 22 x 13
porch 20 x 6

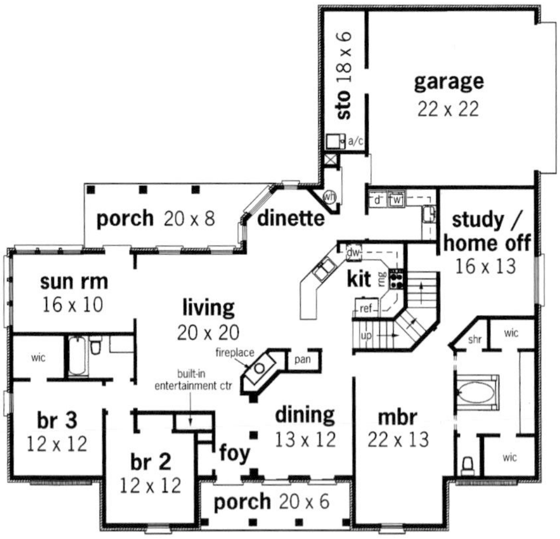

Bonus Area Floor Plan

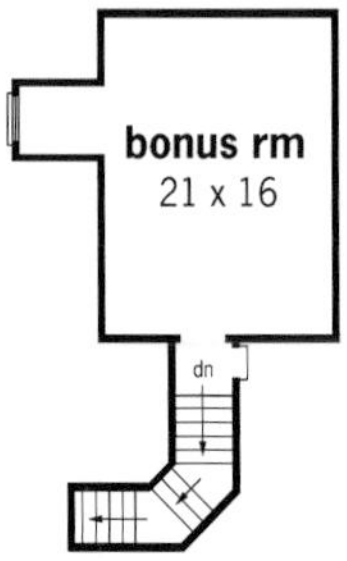

Copyright by designer/architect.

bonus rm 21 x 16

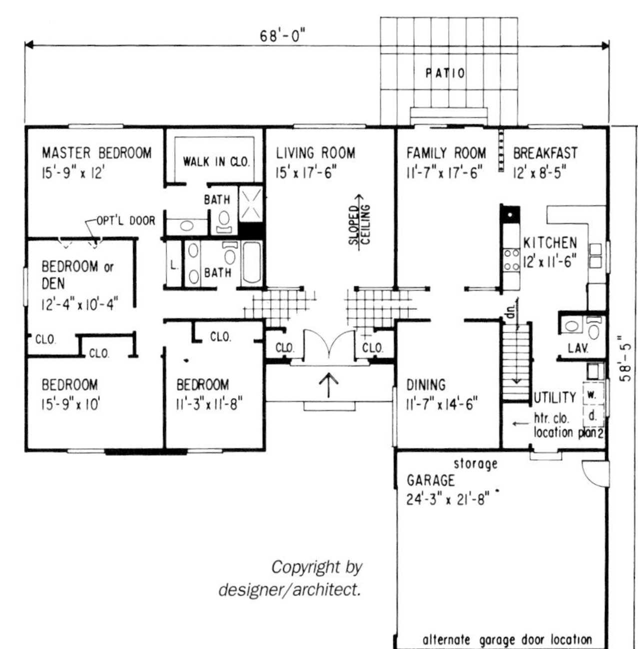

Plan #321371

Dimensions: 68' W x 58'5" D
Levels: 1
Heated Square Footage: 2,305
Bedrooms: 4
Bathrooms: 2½
Foundation: Crawl space, slab or basement
Materials List Available: Yes
Price Category: E

Images provided by designer/architect.

CAD FILE AVAILABLE

Copyright by designer/architect.

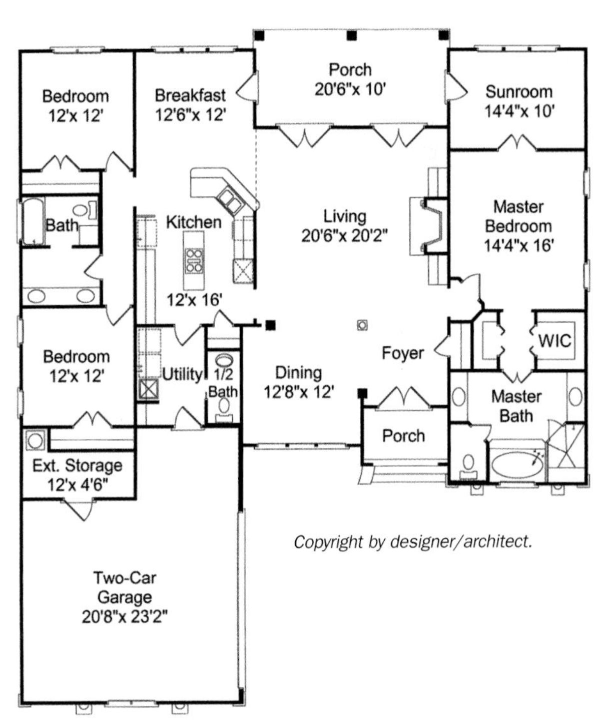

Plan #111017

Dimensions: 61' W x 70' D
Levels: 1
Heated Square Footage: 2,323
Bedrooms: 3
Bathrooms: 2½
Foundation: Monolithic slab
Materials List Available: No
Price Category: F

Images provided by designer/architect.

Copyright by designer/architect.

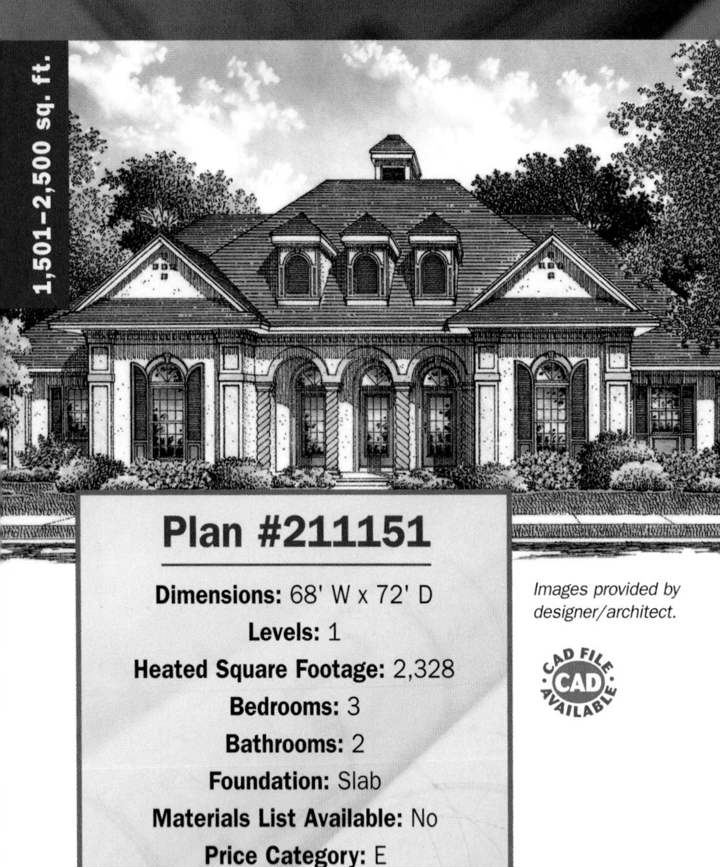

Plan #211151

Dimensions: 68' W x 72' D
Levels: 1
Heated Square Footage: 2,328
Bedrooms: 3
Bathrooms: 2
Foundation: Slab
Materials List Available: No
Price Category: E

Images provided by designer/architect.

CAD FILE AVAILABLE

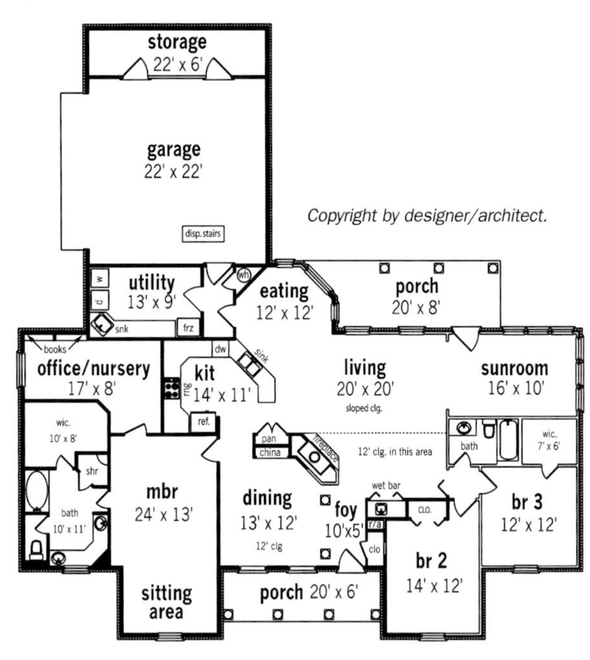

Copyright by designer/architect.

Plan #131045

Dimensions: 81'4" W x 68'3" D
Levels: 1
Heated Square Footage: 2,347
Bedrooms: 4
Bathrooms: 2½
Foundation: Crawl space, slab, or basement
Materials List Available: Yes
Price Category: F

Images provided by designer/architect.

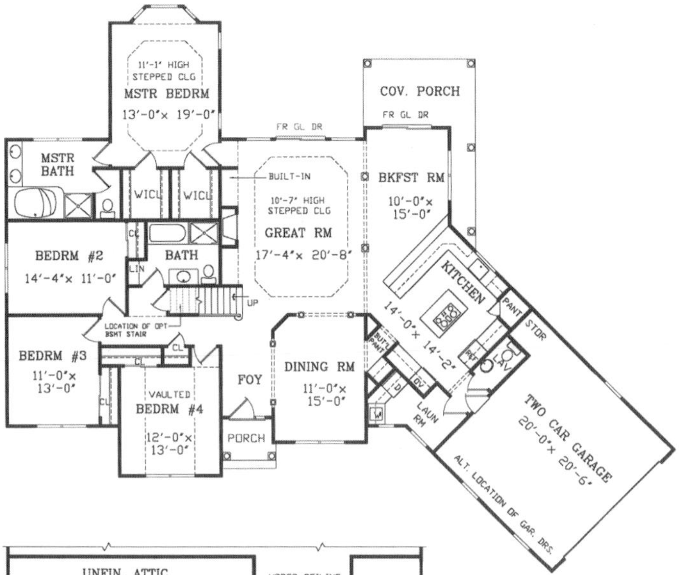

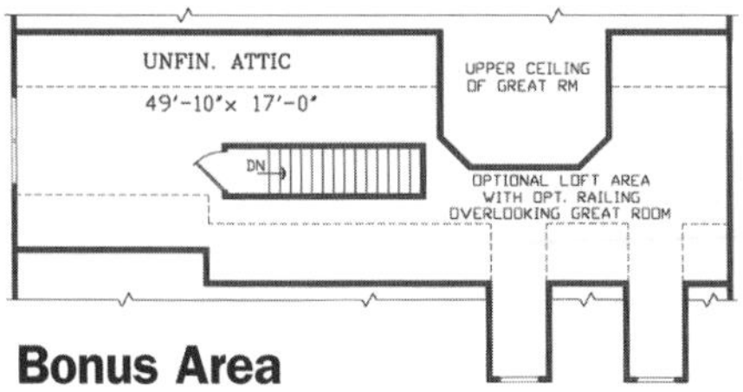

Bonus Area Floor Plan

Copyright by designer/architect.

Plan #191027

Dimensions: 62' W x 42' D
Levels: 1
Heated Square Footage: 2,354
Bedrooms: 4
Bathrooms: 2½
Foundation: Crawl space or slab
Materials List Available: No
Price Category: E

Images provided by designer/architect.

42'-0"

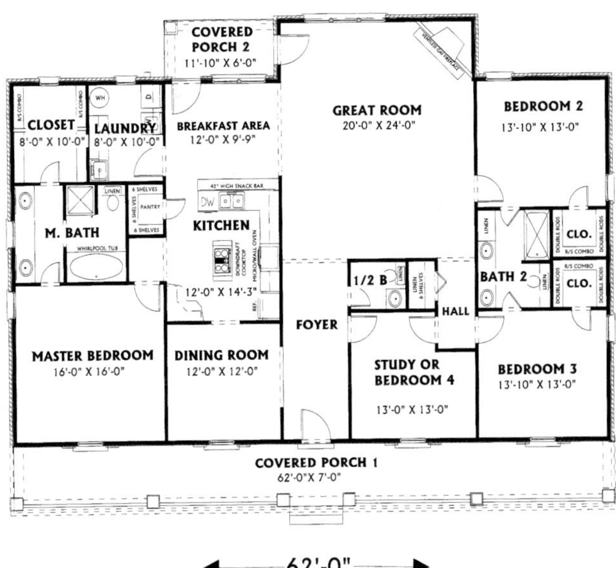

62'-0"

Copyright by designer/architect.

Plan #311022

Dimensions: 73'1" W x 58'6" D
Levels: 1
Square Footage: 2,373
Heated Main Level Sq. Ft.: 2,373
Opt. Bonus Sq. Ft. 1,178
Bedrooms: 3
Bathrooms: 2½
Foundation: Basement, crawl space, or slab
Materials List Available: Yes
Price Category: E

Images provided by designer/architect.

Rear View

Stair Location

Main Level Floor Plan

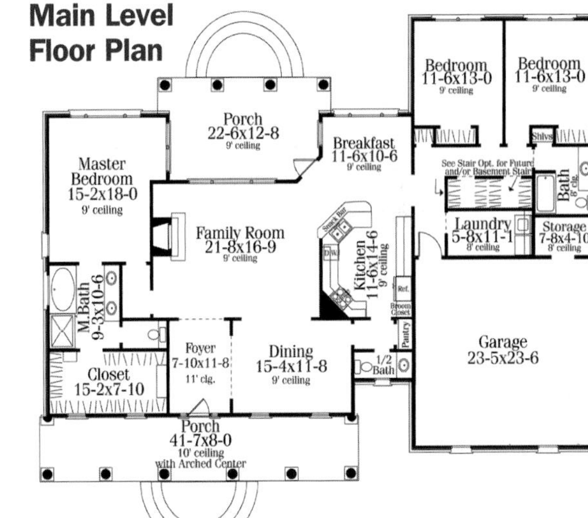

Bonus Area Floor Plan

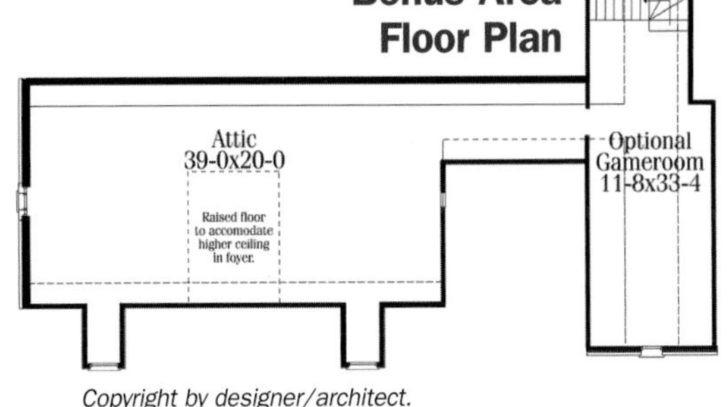

Copyright by designer/architect.

Images provided by designer/architect.

Plan #241001

Dimensions: 65' W x 56'3" D
Levels: 1
Heated Square Footage: 2,350
Bedrooms: 3
Bathrooms: 2½
Foundation: Slab
Materials List Available: No
Price Category: E

Classic, traditional rooflines combine with arched windows to draw immediate attention to this lovely three-bedroom home.

Features:

- Great Room: The foyer introduces you to this impressive great room, with its grand 10-ft. ceiling and handsome fireplace.
- Kitchen: Certain to become the hub of such a family-oriented home, this spacious kitchen, which adjoins the breakfast area and a delightful sunroom, features an abundance of counter space, a pantry, and a convenient eating bar.
- Master Suite: You will enjoy the privacy and comfort of this master suite, which features a whirlpool tub, split vanities, and a separate shower.
- Study: Adjourn to the front of the house, and enjoy the quiet confines of this private study with built-in bookshelves to work, read, or just relax.

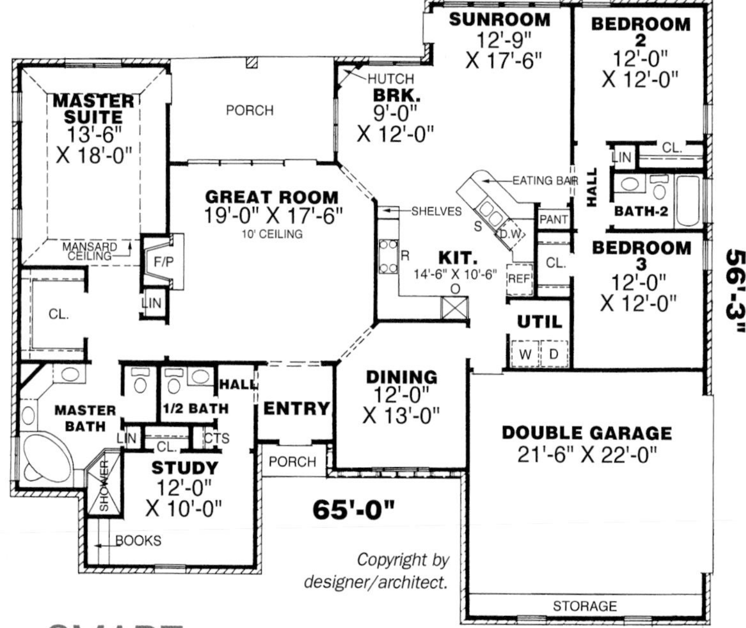

Copyright by designer/architect.

SMARTtip

Kitchen Counters

Make use of counter inserts to help with the cooking chores. For example, ceramic tiles inlaid in a laminate counter create a heat-proof landing zone near the range. A marble or granite insert is tailor-made for pastry chefs. And a butcher-block inlay is a great addition to the food prep area.

Images provided by designer/architect.

Plan #131052

Dimensions: 67' W x 63'10" D
Levels: 1
Heated Square Footage: 2,367
Bedrooms: 2
Bathrooms: 2
Foundation: Crawl space, slab, or basement
Materials List Available: Yes
Price Category: E

The front and back turrets, in combination with the vaulted ceilings and unusually shaped rooms, make this house a treasure.

Features:

- Covered Porch: The circular covered front porch is an endlessly versatile area.
- Dining Room: The shape of this room echoes that of the front porch. Windows let in plenty of light; the ceiling is vaulted; and columns separate the room from the Great Room.
- Great Room: A fireplace, door to the patio, and vaulted ceiling highlight this spacious room.
- Library: Use this room, with its deep bay, as a third bedroom, or turn it into a den or media room.
- Kitchen: The center island and U-shaped counter make this a convenient work space.
- Master Suite: You'll love the turreted sitting room, tray ceiling, two walk-in closets, whirlpool tub, separate shower, and two vanities here.

Copyright by designer/architect.

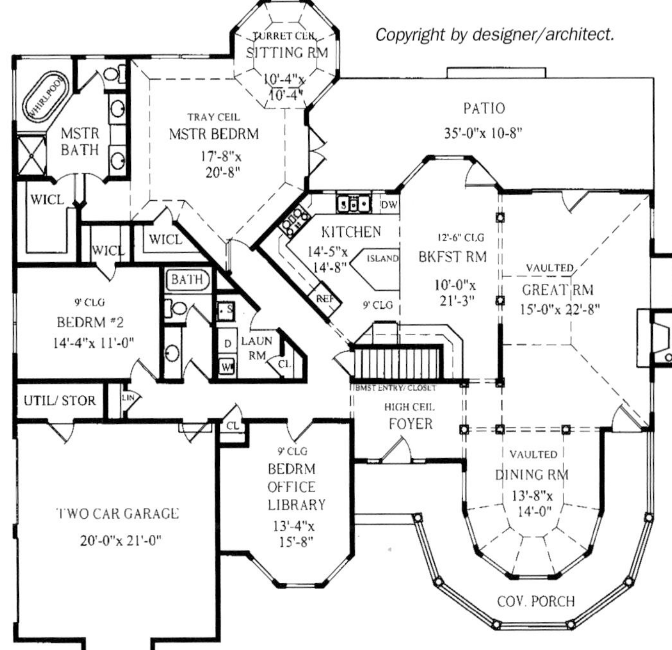

Plan #211009

Dimensions: 72' W x 60' D
Levels: 1
Heated Square Footage: 2,396
Bedrooms: 4
Bathrooms: 2
Foundation: Slab
Materials List Available: Yes
Price Category: E

Images provided by designer/architect.

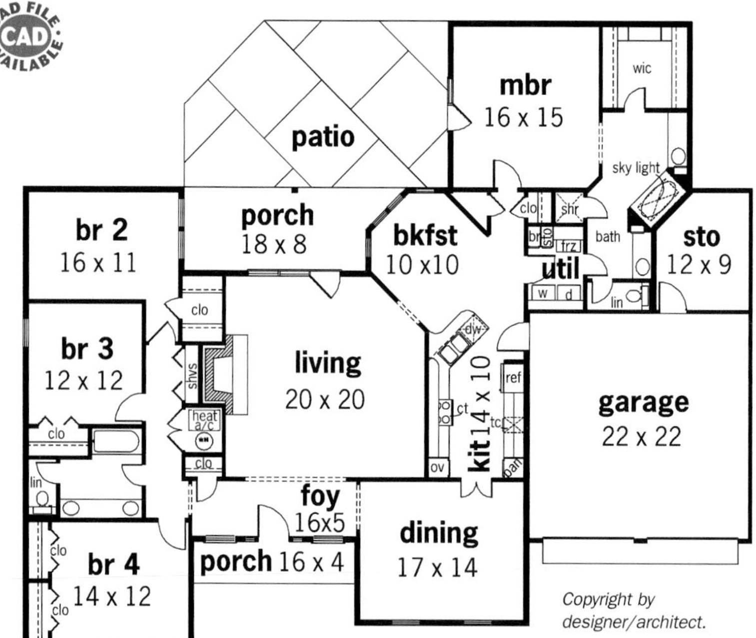

Copyright by designer/architect.

Beautiful arched windows lend a luxurious feeling to the exterior of this one-story home.

Features:

- Ceiling Height: 9 ft. unless otherwise noted.
- Entry: Guests will be greeted by a dramatic 12-ft. ceiling in this elegant foyer.
- Living Room: The 12-ft. ceiling continues through the foyer into this inviting living room. Everyone will feel welcomed by the crackling fire in the handsome fireplace.
- Covered Porch: When the weather is warm, invite guests to step out of the living room directly into this covered porch.
- Kitchen: This bright and cheery kitchen is designed for the way we live today. It includes a pantry and an angled eating bar that will see plenty of impromptu family meals.
- Energy-Efficient Walls: All the outside walls are framed with 2x6 lumber instead of 2x4. The extra thickness makes room for more insulation to lower your heating and cooling bills.

SMARTtip

Ornaments in a Garden

Placement is everything with ornaments in a garden. Some elements are best sitting by themselves. Others are better when they are part of a cohesive whole, perhaps placed in the greenery at a corner or flanking a structure.

Plan #321037

Dimensions: 78'8" W x 50'6" D
Levels: 1
Heated Square Footage: 2,397
Bedrooms: 3
Bathrooms: 2
Foundation: Basement or walkout
Materials List Available: Yes
Price Category: F

CAD FILE AVAILABLE

Images provided by designer/architect.

Come home to this three-bedroom stucco home with arched windows.

Features:

- Dining Room: Just off the entry is this formal room, with its vaulted ceiling.
- Great Room: This large room has a vaulted ceiling and a fireplace.
- Kitchen: A large pantry and an abundance of counter space make this kitchen a functional work space.
- Master Suite: This suite has a large walk-in closet and a private bath.
- Bedrooms: The two additional bedrooms share a common bathroom.

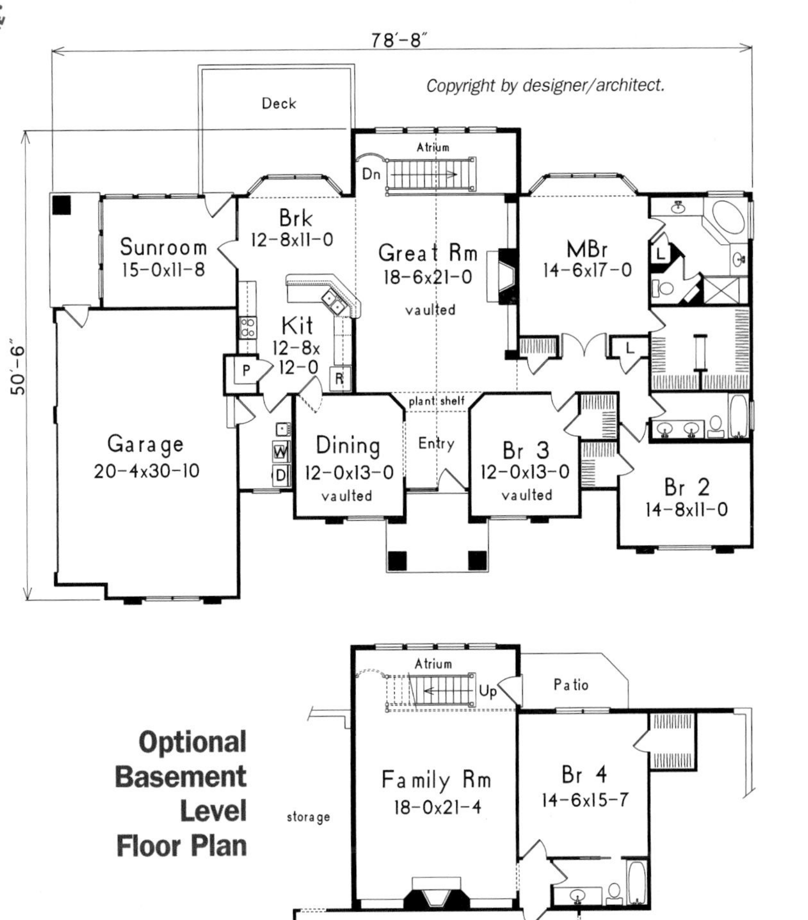

Optional Basement Level Floor Plan

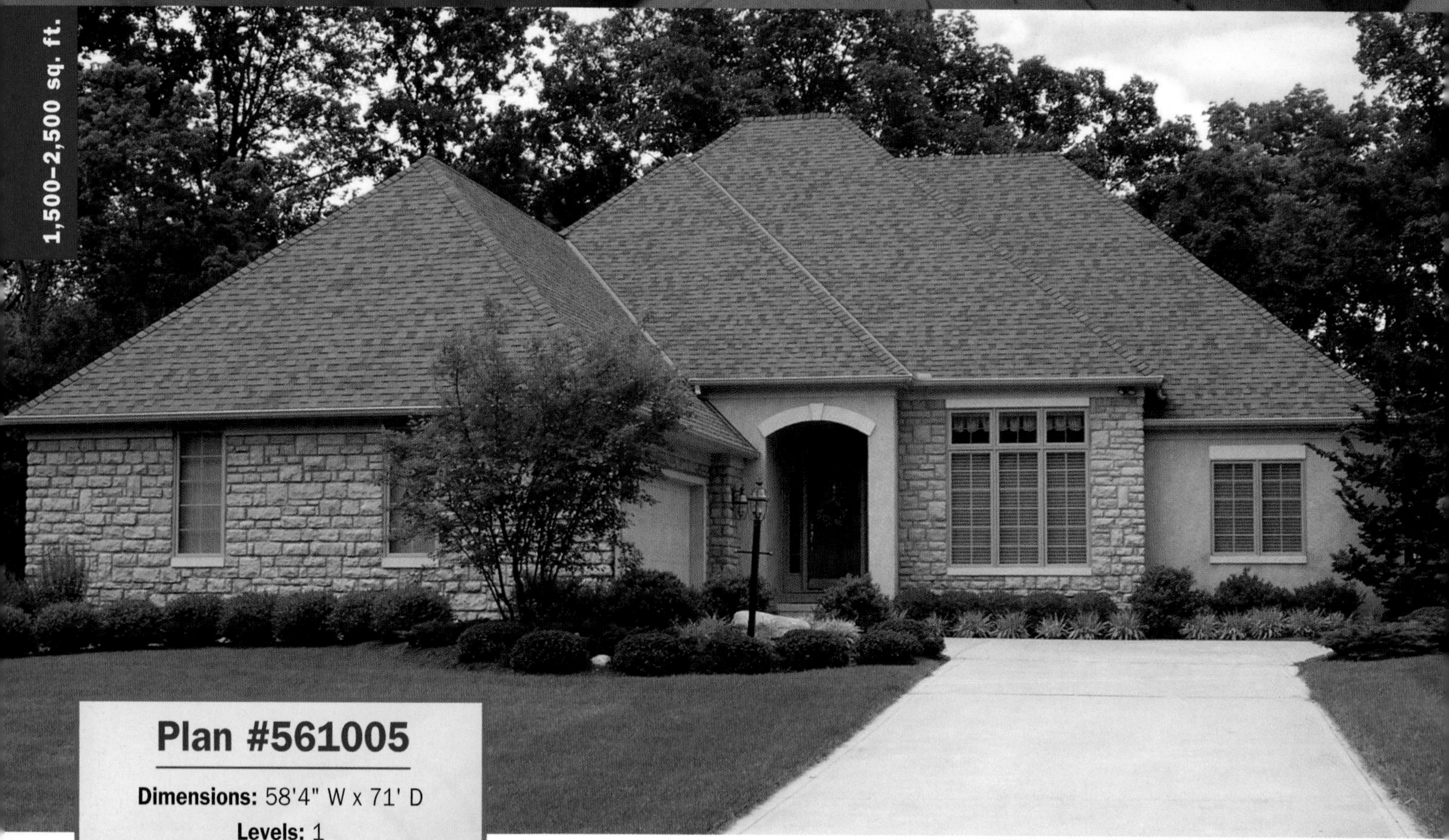

Plan #561005

Dimensions: 58'4" W x 71' D

Levels: 1

Heated Square Footage: 2,358

Bedrooms: 3

Bathrooms: 2

Foundation: Basement

Materials List Available: No

Price Category: E

CAD FILE AVAILABLE

Images provided by designer/architect.

This magnificent farmhouse design, with its traditional front porch and rear screened-in porch, is more than just a home.

Features:

- Great Room: Gather by the glowing fire on cold nights, or expand your entertaining space any other time. This great room is at the center of everything and has plenty of space for friends, family, and anyone else you can think to invite.
- Kitchen: A built-in pantry and ample counter space make a great work area for the family cook and the aspiring chef alike. An open transition to the breakfast area simplifies morning chaos, while a defined separation formalizes the dining room.
- Master Suite: This area is a welcome retreat where you can shut out the frenzied world and simply relax. The attached master bath includes dual walk-in closets, his and her sinks, a standing shower, and a separate tub – perfect for busy mornings and romantic evenings.
- Secondary Bedrooms: These bedrooms boast ample closet space and equal distance to a full bathroom. They're also off the beaten path, creating a calmer space for study and sleep.

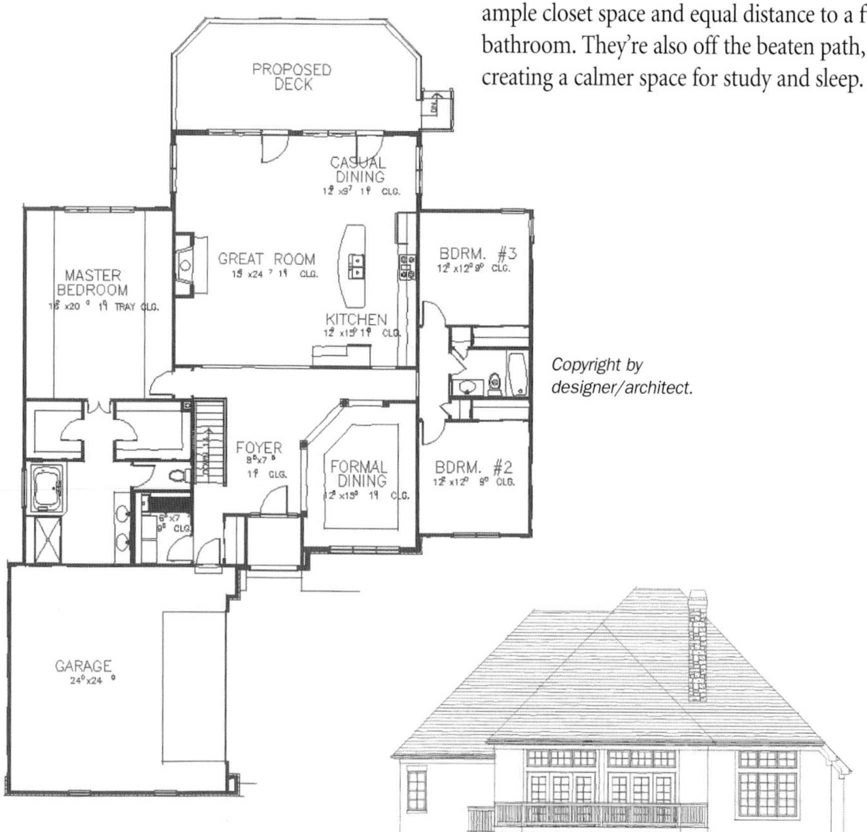

Rear Elevation

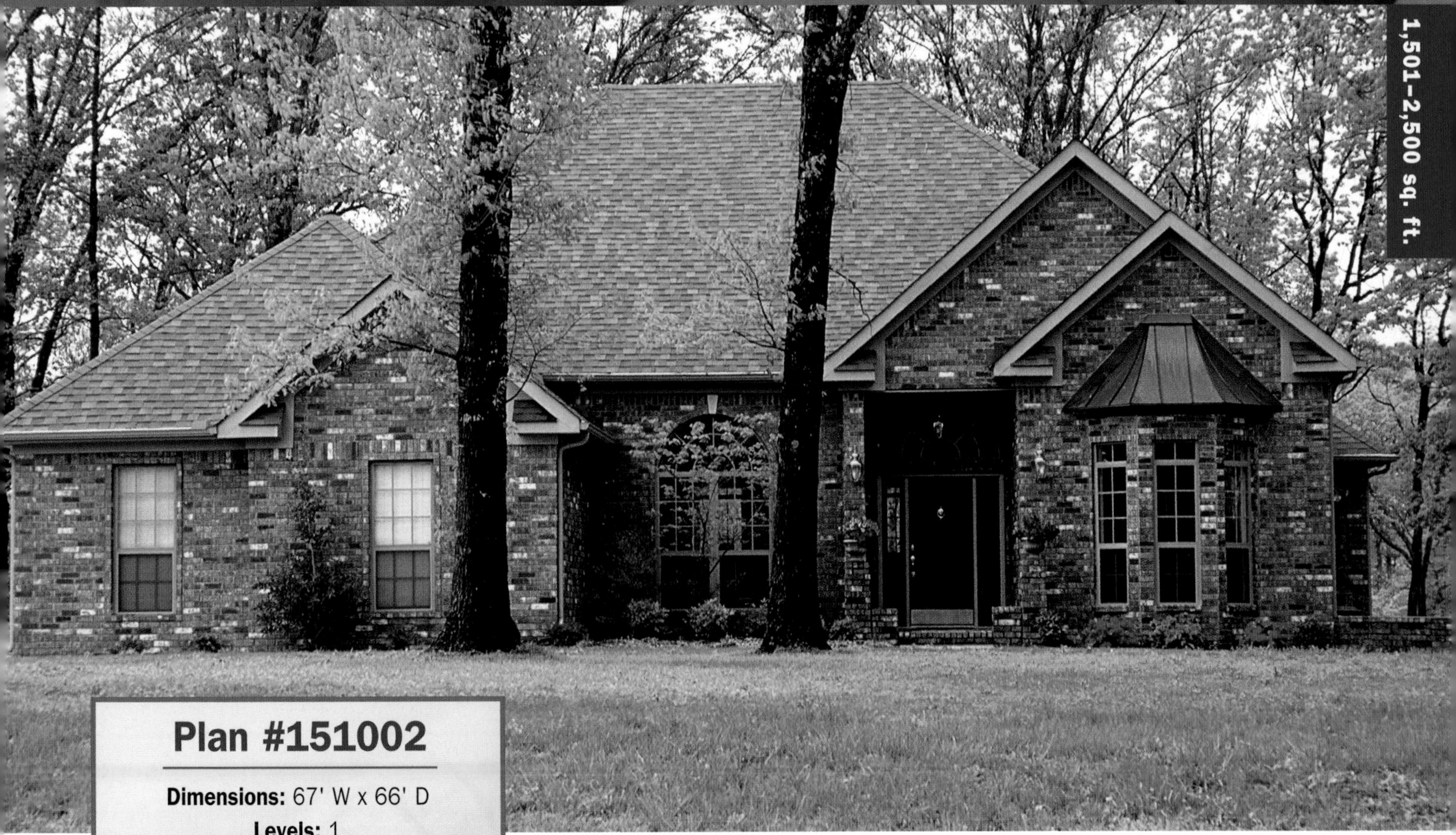

Images provided by designer/architect.

Plan #151002

Dimensions: 67' W x 66' D
Levels: 1
Heated Square Footage: 2,444
Bedrooms: 3
Bathrooms: 2½
Foundation: Crawl space, slab, basement or walkout
CompleteCost List Available: Yes
Price Category: F

This gracious, traditionanl home is designed for practicality and convenience.

Features:

- Ceiling Height: 9-ft. except as noted below.
- Great Room: This room is ideal for entertaining, thanks to its lovely fireplace and French doors that open to the covered rear porch. Built-in cabinets give convenient storage space.
- Family Room: With access to the kitchen as well as the rear porch, this room will become your family's "headquarters."
- Study: Enjoy the quiet in this room with its 12-ft. ceiling and doorway to a private patio on the side of the house.
- Dining Room: Take advantage of the 8-in. wood columns and 12-ft. ceilings to create a formal dining area.
- Kitchen: An eat-in bar is a great place to snack, and the ahndy computer nook allows the kids to do their homework while you cook.
- Breakfast Room: Opening from the kitchen, this area gives added space for the family to gather any time.
- Master Suite: Featuring a 10-ft. boxed ceiling, the master bedroom also has a door way that opens onto the covered rear porch. The master bathroom has a step-up whirlpool tub, separate shower, and twin vanities with a makeup area.

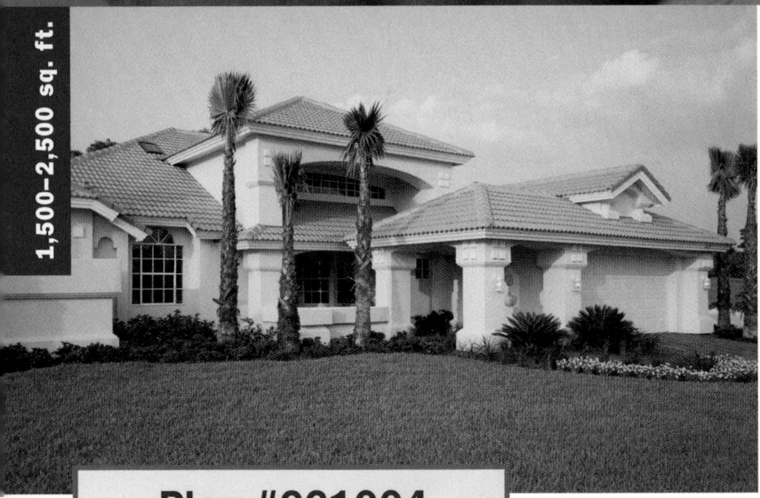

Master Bedroom 16⁸ • 13⁰
Family Room 19⁸ • 15¹⁰
Nook
Living Room 12⁰ • 13¹⁰
Kitchen 16⁴ • 14⁴
Bedroom 2 11⁰ • 11⁰
w.i.c.
Bath 2
Den/Study 11⁰ • 11⁰
Dining Room 11⁸ • 11⁰
Laun.
Bedroom 3 11⁰ • 11⁰
2 Car Garage 20⁰ • 22⁴

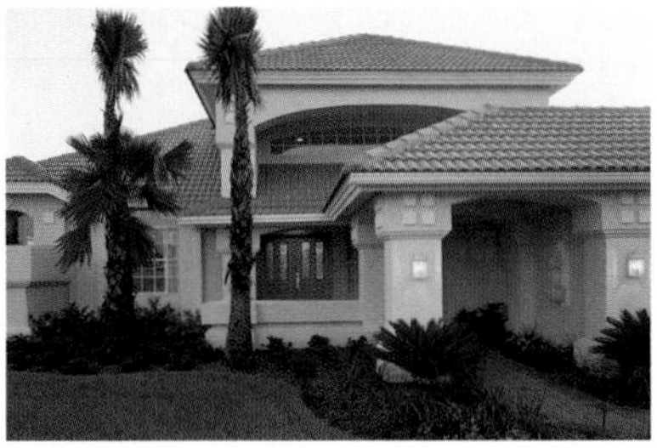

Plan #661004

Dimensions: 60'6" W x 71'8" D
Levels: 1
Heated Square Footage: 2,397
Bedrooms: 3
Bathrooms: 2½
Foundation: Slab
Materials List Available: No
Price Category: E

Images provided by designer/architect.

CAD FILE CAD AVAILABLE

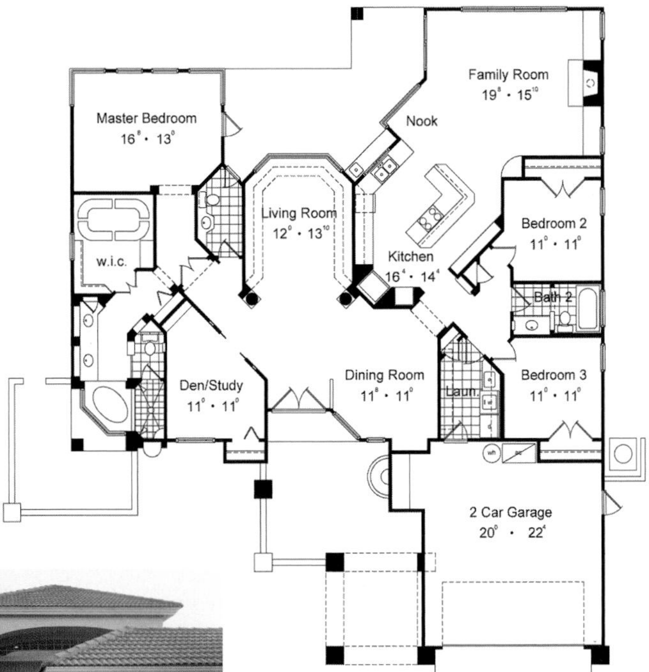

Front View

Copyright by designer/architect.

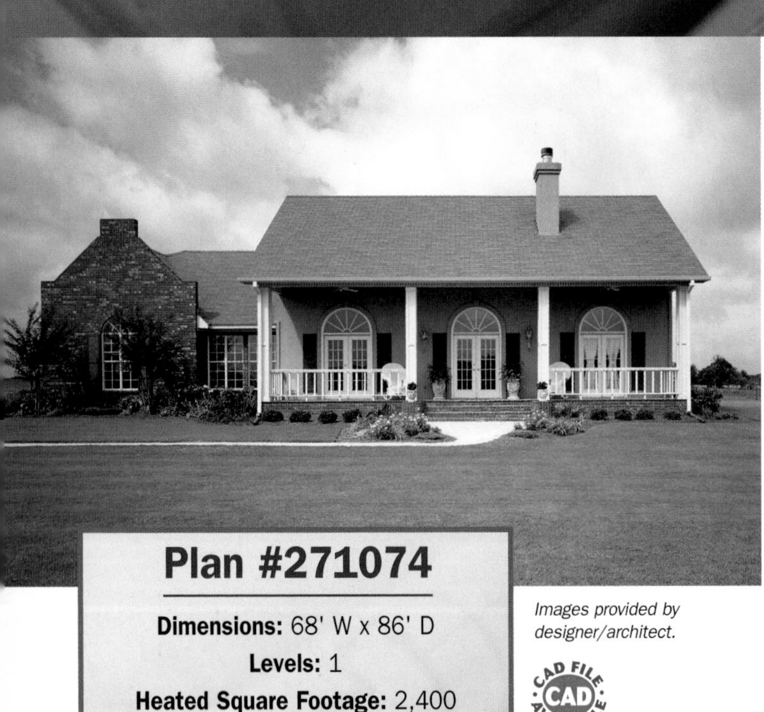

Plan #271074

Dimensions: 68' W x 86' D
Levels: 1
Heated Square Footage: 2,400
Bedrooms: 4
Bathrooms: 3
Foundation: Crawl space or slab
Materials List Available: No
Price Category: E

Images provided by designer/architect.

CAD FILE CAD AVAILABLE

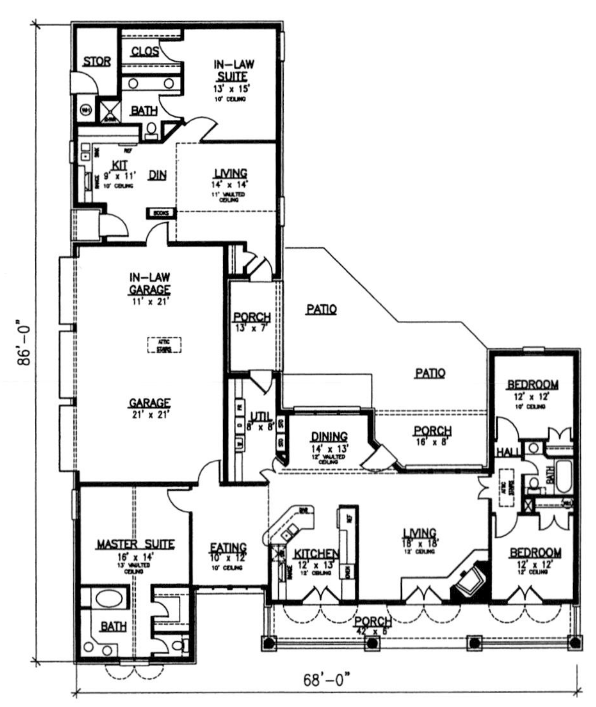

Copyright by designer/architect.

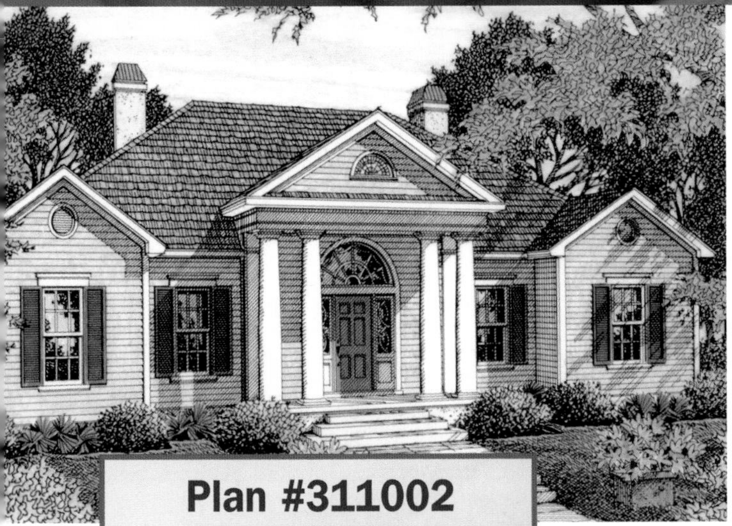

Plan #311002

Dimensions: 56'6" W x 82' D
Levels: 1
Heated Square Footage: 2,402
Bedrooms: 4
Bathrooms: 2½
Foundation: Crawl space, slab, or basement
Materials List Available: Yes
Price Category: E

Images provided by designer/architect.

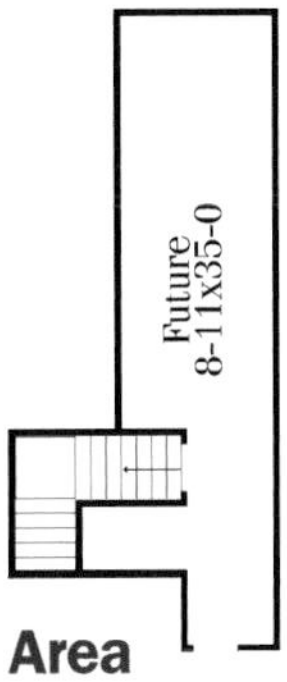

Bonus Area Floor Plan

Copyright by designer/architect.

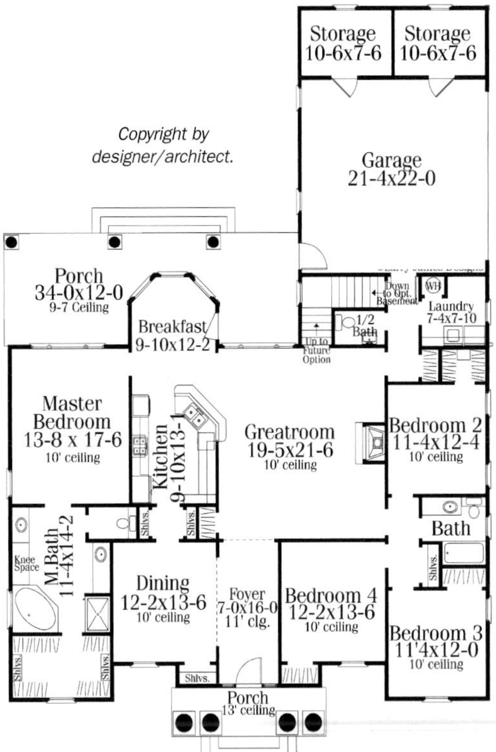

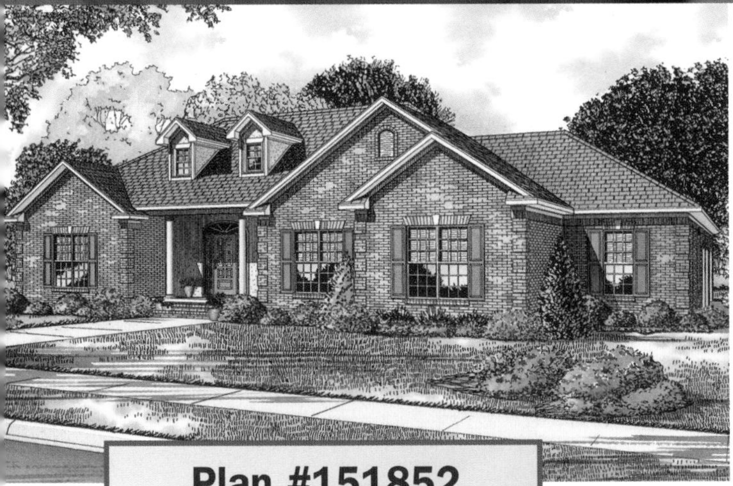

Plan #151852

Dimensions: 70'2" W x 86'8" D
Levels: 1
Heated Square Footage: 2,424
Bedrooms: 4
Bathrooms: 3
Foundation: Crawl space or slab; basement or walkout for fee
CompleteCost List Available: Yes
Price Category: E

Images provided by designer/architect.

CAD FILE AVAILABLE

Copyright by designer/architect.

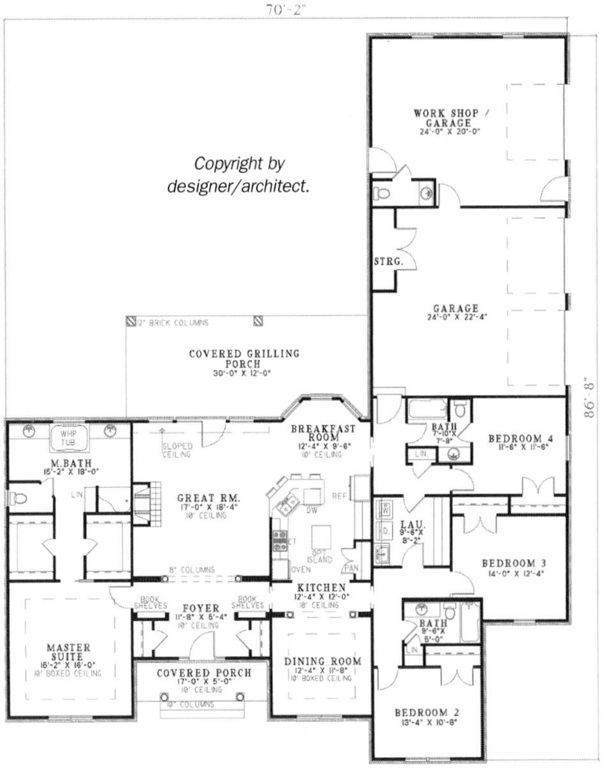

Plan #241017

Dimensions: 74'4" W x 55'4" D
Levels: 1
Heated Square Footage: 2,431
Bedrooms: 4
Bathrooms: 2½
Foundation: Slab
Materials List Available: No
Price Category: E

Images provided by designer/architect.

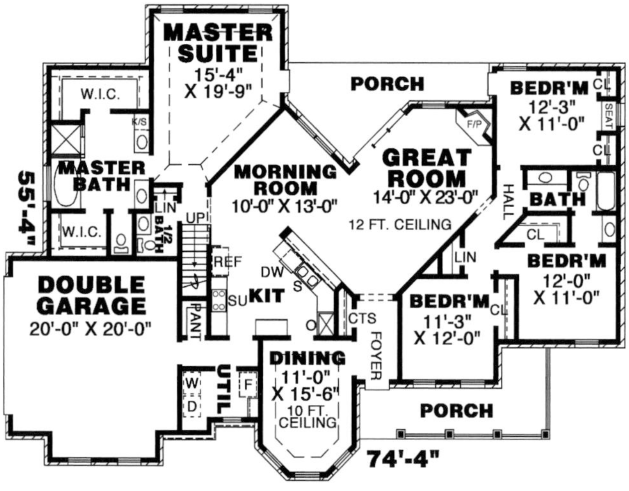

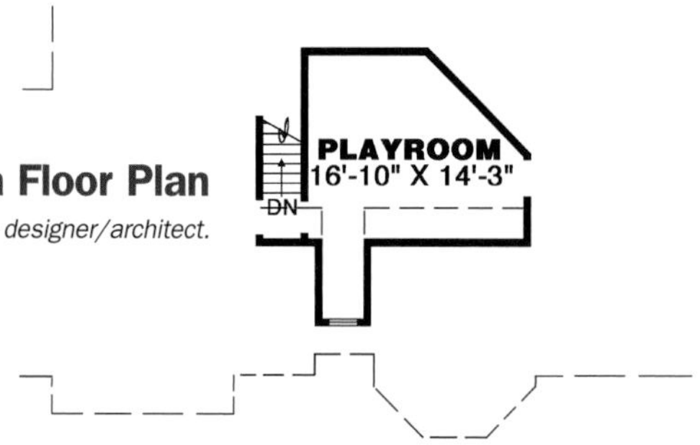

Bonus Area Floor Plan

Copyright by designer/architect.

Plan #351203

Dimensions: 73'6" W x 62' D
Levels: 1
Heated Square Footage: 2,447
Bedrooms: 4
Bathrooms: 2½
Foundation: Basement
Materials List Available: Yes
Price Category: E

Images provided by designer/architect.

CAD FILE AVAILABLE

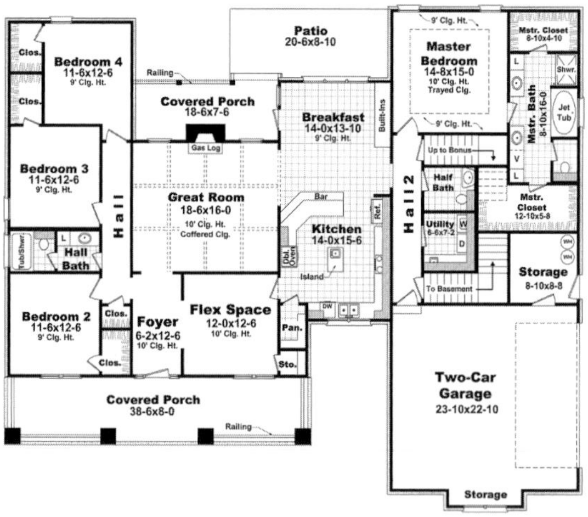

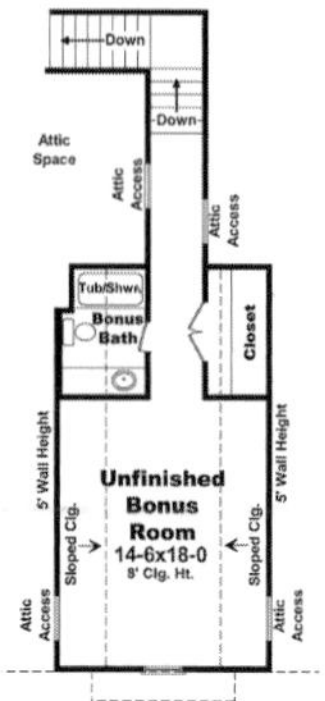

Bonus Area Floor Plan

Copyright by designer/architect.

Plan #321019

Dimensions: 70'8" W x 70' D
Levels: 1
Heated Square Footage: 2,452
Bedrooms: 4
Bathrooms: 2½
Foundation: Basement
Materials List Available: Yes
Price Category: E

Images provided by designer/architect.

CAD FILE AVAILABLE

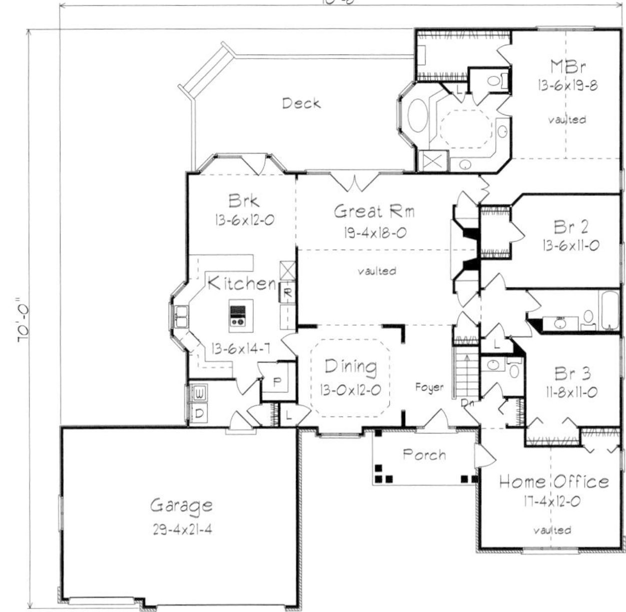

Copyright by designer/architect.

Plan #121053

Dimensions: 66' W x 68' D
Levels: 1
Heated Square Footage: 2,456
Bedrooms: 3
Bathrooms: 2½
Foundation: Basement
Materials List Available: Yes
Price Category: E

Images provided by designer/architect.

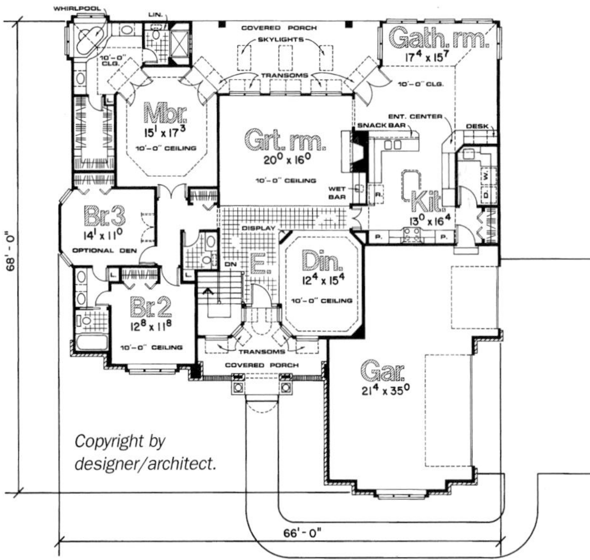

Copyright by designer/architect.

SMARTtip

Installing Plastic Molding

Foam trim is best cut with a backsaw. Power miter saws with fine-toothed blades also work. Larger-toothed blades tend to tear the foam unevenly.

Main Level Floor Plan

Basement Level Floor Plan

Plan #161037

Dimensions: 46' W x 59'4" D
Levels: 1
Heated Square Footage: 2,469
Main Level Sq. Ft.: 1,462
Basement Level Sq. Ft.: 1,007
Bedrooms: 2
Bathrooms: 2½
Foundation: Walkout; basement for fee
Materials List Available: Yes
Price Category: E

Images provided by designer/architect.

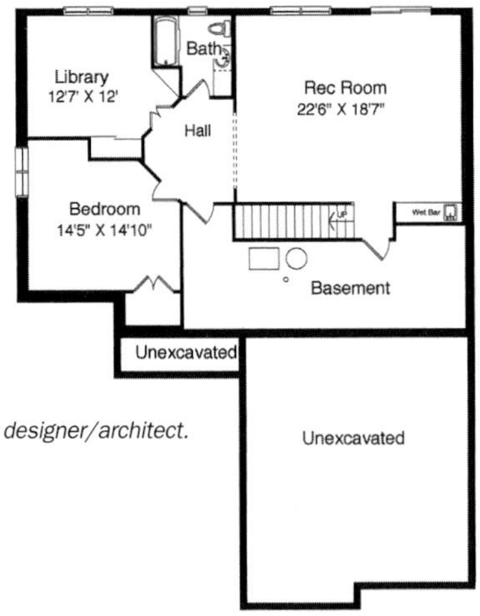

Copyright by designer/architect.

Copyright by designer/architect.

Plan #351088

Dimensions: 66'8" W x 73'2" D
Levels: 1
Heated Square Footage: 2,500
Bedrooms: 4
Bathrooms: 3
Foundation: Crawl space or slab
Materials List Available: Yes
Price Category: G

Images provided by designer/architect.

CAD FILE AVAILABLE

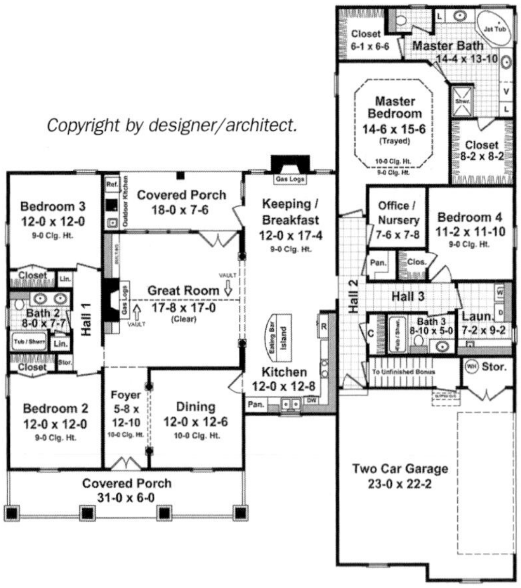

Rear Elevation

Bonus Area Floor Plan

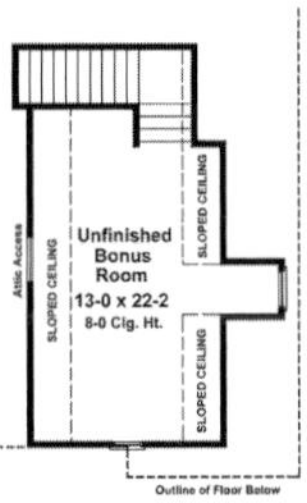

Plan #161196

Dimensions: 59' W x 59'6" D

Levels: 1

Heated Square Footage: 2,469

Bedrooms: 3

Bathrooms: 2

Foundation: Crawl space or slab; basement or walkout for fee

CompleteCost List Available: Yes

Price Category: E

Images provided by designer/architect.

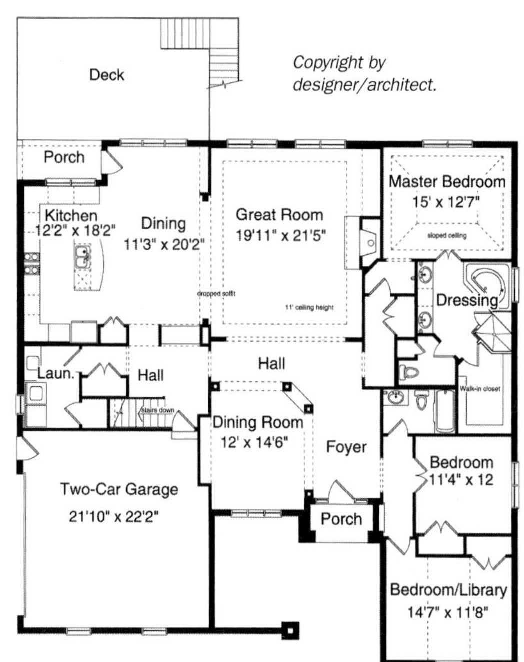

Copyright by designer/architect.

Plan #121003

Dimensions: 76' W x 55'4" D

Levels: 1

Heated Square Footage: 2,498

Bedrooms: 4

Bathrooms: 2½

Foundation: Basement; crawl space or slab for fee

Materials List Available: Yes

Price Category: E

Images provided by designer/architect.

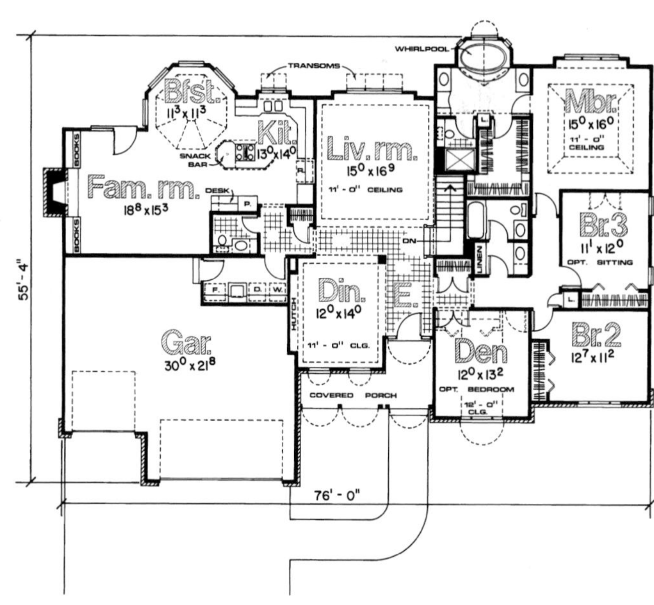

Copyright by designer/architect.

This article was reprinted from *Porches & Sunrooms* (Creative Homeowner 2006).

Porches and Three-Season Rooms

At its simplest, a three-season room or sunroom is a porch modified to keep the weather out. A three-season room protects you from wind, rain, and snow, but it isn't heated or cooled. A sunroom not only keeps the elements out, it offers a heated and cooled environment similar to any other room in your house. If you're looking for a protected spot to get some fresh air, and you don't mind what temperature that air is, consider a three-season room. If you're a sun lover who'd rather not brave freezing cold or oppressive heat to bask in the sunlight, think about a sunroom. In this article we'll look at what goes into creating each of these rooms.

Traditional-style sunrooms, opposite, are often made with standard windows rather than floor-to-ceiling glass.

This manufactured addition could be either a three-season room or a sunroom, depending on the type of glass chosen.

Room Options

You can convert an existing porch to a three-season room by installing glass and screen panels and a storm door between posts or columns. Or you can build a new three-season addition with floor-to-ceiling window-and-screen panels.

Because it is uninsulated and unheated, a three-season room won't get much winter use in cold climates. But on those late fall or early spring days when a porch would be uncomfortably chilly, a three-season room can warm up nicely as radiant heat from the sun is captured in the enclosed space. Where winters are warm, the off season may be the summer, when the uninsulated, unairconditioned space may get too toasty.

Sunrooms are by definition habitable in all seasons, though the demands of insulation, heating, and cooling make them more expensive than three-season rooms. They may be conversions of porches, patios, or decks. They can be custom-

made from the ground up. Or they can be manufactured and installed in a matter of days.

Many sunrooms are highly finished and indistinguishable in style, detail, and furnishings from other rooms in the house. Or they may have a distinctive style all their own.

Whether they are conversions, custom built, or factory made, three-season rooms and sunrooms have many similarities. Their basic structures are often the same. Replace single-pane glass with insulated glass and add insulation to the walls, floors, and roof, and add a source of heating and cooling, and a three-season room becomes a sunroom.

Porch Conversions

Many open-air porches can be converted to three-season rooms. How easily this can be done depends a great deal on how ornate the porch is. It's relatively simple to install window and screen units and a door on a porch that has rectilinear posts and simple railings. Adding windows and a door to a

A manufactured room was cleverly adapted to convert this porch to a three-season room, above and below.

Framing a Porch for Windows

If an opening on a porch is already rectangular and is plumb and level, you can size a custom-built window and frame to fit in that opening, attaching it to the posts, deck or railing, and top beam. Or you can frame new openings to fit standard-size manufactured windows or custom windows of a size you desire. Windows for porch conversions are often housed in wood frames because a carpenter can often make them on site. You can also have aluminum frames custom-built with individual windows and screens made to fit.

If porch openings are irregularly shaped, it's usually more cost-effective to modify the openings than to build oddly shaped windows. This is especially true for windows with moving parts, such as sashes or louvers. Porches with round or molded columns, sloped floors, or elaborate brackets can be framed to accept rectilinear windows, as shown in the drawings at night. Porch decks usually slope away from the house. Openings for windows added along the slope are best framed to create a level bottom because rectilinear windows are much cheaper than trapezoidal ones. Also, glass that rests less than 18 inches above the deck is required by code to be tempered, which will increase the cost. You can frame the opening higher to accommodate standard glass.

Simple Framing for Porch Windows

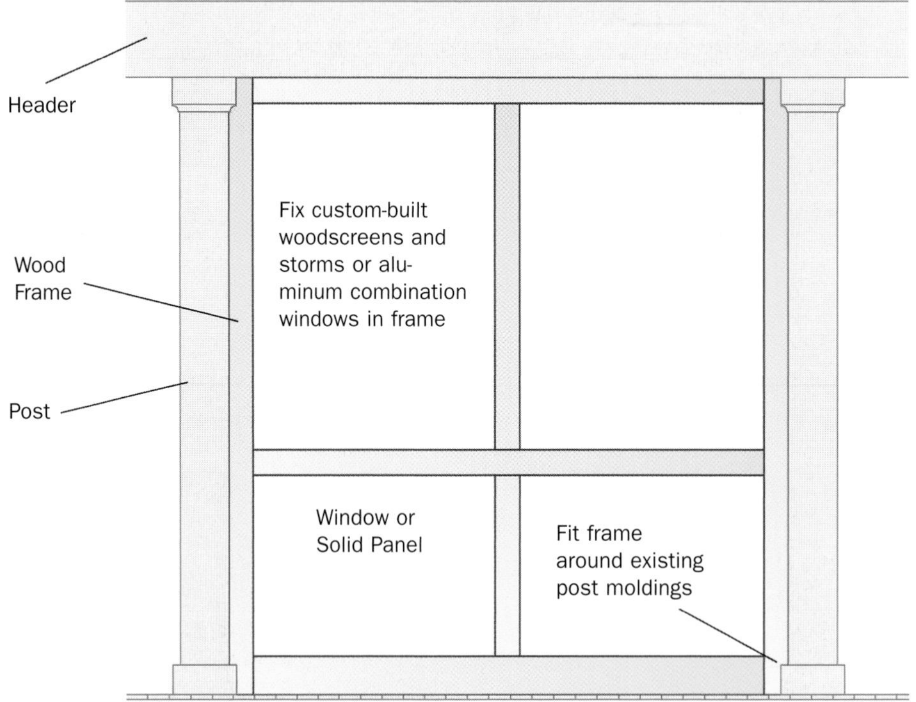

Scribed Framing for Porch Windows

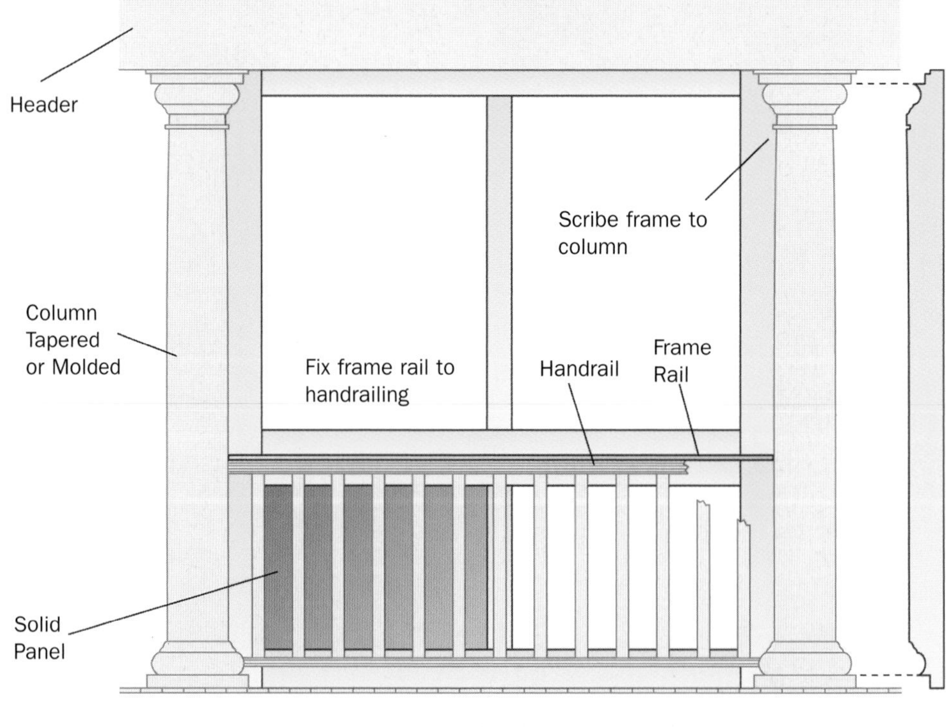

A window frame has been carefully scribed to the Ionic capital and base and the gentle curve of the column shaft in the conversion shown above.

porch that has tapered or heavily molded columns, elaborate brackets, and complex or curved railings requires more thought, more construction skills, and usually more money. (See "Framing a Porch for Windows," left.)

Door, window, and screen units are often much the same for simple and complicated installations alike. The extra cost and installation finesse comes from figuring out how to fill in between rectangular door, window, and screen units and the existing curved and filigreed porch columns and railings.

Converting a porch to a sunroom is a bit more difficult and expensive. Insulated windows and doors are more costly than those with single-pane glass. Insulating an existing porch floor and roof isn't necessarily expensive or difficult, but it may not be terribly effective, either. Nevertheless, charming sunrooms have been made from porches.

Before you consider how to convert an existing porch, make sure it is structurally sound. Check for good footings and foundations; no rotting or deteriorating posts, joists, floor boards, or roof members; and no leaning or tilting. If it's going to cost a lot of money to fix the structure before you convert the space, you should probably tear off the existing porch and build from scratch.

Converting a Deck

A deck is often an ideal site for a three-season room or sunroom addition. Decks are usually located where sun, shade, and wind conditions on your property are optimal. They are usually adjacent to a room in the house that is desirable for connection to a three-season room or sunroom. They may already have a door or sliding door suitable for access to the new room. And they can provide, at the least, a ready-made floor or subfloor.

Before you convert a deck, you'll need to check its footings to see if they are large enough to carry the additional load of walls and roof. A contractor or codes department can help you with the calculations. If the footings are insufficient, you may be able to enlarge them with additional concrete. Or you may need to build temporary supports, tear out the existing footings, and re-pour.

Straight columns are relatively easy to fill in to enclose a porch, right. Turned columns and a railing, far right, make enclosing a porch a more complicated project.

Traditional wooden storm windows and screens enclose this three-season porch conversion, below.

Embedded in the wall, the original porch columns are a striking feature of this converted sunroom, opposite.

Plan #151188

Dimensions: 63'4" W x 59'10" D
Levels: 1
Heated Square Footage: 2,525
Bedrooms: 3
Bathrooms: 2½
Foundation: Crawl space, slab, basement or walkout
CompleteCost List Available: Yes
Price Category: E

Images provided by designer/architect.

This Southwestern-inspired home has a beautiful layout that you will love.

Features:

- Great Room: Opening out from the gallery, this great room is truly at the heart of this home. Built-in shelves and a media center flank a fireplace for a lovely setting.
- Kitchen: This kitchen features plenty of counter space for all of your needs. A center island provides additional space for prepping meals or holding dishes.
- Master Suite: Unwind in this wonderful master suite, complete with a whirlpool tub, a glass shower, separate vanities, and a spacious walk-in closet.
- Secondary Bedrooms: Located near the master suite, two secondary bedrooms are perfect for siblings. A shared bath features a private toilet and bath area.

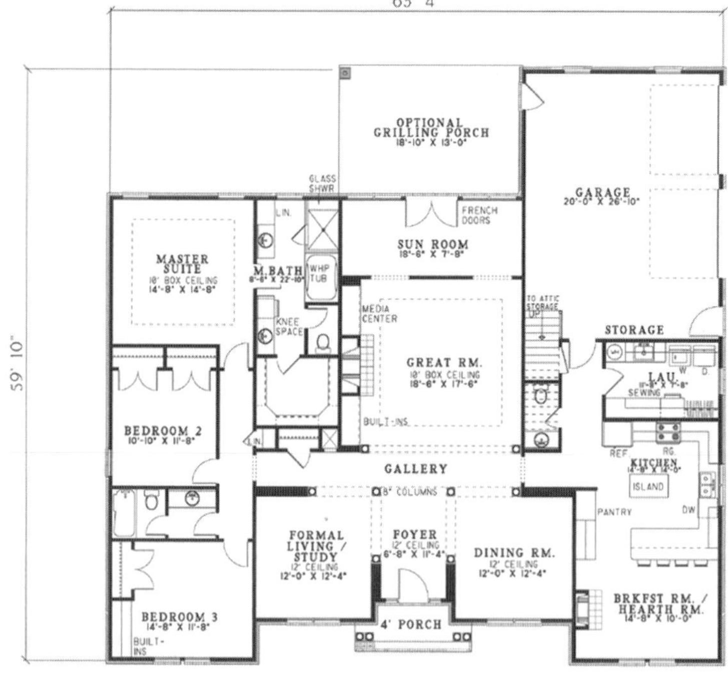

Copyright by designer/architect.

Plan #241008

Dimensions: 65' W x 56'8" D
Levels: 1
Heated Square Footage: 2,526
Bedrooms: 4
Bathrooms: 3
Foundation: Crawl space, slab, or basement
Materials List Available: No
Price Category: E

Images provided by designer/architect.

A covered back porch—with access from the master suite and the breakfast area—makes this traditional home ideal for sitting near a golf course or with a backyard pool.

Features:

- Great Room: From the foyer, guests enter this spacious and comfortable great room, which features a handsome fireplace.
- Kitchen: This kitchen—the hub of this family-oriented home—is a joy in which to work, thanks to abundant counter space, a pantry, a convenient eating bar, and an adjoining breakfast area and sunroom.
- Master Suite: Enjoy the quiet comfort of this coffered-ceiling master suite, which features dual vanities and separate walk-in closets.
- Additional Bedrooms: Two secondary bedrooms, which share a full bath, are located at the opposite end of the house from the master suite. Bedroom 4—in front of the house—can be converted into a study.

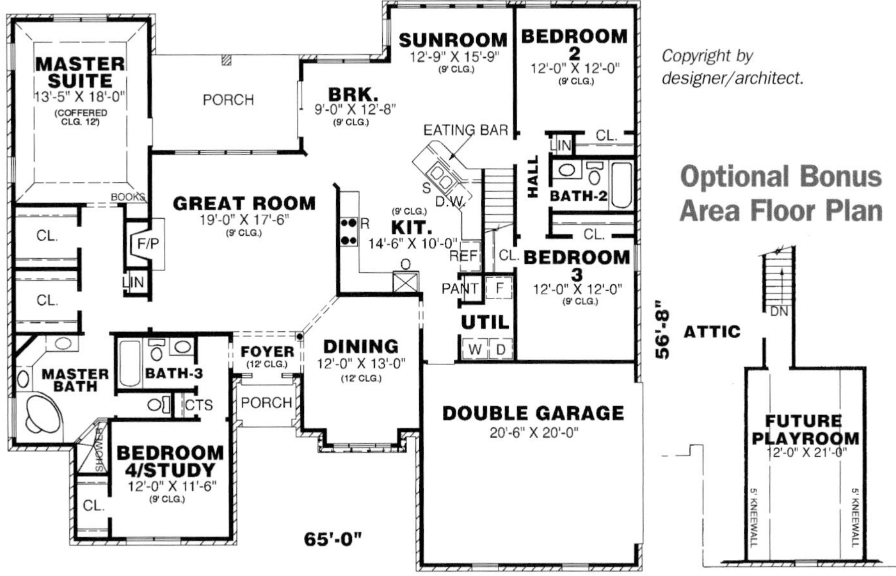

Copyright by designer/architect.

Optional Bonus Area Floor Plan

SMARTtip

Traditional-Style Kitchen Cabinetry

You can modify stock kitchen cabinetry to enjoy fine furniture-quality details. Prefabricated trims may be purchased at local lumber mills and home centers. For example, crown molding, applied to the top of stock cabinetry and stained or painted to match the door style, may be all you need. Likewise, you can replace hardware with reproduction polished-brass door and drawer knobs or pulls for a finishing touch.

Plan #151383

Dimensions: 70'4" W x 57'2" D
Levels: 1
Heated Square Footage: 2,534
Bedrooms: 3
Bathrooms: 2
Foundation: Crawl space or slab
CompleteCost List Available: Yes
Price Category: G

CAD FILE AVAILABLE

The arched entry of the covered porch welcomes you to this magnificent home.

Features:

- Foyer: Welcome your guests in this warm foyer before leading them into the impressive dining room with magnificent columns framing the entry.
- Great Room: After dinner, your guests will enjoy conversation in this spacious room, complete with fireplace and built-ins.
- Study: Beautiful French doors open into this quiet space, where you'll be able to concentrate on that work away from the office.
- Rear Porch: This relaxing spot may be reached from the breakfast room or your secluded master suite.

Images provided by designer/architect.

This home, as shown in the photograph, may differ from the actual blueprints. For more information, please check the floor plans carefully.

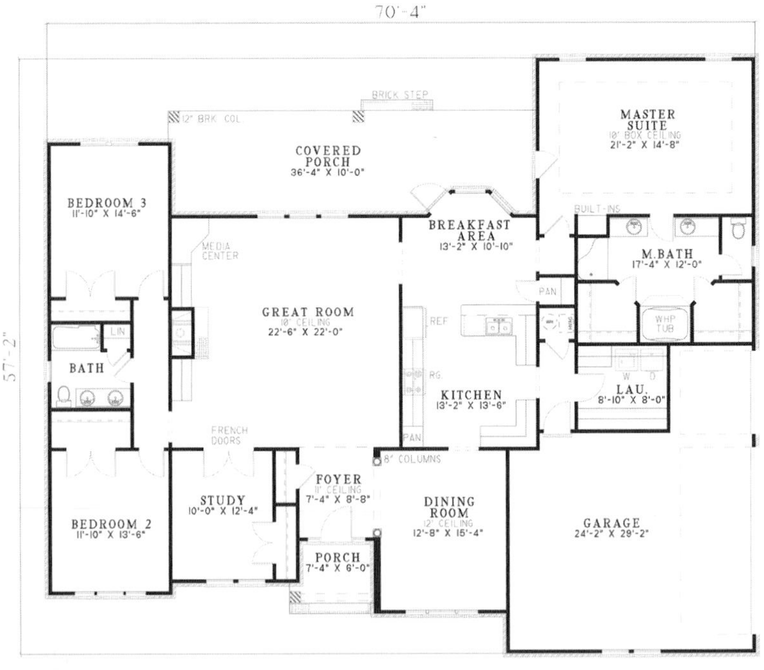

Copyright by designer/architect.

Front View

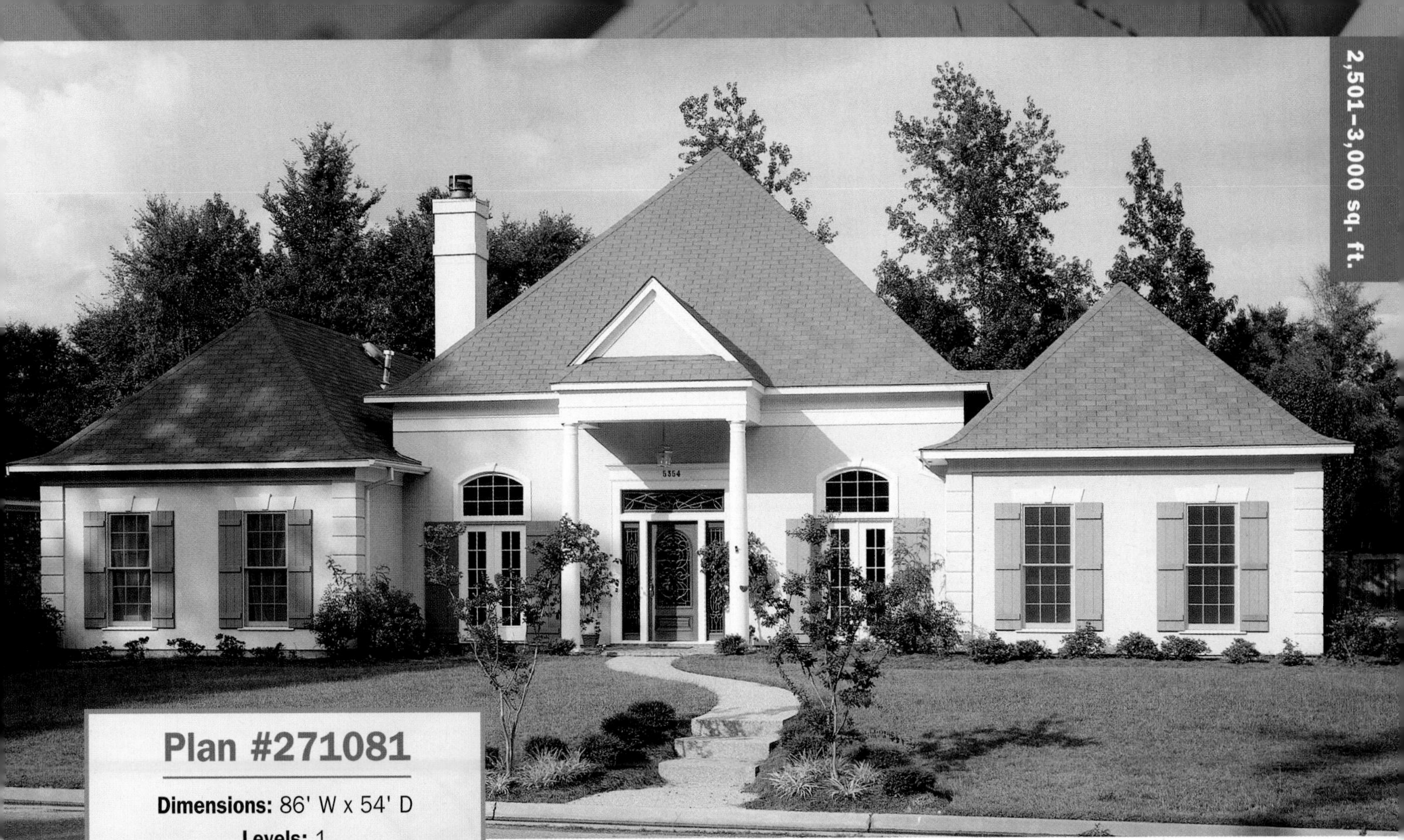

Images provided by designer/architect.

Plan #271081

Dimensions: 86' W x 54' D
Levels: 1
Heated Square Footage: 2,539
Bedrooms: 3
Bathrooms: 2
Foundation: Slab
Materials List Available: No
Price Category: E

This traditional home is sure to impress your guests and even your neighbors.

Features:

- Living Room: This quiet space off the foyer is perfect for pleasant conversation.
- Family Room: A perfect gathering spot, this room is nicely enhanced by a fireplace.
- Kitchen: This room easily serves the bayed morning room and the formal dining room.
- Master Suite: The master bedroom overlooks a side patio, and boasts a private bath with a skylight and a whirlpool tub.
- Library: This cozy room is perfect for curling up with a good novel. It would also make a great extra bedroom.

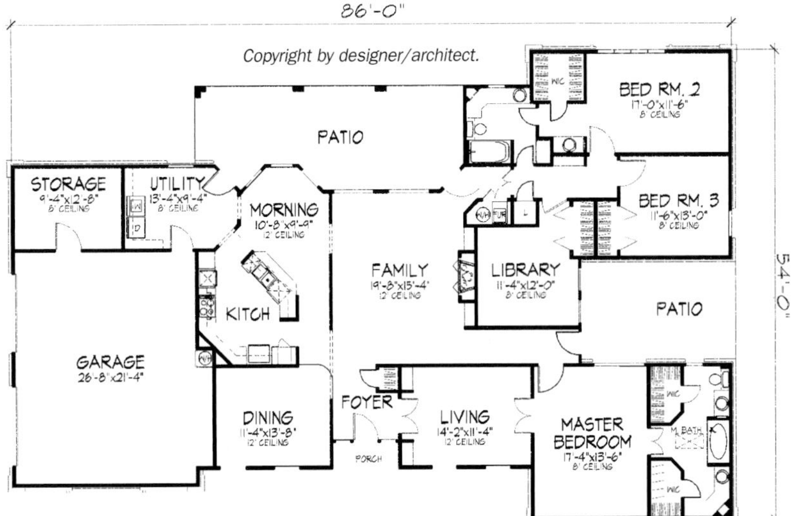

SMARTtip

Determining Curtain Length

Follow length guidelines for foolproof results, but remember that they're not rules. Go ahead and play with curtain and drapery lengths. Instead of shortening long panels at the hem, for instance, take up excess material by blousing them over tiebacks for a pleasing effect.

Plan #151140

Dimensions: 67'2" W x 55'10" D
Levels: 1
Heated Square Footage: 2,525
Bedrooms: 4
Bathrooms: 3
Foundation: Crawl space or slab; basement or walkout for fee
CompleteCost List Available: Yes
Price Category: E

Images provided by designer/architect.

CAD FILE AVAILABLE

Great Room

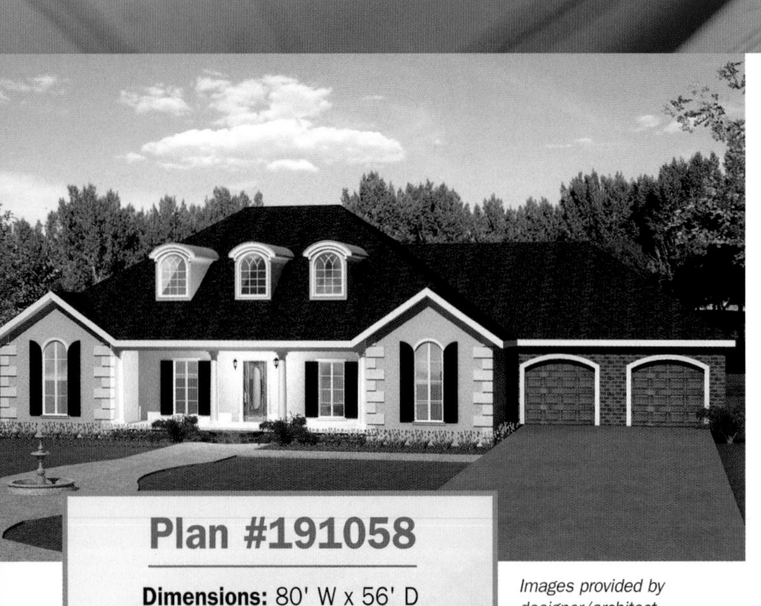

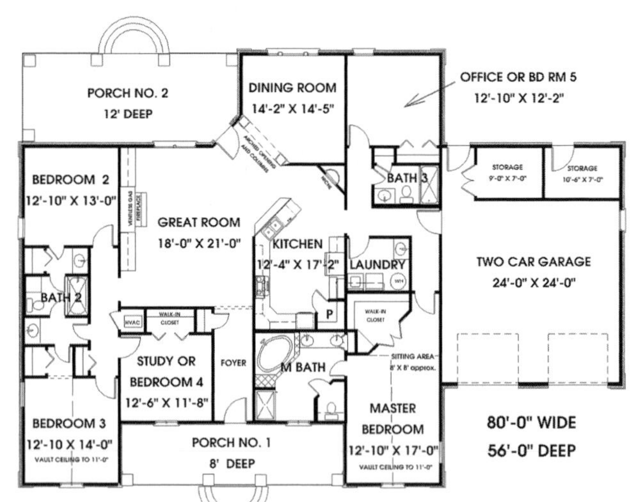

Plan #191058

Dimensions: 80' W x 56' D
Levels: 1
Heated Square Footage: 2,550
Bedrooms: 5
Bathrooms: 3
Foundation: Slab
Materials List Available: No
Price Category: E

Images provided by designer/architect.

Copyright by designer/architect.

Kitchen

Rear View

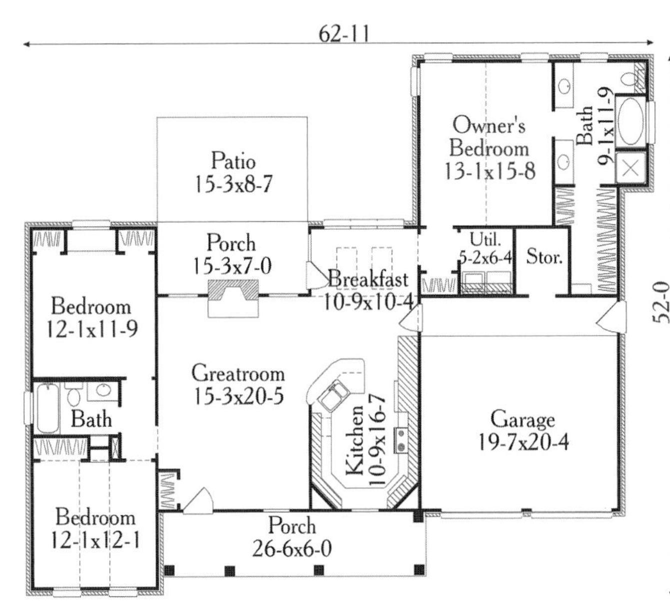

Plan #311050

Dimensions: 62'11" W x 52' D

Levels: 1

Heated Square Footage: 1,606

Bedrooms: 3

Bathrooms: 2

Foundation: Crawl space, slab, or basement

MaterialsList Available: Yes

Price Category: E

Images provided by designer/architect.

Basement Stair Location

Copyright by designer/architect.

Plan #151486

Dimensions: 74'7" W x 70'6" D

Levels: 1

Heated Square Footage: 2,556

Bedrooms: 4

Bathrooms: 3

Foundation: Crawl space or slab

CompleteCost List Available: Yes

Price Category: E

Images provided by designer/architect.

CAD FILE AVAILABLE

Copyright by designer/architect.

Plan #421009

Dimensions: 64'9" W x 59' D
Levels: 1
Heated Square Footage: 2,649
Bedrooms: 3
Bathrooms: 2
Foundation: Crawl space, slab, or basement
Materials List Available: Yes
Price Category: F

Images provided by designer/architect.

Main Level Floor Plan

Alternate Floor Plan

Copyright by designer/architect.

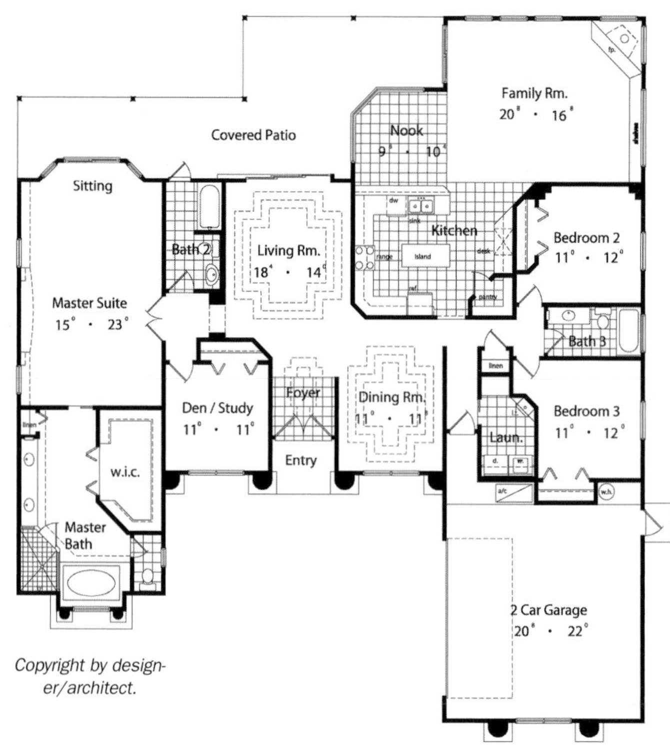

Copyright by designer/architect.

Plan #661007

Dimensions: 66'4" W x 74'4" D
Levels: 1
Heated Square Footage: 2,660
Bedrooms: 4
Bathrooms: 3
Foundation: Slab
Materials List Available: No
Price Category: F

Images provided by designer/architect.

CAD FILE CAD AVAILABLE

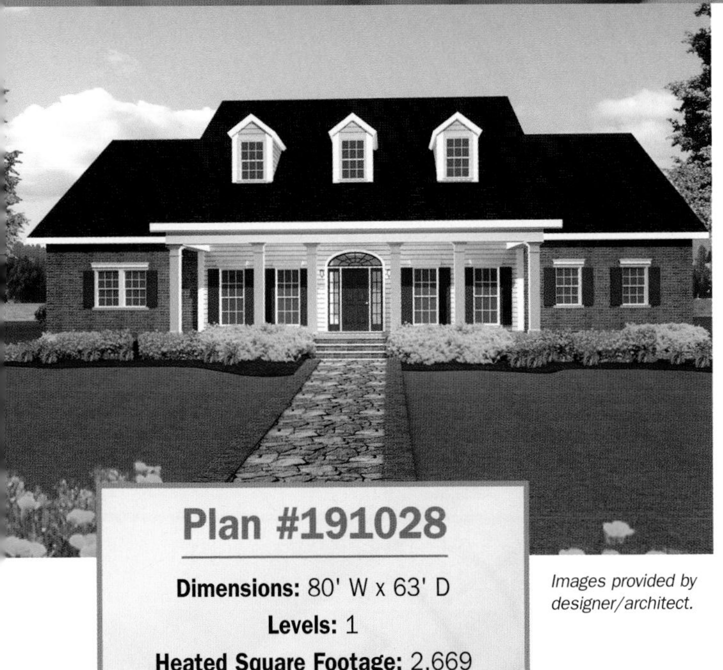

Plan #191028

Dimensions: 80' W x 63' D
Levels: 1
Heated Square Footage: 2,669
Bedrooms: 4
Bathrooms: 3½
Foundation: Slab or basement
Materials List Available: No
Price Category: F

Images provided by designer/architect.

BEDROOM NO. 2 11-8 X 13-0
BATH NO. 2
BEDROOM NO. 3 12-0 X 12-0
COVERED PORCH-2 24-0 X 10-0
BREAKFAST AREA 12-2 X 10-0
HALL
1/2 BATH
LAUNDRY 14-4 X 7-0
MASTER BEDROOM 18-2 X 14-0
GREAT ROOM 21-0 X 22-0
KITCHEN 14-0 X 16-0
TWO CAR GARAGE 21-10 X 26-0
CLO.
CLO.
MASTER BATH
BATH
GUEST BEDROOM 12-0 X 12-0
FOYER
DINING ROOM 14-0 X 12-0
COVERED PORCH-1 36-4 X 8-0

Copyright by designer/architect.

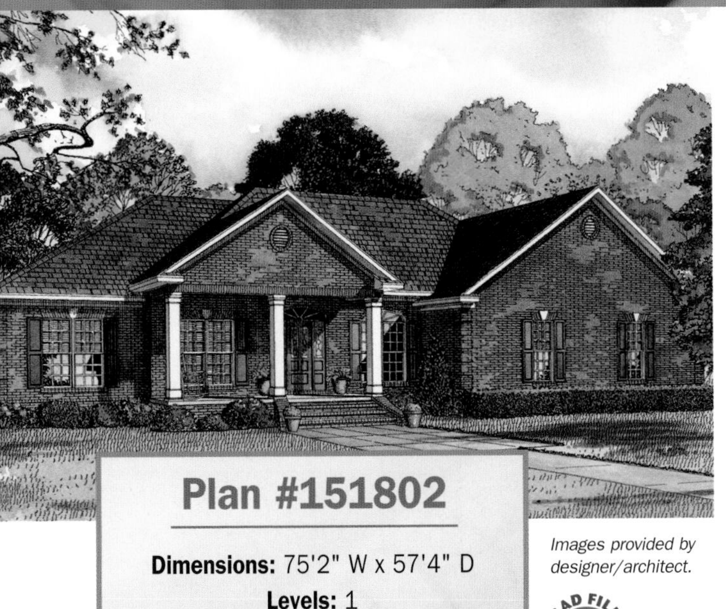

Plan #151802

Dimensions: 75'2" W x 57'4" D
Levels: 1
Heated Square Footage: 2,675
Bedrooms: 3
Bathrooms: 2
Foundation: Crawl space or slab; basement for fee
CompleteCost List Available: Yes
Price Category: F

Images provided by designer/architect.

CAD FILE AVAILABLE

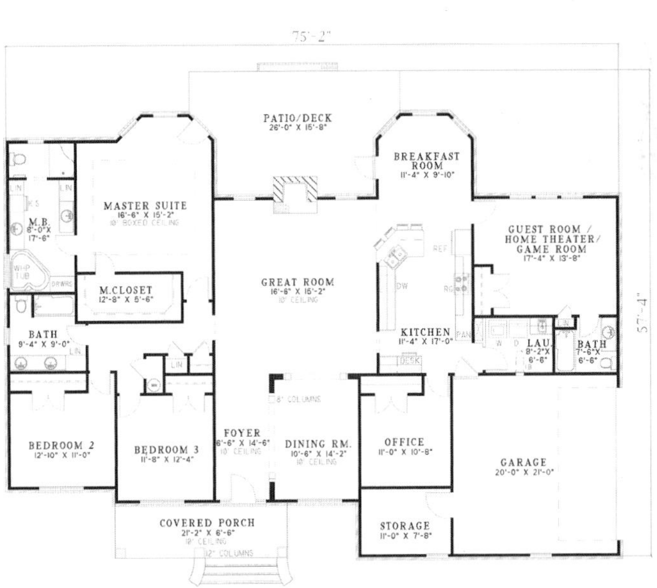

Copyright by designer/architect.

Images provided by designer/architect.

Plan #101013

Dimensions: 72' W x 66' D
Levels: 1
Heated Square Footage: 2,564
Bedrooms: 3
Bathrooms: 2½
Foundation: Basement; crawl space or slab for fee
Materials List Available: Yes
Price Category: F

This exciting design combines a striking classic exterior with a highly functional floor plan.

Features:

- Ceiling Height: 9 ft. unless otherwise noted.
- Family Room: This warm and inviting room measures 18 ft. x 22 ft. It features a 14-ft. ceiling and a rear wall of windows. French doors lead to an enormous deck.
- Kitchen: This unique angled kitchen is open to the hearth room and eating areas, all of which enjoy vaulted ceilings and are surrounded by windows. The hearth room has a TV niche.
- Master Suite: This 19-ft. x 18-ft. master suite is truly sumptuous, with its 12-ft. ceiling, sitting area, two walk-in closets, and full-featured bath.
- Secondary Bedrooms: Each of the secondary bedrooms measures 11 ft. x 14 ft. and has direct access to a shared bath.
- Bonus Room: Just beyond the entry are stairs leading to this bonus room, which measures approximately 12 ft. x 21 ft.—plenty of room for storage or future expansion.

Master Bedroom

Copyright by designer/architect.

Plan #441009

Dimensions: 94' W x 53' D
Levels: 1
Heated Square Footage: 2,650
Bedrooms: 4
Bathrooms: 2½
Foundation: Crawl space; slab or basement available for fee
Materials List Available: Yes
Price Category: F

Images provided by designer/architect.

This home, as shown in the photograph, may differ from the actual blueprints. For more information, please check the floor plans carefully.

You'll love to call this plan home. It's large enough for the whole family and has a façade that will make you the envy of the neighborhood.

CAD FILE AVAILABLE

Features:

- Foyer: The covered porch protects the entry, which has a transom and sidelights to brighten this space.
- Great Room: To the left of the foyer, beyond decorative columns, lies this vaulted room, with its fireplace and media center. Additional columns separate the room from the vaulted formal dining room.
- Kitchen: A casual nook and this island work center are just around the corner from the great room. The second covered porch can be reached via a door in the nook.
- Master Suite: This luxurious space boasts a vaulted salon, a private niche that could be a small study, and a view of the front yard. The master bath features a spa tub, separate shower, compartmented toilet, huge walk-in closet, and access to the laundry room.
- Bedrooms: The two additional bedrooms are located at the back of the plan and share the Jack-and-Jill bathroom.

Copyright by designer/architect.

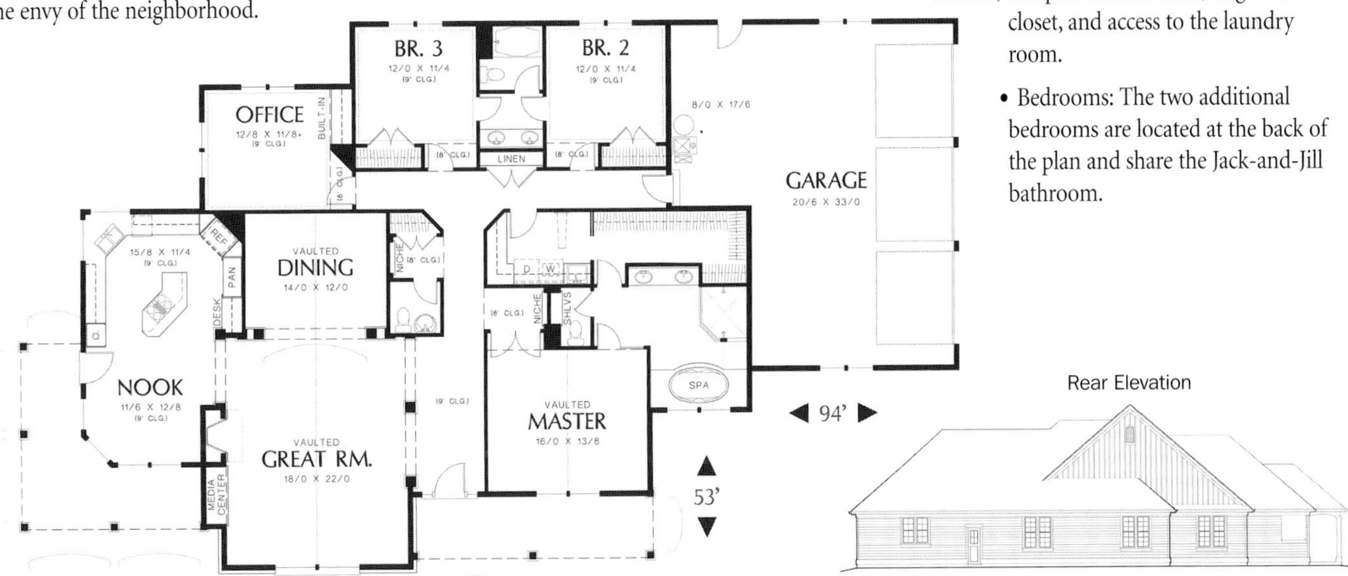

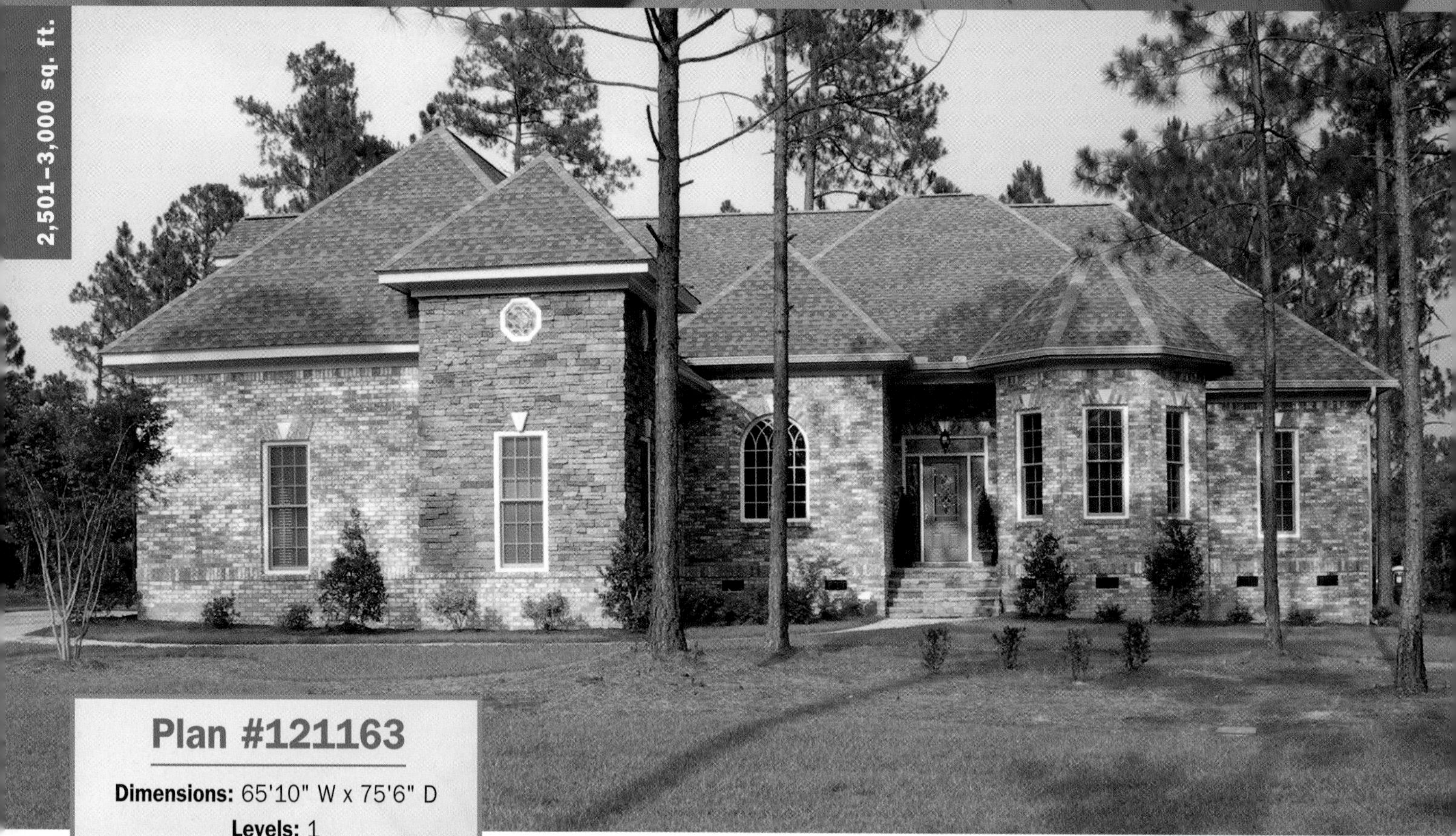

Plan #121163

Dimensions: 65'10" W x 75'6" D

Levels: 1

Heated Square Footage: 2,679

Bedrooms: 4

Bathrooms: 3

Foundation: Slab; basement for fee

Materials List Available: Yes

Price Category: F

Images provided by designer/architect.

CAD FILE AVAILABLE

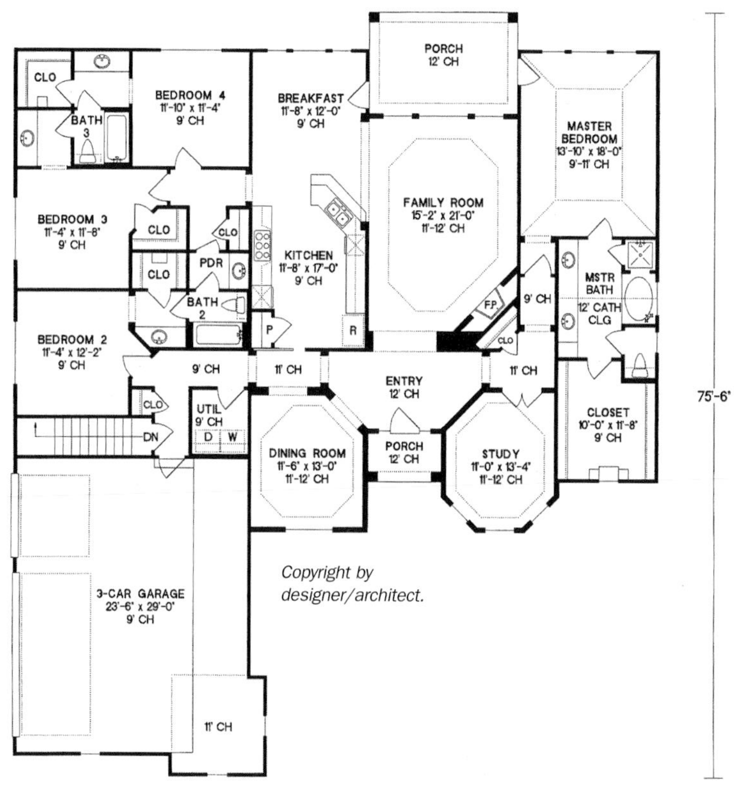

Large rooms give this home a spacious feel in a modest footprint.

Features:

- Family Room: This area is the central gathering place in the home. The windows to the rear fill the area with natural light. The fireplace take the chill off on cool winter nights.
- Kitchen: This peninsula kitchen with raised bar is open into the family room and the breakfast area. The built-in pantry is a welcomed storage area for today's family.
- Master Suite: This secluded area features large windows with a view of the backyard. The master bath boasts a large walk-in closet, his and her vanities and a compartmentalized lavatory area.
- Secondary Bedrooms: Bedroom 2 has its own access to the main bathroom, while bedrooms 3 and 4 share a Jack-and-Jill bathroom. All bedrooms feature walk-in closets.

Copyright by designer/architect.

Plan #211062

Dimensions: 96'6" W x 43' D
Levels: 1
Heated Square Footage: 2,719
Bedrooms: 4
Bathrooms: 2½
Foundation: Slab
Materials List Available: Yes
Price Category: F

Images provided by designer/architect.

CAD FILE AVAILABLE

If you're looking for a beautiful home that combines luxurious amenities with a separate, professional office space, this could be the one.

Features:

- Living Room: Enjoy an 11-ft. ceiling, brick fireplace, and built-in shelving in this room.
- Dining Room: A 2-story ceiling gives presence to this room.
- Kitchen: A breakfast bar here is open to the breakfast room beyond for ease of serving.
- Breakfast Room: A built-in corner china closet adds to the practicality you'll find here.
- Office: A separate entrance makes it possible to run a professional business from this home.
- Master Suite: Separated for privacy, this suite includes two vanities and a walk-in closet.
- Porch: The rear screened porch opens to a courtyard where you'll love to entertain.

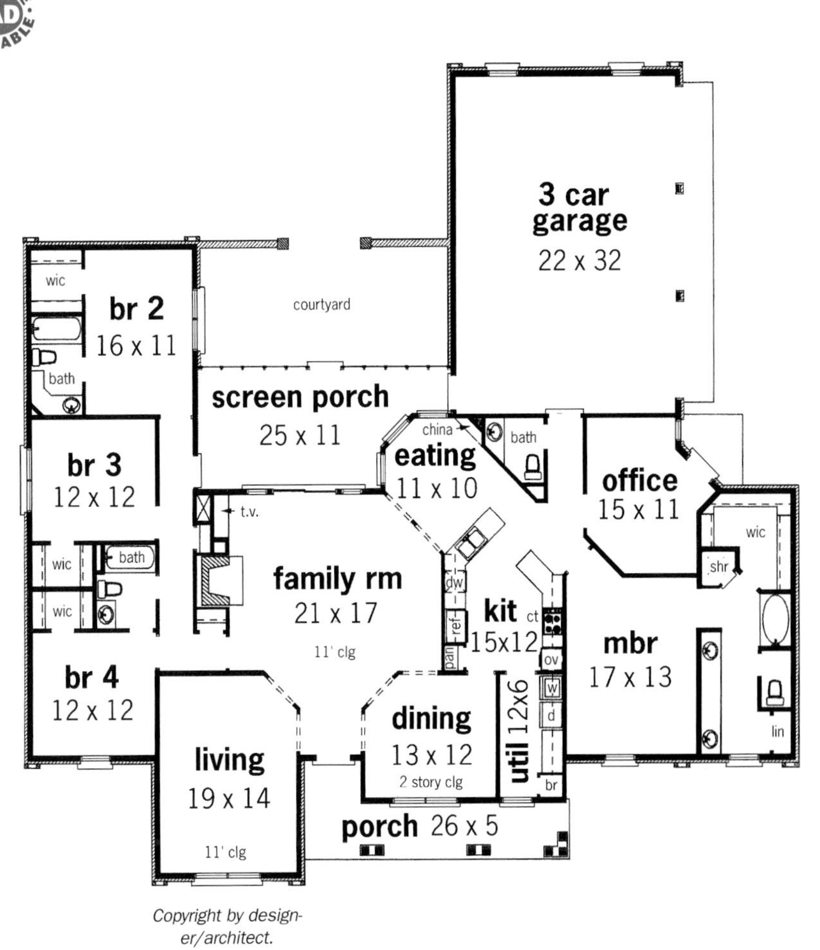

Copyright by designer/architect.

Plan #321027

Dimensions: 72' W x 68' D
Levels: 1
Heated Square Footage: 2,758
Bedrooms: 4
Bathrooms: 2½
Foundation: Basement
Materials List Available: Yes
Price Category: F

CAD FILE AVAILABLE

Images provided by designer/architect.

This stone-and-wood-sided four-bedroom home has country charm.

Features:

- Dining Room: You'll find this high-ceilinged room just off the entry.
- Great Room: This large gathering area has a vaulted ceiling with skylights and a corner fireplace.
- Kitchen: This large kitchen has an abundance of cabinets and opens into the breakfast area with a vaulted ceiling.
- Master Suite: This private area features a vaulted ceiling and a walk-in closet. The master bath has a double vanity and soaking tub.
- Bedrooms: Three additional bedrooms share a common bath.

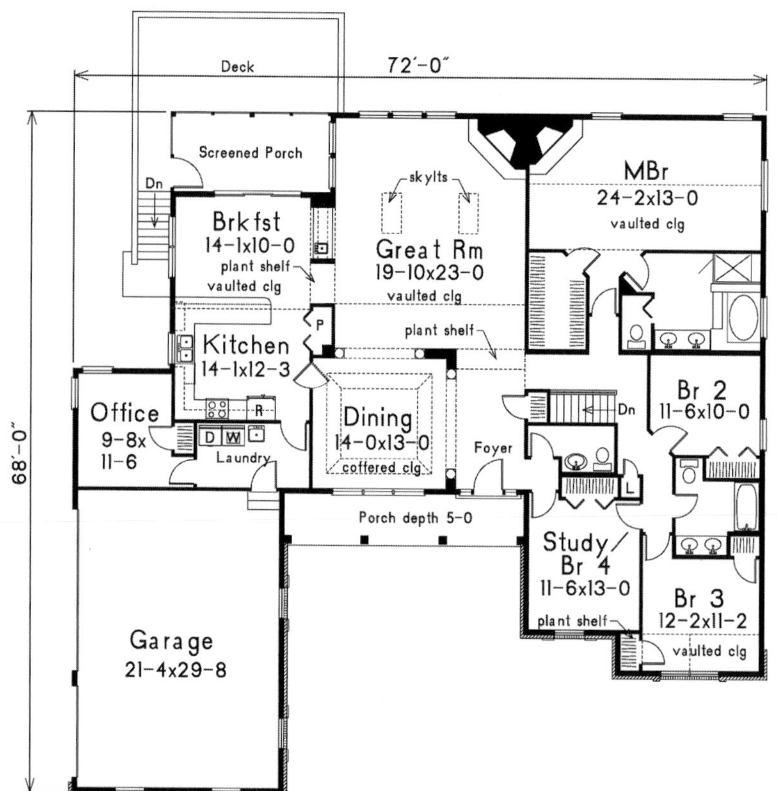

Copyright by designer/architect.

Plan #211011

Dimensions: 84' W x 54' D
Levels: 1
Heated Square Footage: 2,791
Bedrooms: 3 or 4
Bathrooms: 2
Foundation: Slab or crawl space
Materials List Available: Yes
Price Category: F

CAD FILE AVAILABLE

Images provided by designer/architect.

Plenty of room plus an open, flexible floor plan make this a home that will adapt to your needs.

Features:

- Ceiling Height: 8 ft. unless otherwise noted.
- Living Room: This distinctive room features a 12-ft. ceiling and is designed so that it can also serve as a master suite with a sitting room.
- Family Room: The whole family will want to gather in this large, inviting family room.
- Morning Room: The family room blends into this sunny spot, which is perfect for informal family meals.
- Kitchen: This spacious kitchen offers a smart layout. It is also contiguous to the family room.
- Master Suite: You'll look forward to the end of the day when you can enjoy this master suite. It includes a huge, luxurious master bath with two large walk-in closets and two vanity sinks.
- Optional Bedroom: This optional fourth bedroom is located so that it can easily serve as a library, den, office, or music room.

SMARTtip

Types of Decks

Ground-level decks resemble a low platform and are best for flat locations. They can be the most economical type to build because they don't require stairs.

Raised decks can rise just a few steps up or meet the second story of a house. Lifted high on post supports, they adapt well to uneven or sloped locations.

Multilevel decks feature two or more stories and are connected by stairways or ramps. They can follow the contours of a sloped lot, unifying the deck with the outdoors.

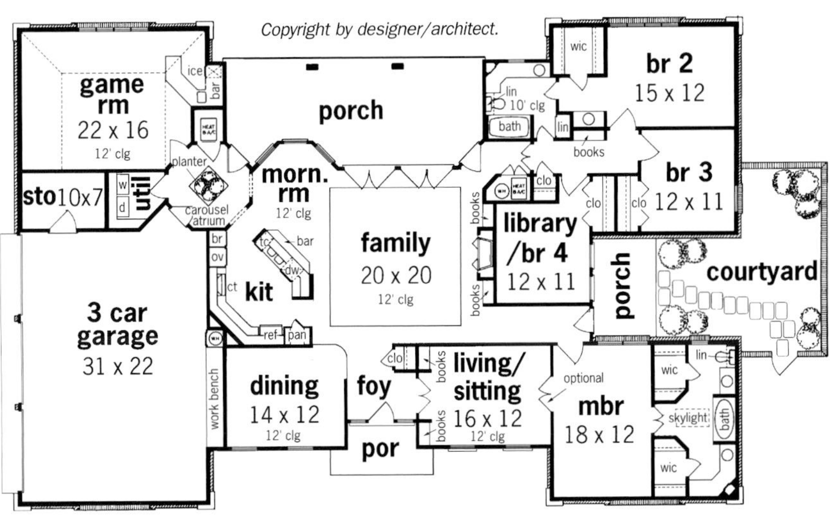

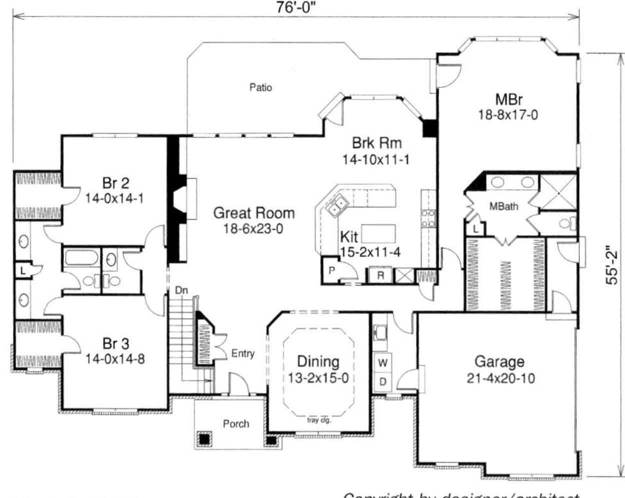

Copyright by designer/architect.

Plan #321007

Dimensions: 76' W x 55'2" D
Levels: 1
Heated Square Footage: 2,695
Bedrooms: 3
Bathrooms: 2½
Foundation: Basement
Materials List Available: Yes
Price Category: G

Images provided by designer/architect.

CAD FILE AVAILABLE

SMARTtip

Decorative Poles

Drapery poles are supported by the brackets fastened to the window frame or wall. The brackets that are provided with the poles generally coordinate and blend in with the pole finish. Brackets can be simple but also decorative. If you opt for a spectacular, attention-grabbing bracket, consider choosing less showy finials for the ends of the pole.

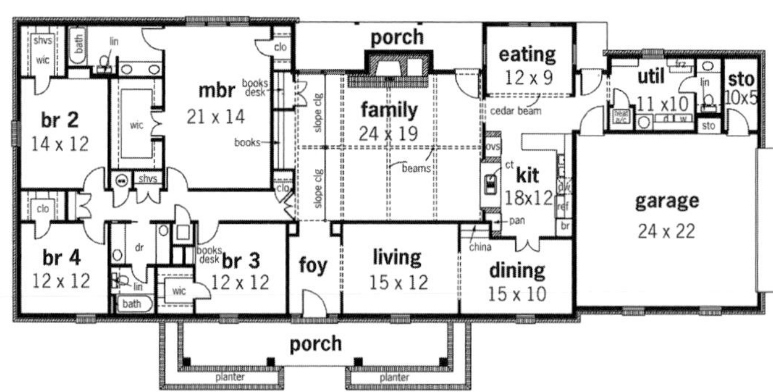

Copyright by designer/architect.

Plan #211155

Dimensions: 96'6" W x 43' D
Levels: 1
Heated Square Footage: 2,719
Bedrooms: 4
Bathrooms: 2½
Foundation: Slab; crawl space for fee
Materials List Available: Yes
Price Category: F

Images provided by designer/architect.

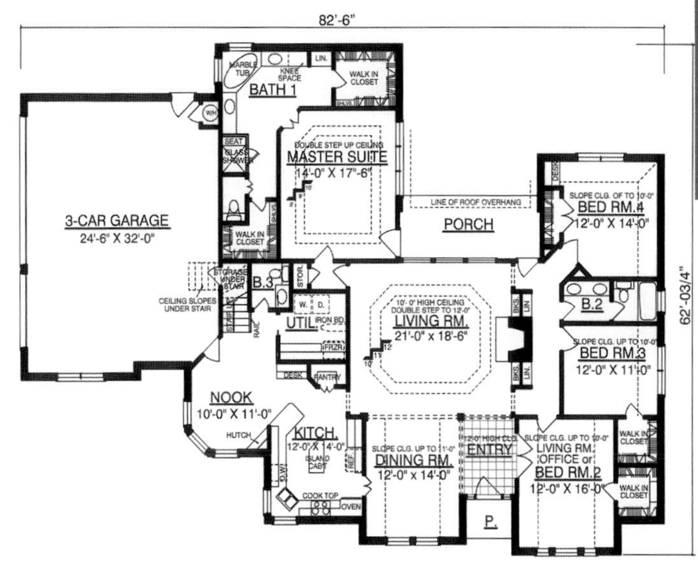

Plan #371095

Dimensions: 82'6" W x 62'0 3/4" D

Levels: 1

Heated Square Footage: 2,725

Bedrooms: 4

Bathrooms: 2½

Foundation: Crawl space, slab, or basement

Materials List Available: No

Price Category: F

Images provided by designer/architect.

CAD FILE AVAILABLE

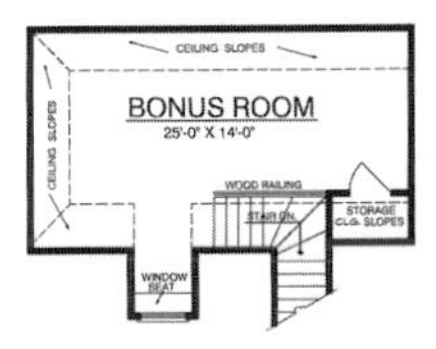

Bonus Area Floor Plan

Copyright by designer/architect.

Plan #111018

Dimensions: 67' W x 79' D

Levels: 1

Heated Square Footage: 2,745

Bedrooms: 4

Bathrooms: 3½

Foundation: Basement

Materials List Available: No

Price Category: G

Images provided by designer/architect.

CAD FILE AVAILABLE

Rear Elevation

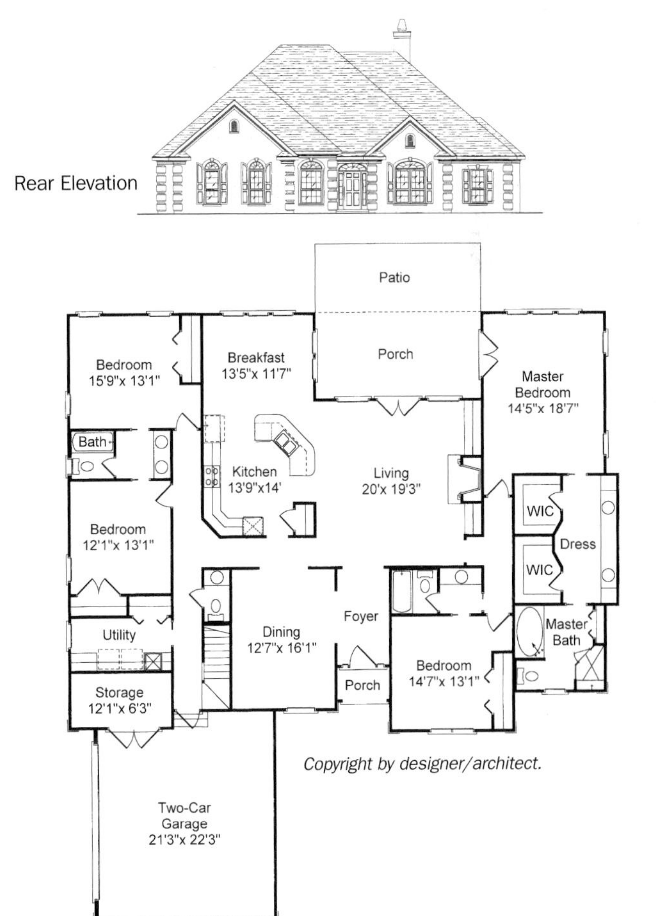

Copyright by designer/architect.

Plan #151594

Dimensions: 65' W x 64'10" D
Levels: 1
Heated Square Footage: 2,760
Bedrooms: 3
Bathrooms: 3½
Foundation: Crawl space or slab; basement or walkout for fee
CompleteCost List Available: Yes
Price Category: F

Images provided by designer/architect.

Bonus Level Floor Plan

Copyright by designer/architect.

Plan #611110

Dimensions: 61'8" W x 74'6" D
Levels: 1
Heated Square Footage: 2,762
Bedrooms: 4
Bathrooms: 3½
Foundation: Slab
Materials List Available: No
Price Category: F

Images provided by designer/architect.

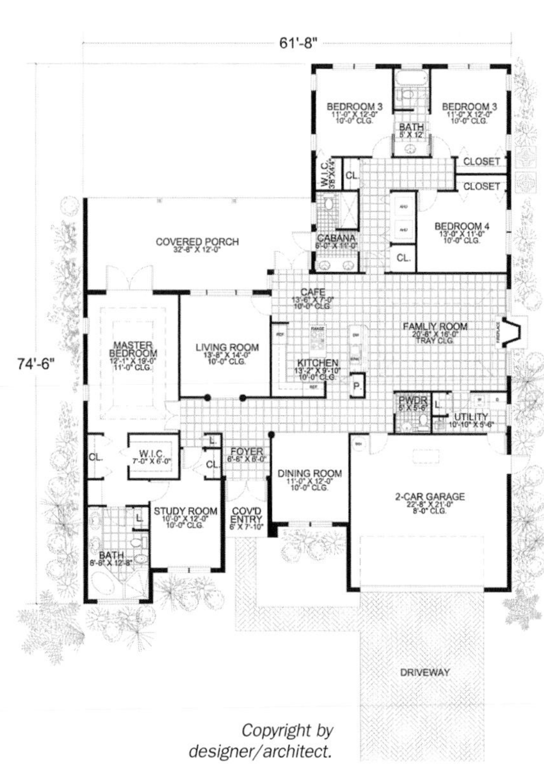

Copyright by designer/architect.

Plan #161224

Dimensions: 87'4" W x 57'4" D
Levels: 1
Heated Square Footage: 2,796
Bedrooms: 2
Bathrooms: 2½
Foundation: Walkout
Materials List Available: Yes
Price Category: F

Images provided by designer/architect.

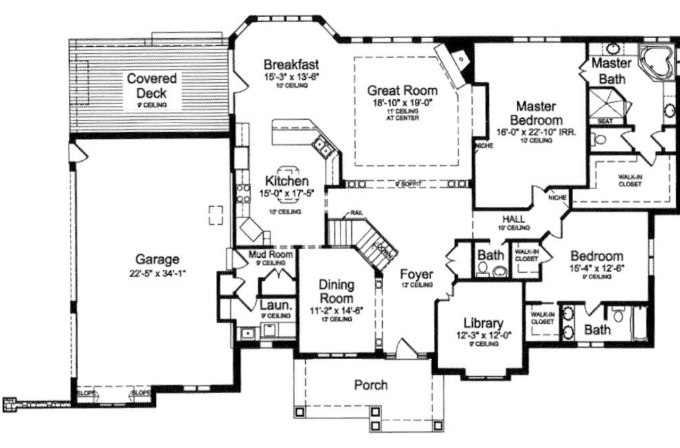

Copyright by designer/architect.

Rear View

Plan #111001

Dimensions: 66'8" W x 76'11" D
Levels: 1
Heated Square Footage: 2,832
Bedrooms: 4
Bathrooms: 2½
Foundation: Crawl space or slab
Materials List Available: No
Price Category: G

Images provided by designer/architect.

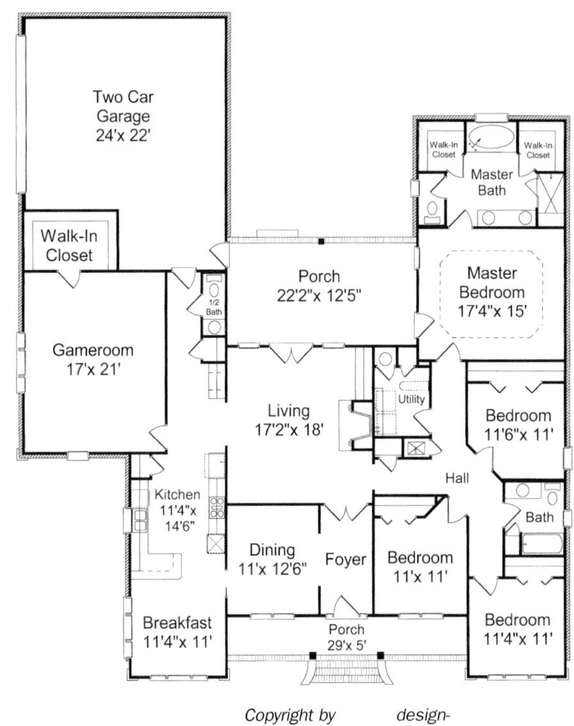

Copyright by design-er/architect.

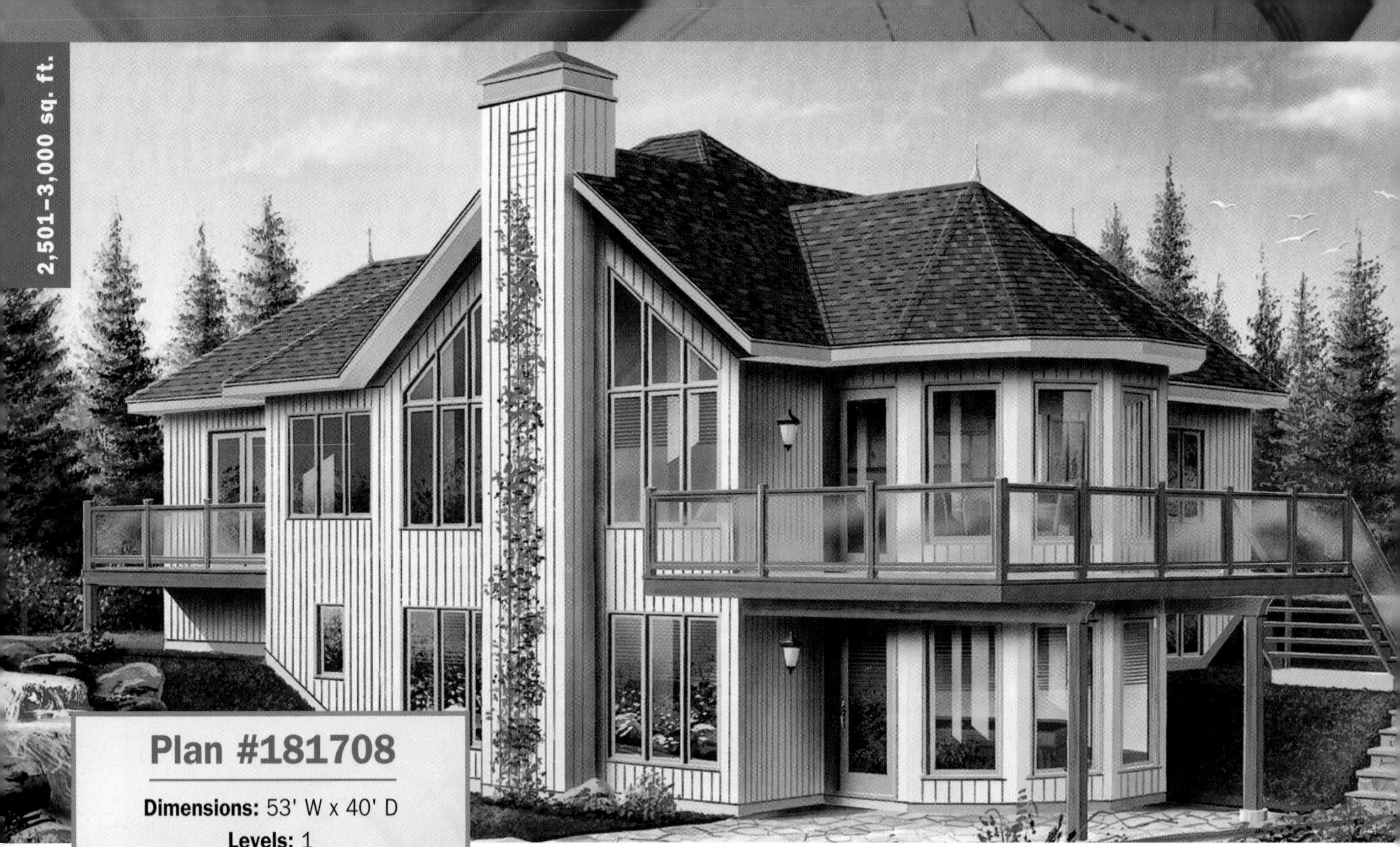

Plan #181708

Dimensions: 53' W x 40' D
Levels: 1
Heated Square Footage: 2,800
Main Level Sq. Ft.: 1,400
Lower Level Sq. Ft.: 1,400
Bedrooms: 3
Bathrooms: 2
Foundation: Basement or walkout
Materials List Available: Yes
Price Category: F

Images provided by designer/architect.

This gorgeous hillside home is designed for comfort and convenience.

Features:

- Great Room: No matter the time of day, this room will be filled with natural light from a sunlit wall of windows or a glowing fireplace.
- Dining Area: Not only does this dining room feature a beautiful bay of windows, but it also adjoins a deck where you might place a small table and chairs for picnic lunches with an elevated view.
- Kitchen: A unique element of this kitchen is the divided snack bar, which flanks the entry to the dining area and curves to provide more open space.
- Bedrooms: Each of these two nicely sized bedrooms has access to a bathroom. The front bedroom opens onto a small private deck.

Main Level Floor Plan

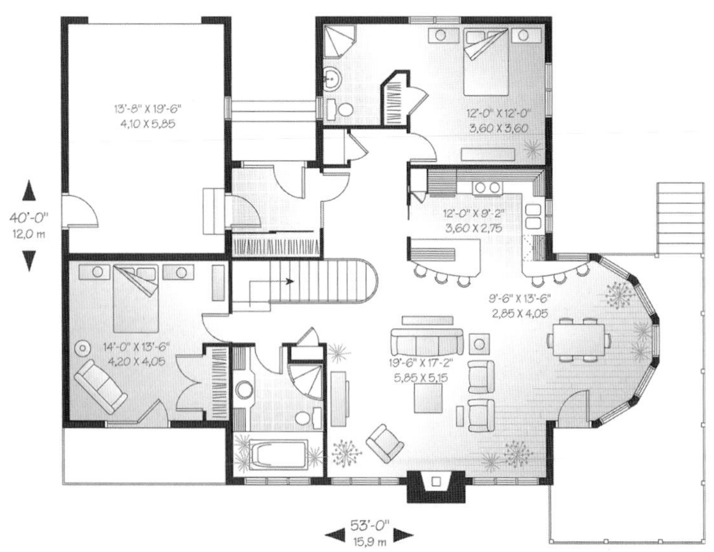

Lower Level Floor Plan

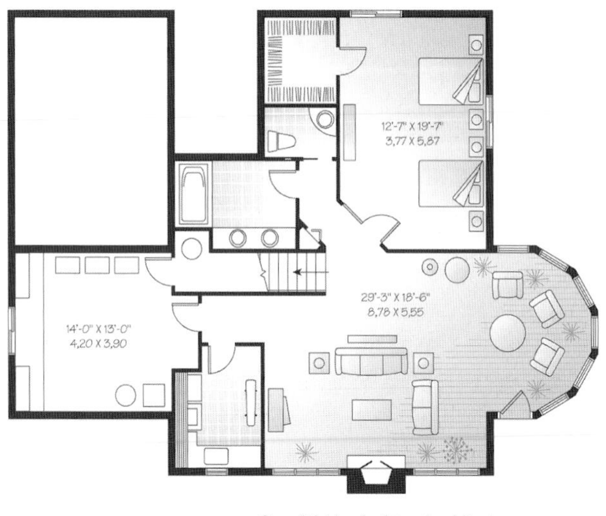

Plan #151057

Dimensions: 73'6" W x 80'6" D
Levels: 1
Heated Square Footage: 2,951
Bedrooms: 4
Bathrooms: 3
Foundation: Crawl space, slab, or basement
CompleteCost List Available: Yes
Price Category: G

Images provided by designer/architect.

The stucco exterior and large windows give this ranch an elegant look.

Features:

- Foyer: Enter the covered porch, and walk through the beautiful front door to this large foyer with entry closet.
- Entertaining: The large great room has a cozy fireplace and built-ins for casual get-togethers. The formal living room, also with a fireplace, is for special entertaining.
- Kitchen: This large U-shaped island kitchen has a raised bar and is open to the breakfast area and the great room. A short step though the door brings you onto the rear lanai.
- Master Suite: This private retreat has a fireplace and a sitting area with access to the rear lanai. The master bath features dual vanities, a whirlpool tub, a glass shower, and a separate toilet room.
- Bedrooms: Three large bedrooms are located on the opposite side of the home to give the master suite privacy. Two bedrooms share a Jack-and-Jill bathroom. The third bedroom has access to a common bathroom.

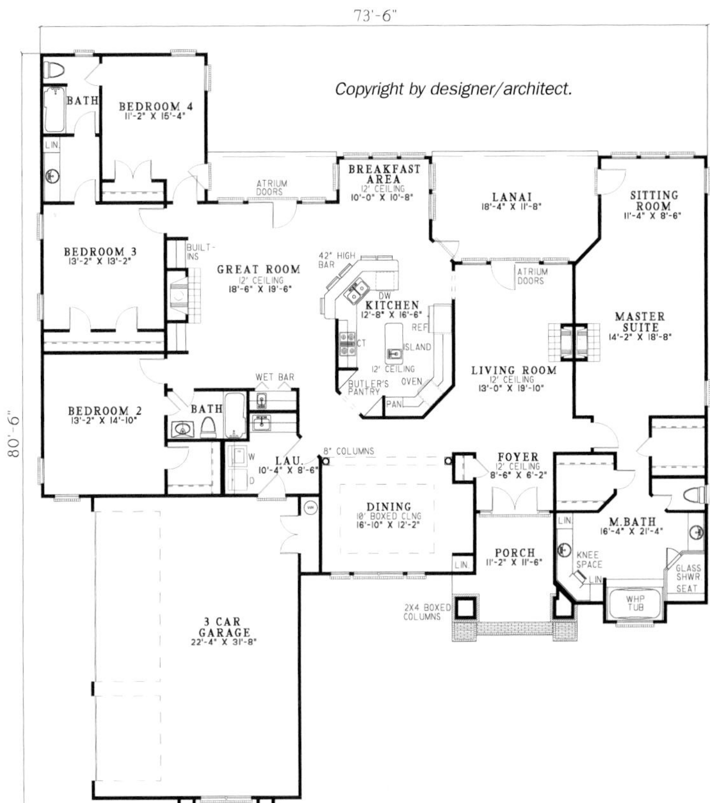

Images provided by designer/architect. Living Room

Plan #111004

Dimensions: 76' W x 85' D
Levels: 1
Heated Square Footage: 2,968
Bedrooms: 4
Full Bathrooms: 3½
Foundation: Slab
Materials List Available: No
Price Category: G

CAD FILE AVAILABLE

If you've been looking for a home that includes a special master suite, this one could be the answer to your dreams.

Features:

- Living Room: Make a sitting area around the fireplace here so that the whole family can enjoy the warmth on chilly days and winter evenings. A door from this room leads to the rear covered porch, making this room the heart of your home.
- Kitchen: An island with a cooktop makes cooking a pleasure in this well-designed kitchen, and the breakfast bar invites visitors at all times of day.
- Utility Room: A sink and a built-in ironing board make this room totally practical.
- Master Suite: A private fireplace in the corner sets a romantic tone for this bedroom, and the door to the covered porch allows you to sit outside on warm summer nights. The bath has two vanities, a divided walk-in closet, a standing shower, and a deluxe corner bathtub.

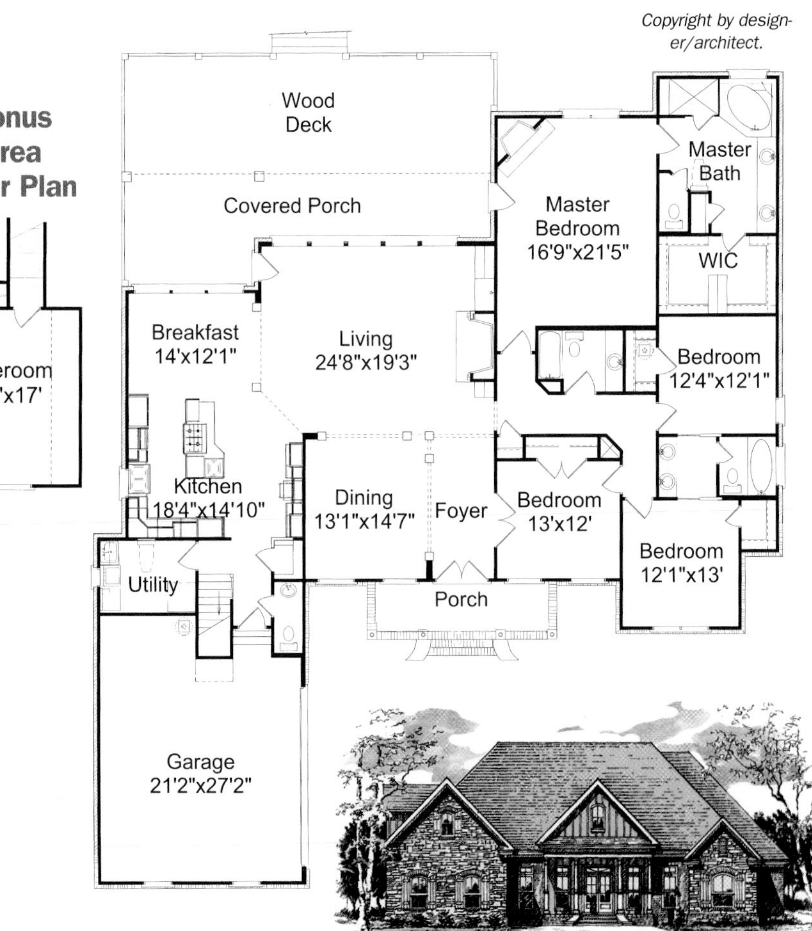

Images provided by designer/architect.

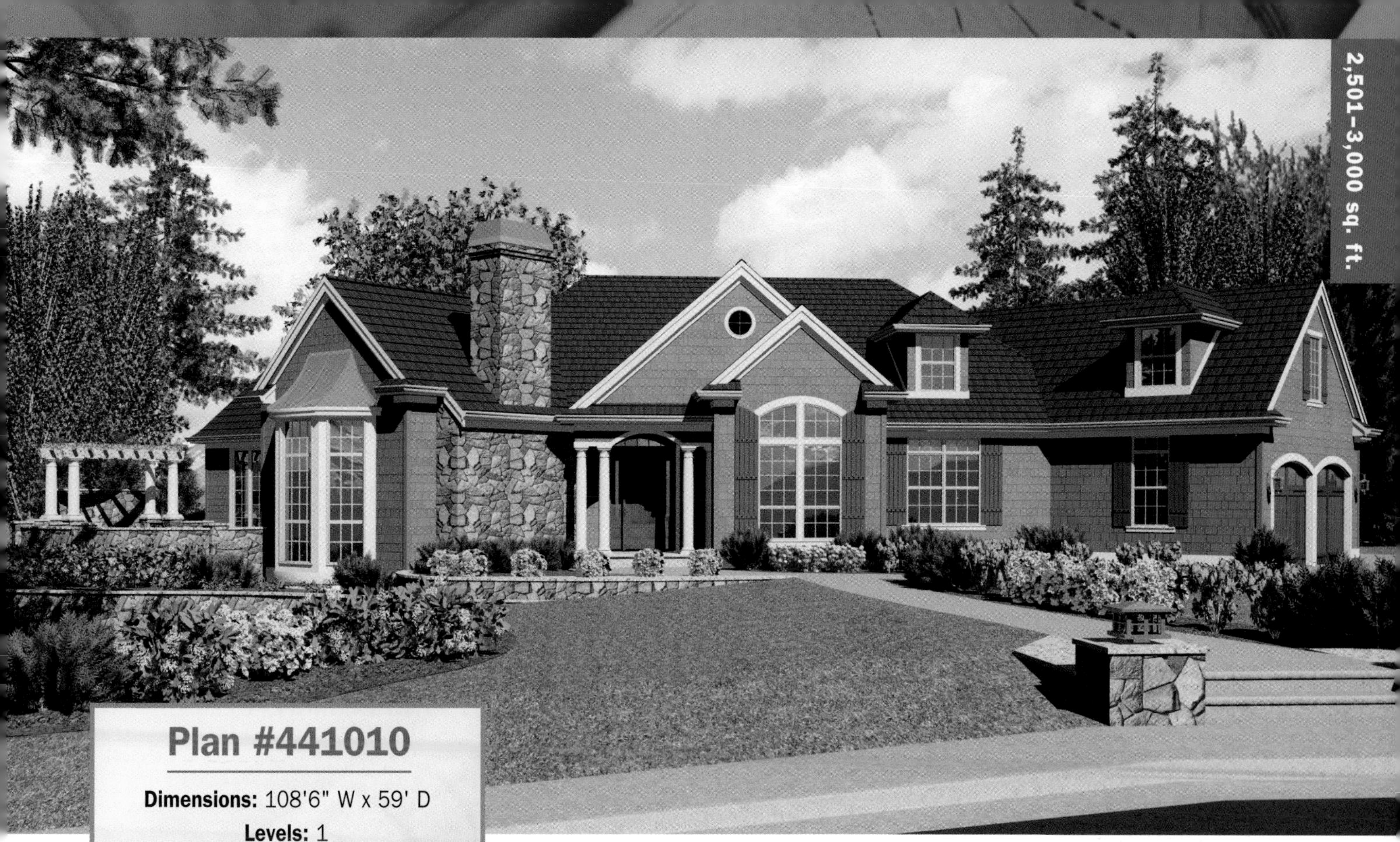

Plan #441010

Dimensions: 108'6" W x 59' D
Levels: 1
Heated Square Footage: 2,973
Bedrooms: 4
Bathrooms: 4½
Foundation: Crawl space; slab or basement available for fee
Materials List Available: Yes
Price Category: F

CAD FILE AVAILABLE

Bordering on estate-sized, this plan borrows elements from Norman, Mediterranean, and English architecture.

Features:

- Great Room: This gathering area features a large bay window and a fireplace flanked with built-ins. The vaulted ceiling adds to the large feel of the area.
- Kitchen: This large island kitchen features a walk-in pantry and a built-in desk. The breakfast nook has access to the patio.
- Master Suite: This retreat features a vaulted ceiling in the sleeping area and access to the patio. The master bath boasts dual vanities, a stand-up shower, a spa tub, and a very large walk-in closet.
- Bedrooms: Two family bedrooms, each with its own private bathroom, have large closets.

Rear Elevation

Copyright by designer/architect.

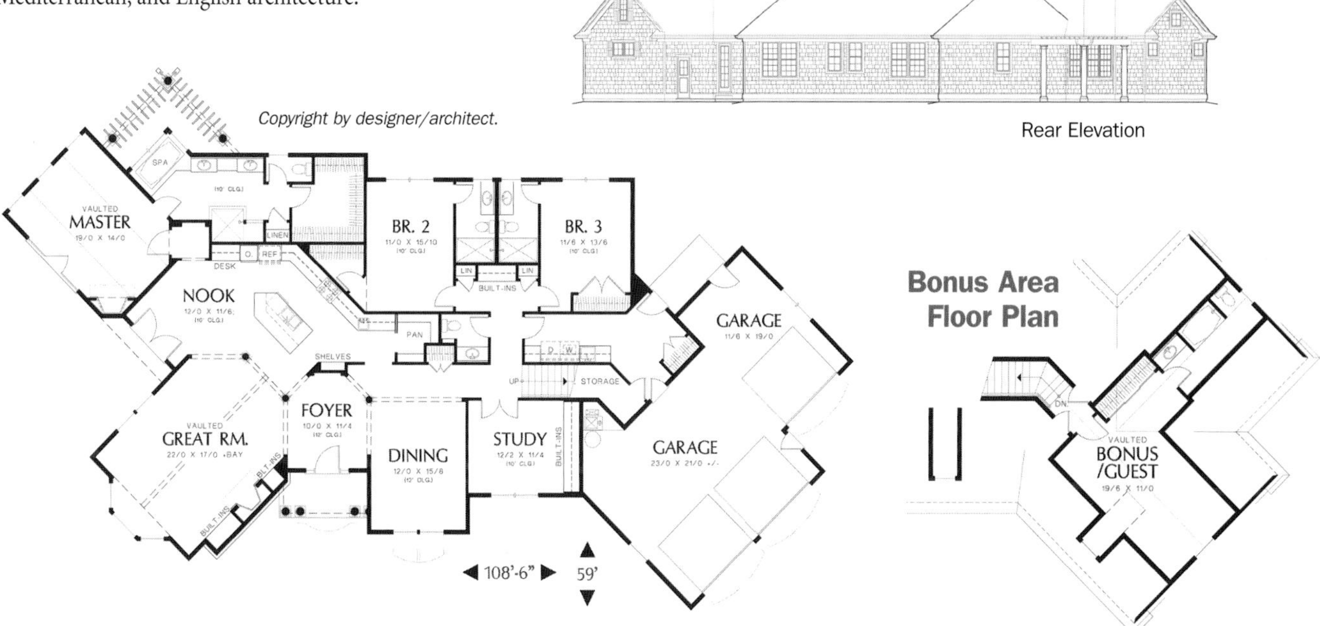

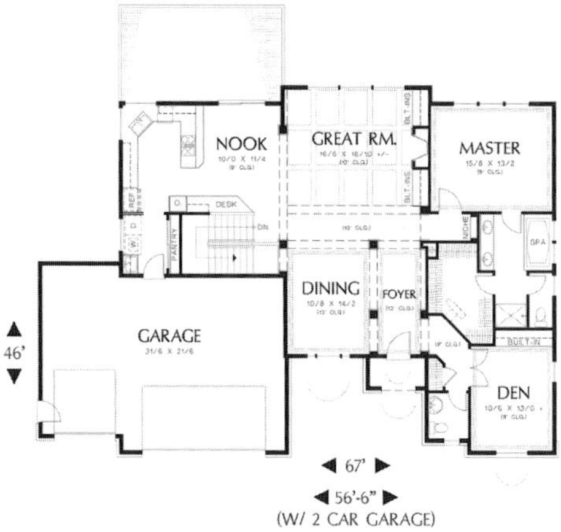

Plan #441011

Dimensions: 67' W x 46' D
Levels: 1
Heated Square Footage: 2,898
Main Level Sq. Ft.: 1,744
Basement Level Sq. Ft.: 1,154
Bedrooms: 3
Bathrooms: 2½
Foundation: Walkout basement
Materials List Available: Yes
Price Category: F

Images provided by designer/architect.

CAD FILE AVAILABLE

Main Level Floor Plan

Basement Level Floor Plan

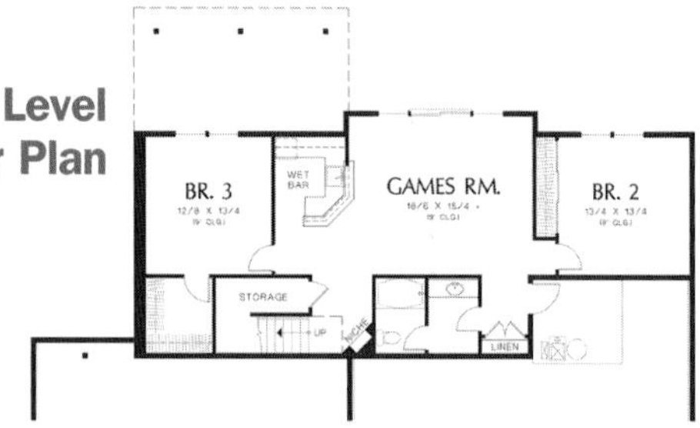

Rear Elevation

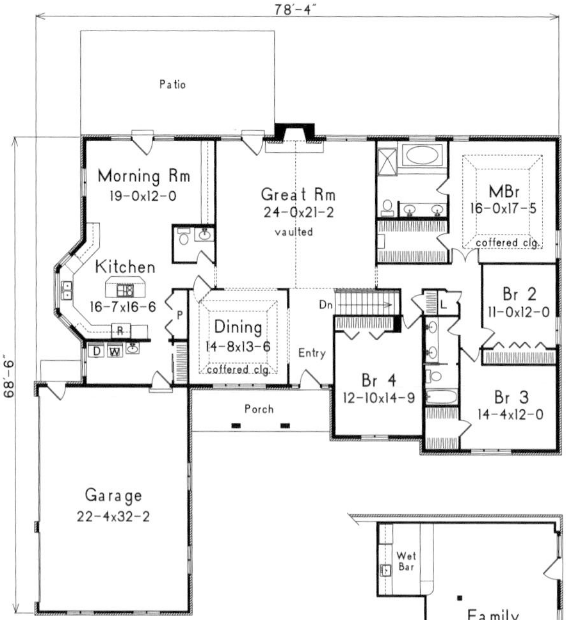

Plan #321036

Dimensions: 78'4" W x 68'6" D
Levels: 1
Heated Square Footage: 2,900
Bedrooms: 4
Bathrooms: 2½
Foundation: Basement or walkout
Materials List Available: Yes
Price Category: F

Images provided by designer/architect.

CAD FILE AVAILABLE

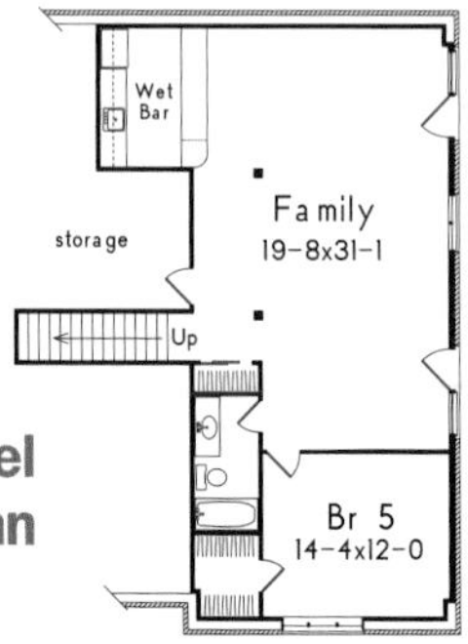

Optional Basement Level Floor Plan

Plan #151845

Dimensions: 84'10" W x 69'4" D
Levels: 1
Heated Square Footage: 3,003
Bedrooms: 5
Bathrooms: 4
Foundation: Crawl space or slab; basement or walkout for fee
CompleteCost List Available: Yes
Price Category: G

Images provided by designer/architect.

CAD FILE AVAILABLE

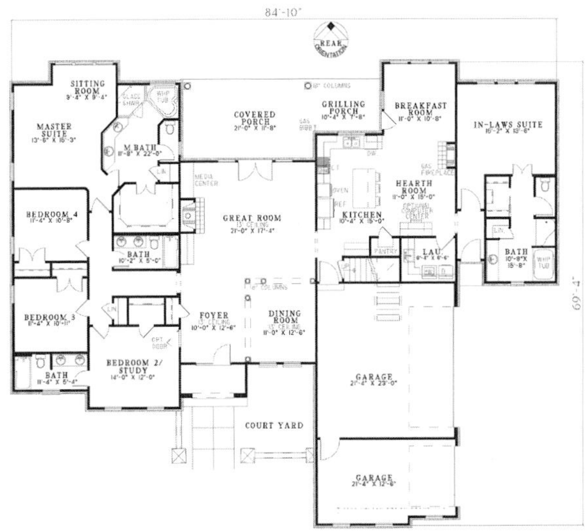

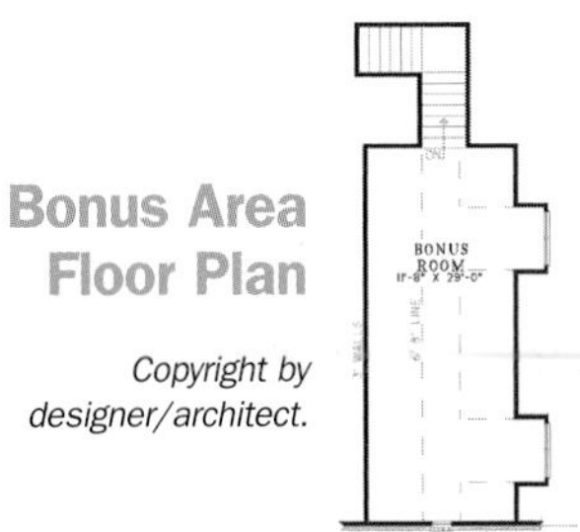

Bonus Area Floor Plan

Copyright by designer/architect.

Plan #151497

Dimensions: 74'2" W x 81'2" D
Levels: 1
Heated Square Footage: 3,021
Bedrooms: 4
Bathrooms: 3
Foundation: Slab
CompleteCost List Available: Yes
Price Category: G

Images provided by designer/architect.

CAD FILE AVAILABLE

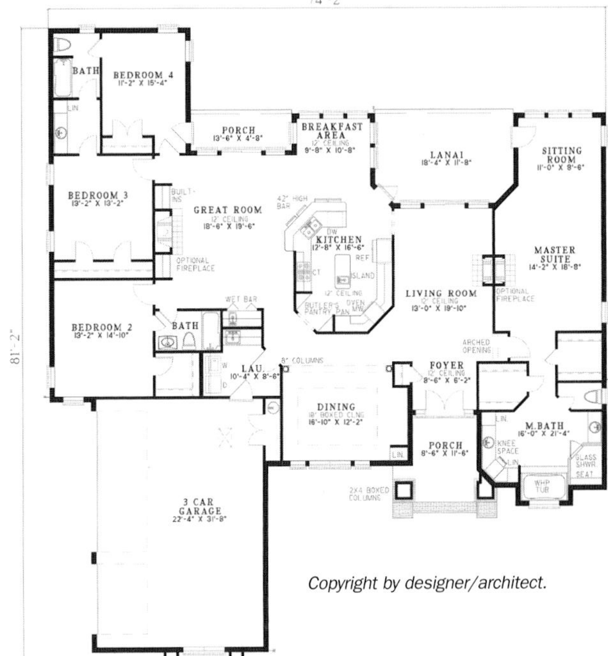

Copyright by designer/architect.

Plan #171013

Dimensions: 74' W x 72' D
Levels: 1
Heated Square Footage: 3,084
Bedrooms: 4
Bathrooms: 3½
Foundation: Crawl space or slab
Materials List Available: Yes
Price Category: G

Images provided by designer/architect.

Impressive porch columns add to the country charm of this amenity-filled family home.

Features:

- Ceiling Height: 10 ft.
- Foyer: The sense of style continues from the front porch into this foyer, which opens to the formal dining room and the living room.
- Dining Room: Two handsome support columns accentuate the elegance of this dining room.
- Living Room: This living room features a cozy corner fireplace and plenty of room for the entire family to gather and relax.
- Kitchen: You'll be inspired to new culinary heights in this kitchen, which offers plenty of counter space, a snack bar, a built-in pantry, and a china closet.
- Master Suite: The bedroom of this master suite has a fireplace and overlooks a rear courtyard. The bath has two vanities a large walk-in closet, a deluxe tub, a walk-in shower, and a skylight.

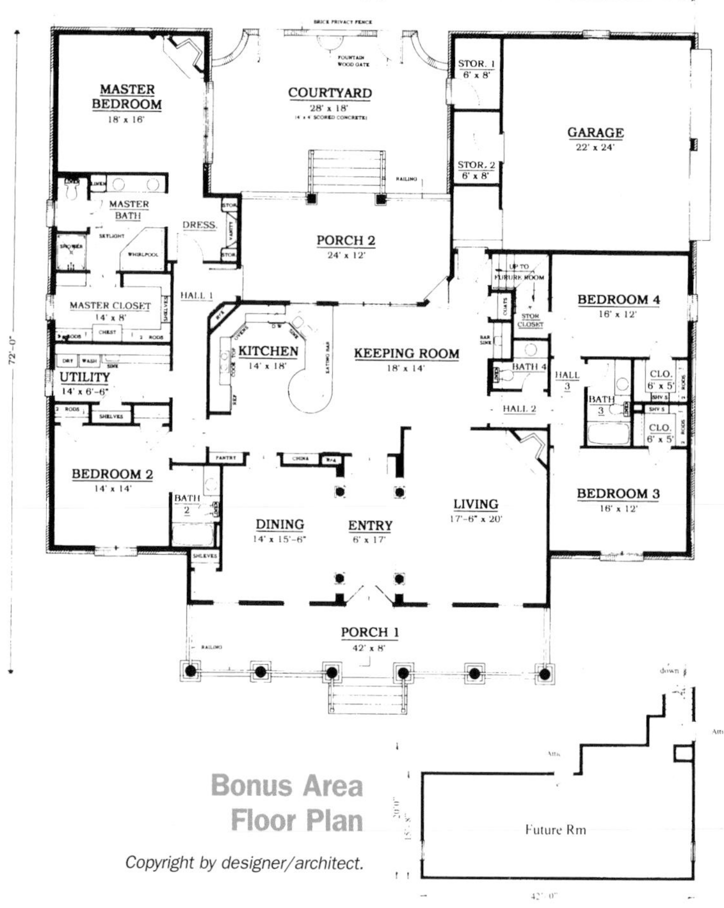

Bonus Area Floor Plan

Copyright by designer/architect.

Plan #541034

Dimensions: 79'6" W x 58'3"D
Levels: 1
Heated Square Footage: 3,162
Main Level Sq. Ft.: 2,113
Lower Level Sq. Ft.: 1,049
Bedrooms: 3
Bathrooms: 3
Foundation: Walkout; basement for fee
Materials List Available: No
Price Category: G

CAD FILE AVAILABLE

Images provided by designer/architect.

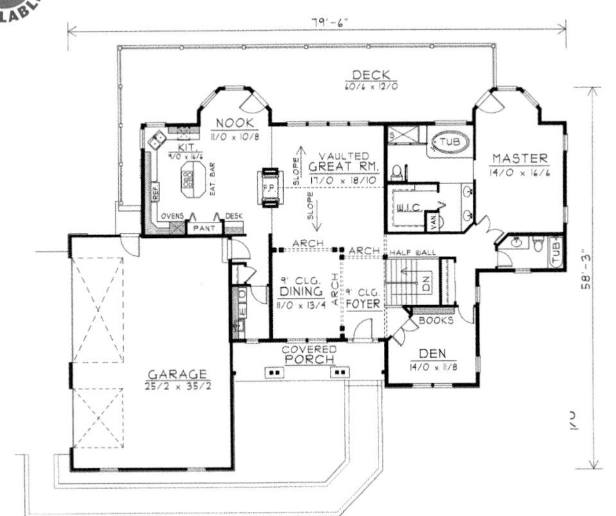

Copyright by designer/architect.

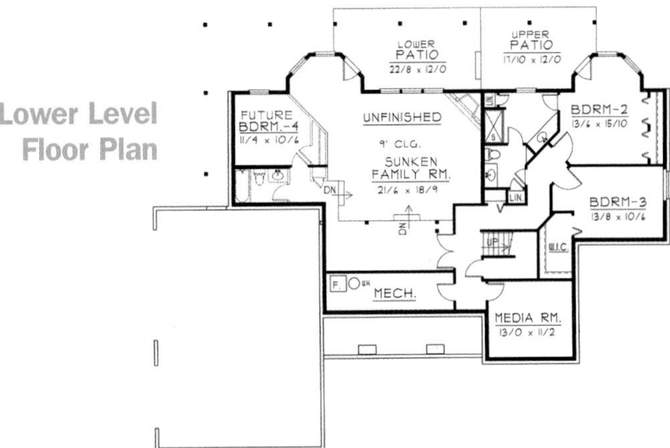

Lower Level Floor Plan

A combination of stone, shutters, and columns blend to create a magnificent exterior.

Features:

- Great Room: A see-through fireplace connects this vaulted gathering area to the kitchen and breakfast nook.
- Den: This den has built-in bookshelves and could serve as an additional bedroom.
- Master Suite: This fantastic suite features an octagonal sitting area. The private bath includes a separate tub and shower, a walk-in closet, double sinks, and a vanity for applying makeup.
- Secondary Bedrooms: Located on the lower level, these two bedrooms share a Jack-and-Jill bathroom.
- Expansion: There is no lack of room to expand as the basement allows for a future sunken family room, another bedroom, and an additional bathroom.

Plan #161056

Dimensions: 86'2" W x 63'8" D
Levels: 1
Heated Square Footage: 3,171
Optional Lower Level Sq. Ft.: 1,897
Bedrooms: 3
Bathrooms: 2½
Foundation: Walkout; crawl space or basement for feee
Material List Available: Yes
Price Category: G

This home is dedicated to comfort and high lifestyle and sets the standard for excellence.

Images provided by designer/architect.

Features:

- Open Plan: A wraparound island with seating is adorned with pillars and arched openings, and it separates the kitchen from the great room and breakfast room. This design element allows the rooms to remain visually open and, paired with a 9-ft. ceiling height, creates a spacious area.
- Great Room: A gas fireplace warms this gathering area, and the wall of windows across the rear brings the outdoors in. The built-in entertainment center will be a hit with the entire family.
- Master Suite: Delighting you with its size and luxury, this retreat enjoys a stepped ceiling in the sleeping area. The master bath features a garden bathtub and an oversized walk-in closet.
- Lower Level: Open stairs introduce this lower level, which mimics the size of the first floor, and, with a 9-ft. ceiling height, offers the same elegant feel of the first floor. Additional bedrooms, a game room, an exercise area, and storage are available options.

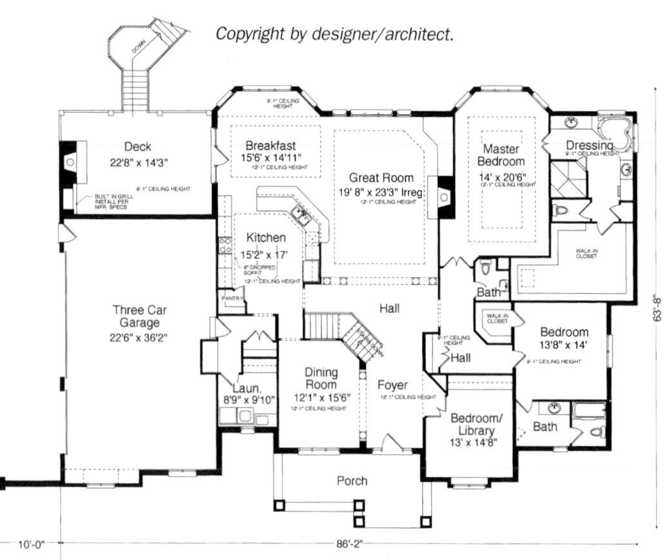

Copyright by designer/architect.

Optional Basement Level Floor Plan

Plan #451321

Dimensions: 65' W x 56'6" D
Levels: 1
HeatedSquare Footage: 3,304
Main Level Sq. Ft.: 1,652
Lower Level Sq. Ft.: 1,652
Bedrooms: 2
Bathrooms: 3
Foundation: Slab or walkout
Materials List Available: No
Price Category: G

Images provided by designer/architect.

If you're searching for an ideal vacation home that's inviting and spacious enough to accommodate loved ones, this is it.

Features:

- Outdoor Living Space: With a covered porch and large open deck, sunbathers and barbecuers alike will enjoy relaxing outdoors.
- Kitchen: This room is perfect for relaxing or enjoying a home-cooked meal.
- Den: This den doubles as an office, or can be converted into an entertainment center for a movie night.
- Master Suite: This luxurious master suite features one of the three large bathrooms in the home.
- Garage: This two-car garage is ideal for multi-car families or those with a lot of sports equipment to store.

Rear Elevation

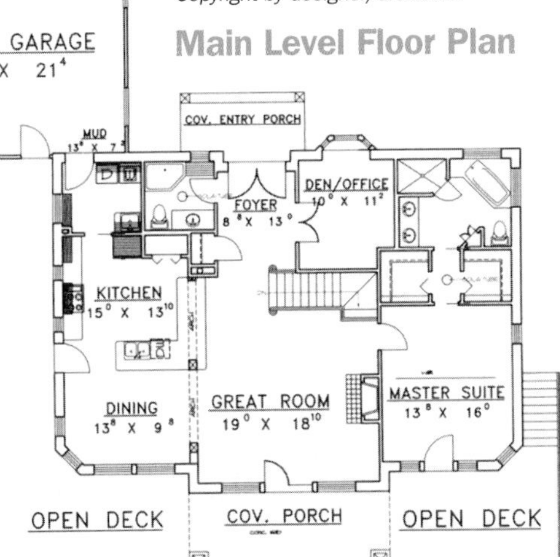

Copyright by designer/architect.

Main Level Floor Plan

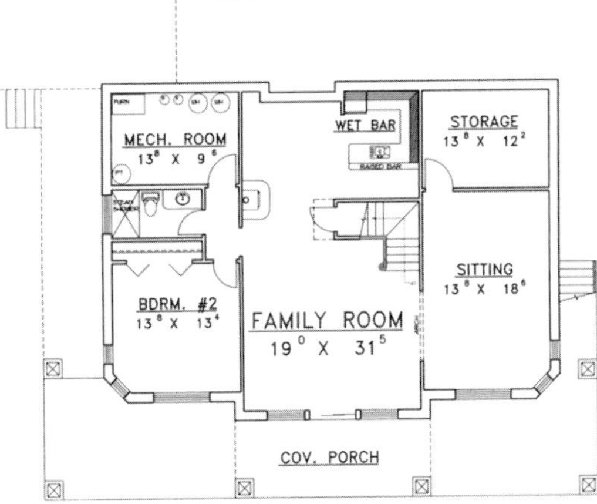

Lower Level Floor Plan

3,001–3,500 sq. ft.

Plan #661193

Dimensions: 64'8" W x 74'8" D
Levels: 1
Heated Square Footage: 3,060
Bedrooms: 4
Bathrooms: 3
Foundation: Slab
Materials List Available: No
Price Category: G

Images provided by designer/architect.

CAD FILE AVAILABLE

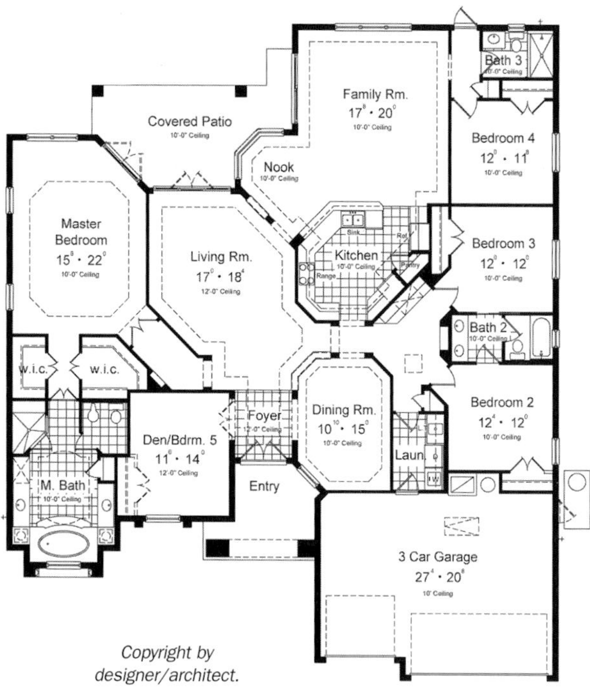

Copyright by designer/architect.

Plan #611181

Dimensions: 78'2" W x 100' D
Levels: 1
Heated Square Footage: 3,455
Bedrooms: 3
Bathrooms: 2 Full, 2 Half
Foundation: Slab
Materials List Available: No
Price Category: G

Images provided by designer/architect.

CAD FILE AVAILABLE

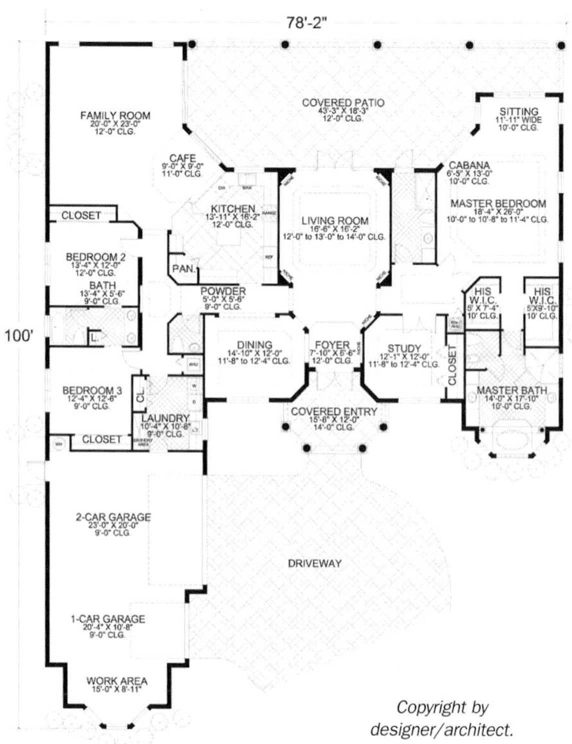

Copyright by designer/architect.

Plan #151060

Dimensions: 80'11" W x 95'8" D

Levels: 1

Heated Square Footage: 3,554

Bedrooms: 3

Bathrooms: 3

Foundation: Crawl space, slab basement, or walkout

CompleteCost List Available: Yes

Price Category: F

Images provided by designer/architect.

CAD FILE CAD AVAILABLE

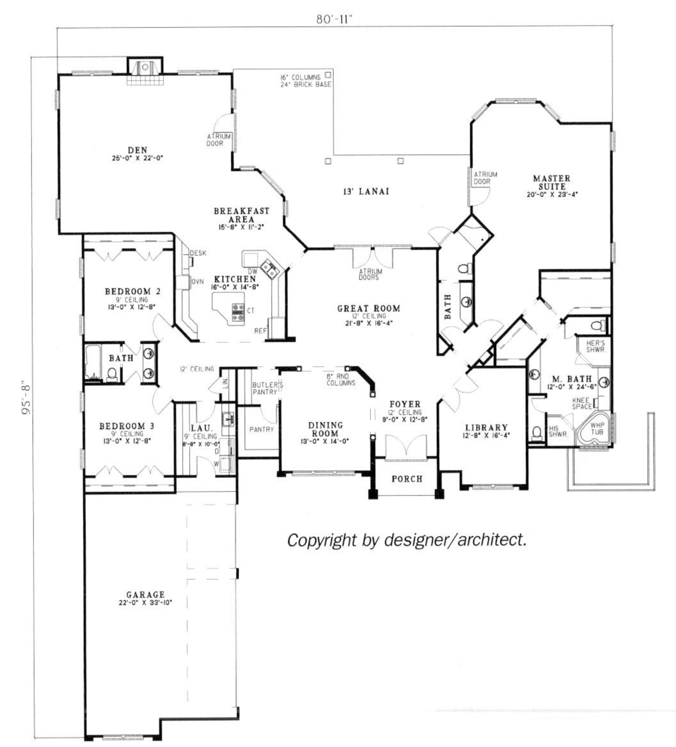

Copyright by designer/architect.

Plan #161028

Dimensions: 84'6" W x 69'4" D

Levels: 1

Heated Square Footage: 3,570

Optional Finished Basement Sq. Ft.: 2,367

Bedrooms: 3

Bathrooms: 3½

Foundation: Basement

Materials List Available: No

Price Category: H

Images provided by designer/architect.

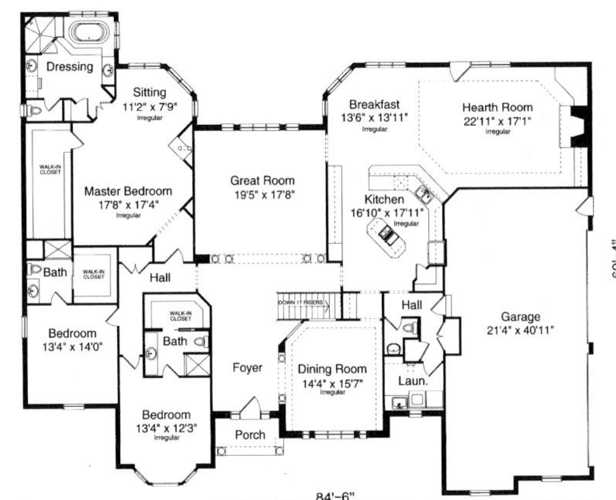

Copyright by designer/architect.

Office 12'10" x 11'8"
Bedroom 12'6" x 14'11"
Raised Bar
Billiards Room 19'8" x 15'11"
Media Area 20'0" x 13'6"
Hall
Bath
Game Room 14'11" x 9'6"
Unexcavated
Basement
Exercise Area 13'8" x 12'5"
Unexc.

Optional Basement Level Floor Plan

Plan #161095

Dimensions: 59' W x 49'8" D
Levels: 1
Heated Square Footage: 3,620
Main Level Sq. Ft.: 2,068
Lower Level Sq. Ft.: 1,552
Bedrooms: 3
Bathrooms: 3
Foundation: Walkout basement
Materials List Available: No
Price Category: H

Images provided by designer/architect.

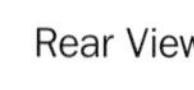

Main Level Floor Plan

Copyright by designer/architect.

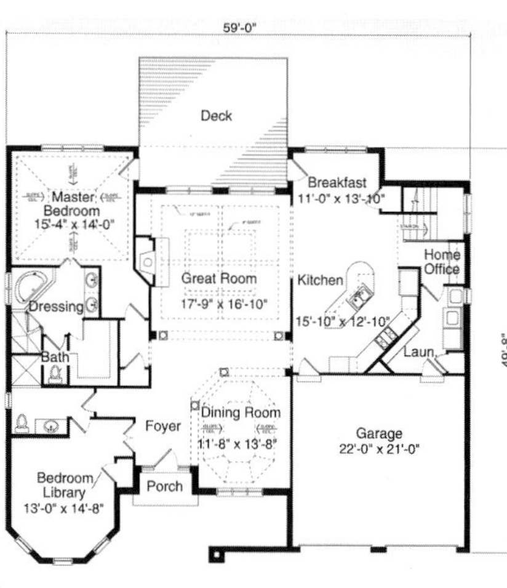

Lower Level Floor Plan

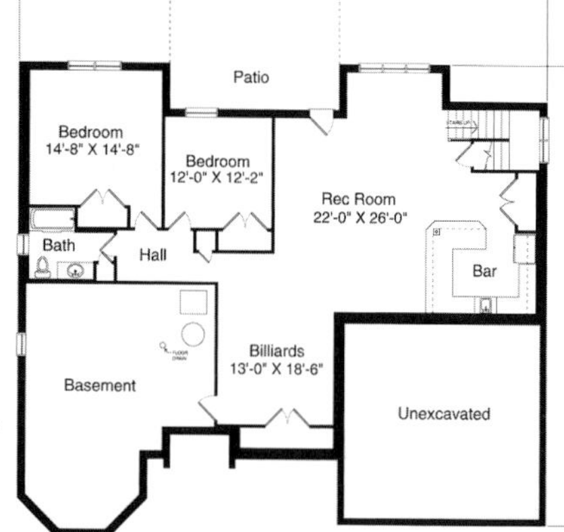

Rear View

Plan #481026

Dimensions: 72' W x 66' D
Levels: 1
Heated Square Footage: 3,837
Main Level Sq. Ft.: 2,374
Lower Level Sq. Ft.: 1,463
Bedrooms: 3
Bathrooms: 2½
Foundation: Walkout basement
Materials List Available: No
Price Category: H

Images provided by designer/architect.

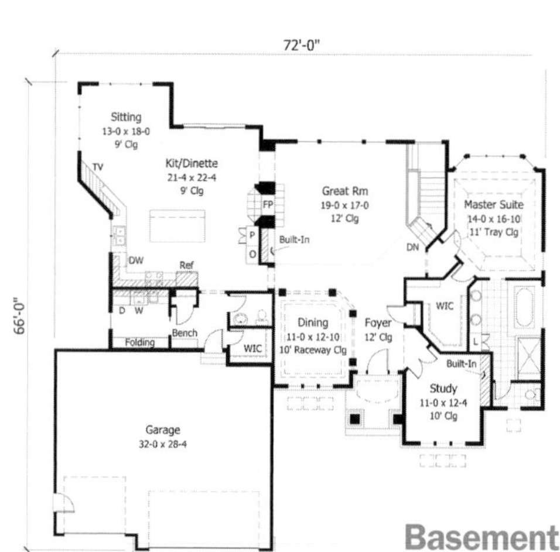

Basement Level Floor Plan

Copyright by designer/architect.

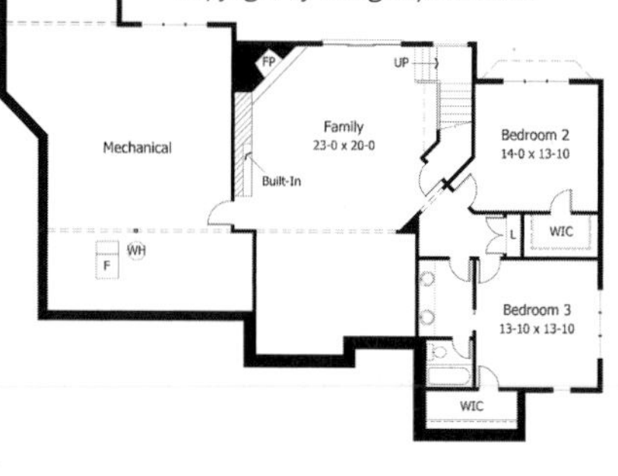

Rear Elevation

Plan #211068

Dimensions: 98' W x 90' D
Levels: 1
Heated Square Footage: 3,960
Bedrooms: 4
Bathrooms: 4½
Foundation: Crawl space
Materials List Available: Yes
Price Category: H

Images provided by designer/architect.

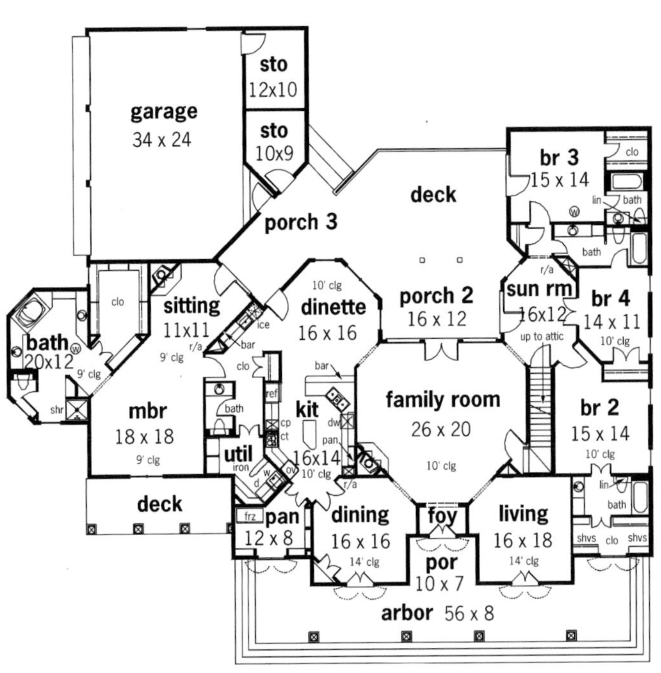

Copyright by designer/architect.

Plan #391049

Dimensions: 78' W x 52'4" D
Levels: 1
Heated Square Footage: 4,064
Bedrooms: 4
Bathrooms: 3
Foundation: Basement
Materials List Available: Yes
Price Category: E

Images provided by designer/architect.

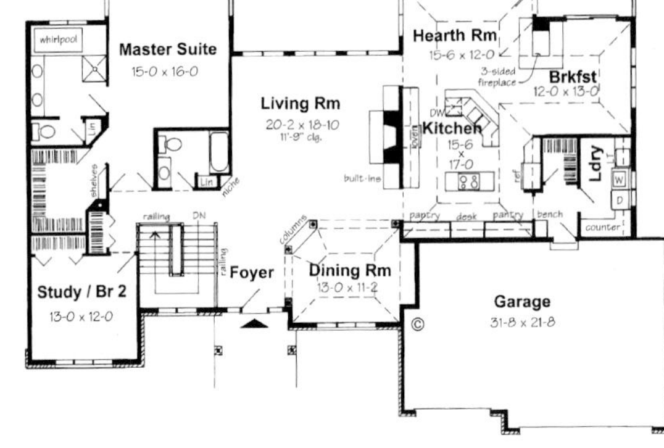

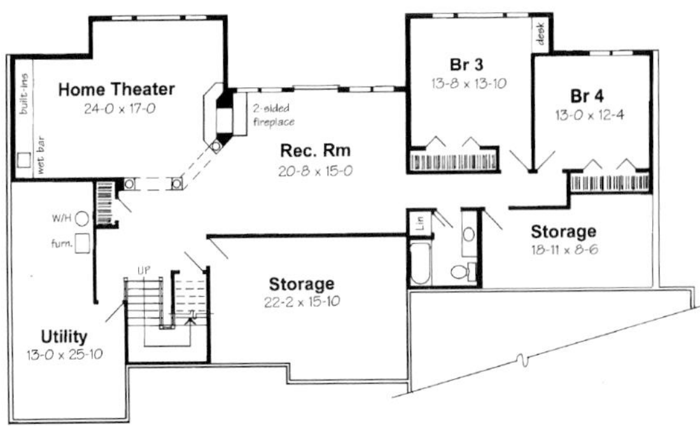

Basement Level Floor Plan

Copyright by designer/architect.

Plan #211067

Dimensions: 96' W x 90' D
Levels: 1
Heated Square Footage: 4,038
Bedrooms: 4
Bathrooms: 4½
Foundation: Crawl space
Materials List Available: Yes
Price Category: I

Images provided by designer/architect.

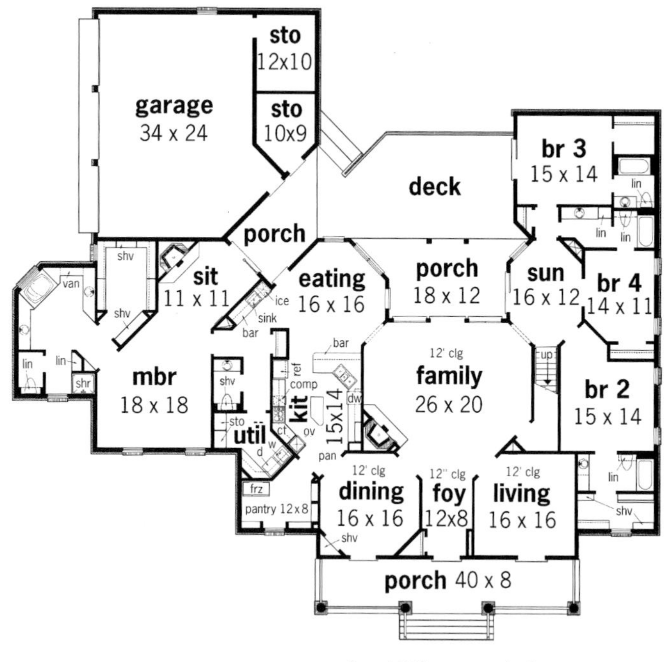

Copyright by designer/architect.

Plan #531020

Dimensions: 74' W x 97' D
Levels: 1
Heated Square Footage: 4,271
Main Level Sq. Ft.: 3,731
Upper Level Sq. Ft.: 540
Bedrooms: 4
Bathrooms: 3½
Foundation: Slab
Materials List Available: No
Price Category: I

Images provided by designer/architect.

CAD FILE AVAILABLE

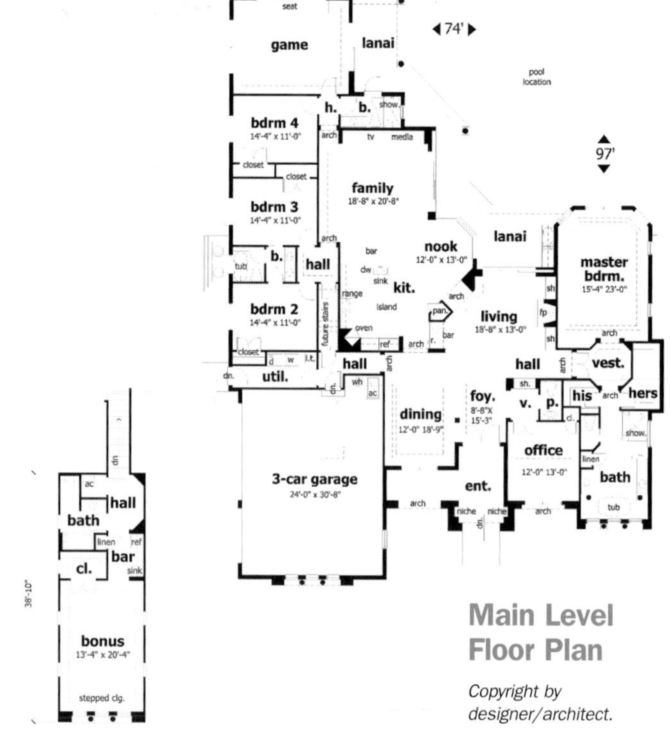

Upper Level Floor Plan

Main Level Floor Plan

Copyright by designer/architect.

Plan #451217

Dimensions: 103'6" W x 53'11" D
Levels: 1
Heated Square Footage: 4,711
Main Level Sq. Ft.: 2,470
Lower Level Sq. Ft.: 2,241
Bedrooms: 4
Bathrooms: 3
Foundation: Walkout basement
Materials List Available: No
Price Category: I

Images provided by designer/architect.

Main Level Floor Plan

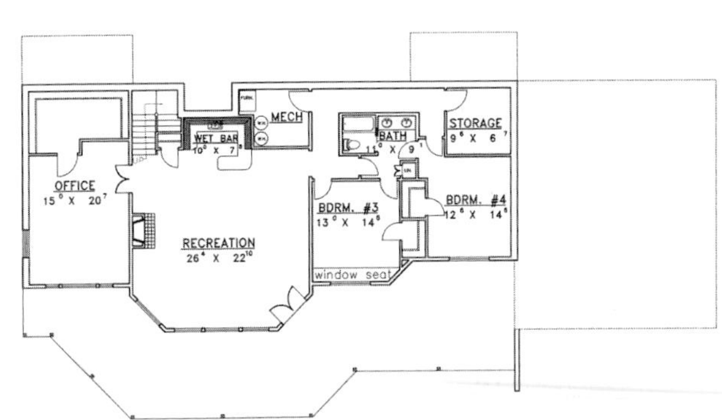

Lower Level Floor Plan

Copyright by designer/architect.

Plan #441212

Dimensions: 81' W x 66' D
Levels: 1
Heated Square Footage: 4,808
Main Level Sq. Ft.: 2,792
Lower Level Sq. Ft.: 2,016
Bedrooms: 4
Bathrooms: 4½
Foundation: Walkout
Materials List Available: Yes
Price Category: I

Images provided by designer/architect.

Main Level Floor Plan

Copyright by designer/architect.

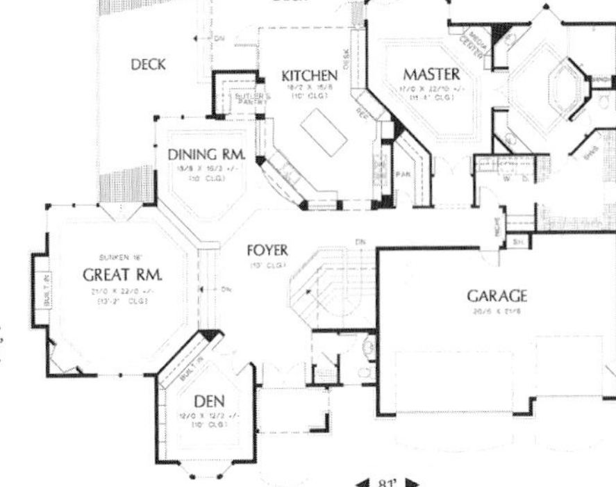

Rear View

Lower Level Floor Plan

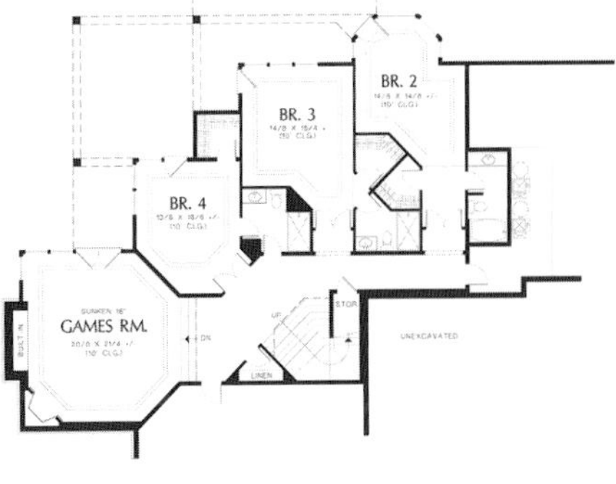

Plan #481028

Dimensions: 86'8" W x 53' D
Levels: 1
Heated Square Footage: 3,980
Main Level Sq. Ft.: 2,290
Lower Level Sq. Ft.: 1,690
Bedrooms: 3
Bathrooms: 2½
Foundation: Walkout basement
Materials List Available: No
Price Category: H

Images provided by designer/architect.

This home, with its Southwestern flair, invites friends and family in for some down-home hospitality.

Features:

- Foyer: A 12-ft-high ceiling extends an open welcome to all. With a view through the great room, the open floor plan makes the home feel large and open.
- Kitchen: This spacious gourmet kitchen opens generously to the hearth room, which features an angled fireplace. A two-level island, which contains a two-bowl sink, provides casual seating and additional storage.
- Master Suite: This romantic space features a 10-ft.-high stepped ceiling and a compartmentalized full bath that includes his and her sinks and a whirlpool tub.
- Lower Level: For fun times, this lower level is finished to provide a wet bar and a recreation room. Two bedrooms, which share a full bathroom, are also on this level. Future expansion can include an additional bedroom.

Rear View

Copyright by designer/architect.

Lower Level Floor Plan

Plan #161093

Dimensions: 70'8" W x 64' D
Levels: 1
Heated Square Footage: 4,328
Main Level Sq. Ft.: 2,582
Lower Level Sq. Ft.: 1,746
Bedrooms: 3
Bathrooms: 3½
Foundation: Walkout
Materials List Available: No
Price Category: I

Images provided by designer/architect.

Detailed stucco and stone accents impart warmth and character to the exterior of this one level home.

Features:

- Great Room: This gathering room, which features a fireplace and a decorative ceiling, offers an extensive view of the rear yard.
- Kitchen: Spacious and up-to-date, this extra-large combination gourmet kitchen and breakfast room is an ideal area for doing chores and hosting family gatherings.
- Main Level: The extravagant master suite, with its private bathroom and dressing area, the library with built-in shelves, and the formal dining room round out the main floor. Accented by a wood rail, the extra-wide main stairway leads to the lavish lower level.
- Lower Level: The two additional bedrooms, adjoining bathroom, media room, billiard room, and exercise room comprise this fantastic finished lower level.

Great Room

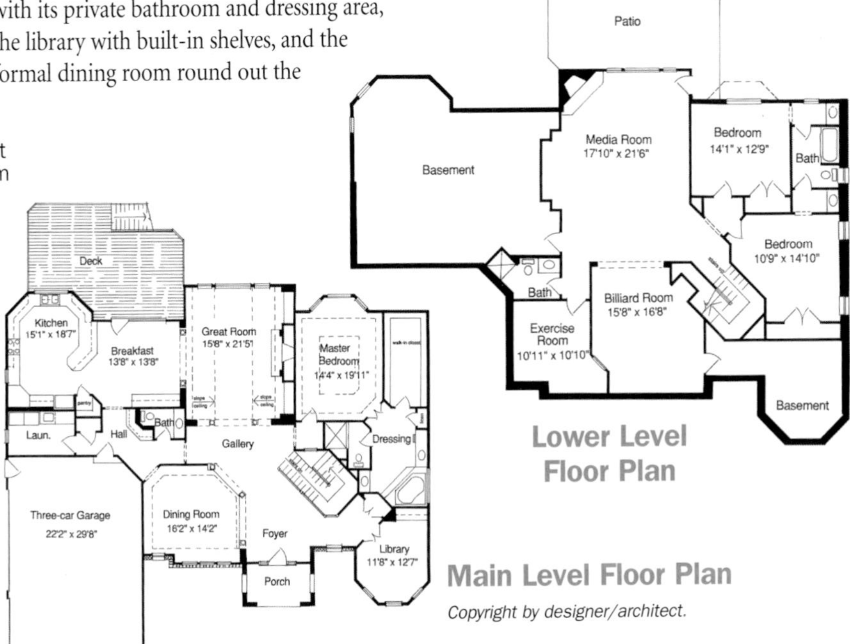

Lower Level Floor Plan

Main Level Floor Plan

Copyright by designer/architect.

Plan #441015

Dimensions: 130'3" W x 79'3" D
Levels: 1
Heated Square Footage: 4,732
Main Level Sq. Ft.: 2,902
Lower Level Sq. Ft.: 1,830
Bedrooms: 4
Bathrooms: 3 full, 2 half
Foundation: Walkout basement
Materials List Available: Yes
Price Category: I

Images provided by designer/architect.

CAD FILE AVAILABLE

An artful use of stone was employed on the exterior of this rustic hillside home to complement other architectural elements, such as the angled, oversize four-car garage and the substantial roofline.

Features:

- Great Room: This massive vaulted room features a large stone fireplace at one end and a formal dining area at the other. A built-in media center and double doors separate the great room from a home office with its own hearth and built-ins.
- Kitchen: This kitchen features a walk-in pantry and snack counter and opens to a skylighted outdoor kitchen. Its appointments include a cooktop and a corner fireplace.
- Home Theatre: This space has a built-in viewing screen, a fireplace, and double terrace access.
- Master Suite: This private space is found at the other side of the home. Look closely for expansive his and her walk-in closets, a spa tub, a skylighted double vanity area, and a corner fireplace in the salon.
- Bedrooms: Three family bedrooms are on the lower level; bedroom 4 has a private bathroom and walk-in closet.
- Garage: This large garage has room for four cars; don't miss the dog shower and grooming station just off the garage.

Main Level Floor Plan

Copyright by designer/architect.

Entry

Lower Level Floor Plan

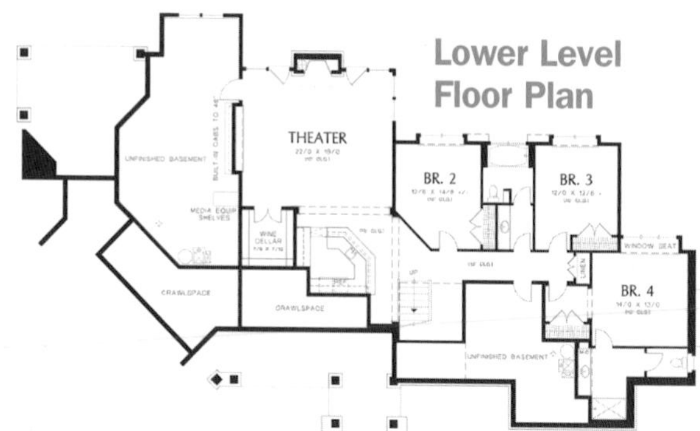

Let Us Help You Plan Your Dream Home

Whether you've always dreamed of building your own home or you can't find the right house from among the dozens you've toured, our collection of Best-Selling 1-Story Home Plans can help you achieve the home of your dreams. You could have an architect create a one-of-a-kind home for you, but the design services alone could end up costing up to 15 percent of the cost of construction—a hefty premium for any building project. Isn't it a better idea to select from among the hundreds of unique designs shown in our collection for a fraction of the cost?

What Does Creative Homeowner Offer?

In this book, Creative Homeowner provides hundreds of home plans from the country's best architects and designers. Our designs are among the most popular available. Whether your taste runs from traditional to contemporary, Victorian to early American, you are sure to find the best house design for you and your family. Our plans packages include detailed drawings to help you or your builder construct your dream house. **(See page 280.)**

Can I Make Changes to the Plans?

Creative Homeowner offers three ways to help you achieve a truly unique home design. Our customizing service allows for extensive changes to our designs. **(See page 281.)** We also provide reverse images of our plans, or we can give you and your builder the tools for making minor changes on your own. **(See page 284.)**

Can You Help Me Manage My Costs?

To help you stay within your budget, Creative Homeowner has teamed up with the leading estimating company to provide one of the most accurate, complete, and reliable building material take-offs in the industry. **(See page 282.)** If that is too much detail for you, we can provide you with general construction costs based on your zip code. **(See page 284.)** Also, many of our plans come with the option of buying detailed materials lists to help you price out construction costs.

How Can I Begin the Building Process?

To get started building your dream home, fill out the order form on page 285, call our order department at 1-800-523-6789, or visit our Web site, ultimateplans.com. If you plan on doing all or part of the work yourself, or want to keep tabs on your builder, we offer best-selling building and design books at creativehomeowner.com.

Our Plans Packages Offer:

"Square footage" refers to the total "heated square feet" of this plan. This number does not include the garage, porches, or unfinished areas. All of our home plans are the result of many hours of work by leading architects and professional designers. Most of our home plans include each of the following:

Frontal Sheet

This artist's rendering of the front of the house gives you an idea of how the house will look once it is completed and the property landscaped.

Detailed Floor Plans

These plans show the size and layout of the rooms. They also provide the locations of doors, windows, fireplaces, closets, stairs, and electrical outlets and switches.

Foundation Plan

A foundation plan gives the dimensions of basements, walk-out basements, crawl spaces, pier foundations, and slab construction. Each house design lists the type of foundation included. If the plan you choose does not have the foundation type you require, our customer service department can help you customize the plan to meet your needs.

Roof Plan

In addition to providing the pitch of the roof, these plans also show the locations of dormers, skylights, and other elements.

Exterior Elevations

These drawings show the front, rear, and sides of the house as if you were looking at it head on. Elevations also provide information about architectural features and finish materials.

Interior Elevations and Details

Interior elevations show specific details of such elements as fireplaces, kitchen and bathroom cabinets, built-ins, and other unique features of the design.

Cross Sections

These show the structure as if it were sliced to reveal construction requirements, such as insulation, flooring, and roofing details.

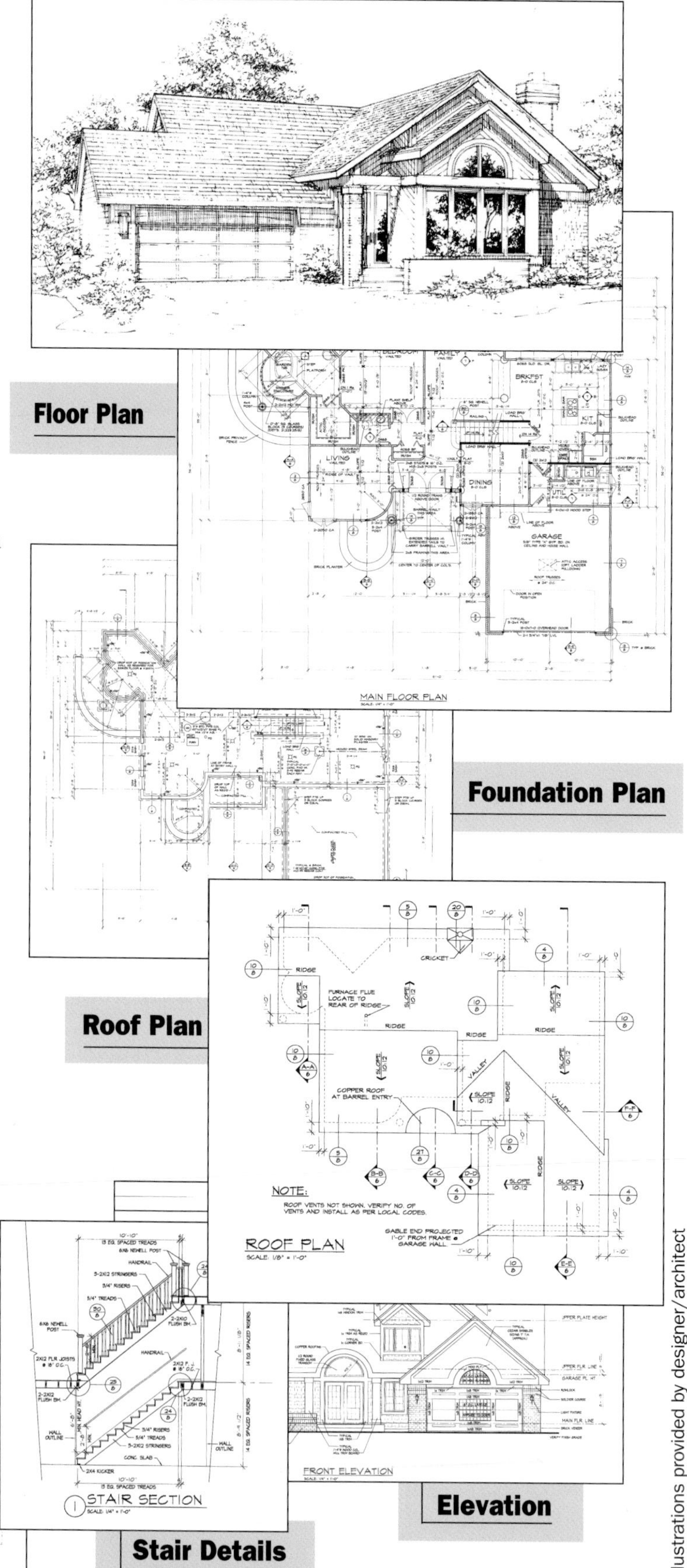

Illustrations provided by designer/architect

Customize Your Plans in 4 Easy Steps

1 Select the home plan that most closely meets your needs. Purchase of a reproducible master, PDF files, or CAD files is necessary in order to make changes to a plan.

2 Call 1-800-523-6789 to place your order. Tell our sales representative you are interested in customizing your plan, and provide your contact information. Within a day or two you will be contacted (via phone or email) to provide a list or sketch of the changes requested to one of our plans. There is no consultation fee for this service.

3 Within three business days of receipt of your request, a detailed cost estimate will be provided to you.

4 Once you approve the estimate, you will purchase either the reproducible master, PDF files, or CAD files, and customization work will begin. During all phases of the project, you will receive progress prints by fax or email. On average, the project will be completed in two or three weeks. After completion of the work, modified plans will be shipped. You will receive one set of blueprints in addition to a reproducible master or CAD files, depending on which package you purchased.

Modification Pricing Guide

Categories	Average Cost For Modification
Add or remove living space	Quote required
Bathroom layout redesign	Starting at $200
Kitchen layout redesign	Starting at $200
Garage: add or remove	Starting at $400
Garage: front entry to side load or vice versa	Starting at $300
Foundation changes	Starting at $200
Exterior building materials change	Starting at $200
Exterior openings: add, move, or remove	$65 per opening
Roof line changes	Starting at $360
Ceiling height adjustments	Starting at $280
Fireplace: add or remove	Starting at $90
Screened porch: add	Starting at $280
Wall framing change from 2x4 to 2x6	Starting at $200
Bearing and/or exterior walls changes	Quote required
Non-bearing wall or room changes	$65 per room
Metric conversion of home plan	Starting at $400
Adjust plan for handicapped accessibility	Quote required
Adapt plans for local building code requirements	Quote required
Engineering stamping only	Quote required
Any other engineering services	Quote required
Interactive illustrations (choices of exterior materials)	Quote required

Note: Any home plan can be customized to accommodate your desired changes. The average prices above are provided only as examples of the most commonly requested changes, and are subject to change without notice. Prices for changes will vary according to the number of modifications requested, plan size, style, and method of design used by the original designer. To obtain a detailed cost estimate, please contact us.

Terms & Copyright

These home plans are protected under the terms of United States Copyright Law and may not be copied or reproduced in any way, by any means, unless you have purchased reproducible masters, which clearly indicate your right to copy or reproduce. We authorize the use of your chosen home plan as an aid in the construction of one single-family home only. You may not use this home plan to build a second or multiple dwellings without purchasing another blueprint or blueprints, or paying additional home plan fees.

Architectural Seals

Because of differences in building codes, some cities and states now require an architect or engineer licensed in that state to review and "seal" a blueprint, or officially approve it, prior to construction. Delaware, Nevada, New Jersey, New York, and some other states require that all plans for houses built in those states be redrawn by an architect licensed in the state in which the home will be built. We strongly advise you to consult with your local building official for information regarding architectural seals.

Before Customization

After

Turn your dream home into reality with

UltimateEstimate

When purchasing a home plan with Creative Homeowner, we recommend you order one of the most complete materials lists in the industry.

What comes with an Ultimate Estimate?

Quote

- Basis of the entire estimate.
- Detailed list of all the framing materials needed to build your project, listed from the bottom up, in the order that each one will actually be used.

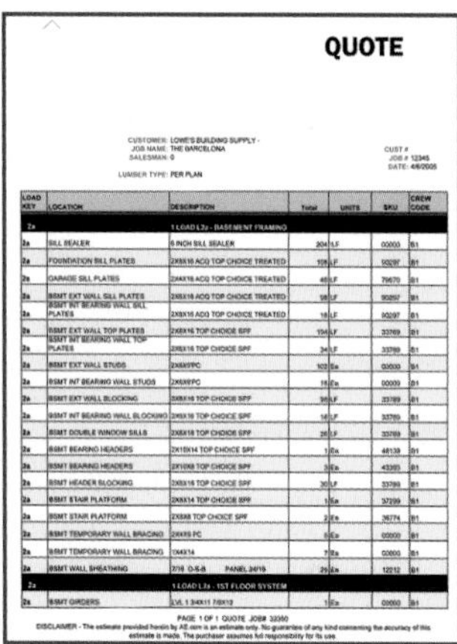
QUOTE

Comments

COMMENTS

- Details pertinent information beyond the cost of materials.
- Includes any notes from our estimator.

Express List

- A version of the quote with space for SKU numbers listed for purchasing the items at your local lumberyard.
- Your local lumberyard can then price out the materials list.

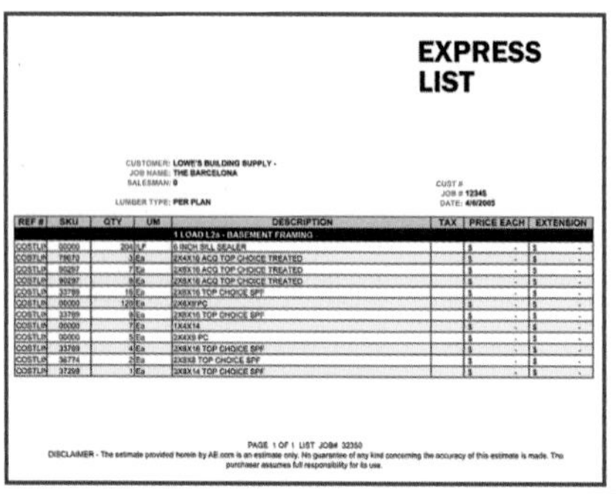
EXPRESS LIST

Construction-Ready Framing Diagrams

- Your "map" to exact roof and floor framing.

Millwork Report

- A complete count of the windows, doors, molding, and trim.

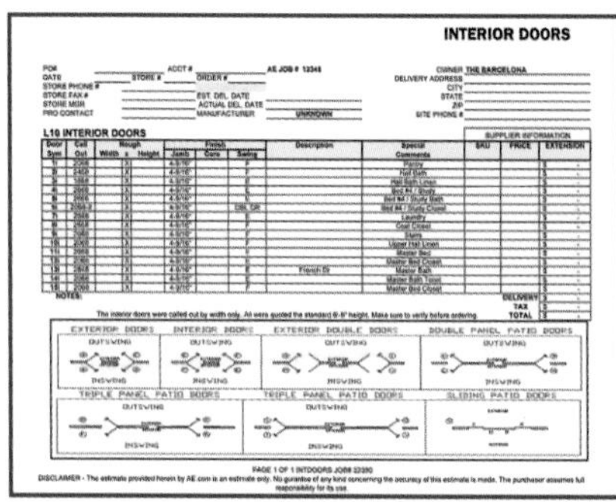
INTERIOR DOORS

Man-Hour Report

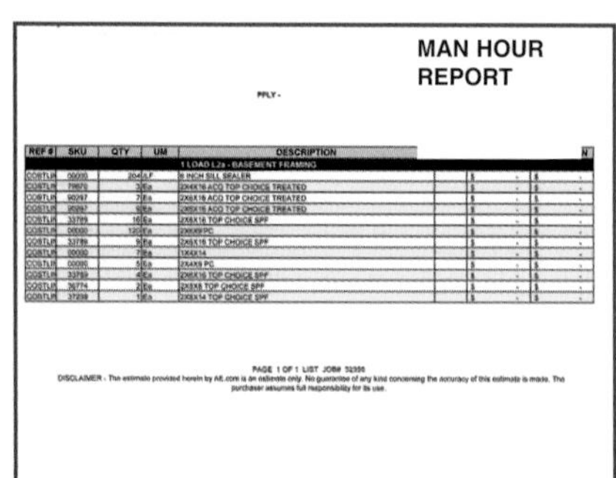
MAN HOUR REPORT

- Calculates labor on a line-by-line basis for all items quoted and presented in man-hours.

2 Why an Ultimate Estimate?

Accurate. Professional estimators break down each individual item from the blueprints using advanced software, techniques, and equipment.

Timely. You will be able to start your home-building project quickly—knowing the exact framing materials you need and how to get them with Lowe's.

Detailed. Work with your local lumberyard associate to select the remaining products needed for your new home and get a final, accurate quote.

3 So how much does it cost?

Pricing is determined by the total square feet of the home plan—including living area, garages, decks, porches, finished basements, and finished attics.

Square Feet Range	UE Tier*	Price
Up to 5,000 total square feet	XB	$345.00
5,001 to 10,000 total square feet	XC	$545.00

*Please see the Plan Index to determine your plan's Ultimate Estimate Tier (UE Tier).
Note: All prices subject to change.

4 What else do I need to know?

Call our toll-free number (800-523-6789), or visit **ultimateplans.com** to order your Ultimate Estimate.

Turn your dream home into reality.

Decide What Type of Plan Package You Need

How many Plans Should You Order?

Standard 8-Set Package. We've found that our 8-set package is the best value for someone who is ready to start building. The 8-set package provides plans for you, your builder, the subcontractors, mortgage lender, and the building department.

Minimum 5-Set Package. If you are in the bidding process, you may want to order only five sets for the bidding round and reorder additional sets as needed.

1-Set Study Package. The 1-set package allows you to review your home plan in detail. The plan will be marked as a study print, and it is illegal to build a house from a study print alone. It is a violation of copyright law to reproduce a blueprint without permission.

Buying Additional Sets. If you require additional copies of blueprints for your home construction, you can order additional sets within 60 days of the original order date at a reduced price. The cost is $50.00 for each additional set. For more information, contact customer service.

Reproducible Masters

If you plan to make minor changes to one of our home plans, you can purchase reproducible masters. These plans are printed on bond or vellum paper that is easy to alter. They clearly indicate your right to modify, copy, or reproduce the plans. Reproducible masters allow an architect, designer, or builder to alter our plans to give you a customized home design. This package allows you to print as many copies of the modified plans as you need for the construction of one home.

PDF Files

PDF files are a complete set of home plans in electronic file format sent to you via email. These files cannot be altered electronically, once printed changes can be hand drawn. A PDF file gives you the license to modify the plans to fit your needs and build one home. Not available for all plans. Please contact our order department or visit our Web site to check the availability of PDF files for your plan.

CAD (Computer-Aided Design) Files

CAD files are the complete set of home plans in an electronic file format. Choose this option if there are multiple changes you wish made to the home plans and you have a local design professional able to make the changes. Not available for all plans. Please contact our order department or visit our Web site to check the availability of CAD files for your plan.

Mirror-Reverse Sets/Right-Reading Reverse

Plans can be printed in mirror-reverse—we can "flip" plans to create a site mirror image of the design. This is useful when the house would fit your or personal preferences if all the rooms were on the opposite side than shown. As the image is reversed, the lettering and dimensions will also be reversed, meaning they will read backwards. Therefore, when ordering mirror-reverse drawings, you must order at least one set of the original plan unreversed. A $50.00 fee per plan order will be charged for mirror-reverse (regardless of the number of mirror-reverse sets ordered). Some plans are available in right-reading reverse; this feature will show the plan in reverse, but the writing on the plan will be readable. A $150.00 fee per plan order will be charged for right-reading reverse (regardless of the number of right-reading reverse sets ordered). Please contact our order department or visit our Web site to check the availibility of this feature for your chosen plan.

EZ Quote: Home Cost Estimator

EZ Quote is our response to a frequently asked question we hear from customers: "How much will the house cost me to build?" EZ Quote: Home Cost Estimator will enable you to obtain a calculated building cost to construct your home, based on labor rates and building material costs within your zip code area. This summary is useful for those who want to get an idea of the total construction costs before purchasing sets of home plans. It will also provide a level of comfort when you begin soliciting bids. The cost is $29.95 for the first EZ Quote and $19.95 for each additional one in the same order. Available only in the U.S. and Canada.

Materials List

Available for most of our plans, the Materials List provides you an invaluable resource in planning and estimating the cost of your home. Each Materials List outlines the quantity, dimensions, and type of materials needed to build your home (with the exception of mechanical systems). You will get faster, more-accurate bids from your contractors and building suppliers. A Materials List may only be ordered with the purchase of at least five sets of home plans.

CompleteCost Estimator

CompleteCost Estimator is a valuable tool for use in planning and constructing your new home. It provides more detail than a materials list and will act as a checklist for all items you will need to select or coordinate during your building process. CompleteCost Estimator is only available for certain plans (please see Plan Index) and may only be ordered with the purchase of at least five sets of home plans. The cost is $125.00 for CompleteCost Estimator.

Ultimate Estimate (See page 282).

Order Toll Free by Phone
1-800-523-6789
By Fax: 201-760-2431

Orders received 3PM ET, will be processed and shipped within two business days.

Order Online
www.ultimateplans.com

Mail Your Order
Creative Homeowner
Attn: Home Plans
24 Park Way
Upper Saddle River, NJ 07458

Canadian Customers
Order Toll Free 1-800-393-1883

Mail Your Order (Canada)
Creative Homeowner Canada
Attn: Home Plans
113-437 Martin St., Ste. 215
Penticton, BC V2A 5L1

Before You Order

Our Exchange Policy

Blueprints are nonrefundable. However, should you find that the plan you have purchased does not fit your needs, you may exchange that plan for another plan in our collection within 60 days from the date of your original order. The entire content of your original order must be returned before an exchange will be processed. You will be charged a processing fee of 20% of the amount of the original order, the cost difference between the new plan set and the original plan set (if applicable), and all related shipping costs for the new plans. Contact our order department for more information. Please note: reproducible masters may only be exchanged if the package is unopened. PDF files and CAD files cannot be exchanged and are nonrefundable.

Building Codes and Requirements

All plans offered for sale in this book and on our Web site (www.ultimateplans.com) are continually updated to meet the latest International Residential Code (IRC). Because building codes vary from area to area, some drawing modifications and/or the assistance of a professional designer or architect may be necessary to comply with your local codes or to accommodate specific building site conditions. We strongly advise you to consult with your local building official for information regarding codes governing your area.

Multiple Plan Discount

Purchase 3 different home plans in the **same order** and receive **5% off** the plan price.

Purchase 5 or more different home plans in the **same order** and receive **10% off** the plan price. (Please Note: study sets do not apply.)

Blueprint Price Schedule

Price Code	1 Set	5 Sets	8 Sets	Reproducible Masters or PDF Files	CAD	Materials List
A	$410	$470	$545	$660	$1,125	$85
B	$465	$540	$615	$740	$1,310	$85
C	$525	$620	$695	$820	$1,475	$85
D	$575	$670	$745	$870	$1,575	$95
E	$625	$730	$805	$925	$1,675	$95
F	$690	$790	$865	$990	$1,800	$95
G	$720	$820	$895	$1,020	$1,845	$95
H	$730	$830	$905	$1,045	$1,900	$95
I	$995	$1,095	$1,170	$1,290	$2,110	$105
J	$1,190	$1,290	$1,365	$1,490	$2,300	$105
K	$1,195	$1,295	$1,370	$1,495	$2,300	$105
L	$1,240	$1,335	$1,410	$1,535	$2,400	$105

Note: All prices subject to change

Ultimate Estimate Tier (UE Tier)

UE Tier*	Price
XB	$345
XC	$545

* Please see the Plan Index to determine your plan's Ultimate Estimate Tier (UE Tier).

Shipping & Handling

	1–4 Sets	5–7 Sets	8+ Sets or Reproducibles	CAD
US Regular (7–10 business days)	$18	$20	$25	$25
US Priority (3–5 business days)	$35	$40	$45	$45
US Express (1–2 business days)	$45	$60	$80	$50
Canada Express (3–4 business days)	$100	$100	$100	$100
Worldwide Express (3–5 business days)	** Quote Required **			

Note: All delivery times are from date the blueprint package is shipped (typically within 1–2 days of placing order).

Order Form

Please send me the following:

Plan Number: ________ **Price Code:** ____ (See Plan Index.)

Indicate Foundation Type: (Select ONE. See plan page for availability.)

❑ Slab ❑ Crawl space ❑ Basement ❑ Walk-out basement

❑ Optional Foundation for Fee ________ $________
(Please enter foundation here)

**Please call all our order department or visit our website for optional foundation fee*

Basic Blueprint Package **Cost**

❑ CAD Files $________
❑ PDF Files $________
❑ Reproducible Masters $________
❑ 8-Set Plan Package $________
❑ 5-Set Plan Package $________
❑ 1-Set Study Package $________
❑ Additional plan sets:
__ sets at $50.00 per set $________
❑ Print in mirror-reverse: $50.00 per order $________
**Please call all our order department or visit our website for availibility*
❑ Print in right-reading reverse: $150.00 per order $________
**Please call all our order department or visit our website for availibility*

Important Extras

❑ Ultimate Estimate (See Price Tier above.) $________
❑ Materials List $________
❑ CompleteCost Materials Report at $125.00 $________
Zip Code of Home/Building Site ________
❑ EZ Quote for Plan #________at $29.95 $________
❑ Additional EZ Quotes for Plan #s________ at $19.95 each $________

Shipping (see chart above) $________
SUBTOTAL $________
Sales Tax (NJ residents only, add 7%) $________
TOTAL $________

Order Toll Free: 1-800-523-6789 By Fax: 201-760-2431
Creative Homeowner (Home Plans Order Dept.)
24 Park Way
Upper Saddle River, NJ 07458

Name ________
(Please print or type)

Street ________
(Please do not use a P.O. Box)

City ________ State ________

Country ________ Zip ________

Daytime telephone ( ) ________

Fax ( ) ________
(Required for reproducible orders)

E-Mail ________

Payment ❑ Bank check/money order. No personal checks.
Make checks payable to Creative Homeowner

❑ VISA ❑ MasterCard ❑ American Express ❑ Discover

Credit card number ________

Expiration date (mm/yy) ________

Signature ________

Please check the appropriate box:
❑ Building home for myself ❑ Building home for someone else

SOURCE CODE **CA426**

Index

For pricing, see page 285.

Plan #	Price Code	Page	Total Finished Sq. Ft.	Materials List	CompleteCost	UE Tier
101004	D	109	4271	Y	N	XB
101005	D	156	4702	Y	N	XB
101005	D	157	4702	Y	N	XB
101006	D	154	4699	Y	N	XB
101008	E	180	4918	Y	N	XB
101009	E	193	5354	Y	N	XC
101011	E	201	5179	Y	N	XC
101012	E	218	5330	N	N	XC
101013	F	250	5966	Y	N	XC
101022	D	162	4917	Y	N	XB
101022	D	163	4917	Y	N	XB
101028	D	151	2272	N	N	XB
101030	E	175	4576	N	N	XB
101033	E	215	2664	N	N	XB
101169	D	168	2495	N	N	XB
101177	D	149	2291	N	N	XB
111001	G	259	4229	N	N	XB
111004	G	262	3855	N	N	XB
111015	F	212	2208	N	N	XB
111017	F	219	2930	N	N	XB
111018	G	257	3279	N	N	XB
121001	D	133	3583	Y	N	XB
121003	E	233	5706	Y	N	XC
121006	C	99	2161	Y	N	XB
121008	C	84	3979	Y	N	XB
121009	B	40	3410	Y	N	XB
121012	B	24	1195	Y	N	XB
121034	E	212	5478	Y	N	XC
121050	D	159	6721	Y	N	XC
121053	E	231	3553	Y	N	XB
121116	E	216	3013	Y	N	XB
121117	D	203	2852	Y	N	XB
121118	C	93	2084	Y	N	XB
121121	C	29	1341	Y	N	XB
121144	B	16	1853	Y	N	XB
121163	F	252	3627	Y	N	XB
121176	D	202	2989	Y	N	XB
121331	G	103	2529	Y	N	XB
131001	D	78	3630	Y	N	XB
131002	D	89	3838	Y	N	XB
131003	C	43	3332	Y	N	XB
131005	D	75	3757	Y	N	XB
131007	D	73	3786	Y	N	XB
131008	C	19	1299	Y	N	XB
131010	D	80	1667	Y	N	XB
131011	E	131	4270	Y	N	XB
131014	C	34	3532	Y	N	XB
131014	C	35	3532	Y	N	XB
131015	E	123	1860	Y	N	XB
131016	E	132	4331	Y	N	XB
131017	C	45	3488	Y	N	XB
131019	F	209	4926	Y	N	XB
131044	E	158	5158	Y	N	XC
131045	F	220	6127	Y	N	XC
131047	D	114	5147	Y	N	XC
131052	E	223	3062	Y	N	XB
151002	F	227	5583	N	Y	XB
151004	E	195	5049	N	Y	XC
151007	C	110	4187	N	Y	XB
151034	D	200	4839	N	Y	XB
151037	C	69	3584	N	Y	XB
151039	B	30	1353	N	Y	XB
151043	E	82	2291	N	Y	XB
151050	F	190	5648	N	Y	XC
151050	F	191	5648	N	Y	XC
151054	C	102	4579	N	Y	XB
151056	D	148	1950	N	Y	XB
151057	G	261	7053	N	Y	XC
151060	F	271	8434	N	Y	XC
151068	D	128	4561	N	Y	XB
151075	D	129	1909	N	Y	XB
151089	E	142	4700	N	Y	XB
151105	D	173	5660	N	Y	XC
151113	D	208	6706	N	Y	XC
151117	D	150	5330	N	Y	XC
151138	C	165	2782	N	Y	XB
151140	E	246	2525	N	Y	XB
151169	C	65	3645	N	Y	XB
151170	E	152	3056	N	Y	XB
151171	D	199	2131	N	Y	XB
151173	C	97	4254	N	Y	XB
151188	E	242	2525	N	Y	XB
151196	C	115	1800	N	Y	XB
151215	C	60	2266	N	Y	XB
151233	D	127	4208	N	Y	XB
151383	G	244	3501	N	Y	XB
151463	C	71	2058	N	Y	XB
151486	E	247	3796	N	Y	XB
151495	D	196	2942	N	Y	XB
151497	G	265	4201	N	Y	XB
151529	B	44	2157	N	Y	XB
151594	F	258	3479	N	Y	XB
151598	D	146	2684	N	Y	XB
151608	C	72	2269	N	Y	XB
151634	E	217	3148	N	Y	XB
151656	D	119	2635	N	Y	XB
151703	D	194	3552	N	Y	XB
151802	F	249	3339	N	Y	XB
151842	D	197	2355	N	Y	XB
151845	G	265	3003	N	Y	XB
151850	D	192	2785	N	Y	XB
151852	E	229	2871	N	Y	XB
161001	C	108	4002	N	N	XB
161002	D	117	4231	N	N	XB
161003	C	63	3512	Y	N	XB
161004	B	28	3193	Y	N	XB
161007	C	77	4043	N	N	XB
161009	C	85	4150	N	N	XB
161010	C	67	3824	Y	N	XB
161013	C	64	3610	Y	N	XB
161014	C	94	4060	Y	N	XB
161026	D	178	4593	N	N	XB
161028	H	271	6861	N	N	XC
161037	E	232	3596	Y	N	XB
161056	G	268	7720	Y	N	XC
161073	D	124	4393	Y	N	XB
161079	B	51	3567	Y	N	XB
161092	D	195	3876	Y	N	XB
161093	I	277	4328	Y	N	XB
161095	H	272	4595	N	N	XB
161115	E	210	4506	Y	N	XB
161196	E	233	3834	Y	N	XB
161224	F	259	6555	Y	N	XC
161249	E	214	5269	Y	N	XC
171001	B	23	1804	Y	N	XB
171004	E	211	3136	Y	N	XB
171006	C	84	2527	Y	N	XB
171008	C	85	2517	Y	N	XB
171009	C	103	2652	Y	N	XB
171013	G	266	5244	Y	N	XC
171015	D	181	3731	Y	N	XB
171023	C	88	3059	Y	N	XB
181021	B	15	2522	Y	N	XB
181148	B	13	2329	Y	N	XB
181153	B	46	1478	Y	N	XB
181159	D	155	1992	Y	N	XB
181216	A	10	910	Y	N	XB
181345	B	12	2235	Y	N	XB
181708	F	260	2800	Y	N	XB
181714	B	18	1244	Y	N	XB
181727	B	30	1800	Y	N	XB
191001	D	203	2156	N	N	XB
191003	C	104	2647	N	N	XB
191004	D	127	2851	Y	N	XB
191009	D	204	3347	N	N	XB
191012	D	198	2123	N	N	XB
191027	E	221	2354	N	N	XB
191028	F	249	5338	N	N	XC
191030	A	9	864	N	N	XB
191032	D	181	3744	N	N	XB
191037	C	72	2562	N	N	XB
191055	D	196	2123	N	N	XB
191058	E	246	2550	N	N	XB
211002	C	105	2696	Y	N	XB
211005	D	161	2844	N	N	XB
211009	E	224	3096	Y	N	XB
211011	F	255	3910	Y	N	XB
211016	B	13	1867	Y	N	XB
211024	B	39	2140	Y	N	XB
211030	D	73	3786	Y	N	XB
211039	D	128	2427	Y	N	XB
211048	D	170	3021	Y	N	XB
211049	D	166	2843	Y	N	XB
211059	E	218	3583	N	N	XB
211062	F	253	3358	Y	N	XB

Index

For pricing, see page 285.

UltimateEstimate

The fastest way to get started building your dream home

Copyright Notice

All home plans sold through this publication are protected by copyright. Reproduction of these home plans, either in whole or in part, including any form and/or preparation of derivative works thereof, for any reason without prior written permission is strictly prohibited. The purchase of a set of home plans in no way transfers any copyright or other ownership interest in it to the buyer except for a limited license to use that set of home plans for the construction of one, and only one, dwelling unit. The purchase of additional sets of the home plans at a reduced price from the original set or as a part of a multiple-set package does not convey to the buyer a license to construct more than one dwelling.

Similarly, the purchase of reproducible home plans (sepias, mylars, or bond) carries the same copyright protection as mentioned above. It is generally allowed to make up to a maximum of 10 copies for the construction of a single dwelling only. To use any plans more than once, and to avoid any copyright license infringement, it is necessary to contact the plan designer to receive a release and license for any extended use. Whereas a purchaser of reproducible plans is granted a license to make copies, it should be noted that because blueprints are copyrighted, making photocopies from them is illegal.

Copyright and licensing of home plans for construction exist to protect all parties. Copyright respects and supports the intellectual property of the original architect or designer. Copyright law has been reinforced over the past few years. Willful infringement could cause settlements for statutory damages to $150,000.00 plus attorney fees, damages, and loss of profits.